The

NATIONAL GOVERNMENT

of the

UNITED STATES

The
NATIONAL
GOVERNMENT
of the
UNITED STATES

48623

WILLIAM ANDERSON

Professor of Political Science

University of Minnesota

NEW YORK: HENRY HOLT AND COMPANY

I pledge allegiance to the flag of the United States of America and to the republic for which it stands, one nation indivisible, with liberty and justice for all.

THE NATIONAL FLAG SALUTE

A nation without a national government, is . . . an awful spectacle.

ALEXANDER HAMILTON,
The Federalist, No. 85.

Preface

What is here presented as a work on *The National Government of the United States* was sketched out many years ago as a course of lectures without thought of publication. On looking over the old outline during the preparation of this book I have been astounded time and again by the great changes that have occurred in the nation's government in the interim.

It is true that many of the old difficulties remain—difficulties connected with national-state relations, executive-legislative relations, the rivalry of parties, and other features of the American political system. To these difficulties, and to the possibility of overcoming or reducing them, much attention is paid in this volume. At the same time great improvements have been made in important parts of the system and the outlook for further progress is not unpromising.

Some readers may think, indeed, that the tone of this volume is unduly optimistic, and that I do not find enough fault. Tested by the standards of those who visualize a theoretically perfect system, any scheme of human government will reveal great defects. Partisans of particular reform measures can always find grievous faults in existing governments to the extent that their own proposals have not been adopted. Such critics as these surely need to be heard and to have their criticisms considered. For the student it is far more to the point, however, to judge a government in its entirety, by comparing it with other political systems that are acually functioning today. When appraised in this way the national government of the United States stands forth as one of the most successful in the world.

My respect for the national government implies no disrespect for or depreciation of the importance of the state and local governments in the United States. Quite the contrary is true. With the present enlarged scope of governmental services there is room and need for all major classes of governmental units, national, state, and local. The competition between them is generally wholesome, and their cooperation in providing joint services has brought great benefits to the people. In fact a volume on state and local governments and their role in the American political system is being prepared to follow this one, and perhaps to be combined with it later in a single volume.

In order to avoid excessive duplication between the parts on national and on state and local government, certain topics that are of great interest at both the national and state levels are dealt with almost entirely in the national government section. Topics that are of primary interest to state and local government are reserved for that part, but a perfect separation of materials is not feasible because of the closeness of the interrelations that exist.

With the publication of this volume on the *National Government*, and the expected early publication of one on *State and Local Government*, there will have been supplied the text materials for courses that are arranged according to the main structural elements or levels in the political system of the United States. My work on *American Government*, now in its third edition (1946), follows functional lines. That is to say, it gives less emphasis to the separate structural elements, and more to the functional integration of the entire system of government. In that work, for example, such a subject as the legislative process, national, state, and local, is dealt with all in one place, whereas in the present treatment Congress is considered in the *National Government* part or volume, while state and local legislatures are studied in the part or volume on *State and Local Government*. For every teacher it is partly a matter of choice and partly one of the requirements of the curriculum as to which approach he shall follow. The goal in each case is the same: a thorough and reasoned knowledge of American political institutions and procedures.

Acknowledgments and thanks for assistance received on this volume are hereby extended to my daughter, Morgia J. Penniman, and to those who shared the laborious task of typing the manuscript, Charlotte Maxey, Barbara Embry, and Louise Olsen.

W. A.

University of Minnesota
March 1, 1946

Contents

x

The

NATIONAL GOVERNMENT

of the

UNITED STATES

CHAPTER 1

Whither National Democracy?

The year 1945 may prove to have been one of the great turning points in all history. In that year the would-be conquerors of the world, Nazi Germany and imperialist Japan, suffered total defeat at the hands of the United Nations, whose attack was spearheaded by China, Great Britain, the Union of Soviet Socialist Republics, and the United States of America, perhaps the greatest military alliance of all times. In the same year atomic energy and atomic bombing came as the culmination of one of the most intensive periods of scientific and technological advances known to man. In that year also came the adoption of the charter of the United Nations, a document designed to combine all the peace-loving nations in a single organization to maintain security and to promote the progress of mankind.

In the new age that stretches out before us all, the peoples of the world are going to be put to tests fully as important and as difficult as those of the six terrible years of war and blood and destruction that went before. Can they maintain international peace and security? Can they fulfill the legitimate yearnings of their peoples for employment, decent incomes, and higher standards of living? Or must new depressions and new wars follow, leading the human race even closer to the brink of destruction?

There will be tests, large-scale and very trying tests, for all the major nations. The material forces of fascism and nazism have been destroyed but their ghosts still stalk the earth, waiting for a new incarnation and a new accession of power. The nations that destroyed the military and economic power of these modern monsters have yet to prove that they can ensure over a long period of time the fruits of their military victory. Much will depend upon how they govern themselves and manage their affairs at home. Democratic government in all nations, large and small, is entering upon a new trial period. The success or failure of democratic processes in the larger nations in the next few generations will have much to do with deciding the fate of the human race.

1

In particular, the eyes of the world are upon the United States. It emerged from the recent war as the greatest military and economic power on earth. Its wartime leadership in world affairs, like its material assistance in the most critical period of the war, was accepted abroad almost without question. Can this nation now measure up to the demands of the age for leadership in peace? Can its government so operate and can it follow so wise a policy at home and abroad as to help lead the whole world to more democratic and more peaceful ways? That is the challenge of the times to the United States of America.

A. AN URBAN, INDUSTRIAL AGE

The United States began its course under the Constitution with a small population, an essentially agricultural economy, a little commerce and less industry. There were no great cities. The tempo of change was relatively slow, as we see it now, and the activities of government were on a small scale. The role of government was conceived of as essentially regulative and negative, not constructive and positive.

This old pattern of life and government has changed tremendously. In relative economic importance agriculture has declined. Although in absolute terms its production is greater than ever, a diminishing percentage of the population takes care of producing the needed foods and fibers. Almost every other economic activity has grown astonishingly since the beginning of the republic. Manufacturing industries, coal and iron and steel, oil and gas and chemicals, textiles and wearing apparel, automobiles and all manner of household equipment; transportation by water, rails, roads, and in the air; communications by telegraph, telephone, radio and postal service; newspapers, periodicals, and books of national circulation; big business in corporate forms; organized labor; powerful pressure groups; a highly urbanized society that demands services from government on an unprecedented scale; a constant flow of inventions and technological changes that force society and government to ever new adaptations and activities—these are some of the characteristics of modern American society even in time of peace. And when war comes as it has twice in thirty years, in its total or all-out form, the pace of change is tremendously increased, while the activity of government is forced up to levels never before thought possible.

Such, in brief, is the type of society in which the present United States government must do its work. The clash of interests, rural against urban, labor against capital, section against section, and all the propaganda, lobbying, and pressure activities that accompany such struggles, make the decisions of government more crucial and dangerous than ever. They also compel the government to do many more things than ever before in order to keep domestic peace and to help satisfy the ever-changing demands for justice between classes and for a rising standard of living. The task is immensely difficult and complicated. Men may well ask whether any system of government can succeed in doing what needs to be done.

B. AN AGE OF INTERDEPENDENCE AMONG NATIONS

Other nations early accepted the United States as one of them. In the beginning years of the republic the United States made foreign alliances and negotiated many treaties with other nations. Then came a period when America's thoughts turned in upon itself, when the development of the continent was all that seemed to matter. A colonial spirit of suspicion against foreigners turned into an attitude of isolationism. The United States people felt that they were different from, and not a little better than, all foreigners. They wanted "no truck with foreign powers" and no outside responsibilities, even though they claimed the right to sail anywhere on the high seas and to do business in all parts of the world.

The idea that the United States could isolate itself from the rest of the world never had solid footing in reason or in experience. It became increasingly illogical as the advance of commerce, transportation, communications, science, and education reduced all effective distances and brought all peoples of the world closer together. The lesson of the interdependence of nations should have been learned at the turn of the century when the Spanish-American War, the annexation of Puerto Rico, Hawaii, the Philippines, and the Canal Zone, the struggle for the Open Door in China, and the Russo-Japanese War drew the United States into action in many parts of the globe. Unfortunately even World War I did not drive the lesson home sufficiently; the nation again tried to turn its back upon the world and to wash its hands of all responsibilities abroad. A selfish and isolationist postwar American economic policy had much to do with bringing on the Great Depression, and that in turn led on to the bloodier and more destructive World War II. This time the lesson seems to have been learned, but at terrific cost. Will it stay learned or will it soon be forgotten? A younger generation, some of whom may read this book, will have much to do with the answer to this question.

One of the first principles of political science is the interdependence of men. Very few can live as solitary savages and none can enjoy the best life possible for men under such conditions. With the world constituted as it is today, the interdependence of nations is the unavoidable corollary of the interdependence of men, if it is not itself a first principle. No nation can isolate itself. None can be safe when any other is threatened with violence to its rights. Said Cain, "Am I my brother's keeper?" Says the modern intelligent statesman, "How can any nation defend itself if it does not act to some extent as its brother nation's keeper?" Do we need to go farther in stressing the interdependence of nations and the impossibility of isolation than simply to refer to the atomic bomb, long-range bombing raids, and the robot bombs with which the nazis so nearly destroyed London?

Once this principle of international interdependence and responsibility is driven home, every nation needs to ask itself whether its own government is so organized and its policies so adjusted as to make possible for it an intelligent, responsible and flexible participation in international affairs. Is the national government of the United States so organized and are its policies so adjusted? Is the mood of its people and of its leaders such that the necessary changes will be made to enable the United States to carry both its internal and its international responsibilities? These are important questions for statesmen and for students. But first, is the United States truly a nation?

C. AMERICAN NATIONHOOD

As we look about the world today we find that there are some sixty or more political units that recognize each other's independence and each of which has its own government. Among them they control all the people and all the habitable area of the earth. Sometimes these entities are called states, sometimes nations, as in the terms "the state system," "the family of nations," and "United Nations."

On closer examination the term "nation" seems to have at least two principal but distinctive meanings. (1) First, as used in the language of international law and international relations, nation has a political significance. It means one of the politically independent peoples that are recognized as separate members of the international state system. In this sense "nation" has nothing necessarily to do with the cultural unity of the people who constitute the population of any particular nation. (2) A second meaning is that of a conscious cultural unity among a people, without regard to whether they are organized and recognized politically as a separate state or nation. Thus there are so-called "national minorities" or distinct cultural groups existing within a number of the independent states or nations of the world.

The United States is certainly a nation in the first sense. Its independent political status was recognized by several nations before the Constitution was adopted. This recognition was accorded to the Union as a whole, not to each of the states separately. Even in the early days of the movement for independence from Great Britain the several colonies (later states) worked together as one through the Continental Congress. In foreign affairs and in war the colonies and states asked for no other status than that of members in a larger entity, the United States of America. They knew that in unity lay their strength and their only hope of independence and international recognition.

Furthermore, the thirteen colonies that became states never had separate, independent standing in their external affairs. Before independence was achieved, they were colonies under the British government. They had powers of local self-government in varying degrees, but they had a common central government whose main offices were in London. The difficulties that the colonies had in dealing separately with a remote central government in which they had no direct representation were in part the motivation for independence. They needed a common central government, but they wanted it to be located in America and to be under their immediate control. Their struggle was an integrating movement at the same time that it was a drive for independence, to unite in America the parts that were being separated from Great Britain. In order to break one bond they created another.

It happened, however, that as colonies they had had separate existences and separate local governments. Distinctive cultural loyalties had been developed around such names as Massachusetts and New York, Pennsylvania and Virginia. It was but natural to continue into the period of independence from Great Britain the loyalties and the separate local governments that had been attached to the colonies of these names. When independence came each colony renamed itself as a "commonwealth" or as a "state."

The latter term was and is rather unfortunate as applied to these entities. The term "state" was one that had been commonly used to designate independent nations like France or Spain—entities with separate international standing. Among the more sagacious leaders in the war for independence there was no thought that each little separate colony could successfully maintain separate statehood in the international sense. But the designation of the now-independent colonies as "states" helped to reinforce the cultural differences that had already developed, and to give the states inflated and unrealistic ideas. The Articles of Confederation, drawn up in 1777 and finally ratified in 1781, even guaranteed the "sovereignty" of the so-called states.

This combination of factors proved to be a real obstacle to the unification of the United States even after the Constitution was adopted. Cultural differences among the states were exaggerated. Many persons held their loyalties to be first to their states and only secondarily to the United States. Actually, except for the institution of slavery in the southern states, there was a high degree of cultural unity, in language, law, religion, origins and traditions.

It would be hard to say when the Americans first came to think of themselves as a nation in a cultural sense. General Washington used the word "nation" as applied to the thirteen states as a whole during the war for independence and his young aide, Alexander Hamilton, employed the term frequently. In overlooking the differences between New Yorkers, Pennsylvanians, Virginians, and so on, these men were probably far ahead of the people generally. Furthermore, they perhaps had in mind primarily the political concept of a nation, as a unit or entity in international affairs. The important thing is, however, that they used the term "nation" for the totality of the people of the thirteen states and that this idea of American nationhood never disappeared but rather grew in strength from that time on.

In the years and decades that followed independence, the feelings for state separatism and sovereignty rose again and again to challenge the movement for national unification. The separatist sentiment was in some cases regional— in the West, in New England, in the South. It was when sectional interests were threatened that states-rightism raised its head most vigorously. On the other side many factors were at work creating the sentiment and the cultural reality of nationhood—wars fought in a common cause, fears of foreign aggression, pride in a common Constitution and central government, the frontier and the westward movement of the people, the common interest in the public lands of the west, the increase of interstate commerce by rivers, roads, and railroads, the freedom to go anywhere to establish a farm or a business, the rise of new means of communication, the coming of millions of immigrants who saw only America and knew not the strife about state rights—yes, these and many other factors worked for national unity and ultimately achieved it.

Many things happened along the way. "The United States" became singular instead of plural. We say "the United States is" and not "are." The Constitution and the flag became symbols of unity that were recognized and revered everywhere. National heroes like Washington and Jefferson were lauded in all states. National services like the post office became established and accepted in all parts of the land.

In short, nationhood in the internal and cultural sense was substantially achieved, although we cannot set an exact date for its beginning. Neither can we say that even today it is perfect in all respects. The Constitution itself perpetuates some practices that emphasize the states rather than the nation. It does not provide for national majority rule in any comprehensive and certain way. Added to this is the fact that there are several national, racial, and religious minorities that have not been fully assimilated or accepted.

D. THE NATIONAL GOVERNMENT

During the war for independence and the years that followed under the Articles of Confederation, the embryonic nation did not have a truly national government. There was no national executive and no system of national courts. The Congress under the Articles of Confederation was not an effective legislative body for national purposes. Its constantly rotating membership was dominated by the state legislatures, which chose the states' representatives in Congress. It had no taxing power, no power to raise and support armies, and in effect no power to enact and enforce laws. After the stress of war had passed it deteriorated rapidly. In the face of domestic violence, interstate tariff controversies, a depreciated currency and a loss of national credit, the Congress was all but helpless. It was this situation that led Hamilton to exclaim in *The Federalist* essays that "A nation without a national government is an awful spectacle."

The men who met in 1787 to frame a new constitution or to strengthen the Articles of Confederation did not intend to wipe out the states; far from it. What they did propose was to set up a new structure, a government for the nation as a whole, and one adequate for all national purposes. In their effort to do this they invented something entirely new in the history of politics—

a strong central government for the people of a group of states; one which rested upon and could reach both the states and the people thereof, and which at the same time left the separate governments of the states in existence to operate within their several territories for all non-national purposes.

This arrangement of two separate governments over the same people was unlike any league or confederation that had theretofore existed anywhere in the world. It was very much as if a substitute had been found for the old central government of the colonies that had operated from London, and had been set up in America to do for the colonies (now states) the same work that the British government had previously done for them all.

There was no name ready at hand for such a new type of arrangement. What should it be called? The framers spoke of the new entity as a "union," and called its central government simply "the government of the United States." This was legally sufficient to distinguish the new over-all government from the governments of the separate states but it was too long an expression for popular use. Something shorter had to be coined. The term "Union government" or "government of the Union" would have been justified by the words of the Constitution. Such an expression was not then adopted and has seldom been used at all.

It was the exigencies of the campaign for the adoption of the Constitution that gave rise to the expression that has since then been most commonly used. From the first the opponents of the Constitution attacked it for setting up a "consolidated government." They meant one that was too highly centralized, one that was a unitary national government. They pictured the "sovereign states" as being in effect wiped out by the new Constitution.

Those who favored the adoption of that document had to overcome this argument. They chose for themselves the name of Federalists. They chose this name with an eye to its propaganda value. They also called their opponents Anti-Federalists, which was probably very unfair. The Federalists placed great stress in their arguments upon the confederate or federative nature of the Constitution, and were at great pains to point out how much the new frame of government actually left to the states. In *The Federalist* essays Hamilton argued that the people of the United States were a nation and needed a strong national government. At the same time he insisted that the Constitution left a great deal of freedom to the states and went no farther than was necessary in giving strength to the central government. Madison in an essay in the same series analyzed separately the "federal" and the "national" features of the new government, and concluded that the Constitution provided a happy mixture of the two.

It was in the debates of 1787-88 over the proposed Constitution, therefore, that the term "federal government" came to be applied to the central or national government. From time to time various persons have pointed out the ineptitude of the phrase "federal government" as applied to the central government of the Union, and many have adopted the term "national government," but without having much effect on popular usage.

Correctly used, the term "federal government" is a general one that refers to any system of government in which the powers and functions of government are divided between a central government and a number of state or provincial governments. In the United States there is such a division and it would be appropriate to refer to the entire United States system of government (including both the central and the state governments) as an example of federal government or as a federal system. But the central government alone is not a federal government.

Neither is the term "federal" justified by any word in the Constitution. As previously stated that document uses the term "Union," not federation or any of its variant forms. The use of the term "federal" to describe the central government of the nation implies that the government has been created by treaty, in this case presumably a treaty among the states, whereas the framers used the word Constitution, which means the basic charter or organization of a single government, and worded the preamble so that the Constitution was ordained by *the people of the United States* and not by the states as such. It would be hard to say how much confusion and misunderstanding have been caused by the use of the term "the federal government" as it is used in this country, but it must have been a great deal.

For the foregoing reasons this book will not use the term "the federal government" to indicate the central government of the United States. Far more appropriate is the term "the national government." This is not because the Constitution uses the term "national" but rather because the United States has in fact become a nation in every important sense of the term and because its central government serves the nation as a whole for every important national and international purpose. The central government is a national government. Let us frankly call it that.

E. LARGE SCALE DEMOCRACY

What about the form of this national government? Whether they fully realize it or not the people of the United States are engaged in one of the most important experiments in human government of all time. A people of 140 millions, occupying an area of 3 million square miles, they are governing themselves and their relations with the outside world according to modern principles of democratic self-rule. Several political philosophers have said that such large scale democracy is simply impossible. Others have said that all governments, even those that have democratic forms, are really governments by the few who head the political organization.

Still others say that the United States is not in form a political democracy but a republic or an example of representative government. At one time, long ago, democracy meant direct rule by people in places so small that all could participate in the assemblies and nearly everyone held some office during his life. In this sense certainly the United States is not a democracy. But times have changed and so has the meaning of the word democracy. Today the word is the accepted term for various forms of popular rule as distinguished from dictatorship and fascism.

Modern democracy can be said to prevail in any country where (a) a large part of the adult citizens are entitled to vote; (b) there is freedom of assembly, thought, speech, and press; (c) the principal policy-making officers of the government are freely elected by the voters at reasonably frequent and regular intervals; and (d) it is settled custom that those who are defeated at the polls will withdraw peacefully from office, while those who are elected will assume office and endeavor to carry on the government in accordance with the public will and the general welfare.

This is a rather long definition of political democracy, but every part of it is important. A considerable portion of the adult citizens must be permitted to vote as a matter of legal right. Countries that permit substantially all men to vote may qualify as democracies, but the situation is more democratic when women are also entitled to the franchise. Freedom of assembly, thought, speech, and press is essential if the people and their leaders are to be able to discuss and criticize the policies of the government and to reach sound conclusions as to men and policies. Free elections, held regularly and not too infrequently, are also necessary, so that the voters who have been informed by public discussion may express their wishes through the election of new officers if they so desire. All parties and elements in the state need to recognize and accept these arrangements, so that when an election has been held, the verdict of the voters will be honestly registered and obeyed, and no party or officer will try to retain power by force after the voters have spoken against them. And then, finally, whoever assumes office is bound to use his official power for the general welfare, as much as possible in accordance with a clearly registered public opinion. Democracy aims at the general good, which includes the welfare of every individual, and it rests upon the notion that in general matters the people know best what is good for them.

To carry on government according to such principles, in war as well as in peace, over a continental area with 140 million people, implies a faith in mankind that very few political philosophers ever held. Many believed that only by superior authority and force could large numbers of people be kept in order. In our day the fascists in Italy and in other lands, and the National Socialists (nazis) in Germany, put forth the doctrines of rule by an "elite class" headed by one man, the dictator or *Führer*, as the only true basis of strong, effective government. Their cruel treatment of their own people as well as of those whom they conquered and despoiled showed how little respect they had for the elemental rights and dignity of man. By decisive defeat in war they were brought to a belated justice and the rotten hollowness of their regimes was exposed. Even now many of their followers remain unchanged in their po litical views, however, while certain persons in democratic countries, though now quiescent, also distrust popular rule and continue to long for dictatorship.

Thus in the hour of military triumph of the democracies over the dictatorships the threat to democratic institutions remains. It is in the very nature of democracies that they must live dangerously. They must permit a maximum of free thought and free speech. They must allow even erroneous and insidious thoughts to be entertained up to the point where there is actual threat of violence against the people and their government. They must have confidence in their ability to put down those who would destroy democracy when the time finally requires such action.

And so the United States stands today as the world's outstanding example of giant democracy. In this sense its system of government is relatively new in the world and almost unique. During past decades of semi-isolation from world affairs the threats to its democratic institutions were not very serious. But is it possible for a nation to be active, strong, and just in its international dealings while operating through democratic processes at home? Can the firmness, power and speed required in international actions be harmonized with the slower and more deliberate democratic processes at home?

F. IS THE NATIONAL GOVERNMENT ADEQUATE TO ITS TASKS?

The United States is a nation in both the political and cultural meanings of that term. It is a great and powerful nation. It exists in an era that puts tremendous demands upon people and government, an age of great industrialization, urbanization, and technological change, an age in which quickened communications and expanded knowledge make every nation closer to every other one. It is a nation in a system of interdependent nations, a system in which each nation has heavy international as well as domestic responsibilities.

This nation has a national government, a single, great, powerful organization for handling all national and international affairs. That government is organized along the lines of a modern representative, elective democracy. Is that government suitably organized and directed to achieve the manifold aims demanded by the people and the times? To what extent is it a truly national government? Can it be kept intelligent, alert, active and vigorous in the protection of the nation's security, the promotion of the people's welfare, and the preservation of the basic civil liberties that make a nation democratic and its government responsible?

These are some of the questions to keep in mind throughout the following discussion of the national government of the United States. Let us approach that government objectively and with critical intelligence, attempting always to avoid excesses of either praise or blame.

CHAPTER 2

Backgrounds of the Union

As of the present time the midpoint in the history of government in the United States is the year 1783, when the treaty of peace with Great Britain recognized and established American independence. Stretching backward from that year lay over 160 years of experience in limited self-government in the colonies, closing with some years of joint effort in the struggle for independence.

THE COLONIAL IMPERIAL RELATIONSHIP

Colonial Government. After the failure of earlier colonizing efforts the British people succeeded in the seventeenth century in establishing colonies in Virginia, Massachusetts Bay, and other points up and down the coast from what is now Maine to Georgia. They also took over Dutch and Swedish settlements in the middle of this stretch of coast. Grants of land were made by the British king or crown to various companies, groups, and individuals so that presently the whole coastal region claimed by the British was divided into separate provinces or colonies.

Since it was impracticable to rule these territories in all matters from London, self-governing powers were conferred upon the several colonies in varying forms and degrees. The most complete powers of colonial self-government were found in Massachusetts, Connecticut and Rhode Island, but Massachusetts suffered a significant loss of power before the end of the seventeenth century. In most of the colonies there was an elective branch of the colonial assembly to which was entrusted considerable control over taxes, expenditures, and general legislation. This branch was the center of nearly every struggle of the colonists for the increase of popular control over the government.

The rest of the officers in most of the colonies represented the Crown of Great Britain. There was first the royal governor who was sent out with instructions from the King and his advisers for the general rule of the colony.

In addition there were other civil and military officers, the judges of the courts, and an executive council to advise the governor and to serve as a sort of second chamber of the assembly (legislature). The members of the council and a number of other officials were appointed by the Crown from among the local residents, but they were attached to the governor and the Crown by a number of ties, social, economic, and religious.

Small, weak, and at first mostly unprofitable, the colonies suffered a great deal in the early years from neglect by the home government. During this period the peoples developed practices of self-government that were later a strength to them and a danger to the bond that held them to Great Britain. On the other hand, the home government in London lacked experience in the administration of colonies and was deterred from doing much about the problem by the great distances involved, the expense, and the apparent lack of any considerable gain to be achieved.

Thus things drifted along in the early decades of colonization in America. The Privy Council, the body of the King's advisers, tried by one method and then another to handle the various requests for official action that came from the colonies. In the meantime a policy of using the colonies for supplying England with raw materials, and of reserving manufacturing and the shipping trade for the home country was developing. Parliament passed certain Acts of Trade for this purpose, and the Privy Council set up a Board of Trade to enforce the regulations, promote trade, and supervise the colonies. This policy aroused many colonial leaders to resistance.

Beginnings of Colonial Union. The home government supervised each colony as a separate unit, but as the colonies grew and their trade and wealth increased the colonial peoples became better acquainted with each other. A common cause, that of resistance to certain obnoxious trade regulations, then drew them closer together. Earlier various forces such as the need for common defense against the Indians had brought about a joint agreement among Massachusetts, Plymouth, Connecticut and New Haven, which lasted for forty years (1643-84) under the title of "the New England Confederation." Fears of Spanish, French, and Indian aggression forced certain leaders in other colonies also to think of a confederation of the colonies for common purposes. During the early and middle part of the eighteenth century several plans were put forth for colonial federation. At one time even the home government favored such a move as a possible means of shifting some of the expense of military defense to the colonies, but the colonial leaders and the home government could not agree on the organization or powers of such a confederation or on who was to control it.

As the leaders in all the colonies became more fully aware of their common interests, the greatest defect in their governmental organization became clear. Their central government was in London, not in America. It was controlled by others, not by themselves. However honest and conscientious the British kings, ministers, and members of Parliament might be, they did not and could not understand the colonial point of view. Furthermore this distant central government dealt with each colony separately. By itself each colony was too small and too poor to resist undesirable British policies. There was obvious need, therefore, for union among the colonies so as to present a united front not only against the home government but also against the Indians or any possible foreign aggressor—Spain or France.

The colonial leaders did not at once think of or insist upon independence. There were obvious advantages in the connection with Great Britain, in defense, in commerce, and in cultural matters. Indeed the division of functions between the government in London and the governments of the several colonies was not unlike that in the present Constitution of the United States. The home government took care of foreign affairs, defense and war, general regulations of commerce, the postal service, coinage, Indian affairs, and the higher judicial courts. This relieved the colonies of much expense and trouble, even though the colonists were not always satisfied with the results. The colonial governments dealt in general with only such matters as fall to the states in present-day American government, and as a result their expenses were relatively small.

There was no great public demand for colonial union until after the middle of the eighteenth century. Each colony had developed its own political organizations, laws, traditions, and culture. Each colonist was a British subject, to be sure, but he felt himself to be a citizen primarily of his own colony, such as Virginia, Pennsylvania, or Massachusetts. There was no distinctly American political bond to draw the colonies together, no American citizenship as such, no common American political organization, no American army or navy or flag. Certain common culture traits were evident up and down the coast— the same language, the same general laws, much the same religion, and similar economic institutions. These provided favorable conditions for ultimate union, but what united the colonies finally was opposition to a series of acts of the British government, both Crown and Parliament. These acts, passed after 1760, imposed upon the colonies new taxes and trade restrictions that appeared to leading colonists to be contrary to their rights and wholly obnoxious.

Colonial Resistance to Home Government. What followed was the organization of political resistance among middle class and popular leaders, first in the separate commercial centers, then in whole colonies, and finally on an inter-colonial basis. Committees of Correspondence carried on the agitation all along the coast, and their exchanges of views resulted in the holding in 1774 of the first Continental Congress. This was a body unauthorized by law; it represented the leaders in the resistance movement in a number of colonies. At least the leading colonists had learned by that time that each separate colony standing by itself was too weak to check the actions of the home government. The need for a united front among the colonies was evident.

With a united front it was hoped that methods of agitation, propaganda, and more or less passive resistance would achieve the desired results. Most of the leaders expected the colonies to remain within the British empire and they hoped to achieve their ends by political means. They were not yet ready either for war or for independence. British mishandling of the situation and the demand for independence by the more extreme resistance leaders in the colonies soon prevented a peaceful adjustment of relations. As early as 1774 the colonial governors were being defied and illegal legislative assemblies, usually called conventions of the people, were set up in several colonies. By 1775 there was virtual independence; the colonial governments had been or were being replaced by new revolutionary states. The War for Independence was about to begin.

The story of central government within the United States, as distinct from that exercised over the colonies from London, presumably begins with the Continental Congresses. The history of these Congresses precedes and merges into the story of the Congresses under the Articles of Confederation.

Washington once said that "influence is not government." Properly speaking the first Continental Congresses had no powers of government whatever. They did not even claim such powers. There was no United States or United Colonies of America, no "continental" political entity for such a body to represent, no "constitution" to give it support. The revolutionary conventions in the several colonies or states could and did more quickly acquire real powers of government than the Continental Congresses. Nevertheless the need for united action was so great and the prestige of the leaders in the early Continental Congresses so high, that the influence of that body soon began to change into the semblance of power. It was looked to for leadership by many persons in all the colonies.

The Continental Congress that met early in 1776 had a number of important decisions to make, all interdependent, of which the following were politically most important:

1. Whether boldly to declare the independence of the colonies (states), or to try by further conciliation to remain within the empire.
2. What steps to take to regularize the government of each colony.
3. How to form a firmer union among the colonies.
4. What measures to adopt to make effective resistance to the British forces.

Separate committees worked upon these matters, and their recommendations, when approved by the Congress, laid several important stones in the foundations of American government, both national and state.

INDEPENDENCE

Resolution of July 2, 1776. Decision upon the first question was reached on July 2, 1776, when a short resolution was adopted declaring that

these United Colonies are, and of right ought to be, free and independent States, that they are absolved from all allegiance to the British Crown, and that all political connection between them and the
State of Great Britain is, and ought to be, totally dissolved.[1]

This is one of the last occasions on which the revolutionary leaders refer to
"colonies." In the same sentence the colonies become "independent States."
On July 4th, when the longer "Declaration of Independence" was adopted,
the present official title, "United States of America," was used instead of
"United Colonies," and thereafter "United States" was the recognized designation.

Formal Declaration of Reasons, July 4. The leaders in Congress did not
think it sufficient to resolve upon independence. "A decent respect to the
opinions of mankind" impelled them to declare to the world the causes that
had led them to the separation. The resultant statement, called the Declaration of Independence, is one of the greatest documents of American political
history and in the whole history of human freedom. It records in classic, terse,
and moving sentences the political theories of the Revolutionary leaders, and
the list of grievances that the members of the Continental Congress put forth
as justifying the separation from England.

Declaration Not Part of Constitution. At the same time it is not a part of
the Constitution or of the law of the land at the present time. However much
a judge may be swayed by its principles, no court in the United States has any
power to give effect to it in its decisions. It summarizes the views of the Continental Congress as to the rights possessed by the colonists as men and Englishmen prior to independence, rights that the king is charged with having
violated. It indicts a king; it does not form a new government or grant any
rights to American citizens.

Political Theory of Declaration. The Declaration of Independence has had
great influence upon the course of American political thinking and undoubtedly upon political developments as well. When Jefferson and his associates
came to write it, they could not discuss merely the drab legal rights of British
subjects that they believed had been violated. Such a statement would not
have had a wide appeal. Instead they asserted the rights of man in general.
People of that time, and particularly in France where the Americans hoped
for support, were tremendously concerned about man in general, or humanity
as a whole. And so in the Declaration the first substantive statement sets out
a philosophy of the rights of man.

We hold these truths to be self-evident, that all men are created
equal, that they are endowed by their Creator with certain inalien-
able Rights, that among these are Life, Liberty and the pursuit of
Happiness.—That to secure these rights, Governments are instituted

[1] Becker, *The Declaration of Independence*, p. 3; *Journals of Congress* (Ford ed.) V,
p. 424.

among Men, deriving their just Powers from the consent of the governed.—That whenever any Form of Government becomes destructive of these ends, it is the Right of the People to alter or to abolish
it, and to institute new Government, laying its foundation on such
principles and organizing its powers in such form, as to them shall
seem most likely to effect their Safety and Happiness.[2]

Here in three pithy sentences is almost the whole theory of popular sovereignty—of what Lincoln later called "government of the people, by the
people, and for the people." The doctrines that government may properly
exist only with the people's consent, that it exists for their service and happiness, and that they may overthrow it or change it at will, are all asserted. Here,
too, is the proposition that man has natural rights, rights prior to or even
superior to any government, and that government exists only to protect these
rights. If to Americans these now seem very commonplace ideas they would
do well to contrast them with the officially approved pronouncements of fas-
cist and nazi writers in Europe in the past two decades.

The Declaration is in one sense the first official national utterance on the
part of the new political unit, the United States of America, whose birth it
proclaimed. Several of the states had, through their own conventions, adopted
their own declarations of independence a month or more before this national
pronouncement, but the outside world and many if not most of the American
people look to the joint declaration of July 4, 1776, as the true beginning of
American independence. And that declaration implied a union of the states
and their peoples into a new political entity, the United States of America,
just as clearly as it announced a severance from Great Britain.

In short the declaration provided a peculiarly American justification, for
independence and self-government. It became a sort of symbol of American-
ism, like the flag, which was designed at about the same time, and which
emphasized American unity with its thirteen stripes and thirteen stars. These
symbols, together with such slogans as "no taxation without representation,"
and "give me liberty or give me death," were unquestionably potent factors
in developing national unity.

CONFEDERATION

The same Continental Congress that adopted the Declaration of Independence and advised the states to adopt state constitutions proceeded also
in 1776 to draw up articles of union between the new-born states. This Congress was itself a body without any known legal powers. Its name suggested
a meeting of ministers from a number of independent states, and it had, in
fact, no power to compel any state to do anything without its own consent.
There was no constitution, no league or treaty among the states, no document

---

[2] See discussion in Becker, *op. cit.*, pp. 24-79.

to which the Congress could refer as giving it any authority or any regular organization. What it did, it did more or less by mutual consent.

The drafting of articles of confederation fell to a committee of the Congress appointed in June, 1776. Delays, interruptions, and disagreements in the committee and later in the Congress prevented the adoption of the Articles by the Congress until November 15, 1777. The document was then referred not to the voters in the several states but to the state legislatures—further proof of the strong position of those bodies. Eight states had ratified them by July 9, 1778, and the Articles were thereafter followed in practice. Legally, however, the Articles were not in effect until all states had approved them, and Maryland, the last of the states to consent, did not sign them until March 1, 1781.

It has been said that if the Articles could have been drafted and adopted promptly in 1776, a considerable measure of power might have been conferred upon the Congress. As the months went by, bickerings developed that prevented this, and presently the members insisted upon asserting in the Articles the sovereignty of the states.

Confederation and Federation Distinguished. The short title of the document adopted is "Articles of Confederation and Perpetual Union." [3] Each state is named separately, from New Hampshire to Georgia. The term "confederacy" is also used, but not "federation"—and it is interesting to note that many years later the southern states, strongly insistent on state rights, when seceding from the Union, called their organization the "Confederate States of America." According to modern usage, a "confederation" is a different thing from a "federation" or "federal union." In each case a number of so-called "states" are drawn into a common organization for common purposes, and in each there is a central agency for common action, but there are certain differences that may be noted as follows: [4]

Confederation or Confederacy	*Federation or Federal Union*
1. States are members, and the central agency rests on them.	1. Both central and state governments rest on the people.
2. Each state has full powers of government, except over external affairs and a few others delegated to the central agency.	2. Powers of government over people divided between central government and states.
3. Central agency not a true government, and it acts internally only through state governments.	3. Has a real central government, acting directly on people.
4. Articles of union more like a treaty than a constitution.	4. A real constitution binds central government, states, and people.

[3] For text of the Articles see H. S. Commager (ed), *Documents of American History,* 1934, pp. 111-16.
[4] See Gettell, *Political Science,* pp. 464-66.

That the union under the Articles of Confederation was legally of the "confederate" rather than of the "federal" type is clearly shown by the article on state sovereignty, which is placed significantly after the first article which merely names the confederacy "The United States of America."

> Article II. Each State retains its sovereignty, freedom and independence, and every power, jurisdiction and right, which is not by this confederation expressly delegated to the United States, in Congress assembled.

Here the word "retains" signifies an agreement that the states already were separately sovereign and independent, while the word "expressly" means that the Congress of the United States could not claim any power not clearly granted in so many words by the Articles.

Central Agencies of the Confederation. "For the more convenient management of the general interest of the United States," the Articles provided for a Congress that was in effect only a continuation of the Continental Congress. In this body each state had one vote, and each elected and supported its own members, from two to seven in number. No member could serve over three years in any six. In practice the legislatures chose the delegates to Congress, and they had power to recall them at any time. Annual meetings were provided for and were held. In nearly all matters the votes of nine states were required to pass a measure in Congress.

Instead of creating a single executive, the Articles provided that the Congress should appoint "a Committee of the States," consisting of one delegate from each, to sit while Congress was not in session, to execute such powers as Congress might designate, but none of the policy-making powers of Congress could be delegated to it.

The provisions for a common judiciary were also rudimentary. The Congress itself had power to provide for special temporary commissions to settle disputes between the states, in a manner not unlike that sometimes provided for settling international disputes; and it also had power to, and did, establish a court of appeals to settle finally, on appeal from the state courts, cases involving ships and goods seized as prizes of war, and also cases of piracies and felonies on the high seas. A number of interstate disputes and prize cases were settled peaceably and lawfully in these several ways.

Powers of Congress. Clearly, the Congress was the only important agency of joint action created by the states under the Articles. Upon it were conferred whatever powers the states gave up in the interests of the common welfare. To the Congress were granted "the sole and exclusive right and power" to declare war, to make peace, to send and receive ambassadors, and to make treaties and alliances; also to regulate the coinage, fix weights and measures, regulate trade with the Indians, establish and regulate post offices, build and equip a navy, appoint all navy officers and the superior army officers, and to make rules for both land and naval forces.

Insofar as the creation of an over-all national government was concerned, the Articles in some respects represented a step backward. The Congress did not receive the power, formerly exercised by Parliament, of regulating commerce among the colonies. It had no clear authority to establish rules for legal tender in the settlement of debts. Thus each state could legally erect tariff barriers against the others, and could make its own legal tender laws. On the important subject of taxation, the states yielded no power whatever to Congress. Every bit of taxing power remained exclusively in the states.

As to finances, the Congress had power "to borrow money, or emit bills on the credit of the United States," "to ascertain the necessary sums of money to be raised for the service of the United States, and to appropriate and apply the same for defraying the public expenses." All expenses incurred by Congress for the common defense or general welfare were to be paid from a common treasury, to be supplied with funds from time to time by the several states "in proportion to the value of all land within each State," and the taxes for this purpose were to be levied by the legislatures of the several states. Except through borrowing, Congress had no power to raise money directly. It could only ask the states to contribute.

Similarly, it had no power to compel men to serve in the army. All it had was the power "to agree upon the number of land forces, and to make requisitions from each State for its quota, in proportion to the number of white inhabitants in such State; which requisition shall be binding, and thereupon the Legislature of each State shall appoint the regimental officers, raise the men and cloath, arm and equip them in a soldier-like manner, at the expense of the United States."

Thus men and money, the sinews of war and government, depended wholly on the state legislatures, the bodies on which the members of Congress themselves depended for their offices. To be sure the states had consented to do their several shares:

> Article XIII. Every State shall abide by the determinations of the United States in Congress assembled, on all questions which by this confederation are submitted to them. And the articles of this confederation shall be inviolably observed by every State, and the Union shall be perpetual.

All these solemn promises were made in the name of "the Great Governor of the World." Here was an experiment in government by compact and consent—but it was the consent of states, not of individual men. The "determinations" and "regulations" adopted by Congress are nowhere called *laws*. The Congress made certain treaties binding on all the people, but it did not enact laws at all in the ordinary sense. Congressional determinations were, of course, strong recommendations to the states, but they could not be enforced by Congress upon individuals. So difficult was it to get the states to do their part in carrying out congressional determinations that Madison, when a member of Congress in 1781, recommended an amendment to the Articles permitting Congress to use the military and naval forces to compel states to abide by its determinations.

It is doubtful, therefore, whether the central organization under the Articles of Confederation was strictly speaking a "government." In but few matters could it reach the citizen by its own legislation. It could not tax him. It could not force him to serve in the army. It could not punish him for violation of the treaties or regulations it made. Indeed, there were no individuals who were subject to its jurisdiction. Each of the states had its own citizens. These had, by the Articles, "all privileges and immunities of free citizens in the several states" and the right to move into any state, and to engage in trade on an equal footing with the inhabitants thereof, but the Congress could not itself enforce this privilege if violated.

The United States were not yet a nation, in short, but thirteen states united in confederation. They were still plural, not singular. Broad-visioned men like Washington, Hamilton, Franklin, and Dr. Benjamin Rush were already speaking of the "nation" and the "national interests," but they were ahead of their time. The words "national" and "nation" were not popular in those days, and do not appear in the Declaration of Independence or in the Articles of Confederation. Jefferson in the Declaration of Independence got as far as to say "one people," but the term men generally used to express American unity was a geographical one—"continental." This word alone was rather inadequate for expressing the many common interests that in fact drew the colonists together.

STATE CONSTITUTIONS AND GOVERNMENTS

The relationship of this new political union to the states and their governments presents an interesting problem. In the turmoil of the transition to independence in 1774 and 1775 revolutionary conventions took over the powers of government in all the colonies except two, Connecticut and Rhode Island, where the old charters and charter governments continued in operation. In all the others there was grave doubt as to the legal status and proper organization of the actual government. Some states so far recognized the leadership of the Continental Congress as to send official requests to it for advice as to what to do to regularize their governments. On May 10, 1776, nearly two months before the Declaration of Independence, Congress advised all the states to proceed to frame and adopt constitutions if they had not already done so.

The state conventions undertook the task at once. By the middle of 1777 ten of them had adopted state constitutions. Rhode Island and Connecticut continued under their old charters, while Massachusetts did not adopt its constitution until 1780, after failing in an earlier attempt. Under these constitutions the states provided for legislatures, governors, certain other officials, and courts. Several of them included also bills of rights and a separation of powers. The actual government of the country, that is, the making and enforcing of laws, the raising and spending of money, and the rendering of public services, was carried on mainly by the states and their counties, towns, and cities.

What was the relationship of Congress to these state constitutions and governments? It is easy to present an argument that each state separately became independent of Great Britain and that each one by itself made its constitution and carried on its government as a "sovereign state." On the other hand Congress was in existence and had declared the independence of "the United States of America" before most of the states got around to separate declarations. Furthermore the states waited for advice from Congress before adopting constitutions. Out of the first view of the facts certain Anti-Federalist and Republican leaders drew conclusions favorable to states' rights and state sovereignty. Out of the other view of the same facts certain Federalists and those who followed their line of reasoning drew definitely nationalistic conclusions. They argued that it was as "United States" that the Americans carried on the war to a successful conclusion, as "United States" that they made treaties and alliances to get aid in the war, and as "United States" that they declared and obtained recognition of their independence and established their territorial claims at the expense of Great Britain. These are facts of historical record, however weak may have been the Continental Congress.

Furthermore the states in carrying on the government of the country made numerous unpopular decisions and mistakes, and both during the War for Independence and in the following years they lost much of their early public support. Business was upset by war conditions, taxes were hard to pay and hard to collect, and the extraordinary demands for men, money and materials to carry on the war created some large state debts and brought turmoil into state finances. A number of states yielded to the demands of the debtor class for cheap money and inflation. Price-fixing measures were adopted to prevent profiteering but were not well enforced. Goods as well as money were made legal tender in several states, and creditors had to accept their pay in such goods or not be paid at all. Interstate antagonisms arose and several states began to build up tariff walls to keep out the goods that were coming in from others. The property rights of men who did not support the war were destroyed and their estates were taken away. In short, business, businessmen and the property-owning classes generally suffered from many restrictions and deprivations.

But it was not alone the conservative business leaders who were disturbed. Jefferson, who was something of a political liberal, was also disquieted and he found the cause of the difficulties to lie partly in the form of the state government. In his famous *Notes on Virginia*, a book dated 1782, he found numerous faults with the Virginia government, of which the most important was the concentration of power in the hands of the legislature.

> All the powers of government, legislative, executive, and judiciary, result to the legislative body. The concentrating these in the same hands is precisely the definition of despotic government. It will be no alleviation that these powers will be exercised by a plurality of hands, and not by a single one. 173 despots would surely be as oppressive as one.[5]

Now, Virginia was rather proud of its constitution. It had a bill of rights, and provision for the separation of powers. In practice, however, it had complete supremacy of the legislature. That body could alter the constitution itself, and at one time, to Jefferson's great distress, it discussed a proposal to set up what he called a dictator.

Decline of Congress. In the meantime, the Congress under the Articles of Confederation was also having a difficult time. Because of its constitutional weakness it was unable to capitalize on the mistakes of the states or to increase its own prestige. From the battlefield Washington wrote with bitterness of its ineptitude in the supplying of men and money. In the postwar period it floundered almost hopelessly in a financial bog, unable to pay off the soldiers, or to meet interest and principal payments on the government debt. The "Continental" paper money it had issued depreciated until it practically lost all value—and "is not worth a Continental" became a by-word. Government bonds sank to but a small fraction of their face value, and new loans could hardly be floated. Attempts to get the Articles amended so that Congress could levy import duties, or levy and collect its own taxes, failed when one or another state refused to ratify. A unanimous vote of the states was necessary for amendment of the Articles.

And so Congress, without hope of increasing its powers, with a constantly changing membership in which the abler men of the country were fewer and fewer, fell into a serious decline after the war. It lost even the moral leadership that it had held in the beginning of the Revolutionary movement. If America was to create an effective union of the states, and a truly national government, the time for a change was clearly coming.

WESTERN LANDS AND TERRITORIAL GOVERNMENT

It was a simple but highly important issue that led the representatives of Maryland in the Congress to decline until 1781 to ratify the Articles. Maryland was a small state with no claims to the great unexploited area beyond the mountains. Her close neighbor, Virginia, had a claim to the land westward "from sea to sea," and other states had similar claims. Maryland feared to enter a confederation in which some of the members might grow tremendously

---

[5] Jefferson, *Notes on the State of Virginia*, 2nd ed., Phila., 1794, p. 170.

in population and wealth while she remained small. Her leaders insisted that the western lands should belong to all, to the whole confederation, and not to only a few. Virginia was particularly reluctant to yield on this point.

In 1780 Congress passed a resolution that paved the way for Virginia's action.[6] It provided that the lands ceded to the United States should be used for the common benefit of all, and said that such lands would be "formed into distinct republican states" to be admitted to the union on an equal basis with the other states. Virginia thereupon evidenced her intent to cede her claims northwest of the Ohio River to the United States, as other states had already done, and Maryland soon after ratified the Articles. By 1783, most of the western lands had been ceded to the United States.

In its closing days, too late to revive its own waning prestige, but not too late for the establishment of the new territorial policy, the Congress enacted the famous Ordinance of 1787 (the Northwest Ordinance).[7]

The purpose of this ordinance was to provide an orderly method of opening the western lands to settlement. It established a temporary government under a governor and certain other officers to be appointed by Congress; arranged for a second stage of territorial government, after the population had passed 5,000, a stage in which the residents would elect legislative representatives; and provided for the ultimate formation of five states within the territory, to be admitted to the union "on an equal footing with the original States in all respects whatever." Thus this momentous document settled the general outlines of the American policy of colonial expansion and territorial self-government, and paved the way for numerous later acts admitting states to the union until it included forty-eight self-governing states, reaching from the Atlantic to the Pacific.

SUMMARY: THE LESSONS LEARNED

One often hears the shallow and cynical assertion that "We learn from history that we learn nothing from history." It would be hard to find a more indefensible generalization. All human knowledge is in a sense historical. It is true that entire populations do not learn all the lessons of the past, and that very few people can simply absorb the truths of the past while doing other things. Knowledge is gained by experience and by effort.

The leaders who carried on the government through the War for Independence and the following years certainly learned a great deal from that experience and from the experience of colonial and state government. They learned the weakness and the insecurity of small states in the presence of large and ambitious ones. They learned the strength that comes from union. They saw the importance of a sound organization of government and the

---

[6] Commager, *op. cit.*, pp. 119-20.
[7] Commager, *op. cit.*, pp. 129-32.

need for an effective executive. They came to appreciate that governments must rest upon the people.

In fact they learned a great deal from the experiences of the colonies and of the revolting states. Not least among the lessons learned were the operations and results of a series of colonial governmental practices and institutions that we have not even attempted to describe. These included the advantages of written charters and constitutions, the role of the courts in keeping governments within reasonable bounds, the doctrine of limited government, the executive veto, and a number of others. The proof that they learned about these things is to be found in what they did very soon to reorganize the union in order to make it serve the national interest more effectively. What they wrote into the new Constitution of the United States in 1787 was not plucked out of the air or, except in small part, out of the books of political theorists. It came from solid experiences, both bad and good.—But all that will come in the next and other following chapters.

REFERENCES

Carl L. Becker, *The Declaration of Independence: A Study in the History of Political Ideas*, New York, 1922.

J. Q. Dealey, *Growth of American State Constitutions from 1776 to the End of the Year 1914*, New York, 1915.

Allan Nevins, *The American States During and After the Revolution, 1775-1789*, New York, 1927.

A. C. McLaughlin, *A Constitutional History of the United States*, New York, 1935.

W. F. Dodd, *The Revision and Amendment of State Constitutions*, Baltimore, 1910.

F. N. Thorpe, *The Federal and State Constitutions, Colonial Charters, and Other Organic Laws*, etc., 7 vols., Washington, D. C., 1909.

H. C. Hockett, *The Constitutional History of the United States, 1776-1826*, New York, 1939, espec. pp. 88-179.

Merrill Jensen, *The Articles of Confederation*, Madison, University of Wisconsin Press, 1940.

John M. Mathews and Clarence A. Berdahl, *Documents and Readings in American Government: National and State*, rev. ed., New York, 1940, pp. 13-34.

A. N. Christensen and E. M. Kirkpatrick, *The People, Politics, and the Politician: Readings in American Government*, New York, 1941, pp. 29-36.

CHAPTER 3

The Constitution Formed and Adopted

FORCES LEADING TOWARD STRONGER UNION

Neither the first state constitutions nor the governments under them, neither the Articles of Confederation nor the central agencies they created, can truly be said to have been a failure. Each was instrumental in doing at least the minimum things that were required to win the war for independence and to establish peace in America. The old problem of over-all organization was still unsolved, however—the problem of creating a national organization of the thirteen colonies (now states) so that they and others later admitted to the union, while continuing to govern themselves in all local matters, could act in unison in the settlement of common difficulties in peace as well as in war. Now the problem had been transferred wholly to America, and people could not evade it.

Need of Stronger Union. A stronger union was clearly needed. Standing by itself, not one of the "sovereign" states was strong enough or big enough. Only as "one people" could the Americans really claim "to assume among the Powers of the earth the separate and equal station to which," in Jefferson's language "the Laws of Nature and of Nature's God" entitled them. Various events of the postwar period strongly emphasized the weaknesses of the American political system. Among the most disturbing of all difficulties to men like Washington, Robert Morris, and Alexander Hamilton were the radical economic movements in the several states. The debtor classes, with their demands for cheap money, for the cancellation of debts, and for the right to use commodities to pay their bills, were everywhere organizing and agitating for their economic panaceas. In 1786 the paper money forces carried the elections in a number of states. In western Massachusetts under the leadership of Daniel Shays, impatient debtors broke out in rebellion against the government of the state.

A Turn to the Right. By this time, however, 1785-86, public sentiment had in general become somewhat more conservative than it had been ten years before. The radical leaders who in 1774-76 had whipped up the sentiment for independence had soon passed from power. To win the war, most of the states had turned to more capable and steadier leaders and organizers. On a small scale, something like a counter-revolution had taken place. Most of the people now wanted to settle down to work and trade. They were somewhat weary of political agitation. They were content to have won political independence, and had no heart to plunge at once into economic and social reforms. What the dominant classes now wanted was a firm government that would pay its debts and keep down the agitators, while the people went forward in the expansion of business and the development of the national domain, now reaching to the almost mythical Mississippi River on the west.

It may be that the conservatives exaggerated the evils of the time, but whether they did or not, they thought they saw foreign trade badly upset, tariffs and trade barriers growing up between the states, depreciation of the currency, public and private credit at a very low ebb, treaty rights being violated, contracts being impaired and property rights destroyed without legal process, the British continuing to occupy posts in American territory, the Spanish refusing to open the Mississippi to commerce, the continental army badly disorganized, and the states too weak and too much influenced by the radicals to give due protection to business and property.[1]

In short, men of substance were beginning to think more in national terms. The war for independence had done much to make one nation of the Americans, but little or nothing had been done to give the nation a common government. One of their leaders, Alexander Hamilton, summarized their views in one pithy sentence: "A *nation* without a *National Government* is an awful spectacle." [2]

STEPS TOWARD A NEW CONSTITUTION

For a few years the conservative leaders thought that by amendment of the Articles enough could be achieved to strengthen the Congress adequately. In particular they urged amendments to authorize Congress to levy and collect sufficient taxes to revive the national credit. Several different amendments to this effect were submitted by Congress to the states. Each failed of passage because the unanimous vote of the state legislatures was required, and in each case at least one legislature refused to give up to Congress any part of its taxing power.[3]

[1] For the background of the movement for the Constitution, see Beard, *The Rise of American Civilization*, New York, 1927, pp. 297-335; Schlesinger, *New Viewpoints in American History*, New York, 1922, pp. 184-99, "Economic Aspects of the Movement for the Constitution"; Hockett, *The Constitutional History of the United States, 1776-1826*, New York, 1939, espec. pp. 153-204.

[2] *The Federalist*, no. 85.

[3] See Nevins, *The American States During and After the Revolution*, pp. 606-63.

Annapolis Convention, 1786. The conservative leaders soon saw that the Congress was not the body to give leadership toward stronger government, and the Articles not the instrument in which to put faith. They proceeded, therefore, to ignore Congress and to start a separate movement for a stronger union. Virginia and Maryland having had occasion to discuss jointly the control of navigation on the Potomac, it occurred to some to suggest a wider conference of the states to discuss commercial regulations.

Resolutions framed in similar language were pushed through nine state legislatures in 1785 and 1786 to provide for the appointment of delegations to a conference at Annapolis in September, 1786, "to take into consideration the trade and commerce of the United States" and for other purposes. It is interesting to note how Congress was ignored in this movement, and to observe in it also a possible violation of the Articles which provided that

> No two or more states shall enter into any treaty, confederation or alliance whatever between them, without the consent of the united states in congress assembled.[4]

Only five states actually sent delegations to the Annapolis convention—too small a number for the action intended—but two leaders, Hamilton and Madison, induced the conference not to adjourn without proposing a new and still more inclusive convention of the states. The report adopted by the convention accordingly urged

> that speedy measures be taken, to effect a general meeting of the States, in a future convention, not only to discuss commercial questions, but also to take into consideration the situation of the United States, to devise such further provisions as shall appear to them necessary to render the constitution of the Federal Government adequate to the exigencies of the Union; and to report such an Act for that purpose to the United States in Congress assembled, as when agreed to, by them, and afterwards confirmed by the Legislature of every State, will effectually provide for the same.[5]

Congress being by this time nearly desperate in its struggle to meet the expenses of the United States as a whole, joined the movement by supporting the call for the proposed convention.

THE FEDERAL CONVENTION

Again the states were called upon to send delegates to a convention, and this time all responded except Rhode Island. All told, seventy-four members were appointed to the convention which assembled in Philadelphia, May 25, 1787, fifty-five attended one or more sessions, and thirty-nine signed the con-

[4] Articles of Confederation, Art. VI, par. 2.
[5] Commager, *op. cit.*, pp. 132-34, gives the proceedings of the convention.

stitution finally proposed. Washington was the choice for presiding officer, and a secretary was also appointed. The latter kept only the barest kind of record for the official journal, and it is from Madison's private notes on the debates (not published until 1840) that most of the knowledge as to what took place is derived. The members were pledged to secrecy, and kept their pledge with remarkable unanimity. Not until the proposed constitution was published did the people generally come to know what had been formulated.[6]

Many published accounts tell of the personnel of the convention. Thomas Jefferson and John Adams were absent on official missions in Europe. Two other great figures of the early revolutionary period, Samuel Adams and Patrick Henry, were not present. Despite these and a few other exceptions the convention contained practically all the important leaders of the times as well as certain persons of less fame and ability. Most of the members had had wide experience in public affairs, and were possessed of practical wisdom, but the convention was noteworthy also for the wide variety of talents it contained. There were scholars, writers, military leaders, lawyers, businessmen, and that venerable sage and wit, Benjamin Franklin. The outstanding members were undoubtedly Washington, Franklin, Madison, and Hamilton, but a large number of men of nearly first rank made the convention the effective working body it proved to be.

PLANS OF FEDERAL REORGANIZATION

Virginia Plan. As the convention members assembled, various plans were put forward for discussion. Two of these were of especial importance—the Virginia or large-state plan presented by Edmund Randolph, and the New Jersey or small-state plan, proposed by William Paterson.[7] The Virginia plan outlined a scheme for a strong new national government, with a two-chambered legislature, an executive, and a judicial department, and with power "to legislate in all cases to which the separate States are incompetent," and to enforce its own laws on individuals. Under this plan the large states would dominate the union, since representation was to be according to population or according to financial contributions to the national treasury. All members of the central government were to be paid liberally from the central treasury, and thus there would be less dependence of the national government on the states. While this plan spoke of correcting and enlarging the Articles of Confederation, it obviously pointed toward a wholly new constitution.

New Jersey Plan. The New Jersey plan was the reply of the small states to the centralizing, strong-government tendencies of the Virginia plan. It built

[6] Among the best short accounts of this famous convention are Max Farrand, *The Framing of the Constitution of the United States*, New Haven, 1913; R. L. Schuyler, *The Constitution of the United States: An Historical Survey of Its Formation*, New York, 1923; and A. C. McLaughlin, *A Constitutional History of the United States*, New York, 1935, pp. 148-97. There are, of course, many other accounts.

[7] Commager, *op. cit.*, pp. 134-38, gives also Hamilton's plan.

upon the Articles and the existing single-house Congress in which votes were by states and the delegations in Congress depended on the states for their pay. It proposed to add an executive to be chosen by Congress, and also a federal judiciary—the latter to have mainly the right to hear appeals from the state courts in certain types of cases. The powers of the central government were to include only the power to tax imports, to levy a stamp tax on documents, and to fix postal charges, plus the power "to pass Acts for the regulation of trade and commerce as well with foreign nations as with each other." All acts made in pursuance of powers vested in Congress were to be "the supreme law of the respective States . . . and . . . the Judiciary of the several States shall be bound thereby in their decisions, any thing in the respective laws of the Individual States to the contrary notwithstanding." [8]

Toward a National Government. Thus the New Jersey plan as well as the Virginia plan made the definite shift to the creation of a national government with power to pass laws binding on individuals. This was a conspicuous omission in the Articles, and on this point there was no serious disagreement in the convention. Both plans agreed also on the creation of executive and judicial branches of the central government. The plans differed on the extent of the power to be granted to the central authorities, and on the composition of Congress and the apportionment of representation in it. The Virginia plan, giving representation in Congress on the basis of population, would have thrown the control of the central government into the hands of the people of the large states; hence the large-state proponents of this plan were willing to give the central government very broad powers. The New Jersey plan held to the old ideas of equal representation of states without regard to population, and of state payment and control of their delegations in Congress. It proposed also to grant much less power to the central government, and to check the latter through having the state courts empowered to interpret and apply the federal laws. Thus the main lines of division within the convention were clearly drawn: large state *versus* small state; strong central government *versus* state sovereignty.

SETTLEMENT OF PRINCIPAL ISSUES

Representation in Congress. A great deal has been written about the so-called "compromises" in the convention. One great compromise there was, and that dealt with the composition of Congress and the basis of representation in it. Over this question the convention nearly broke up—the small states insisting on equality, the large ones on representation in proportion to population. The compromise reached now seems a simple one, but it was very hard for the two parties to accept. The Virginia plan had proposed a two-chambered legislature—the members of the larger house to be elected by the voters in the states in proportion to population or contributions, those of

[8] Commager, *op. cit.*, pp. 136, 137.

the smaller house to be chosen by the members of the other from persons nominated by the state legislatures. Under this plan the state legislatures had no direct control over either house, whereas in the existing Congress, favored by the small states, all members were chosen by and responsible to the state legislatures, and each state had one vote.

Compromise on Congress. In the compromise, two houses were provided. The upper house (Senate) became the direct successor of the old Congress. In it each state was to have just two members, and these were to be elected by the state legislatures. Thus state equality of voting right and state legislative control over members were retained. This house was also to have special powers over treaties and appointments, as in the case of the old Congress, thus giving the small states special weight in such matters. Membership of the larger house (House of Representatives) was then to be apportioned among the states according to population, and the members were to be elected directly by the voters in the states. All revenue measures, which would naturally draw most money from the large states, were to originate in this house in which the large states had greater representation. Since no law could be enacted without the consent of both houses, both large- and small-state members, when they considered the result of the compromise, were persuaded that they had protected all their essential interests, although to the very end of the convention there was some bickering between the two parties. There were many other points, large and small, on which adjustments had to be made, but none on which there was a major compromise such as that described above. Despite differences on political questions, the delegates were essentially united on the issue of protecting property rights and business.

DRAFTING AND SUBMISSION

Committees on Detail and Style. The convention proceeded in its early stages by discussing and adopting rather general resolutions in committee of the whole. When the number of those adopted had become rather considerable, it appointed a *committee on detail* to put its decisions into orderly form. This committee itself naturally introduced a considerable amount of new language, largely drawn from other public documents such as the Articles of Confederation and leading state constitutions. Its draft was then taken up in convention and debated section by section. At this stage there were numerous changes that called for further rewriting of the convention's work. For this purpose a separate committee was appointed, generally called the *committee on style*. Gouverneur Morris of Pennsylvania, a member of this committee, was mainly responsible for the redrafting given to the various sections at this stage. The document that finally issued from this committee was fairly clear, harmonious, and integrated as compared with that emanating earlier from the committee on detail, and so many were the changes in wording that even scholars will probably never know how much the later course of constitutional development was affected by this committee's work. Thereafter the convention made very few changes in the document on which it had labored so long.

A New Constitution Results. The question of submission of the Constitution for ratification troubled the members greatly. Many delegates were under definite instructions to do no more than to submit amendments to the Articles of Confederation. The convention's objective clearly could not be achieved in this way. A wholly new Constitution was being drafted, one in which a distinct central government was being set up with power to make and enforce laws against individuals. To have submitted such a document to the thirteen state legislatures in the hope of unanimous approval would have been sheer folly. But to proceed in any other way was distinctly unauthorized if not clearly revolutionary. The final decision was both bold and novel.

Submission to State Conventions. The convention itself represented a carrying forward of the idea worked out in Massachusetts between 1776 and 1780 of having a separate convention, a·body not charged with other duties, draft and propose a constitution. The same method was applied to obtain ratification of the new Constitution. It was agreed that

> The Ratification of the Conventions of nine States shall be sufficient for the Establishment of this Constitution between the States so ratifying the Same.[9]

The conventions proposed were to be elected separately in the several states. They were to represent the voters, not the legislatures. In setting nine states as a sufficient number to put the new Constitution into operation, the members were planning deliberately to overthrow the "Articles of Confederation and perpetual union between the States"; in appealing directly to the voters as represented in special conventions they were undermining to some extent the legislatures of the states. The new Constitution was not to be a mere treaty, however solemn, among sovereign states; but a "supreme Law" over them, decreed by the voters in conventions, and resting directly upon the people. "WE THE PEOPLE of the United States, . . . do ordain and establish this CONSTITUTION for the United States of America." [10]

RATIFICATION

As requested by the convention, the Continental Congress transmitted the proposed Constitution to the several state legislatures with the request that they arrange for the election and holding of state conventions to consider the proposal. Although under no legal compulsion to do so, the legislatures in all states except Rhode Island were persuaded by the friends of the new plan to make the necessary arrangements to test out the people's attitude toward it.

[9] U. S. Const., Art. VII.
[10] U. S. Const., Preamble.

Finally approved in the convention on September 17, 1787, the Constitution was ratified by the Delaware convention on December 7 of the same year. Several other states followed quickly, and then the ratifications began to come more slowly. By June 21, 1788, nine states had ratified, but two key states, New York and Virginia, still stood out. The opposition seemed to grow stronger with the passage of time, and it was only with great difficulty and by close votes that Virginia and New York were brought into line. North Carolina and Rhode Island remained outside, the former until 1789, the latter until 1790.[11]

It is well known that only a small percentage of the American people were entitled to vote in 1787 and 1788, when the ratifying conventions were elected, and that property qualifications kept many poor persons from participating. It is probably true, also, that on a direct referendum to those then entitled to vote, the Constitution would have been defeated in a number of the states and could not have gone into effect. This is one of the grounds for the statement frequently made that the Constitution is undemocratic—but more of that later.

Arguments Against Ratification. The grounds put forward for opposition to the Constitution covered a wide range. They were in some cases contradictory and at cross purposes. There were, however, two lines of argument important enough to examine. *First* was the opposition to centralization, coming from state and local political leaders and other friends of states' rights. Something of the old revolutionary opposition to a distant central government flared up again in the speeches in the state conventions and in many printed attacks on the Constitution. The friends of the Constitution called themselves "Federalists," which was technically correct, but which put the opposition at a disadvantage. Many of the latter clearly saw that the new Constitution really created a new government, a national government, for many important purposes, and that after its adoption the states would not be the same as they had been.

Second, and closely related, was the charge that there was no bill of rights to protect individuals against this new and potent government. Men pictured the complete wiping out of personal liberties by the new government, and cried out strongly against dictatorship and autocracy.

The obvious answers to these arguments—(a) that some centralization was needed, and (b) that, since the new central government would have only a limited range of powers, it would not be in position to invade personal liberties—were not enough to satisfy the opposition. In several states ratification was obtained only on the understanding that important amendments, including a bill of rights, would be promptly proposed by the new Congress to the states. With these understandings, and with eleven states under "the new

[11] For a more extended account of the ratification, see McLaughlin, A Constitutional History of the United States, pp. 198-223.

roof," the new government was established. Elections were held late in 1788, and between March 4 and April 30, 1789, when Washington was inaugurated at New York, the new government was set in operation.

THE FIRST TEN AMENDMENTS

Bill of Rights. The work of organizing the new government was then only begun. The first Congress faced a tremendous task in the creation of executive departments and a federal judiciary and in devising financial ways and means to launch the new government. This work was well done, but it took so much time that it delayed for some months the completion of one piece of unfinished business connected with the Constitution, namely, the framing and submission of certain amendments to constitute a bill of rights, as demanded by opponents of the Constitution during the struggle over ratification.

Several of the states submitted proposed amendments to Congress for consideration. Madison reduced them in number. Appropriate committees of the two houses then considered the proposals, reduced them further to twelve in number, and Congress submitted these in a group to the state legislatures. Not one of the twelve affected the framework of the national government. Nine dealt with the rights of individuals against the national government. These are the first nine amendments, and they constitute the major part of the national bill of rights. The Tenth Amendment deals with the reserved rights of the states and of the people. The other two, which were not ratified by the states, dealt with the apportionment of members in the House of Representatives, and changes in the compensation of members of Congress. With the adoption of the first ten amendments in 1791 the first great stage of national constitution-making came to an end.

INTERPRETATIONS OF THE MOVEMENT FOR THE CONSTITUTION

Looking back over this great episode in American history, different men have reached divergent and even opposite conclusions as to what was done and why.

1. A Gift from a Benevolent Providence. George Bancroft, the once-popular historian, not only accepted the well-known eulogy uttered by William E. Gladstone,[12] but also implied that some "invisible hand," some higher power leading men on to justice and happiness, guided the pens of those who wrote the Constitution.

> Do nations float darkling down the stream of the ages without
> hope or consolation, swaying with every wind and ignorant whither

[12] Gladstone's dictum was this: "As the British constitution is the most subtle organism which has proceeded from progressive history, so the American Constitution is the most wonderful work ever struck off at a given time by the brain and purpose of man."

they are drifting? or, is there a superior power of intelligence and love, which is moved by justice and shapes their course?

His whole glowing account of the formation and adoption of the Constitution seems to answer, "Yes, there is such a power, and it did help make our Constitution"; but at times he gives some credit also to the "calm meditation and friendly councils" of the men in the convention for a constitution that "excelled every one known before." [13]

2. A Development from the English Constitution. Other historians, looking mainly at the documents and the language used therein, have looked upon the work of 1787 and 1788 as a continuation on American soil of the great Anglo-Saxon struggle for orderly self-government, a struggle that dates back to far beyond Magna Charta.[14] To some of them it has seemed that the English-speaking peoples had special liberty-loving qualities that led them rorward almost inevitably to written constitutions with bills of rights and limits on the powers of government. Bancroft, too, held something of this view. Despite these exaggerations on the part of a few, the student will find that many clauses in both national and state constitutions can indeed be traced back to early English sources and others to colonial practices and experiences.

3. Economic Interpretation. A later group of historians, perhaps best represented by Charles A. Beard, finds the motivation back of the Constitution largely in the economic struggles of the times, and particularly in the drive of the property-owning classes to establish a system of government that would restore value and give adequate protection to their holdings of money, public securities, and land, and to their business enterprises. The various devices that state legislatures had adopted to enable debtors to avoid full and honest payment of their debts—devices that included the wholesale printing of paper money (as in Rhode Island) and the making of goods and even land "legal tender" [15] in the payment of debts—had scandalized the business and industrial leaders of the times, and had seriously disturbed the economic system.

It is Dr. Beard's conclusion that the first real steps toward making the Constitution were taken by a small group of able men personally interested in what they did because of their possession of money, public securities, manufacturing plants, shipping, and trade, and that "a large propertyless mass"

---

[13] *History of the Formation of the Constitution of the United States of America,* 3rd ed., 2 vols., New York, 1883—vol. II, pp. 3, 366-67.

[14] See for example Hannis Taylor, *The Origin and Growth of the American Constitution,* Boston, 1911, pp. 18-19, 70, 243-44, etc.; J. R. Tucker, *The Constitution of the United States,* Chicago, 1899, p. 177; F. J. Stimson, *The American Constitution,* New York, 1908, pp. 21 ff., 131 ff.

[15] "Legal tender" is anything that may legally be offered by one person to another in payment of a debt. It may be gold, silver, paper money, or anything else legally declared to be "legal tender." The states had the power to establish legal tender before the Constitution; now Congress has the power.

of people had no significant part in either the framing or the adoption of the Constitution. Hence the Constitution is "essentially an economic document," designed to protect private property rights.[16]

4. **Socialist Interpretation.** This "economic interpretation" of the Constitution has been given a special twist by various Socialist and Communist writers. Thus a one-time Socialist candidate for the Presidency has described the Constitution as founded "by the rich for the rich," [17] and a well-known Socialist writer, slightly modifying a Marxian formula, says that "the convention was simply a committee representing the commercial and manufacturing classes of the northern and middle states and the southern plantation interests." [18]

Economic Interpretation Analyzed. These varying interpretations of the movement for the Constitution give the student a wide range of choice. Those who have developed the third view outlined above have made out a strong case. The more impartial and objective among them neither praise nor blame the founders for their motives, but test their work rather by its results. Was the movement for a new national government on the whole a wise one, with generally satisfactory consequences, or was it not? They recognize the fact that economic motivation is one of the most common and understandable of human drives to action. Men want peace, order, prosperity, a right to live their own lives in their own way—and they frame governments to these ends. When private property rights are a recognized means to personal security and happiness, men will organize governments to protect those rights. In doing this through the Constitution, the framers found in English and American constitutional documents various devices such as bills of rights, due process clauses, the separation of powers, and others, that they incorporated for their own and other people's protection in the national constitution. Thus the third or economic interpretation does not deny or contradict but supplements the second which sees a continuity of English and American constitutional development.

National Debt and Sound Money Clauses. Among the many clauses that reveal the economic purposes of the Constitution are the following two:

> All Debts contracted and Engagements entered into, before the Adoption of this Constitution, shall be as valid against the United States under this Constitution, as under the Confederation.[19]

> No State shall . . . coin Money; emit Bills of Credit; make any Thing but gold and silver Coin a Tender in Payment of debts; pass

[16] *An Economic Interpretation of the Constitution of the United States*, 1935 ed., New York, especially the conclusions, pp. 324-25. See also A. M. Schlesinger, *New Viewpoints in American History*, pp. 184-99, and H. C. Hockett, *The Constitutional History of the United States*, 1776-1826, especially pp. 180-230.

[17] Allan L. Benson, *Our Dishonest Constitution*, New York, 1924, ch. I.

[18] A. M. Simons, *Class Struggles in America*, 3rd ed., Chicago, 1906, pp. 24-28.

[19] U. S. Const., Art. VI.

any Bill of Attainder, ex post facto Law, or Law impairing the Obligation of Contracts. . . .[20]

It was expected, of course, that under a strong central government the old government bonds (debts contracted) would rise in value and be paid in full. All government bondholders, including those in the convention, would benefit from this. The second clause here quoted aimed directly at preventing state legal tender laws and other cheap-money and contract-avoiding devices. It represents a victory of "sound money" over inflationist ideas.

Were These Provisions Dishonest? The interpretation of motives in human conduct is a very risky and difficult matter. To speak of the framers and the Constitution itself as "dishonest" because the document includes such clauses as these is not warranted.[21] These provisions are forthright and specific. They were published and debated in all the states. On the subject of the debts, for example, the framers might have done something quite different. (1) They could have said nothing in the Constitution about the subject, and have tried to conceal their true purpose which was to have the debts paid. This would have been dishonest. Or (2) they might have inserted a provision for repudiating the debts of the Confederation. Would this have been honest? It is generally accepted that a new government succeeding an old one is responsible for the old debts; and in the long run no government that repudiates old debts can have good credit when it needs to borrow in the future. The whole structure of public and private finance in an individualist system rests upon an honest willingness to meet all obligations as fully as possible.

Opposition Also Desired Protection of Property Rights. It is difficult to believe that the framers of the Constitution were seeking only to enrich themselves; it is also curious that their opponents at the time made so little argument out of the clauses here quoted. It is true that the opposition both in the federal convention and in the state ratifying conventions did not represent fully the poorest classes, but some of them surely stood nearer to the poor than many of those who favored the adoption of the Constitution. Yet even these and other opponents of the Constitution made relatively little of the provisions protecting property rights. Indeed in North Carolina, which came nearest to having manhood suffrage without property qualifications, where the convention represented men rather than property, the real objection to the Constitution was the lack of a bill of rights. From this convention, as from others, came demands for a bill of rights, and specific suggestions as to what the bill should contain. Two clauses that finally entered into the first ten amendments, and that were quickly ratified by the states, are significant of the attitude toward property rights of those who opposed the Constitution. These are:

[20] U. S. Const., Art. I, sec. 10, par. I.
[21] As in Allan L. Benson, Our Dishonest Constitution.

The right of the people to be secure in their persons, houses, papers, and effects, against unreasonable searches and seizures, shall not be violated. . . .[22]

No person shall . . . be deprived of life, liberty, or property, without due process of law; nor shall private property be taken for public use, without just compensation.[23]

These restrictions on the power of the national government, proposed by the opponents of the Constitution, suggest that all classes and practically all individuals at that time desired to have property protected against government interference or seizure. The time was one in which nearly all men believed strongly in the right of private property. Under these conditions surely the framers of the Constitution cannot be condemned for inserting clauses to protect the government's credit and individual property rights.

Popular Participation in Making of Constitution. That the Constitution was undemocratic in the present-day sense cannot be denied. The framers believed in property qualifications for voters, and in representative rather than direct democratic processes. Again in this there does not seem to have been any conspiracy against the people. The framers were not ahead of the times in their views on popular participation in government, but neither were they far behind. There was no popular referendum on the Constitution, but neither was there a strong demand for it. Massachusetts in 1780 was the first state to hold a referendum on a state constitution, New Hampshire followed soon after, but other states were generally unprepared for this procedure.

In deciding to submit the Constitution to state conventions in the several states the framers went as far in the direction of popular participation as the times and the laws permitted. Each state could set its own voting qualifications for electing representatives to the state convention. It is true that the elective franchise was quite undemocratic in most of the states and that only a small part of the people (and that generally the more well-to-do part) could vote in the elections; but the federal convention had no power to override the state laws in this matter.

Constitution a Middle-of-the-Road Document. In short, the Constitution was framed by a group of experienced and practical men, with a national point of view, representing the more prosperous elements in their states, to be sure, but representing also a great deal of the "will for the public good" that existed at the time. Under the whip of fear lest anarchy come to prevail and all the security of orderly government, normal business relations, and private property be destroyed, they did what they could in accordance with the sentiment of the times to ensure the kind of life that they and other Americans hoped to achieve. They did not rush forward toward democracy, but neither did they swing back to monarchy. Their work helped to guarantee

[22] U. S. Const., Amendment IV.
[23] U. S. Const., Amendment V.

the republican institutions already established in the several states, and it did not stand seriously in the way when the states soon after began to move on toward more democratic ways. The upshot was that Americans of all classes within the next generation or two came to revere the Constitution as very few documents in history have been revered. It became a new symbol of national unity and national greatness.

MAIN FEATURES OF THE CONSTITUTION

Whatever one may think about the motives and the forces that brought about the adoption of the Constitution or concerning the merits of particular clauses, in retrospect one can see that it was a great act of political constructiveness and invention. Among the features that were very unusual at the time were these:

1. *Republican Government.* The Constitution was definitely republican both for the nation and for the states. At that time monarchy was the prevailing form of government among all the leading powers, but after their decades of experience with partial self-government and their conflicts with the British royal power, the American people had no stomach for monarchs. And, of course, republicanism opened the door to genuine popular sovereignty.

2. *Written Constitution.* A written constitution for a nation was also something of a novelty. For this there were American precedents in the charters of several of the colonies, in the constitutions of the states, and in the Articles of Confederation.

3. *Federalism.* No doubt the greatest political invention in the new Constitution was federalism itself. Nothing exactly like it had ever existed before. In effect what had been done between 1774 and 1788 was to transfer the central government from London, where it was remote and irresponsible, across the Atlantic to America, where it was set up under a direct responsibility to the people. The new central government was authorized to perform for the whole American people what the British government had previously performed for all thirteen colonies, while the states were left free to do separately what the colonial governments had done. Explained in this way the matter looks very simple, but in fact it was a new sort of thing to have two levels of government operating over the same area and the same people, each empowered to tax and to make and enforce its own laws without interference by the other.

4. *Division of Powers and Limited Government.* To bring about this result it was necessary to define the powers of the central government, and thereby to create a "division of powers and functions" between the central government and the states. This idea of limiting the powers of a central or national government was also very unusual at the time, but it seemed to be necessary as a means of winning support for the adoption of the Constitution. At the

same time the legitimate acts of the central government were made "the supreme laws of the land."

5. *A New National Government.* A new government was also brought into existence in this process, a government for the whole nation, complete with legislative, executive, and judicial departments to handle all important national and international affairs. This was an essential step in the construction of the new federal system. In fact it proved also to be an important factor in unifying the nation.

6. *Separation of Powers.* In creating this new central government the experiment was tried of separating the powers of the government between the legislative, executive, and judicial branches, and enough "checks and balances" were introduced to make possible the preservation of the three branches without preventing their cooperation as parts of a single government.

7. *Amending Provision.* Finally the written Constitution within itself provided for methods by which it could be formally changed.

When all these features have been examined and have been viewed against the background of the types of government then most prevalent in Europe and throughout the world, the Constitution stands forth as undoubtedly one of the most original and constructive political documents of that time and of all times.

How it works, and what defects it has revealed in practice, will be considered more fully hereafter.

REFERENCES

Max Farrand, *The Framing of the Constitution of the United States*, New Haven, 1913.

Max Farrand (ed.), *The Records of the Federal Convention*, 4 vols., New Haven, 1938. The most complete collection to date.

J. Elliot, *The Debates in the Several State Conventions on the Adoption of the Federal Constitution*, etc., 5 vols., Philadelphia, 1836; reprints 1888, 1941.

U. S. Library of Congress, *Documents Illustrative of the Formation of the Union of the American States* (Charles C. Tansill, ed.), Washington, 1927. Notes of Madison and others. Most useful one-volume collection.

A. C. McLaughlin, *A Constitutional History of the United States*, New York, 1935, chs. XIII-XV.

R. L. Schuyler, *The Constitution of the United States: An Historical Survey of Its Formation*, New York, 1923.

C. A. Beard, *An Economic Interpretation of the Constitution of the United States*, New York, 1913, new ed., 1935.

Charles Warren, *The Making of the Constitution*, Boston, 1928.

A. M. Schlesinger, *New Viewpoints in American History*, New York, 1928, especially ch. VIII.

Hastings Lyon, *The Constitution and the Men Who Made It: The Story of the Constitutional Convention 1787*, Boston, 1936.

H. C. Hockett, *The Constitutional History of the United States, 1776-1826*, New York, 1939.

C. B. Swisher, *American Constitutional Development*, Boston, 1943, ch. 2.

Robert S. Rankin, *Readings in American Government*, New York, 1939, pp. 10-32.

John M. Mathews and Clarence A. Berdahl, *Documents and Readings in American Government: National and State*, rev. ed., New York, 1940, pp. 35-48.

A. N. Christensen and E. M. Kirkpatrick, *The People, Politics, and the Politician: Readings in American Government*, New York, 1941, pp. 36-54.

CHAPTER 4

The Constitution and How It Changes

"Constitutional government" is government according to a body of established fundamental laws and customs. The terms "constitutionalism" and "government of laws" convey much the same meaning. Both imply that the government itself is, and recognizes that it is, under a body of "rules of the game" and that it has no right to violate these rules in governing the people. The basic laws that limit the government, like the government itself, exist to protect the individual against arbitrary acts. When the government itself obeys the established rules, there is said to be a "government of laws and not of men."

To most informed Americans this will seem to be a very elementary idea, hardly worth repeating. But "a frequent recurrence to fundamentals" is especially important at this time of world crisis. A strong spirit and a constant practice of constitutionalism are indispensable to the preservation of popular government. The dictatorial regimes that recently threatened the destruction of popular government throughout the world, cloaked their actions in the garb of legality, yet proceeded on the assumption that they were above law, and even above morals.

Constitutionalism and government according to fixed and supreme laws are in the best American tradition of popular government. This is one reason for knowing the framework of basic laws that create and organize the government and define its powers and functions. The citizen needs to know the legal limits on government in order to protect his own rights and the democratic system. Basic laws determine also the rules for the practical operation of government, the division of labor between units of government, the procedures they should follow, and the means of making all parts of a complex mechanism work harmoniously together. Hence, for the best operation of government, legislators, and administrators also need to know the legal foundations and framework.

In the United States there are constitutions and other basic laws applicable to all levels of government. The term "constitution" itself has various meanings.

Constitution in Limited Sense. When a person says "the Constitution" or "the Constitution of the United States" he usually means the written document with its amendments to date, or a little more broadly, this document as interpreted by the courts. When he speaks of "the state constitution" he means the written constitution of a particular state. He does not usually think of statutes, treaties, customs, and other elements as parts of the constitution. In the United States, then, a thing is thought of as "unconstitutional" if it violates the written constitution of the nation or the state as interpreted by the courts. The study of "constitutional law," consequently, is the study almost entirely of judicial decisions interpreting the written constitution.

Constitution: Broad Definition. The constitution of a government in its widest and most correct sense for political science is the entire body of rules, both written and unwritten, legal and customary, that provide for the organization and procedure of the government, define its powers and functions, and set forth the fundamental rights and duties of the individual with respect to the government. In the sense of having such a body of rules, every government has a constitution. Even a dictatorship or an absolute monarchy has some rudiments of a constitution, providing at least a framework of organization under the autocrat. A local government has a constitution in this sense just as a national government has.

Written and Unwritten Constitutions. In no case are all the rules of a constitution set forth in a single written document. The constitution of Great Britain is said to be unwritten, because there is no one central document to which British citizens can point as embodying the main features of their government. The American national government, as well as each of the state governments, is said to have a written constitution, because each has one great document that is called its constitution, although in no case does that document include all the rules.

The fact here noted is not as important as two other differences between the British and the American constitutions. (1) The British constitution recognizes the power of the "king in parliament," in fact of Parliament itself, the legislative body, by ordinary law, to change any part of the constitution. Thus the British constitution stands on the same level as ordinary law, and not legally above such law. In the United States both the national and the state written constitutions are recognized as being above the ordinary law-making authorities, and subject to direct change only by special methods. (2) Because of the supremacy of Parliament in Great Britain, the courts of law do not have the power, and do not venture, to declare "unconstitutional" and illegal any act of Parliament. In the United States the courts have assumed and regularly exercise the power to pass on the constitutionality of acts of Congress, state legislatures, and local governments, i.e., to decide whether any such act involved in a case before them violates the written constitution of nation or state as interpreted by them. If they find an act unconstitutional, they feel obliged to refuse to enforce it.

Legal and Customary Rules. The legal rules of a constitution in the broad sense are those that have the force of law. Most of them will be enforced in the courts of law in cases properly brought before them. Thus the constitutional right to jury trial in certain cases will be enforced by the court in which the trial is to be held, or by a higher court on appeal. In the actual working constitution there are, however, a number of strictly *legal* rules that only the executive or the legislative branch can legally enforce. Such are, for example, the rules as to the qualifications of the members of legislative bodies. These are enforced by the separate houses, and no court unless expressly authorized by the constitution or by a valid law would enforce them, either to seat or to unseat a member.

But, in addition to these *legal* rules, there are customary ones that it would be exceedingly hard for anyone to enforce in case of a breach. For example, the custom was that Presidents should serve for not more than two terms. These customary rules are exceedingly important, and they hold for long periods. However, when the voters elected President Franklin Roosevelt for a third term, and then a fourth, there was no legal way to stop it, or to prevent his serving. In Great Britain the form of the government is largely based on custom.

In a broad sense, then, the *total constitution of a government* includes the following elements:

1. The written constitution, including formal amendments.
2. Important, enduring statutes that organize and regulate major branches, and departments of the government.
3. Court decisions interpreting and applying the written constitution and basic statutes.
4. Less important, but worthy of mention, are the opinions of public attorneys and the rules of major departments insofar as they deal with important matters.

These four elements are all parts of the *law*. Finally there is the non-legal element:

5. The customs and practices that in fact determine the form and operation of the government.

Written Constitution of United States. This document, as originally approved by state conventions in 1787 and 1788, and as amended to date, is both a federal constitution, since it is the basis of the federal union among the states, and a national constitution, since it sets up and grants powers to the national government. Even with its twenty-one amendments it is a document of under 7,000 words.[1] Its first three articles provide, respectively, for the legislative, executive, and judicial branches; a fourth deals with states, interstate relations, and territories; a fifth provides for constitutional amend-

---

[1] For the text of the Constitution see pp. 559-573.

ments; and a sixth contains the famous "supreme Law of the Land" clause. Of the amendments, the first nine and parts of the Thirteenth, Fourteenth, and Fifteenth (Civil War Amendments) constitute a bill of rights for individuals. The document as a whole deals almost entirely with fundamental matters and, among written constitutions, it is to this day a model of clear and comprehensive statement.

This Constitution does not stand by itself. It is only part of an integrated system of laws that includes national statutes and treaties, state constitutions and statutes, and other groups of legal provisions. Nevertheless the written Constitution of the United States is at the very pinnacle of the complex American legal system. It is the keystone of the arch. By its own terms it stands first, and without qualification, among the elements that make up the "supreme Law of the Land."

> This Constitution, and the Laws of the United States which shall be made in Pursuance thereof; and all Treaties made, or which shall be made, under the Authority of the United States, shall be the supreme Law of the Land; and the Judges in every State shall be bound thereby, any Thing in the Constitution or Laws of any State to the Contrary notwithstanding.[2]

This status of priority over other laws was almost necessary to a Constitution that creates a national government and that deals with the highest subjects in government. For these several reasons it may be argued that the power to change this Constitution is the highest law-making power in the United States. We turn next to a consideration of how the Constitution is changed from time to time.

CHANGING THE CONSTITUTION

That constitutions like other laws have to be changed from time to time to keep them abreast of human needs and knowledge is scarcely open to question. What is more debatable and worthy of the closest analysis are the ways in which they are changed. A mainly customary constitution like that of Great Britain appears to be in many ways more flexible and adaptable to changing needs. In the United States the process of constitutional change is more complex and in part more difficult.

Constitutions have been likened to man-made structures such as buildings, and also to natural organisms. The difference is presented by the question: Are constitutions made and changed by man, or do they simply come into existence and then grow and change by natural processes unaided by man, like trees and animals? Neither one of these two processes exactly fits the facts concerning constitutions. Men do not fully control either the material and cultural conditions that give rise to the need for constitutional change,

[2] U. S. Const., Art. VI, par. 2.

or the accumulated background of ideas from which they must draw when they propose to make a change.

Nevertheless the framework of governments and the provisions of constitutions are being changed constantly and consciously and the process of change is largely controlled and directed by men. Almost every change in government can be traced back to the conscious decision of someone. At times there are confusion and apparently aimless growth in constitutions because (a) decisions are made by many different authorities and frequently conflict, or (b) very few men who make decisions are able to predict the full *consequences* of their decisions, so that results follow that neither they nor anyone else had expected.

Changes in the actual or working Constitution of the United States take place in the following principal ways:

1. By the decisions and actions of Congress, the President, the Supreme Court, giving new meanings to old words, broadening or narrowing them, and so on.

2. By Congressional statutes that add to or fill in the details of the written Constitution.

3. By changes in the "customs" or "usages" of the Constitution.

4. By formal amendments to the written Constitution. This is the only method that changes the text of the written document. The other methods achieve changes in the actual Constitution by subtler means.

JUDICIAL DECISIONS AND CONSTITUTIONAL CHANGE

Foreigners generally look upon the power of the Supreme Court of the United States to pass upon the constitutionality of acts of Congress as the most distinctive feature of the American government. They seem to think of the occasional decisions of that court in which Congress is held to be without power to do something, as the most important of all acts affecting the Constitution. As a matter of fact these decisions are important, yet they are only the most striking and dramatic examples of a regular judicial activity that runs from the very lowest courts up through the ranks to the highest court in the land. In the course of this activity every government, local, state, and national, has its acts scrutinized by the courts from day to day, in cases regularly brought before the courts. The whole subject of "judicial review" is so important that a separate chapter is devoted to analyzing it.[3] Here we consider only one question, namely the extent to which judicial decisions make changes in the Constitution.

The fact is that Americans live under "the Law of the Land." Every person, whether an official or a private citizen, is under substantially the same general laws, and subject to the same courts. Anyone who thinks his rights are being violated by any officer of a government may usually, in some legal way, test

[3] See ch. 18, below.

his rights before the courts and obtain a decision. It is hard for the courts to reach and control such high officials as the President or the Congress, but most laws are carried out by lower officers, and these can nearly all be checked in some way by the courts. And so the tax collector, the sheriff, the mayor, the state public utilities commission, the state or local health department, the Postmaster General, or Secretary of the Interior, to give a few examples, are liable any day to be haled into court to show by what right they do certain things. They plead that they are acting under a statute of Congress, or a state statute, or a city ordinance, but the irate citizen contends that this so-called legal enactment is against the constitution, national or state.

In deciding such cases the courts must usually answer "Yes" or "No" to some specific questions. Did the state have the power to pass the tax law in question? Did Congress have the power to depart from the gold standard in paying government bonds? Did the local school have the power to require school children to salute the flag, or does this deny some constitutional right of parents or children? The answer to each of these questions presumably makes a little more clear and sharp the legal powers of all branches of government, their organization, and the procedures they must follow, although actually this is not always the case. Usually the state supreme court settles finally the questions that concern local government and some that concern the state, while the Supreme Court of the United States settles all national questions and such state and local questions as arise under the United States Constitution.

Do the courts in this way "change" the constitution? There are those who assert that they do not. To them the law is an inexorable thing that follows perfect laws of logic to incontrovertible conclusions. The courts, they say, merely "declare what the law is," as when the arithmetic teacher assures the pupil that two and two make four. This view is really too naïve.

Courts are made up of judges, and judges are human beings, fallible like all the rest of mankind, though generally well learned in the law and conscientious to a high degree. They declare what they think the law is, but where no signs point a clear path they naturally say the law "is" what they think it "should be." In short, there is a wide range of choice for the judges in many cases. In exercising this choice they fill gaps in the clauses of the Constitution and help turn the course of government this way or that. Where they merely sustain what the government does, their influence is less perceptible than where they declare its action unconstitutional. To fill a gap is to make a change. In short, the courts undoubtedly make changes in the framework of laws controlling the government of the United States, and thereby they make changes in the actual Constitution.

It is sometimes argued, however, that the courts merely decide particular cases, and that their decisions are binding only in those cases. This appears to be true, but when in any case a court declares an act unconstitutional, the other branches of government usually abide by the decision, discontinue the line of action held invalid, and even in some cases abolish whole departments and functions previously established. Lower courts also abide by the decision in future cases. Furthermore a decision against State A is a precedent to prevent all the other forty-seven states from trying the same thing. Thus a single decision has widespread and long enduring consequences.

ACTIONS BY CONGRESS AND THE PRESIDENT

It would be a mistake to think of the courts alone among the branches of government as having the power to interpret the actual Constitution. Each of the other branches must also construe its own powers under the Constitution. Indeed, before any matter affecting the powers and actions of the national government can get into the courts for decision, one or both of the other departments must have acted. Let us consider, for example, the question of child labor. Congress, on the recommendation of the President, passed two different laws, one to regulate child labor that affected interstate commerce and the other to tax the products of child labor shipped in interstate Commerce. The Supreme Court held first one and then the other act to be unconstitutional.[4] Congress and the President persisted in thinking that the national government had power to regulate this subject. Finally Congress passed the Fair Labor Standards Act of 1938 which forbade the interstate shipment of goods made by child labor. This time the Supreme Court upheld the act of Congress, and reversed its earlier decisions.[5]

There are many other instances of actions by Congress, by the President, or by the two jointly, in which a decision must first be made by them as to their constitutional power to act. This is because the courts of the United States refuse to give "advisory opinions" in advance of action; hence the decision on powers must first be made by the branch that is to take the action. In many instances the question of constitutionality does not get to the courts at all, and in others it does not get there for a long time. Meanwhile the political department's decision thus made stands as the practical interpretation of the Constitution. It is in fact, a part of the actual Constitution until it is changed. If later the appropriate branch of the government changes its view and acts upon a new interpretation of its powers, that in turn becomes for the time being a part of the actual or operative Constitution.

STATUTORY AMPLIFICATION

Even where an express power vested in Congress by the written Constitution is clear and comprehensive, it is still up to Congress to act to put the power into effect. The written Constitution is very short. It provides only very sketchily for the departments of administration and their functions, for

[4] Hammer v. Dagenhart (1918), 247 U. S. 251; Bailey v. Drexel Furniture Co. (1922), 259 U. S. 20.
[5] U. S. v. Darby Lumber Co. (1941), 312 U. S. 100.

the organization and procedure of the courts, and for other important matters such as naturalization, citizenship, and civil rights. When Congress proceeds to enact legislation on these important matters it is, in effect, amplifying the written Constitution, or filling in its details.

Some of these acts that amplify the written Constitution and provide for the actual working organization of the government are nearly as important and almost as enduring as the written constitution itself. The National Judiciary Act, the Interstate Commerce Act, the Civil Service Law, and the Sherman Anti-Trust Law are outstanding examples of important national statutes. True it is that these must conform to the written Constitution as interpreted by the courts. This hurdle once surmounted, they rise almost to the position of parts of the Constitution itself.

THE CUSTOM OF THE CONSTITUTION

That the actual or working constitution of a government is made up in large part of usages and customs is not seriously questioned. How large a part they play in government is not known. They loom very large in the national government, where some of the most important relationships and operations are determined by customary practices. There is good reason to believe that in the government of the future usage and custom will play an increasing role while legalism will decline.

Some examples of national usages that modify constitutional practice without having been enacted as law by anyone are as follows:

1. The practice that representatives in Congress must have residence in their districts; the written Constitution requires only residence in the state.

2. Presidential electors, far from being free agents in balloting for President, as the Constitution seems to imply, are little more than "rubber stamps" for recording the will of the voters who elected them.

3. The method of nominating candidates for the Presidency, and thus in effect of limiting the choice of both voters and electors, is almost entirely a matter of usage.

4. Cabinet members are by custom excluded from addressing either house of Congress, although one exception has been made.

5. The Cabinet itself rests mainly upon custom, not on law.

Some of these usages, such as the methods of nominating candidates for the Presidency, and electing the President, clearly ignore the intention of the framers of the Constitution. Here the provision of the written Constitution is almost a dead letter as a result of custom and usage.

The text of the written Constitution can be changed by formal amendments. Amplifying statutes can be changed by later statutes. Later court decisions overrule or change earlier ones, and change also the meanings of other parts of the Constitution. But how are customs changed? To this no direct and simple answer can be given. A strong personality may override earlier customs with impunity. President Wilson broke with custom (a) when he addressed Congress in person, instead of by written message, and (b) when he went on a mission to a foreign country during his Presidency. Franklin Roosevelt did the same when he broke the two-term tradition. The growth of the party system wrought many important changes in American government, and so too did the strong swing toward democratic control of the government that marked the nineteenth century. United States Senators had in fact become directly chosen by the voters in some states because a militant democracy demanded it, long before the Constitution authorized direct election.

METHODS OF AMENDING THE WRITTEN CONSTITUTION

The methods of changing the actual Constitution that are discussed in the preceding pages leave the text of the written Constitution unchanged, however much they may add to it or modify political usages. The Constitution itself makes definite provision for formal amendments and revisions.

This provision, Article V, is exceedingly important. Its presence in the Constitution was one of the factors in overcoming the opposition to adoption, for if amendments could be made by a regular and orderly procedure there was less reason for rejecting the whole document. As Washington said in a letter to Patrick Henry, at the beginning of the struggle for ratification of the Constitution :

> I wish the Constitution, which is offered, had been more perfect; but I sincerely believe it is the best that could be obtained at this time. And, as a constitutional door is opened for amendments hereafter, the adoption of it, under the present circumstances of the Union, is in my opinion desirable.[6]

The article on amendments reads as follows:

> The Congress, whenever two-thirds of both Houses shall deem it necessary, shall propose Amendments to this Constitution, or, on the Application of the Legislatures of two-thirds of the several States, shall call a Convention for proposing Amendments, which, in either Case, shall be valid to all Intents and Purposes, as part of this Constitution, when ratified by the Legislatures of three-fourths of the several States, or by Conventions in three-fourths thereof, as the one or the other Mode of Ratification may be proposed by the Congress; Provided that no Amendment which may be made prior to the Year One thousand eight hundred and eight shall in any Manner affect the first and fourth Clauses in the Ninth Section of the first Article; and that no State, without its Consent, shall be deprived of its equal Suffrage in the Senate.

[6] Letter of September 24, 1787, quoted in Beck, *The Constitution of the United States*, p. 189, n.

What Are Amendments? It will be noticed that this provision refers only to "Amendments." This term has never been precisely defined. Amendments are commonly thought of as rather minor changes, while the term "revision" generally implies a more complete overhauling, even when it falls short of the adoption of a completely new constitution. On its face, therefore, the Constitution does not seem to provide for either extensive revision or for the proposal of a wholly new constitution. Since this particular question has never been raised under the United States Constitution, no definite answer to it can be given. There is reason to believe, however, that the term "amendments" is broad enough to cover very substantial revisions. It is a frequent practice in legislative bodies to "amend" a bill by striking out all except the title and the enacting clause, and putting in place of the matter striken out a wholly new measure.

Power of Amendment. While the quantitative question of the extensiveness of amendments has not been directly raised, the qualitative question as to the nature of amendments has arisen. The Eighteenth Amendment to the Constitution, prohibiting the manufacture and sale of liquors, was violently opposed by many people. Various cases involving it were carried to the Supreme Court. One contention was that the amendment was so drastic an invasion of the sphere of the states and of individuals and that it so completely changed the character of our government, that it could not be considered an amendment at all.[7] It did not change anything in the Constitution, but added something entirely different to it. These and similar contentions were overruled by the court, and the amendment was wholly sustained.

Express Limit on Amending Power. The amending power is, therefore, not limited by any rule as to the extensiveness of the amendments to be made; or as to the subject matter of amendments except one. The one exception now still effective is stated expressly in the last clause of Article V—"that no State, without its Consent, shall be deprived of its equal Suffrage in the Senate." The Senators might conceivably be reduced to one from a state, or increased to three or more, but each state must have the same number, and they must have equal votes. To this extent the Constitution appears to be a compact among the states, and unchangeable without the consent of all. It is very unlikely, of course, that the Senate will in the near future cast a two-thirds vote to propose an amendment to abandon the equality of the states in the Senate. A national constitutional convention might propose such a change, but then it is very unlikely that three-fourths of the states would ratify the proposal. Some day the question may arise, however, and the demand for the change may be great. Could it then be accomplished, or is this one point on which the Constitution cannot legally be altered?

It has been suggested that it can be done legally by two successive amendments. The first would simply repeal the proviso that now prohibits an amend-

[7] See National Prohibition Cases (1920), 253 U. S. 350, and Leser v. Garnett (1922), 258 U. S. 130.

ment depriving the states of equal suffrage in the Senate. The second would be an amendment to specify the number of Senators from each state, or the ratio in which they should be apportioned. Other measures that would achieve the same substantial results would be (a) a series of amendments taking from the Senate practically all its important powers, but leaving the Senate in existence as an almost functionless organ like the human appendix, or (b) an amendment abolishing the Senate—for equality of representation in the Senate can have no meaning if there is no Senate. Either of these proposals would require a very strong national movement for a one-chambered Congress, and even a large national majority would not be certain to have its way.

Amending Procedure. The *power* to change the federal Constitution is, then, ample for all practical purposes. To be legal under the present Constitution, the amendments must follow the *procedure* laid down, and be approved by the requisite majorities. It will be noticed that the procedure calls for two related steps, (a) proposal and (b) ratification. The proposal is always a national one, being made by Congress or a national constitutional convention. Ratification is a matter that can be effected only by the state legislatures or by conventions in the states. The federal structure of the American governmental system is nowhere more clearly shown than in the necessity for joint national and state action in amending the Constitution.

It has been said that there are four ways of amending the Constitution. This statement arises from the fact that there are two ways of proposing and two of ratifying amendments, and that either method of proposal may be linked up with either method of ratification. The four possibilities are shown in the accompanying diagram.

In fact the first method (proposal by Congress, ratification by the state legislatures), has been used in all cases but one. The Twenty-first Amendment, repealing the Eighteenth, followed the second procedure (proposal by Congress, ratification by state conventions). Methods 3 and 4 have not been used for amendments, but Method 4 is very nearly the same as that used in 1787-88 for the proposal and ratification of the Constitution itself.

METHODS OF AMENDING THE UNITED STATES CONSTITUTION

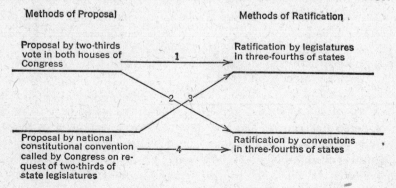

Proposal by Congress. The proposal of an amendment by Congress requires a two-thirds vote in each house. This has been held to mean two-thirds of those present and voting, assuming at least a quorum to be present. It is not necessary to have the affirmative votes of two-thirds of all members, both those present and those absent. Neither is it necessary to send the proposal to the President for his signature. In proposing constitutional amendments Congress is exercising a constituent power, and not a power of ordinary legislation; hence the President's power of veto over ordinary laws and resolutions does not apply. Moreover, his negative to a proposal could do little in most cases except to cause delay, since the measure would already have received the two-thirds vote needed to override his veto.

Proposal by a National Constitutional Convention. Evidently believing that there would be times when Congress would refuse to propose amendments desired by the state legislatures, the framers of the Constitution inserted the clause requiring Congress to call a national constitutional convention whenever requested so to do by two-thirds of the state legislatures. The words of the Constitution, "shall call a convention," imply a strong moral obligation on Congress to act, but it is difficult to see how a reluctant Congress could be forced to do so. Thus far it has failed to act, and although in the past 150 years most of the states have requested the call at one time or another, there has been no such concerted movement of the states at any time as would suggest that sort of united action by the state legislatures that the Constitution seems to contemplate. The requests of the states should clearly come within a reasonably short period of time, and Congress undoubtedly has power to decide what that time shall be.

Whenever a convention comes to be called, Congress will have to designate how it shall be composed, how the members shall be elected, and possibly how they shall vote (whether by states or otherwise), and finally how the convention's proposals shall be ratified, whether by legislatures or by conventions in the states. The convention alone will propose the amendments, few or many as it may see fit, but Congress will have considerable control over its composition and over the process of ratification.

A recent drive by various groups who claim to represent taxpayers, for a constitutional amendment to limit all national income and estate taxes to not over 25 per cent, has taken the form of a demand for a constitutional convention to submit the proposal. In the early stages of the movement a number of state legislatures were induced to petition Congress to call a convention to submit such an amendment to the state legislatures. The proponents argued as if Congress could be forced to call the convention whenever two-thirds of the state legislatures requested it, that the convention would have to approve their proposed amendment, and that it would have to submit it to the state legislatures rather than to state conventions for ratification, since that is what their petition called for. None of these things is required by the Constitution. There is no way by which the legislatures can force Congress to act. If Congress ever does call a convention to propose constitutional amendments that convention will be free to do as much or as little as it sees fit, and to propose only such amendments as it considers wise.

Ratification by State Legislatures. When proposing constitutional amendments, Congress also designates the method of ratification to be used. Twenty-five out of twenty-six proposed amendments have been submitted by Congress to the state legislatures. Of these twenty have been adopted, four rejected, and one is still pending—the Child Labor Amendment. Clearly Congress does not submit amendments until they are urgently demanded and have good prospects of being ratified.

Ratification is not complete until the amendment has been approved by both houses of the legislatures of three-fourths of the states. This is a high majority requirement, since thirteen states can prevent thirty-five from obtaining what they desire. In fact, if only one house in each of thirteen states fails to ratify, the amendment is lost. In one case an amendment failed of ratification because in a single state, perhaps through oversight, only one house passed the resolution for ratification. This amendment, submitted to the states in 1810, provided for the loss of American citizenship by those who accept foreign titles and offices. It was actually considered to have been adopted, and was printed for a time in unofficial editions of the Constitution.

By "the legislature" is meant, of course, the ordinary legislative body of the state. The states that have vested legislative power in the voters to be exercised through the initiative and referendum, or the latter alone, have no power to refer federal constitutional amendments to the voters. The national Constitution fixes upon the ordinary legislatures as the proper bodies to ratify amendments, when so designated by Congress, and the states have no power to change this requirement.[8]

Objections to Ratification by State Legislatures. Those who would make the Constitution even more difficult to amend than it is, have criticized ratification by state legislatures on the ground that a legislature elected before an amendment is submitted by Congress has no mandate from the people to act upon that amendment. Many insist, too, that a legislature in any case is unfitted for this work, since it has many other things to do and also has its own special interests to protect. During the general onslaught on the Eighteenth Amendment it was proposed by several members of Congress to change the amending clause so that after the legislatures had ratified an amendment it should also be submitted to the voters in the states, and that ratification should not be complete until both the legislatures and the voters in three-fourths of the states should have approved. This had the appearance of a democratic proposal, but in fact it would have made it far more difficult even for a large majority of the people to change the Constitution.

Ratification by State Conventions. In addition to the twenty-five proposed amendments submitted to the state legislatures, one, the twenty-sixth to be

[8] Hawke v. Smith (1920), 253 U. S. 221.

proposed, was submitted to state conventions. It was ratified as the Twenty-first Amendment, and its main result was to repeal the Eighteenth or Prohibition Amendment. Those who desired the repeal thought for some time of having the states petition Congress to call a national constitutional convention to propose repeal, but finally concluded that public sentiment was at such a point that Congress would make the proposal to repeal, and that state conventions could be easily elected to achieve the result. In this they were correct. Congress passed the resolution for the repealing amendment and designated state conventions as the proper ratifying bodies. It did not specify how the conventions should be elected or constituted. Each state legislature passed its own law or resolution for this purpose. Some of the state conventions were small, some large. The largest was Indiana's with 329 members; the smallest New Hampshire's with only 10; nearly half had 50 members or fewer. Over half were elected by state-wide votes, some by districts, and a few by a combination of the two.[9]

Convention Method Permits Popular Referendum. The significant feature of the process was that there was practically a nation-wide popular referendum on the prohibition question, and on a constitutional amendment. The Supreme Court had held that an amendment referred by Congress to state legislatures could not be acted on by referendum vote in the states. But under the convention method the situation was different. In each state those who favored repeal of the Eighteenth Amendment put up their lists of candidates for the convention, and the opponents put up rival slates. Usually there was just one slate for each side and the voters had a clear-cut issue on which to vote. As soon as the election was over the issue was settled. In almost every state the candidates pledged to the repeal of prohibition won the election. When the conventions met, the members were already committed to vote for repeal, and did so. They were mere "rubber stamps" to record the election result, and exercised little more freedom of choice than the usual partisan slates of presidential electors.

Problems of Convention Method. A simple way has been found, therefore, to hold a nation-wide referendum on constitutional questions. Several points need to be noted, however. *First*, there is a clear-cut referendum only when a single issue is presented. The voters do not vote directly on the proposed amendment, but on members to a convention. If two or more amendments were submitted at once, the issues would become more and more confused, and the delegates to the convention could not be so definitely pledged. A state might provide in such case an advisory referendum vote on the several questions, but it could hardly be binding in the legal sense. *Second*, when only one amendment is submitted at a time, the convention becomes in no true sense a deliberative body. Its work can be done in an hour or less, by a single

---

[9] See E. S. Brown, "The Ratification of the Twenty-first Amendment," *Am. Pol. Sci. Rev.*, vol. 29, pp. 1005-17; U. S. Dept. of State, *Ratification of the Twenty-first Amendment to the Constitution of the United States*, pamphlet, Washington, 1934.

vote of members already pledged for or against the amendment. This is very far from the theory of the nature of a constitutional convention. *Third*, a number of state legislatures might interfere in the process by refusing to provide for the conventions. This might happen particularly in the case of amendments proposed to transfer powers from the states to Congress. Under its authority to pass laws "necessary and proper" to carry out the powers vested in the national government Congress might meet this situation, but new laws and machinery would probably have to be devised. *Fourth*, in any case the final vote on the amendment is by states, and a three-fourths majority of the states is required.

Beginning with Massachusetts before 1780, the states developed in the next fifty years a theory of constitution making that was based on the following controlling propositions: (a) That a constitution is a higher form of law, above the legislatures and the ordinary laws made by legislatures; (b) That it emanates from the people and should be approved by them; and (c) That a constitutional convention, elected by and responsible to the people for the sole purpose of proposing and submitting constitutional changes, is a better instrument for that purpose than the ordinary legislature.

It must be clear from the discussion above that the pure theory of the making and changing of constitutions by conventions and popular votes has made but little headway in the national field. The ordinary national legislature, Congress, has proposed all amendments to date, and the ordinary state legislatures have been asked to ratify them in all cases but one. In that one exceptional case the state conventions used were simply registrars of the voters' will, and not true constitutional conventions.

Time Limits on Ratification. In proposing constitutional amendments, Congress has recently begun to specify time limits within which amendments must be ratified. The purpose in so doing is to make proposal and ratification a continuous or connected process, so that within a reasonably short period the whole procedure will be completed and there will be evidence of a real meeting of the minds of Congress and the states. Ratifications spread over a period of fifty or more years, for example, would not indicate any real concurrence of opinion among the states at any one time. In proposing the Eighteenth Amendment, Congress set a period of seven years within which time ratification, to be effective, should be completed. The right of Congress to set such a reasonable time limit was sustained by the Supreme Court.[10]

The Child Labor Amendment, submitted to the states in 1924, contained no time limit on ratifications. In 1925 both houses of the Kansas legislature expressly rejected the amendment. Twelve years later both houses approved the proposal, but the vote in the state senate was so close that the opponents promptly applied to the state courts to prevent the secretary of the senate from certifying that it had carried. It was argued not only that Kansas had already rejected the amendment, but also that so long a time had passed since Con-

[10] Dillon v. Gloss (1921), 256 U. S. 368.

gress proposed the amendment that it had lost its vitality. The state supreme court refused to act to stop the certification, and the opponents resorted to the Supreme Court of the United States for a decision favorable to their cause. That court refused to declare either that prior rejection of an amendment prevented later ratification, or that the thirteen years from 1924 to 1937 made such an unreasonably long period that the proposal had lost its vitality.[11] Badly divided on other points, the judges voted 7 to 2 that the question whether a constitutional amendment has been adopted is not a judicial but a political question, and one for Congress, not the courts, to decide. This decision makes clearer than before the tremendous power of Congress over constitutional amendments.

Criticisms of Federal Amending Process. The first twelve amendments were adopted without great difficulty. Indeed the first ten merely carried out the understanding that there would be a bill of rights. Then followed a period of sixty years (1804-65) in which Congress proposed only two and neither was adopted. During the Civil War period the northern-controlled Congress proposed amendments to abolish slavery, and to guarantee Negroes citizenship and the right to vote. These proposals were not only pro-Negro but also anti-state rights and centralizing in their tendency. Southern opposition was so strong that Congress had to resort to very dubious methods, especially in the case of the Fourteenth Amendment, to get them adopted. Whether or not they could be adopted depended on what states and what governments Congress would recognize in the South.

Some years later when farmer and labor groups procured the enactment of state and national laws to regulate business, break up monopolies, and impose a national income tax, and the Supreme Court took a turn to the right and began to invalidate much of this legislation, progressives generally began to complain that the amending process was too difficult, and even their conservative opponents thought they were secure against change through constitutional amendments. Both sides were rather surprised when the income tax amendment (XVI) and the one for the direct election of senators (XVII) were adopted in 1913. Right after World War I came two others, the one on prohibition (XVIII) in 1919 and that on woman suffrage (XIX) in 1920, while in the depth of the Great Depression (1933) came two more—the Twentieth, regulating the terms of the President and Congressmen, and the sessions of Congress, and the Twenty-first, repealing the Eighteenth Amendment. In each case two-thirds of Congress had proposed and three-fourths of the states had ratified the amendments. Thus the amending process seems to be reasonably workable, particularly in times of great stress and agitation. Indeed the opponents of the prohibition amendment thought the process was too easy. The experience with the Child Labor Amendment, submitted in 1924 and still unratified, reveals, however, the difficulty of getting state legislatures to relinquish further power to Congress.

[11] Coleman v. Miller (1939), 307 U. S. 433, 59 S. Ct. 972.

Since the Supreme Court has changed its views on the powers of Congress to regulate interstate commerce and employment connected therewith, the Child Labor Amendment has become much less important. Indeed, as long as the Supreme Court holds its present very liberal views toward the powers of both Congress and the state legislatures, the whole federal amending process will have less significance.

In closing, then, a word may be said about the relationships among the various methods by which the actual Constitution may be changed. The President and Congress will in general be aware of public needs and desires and will tend to interpret their powers as adequate to meet those needs and satisfy those desires. Except in a few matters of organization of government as set up under the written Constitution there will not be much need for national constitutional amendments in the near future unless the Supreme Court starts in once more to invalidate important legislative measures on the ground that they are beyond the powers of the national government. But if the court will recognize the coordinate authority of the other branches of the national government and their special competence to deal with all matters of policy and administration, the nation may go a long time without amending the written Constitution.

REFERENCES

J. W. Garner, *Political Science and Government*, New York, 1932, ch. 18.

R. G. Gettell, *Political Science*, New York, 1933, ch. 15.

W. F. Willoughby, *The Government of Modern States*, rev. ed., New York, 1936, chs. 10 and 11.

H. L. McBain, *The Living Constitution*, New York, 1927, ch. I.

H. W. Horwill, *The Usages of the American Constitution*, London, 1925.

American Academy of Political and Social Science, *The Annals*, vol. 185, May, 1936, "The Constitution in the 20th Century."

C. H. McIlwain, *Constitutionalism, Ancient and Modern*, Ithaca, N. Y., 1941.

F. A. Ogg and P. O. Ray, *Introduction to American Government*, 8th ed., New York, 1945, ch. IV.

S. P. Orth and R. E. Cushman, *American National Government*, New York, 1931, ch. IV.

A. N. Christensen and E. M. Kirkpatrick, *The People, Politics, and the Politician: Readings in American Government*, New York, 1941, pp. 23-29.

J. M. Mathews, *The American Constitutional System*, 2nd ed., New York, 1940, ch. IV.

O. P. Field, *A Selection of Cases and Authorities on Constitutional Law*, Chicago, 2nd ed., 1936, ch. I.

H. V. Ames, "The Amending Provision of the Federal Constitution in Practice," *Proc. of Amer. Philosophical Soc.*, vol. LXIII, pp. 62-75 (1924).

W. F. Dodd, "Amending the Federal Constitution," *Yale Law Journal*, vol. XXX, pp. 321-54 (1920).

L. B. Orfield, *The Amending of the Federal Constitution*, Chicago, 1942.

Justin Miller, "Amendment of the Federal Constitution: Should It Be Made More Difficult?" *Minn. Law Rev.*, vol. 10, pp. 185-206 (1926).

Robert S. Rankin, *Readings in American Government*, New York, 1939, pp. 33-52, 407-12.

John M. Mathews and Clarence A. Berdahl, *Documents and Readings in American Government: National and State*, rev. ed., New York, 1940, pp. 48-60.

CHAPTER 5

The Nation and the States

The national government cannot be viewed as existing all by itself. When the framers of the written Constitution provided for its establishment, they left the state governments intact. In so doing they helped to create a unique dual system of public authority. The national government was designed to serve the general needs of the entire people and the entire territory of the United States, while each state was left to serve its own fraction of the whole. It was recognized that the welfare of the nation depended upon having certain functions handled for the whole people by one central authority; these were accordingly assigned to the national government. Other functions were seen to be of such a nature that each state might deal with them separately and in its own way, to the satisfaction of its own people and without harm to the nation.

DIVISION OF FUNCTIONS AND POWERS BETWEEN NATION AND STATES

What took place, therefore, was a division of the functions of government between the national government on the one hand and the several states on the other. Within the range of its own proper functions the national government and each state government was left free to act upon its own best judgment and through its own officers. It was recognized by the framers that conflicts might arise between the national government and one or more states, and among the states, and provision was made for these contingencies; but it was assumed that ordinarily the national government and each state would go about its work independently and without much conflict with others.

The historical conditions almost necessitated the type of division of functions that was made. Each of the states then in existence had claimed full "sovereignty," except as limited by the Articles of Confederation, and each had proceeded to exercise a considerable range of public functions. On the other hand the Congress under the Articles had only a few functions and each one of these was set forth in express words in the Articles. Consequently the most logical plan for the new Constitution was to state in it the particular functions to be exercised by the new national government and by implication to reserve all other functions to the states. This is, in fact, what was done, and it is doubtful whether the people would have approved any other plan. It is conceivable, however, that the functions and powers of the states might have been enumerated and all the rest have been left to the national government, or that an attempt might have been made to provide separate lists of the functions of both the national government and the states, as was later done in Canada.

Differences Between Articles of Confederation and Constitution. There are several important differences, however, between the Articles of Confederation and the present written Constitution with respect to the division of functions. (1) One is that in the Articles there was the following provision (Art. II, previously quoted): "Each State retains its sovereignty, freedom and independence, and every power, jurisdiction and right, which is not by this confederation expressly delegated to the United States, in Congress assembled." Such a clause, with its boastful claim of state sovereignty and independence, and its crippling attack upon the powers of Congress through the words "expressly delegated," was purposely omitted from the Constitution. Later when Congress drafted the amendments that became the national bill of rights (first ten Amendments to the Constitution, adopted 1791), it was under pressure to propose something similar to the provision quoted from the Articles, but what it submitted to the states was something very different, to wit: "Amendment X. The powers not delegated to the United States by the Constitution, nor prohibited by it to the States, are reserved to the States respectively, or to the people." The words "expressly delegated" were proposed to Congress and rejected. Thus the door was intentionally left open for the national government to exercise "implied powers," a point to be discussed hereafter.

(2) A second difference is this: Under the Articles there was really only one central organ, the Congress. Separate executive and judicial branches did not exist. Consequently all the functions conferred by the Articles upon the central agency were perforce delegated to Congress. Under the Constitution, however, there are three separate, full-fledged branches of government, and to each of them the Constitution grants certain functions and powers. For example, the making of laws is delegated to Congress, the making of treaties to the President, and judicial powers are delegated to the courts. Even to find all the functions and powers expressly delegated to the national government, therefore, it is necessary to read the entire Constitution, and to add together all the separate functions that are delegated to each of the branches.

(3) A third and very important difference is that the Constitution confers upon the central authorities not only certain *functions* but also *actual powers* of government, to make and enforce laws, to collect taxes, to raise armies,

and so on. The latter was not the case under the Articles. Except in foreign affairs the Congress under the Articles was practically without any powers.

Powers and Functions of Government Distinguished. The words "powers" and "functions" as used herein need to be defined. It is customary to speak of the "division of powers" between the national government and the states, but actually there is more of a division of functions than of powers. This fact becomes increasingly clear as governments are called upon to perform more functions than formerly were expected.

Governmental powers are essentially *means* to the ends or purposes of the community. If you send a boy to the market to get some food for dinner you must give him *power or authority* to spend some money, or to buy on your credit, and perhaps to use his judgment about accepting substitutes. His *function* is to get some food for you; that is the *end or purpose* for which you send him. But he must have the power or authority necessary to achieve the purpose or to perform the function, and this power is only a *means* to the end.

All governments, big and small, wherever they may be, exercise practically the same powers or means, although the definitions may differ somewhat from place to place. First come the internal *powers of compulsion*, including (a) the *taxing power*, (b) *eminent domain*, (c) *police power* (or the general power to regulate both persons and things), (d) *civil and military draft*, and (5) *penal power* (the power to punish persons for violations of duty). These powers are available to governments in all countries. In addition there are certain *external powers of compulsion*, notably the *power to make war*. Then there are powers of government that do not necessarily involve compulsion upon anyone, such as the powers to render services, to own and use land and buildings, to employ help, and so on, like any business, and also to make treaties and other agreements with other governments.

All these powers are primarily the *means* used by government to perform public functions. A government does not tax merely for the sake of taxing, but mainly to get revenues to pay for necessary public services. A treaty is not an end in itself but a means to peace or trade or some other desired end.

The powers are distinguished from each other by the manner in which they affect persons and property, by *taking* property into public possession, or *regulating* speed on the highways, or *penalizing* offenders. But in a sense they are all parts of one great power—the power of government over all persons and things within its jurisdiction.

Governmental or public functions, on the other hand, are the *immediate ends or purposes* for which governmental powers are employed. A function in this sense is simply some duty to be performed, or some service or activity to be carried out in the public interest. Of these functions there is today a long and growing list, including national defense, preservation of law and order, public health, public education, roads and public works, social security, and many more. They all contribute in turn to the more remote ends or purposes of government—"the general welfare" or "the good life."

It may be said, then, that *governmental powers are primarily means*, whereas *governmental functions are mainly the immediate ends* or *purposes* for which the powers are used. The framers of the Constitution saw that the Articles of Confederation imposed a number of *functions* on the Congress of that day but gave it practically *no powers* to perform these functions. In effect it could only recommend action to the member states. In the minds of many persons this was the chief defect of the Articles, and the framers of the Constitution fully intended to make a national government *with powers adequate to the performance of its functions*.

Alexander Hamilton stated in *The Federalist*, No. 31, that it was axiomatic "that the means ought to be proportioned to the end; that every power ought to be commensurate with its object; that there ought to be no limitation of a power destined to effect a purpose which is itself incapable of limitation." And again, "A government ought to contain in itself every power requisite to the full accomplishment of the objects committed to its care, and to the complete execution of the trusts for which it is responsible, free from every other control but a regard to the public good and to the sense of the people." [1]

But while this distinction between powers and functions ("objects," "trusts") was fully recognized, when it came to listing the things that the new national government was to be authorized to do, powers and functions, means and ends, were almost indiscriminately run together and there was no systematic coverage of all the essential means or powers. As practical men the framers put down only the essentials, and only as much as they thought the people would approve, and left the rest to be worked out later. Actually their phrasing was broad enough to imply a number of national powers that they did not state expressly.

Functions Expressly Delegated to National Government. The original Constitution clearly authorizes the national government to provide for the following functions (services, objects, purposes):

1. National defense and war
2. Foreign relations
3. Government of territories not in any state
4. Regulation of commerce with foreign nations, with the Indian tribes and among the several states
5. Naturalization
6. Bankruptcy laws
7. Coinage of money and regulation of its value
8. Fixing standards of weights and measures
9. Postal service (post offices and post roads)
10. Granting and protection of patents and copyrights
11. Guaranty of republican form of government to the states

[1] See also the remarks in *The Federalist*, nos. 15, 23, and 30.

12. A federal court system, and adjudication of disputes between states, citizens of different states, etc.

Later amendments have conferred on the national government powers to prevent slavery, regulate citizenship, and to protect citizens against discrimination on grounds of race, color, and religion.

A number of minor matters not covered in the foregoing summary are also authorized.

Powers Delegated to National Government. The written Constitution is incomplete and unsystematic in stating the *powers* (as distinct from the functions) of the national government. A listing under appropriate headings reveals the following:

1. *Taxing power.* This power is most fully and completely conferred upon the national government but without any corresponding prohibition against the states. "The Congress shall have Power to lay and collect Taxes, Duties, Imposts and Excises, to pay the Debts and provide for the common Defence and general Welfare of the United States." (Art. I, sec. 8, par. 1.)

2. *Eminent domain,* the power to take land and other things for public use and purposes is not expressly stated in the original Constitution. In Amendment V, however, adopted in 1791, it is provided negatively "nor shall private property be taken for public use, without just compensation." This proviso seems to assume that the national government has the power of eminent domain.

3. *Police power* or the general power of regulation over persons and things is not as such delegated to the national government. However some portions of it are delegated as in the power of Congress "to regulate Commerce with foreign Nations," etc.; "to establish a uniform Rule of Naturalization, and uniform Laws on the subject of Bankruptcies," etc.; to "regulate the Value" of money; and so on. Most important in this connection is the last paragraph of Article I, section 8, the power of Congress "to make all Laws which shall be necessary and proper for carrying into Execution the foregoing Powers, and all other Powers vested by this Constitution in the Government of the United States, or in any Department or Officer thereof." This blanket authorization or something like it might have been enough to delegate to the national government all powers of every kind needed by it to carry out its functions, but then why were other specific powers stated?

4. *Civil and military draft,* or the compulsory taking of personal services for public purposes is a power that was not expressly stated in the Constitution. It had to be implied from other clauses such as the power "to raise and support armies."

5. *Penal power,* or the power to punish persons for violations of law, is expressly stated with respect to counterfeiting, "Piracies and Felonies committed on the high Seas, and Offenses against the Law of Nations." What about punishments in other cases? The power to provide these must be implied

from other provisions, and perhaps especially from the "necessary and proper" clause quoted above.

Enough has been said to show that there is some incompleteness and confusion with respect to the *powers* conferred upon the national government. Much was left to implication instead of being expressed.

With respect to certain of the functions and powers delegated to the national government the framers of the Constitution decided to make them exclusively national. In order to achieve this end they expressly provided in Article I, section 10, against the states doing certain stated things that elsewhere in the Constitution were delegated to the national government. "No State shall enter into any Treaty, Alliance, or Confederation"; "coin money"; etc. Also "No State shall, without the Consent of the Congress, lay any Imports or Duties on Imports or Exports, . . . [or] lay any duty of Tonnage, keep Troops, or Ships of War in time of Peace, . . . or engage in War, unless actually invaded, or in such imminent Danger as will not admit of delay."

These prohibitions against the states clinch the fact that the corresponding grants of power to the national government are exclusive. But what about other powers and functions delegated to the national government, without a parallel prohibition against the states? May they be exercised or performed by either the nation or the states, or by both at the same time? To this question, and others like it, the written Constitution gives no direct answer, and the "supremacy clause" is not alone sufficient to tell what will be decided.

RULES FOR CONSTRUING NATIONAL POWERS AND FUNCTIONS

Hamilton v. Jefferson. It was not long after the new national government was set up before the question arose as to the powers of the national government. Hamilton, as Secretary of the Treasury under President Washington, proposed that Congress incorporate a Bank of the United States to facilitate the work of the national government in carrying out some of its delegated powers and functions, i.e., to levy and collect taxes, to borrow money, to regulate the coinage, to regulate commerce, and to provide for the common defense. He presented his plan to the President.

Jefferson, as Secretary of State, and Madison, in Congress, opposed the project, and argued that it was unconstitutional. They took the line of strict construction. (1) The power to incorporate anything was not delegated to Congress. (2) None of the general clauses of the Constitution was broad enough to authorize this incorporation. (a) The power "to lay and collect taxes" to provide for "the general welfare of the United States" is not a power of Congress to do anything it pleases for the general welfare, "for the laying of taxes is the *power*, and the general welfare the *purpose* for which the power is to be exercised." (b) The power "to make all Laws which shall be necessary and proper for carrying into Execution" the powers of the national government, was deemed by Jefferson not to apply, since all the powers could be carried into effect without the bank, and hence the incorporation of the bank was not *necessary*. The word *"necessary"* was to be taken in its strict sense, he thought; for if Congress could exercise every power that it thought *convenient* for national purposes, the attempt in the Constitution to enumerate its powers was just a waste of words.

Hamilton took a decidedly different view of the matter. The essential issue was the right of Congress to create a corporation. Conceding that the national government is one of delegated and enumerated powers, he nevertheless argued

> (1) That every power vested in a government is in its nature *sovereign*, and includes by *force* of the *term* a right to employ all the *means* requisite and fairly applicable to the attainment of the ends of such power. . . . (2) [That] it is unquestionably incident to *sovereign power* to erect corporations . . . in *relation* to the *objects* intrusted to the management of the government. . . . Thus a corporation may not be erected by Congress for superintending the police of the city of Philadelphia, because they are not authorized to *regulate* the *police* of that city. But one may be erected in relation to the collection of taxes, or to the trade with foreign countries, or to the trade between the States, or with the Indian tribes; because it is the province of the federal government to *regulate* those objects and because it is incident to a general *sovereign* or *legislative* power to regulate a thing, to employ all the means which relate to its regulation to the best and greatest advantage. . . . (3) That there are "implied" and "resulting" powers, as well as express ones, and (4) that the powers contained in a constitution of government, especially those that concern the general administration of the affairs of a country, its finances, trade, defence, etc., ought to be construed liberally in advancement of the public good.[2]

Marshall and Supreme Court Adopt Hamilton's Views. The opposing views have probably never been better stated than in these two papers by Jefferson and Hamilton on the question of the bank. Congress adopted Hamilton's proposal, and the bank existed and functioned to the end of its charter period without legal contest against it. When the Second United States Bank was chartered, however, Maryland passed an act to tax its Baltimore branch, and the question arose whether the tax was constitutional. The attorneys for Maryland raised the counter-issue whether the bank itself was legal. The resulting decision in McCulloch v. Maryland (1819) is perhaps as important as any decision ever rendered by the Supreme Court.[3] Chief Justice Marshall wrote

---

[2] Commager, *Documents of American History*, pp. 156-60, gives the gist of the debate between Hamilton and Jefferson.

[3] 4 Wheaton (U. S.) 316. See also Commager, *op. cit.*, 213-20, and Cushman, *Leading Constitutional Decisions*, 7th ed., 1940, pp. 9-20.

the opinion of the Court, and in it he took over most of Hamilton's line of argument, given above, and set the course of constitutional construction in general toward a liberal view of the powers of the national government. This famous decision may be summarized as follows:

1. *A People's Constitution.* It was "the people" and not the states that established the federal Constitution and created and delegated powers to the national government. Hence the Constitution is binding on the states.

2. *National Laws Supreme.* "The government of the United States, though limited in its powers, is supreme within its sphere of action," and "its laws, when made in pursuance of the constitution, form the supreme law of the land."

3. *Implied Powers.* Unlike the Articles of Confederation, the federal Constitution does not exclude the central government from exercising "incidental or implied powers." Even the Tenth Amendment, adopted for the purpose of reserving to the states the powers not delegated to the national government, does not say that Congress shall have only those powers "expressly" delegated to it. It was the intention to permit Congress to use the means requisite to the carrying out of its enumerated powers and functions.

4. *Resultant Powers.* "Although, among the enumerated powers of government, we do not find the word 'bank' or 'incorporation,' we find the great powers to lay and collect taxes; to borrow money; to regulate commerce; to declare and conduct war; and to raise and support armies and navies. The sword and the purse, all the external relations, and no inconsiderable portion of the industry of the nation, are intrusted to its government. . . . Now it may, with great reason, be contended, that a government, intrusted with such ample powers, on the due execution of which the happiness and prosperity of the nation so vitally depends, must also be intrusted with ample means for their execution. . . . It is not denied that the powers given to the government imply the ordinary means of execution."

5. *Divided Sovereignty.* "The creation of a corporation, it is said, appertains to sovereignty. This is admitted. But to what portion of sovereignty does it appertain? Does it belong to one more than to another? In America, the powers of sovereignty are divided between the government of the Union, and those of the States. They are each sovereign, with respect to the objects committed to it, and neither sovereign with respect to the objects committed to the other."

6. *Necessary and Proper Clause.* But the Constitution itself, in the clause concerning the making of all "necessary and proper" laws had made clear the right of Congress "to employ the necessary means for the execution of the powers conferred on the government." And the word "necessary" is not to be given a rigid definition, for "we find that it frequently imports no more than that one thing is convenient, or useful, or essential to another. To employ the means necessary to an end, is generally understood as employing any means calculated to produce the end, and not as being confined to those single means,

without which the end would be entirely unattainable. . . . We think the sound construction of the Constitution must allow to the national legislature that discretion, with respect to the means by which the powers it confers are to be carried into execution, which will enable that body to perform the high duties assigned to it, in the manner most beneficial to the people. Let the end be legitimate, let it be within the scope of the Constitution, and all means which are appropriate, which are plainly adapted to that end, which are not prohibited, but consistent with the letter and spirit of the Constitution, are constitutional. . . ."

In conclusion, then, the court sustained the act of Congress incorporating the bank as a means or instrumentality of the national government, and held that Maryland's attempt to tax the bank was unconstitutional and void.

Express, Implied, and Resultant Powers. Under this line of reasoning, followed and developed in later decisions, the national government has (a) the functions and powers expressly granted to it by the words of the Constitution; (b) the implied power to use the means deemed by Congress most appropriate to carry out each granted power; and (c) "resulting" or "resultant" powers, not implied in or incidental to any one granted power, but resulting from a set of conditions in which a group of powers are involved. Hamilton explained the latter type in his paper on the bank.

> It will not be doubted, that if the United States should make a conquest of any of the territories of its neighbours, they would possess sovereign jurisdiction over the conquered territory. This would be rather a result from a whole mass of the powers of the government, and from the nature of political society, than a consequence of either of the powers specially enumerated. . . .[4]

Are There Also "National Powers"? Another doctrine that has begun to appear in the decisions of the court asserts (d) that the United States is one nation for all external and international purposes; that all power over external affairs has been denied to the separate states; and that consequently "as a nation with all the attributes of sovereignty, the United States is vested with all the powers of government necessary to maintain an effective control of international relations."[5] In a more recent decision[6] the matter has been put as follows:

> It results that the investment of the federal government with the powers of external sovereignty did not depend upon the affirmative grants of the Constitution. The powers to declare and wage war, to conclude peace, to make treaties, to maintain diplomatic relations with other sovereignties, if they had never been mentioned in the Constitution, would have vested in the federal government as neces-

[4] Commager, op. cit., p. 157.
[5] Burnet v. Brooks (1933), 288 U. S. 378, 396.
[6] U. S. v. Curtiss-Wright Export Corporation (1936), 299 U. S. 304, 318.

sary concomitants of nationality. . . . As a member of the family of nations, the right and power of the United States in that field are equal to the right and power of the other members of the international family. Otherwise, the United States is not completely sovereign.

The importance of this doctrine lies largely in its possible development in the future. As nations become increasingly interdependent and must perform more functions together, by international action, the government that wields international power must become increasingly dominant over its state and local subdivisions. From an internal viewpoint the doctrine that there are *national powers* that are *independent of the Constitution* gives a final blow to any thought of strict construction to the powers of the national government. The strict constructionist view holds that the national government must look into the written Constitution for every one of its powers and functions, that the Constitution is the sole source of national powers. But the doctrine of "national powers" finds in nationhood itself an independent source of powers, a source outside of and beyond the Constitution. It says in effect that the national government as sole representative of the nation has all the powers, and therewith a control over all the functions, that are in its judgment necessary for national and international needs. That this includes the legal authority to override the states even in matters that have heretofore been left to their discretion is no longer open to question. International policy and necessity must be controlling over all internal arrangements.

CONSTRUCTION OF STATE POWERS AND FUNCTIONS

It was unquestionably the intention of the framers of the Constitution to confer upon the national government all the functions and powers necessary for the national safety and welfare and to leave to the states all the other functions of government together with the powers or means necessary to carry out those functions. The Tenth Amendment, adopted along with others in 1791, made this intention explicit.

"The powers not delegated to the United States by the Constitution, nor prohibited by it to the States, are reserved to the States respectively, or to the people."

Many persons thought this amendment to be superfluous, and in fact it has had very little influence upon either state or national activity. However, the principle stated in this amendment makes it clear that a state does not need to look into either the national or its own state constitution to find a catalog of the things that it may do as a state. The functions and powers of the state are not listed and enumerated. The national Constitution obviously puts some *restrictions* upon the states, and each state constitution puts some limits and prohibitions upon the government of that state. In all other respects the state government of any state is free to go ahead with anything that it desires to do without pointing out any specific authorization in either the national or the state constitution. If it is not forbidden, it may be done.

It would appear, therefore, that between them the national and state governments should be able to accomplish any purpose that seems necessary to them or to the people. There should be *complete coverage* of the whole range of governmental functions and a full complement of all the powers needed to perform them. State and national governments have gone ahead upon this assumption. Urged on in recent decades by a realization of new public needs that arose out of industrialization, the growth of cities, the insecurity of agriculture, the destruction of natural resources, and technological advances, both the national and state governments have added greatly to the range of their functions and services.

In fact, however, things have not worked out smoothly in all instances. When two men stake a claim upon the same piece of land or two governments in a federal system try to tax or regulate the same things, there is likely to be trouble, and so there has been. There have been actual conflicts between the national government and the states. In addition the Supreme Court at one time held certain attitudes toward the activities and the relations of national and state governments that created additional difficulties.

Conflicts of Interests. Since the people of the states are also the people of the nation, it might be thought that there would be complete harmony or community of interests between national and state governments, but experience reveals many points of conflict between them. For example, (1) the party that controls Congress never really represents the whole nation. Sometimes the interests of the northern and western states will dominate Congress, while southern interests are in a minority; at other times the South, Middle West, and Far West will be in control and the Northeast will be out of power. In such cases the minority states will probably be controlled by the party that is in a minority in Congress, and will be strongly opposed to the national policy. This has been observed in the cases of slavery, the tariff, and many less important issues. (2) When the national government levies income taxes, the bulk of which are paid in a few eastern states, and then turns around and spends a large part of the money thus obtained for roads and relief work in the poorer states of the West and South, the conflict of interests is very clear. From the poorer states come practically all the demands for federal aid; from the wealthier comes the opposition. (3) The national regulation of railroad rates has meant raising rates in some states above what they need to be there, in order to give interstate railroads enough income so that they can afford to give the same rates and service in other states where, because of high costs, the rates should be somewhat higher. (4) To get enough revenue, both national and state governments tax a number of the same things such as gasoline, tobacco, incomes, and inheritances, with resultant conflicts, inconveniences and reduction of revenue to both. (5) In such important matters as the regulation of railroads, utilities, banking, and insurance, expansion of national activity means reducing the importance and may mean eliminating the jobs of state officials. The opposition of state officeholders to such expansion is, therefore, easily understandable. In their annual conferences the governors of the states never fail to berate the national government for its encroachments upon the states.

On the other hand it must be remembered that many states have urged the national government to help them out and to undertake functions that were too big and too expensive for them to handle alone. The national government has greater financial resources, it can command the services of the best experts, and it has a good reputation for administrative honesty and efficiency. Therefore the states have on the whole welcomed federal aid and guidance in road building and in public relief work, and have benefited from the regulatory work, research, and other activities of the national government.

Supreme Court Attitudes, Old and New. In a number of cases recently the states, or some of them, have appeared as parties in the federal courts in cases designed to prevent the national government from undertaking or continuing a public function. They have in this way protested against its control over rivers and its intervention in the regulation of insurance companies. In such cases the Supreme Court is called upon to decide between the nation and the states, and thus to draw the lines between national and state powers in various fields.

In many other cases since about 1870 private persons, either individuals or corporation, have applied to the courts to prevent either the national government or some state from enforcing some new tax law or some regulation or taking of their business or property. Their contention has usually been that a particular action of government was unconstitutional or beyond the powers of the government in question. During this period and down through 1936 the Supreme Court frequently took a very limited view of national or of state powers, and invalidated the legislation in question. Its attitude in some of these cases (and it was not always the same attitude) may be summed up as follows:

It tended to look upon the national government and the states as natural competitors for power, as antagonists in a struggle. A conflict of interests was assumed to exist, even though no representative of the state or national government was present in court to raise the question. Closely related to this was the idea that both the national and state governments could not exercise the same power (except in some fields of taxation). Therefore, if a power had been granted to the national government (like the power to regulate interstate commerce) or reserved to the states, the other government could not exercise it even though the first was not doing so. Assuming unquestioningly its own power of mind reading, the court asserted, for example, that "the silence of Congress" in not forbidding or regulating some phase of interstate commerce meant that Congress wanted it left unregulated by anyone, and the states were thereby excluded. It was an "either-or" matter, and the court did not accept the idea that both might regulate the same thing more or less cooperatively or alternately.

Also important was an attitude of the majority of the court against government intervention in fields relating to property, contracts, labor, and business in general. Sometimes it was a state, and sometimes the national government, that was trying to do something, but whichever it was this attitude of the court frequently led to decisions that the proposed action was unconstitutional. It was beyond the commerce or taxing power, or it took property without due process of law.

As a result of these judicial attitudes many measures, both national and state, were declared to be unconstitutional. In fact, instead of the national and state governments being able between them to achieve every purpose of government, there developed a sort of "twilight zone," a "no-man's land" between the national government and the states, an area in which neither could act effectively. This was also called "the sphere of anarchy," in which business could do as it pleased. Child labor, for example, could not be effectively suppressed by either nation or state or by the two together for a number of years.

Since 1937 the Supreme Court has reversed the old attitude on all these points. Its construction of the powers of the national government and of the states is more liberal than at any time since the days of Chief Justice John Marshall. It is not opposed to government activity; it does not assume that there is a necessary conflict between the nation and the states, but stresses rather their common interests and their cooperation within the federal system. It does not view the powers and functions of government as a fixed and limited number or amount; it does not believe that if the nation has more there must be less for the states. On the contrary it sees, what in fact is true, that as the nation leaves behind the days of *laissez faire* and enters an era of greater socialization, both the national government and the states may increase their functions at the same time without necessary conflicts. The court no longer holds that a particular function must be *either* state *or* national and cannot be both; instead it emphasizes that many functions are *both national and state*. They require the support of both if the best result is to be obtained.

The new keynote is interdependence and cooperation. There is room and there is work within the federal system for both the national government and the states. Both can become more important in the life of the people at the same time. Both are necessary in the federal system, and each must learn to be tolerant and cooperative toward the other. The emphasis is no longer upon national-state rivalry and struggle for constitutional rights but upon functional cooperation in the interest of the general welfare.[7]

[7] See for example the decision by Justice Cardozo on the Social Security Act, in Steward Machine Co. v. Davis (1937), 301 U. S. 548.

METHODS OF NATIONAL-STATE ADJUSTMENT AND
COOPERATION

Conflict and cooperation are only different phases of the complex relationships between the national government and the states. Disagreement over particular matters does not prevent genuine collaboration in others, and even disagreements give way in time through processes of discussion and compromise to a new adjustment of interest.

In the United States the harmonizing of national and state interests is accomplished in a number of ways. (1) Public opinion, as developed through education, the press, the radio, and countless organizations of citizens, is a very important factor. It has become increasingly favorable to national action and to national-state cooperation. (2) The political parties also have the role of harmonizers of national and state interests. (3) Congress and the President are continuously aware of the problem of state relations and have adopted many measures that have been favorable to state interests. Noteworthy among these is the system of federal aid to the states for such functions as highways, social welfare and relief, and agricultural education. (4) The governors and legislatures of the states, various organizations that represent them such as the Governors' Conference and the Council of State Governments, and numerous state officials and their organizations in many fields of public service participate in the process of adjustment. In time of war they are particularly cooperative with the national authorities. It was the states that took over, in the early days of World War II, the administration of selective service, the rationing of tires and gasoline, and civilian defense activities. All these might otherwise have fallen on the already overburdened national government.

(5) Finally, when state claims of right against the nation, or national claims against states, need to be settled judicially, ways can usually be found to get a hearing in the federal courts and ultimately in the Supreme Court of the United States. This has always been a court of high ability and integrity, and one sworn to uphold the Constitution of the United States. Its views have in general been nationalist, but it has never failed to accord a fair hearing to the states or to uphold their rights and powers as fully as it could.[8]

National Supremacy. When any case comes before the courts in which any person, including any state, alleges a conflict to exist between an action, law, or treaty of the national government on the one side, and a state action or law on the other, the court finds a sure guide laid down for it in the United States Constitution. The second sentence of Article VI reads as follows:

> This Constitution, and the Laws of the United States which shall
> be made in Pursuance thereof; and all Treaties made; or which shall
> be made, under the Authority of the United States, shall be the

[8] See O. P. Field, "State versus Nation, and the Supreme Court," *Am. Pol. Sci. Rev.*, vol. 28, pp. 233-44 (1934).

supreme Law of the Land; and the Judges in every State shall be
bound thereby, any Thing in the Constitution or Laws of any State
to the Contrary notwithstanding.

If the national government's law or treaty is within the constitutional powers of that government, it must prevail over anything the state may enact or
do. This will apply also to any legal actions taken by any person under the
national law or treaty. Even though the state might have had power to do
what it did in the absence of a national law or treaty, the fact that such a
law or treaty exists and is valid is enough in case of conflict to set aside the
state law and any action thereunder.

There was a time when the Supreme Court of the United States seemed
to take a different view on this. It developed a doctrine that was called "dual
federalism." It seemed to say that national and state actions stood upon the
same level, so that the reserved powers of the states operated as a check upon
the delegated powers of the nation. Thus a national tax was held invalid for
no other reason than that it was to be spent to achieve a purpose of regulation
in agriculture which, said the Court, could legally be accomplished only by
the states. This doctrine, which goes directly contrary to the supremacy clause
quoted above, has now been repudiated by the court. National supremacy has
been restored with respect to all laws, treaties, and actions thereunder, that
are within the powers of the nation, no matter what the effect thereof may
be on the states.

REFERENCES

E. S. Corwin, *The Twilight of the Supreme Court*, New Haven, 1934.
——, *The Commerce Power versus State Rights*, Princeton, 1936.
——, "National-State Cooperation—Its Present Possibilities," *Am. Law School
Rev.*, vol. 8, pp. 687-706 (1937).
A. F. Macdonald, *Federal Aid*, New York, 1928.
V. O. Key, Jr., *The Administration of Federal Grants to the States*, Chicago,
1937.
Jane Perry Clark, *The Rise of a New Federalism*, New York, 1938.
F. A. Ogg and P. O. Ray, *Introduction to American Government*, 8th ed.,
New York, 1945, chs. V-VII.

CHAPTER 6

United States Citizenship

Nations are composed of people. The final and indivisible unit in any nation is the individual man, woman, or child. This is as true of the United States as of any other nation. We should not permit the federal structure of the government to conceal or minimize the fact that "We the people of the United States" ordained and established the Constitution and are inescapably responsible for the success of the nation in every way. It is not forty-eight states but 140 million people who make up the nation.

To understand fully the American people and their capacity to operate successfully a national government in a world of nations it is important to know a great deal about their character, history, and achievements; their national outlook and modes of thought; their social organization and standards of life; their racial and sectional groupings; their industries and employments. Unfortunately this book, which deals with government, cannot explore these important matters at all adequately. What we can do is to examine briefly who are the citizens of this nation from the legal and practical viewpoints, and to show something of their governmental rights and responsibilities. Who are the people that make up the nation?

CITIZENS AND NATIONALS DEFINED

The Constitution uses the terms "Citizens of each State" (Art. IV, sec. 2) and "citizens of the United States" (Amend. XIV). On the other hand the nouns "national" and "nationality" are terms of international law that were taken over into the new "Nationality Code" enacted by Congress in October, 1940.[1] This law says that "The term 'national' means a person owing permanent allegiance to a state" such as the United States. There are two classes of nationals: citizens and non-citizens. All other persons may be called non-nationals.

[1] Nationality Code of 1940 (*U. S. Code Annotated*, Title 8, ch. II, secs. 801-10).

74

The inhabitants of the "outlying possessions," such as the Philippine Islands, Guam, and Samoa, are in general nationals of the United States but not citizens; whereas the inhabitants of the territories, Alaska, Hawaii, Puerto Rico, and the Virgin Islands (now considered as parts of the United States for nationality and citizenship purposes), are in most cases both nationals and citizens in the same way as the inhabitants of the forty-eight states and the District of Columbia.

"Citizen" is a less inclusive term than "national." Citizenship signifies full membership in the body politic of a nation or state. It is a term of constitutional or internal law, within the particular country, since every national state determines citizenship according to its own constitution and laws. What does this membership imply? How is it acquired and how is it lost? What rights and what duties does citizenship carry with it?

Citizenship a Constitutional Right. Frequently one reads that citizenship is a mere "privilege," implying a sort of temporary and limited right that can be taken away by the government, like the privilege of operating a restaurant under license, or of practicing some vocation or profession. With respect to the great majority of American citizens, this view is not correct, and is contradicted by the words of the Fourteenth Amendment to the national Constitution:

> All persons born or naturalized in the United States, and subject to the jurisdiction thereof, are citizens of the United States and of the State wherein they reside.

By that provision of the Constitution every person who is a citizen by birth or naturalization in the United States has a constitutional right to his citizenship—a right that is protected by laws and courts, and that cannot be taken away from him legally except as the result of his own actions in relinquishing or forfeiting it, or by another constitutional amendment. The sort of thing that happened in Germany in 1935, when Jews were deprived of their citizenship by decree, *might* happen in the United States, but it could not happen without a change or a violation of established constitutional rights.

Citizenship and Suffrage Not the Same. Ancient Greek writers like Aristotle thought of citizenship as implying full right to participate in public affairs. "He who has the power to take part in the deliberative or judicial administration of any state is said by us to be a citizen of that state, . . ." [2] Even certain recent writers evidently hold this view. "As distinct from aliens, serfs, women and children or other members of the community who are passive subjects rather than active partners, citizens enjoy a certain reciprocity of rights against, and duties toward, the community." [3] These views are not in accordance with the law of citizenship in the United States. Here men, women, and children are equally citizens of the United States. But "suffrage," or the right to vote

[2] Aristotle's *Politics*, Bk. III, secs. 1-5.
[3] Encyc. of Soc. Sci., vol. 3, p. 471.

in public elections, does not belong to all citizens. For example, persons under twenty-one born in the United States are citizens but may not legally vote except in Georgia, where the voting age is now eighteen, while many citizens over twenty-one are excluded from voting by other legal regulations.

DEVELOPMENT OF CITIZENSHIP LAWS

In the colonial period of American history most of the people were British nationals and had also a subordinate sort of citizenship in their particular colony. With the establishment of independence, each state had its own citizens, and there was legally no national citizenship of the United States. The Articles of Confederation definitely recognized state citizenship and also accorded to state citizens a right of interstate travel and trade. Even the original Constitution of the United States did not provide outright for national citizenship although it did provide for Congress to establish a "uniform rule of naturalization." The famous Dred Scott decision, which denied the claims of a Negro to freedom and citizenship, even though he had lived for a time in non-slave territory, showed that state and national citizenship both existed, but it also revealed a great confusion of ideas concerning the law of citizenship. Each of the nine Supreme Court justices wrote a separate opinion to explain his views.

The Fourteenth Amendment. In 1868 the states ratified the Fourteenth Amendment to the United States Constitution. It was designed among other things to overcome the confusion about citizenship revealed by the Dred Scott case and to confer citizenship on the Negroes, who had recently been freed from slavery. Its essential clauses on citizenship are as follows:

> Sec. I. All persons born or naturalized in the United States, and subject to the jurisdiction thereof, are citizens of the United States and of the State wherein they reside. No State shall make or enforce any law which shall abridge the privileges or immunities of citizens of the United States.

This amendment clearly does several things. (1) It makes a broad and definite though not exhaustive rule as to who are United States citizens. (2) It puts national citizenship ahead of state citizenship, i.e., makes it "paramount and dominant," as to all persons born or naturalized in the United States. Whereas at one time national citizenship was secondary and depended on state citizenship, since 1868 state citizenship has depended on national citizenship and has been secondary to it. (3) One who is a United States citizen by birth or naturalization in the United States need only reside in a state to become a citizen of that state.

Since 1868 there have been additional changes in the law of citizenship through statutes and treaties, culminating in the comprehensive "nationality code" of October, 1940. This code has been modified in minor details during the defense and war period by provisions for the citizenship of former Americans who served in the armies of our allies, and of aliens who served in the United States armies.

STATE CITIZENSHIP

Dual Citizenship. As a result of historical developments, and by clear intention of the Fourteenth Amendment, a person can be a citizen of the United States and a citizen of the state in which he resides. This creates the situation known as *dual citizenship*, which signifies that a person is both a citizen of the United States and a citizen of a particular state. Those citizens of the United States who reside (i.e., have domicile) in the District of Columbia, in a territory, or abroad, or who from some other cause lack residence in any of the forty-eight states, have national but not state citizenship. All other citizens of the United States—and this means over 98 per cent of them—have their residences in the states, and therefore have dual citizenship. Of course, national citizenship completely overshadows and dominates state citizenship for most persons, and few even stop to question seriously whether they are citizens of a particular state. Nevertheless the two citizenships are legally separate and distinct.

Present State Citizenship Laws. State citizenship is today a much neglected subject. The state constitutions make very few provisions for it, and practically the same is true of present state statutes. State laws and constitutions contain some provisions limiting the rights of aliens, meaning aliens with respect to the United States as a whole; and they make various provisions also that for voting, officeholding, and other purposes "residents" only shall be qualified. The Vermont constitution speaks also of "freemen," meaning citizens, but where the term "citizenship" is defined in state laws and constitutions the wording usually follows almost exactly that of the Fourteenth Amendment. In fact, there seems to be no important case today in which a state defines state citizenship so as to create a body of state citizens who are not also United States citizens. Since the decision of Chirac *v.* Chirac in 1817, the states have apparently abandoned all attempts to have separate naturalization laws.[4] Where state courts now engage in naturalization work, they do so as agents of the national government under the United States naturalization laws. They admit persons to United States, not to state, citizenship.

Rights of State Citizenship. State citizenship, as distinct from national, was recognized in the original United States Constitution, and still is so recognized, by the so-called "comity clause."

> The Citizens of each State shall be entitled to all Privileges and Immunities of Citizens in the several States.[5]

[4] Chirac v. Chirac (1817), 2 Wheaton (U. S.) 259.
[5] U. S. Const., Art. IV, sec. II.

The privileges and immunities guaranteed by this section, although they will never be fully known, have been defined in part by judicial decisions. Essentially the guaranty is one of equality. The citizens of any state when in another state are entitled to equal treatment with the citizens of the latter state in certain important matters. They may legally acquire property rights, make contracts, engage in ordinary lawful labor and business, and obtain the protection of courts and law-enforcing agencies on an equal basis with citizens of the state concerned and in conformity with its laws. Thus with respect to these so-called "fundamental" *civil* and *economic* rights, no state may discriminate against citizens of other states in favor of its own.

Political Rights. At the same time, in certain *political* matters, including the right to vote and to hold state or local public office, states may and do discriminate in favor of their own citizens. This favoritism goes even farther in many cases. Thus to obtain employment in the service of a state or local government one is also required in most places to be a local resident or citizen. Similarly in the licensing of persons for the practice of such public professions as law and medicine, residence or citizenship in the state is frequently required; and in businesses where public regulation must necessarily be strict, as in the sale of liquor, and of stocks and bonds, similar requirements have been upheld.[6]

Rights in State Domain and Institutions. Each state has also certain *rights in its own domain* that it holds for the special advantage of its own citizens. Wild game and fish, for example, belong in a sense to the state, and it is customary for the states to charge higher hunting and fishing license fees to non-residents than to its own citizens. The states also charge non-residents higher tuition than residents in state colleges and universities, and permit only residents to be admitted to their hospitals and asylums except in emergency cases. Persons who are afflicted with contagious diseases are frequently turned back by one state to the state of residence, a thing that may not legally be done with citizens of the state itself.

In short, there are a number of rights that a state can grant to its own citizens or residents that it may and does legally deny to non-residents, or grant to non-residents only on more difficult terms than those imposed on residents. These advantages given to the citizen in his own state constitute the special rights of state citizenship. Taken all together, they amount to a considerable difference in rights between citizens and non-citizens of the state. The transient and the temporary sojourner are everywhere under some special handicaps.

But none of these preferential arrangements can legally affect the rights of national citizenship, nor does state citizenship as such have any significance of which any foreign nation needs to take notice. In international dealings it is only national citizenship, or nationality, that counts.

[6] See Roger Howell, *The Privileges and Immunities of State Citizenship.*

THE ACQUISITION OF UNITED STATES CITIZENSHIP

Natural Born and Naturalized Citizens. The Constitution speaks in one place of "natural born" citizens of the United States, and elsewhere it mentions "naturalization." The first clearly refers to the acquisition of citizenship by birth, and the second to the conferment of citizenship on persons who are not citizens by birth.

Citizenship by Birth. Citizenship by birth may be acquired either (a) by birth in a certain place, or (b) by birth to certain parents. Various nations have followed one or the other, or both of these two different rules concerning citizenship by birth. Where the law provides that all persons born within the territory of a state and subject to its jurisdiction are citizens, the rule is designated as *jus soli*, or law of the soil or place. Where the law is that children born of citizen parents are citizens of the state regardless of where the parents chance to reside at the time, that state is said to follow the rule of *jus sanguinis*, or law of the blood or parentage.

Citizenship by Birth in the United States. By the Fourteenth Amendment, previously quoted, all persons born in the United States and subject to the jurisdiction thereof are citizens of the United States. It matters not in these cases whether the parents are citizens, or even whether they are eligible to become citizens. Birth within the United States is enough. The words "in the United States" have never been fully defined, but in practice the so-called "incorporated territories," Hawaii, Alaska, Puerto Rico and the Virgin Islands, are included with the forty-eight states and the District of Columbia. In practice, too, persons born on foreign vessels in territorial waters of the United States are so considered, but persons born to non-American parents on American ships on the high seas are not considered to have been born in the United States for the purposes of citizenship.

"Subject to the Jurisdiction" Defined. Persons born in the United States must also be "subject to the jurisdiction thereof" in order to have their citizenship by birth in the place. Before 1924 tribal Indians born in the United States were not considered to be subject to the jurisdiction of the United States, and hence not citizens by birth. Likewise children born in the United States into the families of foreign diplomatic representatives (ambassadors and ministers and their official staffs) are not subject to United States jurisdiction, but the reverse is true of children born here into the families of foreign consuls, since the latter do not have the same immunity as diplomatic representatives. If it should happen that some day some part of the United States, or some territory such as Hawaii, or Alaska, were occupied by a foreign enemy, children born to such enemy during the occupancy of this territory would also not be "subject to the jurisdiction" of the United States, and hence would not be citizens by *jus soli*.

Citizenship by Birth to Citizen Parents Outside the United States. The Constitution refers to but does not define "natural born" citizens. Also it makes no provision respecting the citizenship of children born of American parents outside the United States. The citizenship of such persons depends, therefore, almost wholly upon statutes and treaties. In the first general naturalization act (1790) children born to American parents outside the United States were given United States citizenship, but later for over fifty years (1802-55) the law stood in some confusion. In 1855 Congress enacted that children born outside the United States would be citizens if the father were a citizen at the time of their birth.[7] With occasional modifications this has continued to be the law. Under the 1940 law, if both parents are citizens a child born outside the United States or any outlying possession is a citizen if one parent has resided in the United States or an outlying possession. The same is true where one parent is a non-citizen national and the other a citizen who has resided in the United States or an outlying possession. But where one parent is an alien and the other a citizen, the latter must have resided ten years (five after the age of sixteen) in the United States or an outlying possession, and in addition the child, to gain citizenship, must reside in the United States or an outlying possession five years between the ages of thirteen and twenty-one and beginning before sixteen.[8] The purposes of these requirements are to give some reality to the citizenship of persons who are born abroad, and to reduce the nation's obligations to protect such foreign-born persons.

Citizenship by Naturalization. In addition to "natural born" citizens (i.e., citizens by birth in the United States and those born elsewhere to citizen-parents as defined above), there are citizens by naturalization. These are persons who began life without United States citizenship and who acquired it by complying with the law on the subject. Independently of such laws no person has a legal right to acquire the citizenship of any country. There is no international law creating such a right. In the United States, however, any person who has in good faith and in compliance with law become a citizen by naturalization has thereafter, under the Fourteenth Amendment, a constitutional right to his citizenship equal to that of any citizen by birth.

Naturalization in Connection with Annexations. When a nation annexes any territory not previously possessed, the inhabitants other than resident aliens become "nationals" of the annexing state. Options may be given to them to take or retain some other allegiance, but if they do not make this choice they will be presumed in international law to be nationals of the nation that annexes their territory. But the mere act of annexing a territory does not make its inhabitants "citizens" of the United States. This requires separate and distinct action, either at the time of annexation or later, and

---

[7] 10 Statutes at Large, 694.
[8] U. S. Code Annotated, Title 8, ch. II, sec. 601.

such action may never be taken. The treaty of 1803 for the purchase of Louisiana provided that

> The inhabitants of the ceded territory shall be incorporated in the Union of the United States, and admitted as soon as possible, according to the principles of the Federal Constitution, to the enjoyment of all rights, advantages and immunities of citizens of the United States. . . .[9]

The treaty of 1819 for the annexation of Florida contained a similar clause. Later treaties for acquiring the California region, Puerto Rico and the Philippines left questions of citizenship to be decided by Congress.

Collective Naturalization. For the Negroes in the United States in 1868, the Fourteenth Amendment was a great act of collective naturalization. On several occasions Congress has also made large masses of persons citizens by single acts of its own without requiring the individuals concerned to do anything. When territories were raised to statehood and admitted to the Union, and when the free state of Texas was admitted, the free white inhabitants were made citizens *en masse*. There are a number of other important examples. Thus tribal Indians born in the United States were made citizens by an act of Congress in 1924. Former citizens of the Republic of Hawaii and the white inhabitants of Alaska became citizens when these territories were "incorporated into" the United States. After an experiment with a "citizenship of Puerto Rico," Congress provided that such persons as were Puerto Rican citizens should become United States citizens. The 1940 law completes the process of naturalizing persons born in Puerto Rico since 1899. The Danish subjects in the Virgin Islands, which were acquired in 1917 from Denmark, and all persons born there since the acquisition, were made United States citizens in 1927, except for such persons resident there in 1917 as chose to retain their Danish citizenship. These are all cases of collective naturalization, and such collective acts are just as effective as naturalization of any other kind.

Naturalization Laws and Regulations. The Constitution empowers Congress to establish a "uniform rule of naturalization." As a matter of fact such a thing as a uniform rule does not exist. Congress has not only, on numerous occasions, provided for collective naturalization of large groups of people as noted above, but has also from time to time made separate provision for special groups of persons, and has even passed some statutes to grant citizenship to particular persons named in the acts. As a result the citizenship and naturalization laws are very complicated.[10]

Voluntary Individual Naturalization. An important part of the present law on naturalization is that which provides for voluntary individual naturalization of immigrants who have come to the United States for the purpose of

[9] See Commager, *Documents of American History*, pp. 190-91, for an abbreviated text of the treaty.

[10] See 1940 act in *U. S. Code Annotated*, Title 8, ch. II, secs. 701-47.

permanent settlement. The registration of aliens under the Alien Registration act of 1940 revealed that there were then nearly 5 million aliens in the United States, more in fact than the census of the same year had reported. But there were over 7 million foreign born persons in the population that year who had become naturalized.

Immigration Restrictions. Following paragraphs will show how careful Congress has been to provide that only persons who are really fit for it shall acquire United States citizenship by naturalization. But before the naturalization process can begin for any person he must first gain legal entry to the country. At this point the restrictions are even greater. The present national policy and laws on immigration are almost the reverse of what they used to be when population was needed to settle and develop the country. Then the nation's doors were open wide to practically all comers, and especially to the peoples of Europe. Now the laws not only exclude as immigrants practically all members of races ineligible to citizenship, and all persons who are mentally deficient, paupers, diseased persons, criminals, anarchists, contract laborers, and many other groups, but in addition the laws set definite annual quotas for each country from which quota immigrants are permitted to come. These quotas do not apply to Canada or the Latin American states but do apply to other nations throughout the world.

The minimum quota for any country with a quota is 100. All other quotas are controlled by the "national origins" principle, each quota being in proportion to the number of persons from the particular country already in the United States in 1920. Great Britain and North Ireland have the largest quota, over 65,000 a year, and the total of all quotas is under 154,000. In fact the net immigration into the United States for a number of years has been far less than the permissible maximum. The sifting out of immigrants takes place both abroad, under the supervision of United States consuls, and in the United States under the watchful eyes of the Immigration and Naturalization Service.

Who Are Eligible to Naturalization? Under the present general law, only "white persons, persons of African nativity or descent, and descendants of races indigenous to the Western Hemisphere" are entitled to become naturalized American citizens. Persons of the so-called yellow and brown races are in general excluded therefrom but Filipinos who have rendered honorable service in the United States military forces have the privilege of naturalization under special provisions of law. During World War II, also, the bars were let down for a small annual quota of Chinese, and those Chinese who are admitted may acquire citizenship. In wartime alien enemies may not begin the process of naturalization, but those who are far enough along may complete the process. Persons who have deserted from the United States military or naval forces, and enrollees who flee from the country to escape the draft, shall upon conviction be ineligible to become citizens.

Residence Requirements and Procedures. Any person eligible to become a citizen must (1) obtain lawful entry to the United States and establish a permanent residence; (2) make formal "declaration of intention" to become a citizen, before the clerk of a court authorized to naturalize persons: (3) reside continuously at least five years in the United States and at least six months in the state where he applies for naturalization, immediately preceding his application; (4) file his petition for naturalization not less than two nor more than seven years after his declaration of intention; (5) submit to a preliminary hearing before an officer of the Immigration and Naturalization Service; (6) wait at least ninety days after the filing of his petition before his final hearing in court when (7) he must attend such hearing and answer such questions as the judge puts to him. Thus the ordinary minimum period of residence is now five years and ninety days before a certificate of naturalization can be issued.

Special Tests and Requirements. The original naturalization statute of 1790. about a half page in length, permitted any free white alien of good character who had resided in the United States for two years to become a citizen by taking an oath before a court of record to support the Constitution. Then, and for over a century afterward, the United States wanted immigration, and it made citizenship easy for the alien to acquire. A great change in policy is revealed not only in the present immigration laws, with their quotas and other restrictions, but also in the laws on naturalization. Among other requirements the applicant for citizenship today must (1) be able to speak English, if physically able to speak at all; (2) not be an anarchist (that is, a disbeliever in all organized government) or a member of any organization holding such views; (3) not be a believer in, or a member of an organization that believes in, or participate in the financial support or printed advocacy of any of the following: (a) anarchism, as noted above, (b) overthrow by force or violence of the United States government, (c) assaulting or killing of the officers of the United States government or any other organized government, (d) unlawful damage, injury, or destruction of property, or (e) sabotage; (4) be of good moral character, as attested by two credible witnesses; (5) "renounce absolutely and forever all allegiance and fidelity to any foreign prince, potentate, state, or sovereignty," and renounce all hereditary titles and titles of nobility; and (6) take oath "to support and defend the Constitution and the laws of the United States against all enemies, foreign and domestic, and to bear true faith and allegiance to the same. . . ." [11]

Some years ago several judges interpreted the oath required in naturalization cases to include the pledge to bear arms in defense of the country. Under this ruling a woman over fifty years of age, a wartime nurse, a clergyman, and a professor in a divinity school, all pacifists, or conscientious objectors, were denied naturalization. The Supreme Court, by divided votes, sustained these decisions, although the minority pointed out how valuable a group of citizens

[11] *U. S. Code Annotated*, Title 8, ch. II, secs. 704-09, 731, 732, 735.

the United States had in the Quakers and other conscientious objectors.[12] Saying that the oath set forth in the statutes does not mention the bearing of arms, the Court in 1946 reversed its earlier decisions.[13]

Effect of Naturalization. Any person who has been lawfully naturalized and who shows by his conduct an intention to live up to his obligations as a citizen acquires a right to citizenship equal to that of one born in the United States. Furthermore children born outside the United States, if still under eighteen years of age and residing in the United States when both parents have become citizens, automatically acquire citizenship by the naturalization of the parents. Children over eighteen, and the husband or wife of one who becomes naturalized, must themselves go through the procedure of naturalization.

Naturalization Courts and Administrative Agencies. Exclusive jurisdiction to naturalize persons as citizens of the United States is conferred upon United States district courts in the states, the territories, and the District of Columbia, and on state and territorial courts of record whose jurisdiction is unlimited as to the amount in controversy, in their several districts. The process of naturalization is a judicial one, but at the same time the increasing complexity of the law, the need for special knowledge and investigation of cases, and the existence in the Immigration and Naturalization Service of a body of experts, have led Congress and the courts to rely more and more on this administrative agency for enforcement of the law. The service is now in the Department of Justice. It investigates all applicants for naturalization and has charge of all matters relating to immigration, naturalization and the revocation thereof, and the registration of aliens.

Revocation of Naturalization. When the United States confers citizenship upon any alien it is presumed that he has complied with the law in good faith and has told the truth about himself on all important points. If it is later discovered that he did not do this, but obtained his papers by fraud, then his acquisition of citizenship is presumptively invalid and may be revoked. Furthermore if within five years after naturalization a person returns to his former country, or goes to another country and takes up residence there, he will be presumed to have had no intention of becoming permanently a United States citizen and his papers may be canceled unless he can prove his good faith in acquiring citizenship. The burden of proof is on him. Cases have arisen recently in which the United States Department of Justice has attempted to get a revocation of the naturalization papers of certain communists. The Department took the position that the Communist Party believes in the overthrow of the United States government by force and violence, and that no one who belongs to that party can conscientiously become an American citizen. In a leading case of this kind the Supreme Court ruled that mere membership in the Communist Party is not enough to prove a person's inten-

---

[12] See the following Supreme Court decisions: U. S. v. Schwimmer (1929), 279 U. S. 644; U. S. v. Bland (1931), 283 U. S. 636; U. S. v. Macintosh (1931), 283 U. S. 605.

[13] Girouard v. U. S. (1946), 66 S. Ct. 826.

tion to aid in overthrowing the government by violence. Similarly expressions of sympathy for Hitler and the nazis were held to be insufficient in themselves to justify revocation of citizenship.[14]

CITIZENSHIP OF WOMEN

The custom in most countries, and that previously followed in the United States, was to consider the family as a unit for purposes of allegiance, with the husband and father as the controlling member. Thus the wife on marriage took the nationality of her husband, and the children acquired the same allegiance at birth.

Following the adoption of the woman suffrage amendment (the Nineteenth) in 1920, Congress proceeded to make a series of changes in the law, aiming at the ultimate goal of equal citizenship rights for men and women, and to some extent making citizenship an individual and not a family matter. Formerly an American woman lost her American citizenship and presumably gained that of her husband on marrying an alien, whereas a foreign woman marrying an American acquired United States citizenship. Today neither of these things takes place. An American man marrying a foreigner, or an American woman marrying a foreigner, may renounce United States citizenship if he or she so desires. Without definite renunciation no change of citizenship occurs—except where, in the case of women, one needs to affirm one's American citizenship in order not to acquire dual citizenship. Furthermore the children born abroad in these cases of mixed marriage may acquire United States citizenship through either an American father or an American mother. Foreigners who marry Americans can be naturalized by a simplified process after three years of residence, except that a foreigner ineligible to citizenship could not be naturalized in any case. A method is also provided for naturalizing former American women who lost their citizenship through marriage under the previous laws.

FORFEITURE OF CITIZENSHIP

American Interest in Expatriation. Nationality and citizenship are civil and legal statuses, and are not inherent in any individual merely because he is a human being. Consequently either or both of these statuses may be acquired, and they may also be lost or forfeited, according to law. The people of the United States, feeling that they needed immigrants in large numbers to develop the country's resources, and knowing that foreigners would not flock here unless assured that they could acquire American citizenship and protection, stood firmly throughout the nineteenth century for the right of immigrants to give up their foreign allegiance and to acquire United States citizen-

[14] Schneiderman v. U. S. (1943), 320 U. S. 118; Baumgartner v. U. S. (1944), 322 U. S. 665.

ship. Disputes arose, however, with those foreign countries that denied the right of their subjects to renounce their allegiance. This was certainly one of the issues in the War of 1812 with Great Britain, but it was not until 1868 that Congress formally declared by law the policy of the American government to uphold the right of expatriation.[15] The provisions of the Nationality Code of 1940 on this matter may be summarized as follows:

Any national of the United States, whether by birth or naturalization, loses his nationality (and citizenship) by any of the following methods: obtaining naturalization in a foreign state; taking an oath of allegiance to such state; entering its armed forces (unless expressly authorized by United States law); holding an office in a foreign state usually reserved for its nationals; voting in a foreign election or plebiscite; making a formal renunciation of American nationality; and deserting from military or naval service or committing treasonable acts against it, as proved in a proper court. The older citizenship law forbade expatriation in time of war, but not so the Nationality Code.

So-called Loss of Citizenship for Crime. There is a popular theory, also, that individuals "lose their citizenship" as a result of conviction for ordinary crimes, and that the President in federal cases and the governors in state cases have power to "restore citizenship" to such persons. What is meant by this? The cases of deserters in wartime and of those who commit treason are clear. If they are convicted they lose their nationality and with it their citizenship. For other crimes against the United States there is no such penalty. However, state constitutions and laws generally disqualify persons who have been convicted of serious crimes from voting and from holding public office. It is the restoration of these rights of voting and of officeholding that is achieved by the appropriate pardon.[16] Citizenship itself is not lost through conviction of ordinary crimes.

STATUS OF NON-NATIONALS

Declarants. The alien who has come to the United States to reside and who has formally declared his intention to become a citizen is generally called a "declarant." He is not yet a citizen, but still definitely an alien. Should he return to his native country, or go to some other, before completing his naturalization, the United States government would as a rule give him no protection. Should he, while in the United States, commit any crime, develop immoral tendencies, become a public charge, or refuse to perform public duties, he would be liable to deportation like any other alien.

Aliens. Aliens are persons whose permanent allegiance is owed to some other country than that in which they reside. Under the United States Constitution aliens who are lawfully within the country, being "persons," cannot be de-

---

[15] See *U. S. Code Annotated*, Title 8, ch. I, secs. 15, 16.
[16] *U. S. Revised Statutes*, secs. 1996-98. And see E. S. Brown, "The Restoration of Civil and Political Rights by Presidential Pardon," *Am. Pol. Sci. Rev.*, vol. 34, pp. 295-300 (April, 1940).

prived of life, liberty, or property without due process of law. Now that the meaning of "liberty" under the Fourteenth Amendment is being enlarged from time to time by judicial decisions that hold it to include such rights as freedom of speech, assembly, and publication, the rights of aliens among others are being gradually increased. They, too, as persons, have the rights to freedom of speech, press, and religion.[17]

Certain duties are also imposed on aliens. They have what is called "temporary allegiance" to the United States while here, and are obligated to observe the laws and to assist in enforcing them, as are citizens. They may not be compelled to render military service, since this is an obligation that falls especially on citizens.

The restrictions upon them are not to be ignored, however.[18] Even after entering under the present strict immigration laws, they are in the United States entirely by sufferance, and may be deported by the authorities for various breaches of law. The record of deportations in the years following 1918 is an astounding one. Since late 1940 every alien in the United States aged fourteen or over has been required to register and to be fingerprinted, and each must keep the Commissioner of Immigration and Naturalization informed as to his whereabouts and changes of address.[19] Furthermore, Congress has recently been especially insistent upon the deportation of alien communists, German Bundists, and others who preached overthrow of the American system of government by violence or who practiced sabotage. The Department of Justice has attempted to enforce the acts of Congress but the Supreme Court has prevented extreme action by insisting that aliens, like others, are entitled to due process of law.[20]

If not protected by treaties between the United States and their home country, aliens may be forbidden to acquire lands and to organize corporations for land holding or other business purposes, to engage in certain public professions, to hold public employment, to receive public relief, or to enter certain businesses that require special licenses and special police supervision. In practice, the restrictions against foreigners are relatively fewer and less burdensome than might be expected. Attempts by the states in certain cases to prevent aliens from obtaining work in private industry have been held unconstitutional, and many states by positive constitutional provisions give aliens the

same rights of land ownership as citizens. It is usually only aliens ineligible to citizenship who are forbidden by the states to become landowners.

[17] Bridges v. California (1941), 314 U. S. 252.
[18] See F. A. Cleveland, *American Citizenship*, chs. VII-XII; for a different view see a clever article by Don Layne, "Why Become an American Citizen?" in *The American Mercury*, vol. LI, pp. 179-84 (1937).
[19] Act of June 28, 1940, ch. 439, 54 Stat. 673.
[20] Bridges v. Wixon (1945), 326 U. S. 135.

MULTIPLE NATIONALITY

Conflicts in Laws on Nationality. As long as a system of independent national-states exists, it is logical that every human being should have allegiance to one and only one state—one nationality, and one only. Unfortunately, different states have conflicting rules of citizenship, and as men and women move in large numbers from one country to another, many mix-ups occur. There are numerous cases in which an individual has the legal right to two or more national allegiances, or in which two or more states may claim his allegiance and his services. The most common causes of this "multiple nationality" are probably these three:

1. When emigrants from a country that follows the rule of *jus sanguinis* move to a country that adheres to the rule of *jus soli*, their children born in the latter country are claimed as citizens by both. One claims them because of place of birth, the other because of their parentage.

2. When emigrants from a country that denies its nationals the right of expatriation become naturalized in another country, the former country still claims them as citizens, but so does the latter.

3. When a woman citizen of a country that gives women their own citizenship status marries a citizen of a country in which the wife automatically takes the citizenship of her husband, both may claim her allegiance.

Difficulties Resulting from Multiple Nationality. Persons having "multiple nationality" frequently find themselves in difficulty when traveling in their homeland. They may be held for military service, or subjected to punishment for evading other obligations of citizenship. A material reduction of the difficulties arising from multiple nationality can be brought about only by the nations agreeing to treaties establishing more uniform laws of nationality than now prevail. In the years of international cooperation that lie ahead there may be substantial progress in this direction. In the meantime, the foreign representatives of the United States, both consular and diplomatic, annually adjust many cases of multiple nationality by negotiation. The national government is obligated to protect American citizens abroad, and does so to a very considerable extent .

Most troublesome of all, perhaps, are the cases of persons who come to the United States, are naturalized here, and shortly after return to the home country, expecting then the protection of the United States. To reduce somewhat the difficulties in the latter cases, as noted above, the law now provides a means of canceling the naturalization certificates of such persons. This law also authorizes American diplomatic and consular officers abroad to presume that naturalized persons who have gone back to their native country and lived there two years, or to any other country and lived there five, have given up their citizenship. This does not finally settle the case, but it puts the burden of proof on the naturalized citizen.

THE POSITION OF STATELESS PERSONS

Causes of Statelessness. If the lot of the person having "multiple nationality" is sometimes difficult, that of the "stateless person" is even more so. His predicament is that he has no country that claims his allegiance or that will give him citizenship status. This situation often results from his own bad faith or mistakes, but sometimes it results simply from the operation of conflicting nationality laws. The same laws that give two or more allegiances to some persons deprive others of any citizenship whatever. Many persons lost citizenship under the Hitler regime in Germany and in the wars and conquests that that regime promoted. The United States became a haven for a considerable number of such stateless persons during World War II.

A careful student of this problem has listed dozens of ways in which persons may become wholly stateless, and it is known that many stateless persons exist.[21] They cannot get passports to go abroad, but they can be deported if any place can be found that will receive them. In other ways, too, they constitute a special problem for the naturalization authorities.

CHANGING POLICIES AND PROBLEMS

The foregoing pages recount, in a manner all too sketchy, one phase of the struggles of a people toward a truly national policy on citizenship. At first the several states controlled admission to citizenship. Even the original Constitution did not clearly establish citizenship as an unequivocally national status. State loyalties and state resistance had first to be overcome. True nationhood was yet to be attained.

At the same time there was a general desire for more population, to make the nation grow in numbers and in wealth, to develop the vast reaches of the west and the almost unlimited natural resources. Immigration was encouraged. Land ownership, citizenship, and the right to vote were made easy for the foreigner to obtain in the United States. Foreigners came in great numbers to the land of opportunity and, despite some scattered friction between them and the native born, there was little effort made to obstruct their entry or their naturalization.

Indeed the first great issue over citizenship did not concern any foreign born persons, but a large unassimilated minority of long standing, the Negroes. The Dred Scott case with its confusing decision revealed how ambiguous was the citizenship law of the United States and how far short it fell from being a national law. The Fourteenth Amendment, following the war between the states, represented a powerful and in some respects idealistic effort to establish equal citizenship rights for all Americans, a truly national citizenship if

[21] Catheryn Seckler-Hudson, *Statelessness; with Special Reference to the United States,* Washington, 1934.

not a brotherhood of men, without regard to race or color. It had some effect, particularly in the direction of breaking down state lines and loyalties, but it took a long time even to achieve this much.

In the meantime the bungling and the violence that characterized the re-construction of the southern states after the war, revealed how deep-seated was the racial cleavage in the South. For the time being equal citizenship rights and social or economic acceptance for the Negroes were simply out of the question. Then, too, as industrialization advanced in the North, as labor became more conscious of its interests, and as more immigrants settled in the cities and became competitors for jobs, there was increasing anti-foreign agi-tation. There were drives against the easy immigration and naturalization laws and against granting aliens the right to vote. A new wave of restrictions against foreigners reached a high point during and just after World War I. The old national policy of the United States as a haven for all men had been reversed.

When this great change took place, the United States people awoke to find that despite the Fourteenth Amendment and the national citizenship laws, the nation was still far from being perfectly united. There still are racial and national minorities such as the Negroes, the Japanese-Americans and the Mexicans, who do not in fact receive full citizenship rights. Anti-Semitism also flourishes in many places, along with other examples of intolerance towards groups on religious and other grounds.

These brief observations only emphasize the fact that perfect national unity and equality of rights among the whole American people have not yet been attained. The law of national citizenship and of equal protection for all persons sets a very high standard. It is for future generations to demonstrate whether or not the facts can be raised up to the standard of the law.

Those who endeavor to bring about greater equality of civil rights among citizens face certain issues of democratic methods. One is the question as to how much can be achieved by laws and law enforcement, and how much must be left to the slower processes of education. There are already a number of pertinent constitutional provisions and statutes and no one can say in advance how much more would be achieved if additional laws to equalize civil liberties were to be enacted.

Granting that some new laws are necessary, the next issue is whether they shall be enacted and enforced by the national government or by the states or by the two together. The methods of national enforcement that have been tried up to now have not been notably successful, and on the other hand certain states have been very reluctant to act at all. There seems to be a need in this field for the invention of new devices of national-state coopera-tion on a program of protecting citizenship and the rights that pertain to it.

REFERENCES

Luella Gettys, *The Law of Citizenship in the United States*, Chicago, 1934.

F. A. Cleveland, *American Citizenship as Distinguished from Alien Status*, New York, 1927.

Catheryn Seckler-Hudson, *Statelessness; with Special Reference to the United States*, Washington, D. C., 1934.

U. S. Code Annotated, Title 8, including Nationality Act of 1940.

C. H. Maxson, *Citizenship*, New York, 1930.

A. J. Lien, *Privileges and Immunities of Citizens of the United States*, New York, 1913.

Roger Howell, *The Privileges and Immunities of State Citizenship*, Baltimore, 1918.

F. A. Ogg and P. O. Ray, *Introduction to American Government*, 8th ed., New York, 1945, ch. VIII.

N. Alexander, *Rights of Aliens under the Federal Constitution*, Montpelier, Vt., 1931.

S. P. Breckenridge, *Marriage and the Civic Rights of Women; Separate Domicil and Independent Citizenship*, Chicago, 1931.

J. M. Mathews, *The American Constitutional System*, 2nd ed., New York, 1940, ch. XXI.

A. N. Christensen and E. M. Kirkpatrick, *The People, Politics, and the Politician: Readings in American Government*, New York, 1941, pp. 184-207.

CHAPTER 7

The National Electorate

Perhaps the title of this chapter should be in the form of a question: To what extent and in what sense is there a national electorate in the United States? How is the composition of the electorate determined, and what are its tasks? To what extent does the national government control in such matters, and how much is left to the states? Is the nation at the mercy of the several states with respect to the establishment of a democratic suffrage?

The close integration of the national and state governments in the American system is nowhere better revealed than in matters relating to the suffrage, nominations, and elections. Here we find not two separate, independent bodies of law, one for national and the other for state purposes, but rather one great mass of state laws that serve both the national government and the states. The registration of voters and the conduct of elections in such states are a unified process directly under state laws and control. There are a few national constitutional principles and a small body of national laws, however, that control the election process with respect to national elections, and it will be necessary to explain their relationship to the whole process.

THE RIGHT TO VOTE

The ballot as developed for public elections in the United States is a sheet of paper on which the legal voter is authorized to mark his choices among candidates for public office and on public measures, and which he is entitled to have counted so as to give effect to his choices. The right of any individual to cast a ballot in public elections is designated by various terms such as (a) the suffrage, (b) the elective franchise, (c) the right to vote, and (d) the right of the ballot. Those having this right are spoken of in the aggregate as voters, electors or the electorate. The process of marking and casting ballots is called voting, electing, or balloting.

Popular Sovereignty and Suffrage. In the United States political sovereignty is vested nominally, and to a large extent really, in the people. Constitutions, both national and state, are adopted in the name of the people, and are generally considered as emanating from them. Most of the state constitutions contain provisions like this:

> Government is instituted for the security, benefit and protection of the people, in whom all political power is inherent, together with the right to alter, modify, or reform such government whenever the public good may require it.[1]

This is a typical expression of popular sovereignty. It is followed in all state constitutions by provisions for popular election of public officers. But the term "the people" is vague and undefined. If elections are to be conducted in an orderly manner there must be some definition of what people are entitled to vote at public elections. Hence "the people" who at least nominally establish the state constitution designate *some* of the people to act as legal voters. The right to vote is established, defined, and regulated by both constitutions and statutes.

Development of the Suffrage. The suffrage laws of the states were not enacted all at once in their present form. In each state there has been a development that can be read in successive constitutions, constitutional amendments, and statutes.[2] The changes from colonial times to the present have been substantially these: (1) Requirements that a person must own a certain amount of property in order to be able to vote have been almost wholly wiped out. (2) Religious tests have all been abandoned. (3) Where once there were different voting qualifications in some states for city officers, for the lower and upper houses of the legislature, and so on, today there is almost complete unification of the requirements *within each state*, so that in any community the same list of voters will suffice for almost any election, national, state, or local. Since there are forty-eight states, however, nation-wide uniformity of requirements does not exist. (4) In this unification of requirements within each state, state control has been almost complete. The power of local governments to define their own electorate has nearly disappeared, and the national government has interfered up to now primarily to ensure voting rights to Negroes and women. (5) The electorate has been greatly increased in proportion to population. Whereas some of the colonies had as few as 5 per cent of their people eligible to vote, today there are communities where well over half the population are registered voters. (6) Beginning about a century ago a number of states permitted alien residents to vote, but at present citizenship is a requirement for voting in every state. (7) The number of officers subject to popu-

[1] Minnesota Const., Art. I, sec. I.
[2] See especially A. E. McKinley, *The Suffrage Franchise in the Thirteen English Colonies in America*, and K. H. Porter, *A History of the Suffrage in the United States*.

lar election, and the number of measures on which voters may act, has increased greatly since colonial times.

The Right to Vote in State Elections. Each state has the power to determine for itself what persons may vote in its state and local elections. It is in the state constitutions, therefore, and in the state statutes that the qualifications for voting are set forth. Since the state constitution is read as a limitation on the powers of the state legislature, the latter is not ordinarily allowed to change the voting qualifications provided by the state constitution, or to add to or subtract from those qualifications. It has been generally held, however, that a registration requirement is not an additional qualification, but only a means of proving what persons are eligible to vote.[3]

The Right to Vote in National Elections. The foregoing paragraph relates to state and local elections. With respect to national elections the situation is different. The states do not confer the right to vote for members of the two houses of Congress; they do not do so because they have no power to. It is the Constitution of the United States that confers this right. For convenience, however, the framers of the Constitution decided not to establish an entirely separate list of national voters in each state. Instead it was provided that "the Electors in each State [for members of Congress] shall have the Qualifications requisite for Electors of the most numerous Branch of the State Legislature." (Art. I, sec. 2, par. 1; Amend. XVII, par. 1.)

This means that there is a body of national voters for electing members of Congress, but that the qualifications of these voters in any state are those set by the state for the lower house of the state legislature. Anyone who qualifies as a voter for the lower house of the state legislature has a right conferred on him by the national Constitution to vote for both Representatives and Senators in Congress. This right can be protected and enforced by the national government, and any act by a state or by its officers to prevent qualified persons (Negroes, for example) from exercising this right is illegal and punishable, under Acts of Congress.[4]

The situation with respect to the choice of Presidential Electors is somewhat different. On this the Constitution provides that "Each State shall appoint, in such Manner as the Legislature thereof may direct, a Number of Electors" to participate in the election of the President and Vice President. (Art. II, sec. 1, par. 2.) This is a direct delegation of power by the Constitution to the state legislatures. It is not even required that the Presidential Electors be chosen by popular vote. The Supreme Court has said that these Electors are state officers and not officers of the United States. Actually they perform no function of the state government. A better interpretation would seem to be, therefore, that for the choice of Presidential Electors the state legislatures have been made agents of the nation. It is their duty to see to it that Presi-

---

[3] See J. P. Harris, *Registration of Voters in the United States*, 1929, ch. XII.
[4] See *Ex parte Yarborough* (1884), 110 U. S. 651; Lane v. Wilson (1939), 307 U. S. 268; U. S. v. Classic (1941), 313 U. S. 299.

dential Electors are chosen. If they delegate this function, as they all have, to the voters in their states, those voters also exercise a national function, that of assisting in filling the two highest elective offices of the national government. Consequently Congress may regulate Presidential elections at least to the extent of prohibiting any corrupt and excessive campaign expenditures. As the Supreme Court said about this, "To say that Congress is without power to pass appropriate legislation to safeguard such an election from the improper use of money to influence the result is to deny to the nation in a vital particular the power of self-preservation." [5] Here, be it noted, a doctrine of national "power" of self-preservation is invoked to uphold an act of Congress. Furthermore, since the same body of voters elects both members of Congress and Presidential Electors, and at the same elections, the power of Congress would seem to be about the same with respect to both.

The Poll Tax Issue. The question of the power of Congress to control the electorate that chooses members of Congress and Presidential Electors has come up in connection with the poll tax issue. Several states in the South not only set up qualifications of citizenship, age, residence, and literacy for all who wish to vote, but also still require each qualified individual to pay a poll tax before voting. Have the states the power to do this? May Congress forbid the collection of the poll tax as a prerequisite for voting in national elections? Those who oppose the poll tax and who favor an act of Congress to forbid it reason as follows:

For the election of members of Congress the national Constitution creates an electorate that has the same "qualifications" in each state as are set up in the state for electing members of the state's lower house. The states are empowered to set genuine *qualifications* for such voters, but that means only such tests as determine their actual competence, capacity, or fitness. A poll tax, they say, is not of this nature. It tests or proves no capacity or quality. A person who pays it is not necessarily any more fit to vote than one who does not. It is simply an arbitrary obstacle or prerequisite. When applied to persons otherwise qualified to vote for members of Congress, it is a state tax for state benefit upon the exercise of a national right. It is, therefore, unconstitutional, and Congress may forbid it by law.[6]

This line of argument was not presented to the Supreme Court in 1936-37 when the court upheld a Georgia state poll tax.[7] In that case no act of Congress was involved, and the court upheld the state tax not as a qualification for voting but as a "prerequisite" and a "familiar and reasonable regulation long enforced in many states." Some of the members of the present Supreme Court would be likely to favor the new anti-poll tax argument. Certainly if the nation as a whole is to have any real control over the election of its Con-

[5] Burroughs v. U. S. (1934), 290 U. S. 534.
[6] See: *H. R. 7, the Anti-Poll Tax Bill is Constitutional,* a pamphlet issued by National Committee to Abolish the Poll Tax, Washington, about 1943.
[7] Breedlove v. Suttles (1937), 302 U. S. 277.

gress there must be some limit upon the power of the states to set up arbitrary and irrelevant obstacles to voting. Under its power to enact laws "necessary and proper" to carry out the Constitution, Congress must have the authority to define in a broad and reasonable way what are appropriate "qualifications" for voting in national elections.

Soldiers' and Sailors' Right to Vote. Another issue arose during World War II concerning the power of Congress over voting. Many men had entered the service and had been sent to foreign lands just before they reached voting age. It was difficult for all and nearly impossible for some to get registered in their own states. Could Congress set up a general rule to help these men get the right to vote even though it contravened state laws? This issue did not come clearly to a head. There is little reason to doubt, however, that under its various war powers, including that "to raise and support armies" Congress may protect the political rights of men in military service just as it looks out for their civil and economic rights, even to the extent of overriding state laws. Its failure to do so fully during World War II was not due to any lack of constitutional power but rather to a strong state-rights feeling in Congress and to a fear that national regulation of elections to this extent would enable the nation's executive, the President and Commander in Chief, to dominate the entire election process.

Negro Suffrage and Woman Suffrage. It may be argued of course that, if the thing is important enough, the national government should proceed by constitutional amendment to do something about the poll tax and the soldiers' vote. There are two precedents for this, the Fifteenth Amendment, adopted for the benefit of the Negroes, which forbids any state to deny or abridge the right of citizens to vote "on account of race, color, or previous condition of servitude" and the Nineteenth or woman suffrage Amendment which forbids such denial or abridgement "on account of sex." These two amendments were important steps toward making the suffrage laws uniform throughout the nation; they do not expressly authorize women and the people of all races and colors to vote but they do forbid discriminations against women and Negroes as such. Furthermore they apply to state and local as well as to national elections. It was probably necessary to have these particular constitutional amendments to achieve these purposes. On the other hand it is very doubtful whether constitutional amendments are needed either to eliminate the poll tax requirement in national elections or to authorize Congress to provide full protection for the rights of soldiers and sailors to vote. Moreover the failure of the Fifteenth Amendment to ensure the voting rights of Negroes suggests that another amendment might be equally ineffective.

Grandfather Clauses and White Primary Laws. General and genuine tests of the ability of individuals to vote intelligently are not forbidden by the Fifteenth and Nineteenth Amendments even though in fact such tests may exclude more Negroes than whites or more women than men from voting. Conversely, direct discriminations by the states against Negroes as such are invalid. For example, the Oklahoma constitution of 1910 established a reading and writing test for voters, but exempted from this test any persons who themselves, or whose lineal forebears (father, grandfather, etc.) were entitled to vote anywhere on January 1, 1866. Other southern states had similar provisions. Since only whites had had the right to vote at the time specified, these so-called "grandfather clauses" meant that Negroes but not whites had to take the reading and writing test. This was held invalid as directly contrary to the Fifteenth Amendment.[8] The Oklahoma legislature thereupon enacted (a) that all who had been qualified to vote in 1914 should continue to be so, and (b) that others must register between April 30 and May 11, 1916, a period of twelve days. When a Negro who failed to get registered at the time was later excluded from voting, he sued for damages under the United States statutes. The Supreme Court upheld him, declaring that this Oklahoma legislation put discriminatory burdens on Negroes and was invalid.[9]

In another attempt to exclude Negroes from voting, Texas and other states passed "white primary" laws under which only white persons were permitted to vote in Democratic party primary elections in the state. Primaries are preliminary public elections for choosing candidates for later election to office, and Democratic party primaries are in many respects more important than the final elections in the South. In a decision upon the Texas statute the Supreme Court held the primary to be an important part of the election process, and held that the act excluding Negroes was an act of the state which denied to them the "equal protection of the laws" to which they are entitled under the Fourteenth Amendment.[10] Thereupon Texas repealed the invalid statute, and thus left it to each political party in convention to make its own rules of membership. When the party then, by act of the party convention, limited party membership and participation in party primaries to white persons, the Supreme Court at first held that this was a party action, not the state's action, and that therefore it was not forbidden by either the Fourteenth or Fifteenth Amendments which forbid state but not private actions.[11]

Later the Supreme Court had another case before it in which a Texas political party, conducting a primary election under state laws, excluded a Negro from participating. On this occasion the court reversed its former decision. It held not only that a primary election is a part of the election process but also that where a political party acts under state authority and performs important services for the state in the conduct of the primary, it acts as an agent of the state. Thus the party's discrimination against Negroes under such circumstances is the action of the state and is unconstitutional.[12]

The foregoing paragraphs reveal an increasing interest of the national government not only in the right of citizens to vote in national elections, but also

[8] Guinn v. U. S. (1915), 238 U. S. 347.
[9] Lane v. Wilson (1939), 307 U. S. 268.
[10] Nixon v. Herndon (1927), 273 U. S. 536.
[11] Grovey v. Townsend (1935), 295 U. S. 45.
[12] Smith v. Allwright (1944), 321 U. S. 649.

in gaining for all citizens equal rights of participation in all elections, without arbitrary discriminations. It is settled also that the national government has ample legal authority to achieve a fair degree of equality for all citizens in voting whenever it so desires. As things stand today, however, the national government still leaves it mainly to the states to define and to enforce proper qualifications for voters. While this situation continues there is likely to be a continuation of discrimination against Negroes and other minority groups. It does some good, undoubtedly, for the Supreme Court to continue to lecture to the states on this subject, but until Congress and the national administration take more positive and constructive steps, little change is likely to take place.

PRESENT LEGAL SUFFRAGE QUALIFICATIONS

There are today throughout the United States only three general requirements for the suffrage, namely, (a) citizenship, (b) adult age, and (c) residence in the place of voting. Supplementary to these in certain states are several others, including (d) literacy tests, (e) tax-payment, (f) registration, and (g) certain more or less standard disqualifications for crime, insanity, etc., that affect relatively small percentages of the people.

Citizenship. As already indicated, citizenship does not carry with it automatically the right to vote. Millions of American citizens are without the franchise because they are not yet of age, or because they lack some other particular qualification such as sufficient length of residence in the place of voting. There is also no rule of the United States Constitution forbidding states to give the franchise to aliens. In the first state constitutions the right to vote was conferred on "inhabitants" or "residents"; the word "citizens" was not ordinarily used. Under the liberal immigration rules of the times, many foreigners entered the country, acquired residence and the necessary property, and soon qualified as voters, with or without naturalization.

Anti-Alien Movements. At first little attention was paid to this circumstance of foreigners voting, since property ownership was considered more important than citizenship. In time, however, a clear-cut issue was presented. In the two decades before the Civil War an "American" or "Know-Nothing" party arose to denounce the practice of letting foreign-born persons vote and hold office. "America for Americans" was one of their slogans. In the New England and Middle Atlantic states they were especially bitter in their denunciations of the Irish and other immigrants who were enrolled by partisan election officers and brought to the polls to vote in large numbers. As a means of keeping these immigrant elements from dominating the elections two requirements were advocated: *first*, that only citizens should be permitted to vote, and *second*, that there should be a literacy test, since many of the foreign born were wholly unlettered. The Louisiana constitution of 1812 seems to have been the first definitely to require citizenship, but most eastern and southern states later did the same. Connecticut in 1855, aiming directly at the illiterate foreign born, required voters to be able to read the constitution or laws, and in 1857 Massachusetts followed suit.

Declarants as Voters. While this anti-alien movement was strong in the East, certain middle-western territories and states, desiring an influx of immigrants, offered the right to vote to persons who had merely declared their intention to become citizens. Wisconsin was the first to extend this privilege (1848), but the movement spread in the Middle West and South, so that a third of the states permitted declarants to vote. It was possible, of course, for an immigrant to declare his intention to become a citizen almost immediately on settling in this country. He remained an alien, legally, and in fact, and if he could already vote he had less incentive than otherwise to complete his naturalization. For this and other reasons, the agitation against aliens voting was revived, and within a few years after World War I this voting had been abolished in all states. Citizenship is now a requirement in all states, but this does not mean that no aliens now vote in the United States. There are so many persons who do not clearly know their status, so many instances in which the facts as to citizenship are confused, and there is such laxity in the enforcement of the registration and election laws in many places, that there probably are tens of thousands of cases of actual alien voting.

Age as a Qualification. Although recognizing differences between males and females with respect to age of consent to marriage and for other purposes, the common law hit upon twenty-one years as the age when both sexes reach full adult status for most legal purposes. For voting purposes several American colonies and states experimented a little with other ages, but finally all states accepted twenty-one years as the age at which the voting right, and the right to hold public office, begin. Georgia has recently departed from this standard by lowering the voting age to eighteen.

Residence as a Qualification. When "freemanship" or property ownership in a place qualified a person as a voter, actual residence in the place was not required. Later when these evidences of a "stake in the community" were dropped from the suffrage qualifications, residence in the place received more and more emphasis. Today some specific period of residence within the state, and within the county or voting district or both, is a requirement in every state. (1) The most common period of residence *within the state* is one year (32 states), but five states (4 southern) require two years, and 11 others require only six months. (2) *Within the county* the requirements vary from thirty days to one year—six and three months being among the most common requirements. (3) *Within the voting precinct* from ten to thirty days are usually required, but the requirements run as high as one year. The importance of residence requirements to the individual voter cannot easily be overemphasized. In urban places, particularly, hundreds of thousands are prevented from voting every year because of failure to establish the necessary residence. They move from precinct to precinct, from ward to ward, even from city to city, in large numbers each year.

What Is Residence? "Residence" is a legal term that is defined somewhat differently in the various states. Furthermore, residence for voting purposes may be different both in nature and in length from residence for purposes of marriage or divorce, for the obtaining of business or hunting licenses, and for other purposes. In general, however, residence depends upon (a) certain facts, (b) the intention of the individual, and (c) the laws of the state controlling both.

Intention, from the individual's point of view, comes first. The adult, self-supporting individual has a very considerable range of choice with respect to place of residence—minors and dependents very much less. Intention is a personal matter, but it must be a clear and definite intent to make a certain place his residence permanently, or for a definite and fairly long period of time, with no immediate intent to move away.

Facts. Everywhere the law requires that certain facts support the intention, since intention alone does not establish residence in a place where one has no abode. The laws vary, but usually one must have a rented room, apartment, lodging arrangements, house, or at least the privilege of returning to the residence of some near relative, to constitute the factual tangible evidence of residence. Unmarried persons living with their parents have their residence with them. Continuous habitation of the place of abode is not required. Thus traveling salesmen, itinerant workmen, and others whose work or pastimes keep them moving from place to place are entitled to have some place that they consider to be their home as a place of legal and voting residence, but if challenged by the election officials, they may be compelled to show tangible evidence of actual residence in the place.

The *law* is a factor in each state in fixing the rules of residence for every person. The intention that one has must be such as the law approves. Thus on the question of intention, one may not legally have the intention to have two or more voting residences. "One man, one voting residence," and "one man, one vote" have come to be accepted rules in all American states. The person with a town house and a country house, for example, may not have voting residence at both places. In most states college students may not acquire voting residence in the college town if they get their support from parents or guardians living elsewhere, and if they think and speak of the latter place as "home." Likewise workmen on a temporary construction job, soldiers and sailors stationed in forts and barracks, inmates of poorhouses, and other groups are generally held by law not to acquire voting residence where thus temporarily located, although "absent voting" laws may enable them to mail ballots to their home districts.

Literacy Tests. Connecticut and Massachusetts when they introduced literacy tests for voting before the Civil War were aiming to reduce the political power of the foreign born. After the Reconstruction, when the whites in the southern states were endeavoring to eliminate Negro voting, they also placed literacy tests in their state constitutions. Today such tests exist in twenty states, and the number is slowly rising. Generally speaking, in the South the literacy test is alternative to some other test and not additional; if one owns a certain amount of property, he need not pass the literacy test. Elsewhere it is an independent test, additional to all others.

In its most common forms the test requires the applicant for registration as a voter to read some part of the national or state constitution in English, and to write his name; in the South he is more generally required "to read and write" some article of the Constitution. The test is usually given by the election authorities at the time of registration, and is therefore often given by persons who are themselves nearly illiterate, and who are interested as partisans in increasing the number of registered voters of their own party, and in holding down the number of others. In New York the determination of a person's literacy for suffrage purposes is made by the public school authorities, who conduct standard tests at regular and frequent intervals. Furthermore, all persons who have completed the fifth grade in an approved school are exempted from the special test. If the literacy test is meant to be fairly and intelligently applied, this New York plan would seem to be far superior to the usual political method of enforcement.

Tax-Payment Tests. In a declining number of the states, mainly in the South, there is a tax-payment test added to other requirements. It consists usually in the payment of an annual poll tax of from $1 to $2, the receipt for which must be shown either at the time of registration or at the election. This, as previously indicated, is an effective way of keeping many poor whites and Negroes from voting. It lends itself to various political "rackets," such as providing party funds to pay the poll taxes of voters who will "vote right." As actually administered, therefore, it does not achieve the supposed result of keeping only the shiftless from the polls.

Registration Requirements. As stated above, registration is in a sense not an additional suffrage qualification, but a means of proving that one has the required qualifications. It is particularly needed in large cities to prevent wholesale voting by persons who are not legal voters. It is extended over the entire area of more than half the states, but is lacking in the rural portions of many states. In the South, registration of voters by white election officials is one of the most effective means of keeping Negroes from voting. Everywhere the necessity of registering before voting has the effect of keeping careless and indifferent citizens from the polls.

The Negro's Right to Vote. While none of the foregoing prerequisites and qualifications for voting seems to be wholly unreasonable, it is clear that if they are enforced in a partial and arbitrary manner their cumulative effect can be very restrictive. It is no mere accident that most of the Supreme Court decisions involving the constitutional right to vote have concerned Negroes.

The Fourteenth Amendment having established the citizenship of Negroes, the Fifteenth Amendment was placed in the national Constitution in the attempt to guarantee to them the right to vote. During Reconstruction days, about 1865 to 1876, the Negro vote dominated certain southern states, but thereafter white supremacy was rapidly restored and within a generation Negroes were almost wholly eliminated from the electorate in the deep South while farther north, through Tennessee, Kentucky, and West Virginia, Negro voting was and is more generally tolerated. In the true North there is relatively little discrimination and in fact much scrambling of the parties to get the Negro vote. It is where Negroes are most numerous, where they might win elections, that they find it most difficult to vote.

The states in the far South have worked out a series of measures that rather effectively prevent voting by Negroes. These may in spirit violate the Fifteenth Amendment, but in form they are not directed against men on account of their "race, color, or previous condition of servitude." They follow other lines, and it is the cumulative effect of many provisions rather than that of any single one that produces the result. At first it was intimidation that drove and kept the Negroes from the polls. Later the whites legalized their supremacy by constitutional and statutory acts. The "white primary" regulations of the Democratic party in a number of states; the educational tests as enforced by white election judges; the poll tax requirement; the necessity for registration long in advance of the election; and the general sentiment of the dominant race against Negro voting are almost completely effective.[13]

Common Disqualifications. In practically all states there are certain specific disqualifications such as: (1) *Conviction of crime.* Various states stress crimes against the election laws, bribery, felonies and "infamous crimes," perjury, and others. The governors and pardon authorities usually have the power to restore the right to vote after the completion of a sentence or along with the issuance of a pardon. (2) *Serious mental incompetency* such as insanity, idiocy, and incapacity to handle one's own affairs, as determined by a court. (3) *Paupers* are also disqualified in about a dozen states. By "pauper" in this case is presumably meant one who is chronically so unable to provide for himself, in good times as well as in depressions, that he must depend on public aid. During the severe depression in the 1930's, various conservative groups including the National Association of Real Estate Boards advocated the barring from the suffrage of all persons then on relief—numbers running into the millions and taking in a large percentage of the adults in a number of states. The public at large recognized, however, that most of those then on relief were normally competent and self-supporting persons who would again become producers as soon as employment was offered. It is significant of deep cleavages in public opinion that such a proposal to disfranchise the unemployed could be made.

[13] See Kent, *The Great Game of Politics*, pp. 314-19; Lewinson, *Race, Class and Party*; Myrdal, *An American Dilemma*, vol. I, part V.

NATURE AND CONTENT OF THE RIGHT TO VOTE

Suffrage a Legal Right. Any person who can qualify under the suffrage provisions of the constitution and laws of his state is legally entitled to be a voter. The right is one protected by law and enforceable by courts and the regular law-enforcing agencies. It is incumbent on the individual, when confronted with illegal attempts to prevent his voting, to apply to the proper courts to protect his right.

Is It Not Also a Duty? The typical American's attitude is that voting is a right that he may exercise or not as he sees fit. He assumes that the right to vote includes the right not to vote. Many laws are also based on this theory. All persons who abstain from voting are expected to acquiesce in the decision of those who go to the polls, no matter how few they are. Practically this rule is almost indispensable, for without it those who abstain from voting might paralyze the actions of government by their inaction. At the same time it needs to be recognized that voting at public elections is one of the most important of the steps in the democratic process of government. If voters may at will neglect their duty, then the public loses the thought and the services of those who abstain, while an undue weight is given to those who have a special interest in acting. In short, the right to vote carries with it logically the duty to vote and to vote as intelligently and as disinterestedly as possible.

Compulsory Voting. Nevertheless the American people have not moved toward making voting compulsory. A Missouri supreme court decision of 1896 held such a law to be unconstitutional, as an infringement of the "sovereign right of suffrage." Compulsory voting measures submitted to the voters in several western states have been rejected. Two state constitutions (Massachusetts and North Dakota) authorize the legislature to penalize non-voting, but no laws have yet been enacted under these provisions.

Non-Voting. In the total there is probably more voting year by year in the United States than in any other two or three countries, with the possible exception of Russia. Elections are more frequent here, and they cover more offices and measures. Nevertheless the proportion of people voting is higher in some countries than here. In the "no third term" election of 1940, when the nation cast its largest total vote to date, just about 50,000,000 people cast ballots for Presidential electors, but this was less than 38 per cent of the population, and less than two-thirds of the 80 million citizens over 21 years of age in 1940. In 1944 the total was about 4 million less. One potential voter in every three fails to vote even at Presidential elections. This ratio is not uniform over the whole United States. In the South, the important decisions are made in the white controlled primaries, and the final election is attended by relatively few voters since the result is almost a foregone conclusion. Hence in these states the ratio of votes to population falls to about 8 or 10 per cent and has gone as low as 5 or 6 per cent. In certain northern states, on the other hand, the ratio rises to over 40 per cent of the population and to perhaps 75 per cent or more of the potential electorate.

Content of Right to Vote. The right to vote has a constantly varying content. It includes generally the right to vote for all public officers who are elective within the district where the voter resides. Presidential electors, Senators, and Representatives in Congress, governors, and state legislators are everywhere included in the list at the present time. Beyond these are varying numbers of state administrative officers, judges of state and local courts, and officers of local governments. In most states, also, the right to pass upon new constitutions and constitutional amendments is included, while many states have added the right of the voters to pass upon a variety of state and local measures, and even the power to recall elective officers from office before their terms expire. Primary elections, at which candidates are nominated for later election, should also be listed as important.

Under the constitutional division of functions between the national government and the states it has been left mainly to the states to determine the functions of the electorate. The Constitution requires the popular election of only Senators and Representatives in Congress. From time to time there have been proposals for the popular election of national department heads and of the nation's representatives in certain international organizations, as well as for a national referendum on going to war. These proposals seem to be so lacking in practicality and so likely, if adopted, to bring disunity into the national government that they have not received serious consideration. The proposal for the direct popular election of the President and Vice President, on the other hand, would, if adopted, make little or no change in the present functions of the nation's electorate.

REFERENCES

A. E. McKinley, *The Suffrage Franchise in the Thirteen English Colonies in America*, Philadelphia, 1905.

K. H. Porter, *A History of Suffrage in the United States*, Chicago, 1918.

J. P. Harris, *Registration of Voters in the United States*, Washington, 1929, chs. I, III, XII.

A. J. McCulloch, *Suffrage and Its Problems*, Baltimore, 1929.

Paul Lewinson, *Race, Class, and Party: A History of Negro Suffrage and White Politics in the South*, New York, 1932.

Frank R. Kent, *The Great Game of Politics*, Garden City, N. Y., 1923.

E. M. Sait, *American Parties and Elections*, New York, 1927, chs. I-III.

F. A. Ogg and P. O. Ray, *Introduction to American Government*, 8th ed., New York, 1945, ch. X.

A. N. Holcombe, *State Government in the United States*, 3rd ed., New York, 1931, ch. VII.

F. A. Cleveland, *Organized Democracy*, New York, 1913, chs. X-XII.

C. E. Merriam and H. F. Gosnell, *Non-voting, Causes and Methods of Control*, Chicago, 1924.

H. F. Gosnell, *Getting Out the Vote: An Experiment in the Stimulation of Voting*, Chicago, 1927.

R. C. Martin, "The Municipal Electorate: A Case Study," *Southwestern Social Science Quarterly*, vol. XIV, no. 3, December, 1933.

L. H. Bean, *Ballot Behavior, A Study of Presidential Elections*, Washington, 1940.

Gunnar Myrdal, *An American Dilemma: The Negro Problem and Modern Democracy*, 2 vols., New York, 1944, espec. vol. I, part V.

John M. Mathews and Clarence A. Berdahl, *Documents and Readings in American Government: National and State*, rev. ed., New York, 1940, pp. 168-73.

A. N. Christensen and E. M. Kirkpatrick, *The People, Politics, and the Politician: Readings in American Government*, New York, 1941, pp. 208-38.

CHAPTER 8

The Substance of American Politics

COMMON AND CONFLICTING INTERESTS

The United States is a nation of 140 million people with over 80 million potential voters. As one people they have many things in common, such, for example, as language, institutions, history and traditions, government, law, foreign policy and defenses, highways and waterways, and a great array of public facilities. Living in one country together and dependent upon its natural resources and other advantages, they have more reasons for national unity than for differences.

At the same time there are within the nation diverse and competing interests. Spread over a great area; living some in great cities, others in smaller places, some in prosperous farming areas and others in poorer sandy, mountainous or cut-over districts; dependent upon different employments and concerned with different material interests; having divergent views as to what the public policy should be on many different issues—the various groups who compose the nation naturally have many grounds for political disagreement.

One of the principal causes for controversy is public policy with respect to economic matters. Governments have tremendous power through their laws and their policies in administration to affect property rights, the wages of labor and the return on capital, the prices of agricultural and other products, the rates of railroads and utilities, and the jobs and incomes of practically all the people.

This influence of government in the economic realm is not the only factor that makes it important, but it is something that is ever present. On the other hand the great vested economic interests in such fields as manufacturing, commerce, banking, railroads, and utilities, the forces of labor and of agriculture, the professions, teachers, and civil servants—these are all important elements in the nation's political structure and functioning. Furthermore there are sectional economic interests that must be reckoned with in politics—the Northeast, the South, the Far West; the cotton farmers, the grain growers, the cattle raisers, the coal, iron, and oil industries, and so on—each more or less dominant in some region.

At the present stage in world development there is one issue that makes the role of government in the economic life of the United States of outstanding concern. The nations of the world stand more or less divided and still partly uncertain whether they shall follow the system of complete public ownership and management of all production of goods and services, as exemplified in the USSR, or the system of private capitalism and free enterprise of which the United States is now the outstanding example. The drift in recent years seems to have been toward the Russian system; much of Europe may go a considerable distance in that direction in the years ahead. In what direction and how far shall the United States go in the public ownership and control of business, labor, and agriculture in the postwar decade? There is no more burning issue in the politics and government of this nation today.

The struggle of various political parties, pressure groups, and individuals over this major issue is a large part of the substance of American politics. In fact, among a people who are strongly united as one nation, who have more common interests than they have conflicting interests, politics is one of the principal methods of settling economic and other grievances and disagreements. It is a method of harmonizing and adjusting differences without resort to violence and without fundamental change in the system of ordered liberty and constitutional government.

INTEREST GROUPS AND ORGANIZATIONS

It is characteristic of American democratic methods that there is almost unlimited freedom of association for any lawful purpose. If even a mere handful of people in any neighborhood or region, or in any trade, industry, or branch of agriculture, feel that they have grievances and believe that they can improve their lot by forming an association, they are free to go ahead. This right of free association goes hand in hand with freedom of speech, press, and religion, the right to agitate and propagandize for their particular cause, and to petition the public authorities for the redress of grievances. By statutes, both national and state, the rights of organization have been extended and strengthened in the interests of farmers, laborers, cooperatives, churches, and other groups.

As a result of this freedom and encouragement to organize, and of the people's needs and capacity for organization, there are countless local, state, and national groups that are today in position to give their views to the public and to the government. Almost every conceivable interest has its association, its headquarters, and its spokesmen. Practically all these associations participate more or less in the political discussions of the nation insofar as they concern their own interests and membership. Among the more powerful organized interests are those in

(1) *Agriculture* (The American Farm Bureau Federation, The National Grange, The National Farmers' Union, and many special associations in dairying, cattle raising, sugar growing, etc.);

(2) *Labor* (The American Federation of Labor, The Congress of Industrial Organizations, The Railroad Brotherhoods, and others);

(3) *Industry, Commerce, and Finance* (Chamber of Commerce of the United States, National Association of Manufacturers, American Bankers Association, Association of American Railways, and so on through a long and imposing list);

(4) *Professions* (American Bar Association, American Medical Association, National Education Association, etc.).

In addition to these associations that are strongly motivated by economic considerations there are countless others in which the economic motive plays a smaller role. It must not be forgotten that men are moved to action by many motives, which vary from time to time and are somewhat different from man to man. It is one of the glories of a free and democratic life that it enables men to satisfy desires for non-material ends. Religion, patriotism, humanitarianism, the love of music, the arts, education, and science, the urge to promote public health and to relieve human distress, these are among the finest expressions of human motivation. Corresponding to each of these motivations there are many associations that work actively in public affairs. These also might be called "pressure groups," because they do bring their influence to bear on public leaders and officials, although their aims are largely or wholly unselfish.

In considering all these organized groups that participate actively in the political life of the country it is interesting to note how many of them are truly national. Although local, state, and regional groups are naturally more numerous, there is today an almost complete coverage of major interests by national associations. This is a relatively recent development. Very few national associations go back as much as seventy-five years to a time before the Civil War. In fact the great majority seem to have been organized on a national basis in the last forty or fifty years—an evidence of how recent has been the development of a cultural and economic nationalism in the United States.

GROUP PROPAGANDA AND PUBLIC OPINION

Groups and associations work in a variety of ways to achieve their several purposes. One method is that of propagandizing and educating the public, through newspapers, periodicals, advertisements, radio talks, pamphlets and innumerable other channels. These are not the only sources from which the people learn, but they are nevertheless exceedingly important in *the democratic process of harmonizing interests and meeting human needs*. That process is an ever-changing one, of course, and one in which the rise and fall of organizations is an interesting factor.

Going back to the beginning of the organization itself, the democratic process as seen from its own vantage point, is somewhat as follows:

(1) First, certain individuals, or even a single one, feeling a certain need or having some grievance, begin to talk about it. (2) This soon results in the formation of a special interest group or organization which, though purely local at first, may soon spread till it covers the state or the nation. (3) These groups put forward their ideas first within the circle of those directly concerned and later to a wider public. They want to get the people generally and the government to espouse their cause. (4) As a result their ideas get taken up for discussion in public meetings, newspapers, pamphlets, radio broadcasts, and many other ways. (5) At this point a more general or "public" opinion begins to form as to their claims and ideas. (6) If the matter is one calling for public or governmental action, candidates for public office, political leaders and parties may be induced to espouse the new proposals. If this is done the next steps are (7) the nomination and election of public officers to carry out the idea, and then the regular processes of government, which are (8) legislation, (9) administration, and (10) adjudication, naturally follow. Thus the idea of a single citizen as to old age pensions or a local public improvement, or the demand of the wool growers for a protective tariff, or of organized labor for the right to organize their own unions, for example, may become in time an established policy and function of the government.

It is a mistake, of course, to think of the process ending at this or any other point. No general public policy is ever settled absolutely and for all time. Opposition arises and must be met. Changes in circumstances call for changes in laws. Moreover the laws do not enforce themselves, so that it is necessary for interested groups to be forever on the alert to protect their interests. Thus it comes about that organized groups have a continuing usefulness although the work that they do is ever-changing.

No one could assert that all organizations of the types mentioned above work always for the public good. It is unwise to idealize the often fierce and unscrupulous competition of interest groups. Some of them are clearly selfish in a number of their demands. It is essential to the democratic process, however, that every one should be heard. What is more, the greatest public good is attained when the largest number of individuals and groups are satisfied, and the mere fact of being given a hearing and fair consideration is one of the greatest satisfactions of the democratic process.

Public Opinion. In the foregoing summary of the democratic process of government the term "public opinion" was used. What is this thing and what importance has it in the process? To some it suggests that there is a "public" or a "group mind" distinct from the minds of individuals. Modern psychology is very skeptical of this notion. It is only individuals that truly have minds and opinions, but when many individuals hold the same idea or opinion, it has a potency that it otherwise would not have. A public opinion may be defined then as an idea or opinion concerning a public matter held by a considerable number of persons in the same community or country. Presumably to be effective it should be held by a majority, but that may not always be the case.

Some ideas like respect for law and order, for the rights of private property, and for the American flag have been held so long and by so many persons as to be traditional. One hardly needs to give reasons for such views. An overwhelming public opinion supports such ideas along with free public education and the separation of church and state. As to other ideas the favorable majority may not be so impressive, and when new proposals are put forward it is always a question as to whether a majority public opinion will ever be obtained— and if once attained, as in the case of prohibiting the liquor traffic, whether it will hold for any length of time.

Importance of Public Opinion. Writing over fifty years ago, James Bryce expressed the view that public opinion was the ultimate force in the United States and the real ruler of the country.[1] Bryce was not original in this. De Tocqueville had emphasized it fifty years before Bryce, and Alexander Hamilton fifty years before that. Neither is this the only theory as to the ruling power in America. Some have asserted popular sovereignty or the rule of the people in a direct sense; others have asserted that the "invisible government" of party leaders and bosses rules the United States; and some have said that the American government is controlled by "big business," or "privileged business" or "Wall Street." If words mean anything these statements cannot all be true.

In any case the idea of rule by public opinion was rather long neglected, but with the rise of the study of psychology and the development of research into men's attitudes and opinions, the idea has been revived. Today there are many scholars, public officials, and businessmen who emphasize the reality of rule by public opinion. Many of them are engaged constantly in plying people with "straw ballots," questionnaires, and interviews, to learn what people think, what they like to buy, and how they intend to vote. Polls of public opinion and efforts to measure attitudes have in little more than a decade become matters of daily comment in the press and of full-time employment for many persons. The scientific principles of sampling and polling opinions have been well advanced within the past generation.

Sources of Individual Opinions. "Public opinion" is to be discovered, then, by finding what the majority of individuals think, or say they think. But before too much weight is given to public opinion as the real ruler of America, the question should be asked: "How do individuals get their opinions and attitudes?" Are they generated spontaneously within the individual mind, or does the individual get his ideas from outside? There is little doubt but that the streams of ideas and suggestions that constantly pour in upon the individual are somehow modified within him by the stock of ideas, attitudes, and prejudices that he already has. No two persons get from a speech or an advertise-

[1] James Bryce, *The American Commonwealth*, Pt. I, ch. I, and Pt. IV.

ment exactly the same impression. This factor aside, however, it is clear that people get their ideas and opinions very largely, if not entirely, from their environment. From early family life, community traditions, schools, newspapers, magazines, books, the radio and the movies, roadside billboards and campaign speeches, advertisements and handbills, the suggestions made by friends and others, come the ideas and attitudes that men call their own.

Propaganda in the Formation of Opinion. This being the fact, it did not take politicians long to learn that *opinions can be created*. Over two thousand years ago Plato in the *Republic* showed how by censorship and allegories young and old could be taught to believe what the rulers thought they should believe. No doubt there was organized propaganda even earlier. In modern times propaganda, which may be defined as the spreading of ideas that men want other people to believe, regardless of whether they are true or not, has become one of the chief weapons of all organized groups, including the state itself. Under dictatorships the right to propagandize becomes practically the monopoly of the government; everyone else must submit to censorship. Where speech, press, and radio are free, every group and every individual may engage in propaganda, i.e., may participate in forming the opinions of others to conform to a desired pattern. Propaganda is, therefore, a continuous factor in the making of opinions, and under its influence people are constantly, though sometimes unconsciously, changing their attitudes and ideas.

Resistance to Propaganda. The power of groups and interests to create favorable opinions is not unlimited. There are many individuals who read little or nothing, who seldom listen to the radio, and who are not reached by other agencies of propaganda. Others have their minds closed by prejudice or early conditioning, and are almost impervious to new suggestions. The most educated groups in the community are highly sensitive and resistant to certain kinds of propaganda, especially of the commercial kind. Then, too, rival interests provide conflicting propaganda, so that one side to some extent cancels the work of the other.

Propaganda and Other Causes of Changes in Opinion. Nevertheless, there is constant change in the opinions of the people. Sometimes it is very slow; at other times it comes with surprising rapidity. The remarkable change of opinion on national prohibition between 1919 and 1933 is a case in point. Advances in science cause some of the change, particularly when the new knowledge is applied in the development of some great industry, such as automobiles or the radio. Natural calamities are often potent; the great drought of the 1930's changed many ideas as to the proper land policy for the United States. There are other causes, too, and among these propaganda must be counted as one. So important indeed has propaganda become that every large organization, including government departments, national associations, large interest groups, and great single industries, maintain their public relations or publicity departments. The form in which the reports of their activities go out to the public is exceedingly important—important because they can create a favorable or an unfavorable public opinion.

Influence and Importance of Public Opinion. It appears then that public opinion is not an independent, self-operating and self-generating force in the community. On the contrary, it is something that can be created, within limits, by interest groups of all kinds. It is a *result* as well as a *cause*. It is but one of a series of steps or forces in the democratic process as a whole. It is important, or at least the "prevailing opinion" is important, because it marks, or sets, the main lines of public policy. But, of course, there are countless little acts of all branches of government about which there simply is no public knowledge or interest, minor details to which the public is indifferent. In the decisions on many such matters, special interests of all kinds have their say—men demanding pensions, corporations claiming tax refunds, and countless others of similar nature.

How Opinions Are Expressed. There are many ways in which opinions may be expressed, opinions of individuals, of groups, of popular majorities. It is unnecessary to list all the ways of expressing opinion, but at least the methods most commonly used by individuals and groups in their attempts to influence the government should be noted.

1. *Legally Binding Expressions of Opinion.* Some expressions of opinion are public, legally authorized, and more or less binding on the appropriate branches of the government. These include both the primary elections at which candidates for public office are nominated, and the final elections at which public officials are chosen. While it is not always clear what the mandate of the people is in turning out some officials and electing others in their places, campaigns usually bring out some differences of policy sufficiently so that the vote for the winning candidates can be interpreted as giving public approval to their policies. Included also under this heading would be referenda, or elections directly on public measures: state constitutions, constitutional amendments, statutes, and local charters and ordinances. The initiative and referendum may properly be considered as means of ascertaining public opinion in legally binding form.

2. *Unofficial Expressions of Opinion.* Other expressions of opinion are more or less private, unofficial, not binding on the government, and representative usually of the views of minorities. Under this heading would come resolutions adopted at mass meetings, the petitions of organizations, the statements made by lobbyists for such organizations, letters, and telegrams to public officials (often sent at the solicitation of propagandists), visits of delegations and individuals to their representatives and to government departments, unofficial straw votes, letters to the newspapers, newspaper editorials, and a host of others. These require a great deal of sifting, for often they represent the views of "cranks" and "lone wolves" who in no sense voice a generally held opinion.

A fundamental difference between the two classes of expressions of public opinion appears upon analysis. The first group includes only decisive expressions of a sort of public or majority will. They are decisions in legal form and binding upon the government. They take place in the regular course of governmental operations, and will be considered in their appropriate places. The second group of expressions of opinion take place mainly outside of government and are directed to it. They are expressions of individual and group opinions and they fall far short of being public and general.

Polls on Candidates. In recent years, as mentioned above, so-called "straw votes" and "polls of public opinion" have come into great prominence, particularly at the time of Presidential election campaigns. A straw vote may be defined as an unofficial sampling of the voters' voting intentions prior to the regular election. It is usually confined to high offices, such as President and governor. A poll of opinion is an unofficial sampling of people's opinions on some question of public concern. It is different from an attitude study, which is usually a more refined analysis of all shades of opinion on a question.

Straw votes had been tried in many cases early in the century by newspapers, politicians, gamblers and others who wanted to know in advance how an election was likely to go.[2] *The Literary Digest,* a weekly magazine, conducted the first great poll on a Presidential election in 1916, and repeated it every fourth year thereafter through 1936. Despite the crudity of the mail-ballot method used, the poll was fairly successful as a means of predicting the general outcome of the election until in 1936, when it went completely wrong. Since then the *Digest* has ceased publication. In the 1936, 1940, and 1944 elections, *Fortune* magazine, the American Institute of Public Opinion (Dr. George Gallup) and other organizations conducted polls of considerable significance and predictive accuracy. Both of the polls just mentioned use the interview method on small carefully selected samples of people. In 1940 both tended to underestimate the Roosevelt or Democratic vote in the North but the *Fortune* poll overestimated the Democratic vote in the South sufficiently to reach the figure of 55.2 per cent, which was just .2 per cent over the 55 per cent vote Roosevelt received.[3] State by state the Gallup poll was very close to the actual results, but its national average was 2.4 per cent below the actual Roosevelt vote. In 1944 the general results of these two polls were much the same as in 1940.[4] Many persons have expressed concern lest these polls have an undue influence on voting and become subject to manipulation by the parties. There is as yet no important evidence of any such results in the polls mentioned, but some polls that have been conducted by partisan groups have shown surprising distortion.

Polls on Issues. In addition to the polls on candidates for high offices, both *Fortune* magazine and the American Institute of Public Opinion, as well as other agencies, sample the opinions of people on a wide variety of public

---

[2] Claude E. Robinson, *Straw Votes,* 1932: *ibid.,* "Recent Developments in the Straw Poll Field," *Pub. Opin. Quar.,* vol. I, pp. 45-56 (1937).

[3] See Daniel Katz, "The Public Opinion Polls and the 1940 Election," *Pub. Opin. Quar.,* vol. 5, pp. 52-78 (1941).

[4] *Ibid.,* "The Polls and 1944 Election," *Pub. Opin. Quar.,* vol. 8, pp. 468-87 (1945).

questions. Because no election follows these polls, as a rule, it is not easy to know how accurate they are in testing the people's views. Much depends on the sample chosen from the population, on the way in which questions are put, and on the ability of the interviewers.

Suffice it to say that many public leaders including high officials and legislators are coming to rely more and more on such polls as guides to the public mind, and are gauging their actions accordingly. In this way, perhaps, public opinion is becoming even more influential than in the past.[5] Officials may to some extent ignore the pressure of a particular group when assured that general opinion is opposed to what the group wants. There is evidence, too, that the force of external events is making American public opinion more truly national instead of sectional or local.

REFERENCES

C. A. Beard, *The Economic Basis of Politics*, New York, 1928.

E. P. Herring, *Group Representation Before Congress*, Baltimore, 1929.

A. N. Holcombe, *The Political Parties of Today*, 2nd ed., New York, 1925.

——, *The New Party Politics*, New York, 1933.

——, *Democracy in a Planned Society*, New York, 1935.

——, *The Middle Classes in American Politics*, Cambridge, Mass., 1940.

Jerome Davis, *Capitalism and Its Culture*, New York, 1935.

S. McKee Rosen, *Political Process: A Functional Study in American Government*, New York, 1935.

The Federalist, espec. no. 10, by Madison.

A. A. Berle and Gardiner C. Means, *The Modern Corporation and Private Property*, New York, 1933.

Peter H. Odegard and E. Allen Helms, *American Politics: A Study in Political Dynamics*, New York, 1938.

Pendleton Herring, *Public Administration and the Public Interest*, New York, 1936.

——, *The Politics of Democracy*, New York, 1940.

Temporary National Economic Committee, various monographs such as no. 11, *Bureaucracy and Trusteeship in Large Corporations*, 1941; and no. 26, *Economic Power and Political Pressures*, 1941.

James Bryce, *The American Commonwealth*, New York, 1908 ed., vol. II, part IV.

Walter Lippmann, *Public Opinion*, New York, 1922.

——, *The Phantom Public*, New York, 1925.

A. L. Lowell, *Public Opinion and Popular Government*, New York, 1926.

——, *Public Opinion in War and Peace*, Cambridge, Mass., 1923.

A. B. Hall, *Popular Government*, New York, 1921.

[5] For current summaries of these polls see *Pub. Opin. Quar.*

W. B. Graves, *Readings in Public Opinion: Its Formation and Control*, New York, 1928.

Peter Odegard, *The American Public Mind*, New York, 1930.

C. E. Robinson, *Straw Votes*, New York, 1932.

Bessie Louise Pierce, *Citizens' Organizations and the Civic Training of Youth*, New York, 1933.

The Public Opinion Quarterly.

Harwood L. Childs, *An Introduction to Public Opinion*, New York, 1940.

Harold D. Lasswell, *Democracy Through Public Opinion*, 1941.

William Albig, *Public Opinion*, New York, 1939.

Leonard W. Doob, *Propaganda—Its Psychology and Technique*, New York, 1935.

Elmer E. Schattschneider, *Politics, Pressures, and the Tariff*, New York, 1935.

A. N. Christensen and E. M. Kirkpatrick, *The People, Politics, and the Politician: Readings in American Government*, New York, 1941, pp. 239-64.

Lindsay Rogers, "Do the Gallup Polls Measure Opinion?", *Harper's Magazine*. vol. 183, pp. 623-32 (Nov. 1941).

V. O. Key, Jr., *Politics, Parties, and Pressure Groups*, New York, 1942.

George Gallup and Saul Forbes Rae, *The Pulse of Democracy: The Public Opinion Poll and How It Works*, New York, 1940.

Hadley Cantril, *Gauging Public Opinion*, Princeton, 1944.

CHAPTER 9

American Political Parties

All forms of truly popular or democratic government imply the existence of political parties and the freedom of the people to organize and to operate them. The United States has been no exception to this rule. The importance of parties in the democratic process of government appears more and more clearly as the operations of government become more numerous and complex.

The word "party" implies divisions among the people, a division into parts or parties. Therefore the phrase "a one-party state," meaning a state or nation in which only one "party" is permitted, is a misnomer. The so-called party is only an oligarchy, a class dictatorship, since it is according to human nature that if freedom were permitted there would be more than one party. Indeed, for democratic government it is necessary to have several parties and the continuing freedom of the people to alter or abandon existing parties, to organize new ones, and to utilize parties freely, in their efforts to gain control of the government.

Political Party Defined. A *political party* in a democracy is a body of individuals organized to gain control of the government by peaceful, political methods, and to use that control to promote the general welfare by constitutional means according to its own program. The program need not be entirely public and unselfish; a party is still a party even if one of its aims is to get and hold public jobs for its own members.

Party Aims and Principles. The primary aim of a political party is to gain control of the government by peaceful, political methods. This means in practice that parties present slates of candidates for public office and endeavor to get them elected. This is the characteristic function of political parties, and it distinguishes them from the "pressure groups," "blocs" and other politically active organizations that were discussed in the preceding chapter. A pressure or "interest" group is generally a body of individuals organized to promote by publicity, agitation, and pressure, some special interest of its members, such as their line of business or a single type of reform. A "bloc" in American political parlance is a group of legislators in Congress or a state legislature organized without regard to party lines to carry through the legislative program of some interest group. As a rule neither a pressure group nor a bloc puts up its own candidates for office, but many pressure groups make known their preferences among the party candidates. By this test the national citizens' Political Action Committee, for example, is a pressure group rather than a party.

Another characteristic of a true party is its loyalty to the constitution. It proceeds by means of persuasion, education, and propaganda rather than by violence, and it aims to work within the existing constitution, at least until the constitution can be changed by lawful methods. This means that, if it wins the election, it will so conduct itself in office as to preserve the right of free elections, and not to prevent the opposition from ousting it after the latter wins some subsequent election. If it loses an election, it will struggle along as a "loyal opposition"—loyal to the constitution and to the principle of majority rule—and be prepared to take office again whenever it wins. *This is the fundamental understanding of all democratic government by parties.*

Party government had been long developing in England and America before this principle was fully understood. George Washington in his Farewell Address strongly denounced "the Spirit of Party generally" and warned that

> However combinations or associations of the above description may now and then answer popular ends, they are likely, in the course of time and things, to become potent engines, by which cunning, ambitious, and unprincipled men will be enabled to subvert the Power of the People, and to usurp for themselves the reins of government, destroying afterwards the very engines which have lifted them to unjust dominion. . . .

In the light of what happened in Italy and Germany these words have a prophetic ring, and Americans should not deceive themselves into thinking that "it cannot happen here." Every group claiming to be a party and demanding the right to a place upon the ballot should be subjected by the voters to a most careful analysis of its nature and purposes. Revolutionary factions, groups whose avowed or concealed true aim is to overthrow democratic methods and to set up a dictatorship, have no moral right to a place on the ballot. At the same time it may be wiser to tolerate them and expose them than to forbid them to take part in elections.

True political parties, be it further noted, are essentially private organizations. They are today much regulated by law, and they perform some truly public functions, yet they are not formally a part of the government. Insofar as the nation or state delegates functions to them, however, the party acts as a responsible public agent, but the public as a whole is ultimately responsible for what is done.[1]

[1] See decision in Smith v. Allwright (1944), 321 U. S. 649.

Parties Become National. From the beginning of American history, parties and pressure groups have appeared from time to time as actors of important roles. They existed in a sense in each of the colonies and continued through constant changes in the states. Then as common problems arose and governmental organization began to overlap state lines, national parties began to emerge. The committees of intercolonial correspondence which paved the way for the Revolution represented a national party in the process of formation. Ever since that time there have been national parties with national names, composed of state parties of the same names, and the latter in turn have had their local subdivisions in the counties, cities, villages, towns, and voting precincts. Here and there on occasion one finds separate state parties, i.e., parties that are not constituent elements of a national party, and also municipal parties that are not parts of any state or national party. These are exceptions to the general rule, however, and are likely to be temporary, for they violate the principle of economy of effort. It is much easier and simpler for lay citizens, and for politicians, too, to belong to or support just one party for national, state, and even local purposes. The specific issues may be different at different levels of government, but the lines of cleavage will be much the same.

Unity of Parties Through All Levels of Government. This integration of parties, from the national level down to the smallest voting precinct, has been one of the most important factors in unifying the nation, just as it continues to be a potent force in bringing about the cooperation of national, state, and local governments in common endeavors. From the viewpoint of the party leaders and workers, the problem of government is a unified one. There is a program to be carried out, and whether it is done by national, state, or local authorities, or by a combination of them is to some extent a matter of indifference. Likewise, when the party worker is to be rewarded with a public position, he is not always deeply concerned whether it is in the national, state, or local government. By operating as part of a state and national party, a local party organization will have an opportunity to obtain patronage and positions for its members and supporters at all governmental levels, assuming that the party has been victorious at all levels.

No attempt will be made here to write a history of American parties. That subject is familiar to all who know the history of the United States.[2] For convenience of reference only, the following periods of major party history may be noted:

1. 1788-1800, Federalist supremacy and organization of Republican opposition
2. 1800-1828, Democratic-Republican supremacy
3. 1828-1860, Democratic supremacy, with Whig and other opposition

---

[2] For brief summaries of American party history see E. M. Sait, *American Parties and Elections*, rev. ed., 1939, chs. X, XI; H. R. Bruce, *American Parties and Politics*, rev. ed., 1932, chs. IV-VII; P. H. Odegard and E. A. Helms, *American Politics*, chs. II-IV.

4. 1860-1872, Republican supremacy, Civil War, and attempted Reconstruction
5. 1872-1896, Republican supremacy, strong Democratic opposition
6. 1896-1912, Republican ascendancy assured
7. 1912-1920, Democratic victory, World War I, and reaction
8. 1920-1932, Republican "return to normalcy," prosperity, and depression
9. 1932-   , Democratic "Roosevelt revolution," New Deal, World War II and its aftermath.

This tabulation refers only to the major parties. Various minor parties have arisen from time to time, and have added much to the interest of campaigns without ever gaining the principal national offices.

PARTY MEMBERSHIP [3]

Nature of Membership. A party is a voluntary association of individual members. As a rule these members are citizens and voters, although unnaturalized foreign-born persons are sometimes active in party affairs. But are all those who vote the party ticket truly party members? This question is particularly pertinent with respect to the two major parties, the Democrats and the Republicans. In 1940 Franklin D. Roosevelt received over 27,000,000 votes for the Presidency: were all these cast by Democratic party members? Obviously not, for in the Congressional and state elections the distribution of votes as between Democratic and Republican candidates was in many cases quite different. There are millions of voters who vote independently, and who would not admit having a membership in any party.

Regular Party Voters. But what about the millions who regularly vote the ticket of one party: are not they members of the party? In a vague sense, perhaps they are, but their bond of membership is certainly a slender one. A member in any other organization would normally go through a formal step of joining the organization, and would attend meetings and participate in the work done. He would serve on committees, or do some other service for the group. In the case of most Democrats and most Republicans, this is not true at all. Being a Democrat or a Republican is about the most casual thing in the world. There is no act of joining the party, no pledge to uphold the party and its principles, no payment of dues, and little or no performance of party functions. If this be membership, it is certainly a very attenuated thing.

Real Participant Members. Clear thinking on this subject would seem to require a different view of membership. The latter would be limited to those

[3] For a discussion of laws and court decisions on party membership see Clarence A. Berdahl, "Party Membership in the United States," *Am. Pol. Sci. Rev.*, vol. 36, pp. 16-50, 241-62 (1942).

who actually participate in the work of the parties. As a minimum there should be membership in a political club affiliated with the party, attendance upon club and party meetings and caucuses, and some participation in the party's work. For these reasons it seems better to think of the person who merely votes the party ticket as one of the unorganized body of voters, as a supporter and not a member of the party, even though he officially registers for voting as a Democrat or Republican, and to think of the party as being composed of only those who are definitely organized, i.e., participants in the work of the organization in some other sense than merely as voters. Neither of the major parties would consist of much more than a million members, under this view, if indeed either has that many.

Membership in Minor Parties. The minor parties are in a somewhat different position, but the same reasoning may be applied to them. The Socialist party candidate for the Presidency received 267,000 votes in 1928, 884,000 in 1932, 187,342 in 1936, and 99,557 in 1940, and 80,500 in 1944. Certainly party membership did not fluctuate in this way. Indeed, the smallest of the five votes represented far more than the party membership, for the Socialist party has a definite enrollment of members with payment of small dues, and the membership figure reported in 1934 was only 22,861. Nevertheless the minor parties differ from the major parties in this, that they are composed of zealous workers who are not afraid to face public opprobrium in working for what they consider a worthy cause. Hence they have probably a larger proportion of actual members to votes cast than do the major parties. They have, also, a definite enrollment of members as a general rule.

BASES OF PARTY DIVISIONS

What is it that induces men to vote for different political parties? Why are some men and women Republicans, others Democrats, and others members or supporters of some particular minor party? There appear to be three broadly different lines of explanation: *first*, those based on economic considerations; *second*, those that consider other environmental factors; and *third*, those that are based upon the supposed inherent or innate dispositions of individuals.

1. Economic Bases of Parties. James Madison in the famous tenth essay of *The Federalist*, while recognizing other causes of faction or party, asserted:

> The most common and durable source of factions has been the various and unequal distribution of property. Those who hold, and those who are without, property have ever formed distinct interests in society. Those who are creditors, and those who are debtors, fall under a like discrimination. A landed interest, a manufacturing interest, a mercantile interest, a moneyed interest, with many lesser interests grow up of necessity in civilized nations and divide them into different classes, actuated by different sentiments and views. The

regulation of these various and interfering interests forms the principal task of modern legislation, and involves the spirit of party and faction in the necessary and ordinary operations of the government.

This classic statement presents, as a matter of fact, two different phases of the economic interpretation of parties. On the one hand there is the struggle between the "haves" and the "have-nots," a vertical struggle between different classes in the same community. This "class struggle," of which Socialist and Communist writers have made so much, can take place in any city, state, or nation, no matter how small or how large. Recent studies of the American electorate have revealed that "social-economic status" (level of income, education, property ownership) is an important criterion that distinguishes Republicans from Democrats generally.[4]

But in a country of any considerable extent, there are also sectional or regional interests *within* the class of the "haves," as well as somewhat similar divisions geographically among the "have-nots." In the United States concentrations of manufacturing, mining, commerce and finance, wheat farming, corn-and-hog farming, dairying, and cotton farming, for example, are found in different sections of the country. Now these different sections do not have identical interests. Mine owners in some areas, manufacturers in others, and farm owners in still others, all members of the class of those who own property, come into frequent conflicts over the prices at which their products and services are to be exchanged, while different groups of farmers also come into conflict because they produce rival and competing products. Some sectional interests benefit from a protective tariff, others lose by it. Professor A. N. Holcombe has made a very impressive presentation of the sectional character of American party divisions, without neglecting the effect of the struggle between upper, middle, and lower classes.[5] Broadly speaking, the sectional analysis is primarily a *description* of how voters vote by regions and not an explanation of *why* they do so. Neither wheat farmers nor cotton farmers have benefited appreciably from a protective tariff, but the wheat farmers have generally supported the party that upholds a high tariff, while cotton farmers have voted in the opposition. Furthermore, wheat farmers on adjoining farms vote opposing tickets, while Negro cotton farmers, when given a chance, vote against the party of their white cotton-raising neighbors. Thus, living in the same place and even working at the same thing do not necessarily make men vote the same way.

2. **Non-Economic Factors Inducing Party Support.** Professors Merriam and Gosnell, in a more eclectic treatment of American parties,[6] group "class divisions" and "sectionalism" along with "race and creed" under a single broad

[4] Dewey Anderson and Percy E. Davidson, *Ballots and the Democratic Class Struggle.*
[5] *Political Parties of To-day*, New York, 1924; *The New Party Politics*, New York, 1933; and ch. I in *The American Political Scene*, ed. by E. B. Logan, New York, 1936.
[6] *The American Party System*, chs. I, II.

heading in their analysis of the "elements in the composition of the party," and then proceed to find four other factors as well, namely: "hereditary allegiance"; leadership and personalities; the continuing "organization" of the party; and common principles and policies. Why should southern Negroes be practically all Republicans and southern whites nearly all Democrats? Partly there is the antagonism of race, which of course has some economic basis, too; and partly there is the "hereditary allegiance" of Negroes, even unto the third and fourth generation, for the party that freed them, and the hereditary allegiance of southern whites to the party of their fathers. Many men and women are, so to speak, born into certain parties, north as well as south, and remain there, i.e., continue to vote for the same party name or label, long after their economic interests have changed. Leadership, too, is important. The leadership of Theodore Roosevelt drew millions of former Republican supporters into the ranks of the Progressive party in 1912; the leadership of Franklin Roosevelt induced other millions of so-called Republicans to vote the Democratic ticket.

Then, too, the party organization is always at work, and hard at work in the "close states," to keep voters in line, while the organization itself, i.e., the true membership of the party in the strict sense discussed above, supplies a considerable fraction of the total vote cast for the party. A part of this membership has little other motivation than to be with the winning party so as to be able to share in the offices and political power. Those politicians who aim primarily at office-holding can be Democrats, Republicans, or anything else, provided the party offers a good chance to win.

Principles and Policies. Common principles and policies have a considerable weight with the more idealistic elements in the community. There are many fairly independent voters who, without regard to their own economic interests, will vote for a party's candidates because the party offers civil service reform, or a certain foreign policy. This is a factor in the voting of many people that cannot be neglected. The old-fashioned cynical party boss who thought that every man had his price and that material gain was the only human motivation was confounded many times and is definitely less powerful than he was.

3. Innate Qualities or Dispositions. Other writers, including A. Lawrence Lowell, late president of Harvard University, have found the tendency of men to go into different parties to be deep-planted in their dispositions.[7] President Lowell grouped men first into two major groups, depending on whether they were generally contented or discontented with the world and their place in it. Each of these groups, the contented and the discontented, he divided again into two parts, according to whether the individuals are disposed to be sanguine, i.e., hopeful of improving their lot, or not sanguine. Thus he arrived at a normal four-fold party division among men, as follows:

[7] *Public Opinion in War and Peace*, Cambridge, Mass., 1923, ch. VII.

1. Discontented and hopeful,   Radicals.
2. Contented and hopeful,   Liberals.
3. Contented and not sanguine,   Conservatives.
4. Discontented and not sanguine, Reactionaries.

A governing combination of the first two would be progressive, of the last two unprogressive; while a combination of the second and third would be stable, and one of the first and fourth would be unstable.

This is only one theory of party divisions based on human attitudes and psychology. All such theories suggest that party divisions may be largely irrational. To think of men as knowing perfectly their own interests and then acting accordingly, in a wholly rational way, is absurd in the light of modern knowledge of human behavior. Two workers in identical positions at adjoining machines may be one a Republican, the other a Socialist. The explanation of their party affiliations and political attitudes is not easily found, and very seldom is it a single, simple explanation.

PRESENT PARTIES AND ACTUAL DISTRIBUTION OF STRENGTH

Present Parties. The major parties in the United States today are the Democratic and Republican. The minor parties active in national politics are the Socialist, Communist, Socialist-Labor, and Prohibition, plus the more localized American Labor party, associated with the CIO. The Political Action Committee of the CIO is not a separate political party.

Dominance of Major Parties. How completely the two major parties dominate the country as a whole may be shown by the votes for Presidential candidates and the number of members elected to Congress.[8] In 1940 Roosevelt received 54.7 per cent of the total, Willkie (Republican) 44.8 per cent, and all others combined less than one-half of 1 per cent. The 1944 results were substantially the same. This is the normal situation, although temporary party splits in 1924, when many Democrats and some Republicans voted for La Follette, and in 1912, when the Republican party was split by the secession of the Progressives following Theodore Roosevelt, resulted in three parties dividing the bulk of the vote for the Presidency.

The same situation appears even more strikingly in the distribution of party strength in Congress. Since before World War I in the two houses, with 531 members together, there have never been more than nineteen members belonging to parties other than the two major ones, and normally there are less than ten such members, or less than 2 per cent. Of the seven in the 1941-42 Congress, four were Progressives (Wisconsin) and one each Independent, Farmer-Labor, and American Labor. In the 79th Congress, 1945-46, only one

[8] *The World Almanac,* issues of 1945 and earlier years, supplies many of the figures that follow.

Senator and two Representatives were listed as Independents. Nominally, at least, all the other members are Democrats and Republicans.

Minor Parties. A series of minor parties that together poll so small a percentage of the total national vote may not seem to be worthy of discussion. Their importance is, however, considerably greater than their numbers would suggest. As propagandists for new ideas they are relatively much more active than the major parties. Their ideas, furthermore, are sometimes taken over by the major parties. Since most of the minor parties are rather "to the left" of, that is more radical than, the major parties, there is always the chance that they will unite to form a new left-wing combination.[9]

The Weaknesses of Minor Parties. The history of the several minor parties reveals the most important obstacle to the success of such a coalition. That obstacle is the constant tendency toward internal dissension and schisms within each of the minor groups, as well as a strong habit of denouncing each other. The Communists have been split between Stalinists and Trotskyites, the Socialists between right- and left-wing groups, and the state Farmer-Labor parties have not cooperated with the national organization of that name. Most of these parties lack the backgrounds, the traditions, and the network of local workers and organizations that would give them stability. Whenever they build up strong state or local organizations, as in the case of the parties in Wisconsin and Minnesota, their interest in holding onto the offices they have attained helps to prevent them from going off on strong crusading movements with groups in other states.

The membership of the Communist and Socialist groups seems to be concentrated especially in a few large cities, notably in New York, Detroit, and Chicago, and it is composed largely of wage earners, among them many of foreign birth. The mid-western Farmer-Labor and Progressive parties of recent years also include many city wage earners of the unionized and more class-conscious group and considerable numbers of the poorer and more discontented farmers. There are many difficulties, of course, in keeping farmers and laborers working together in harmony, for their interests often conflict, but the many predictions of the break-up of these parties from this cause have not been fully realized.

Areas of Major Party Strength. In the election of 1932, Franklin Roosevelt carried all but six states: Pennsylvania, Delaware, Connecticut, Vermont, New Hampshire, and Maine. In the tidal wave of votes that re-elected him in 1936, only Maine and Vermont stood by the Republican party. In the face of such a nation-wide sweep to the Democratic side, it looked as if the old information as to the distribution of party strength was no longer valid, while the increase in the Democratic percentage of the vote from 40 per cent in 1928 to over 60 per cent at its peak in 1936 upset the previous close balance between the parties. The 1940 election showed the beginning of a swing in the other direc-

[9] See J. R. Starr, "Labor and Farmer Groups and the Three-Party System," in *Southwestern Soc. Sci. Quart.*, vol. XVII, no. 1 (June, 1936).

tion, with the Democrats getting 55 per cent of the vote and the Republicans coming back to carry ten states, but even so the Democratic preponderance was still very great. In 1944 the Democratic recession continued, although its percentage of the vote for President (53.8) still gave it a safe margin over the Republicans (46.1).

Prior to the great shift of voting strength to the Democrats in 1932 and 1936, the Republicans were almost sure to carry, in a Presidential election, all the New England, Middle Atlantic, and North Central states as far west as the Dakotas, Nebraska, and Kansas, with a few Mountain and Pacific Coast states. They could also occasionally pick up some border states, like Kentucky and Tennessee. At the same time the Democrats normally carried city and Congressional district elections in some of the larger cities of the northeast, notably in Boston, New York, and Baltimore, and state elections from Maryland to Massachusetts frequently went to the Democrats. Ohio and Indiana were also "close states" that in a number of elections went to the Democrats. Curiously the larger cities from St. Louis and Chicago to Pittsburgh and Philadelphia, including Cleveland and Cincinnati, usually went Republican, while other cities of the northeastern section leaned to the Democratic side. In the same period the Democrats were usually sure to carry the states from Virginia and Tennessee south and west as far as Texas and Arkansas, had an even chance in some of the Mountain states, and a better than even chance in a few border states like Maryland, Kentucky, and Oklahoma.

On the whole the Democratic party was the minority party from the Civil War on; the elections of Cleveland (1884 and 1892) were exceptional, while Woodrow Wilson was elected in 1912 as a result of the Republican-Progressive split. There was little or nothing "in the cards" to foretell the tremendous effect of the Great Depression on people's political thinking and the resultant sweep to power of the Democratic party in 1932. Indeed, some persons thought that the party was on the way to extinction after the serious defeats of 1920, 1924, and 1928. The party's success through four Presidential elections, 1932, 1936, 1940, and 1944, was no doubt attributable in large part to the leadership of Franklin Roosevelt, but that is not the whole explanation.

Present Elements in Democratic Party. The facts are that President Roosevelt had the support of the great majority of wage earners in the cities, and also of a large percentage of farmers throughout the country, together with a very considerable sprinkling of support from business and professional men. In a sense the Democratic party became a national party of farmers and laborers, although it contains other elements. In the "Solid South" the great majority of whites vote with the Democrats, without regard to economic status, while in the North even considerable numbers of Negroes have supported the party. Large bodies of new voters who normally would have voted the Republican ticket began to vote for Franklin Roosevelt, and many of them may continue to support the Democratic party under other leaders. In addition, the straw polls show that millions of persons with whom the depression dealt so hard that they had to accept government assistance or work-relief, apparently have been giving their votes to the Democratic party, although a number of them had slipped away from the party by 1944.

Future of the Republican Party. In a way, the elections of 1932 and 1936 represented as great a shift in political power as the election of 1800, that brought Jefferson and the Democratic-Republican party to power, and that of 1828, bringing in Andrew Jackson and his militant Democratic followers. The election of 1800, for example, spelled the ultimate demise of the Federalist party. Following the 1936 elections many Republican party leaders were so discouraged over the prospect of reviving the party that some even proposed that its name be changed and that it be completely reorganized. Obviously this was showing undue fright and discouragement, as the 1940 election results revealed. Temporarily the center of political power has moved to a lower economic level and has found a broader base in the Democratic party. But that party has its own internal difficulties and is likely to suffer from defections. Meanwhile a conservative party that could poll nearly 17,000,000 votes in 1936, and 22,000,000 in 1940 and 1944 is far from dead.

THE FUNCTIONS OF POLITICAL PARTIES

Constitutions Fail to Provide for Political Functions. The written Constitution of the United States, as of all democratic states, failed to provide for the performance of certain essential functions in the democratic process. It was left to the people more or less spontaneously to provide for the nomination and election of officers and the attainment of majority rule. Practically all the steps of forming public opinion and of providing leadership for the people in the electoral process were left unregulated. In the national Constitution the formal steps in electing the President and Vice President were rather fully stated, but not the informal, initiatory steps.

These omissions were not due to any oversight. Madison, Hamilton and others were fully aware of the need for parties to run popular governments. They had all experienced this fact in the government of the colonies and the states. But they knew also that the whole apparatus of nominations for office and other party work should be as fully as possible in the hands of the people and not be under the control of government officials, lest the latter be tempted to use their power to perpetuate themselves in office.

The need of parties to operate the new national Constitution was apparent almost from the beginning. It was not long, indeed, before they had begun to exercise a considerable number of functions. These have continued, through constant modifications, down to the present day. They may be summarized as follows:

1. Selection and Nomination of Candidates. The *selection of candidates for elective public offices* and for some appointive offices falls largely on the parties. It is highly important to have organized parties nominate candidates for elective office for the simple reason that, if majority rule is to be attained even approximately, the number of candidates presented for an office must be small. From this point of view the fewer the parties, the better the result. If three or more parties present candidates for the same office, the chances that any one will have a majority vote are thereby reduced. At the national level there are only the Presidency and Vice Presidency to be filled by election. Candidates for seats in Congress and for various state offices are nominated by the parties in the respective states, while candidates for local office are nearly everywhere locally presented. Thus the national parties have each really just two important nominations to make, those for the Presidency and Vice Presidency.[10]

2. Marshaling and Leading of Interest Groups. A major party is supported by a coalition of interests rather than a single interest. Here again it is to be distinguished from the pressure group or bloc, which usually represents part or all of but a single interest such as labor or agriculture. The work of *marshaling various interests into a single party, and leading them to political victory* are the true functions of the major party, but they are functions so unobtrusively performed that even most supporters of the party are not aware that they are done. Tradition and habit are helpful to the party leaders in keeping various elements within the fold of the party, but from time to time group interests shift, as revealed in the national elections of the 1930's when the liquor interests, most of the labor groups, and many farmers were brought over to support the Democratic party. Just how these shifts are engineered is a matter that is not recorded. There are frequent consultations and agreements between the leaders of interest groups and the real party leaders with respect to legislative and administrative policies. The leadership qualities of a party's candidates are also of great influence in drawing new elements to support a party.

3. Formulation of Policies and Platform. In connection with this function arises another one, that of *formulating the party's policies and platform.* Formally this is done at the conventions of the party, and to some extent it is actually done there. Representatives of the major interest groups are likely to find their way to national and state party conventions, to see to it that the platform "planks" or provisions that most nearly concern them are such as they desire. They even come with sections fully formulated for insertion in the platform. Each major party endeavors, within the framework of its other commitments and its ideology, to appeal to each large section and interest group. As a result major party platforms look and read somewhat alike. Indeed, it is often charged that they do not differ enough to give the voters a clear-cut choice. This results of necessity from the nature of the major parties: they represent coalitions of interests; they must satisfy all the larger bodies of voters as nearly as possible; but as each party's body of supporters usually contains conflicting elements, it is often necessary to hedge about

[10] See ch. 10.

and qualify their promises to the various groups so as not to antagonize other groups. To be all things to all men is not an easy role. Minor parties, especially those of the left like the Communists and Socialists, are quick to point out the ambiguities and the half-promises in the major party platforms, and to show that their own platforms are clear and decisive. This is all well enough for parties that do not expect to win office and that have no responsibility to various large interest groups.

4. **Campaigns to Win Elections.** Having candidates, a program or platform, and a coalition of interests behind it, each major party proceeds to its next function, that of *winning elections.* This involves a variety of subsidiary activities: keeping the voters lined up; getting them registered; propagandizing them through speeches, handbills, newspapers, private conferences and many other media; getting them out to vote on election day; watching the polls; and seeing that in the count of votes the party suffers no disadvantage. In order to win elections reasonably frequently, the party workers find in some states and cities that they must be ever vigilant and active. Party workers, responsible for particular precincts, must know their voters, keep in touch with them, help them in little affairs with the police, the courts, the tax collectors, the welfare and relief authorities, and other branches of the government, and show an interest in their homes and their jobs. Where the parties are most thoroughly organized, the party workers are always "on the job," available to their constituents at any time.

5. **The Winning Party's Function in Governing.** If the party is successful in the elections, if it wins partial or complete control of the government, its next problem and function is that of *governing.* True enough, it is the legally elected officers who govern in the formal sense, but as they are members of the party, and hold office as a result of the party's support, and want to be re-elected with its aid, they work with the party in carrying out their legal functions. To this end legislative and executive leaders of each party have many conferences with each other and with the other party leaders who hold no public office.

Co-ordination of Government Efforts. The peculiar form of the American system of government, with its division of powers between the national government and the states, and its separation of powers between legislative, executive, and judicial branches at both state and national levels, creates a special problem of government for the major parties. That problem is to develop a certain amount of teamwork among the constituent parts of the federal system so that unified programs can be carried out. In the governmental system itself there is no single center of power; even the President's office does not comprise everything; consequently there is no assurance of cooperation among all the elements in the formal structure. It is for this reason that local leaders are constantly conferring with state leaders, and the latter with national leaders, to attain national and state cooperation, while at all levels the party leaders are bringing about agreements between the legislative and executive branches to achieve common objectives. This is one of the major tasks in the whole conduct of government.

6. Functions of the Defeated Major Party. If unsuccessful in the elections but still possessed of minority representation in the legislative body, a party has the function of *criticizing* the majority party, continuing its *negotiations* to promote the interests it represents and *preparing itself for governing in the future*. Its duty of criticism is to subject all the proposals of the majority party to discussion and debate with a view to disclosing their weaknesses and their possible ill effects. Frequently the majority will compromise to some extent in putting through its policies, for it cannot afford to antagonize any interest groups whose support it may some day wish to have. Then, too, the majority party is frequently internally divided, so that at times the minority can win over enough majority party members to defeat the government's proposal. Time and again after about 1908, Democratic minorities in Congress combined with enough "progressive" members of the Republican majority to defeat the majority party's proposals. More recently Southern Democrats in Congress have combined with the Northern Republican minority to defeat measures of the Democratic administration.

All the time the minority party must continue to tell the public about the mistakes of the majority, and thus build up an atmosphere of public thinking that is favorable to the return of the minority to power. Along with this the minority must do what it can to maintain the loyalty of its supporters through the lean years when out of office.

Major Party Function Not to Create New Opinion. From what has been said above it follows that the creation of opinion in favor of new public policies is not one of the primary tasks of a major party. Interest groups, reform organizations, and individual leaders assume the functions of educating the people and of getting them to favor new measures that are needed for the national welfare. The President, members of Congress, and other public officials also have this responsibility. It might be said, too, that the major party that is out of office has the opportunity to offer an alternative to the policies of the party in power, and to that extent it becomes a leader of opinion. But the major party in power, as a party, is loaded down with too many obligations to different groups to undertake to lead public opinion in new directions. Almost of necessity this weakens the party's hold upon its supporters because time brings changes and the need for new measures. It requires unusually astute leadership for any party in power so to modify its program from time to time as to meet all the changing demands of its supporters.

Minor parties, on the other hand, have the function of leadership in matters of opinion and policies. They are organized to espouse new causes, such as prohibition of the liquor traffic, government ownership of railroads and utilities, or what not. They gain votes to the extent that their ideas appeal to the public. If they become large enough to be important, one of the major parties is likely to accept part of their program in the hope of gaining their votes.

Thus in the 1890's the Free Silver movement and the Populist party were drawn into the Democratic party and soon ceased to have an independent existence.

PARTY ORGANIZATION

The form of the organization of a party is largely conditioned by two factors: the functions the party has to perform, and the form of the government within which it operates.

Organization of Minor Parties. As previously noted, major and minor parties have rather distinct functions. The minor party is as a rule interested in a single class, or it is devoted to a single principle. Its function is to engage in propaganda to spread these principles among the people. This it can do by direct appeal for the principles on their own merits, and by criticizing the work of the parties that are carrying on the government. It does not, however, need extensive organizations to get out the vote, or to keep voters lined up with the party, nor does it need to prepare itself for governing in the immediate future. Thus the form of its organization can be very much the same as that of any propagandist group. It needs a central committee and headquarters; it needs small unit organizations here and there; it needs to select its members rather carefully with respect to their views; it needs to have speakers and a press. At the present time the nation is so large that it presents formidable obstacles to the efforts of any minor party to reach all sections and all the people.

Organization of Major Parties. The major parties have functions comparable to those of the minor parties, and have in addition numerous functions connected with regimenting the voters, governing when in power, and opposing the government when out of power. It follows that the organization of the major parties must consist of various parts that conform more or less to the different divisions of the government itself and to the functions to be performed. The party organization within legislative bodies will be dealt with in connection with legislative organization. Other parts of the party's machinery may be designated as follows:

1. The *formal organization*, which conforms to the state law (if any), and to the regulations of the party itself. This formal organization, again, consists of (a) the permanent organization, which carries on continuously, and (b) the temporary organization, which is set up for the nomination of candidates and for carrying out a particular election campaign, and which goes out of existence when these tasks are ended.

2. An *informal organization* of the real leaders frequently stands behind the formal party organization in the states, counties, and cities. Here will be found the "boss" if there is one, or the "machine," and all those who wield the greatest influence and decide many matters relating to the various interests that support the party.

Thoroughness of Party Organization. Major party organization exists at every level, from the nation down to the voting precinct, which is the smallest subdivision for voting purposes. The permanent organization of each major party includes a national committee, as well as Congressional and Senatorial committees; a state central committee in each state; county committees, as well as some congressional district and legislative district committees in some places; city, village, and town committees; and finally precinct committees, leaders, and workers. This thoroughness of organization is characteristic of the major parties, not of the minor ones; and even in the major parties there are large gaps at the lower levels, especially in states where the victory of one party is so nearly certain that detailed organization and hard work are not needed by the stronger and are futile for the weaker party.

Federal Organization of Major National Parties. It is a notable fact that the two major parties are *national* in name, sentiment, and tradition, and that their members and supporters think of themselves as belonging to national parties. A Democrat considers himself a Democrat wherever he moves and in whatever state he lives. On the other hand both Democratic and Republican party organization is distinctly *federal*, if not confederate, rather than national in its form. The state is the unit upon which each party depends, and the national organs of the party, whether national conventions or committees, have relatively little power over the state organizations. Party members and supporters, also, have their allegiance to the state party organization or to a more local one, but not to the national party organization. Some of the major factors in this situation may be spelled out as follows:

1. *State Units of Party Differ Greatly.* Each major national party is a gathering under one name and one emblem (elephant or donkey) of extremely different state parties. The Republican party in North Dakota may be captured, as it was, by the Nonpartisan League, and be forced into schemes of state socialism; in some states it may be a definitely middle-of-the-road party; and in New York or Pennsylvania an outright conservative party. Nevertheless, each state party that under the laws of its own state has a right to use the name "Republican" is the Republican party thereof. The national committee has no power to rule it out.

2. *State Laws Regulate Parties.* The regulation of parties is almost entirely by state laws and party rules. Congress has not seen fit to regulate the work of the national parties even to the extent that it has the power to do so. Since it is states that make the basic laws for party organization, and state parties organized under these laws that make the remaining rules, national conventions and committees have little power, and no legal authority, to do anything but accept the laws of the several states.

3. *State Parties and National Ticket.* In a few cases, state parties have refused to support the national party nominees for President and Vice President. In such cases there is little that the national party leaders can do about it

except to attempt to heal the breach and wait for better days and more acceptable candidates.

4. *National Party Rules Recognize States.* The rules of the national parties recognize the state parties as their constituent units at almost every turn. In the national committee the states are represented equally, as in the Senate. In the national convention state delegations are treated as units for most purposes except the actual voting for candidates by both the Democrats and the Republicans. The principal committees of both conventions represent the states equally and their members are designated by the state delegations.

5. *No National Bosses.* While there are state bosses and state party machines, there is no national party boss in either party, and in a sense there never has been. Mr. Mark Hanna, who managed the McKinley campaigns, came as near to being a national boss as any leader the country has ever known, and James J. Farley, who handled the first two Franklin Roosevelt campaigns, was certainly an influential leader, but neither was really a national party boss. This results in part from the assumption of leadership by the Presidents and the candidates for President in recent decades. When the latter do not attempt, or attempt and fail, to become the real party leaders, the dominant group of party members in the Senate sometimes assumes the function in part. No party leader, not even a popular President himself, can successfully pull the party strings in all the forty-eight states, in order to defeat his opponents or to help his friends.

6. *Aid by National to State Parties.* The national parties, like the national government, being able to raise money easier than the state units, have found it necessary to buy support for the national ticket in some states, and to some extent in all, by a system comparable to federal aid. It is the national party treasury that pours money into the states for the campaign, and that gives assurances of federal appointments to state and local party workers. The Hatch Act, by limiting national party campaign expenditures to 3 million dollars, may reduce this federal party aid to state parties but will not eliminate it entirely.

These federal characteristics of the organization of the major American political parties have a profound influence upon the entire system of American government. They prevent the national parties from controlling not only the party membership but also their representatives in Congress. They are an obstruction to true majority rule within the party. They compel the party in power to be very careful before it acts to see that a majority of the states as well as a majority of the people go along with them on policies. This makes for slower action and many compromises. It delays the true nationalization of the government.

Rise of Formal Party Organization. Party organization in the early days of the republic was a loose, incomplete, and experimental thing. Lacking other suitable machinery for the purpose, the several parties at one time permitted their members in Congress to nominate candidates for the Presidency. As the reaction against legislative control over the executive increased, there arose a popular agitation against these nominations by legislative caucus. A system of county and state conventions for nominating candidates for state office having developed, in 1831 the first distinctive minor party, the Anti-Masonic, held the first national party convention to nominate candidates for President and Vice President. The other parties quickly followed suit, as the new method was considered to be much more democratic than the older one. For over a century now, the party nominating convention has been known and used.

National Convention's Powers. At the present time the national party convention, held once every four years to nominate candidates for the Presidency and Vice Presidency, and to adopt the party platform, is recognized as the highest organ of the national party. It is in a sense a "constituent" body, since it has the power to make and change the party's constitution. It is also a legislative and a nominating body, with incidental judicial functions within the framework of party activities. All these powers and functions come to it from the fact that it is recognized as the most representative body that the national party ever assembles in one place. Its composition will be discussed later.

Composition of National Committee. Subordinate to the national convention is the national committee of the party. It was originally a committee to conduct the national campaign for the Presidency and Vice Presidency. Later it developed into a permanent executive committee for the national party, a committee whose functions are continuous, and are only increased at the time of the convention and the campaign. The committees of both parties consist today of a man and a woman from each state from the District of Columbia and from each of the territories—plus also, and this is very important, a chairman appointed by the party candidate for the Presidency. Thus the total membership runs to over a hundred, and except for the territorial representation, and the equal representation of men and women, the committee is very much like the Senate in size, in state equality, and in having a chairman imposed upon it from the outside.

States Select Members of National Committee. In theory the national party convention appoints the national committee, and the old rule was that each state delegation to the convention nominated its quota of members and the convention ratified them. The convention still goes through this form, but in fact the state laws in most states now provide for the election. Today the state delegations to the convention select the state's national committee members in about a third of the states; state conventions do it in another third of the states; and the remaining states use either the direct primary method of selection, or permit the state central committee to appoint.[11] Whatever method is used, the national party convention accepts the result.

Functions of National Committee. As a body the committee does very little except during the Presidential election year. Then it meets several times to arrange for the nominating convention and to help plan the party cam-

[11] See E. B. Logan (ed.), *The American Political Scene*, p. 55.

paign. The actual management of the campaign is left to the chairman, who is appointed soon after the convention by the party's Presidential candidate. To him is assigned also most of the work of supervising the permanent office and publicity bureau which each party now maintains between elections. In their several states and territories the members are very useful, however, in keeping posted on party affairs and prospects, in keeping in touch with the local workers, in answering inquiries from party headquarters, and in handling certain patronage questions, particularly when the party is in power. As a rule they are not members of the state central committee, but they keep in close touch with it.

Congressional and Senatorial Committees. As the national parties are primarily interested in the election of the President of the United States, so the work of the national committee turns largely around the nomination and election of the President. The committee has little or nothing to do directly with legislative policies, or with the membership of Congress. After all, Senators and Representatives are nominated and elected in and by the several states. The need of party work on behalf of candidates who seek to oust from their seats members of the opposing party, has given rise to two additional committees, national in scope, and attached to the national party machinery. These are, for each party, the Congressional Committee and the Senatorial Committee, the first for the House, the latter for the Senate. Each is made up of party members in the house concerned, and is responsible for aiding in the election of party members to its own house. Each maintains a permanent organization, and cooperates closely with the national committee during the campaign. The latter, in turn, usually allocates to them the bulk of the funds needed for their campaign efforts.

The Senatorial Committee is usually a small one, consisting of six or seven Senators, elected for two-year terms by the party conference or "caucus" in the Senate. The Congressional Committee of each party is generally larger, and in the case of the Republicans it includes Representatives from each state that has one or more Republican Representatives. The aim is to have one member from each state, but where the party has no Representative in Congress from a state this necessitates the selection of a former member or other suitable person resident in the state.

Legal Recognition of State Parties. State like national party organization was at one time entirely a matter of party rule and custom. State parties are still private and voluntary in the sense that a man may join one or not join as he sees fit, but in other respects they have been woven rather closely into the whole system of public nominations and elections, and many features of their organization and procedures are now regulated by law and in that sense are not voluntary.

Position of State Party Convention. The state party convention was at one time everywhere the chief governing organ of the state party—a constituent, legislative, and nominating body, as in the case of the national party convention. It is still so in a number of states, as revealed in a recent important Supreme Court decision upholding the power to exclude Negroes from the Democratic primaries in Texas.[12] Today, however, the state laws so generally regulate matters concerning nominations and elections that it is not surprising to find the state party convention practically non-existent in some states, especially where the direct primary is used for all important state-wide nominations, and to learn that in other states it has been shorn of many of its former powers.

State Central Committees. With the decline in power of the state party convention, the state central committee has risen to the position of the most important organ of the major state parties. These state central committees are chosen by the members and supporters of each party as provided by law, i.e., either by direct primaries, or by party conventions held in accordance with the law. Minnesota authorizes the party candidates for state-wide offices, for the United States Senate, and for Representatives in Congress, to meet on a certain day and elect a party central committee of such size as they desire. There is no uniformity in the size of state committees; they range from eleven in Iowa to over five hundred in California.[13] The larger committees are naturally forced to appoint small executive committees to do most of the work, but of course it is the chairman, usually elected by the committee, who is the center of party activity. With him rests the supervision of the party headquarters and the management of the campaigns. If he is, as in some states, the national committeeman and a party worker of long experience as well, his position is a very powerful one. Other members of the state committee are also experienced party workers—ward, city, and county leaders in the main.

The state central committees are the true centers of power in both major national parties. Naturally the Republican state committees are of little importance in the "Solid South." In many states, however, the two committees are very nearly of equal power, with the fortunes of war and the spoils of office going first to one and then to the other. To have control over the state central committee is to wield great power in all party affairs.

County Committees. Also important are the county committees, the next lower tier in the party's organizational pyramid. There are over 3,000 counties in the United States, and they cover practically the entire national area. Over a thousand of these are in the South, and here the Republican committees are relatively unimportant. In the remaining counties, both parties are likely to be well organized, and all told there must be close to 5,000 active county committees in the two parties, the Democrats having the larger number today. Their members are chosen either as required by state law, at regular primary elections or in party conventions, or they are chosen according to party rules,

---

[12] Nixon v. Condon (1932), 286 U. S. 73; and see also Grovey v. Townsend (1935), 295 U. S. 45. On the main points at issue these decisions were overruled by the decision in Smith v. Allwright (1944), 321 U. S. 649, but the discussion with respect to the position of the party convention in the party is still valid.

[13] E. B. Logan, op. cit., p. 60.

at caucuses or otherwise. In theory there is choice by the rank and file of the party, but in fact the situation seems to be very different. Time and again state central committees, of the "out" party in particular, have to step in to reorganize and rejuvenate the county committees, and in such cases the state party leaders practically hand-pick the county committees. In many places also the voters show so little interest in the make-up of the county committee that they neglect to appear at party primaries and caucuses, and thus leave the choice to the regular party workers.

City and Ward Committees. As a result of the great growth of cities, city and ward committees have also become necessary to reach a majority of the voters of the country. In the larger cities, where the parties are well organized, the city and ward committees are more virile and active than the county committees, and are largely independent of their control.

Precinct Organization. At the base of the pyramid of party organization are the precinct committees, consisting of party workers, both men and women—ostensibly chosen in most places by the voters of the party in a primary or caucus, but actually in many cases the choice of the county organization or the county chairman. The committee may consist of only two members, a man and a woman, or it may contain three or more, with one recognized as the head. There have been various estimates as to the number of these committees in the United States. The voting precincts in the entire country number about 120,000, and it has been estimated that if each party has one, two, three or some other number of workers in each precinct, the total number of workers in these precinct organizations will run anywhere from 250,000 to well over 1,000,000, depending on the enthusiasm of the estimator. As a matter of fact, no one knows how many there are, or how regularly they are employed in party work. In many rural districts the local clerk, assessor, or tax collector may be a party worker incidentally, in his spare hours. Similarly in one-party regions, like the South, precinct work is not as important as in the doubtful or evenly divided states. The most active party work is to be found unquestionably in certain large cities such as New York, Philadelphia, Boston, Chicago, and the like. In most of these cities, many of the party workers are employed by the city, county, or state, and are giving at least a little public service for their salaries along with services for the party.

Precinct Workers and Their Tasks. Whatever the numbers of these workers, and whether they give full time or only part time to their partisan duties, the basic work of keeping the voters loyal to the party is done by the precinct organizations and workers, called captains, lieutenants, or leaders. To many persons of refined esthetic and ethical sensibilities, the "ward heeler" or precinct worker is an ignoble person, a sign of political degeneracy, but to the party leaders and bosses there are rarely enough of them. The work they do is often sordid enough, but the point is that they meet human beings on the levels at which they live and have their being, and try to do the little things for them that are needed to adjust them to our civilization. They get them out of jail, or help them find jobs, or straighten out their tax problems, in personal and friendly ways.[14]

Recent developments have somewhat weakened these local party workers or at least diminished their influence. The growth of strong farmers' organizations, labor organizations, and even cooperatives have provided millions of voters with new local organizations and a different sort of political leadership from the local unit to the national level. The Farm Bureau Federation may be taken as one example, but the CIO—Political Action Committee and National Citizen's Political Action Committee are equally colorful and active organizations.

Power of Formal Organization. How real and how important is this elaborate formal organization of the major parties from the national conventions down to the precinct workers? Are these various committees and conventions the real masters of the political parties? One hears that behind the scenes there is something more, something that shows its hand but seldom and very little. In short, where are the "boss" and the "machine" about which all Americans have been told so much? In providing by law for the election of the various party committees by the party voters, state legislatures tried hopefully to give the latter a real control over party policy and nominations, to bring the control out in the open and put it into the hands of persons chosen by the rank and file, and thus to put an end to the "invisible government" of the boss and the machine. In fact the situation seems not to have been greatly changed. The voters may have wished at one time to be saved from boss rule, but they did not continue to wish it hard enough year in and year out to attend party primaries and caucuses and to keep close watch on what was done. Not only did they not show sufficient interest, but it appeared also that they needed leadership, guidance, the advice of specialists. The leadership appeared spontaneously from among those who saw the possibilities of gaining power and a living from political work. But the leaders in turn, to make fairly sure of success, needed organization to keep the voters in line. Thus, without regard to what the statutes said, or even in strict conformity to them, leadership appeared and created organizations to regiment the voters to their ends, the ends being power over the electorate and remuneration for the workers and leaders. The true leaders see to it that in the great majority of cases the persons elected by the voters to the party committees are persons acceptable also to the leaders who aim to control the voters through them. Thus there seems, indeed, to be truth in Robert Michels' so-called "fundamental sociological law of political parties," to wit:

> It is organization which gives birth to the dominion of the elected over the electors, of the mandataries over the mandators, of the delegates over the delegators. Who says organization says oligarchy.[15]

[14] E. B. Logan, op. cit., ch. III, "The Politician and the Voter," by J. T. Salter.

[15] *Political Parties: A Sociological Study of the Oligarchical Tendencies of Modern Democracy.* New York, 1915, p. 401.

Necessity of Leadership. It is indeed a little surprising that men should have thought that in the field of politics, alone of all branches of human endeavor, the mass of the voters would be able to lead, and that there would be no need of political specialists and leaders. The new devices of direct election of party committees may have some value when the voters go on strike, or rise in revolt against misgovernment. The bosses cannot have everything their own way all the time, but generally speaking they are left undisturbed by the voters of the party.

Informal Party Organization. Thus, whether the elected committeemen are the leaders themselves, self-nominated and approved by the handful of party workers who attend primaries and caucuses, or whether figureheads are put up as committeemen while the real leaders remain in the background, in every place where party organization is at all strong, there is an informal party organization, an organization that cannot be described, that includes bosses in some places, machines in others, sometimes an outstanding state governor, or a mayor—all told, a group that actually makes the political processes operate. The formal party organization may or may not be the real thing in any particular place.

Political Rewards and the Spoils System. Those who exercise political power naturally expect rewards in the forms of money and power, although some of them must get great satisfaction, too, out of the sense of having served the public. To wield control over an organization of men and women, and to go up the ladder from precinct and ward to county or even state political leadership for a major party must bring considerable satisfaction. As the leader and his followers must live, there must be financial rewards as well. Many are content to be on the public payroll in respectable capacities, and so there is a spoils system for filling the public payrolls with party workers. The civil service laws that attempt to enforce the merit system stand in the way unless they can be manipulated, as sometimes happens. But beyond the list of jobs available for party workers there is a considerable party income from campaign contributions and other more secret gifts or payments for public services rendered, in order to take care of the many party workers who do not get on the public payroll. This problem, and that of party funds, will be dealt with elsewhere.

REFERENCES

E. M. Sait, *American Parties and Elections*, New York, rev. ed., 1939, espec. chs. VI-XI, XIV-XVII.

R. C. Brooks, *Political Parties and Electoral Problems*, 3rd ed., New York, 1933.

E. B. Logan (ed.), *The American Political Scene*, New York, 1936, chs. I-III.

H. R. Bruce, *American Parties and Politics*, rev. ed., New York, 1932.

C. E. Merriam and H. F. Gosnell, *The American Party System*, 3rd ed., New York, 1940.

A. N. Holcombe, *Political Parties of To-day*, New York, 1924.

Stuart Lewis (ed.), *Readings in Party Principles and Practical Politics*, New York, 1928.

F. R. Kent, *The Great Game of Politics*, New York, 1928.

Pendleton Herring, *The Politics of Democracy*, New York, 1940.

Peter H. Odegard and E. Allen Helms, *American Politics*, New York, 1938.

John M. Mathews and Clarence A. Berdahl, *Documents and Readings in American Government: National and State*, rev. ed., New York, 1940, pp. 131-61.

A. N. Christensen and E. M. Kirkpatrick, *The People, Politics, and the Politician: Readings in American Government*, New York, 1941, pp. 265-99.

Dewey Anderson and Percy E. Davidson, *Ballots and the Democratic Class Struggle*, Stanford University, California, 1943.

V. O. Key, Jr., *Politics, Parties, and Pressure Groups*, New York, 1942.

E. E. Schattschneider, *Party Government*, New York, 1942.

Wilfred E. Binkley, *American Political Parties, Their Natural History*, New York, 1943.

CHAPTER 10

The Nomination and Election of the President

At the apex of the elaborate pyramid of elective offices in the United States stands the Presidency of the United States. Not alone the tremendous power of the office and the great influence that the President may wield, but also the great hopes and the affection that the people attach to the holder of this office, make it the greatest election prize in the United States. It is not surprising that the highest objective of every political party should be the winning of this office nor that the contest for it between the parties should be the most exciting, colorful, and expensive of all elections.

To the student of politics the election of the President is an event of outstanding interest because of the uniqueness of the method of election. That method was an experiment and an invention when it was established, and no other nation has really duplicated it. The experiment did not work out as expected, and yet the method that has developed has in the past 160 years produced, on the whole, many distinguished heads of the state—along with some mediocre ones. This is not to say that the method of choice is alone responsible for either the good or the bad results.

Proposed Methods of Election. When the Federal Convention members agreed that there should be a President of the United States, the question arose as to how he should be chosen. In the Virginia plan it was proposed that he be elected by the Congress, and this plan was twice agreed to by the convention. Those members who, on the basis of both theory and the experiences of the states, were afraid of legislative domination over the executive thought this would not do. There was a proposal from Elbridge Gerry of Massachusetts that the national executive be chosen by the state executives, each having an equal vote. This also was rejected.[1] James Wilson of Pennsylvania, not usually considered to have had very democratic leanings, then seriously proposed direct election by the voters. "Experience," he stated, "par-

[1] Charles C. Tansill (ed.), *Documents Illustrative of the Formation of the Union of the American States*, 1927, p. 179.

ticularly in New York and Massachusetts, showed that an election of the first magistrate by the people at large, was both a convenient and successful mode." [2] When this was put to a vote, only the Pennsylvania delegation voted for it. Luther Martin of Maryland, a state in which the governor was then chosen indirectly by a body of special electors, moved "that the executive be chosen by electors appointed by the several legislatures of the individual states." [3] This suggestion was rejected but later revived, modified, and then adopted.

Original Plan of Election. The electoral plan adopted by the Convention and written into the Constitution was as follows: Each state was to appoint, "in such manner as the legislature thereof may direct," a number of Presidential electors equal to the number of Senators and Representatives from that state in Congress. To prevent Congressional domination of the election and of the President, however, no member of Congress nor any officer of the United States could serve as an elector. The electors were to meet in their respective states, not as one body at the national capital, and were to cast their ballots for two persons, i.e., each elector was to have two votes, to be given to different persons, at least one of whom should not be a resident of his own state. These votes were then to be sent to the national capitol, where the president of the Senate (the Vice President of the United States) was to open them in the presence of the two houses. The person with the largest number of votes, if a majority of the total number of electors, was to be declared President of the United States, and the person with the next highest number was to be Vice President. In case two persons had a majority but were tied, or in case no one had a majority, the House of Representatives was to make the final choice, and where no one had a majority, its choice was limited to the five highest candidates. In the voting in the House, each state delegation was to have one vote, and a majority of states was necessary to the election of the President in these cases. After this, the next highest candidate was to be declared to be Vice President, but if two were tied for next place, the Senate was to make the choice for this office.

How was it expected that this plan would work? From the debates in the convention a few points are indubitably clear. *First*, since no provision was made for a system of nominations, preliminary to the choice of the President by the Presidential electors, the delegates either did not think of this problem at all, or else they considered a provision on the subject unnecessary or unwise. *Second*, the delegates seemed to think that the Presidential electors in each state would make careful and deliberate choices, without real partisanship. They expected each state to put forward "favorite son" candidates and they did not foresee how active the national political parties would be in the choice of candidates for President and Vice President. *Third*, nearly all the delegates expected that the Presidential electors would only occasionally give

---

[2] Charles C. Tansill, *op. cit.*, pp. 134, 393.
[3] *Ibid.*, p. 395.

a majority to any one candidate, and consequently they thought that the election would in most cases be thrown into the hands of Congress, where many thought the choice ought to be. *Fourth*, as between the House of Representatives and the Senate the convention majority favored election of the President by the House, since the Senate was already endowed with sufficient power over the President through its right to veto Presidential appointments and to reject treaties. *Fifth*, the majority also favored a fairly short term for the President, but without any restrictions on the number of terms he could serve. Re-elections were expected and favored.

First Election Raises Questions. The original method of election operated through the first four Presidential elections. In the first election, held on the first Wednesday in February, 1789, there were no formal nominations. Almost everyone expected Washington to be elected, as he was. The real problem concerned the Vice Presidency.[4] Virginia being in line for the Presidency, New England seemed entitled to the next highest office, and John Adams was the logical candidate. There was no real danger that he would get the votes of all the electors, but Hamilton, the great political manipulator, was so anxious that Adams should not rival Washington in votes that he wrote many private letters to prevent it. When the votes were opened, Washington had sixty-nine, the full number of the electors chosen, and Adams was next, but with only thirty-four. This was not even a majority, but under the rule of the next highest, he was elected Vice President. Thus the very first election revealed one difficulty with the method of election: the electors could not designate one person to be President and another to be Vice President. If two candidates received equal numbers of votes and majorities, even though the intention was to make one President and the other Vice President, the question would be thrown into the House of Representatives for decision. Only the action of parties and leaders and a certain amount of wire-pulling behind the scenes could prevent tie votes in certain cases.

How Electors Were Chosen. But how were these first Presidential electors chosen? Popular election of the electors was provided for, and was successful in four states, Massachusetts, Pennsylvania, Maryland, and Virginia. New Hampshire also held such an election, but as no one received the majority required by law, the legislature had to make the final choice. Elsewhere the legislatures kept the power in their own hands, and in New York a squabble between the houses resulted in a failure to appoint any electors. North Carolina and Rhode Island were not yet in the Union; thus only ten states actually cast ballots in the first Presidential election, and only half of them permitted the voters to choose, or to try to choose, the electors.

The next election went off more smoothly, and with little difficulty. But parties were already forming, and democratic ideas were abroad in the land. The state legislatures were bombarded with demands to permit the voters to

[4] See Minnigerode, *Presidential Years, 1787-1860*, for brief accounts of the politics of the first Presidential elections.

choose the Presidential electors. At first they yielded but slowly, but as the suffrage came to be widened, the movement accelerated. The last state to make the change to popular election was South Carolina whose legislature continued to choose the electors down to the time of the Civil War.

Rise of Parties and Caucuses. National political parties were definitely taking shape even during Washington's administration. To get the united support they needed for their candidates, factional leaders in Congress called party caucuses as early as 1796, to nominate their candidates for the Presidency and the Vice Presidency. Hamilton was the off-stage guiding genius for the Federalists. Jefferson was both the leader of his party and a candidate for the Presidency. In 1796 he lost to John Adams by three electoral votes; in 1800 he won over Adams by a narrow margin as the result, principally, of the shift of New York from the Federalist to the Republican side.

Election of 1800. These elections showed increasingly the defect involved in not permitting the electors to designate their choices specifically for the two offices. In 1800 Hamilton had to promise Pinckney of South Carolina that he should be run equally with John Adams on the Federalist ticket, so that both would have the same chance at the Presidency. In the same election, Burr insisted on an equal chance with Jefferson for Republican party support. This agreement was made, since Jefferson's party badly needed the support of Burr, an effective Tammany leader who was building up the Republican organization in New York City, Hamilton's Federalist stronghold. There was little doubt that the Republican voters intended Jefferson to be President, and Burr to be Vice President, and there seems to have been a plan to have one Republican Presidential elector in South Carolina cast his second vote for somebody else than Burr. This was not done. Burr and Jefferson both received exactly the same number of votes, and the final choice between them was thrown into the House of Representatives. There the Federalists were still strong, and the feeling against Jefferson was so violent that, had Burr done anything to make an agreement with them, he could have been elected President over Jefferson. Hamilton insisted that Burr was the more dangerous man, but the House had to vote thirty-six times before Jefferson was chosen President over Burr, the final vote being ten states to four.

Method of Election Amended. This experience showed the need for changing the electoral procedure. A constitutional amendment was promptly submitted by Congress and adopted by the states in time for the 1804 election. Under this amendment, the Twelfth, which still controls the method of election, the electors now vote separately for President and Vice President. A majority of the total number of ballots is needed for election to either office. If no candidate has a majority for the Presidency, the House of Representatives makes the choice from the three highest candidates; the vote is by states, and a majority of the states is necessary to elect. A similar rule is provided for the Vice Presidency, except that in this case the Senate elects, and each Senator has one vote.

The Twelfth Amendment also provided that in case the House should fail to elect a President by March 4th, then the Vice President should act as President as in other cases of vacancy. It was not clear whether the House could later elect a President within the four-year term. The Twentieth Amendment, adopted in 1933, sets the beginning of the President's term at January 20th, and provides that if a President has not been chosen, or if one elected has failed to qualify for the office, by the date set, the Vice President elect shall serve as President only until the latter has been elected and has qualified. A Vice President elect is to become President only in case of the death of the President elect.

Congressional Caucuses and Party Conventions. From 1804 to 1824, Presidential elections went along rather smoothly. The Federalist party was dying; the Republicans had almost everything their own way; and one Virginian passed the Presidency on to another, Jefferson to Madison, Madison to Monroe. Nominations were made by the party caucuses in Congress. In the meantime the rise of manhood suffrage was leading steadily to the adoption of popular election of Presidential electors, and the characteristics of the present-day system of Presidential elections were beginning to appear. The next great step in the development came with the ending of nominations by Congressional caucuses and the adoption of national nominating conventions. This, as already noted, came in 1831 and 1832.

Changes Made in Fifty Years. Thus within fifty years not only did the Presidency itself undergo great changes, but the method of election was almost completely altered. The choice of President and Vice President, instead of going regularly to Congress for decision, went there only twice before Jackson, in 1800 and 1824, and has never gone there since. Direct election by the voters had become almost a reality, and has continued to be so. The Presidential electors, instead of being independent in their choice, and careful and objective in making their decisions, have become the tools of party. They automatically vote for the candidates of their own party.

Like other American public elections, the election of the President and Vice President naturally divides itself into two parts, that which is official or provided for by law, and that which is outside of the written laws and Constitution. This unofficial part has arisen and been developed so as to meet fully all the legal requirements, and the two sides of the process dovetail into the appearance of a single process with remarkable precision. The unofficial part of the process provides amply for one phase of the election that the Constitution wholly neglected, namely, the nomination of candidates. This part of the process is also more clearly national than the formal election procedure. The nominations are made in national nominating conventions by national political parties.

THE NOMINATION OF CANDIDATES

Preparations for National Conventions. About the first of the year in which a President is to be elected, the national committee of each major party meets in Washington and issues a call for the forthcoming national convention of the party. The description of the procedure that follows applies to both party conventions, except where otherwise noted. The call stipulates the time and the place of the forthcoming national convention, and calls upon parties in the states and territories to select their quotas of delegates to attend. The Republican convention usually takes place first, sometime in June or July, while the Democratic convention usually follows a few weeks later. The convention city is chosen with regard to the facilities available, such as a good convention hall and adequate hotels; the location of the city with regard to the possibility of swinging extra votes to the party; its location with respect to the residences of the leading candidates for nomination, so as not to give any candidate an undue advantage over others; and the liberality of its local political and business leaders in putting up the money needed for convention expenses.

Apportionment of Delegates up to 1924. The call states also the rules as to the number of delegates and alternates to which each state and territory is entitled. For a long time both parties maintained substantially the same rule on this point: each state was entitled to two delegates for every Senator and Representative from the state in Congress, plus an equal number of alternates. Thus in the Democratic convention, certain northern states that the party had not carried practically since the Civil War were permitted to have delegations that outnumbered many southern states that had voted the Democratic ticket almost unbrokenly. Even more striking was the situation in the Republican conventions, where states from the solid Democratic South had delegations that could outvote many northern states that regularly gave majorities for the Republican ticket. The vice in this arrangement appeared most clearly when a Republican President was up for renomination. Such a President controls the southern Republican delegations, and can use them to help assure his own renomination. He controls them, of course, because for over three years as President he has controlled appointments to numerous federal offices in the southern states, and has been giving them to partisan supporters who constitute an influential part of the small Republican vote in those states. When Theodore Roosevelt in 1912 tried to get the nomination away from President Taft, he carried the delegations in a number of northern and western states, but was unable to overcome the advantage that Mr. Taft had in his control over the southern delegations. The result was not only a split in the Republican party, and the defeat of both Taft and Roosevelt by Woodrow Wilson, but also a renewed demand by the Republican party units in the northern states that there be a new basis of representation in the convention.

Present Apportionment Rules. Since 1924 the Republicans have had a different division of delegates, but the Democrats kept their old rule until 1940. The similarities and differences are shown in the accompanying table. It will be noted that while each party gives every state some representation, the Republican party has rules for scaling down the representation from states that cast relatively few Republican votes, and for increasing the numbers of delegates from states carried by the Republicans. From early days and through the 1940 convention the Democratic party used a uniform rule for all states, no matter how great or how small was the chance of the party carrying any particular state. The new Democratic formula, adopted in 1940 and effective in 1944, merely adds two delegates from each state that has gone Democratic in the preceding Presidential election.

Rules for Apportioning Delegates to Democratic and Republican
National Conventions

DEMOCRATIC	REPUBLICAN
1. Four delegates at large from each state.	1. The same.
2. Two additional delegates at large for each Representative at large in Congress from each state.	2. The same.
3. Two additional delegates at large from each state that went Democratic in the preceding Presidential election.	3. Three additional delegates at large from each state that cast its electoral vote or a majority thereof for the Republican nominee for President in the preceding Presidential election.
4. Two district delegates from each Congressional district in each state.	4. (a) "One district delegate from each Congressional district casting one thousand votes or more for any Republican elector in the last preceding Presidential election or for the Republican nominee for Congress in the last preceding Congressional election." (b) "One additional district delegate from each Congressional district casting 10,000 votes or more for any Republican elector in the last preceding Presidential election or for the Republican nominee for Congress in the last preceding Congressional election."

DEMOCRATIC	REPUBLICAN
5. Three delegates each from the District of Columbia, the Philippines, Hawaii, Puerto Rico, Alaska, and the Canal Zone; two delegates from the Virgin Islands.	5. Three delegates each from Alaska, District of Columbia and Hawaii; and two additional delegates if the delegate to Congress elected at the last preceding election was the Republican nominee. Two delegates at large each for Puerto Rico and the Philippine Islands.

Both parties provide for the election of alternates to the full number of the authorized delegates from each state.

These rules tend to give each major party a national nominating convention of over one thousand regular delegates and about the same number of alternates. Even these large numbers are increased (a) when competing delegations from certain states are both seated and (b) when certain states send more delegates than they are entitled to, under rules that give each one a seat but only a fraction of a vote.

The new rules of apportionment are an interesting evidence that the nominating conventions are becoming more national and more representative of people as such than of the states. They are also an admission that the major parties do not necessarily have voting strength uniformly throughout the nation. The Republican deficiency in the 'Solid South" even raises the question as to how national the party is.

Election of Convention Delegates. The state central committee of each party in a state must see to it that the right number of delegates is duly elected. There are two principal ways in which the convention delegates can be chosen. In about a third of the states, including some of the largest (New York, Pennsylvania, Illinois, Ohio, California, Massachusetts, and New Jersey), the delegates (except certain delegates at large) are chosen at direct primaries, as required by state law.[5] In the rest, the state party conventions elect the state's delegates at large, while Congressional district delegates to the national convention are chosen either by Congressional district conventions or by the state convention.

Decisions on Contested Delegations. When the delegates and the leaders who are working for the several candidates for nomination arrive at the conventions, certain steps have already been taken. The national committee of the party has arranged for a convention hall, has provided a temporary chairman and other officers for the convention, and has prepared a preliminary list of delegates. From a number of states, especially where conventions are used to elect the delegates, there will be several rival delegations representing dif-

---

[5] See Merriam and Overacker, *Primary Elections*, pp. 359-404, for a brief summary of state primary laws as they stood in about 1927.

ferent wings of the party. Which delegation is to be seated? For purposes of temporary organization, the national committee must make this decision, so that all states can be represented; but this may be the vital decision, for upon a few disputed delegations may depend which faction of the party shall get control long enough to rule out the opposition and get its candidates nominated. In some cases the decision of a contest can be made by simply asking: Which delegation was elected in accordance with the party's rules? In other cases the national committee may try a compromise arrangement whereby both delegations are seated, but each delegate has but one-half vote.

Convention Hall Arrangements and Preliminary Steps. Proceeding under the rules of the last national convention, the convention swings into action under its temporary officers. Picture a great convention hall, gaily decorated with flags, banners, emblems of all kinds, and pictures of past Presidents and party leaders. On the main floor are more than a thousand regular delegates, grouped by states, each with its banner and name, and just behind them another thousand alternates. At the main platform in front are the presiding officer and other officials; flanking them, or located in other parts of the hall and balcony, are the hundreds of representatives of the press, the cameramen, and the radio operators. Overflowing the hall and the balcony, especially during the more exciting hours, are the thousands of spectators who have been able to obtain tickets of admission. It is difficult to imagine an arrangement less conducive to calm thought and deliberation. More than anything else it is a monster "pep fest," such as college boys would like to stage on an equal scale before a football game. The partisans have gathered not only to nominate a candidate but also to have an exciting time, to impress the country, and to build up their own enthusiasm and confidence in their cause. The "keynote address" of the temporary chairman is only the first "rouser" of the meeting, and it is intended for the country as a whole just as much as for the delegates. Indeed, all the proceedings go out over the radio and through the press, which do not stint the time and space they allow. Very few if any occasions are as good news copy as a national convention.

The Four Principal Committees. After the keynote, the four principal committees of the convention are appointed: those on credentials, on resolutions (platform), on rules, and on permanent organization. There is a roll call of the states, and the chairman of each state delegation arises in turn and presents the names of the four delegates from his state to serve one on each committee. The committees get to work at once, while the convention marks time. The committee on credentials takes up the work of passing on contests between delegations and, because time is limited, it usually accepts the decisions of the national committee. The temporary roll is then made permanent by vote of the convention.

Rules and Organization. The committee on rules generally recommends adoption of the rules of the past convention, but occasionally changes are proposed, as in the matter of the apportionment of delegates at future conventions, and the change of the two-thirds rule recently made by the Democratic party. Likewise, the committee on permanent organization soon proposes the list of names of the permanent officers of the convention. The permanent chairman is, of course, most important. The man selected for this post is generally associated with the candidacy of the leading candidate. For the rest, the committee usually proposes to make permanent most of the temporary officers.

Framing the Platform. With its list of members finally settled, its rules established, and its permanent officers elected, the convention is ready for its next work, which usually relates to the platform. By this time the committee on resolutions has probably had some difficult sessions, day and night, trying to work out a platform that will satisfy the conflicting demands of the various labor, agricultural, industrial, commercial, and sectional interests. Sometimes, also, powerful individual leaders can be satisfied and be persuaded to support the party ticket only by concessions in the platform.

Development of Party Platforms. Jefferson and other leaders had in earlier days drawn up summaries of their personal political beliefs, but not until the Democratic convention of 1840 did a national party convention formally adopt a statement of its creed and aims. This first platform can be printed on a page and a half of a book of this size. Since that day a century of national party platform-making has produced enough to fill a very substantial volume.[6] In 1900 there were eight national platforms, partly due to splits in both Republican and Democratic parties; usually there are at least four or five, but only those of the major parties are given much attention. The latter tended for a long time to become longer and less specific, so that they frequently filled up fifteen or twenty pages of print. They were not platforms to stand on, but elaborate constructions of falsework, with much "gingerbread" and other ornamentation to attract the eye and to conceal the solid timbers, and real economic interests, that hold the party together. More recently they have tended to become somewhat briefer and more specific, but they still have some of the old characteristics.

Can Platform-Making Be Improved? The vital difficulty, as previously indicated, is one that no major party can overcome and still continue to be a major party. Each is supported by a variety of interests, more or less opposed in their desires, and no party can afford to lose the help of any important interest. There is another difficulty, also, to which both former President Hoover and the late Governor Alfred E. Smith have called attention. In the hurly-burly of a short and tumultuous national party convention, there is not the time to do the work well, nor is the atmosphere conducive to the careful thought that is needed. Mr. Smith recommended that the platform committee be appointed so early that it could meet before the convention and work

---

[6] See Kirk H. Porter (ed.), *National Party Platforms*, New York, 1924, for all important platforms from 1840 to 1924, inclusive.

out carefully the party's platform.[7] This assumed that the usual type of convention delegate is capable of doing the work. Following the 1936 Republican defeat, Mr. Hoover recommended that the party should meet in convention during 1938, the "off year," and formulate a declaration of constructive national principles infused "with intellectual and moral integrity, with human sympathy, with idealism and emotion."[8] It has also been suggested that each of the national parties should maintain a permanent research organization, not one staffed by superannuated newspaper writers and lame duck politicians, but one composed of mature, active, competent experts in a number of lines, and that these should be continuously studying the problems facing the party and the nation, and should be constantly formulating policy statements, not for publication, but for submission to the party leaders in the national committee and in the administration, so that during the years between campaigns the materials for the next platform will be accumulating. In any case, the committee on resolutions now does what it can to formulate a platform; it brings its product to the convention before the nominations are made, and moves its adoption. Minority factions frequently arise to propose substitute resolutions, but as a rule what the committee has drawn up is adopted by the convention.

Marking Time. Several days of the convention have now passed, and the main work still lies ahead. In the meantime many of the delegates have been getting restless and demonstrations in favor of particular candidates have taken place from time to time to alleviate the tedium. Most of the delegates have really nothing to do, and the alternates have even less. Out of over a thousand delegates, about two hundred are needed on the four principal committees, and two of those committees are not really time-consuming. The rest of the delegates smoke and chat, wander out in the lobbies to meet friends, go to lunch to be introduced to leaders from other states, and generally occupy their time in getting acquainted and in being amused. The value of the convention as a meeting place for partisans from all states, a place for getting the feeling of party unity, has not been sufficiently emphasized.

Leaders Active in Negotiations. While the majority of the members have little to do, the state and national leaders are conferring with a view to deals on the final nomination. This is not true where the nomination is a foregone conclusion, but where there is doubt, where there are many candidates, and many pledged delegations, some sort of final compromise is necessary. "Favorite son" candidates from the several states must be given their short runs. "Dummy candidates" must be eliminated, and "dark horse" candidates, i.e., those who have kept in the background but may be available for the final nomination, must be shown in private to the leaders of the state delegations.

[7] See E. B. Logan (ed.), *The American Political Scene*, p. 139 (article by H. R. Bruce, citing A. E. Smith, *The Citizen and His Government*, New York, 1935, pp. 117, 118).

[8] "The Crisis and the Political Parties," in *The Atlantic Monthly*, vol. 160, pp. 257-268, espec. 268 (Sept., 1937).

And so behind the scenes, even early in the convention, there is much dickering, bluffing, cajoling, and persuading.

Situations differ tremendously, of course, and the leaders must conform to them to some extent. For the party in power there is one situation; for the "outs" there is another. A President in his first term is almost entitled to a renomination. Seldom does a party dare to admit it made a mistake in electing him in the first place, while the men whom he has appointed to offices throughout the land form an almost solid phalanx of partisan supporters in his drive for renomination. As a rule, then, other potential candidates in that party must hold back for another four years. But when a President is finishing a second term, and finally reaches a point where he can safely declare that he will not be a candidate for a third term, the rush of candidates begins.

In the "out" party there is more freedom of candidacy at all times. A former President, later defeated for re-election, may have little or no claim. One who has been defeated as a candidate without ever having been President suffers from an even heavier handicap. The party's defeat can be charged to him, while many think that they can reorganize the party, give it a new orientation in policy, and lead it to victory. But often they too must wait, since the party in power may be too strong to defeat at the next election. There is little glory and no profit in accepting a nomination, even for the Presidency, when defeat is almost certain.

Nominating Speeches and Demonstrations. Finally the time has arrived for the nominations. The roll of the states is called, alphabetically, and as Alabama is called first, one of its delegates arises either to nominate some candidate, or to yield Alabama's time to some other state whose delegation leaders wish to nominate a candidate favored also by the Alabama delegation. State after state is called upon; speech after speech is made; there are many seconding speeches as well as original nominations. The conventions have developed a peculiar type of oratory in which each speaker tries to say everything good he can about his candidate without naming him until at the very end. Everyone knows, of course, whom the speaker has in mind, but that he must refrain from naming him as long as he can since the name is the signal for a demonstration upon the floor by the candidate's adherents. Suddenly, as the magic name is given, a din breaks forth. Horns, drums, and other sound-making devices suddenly appear, and the most enthusiastic delegations begin a noisy demonstration, marching up and down the hall cheering their candidate and trying to impress the rest of the convention. This may last only a few minutes for unimportant "favorite sons," but it may last upwards of an hour for the leading contenders. In this way the larger part of a day may be used up, speeches being followed by demonstrations, and these in turn by more speeches.

Procedure in Voting. Then the voting begins, and the convention is at its climax. Candidates for renomination are usually nominated on the first ballot. Another demonstration then follows, and the work of the convention is nearly over. In most cases the "out" party requires a number of ballots to determine its nominee, and sometimes the balloting drags on interminably. There are times when the rival factions in the party do not easily compromise. In 1912 the Progressives withdrew from the Republican convention entirely, while in 1924 the Democrats took 103 ballots before the convention agreed on the nomination of John W. Davis, a man of obvious ability, but one for whom neither faction had any enthusiasm.

Preference Primaries and Delegate Pledges. When it comes to voting many delegates find that they are not entirely free agents. In numerous cases those who have been chosen by state and district party conventions are under instructions from those who elected them to vote for a certain candidate for the Presidency. Also a good many states have Presidential preference primary laws, dating back to the Progressive era before World War I.[9] Under such laws the voters will have expressed their preferences among candidates, and the delegates are directed by the law to give their support to the popular preference as expressed in the primary. Under the South Dakota law the delegates from that state to a national party convention are required to vote up to three times for the people's choice before switching their votes to another candidate. Other laws simply call on the delegates to support the popular choice.

When the Presidential preference primary laws were adopted a generation or more ago, they were looked upon as being important means for defeating the bosses and for ensuring a truly popular control over Presidential nominations. They have not worked out that way, and there is no way in which their requirements can be enforced. That the delegates sent to national conventions ought to be aware of the people's preferences among candidates for the Presidency, goes without saying. But a preference expressed by a sprinkling of party voters who go to the primaries or caucuses in April or May, may be inaccurate at the time, partly because some of the leading candidates have not yet declared themselves, and may have little relevance to the situation the delegates face at the national party convention in June or July. The political situation may have changed; some candidates may have withdrawn, others may have been discredited, while new ones have arisen or come to the fore that were not before the voters at the primaries. An unofficial poll like that of the American Institute of Public Opinion could be a more reliable and up-to-the-minute indication of voter preferences.

Majority, Two-thirds and Unit Rules. Under Republican party rules, a majority of all the delegates has always been sufficient to nominate a candidate for the Presidency or Vice Presidency. This has facilitated quicker decisions in its conventions. For many years the Democrats had a two-thirds rule, but this was accompanied by a state "unit rule." Under the latter, each state delegation took its own vote first, and then, if the state delegation so voted, the entire state vote was cast by its leader as a unit for the candidate who had

---

[9] See Overacker, *The Presidential Primary*; also Merriam and Overacker, *op. cit.*, ch. VII.

a majority of the delegation. This might also be required by the state convention when it sent its delegation to the national meeting. With the rise of the primaries, however, and the direct election of some delegates by Congressional districts, pledged to support particular candidates, it became unreasonable to enforce the unit rule in the national convention. More and more of the states permitted their delegates to vote as individuals. As the unit rule broke down, the two-thirds rule became increasingly unreasonable. In the 1936 convention, where Franklin Roosevelt's renomination was assured by a practically unanimous vote, the two-thirds rule was finally repealed.

Nominating the Vice Presidential Candidate. With the nomination for the Presidency made, attention is turned to the second place on the ticket. Much the same procedure is followed as in nominating the Presidential candidate, and the leaders who have arranged for the latter have not been unmindful of the second position on the ticket. It frequently goes to a man who represents a different section of the country, or a different faction in the party. A Dry and a Wet, a Conservative and a Liberal on the same ticket are not unusual. Among the Democrats, a northerner is usually the Presidential candidate, with sometimes a southerner to balance the ticket. Otherwise, the candidate for the Vice Presidency is taken from a so-called "doubtful state," a state that either party may carry, just as the Presidential candidate also is in many cases, the thought being that the additional votes for a local resident for high national office may be enough to give the party victory in that state. Because these considerations as to availability and vote-getting capacity are so important, it is very rarely that a major party convention nominates for the Vice Presidency a man of outstanding ability. In 1940 Franklin Roosevelt and his advisers practically dictated the nomination of Henry Wallace to be the Vice Presidential candidate of the party, but in 1944 Mr. Roosevelt kept hands off, and Mr. Truman became the nominee over Mr. Wallace.

Electing the New National Committee. One other bit of business the convention has to do: that is to form a new national committee. In theory the convention elects this committee; in fact each state delegation at the convention selects one man and one woman from its own ranks or from the state party for these positions, and the Presidential candidate chooses the chairman. With these things done, the convention adjourns *sine die*, leaving the new national committee to run the campaign and to carry on party affairs for the next four years.

Criticism of National Party Conventions. Everyone who has candidly examined the work of the major party national conventions has found something in them to condemn. They are too large, too turbulent, too brief for careful deliberation on party policies and candidates. Most of the members have no real part in the work that is done, and no true conception of responsible party action. Many are unduly influenced by the excitement of the occasion and by the flamboyant oratory.

Surely some way can be found to make the work of national conventions more rational and deliberative than it is, say the reformers. No doubt they are right, too, for these quadrennial spectacles are not such as to increase one's respect for the processes of democratic politics. A smaller body, meeting for a longer period and under quieter circumstances and a sense of real responsibility, with adequate preparation of information about men and platforms in advance, might do a much better job. In some cases, too, no doubt it could nominate abler leaders. Nevertheless, such as it is, the national convention is the outgrowth and expression of American party politics as it is. Improvement will probably have to come from within.

THE PRESIDENTIAL ELECTION CAMPAIGN

Following formal notification to the candidates of their nominations, and their speeches of acceptance, the campaign really begins in late July or in August. The national party chairman takes charge, and with the aid of the national committee gets a treasurer and other officers, begins to set up offices in the East, in the Middle West, and perhaps in the Far West, arranges for the collection of funds, for the recruitment of speakers, for the use of the radio, newspapers, billboards, and other media of publicity, and in general tries to put "punch" into the party organization that is to carry the burden of the work. Space will not permit an adequate consideration here of all that is done, and with what purposes and results. This is, furthermore, the sort of thing that everyone gets an opportunity to observe more or less closely, every four years.

FINANCING THE CAMPAIGN

Many Americans have expressed great concern in recent decades over the increasing expenditures on Presidential and other elections. Congress and the state legislatures, within their respective spheres, have enacted numerous statutes on the subject of party financing and campaign expenditures without much success in reducing the total amounts raised and spent.

The legislation has been directed at a number of supposed evils such as these: (1) Excessively large total expenditures by political parties, political committees, and individual candidates; (2) improper sources and methods of raising funds, including contributions from corporations and labor unions, and assessments upon public officers, employees, and relief recipients by political parties; and (3) improper expenditure of funds, usually listed under the headings of corrupt and illegal practices. Most of the legislation emanates from the state legislatures, but there is a small body of national laws as well. Under one of the most recent of these no political party may spend more than $3,000,000 in any Presidential campaign.

It has been found difficult to enforce such legislation, partly because astute leaders in various parties and pressure groups are so ingenious in finding ways to raise and spend money without violating the laws, and partly because the personnel and funds provided from public treasuries for enforcing such laws are usually wholly inadequate. Estimates by reliable authorities indicate that as much as $40,000,000 is probably spent through various channels upon a single Presidential campaign.

Are such expenditures excessively high and do they indicate a danger that the Presidency may be bought by the largest campaign fund? Distributed over a population of nearly 140 millions, an expenditure of $40,000,000 in one campaign amounts to about 35 cents per capita, and nearly 50 cents for each potential voter. Considering the extent of the country and the expense of such media as newspapers and the radio for reaching the public, and the rise of costs generally in recent times, such a total amount of expenditure by two major parties over a period of four months or more does not seem grossly excessive. Furthermore it is a known fact that in recent Presidential campaigns the party that spent most was the loser in the election.

Nevertheless the legislation in this field represents a wholesome attitude and it is not unlikely that whenever the abuses in campaign financing become intolerable, means will be found to improve the laws and to enforce them more effectively.

THE ELECTION OF PRESIDENT AND VICE PRESIDENT

Presidential Electors. Legally the election of the President and Vice President is not by the voters at all, but by the Presidential electors. In all states the laws now permit the voters to choose these electors, and in fact the electors do just what is expected of them, i.e., they vote for the candidates of their own party for the two offices. Thus the election seems like direct election by the voters; the electors seem to be just "rubber stamps." Nevertheless, the legislature in any state can at any time legally provide a different way of choosing Presidential electors; it could even choose the electors itself, or set up a special body of voters to choose them. Election by the electors is not the same as election directly by the voters, as will be seen below; and the electors are not *legally* bound to vote for the party candidate.

Presidential electors are, of course, an entirely different body from the delegates who go to the national convention, although some individuals may be both delegates and electors in the same year. Each state is entitled to as many electors as it has Senators and Representatives in Congress. They are nominated for each party by the state party convention or the state central committee, according to the law in the particular state.

Forms of Ballots Used. The names of the candidates for Presidential electors appear as a rule in party groups on the state ballot for the November election. In a few states, the voter must vote for each one separately, and does not even have the benefit of the names of the Presidential and Vice Presidential candidates to guide him. This is a rather absurd and awkward arrangement. It can work successfully only in states where one party is overwhelmingly stronger than all others, as in the "Solid South." Elsewhere the ballot is so printed that the names of the party candidates for President and Vice President are bracketed with those of the persons nominated by the party for Presidential electors. The instructions on the ballot then permit the voter to make a single X in order to vote for the entire group. A number of states have gone so far as to eliminate the names of the candidates for electors entirely from the ballot; the voter simply puts his mark after his choice (singular) for President and Vice President.[10] The names of the party nominees for electors are then on file with the secretary of state, who notifies the winning group. Thus the voter thinks he is really voting for the candidates for President and Vice President, when he is only choosing electors.

Plurality or Minority Elections. The party getting the highest vote in the state, even though not a majority, elects its entire slate of Presidential electors; the state's electoral vote at present is not split, and minorities get no representation. When three or more parties are strong contenders for victory, the winning party may have a mere plurality of popular votes in a number of states, and even a mere plurality in the national vote, as in the case of Woodrow Wilson in 1912. There have been cases, indeed, when with only two important parties in the field, the winning party had fewer popular votes than the loser, as in 1888 when Grover Cleveland (Democrat) was defeated by Benjamin Harrison (Republican). Legally, then, the important thing is not who gets the largest popular vote, but who gets the majority of the electoral votes. Since there are today 96 United States Senators, and 435 members of the House, the total number of Presidential electors is 531, and the majority necessary to elect is 266. New York has the largest number, 47, or nearly one-tenth of the total. Five states have only three each, and the average for the states is eleven. On a strict population basis, the small states are greatly over-represented. The twelve most populous states, all in the Northeast except California, Texas, and North Carolina, have, on the other hand, more than half of the electors, and if the three named be excluded, the states of the Northeast, with Minnesota-Iowa-Missouri as the western fringe of that region, also have more than half of the total.

Electors Meet in States. Although the choice of Presidential electors is in the hands of the states, Congress has set the time of their election and both the time and method of casting their votes for President and Vice President. Under this legislation [11] the governor of each state is supposed to transmit to the Secretary of State in Washington, immediately after the November election, the names of the chosen Presidential electors. If there is any legal dispute as to who was elected in the state, it may be settled by the state in accordance with its own laws, and if the decision is made six or more days before the electors are supposed to meet, the decision is final and binding on Congress.

[10] See L. E. Aylsworth, "The Presidential Short Ballot," Amer. Pol. Sci. Rev., vol. XXIV, pp. 966-70 (1930).
[11] U. S. Code of Laws, Title 3, ch. I.

The electors then meet in their several states (by state law, at the state capitals), on the first Monday after the second Wednesday in December, and cast separate ballots for President and Vice President. Then the electors transmit to Washington certificates showing the several votes cast by them, together with a certificate from the governor showing their own election. The Secretary of State publishes these, and also transmits copies to the two houses of Congress.

Congress Counts the Ballots. Congress meets in joint session for the count of the electoral votes on the 6th day of January, with the President of the Senate (Vice President of the United States) presiding. The ballots from the states are opened, and are counted by tellers from the two houses. Objections are called for in connection with each state's vote, and the law provides for a method of procedure in case of disputed ballots. There has been no important case since 1876. The announcement of the result of the election, and the inauguration of those elected are formalities to which no attention need be given. The oath of office taken by the President at the time of his inauguration is that prescribed by the Constitution.

Vacancies and Succession to Office. The original clause in the Constitution on vacancies and succession reads as follows:

> In Case of the Removal of the President from Office, or of his Death, Resignation, or Inability to discharge the Powers and Duties of the said Office, the same shall devolve on the Vice President, and the Congress may by Law provide for the Case of Removal, Death, Resignation, or Inability, both of the President and Vice President, declaring what Officer shall then act as President, and such Officer shall act accordingly, until the Disability be removed, or a President shall be elected.[12]

"Removal" of the President could come, presumably, only through impeachment. The one attempt to remove a President in this way, that involving President Johnson in 1868, was a failure. "Death" would be proved by a doctor's or coroner's certificate. "Resignation" of the office has never taken place, but Congress has enacted that a resignation or "refusal to accept" the office can be evidenced only by a written instrument, signed by the one resigning or refusing the office, and deposited with the Secretary of State. "Inability to discharge the Powers and Duties" of the office has not been defined. No doubt Congress has power to enact legislation to define and determine such inability, but it has not done so. A President can be very sick, and largely incapacitated, as Woodrow Wilson was for over a year, and still hold office. Congress has enacted that in case both President and Vice President are dead, out of office, or unable to perform the duties thereof, certain cabinet members in order—Secretary of State, Secretary of the Treasury, etc.—"shall act as President until the disability of the President or Vice President is re-

[12] U. S. Const., Art. II, sec. I, par. 6.

moved or a President shall be elected." [13] Clearly, then, the Constitution and the laws provide adequately for succession to the Presidency in case of death, and the people noticed, following the death of President Roosevelt in 1945, how promptly and smoothly the office, transferred to the Vice President, goes right on, with scarcely a pause.

Other Problems Relating to Succession. A person designated by popular vote at the November election to the office of either President or Vice President may happen to die or become disqualified before the electors cast their votes for him, or after their vote is cast and before it is counted by Congress, or after the count and before he can take office on January 20th. These contingencies were not covered in the original Constitution, but are dealt with in part by the Twentieth, or "Lame Duck," Amendment (1933):

> Sec. 3. If, at the time fixed for the beginning of the term of the President, the President elect shall have died, the Vice President elect shall become President. If a President shall not have been chosen before the time fixed for the beginning of his term, or if the President elect shall have failed to qualify, then the Vice President elect shall act as President until a President shall have qualified; and the Congress may by law provide for the case wherein neither a President elect nor a Vice President elect shall have qualified, . . .[14]

But when does one become a "President elect"? At the November general election, or after the electors have voted, or after Congress has counted the electoral vote? Here is a new term in the Constitution, and one for which there is no definition. Furthermore, the amendment does not cover the case of a candidate dying after he has been nominated by a national convention and before the November election. Presumably the national convention of the party could be reassembled if there were time enough, or the national committee could act to select another candidate, but there is little to indicate what would be done. Finally, if it is assumed that there is no President elect until after the Presidential electors have cast a majority vote for a candidate, then the interval between the November popular election and January 6th is also not provided for.

Proposals for Direct Popular Vote on President. All these many difficulties and complications in the process of electing a President, but more than all the thought that Presidents can be elected without having a popular majority, have led to a number of proposals to have the President and Vice President elected directly by the voters. No real progress in this direction has been made, largely for the reason that no one can find a formula that fits the present situation. If a nation-wide majority were required, the southern states would be at a great disadvantage. As they generally exclude Negroes from voting, and settle most of their election contests at the primaries, their votes at the

---

[13] U. S. Code of Laws, Title 3, ch. I, sec. 21.
[14] Sec. 4 of this amendment also has some bearing on the matter.

final election are very small. A uniform national suffrage and election law would seem to be needed for a national vote on the Presidency. Furthermore, all small states would lose proportionately, under such a plan, while the larger states would gain in influence in the elections. Nevada with less than 120,000 population (1940) has three Presidential electors, while New York has 286,800 inhabitants to every elector it controls. On the population basis, such a disproportion cannot be justified, but certainly the smaller states would strenuously oppose any change. To this extent, therefore, the method of electing the President is federal, not national. The will of a national majority can be defeated under the present plan.

There are other possible alternatives besides that of a direct, nation-wide vote for President, but there will not be space to discuss them. After all, the system of nominating candidates is as much to be condemned as the system of election, awkward and uncertain as the latter is. The tendency of the politicians who control the conventions to reject some of the ablest candidates for the Presidency, to take instead "available" men, i.e., those who they think can be elected without regard to personal ability, and to favor New York, Ohio, and other so-called "doubtful" states over other states in the making of nominations, are defects as important to overcome as those of the Presidential electoral system. Both sides of the Presidential electoral process need to be remedied at the same time in accordance with some unified plan.

REFERENCES

R. C. Brooks, *Political Parties and Electoral Problems*, 3rd ed., New York, 1933, chs. VI, VII, XI, XII.

E. M. Sait, *American Parties and Elections*, New York, rev. ed., 1939, chs. XX-XXIII.

H. R. Bruce, *American Parties and Politics*, rev. ed., New York, 1932, chs. XIII, XIV.

E. B. Logan (ed.), *The American Political Scene*, New York, 1936, ch. IV.

C. E. Merriam and Louise Overacker, *Primary Elections*, rev. ed., Chicago, 1928, ch. VII and Appendix A.

Louise Overacker, *The Presidential Primary*, New York, 1926.

F. R. Kent, *The Great Game of Politics*, New York, 1928.

P. O. Ray, *An Introduction to Political Parties and Practical Politics*, 3rd ed., 1924, chs. VIII, X.

Herbert Agar, *The People's Choice*, New York, 1933.

Edward Stanwood, *A History of the Presidency from 1788 to 1897*, 2 vols., rev. ed., Boston, 1928.

D. W. Brogan, *Government of the People*, New York, 1933, parts nine and ten.

Meade Minnigerode, *Presidential Years*, 1787-1860, New York, 1928.

L. T. Beman (ed.), *Abolishment of the Electoral College*, New York, 1926.

Kirk H. Porter, *National Party Platforms*, New York, 1924.

R. V. Peel and T. C. Donnelly, *The 1928 Campaign, An Analysis*, New York, 1931.

——, ——, *The 1932 Campaign, An Analysis*, New York, 1935.

Pendleton Herring, *The Politics of Democracy*, New York, 1940, espec. ch. 16.

Peter H. Odegard and E. Allen Helms, *American Politics*, New York, 1938, espec. chs. XVI-XIX.

Louis H. Bean, *Ballot Behavior, A Study of Presidential Elections*, Washington, 1940.

Robert S. Rankin, *Readings in American Government*, New York, 1939, pp. 106-36.

John M. Mathews and Clarence A. Berdahl, *Documents and Readings in American Government: National and State*, rev. ed., New York, 1940, pp. 207-45.

A. N. Christensen and E. M. Kirkpatrick, *The People, Politics, and the Politician: Readings in American Government*, New York, 1941, pp. 312-36.

Cortez A. M. Ewing, *Presidential Elections, from Abraham Lincoln to Franklin D. Roosevelt*, Norman, Okla., 1940.

V. O. Key, Jr., *Politics, Parties and Pressure Groups*, New York, 1942, espec., chs. 14, 15.

CHAPTER 11

The Structure and Membership of Congress

THE BICAMERAL PRINCIPLE

The structure of the Congress of the United States, which is the legislative branch of the national government under the Constitution, reflects two major influences, one negative, the other positive. On the one hand many members of the Constitutional Convention had served in the Congress under the Articles of Confederation and all had observed its actions and appraised its weaknesses. The Articles provided for a single-chambered Congress that would represent the states as such; kept the delegates dependent upon the state legislatures for their pay, for their instructions, and for their very memberships in Congress; and prevented any member from serving long enough or continuously enough to become thoroughly competent. Terms were for a single year, and no member could serve more than three years in any six. A state could at any time fail or decline to send delegates to Congress. In addition to these obvious structural weaknesses the Congress of that day was so lacking in power that it sometimes looked more like an international congress than a legislative body. This was clearly a model to avoid. On the other hand the framers of the Constitution had before them the examples of the English Parliament and of the colonial and state legislatures. These were bodies with true legislative powers, and with two houses that were based on different principles of representation. Although far from perfect the English Parliament and the state legislatures were reasonably representative and effective legislative bodies. There was no serious doubt at any time but that the majority of the framers of the Constitution wanted such a legislature for the United States as a whole.

Historical Reasons for Bicameralism. Bicameralism in the British Parliament developed as a means of giving separate representation to different social and economic classes, particularly the landed nobility on one side and the commoners in the towns and counties on the other. In the colonies there were the interests of the settlers and those of the Crown and governor. The former received representation in the assembly, while the governor or Crown appointed the council, a separate body. In the first state constitutions there were some cases of representation of the larger landholders in the upper house and of the poorer classes in the lower.

Large and Small State Compromise. Aside from these precedents for bicameralism and the natural desire of many men in the Federal Convention to follow precedent, there was one controlling reason why Congress was made a two-chambered body. The small states wanted all states to have equal representation, while the more populous states desired representation in proportion to their population. Neither party was strong enough to carry its point in the convention; and a compromise was effected whereby each state has equal representation (two members) in the Senate and representation substantially according to population in the House of Representatives. Under this arrangement neither small states nor large states can impose their will upon the other group. The debates over the Constitution brought out several additional reasons why the Congress should be made bicameral.

1. *The Senate as Executive Consultative Body.* In the first place, the Senate was to be a small house capable of advising and assisting the President in executive matters and on treaties. The first Senate was small enough for this purpose, but when President Washington attempted to meet with it for consultation on a proposed treaty, the Senators listened but refused to confer, preferring to send the matter first to a committee, and the President left them in indignation.[1] Attempts at direct consultation ended then and there. Since that time the Senate has become a much larger body than even the first House of Representatives so that such consultation between the President and the entire Senate has become much more difficult, and is not attempted.

2. *The Senate as Representative of Wealth.* A number of the framers of the Constitution hoped also that while the House represented the people, the Senate would represent wealth and property interests, just as certain state senates were then supposed to do. John Dickinson "wished the Senate to consist of the most distinguished characters, distinguished for their rank in life and their weight of property; and bearing as strong a likeness to the British House of Lords as was possible." [2] Other leaders concurred in this view, and the Senate was made elective not by the people but by the state legislatures. Thus the expected radicalism of the lower house was to be checked by the conservatism of the upper. For some decades perhaps this was the character of the Senate, but even before the direct election of Senators, the Senate began to show signs of liberalism equal to that of the House, and more recently the House has on a number of occasions been the check upon the more advanced Senate.

[1] McLaughlin, *A Constitutional History of the United States*, pp. 249-50.
[2] Rogers, *The American Senate*, pp. 17-18.

3. *The Senate as Representative of States, Not People.* Even the hope that the Senate would represent states while the House represented people has been disappointed. According to this theory the Senate would stand for state rights against national encroachments, while the popular House would seek national action for the solution of public problems. In fact the Senate, with a majority from the poorer and less populous states, has frequently been a leader in proposing federal aid bills and other nationalizing measures, while the House has concurred rather reluctantly. Clearly the Senate can be no less nationalistic than the House.

4. *The House as Initiator of Tax Measures.* Finally, the provision of the Constitution that "All Bills for Raising revenue shall originate in the House of Representatives; but the Senate may propose or concur with Amendments as on other Bills," [3] adopted in the hope of keeping the control of tax measures vested firmly in the more popular House has become almost a dead letter through the Senate's practice of "amending" House bills by substituting its own measures for them.

It is evident that these four additional reasons for having two chambers were *a priori* rationalizations rather than propositions based on solid experience. All four contentions have been shown to be untenable in practice. Even the argument that it is well to have two houses in order to have two separate, independent considerations of every bill, is no longer as persuasive as it used to be. There is still a great deal of hasty and ill-digested legislation.

Relative Position of Senate and House. The dominant position of the United States Senate over the lower house, though not expected by the framers of the Constitution, is now generally accepted. Election to the United States Senate is considered a higher goal even than that of election to the governorship of the state, with few exceptions. This results from many factors, among which may be named: (a) the longer term of the Senators, (b) the power that they have in treaty matters, (c) their power to approve or reject appointments proposed by the President, (d) the established prestige of the Senate arising out of its having had many famous members in the past, and (e) the smaller size of the Senate and the correspondingly greater importance of each vote in that body. The greater freedom of debate in the Senate is also worthy of mention.

How long the Senate will continue to hold its present position as the more important of the two houses no one can say. Many factors need to be considered. Upper chambers in other countries have gone into a sort of decline. In this country much will depend upon the capacity of the Senate to make itself into a more effective and responsible national governing body.

The Size of Congress. When all the original thirteen states had joined the Union, the Senate had 26 members and the House of Representatives had 65. As the number of states increased and the nation's population grew larger both houses increased in size. There were a few instances of small reductions

[3] Art. I, sec. 7, par. 1.

in the size of the House of Representatives as a result of reapportionments, but for over a century the tendency was strongly upward. When the reapportionment following the 1910 census brought the House up to 435 members, public opinion and the judgment of Congress itself insisted upon a halt. At about the same time the admission of Arizona and New Mexico (1912) increased the size of the Senate to 96. There has been no increase in either house since that time.

Both houses are far larger in size than the framers of the Constitution had in mind. When a Senate of 96 is contrasted with one of 26, or a House of 435 with one of 65, it becomes clear that the methods of doing business must be considerably different and that the need for rules and discipline will have increased considerably. On the other hand the original 26 Senators represented on the average only 150,000 citizens each (average state about 300,000) and the 65 House members only about 60,000 each, whereas today the average Senator represents nearly 1,400,000 persons (average state about 2,800,000) while the average house member represents over 300,000. These constituencies are very large by foreign standards. An exception is found in the Supreme Soviet of the USSR where the basis is 300,000 population for each deputy and the total membership is 647. The British House of Commons has 615 members with average constituencies of about 70,000, while the Dominion of Canada with less than one-tenth the population of the United States has 245 members in its House of Commons, or one member for about every 50,000 people.

Can the Senators and Representatives in the United States Congress truly represent such large numbers of people? Can they truly represent them in a legislative capacity and at the same time perform all the other services that constituents expect of their representatives? On the other hand could two houses that are much larger than the present ones effectively carry on the business of Congress? To answer any of these questions it will be necessary to consider, as we do in the next chapter, what is the true role of Congress.

THE QUALIFICATIONS OF MEMBERS

Qualifications of Congressmen. While in general any voter is eligible to elective office in the United States, certain special qualifications and disqualifications are laid down in the national Constitution for eligibility to Congress. It is provided that members of the House of Representatives in Congress must be 25 years old, citizens of the United States for 7 years, and residents of their states when elected.[4] The corresponding qualifications for Senators in Congress are 30 years of age and 9 years a citizen.[5] It is also provided that "no Person holding any Office under the United States, shall be a Member of

---

[4] Art. I, sec. 2, par. 2.
[5] Art. I, sec. 3, par. 3.

either House during his Continuance in Office." [6] It is generally agreed that neither Congress nor any state may by law add to or subtract from these qualifications. Each house is the judge of the elections, returns and qualifications of its own members, and each may expel a member by a two-thirds vote.[7]

With these unquestioned powers of control over its own membership, each house of Congress has at times in fact set up additional qualifications, not by general rule but by its refusal to seat members-elect. The House has refused to seat a Mormon who practiced polygamy (Mr. Roberts of Utah) and a Socialist who was under conviction for obstructing the prosecution of World War I (Mr. Berger of Wisconsin). Likewise the Senate has denied seats to members-elect whose primary and campaign expenditures were excessively large in the Senate's judgment and whose campaign funds came in large amounts from supposedly tainted sources. On the other hand the Senate in one case seated a member who was under thirty years of age (Senator Clay of Kentucky), but in a more recent case the under-age person (Senator-elect Holt of West Virginia) was urged to and did wait some months until he became thirty before presenting himself before the Senate. In none of these cases did Congress attempt to lay down a general law for future guidance.

A tremendous controversy raged for a time during the Coolidge administration over the Senate's assumption of power to refuse to seat members-elect, as in the case of Frank L. Smith of Illinois. The opponents of the Senate majority argued that to refuse to seat a Senator-elect from any state was equivalent to denying a state equal representation in the Senate, contrary to the Constitution.[8] Since each house is the exclusive and final judge in such matters, and since no court would take jurisdiction in a case to compel either house to seat the person elected, the protests came to nothing.

Contested Elections. Each house in Congress has the power to decide contested election cases, i.e., cases in which two or more persons claim to be legally elected from the same state or district. In England and in several other countries these questions are settled by the courts, in a judicial manner. It is somewhat doubtful whether Congress could legally delegate this power to the courts. In any case it has not attempted to do so. Each house appoints one or more election committees to which such contests are referred. Congress has also enacted legislation to govern contests in the House of Representatives, and every person claiming to have been elected to that body must conform to this legislation in contesting the election of the person who received the certificate of election. The latter is usually seated temporarily by the House. The committee in each case has, of course, a majority of its members from the party that controls the House, but the common assumption that in these cases a Republican House always seats the Republican claimant and a Demo-

---

[6] Art. I, sec. 6, par. 2.
[7] Art. I, sec. 5, pars. 1, 2.
[8] See the documents in the case of Senator-elect Frank L. Smith of Illinois in Mathews and Berdahl, *Documents and Readings in American Government*, pp. 296-303; also J. M. Beck, *The Vanishing Rights of the States*, New York, 1926.

cratic chamber always seats the Democrat is wholly erroneous. Most of the cases are settled in accordance with law and precedents, and party votes determine the question only in certain marginal, doubtful cases. But even in these few cases, it would avoid much public criticism of Congress if an impartial judicial body could decide them.

TERMS AND TENURE OF MEMBERS

It was intended by the framers of the Constitution that the Senate should be a small but stable and slow-changing body, while the House was to reflect more fully and more quickly the changes in public opinion. The terms of Senators were fixed at six years (one-third to come up for re-election every second year) and the terms of Representatives were set at two years. Little objection has been raised to the length of Senate terms; when considered by themselves they do not seem to be either too long or too short. On the other hand the terms of House members are much too brief. A Representative has only well begun his work following his election before he has to prepare for another election. Elected in the fall of 1946, for example, he takes office in January, 1947, soon begins to hear rumors of rival candidates who are going to try for his seat, and by late 1947 or early 1948 must begin to prepare for the primaries or conventions in which he hopes to be renominated, and then, if nominated, must plunge into the campaign for the fall election in 1948. This gives him too little opportunity to work at the business of being a useful Congressman, and requires him to give an undue amount of attention to the business of getting nominated and elected. There is no way to avoid this except to provide longer terms.

Terms Do Not Coincide. But the terms of Senators and Representatives cannot be considered by themselves, nor is the length of terms in years the only important consideration. Congress is only one branch of the national government. The President and the executive branch as a whole must also be considered. The legislative and executive branches need to work together if the government is to be a responsible government and to operate in accordance with public wishes. The coincidence of elections is therefore another factor to be considered, since men elected all at one time in a clear-cut campaign between two parties are more likely to cooperate than men who are elected at different times and upon different issues.

Because the Senators were originally chosen by the state legislatures there was no thought of gearing their elections to those for Representatives, which come every second year, or to that for President which comes once in four years. When direct election of Senators was established in 1913, and the nation moved that much nearer to direct popular control of the government, the awkwardness of the arrangement of House and Senate terms became more clear. Since only one-third of the Senate seats are filled at the election when a President is being chosen, the other two-thirds being "hold-overs," it is possible for a President to face at once an adverse party majority in that body. Furthermore, since all the positions in the House of Representatives are subject to change every two years, a President often finds his administration blocked by a hostile House majority during the second half of his four-year term. It is here suggested that, if all Senators and Representatives were elected in the Presidential election year and all for four-year terms, the winning party could almost certainly control both the legislative and executive branches for a four-year period. This is a long enough term for a national party to begin to put its policies into effect. The normal term in the leading parliamentary countries is five years. Furthermore if all the candidates of a party, for the Senate, for the House, and for the Presidency, had to stand shoulder to shoulder in a joint campaign, the chances of their adopting a common policy and accepting a joint responsibility would be greatly increased. There are many departures from this standard in the off-year elections and especially among the candidates for the Senate.

It may be argued, of course, that shortening the terms of Senators to four years will result in more rapid turnover and shorter terms of actual service. There is little reason to expect this result. Four years is a fairly long term. Furthermore, the practice of re-electing members is a very common one and it applies to both houses. Although elected for only two years at a time House members in many cases succeed in getting re-elected about as well as Senators, and there are many records from both houses of men having served from twenty up to over thirty-five years. Thus it is clear that the shorter terms in the House are no bar to long service.

PRIVILEGES AND IMMUNITIES

Freedom from Executive Interference. In the development of the English Parliament, and in its long struggle to wrest control of the government from the Crown, it became very important to procure freedom for the members from interference by the king, and by the executive officers and courts that he controlled. The result was the development of certain claims of members to privileges and immunities against outside interference. In the colonial assemblies in America similar claims to freedom for legislators were asserted. Some of these claims were written into state and national constitutions. The national Constitution provides that:

> They [the Senators and Representatives] shall in all Cases except Treason, Felony and Breach of the Peace, be privileged from Arrest during their Attendance at the Session of their respective Houses, and in going to and returning from the same; and for any Speech or Debate in either House, they shall not be questioned in any other Place.[9]

[9] Art. I, sec. 6, par. 1.

This means, of course, that no member may be tried in any court for libel, slander, defamation of character, or other similar offense on account of words spoken in debate in the house. There is no protection here for the member who commits a crime inside or outside of Congress, or even for one who becomes drunk and disorderly, or who drives his automobile recklessly. Neither can the member, as a rule, claim protection beyond what the Constitution states. He may speak freely in the house and even in committee, and his words may be issued by regular legislative publications without his becoming liable to suit. This privilege is very important if the effectiveness of representative government is to be maintained. But the member has no immunity against suit for libeling or slandering a person outside of his duties as a member.

SALARIES AND EXPENSES

Payment of Salaries. In every country as political power has been transferred from the wealthier classes to the masses of the people, there has been a tendency to establish salaries and to allow expenses for legislators. Members of the British House of Commons received no salaries until 1911; members of English borough (city) and county councils are still expected to serve without pay. The great democratic movement in the United States early demanded that compensation be given to all those who served the public as legislators or in other official capacities, in order that poor men as well as rich might serve, and in order to attach all officials to the public interest instead of having them dependent upon and responsible to private patrons. The Virginia plan in the convention of 1787 called for the payment of "liberal stipends" to the members of the "national legislature." Members of Congress arranged for payment of their salaries from the beginning. In 1789 they received small amounts per diem, and later annual salaries, which have since been increased. Today the salary for all members is $10,000 per year, plus allowances for travel expenses and secretarial help. This rate of pay is obviously calculated on the basis of full-time employment, for indeed that is almost inevitable where sessions are annual and of uncertain length and and where distances are long. There is no additional pay for special sessions. Recent increases in the cost of living and in the general salary and wage level of the country, coupled with an appreciation of the value of the services rendered by Congressmen, has led to a strong public demand for a further increase in the salaries of Congressmen.

Abuses in Congressional Expenditures and Appointments. It never looks well, of course, for Congressmen to increase their own salaries, and a recent attempt by Congress to provide pensions for its members was so strongly condemned in the press that Congress quickly repealed its own action. Indirect increases of salaries through nepotism and excessive mileage and expense accounts are also generally condemned outside legislative halls. Nepotism in this case consists in the appointment of a wife, son, daughter, or other close relation of a member as his secretary or to some other position on his own staff or in bringing about his or her appointment to some other position in the control of Congress, with resultant increase of the total family income. This may be justifiable in some cases, but it has an appearance of evil that is hard to dispel. Similarly, the very liberal rates allowed for travel receive much public condemnation. Congress has been improving its regulations on these matters, and at the worst it cannot be said that these expenditures add much to the tax burden. The vice lies rather in the fact that legislators who expect a high standard of economy and purity in administrative officers, themselves often set a rather low standard. They put weapons into the hands of cynical critics of all representative institutions.

Congress and the Franking Privilege. Members of Congress are also much criticized for the use and the abuse of the "franking privilege." This is the right, established by law, of each member to send letters and publications of an official nature through the mails without payment of postage. The charge is made, not without reason, that some members use this privilege as a means of circulating their campaign literature. A speech delivered in Congress, or read into the record, may be printed at the members' expense, but is then mailed out by the hundreds or thousands without payment of postage. Members justify this by pointing out that when their duties keep them so long in Washington each year, they have no other means of keeping in touch with their constituents or of keeping them informed. They feel that they are at a disadvantage as compared with their political opponents who are at home talking to the voters. These opponents, on the other hand, argue that the franking privilege gives the incumbent a great advantage in the campaign over those who are not members of Congress. A definite postage allowance for each member, varied for Senators in accordance with the population of their states, might be a more defensible arrangement than the franking privilege.

Total Expense of Congress. The first annual budget of the entire national government (1789) was about $3,000,000. In recent years the expenditures for maintaining Congress alone have been about $20,000,000, including the Capitol building and Library of Congress expenses. In view of this contrast it is hard to believe that the expenditures on Congress have increased less than those for the rest of the national government, and that the maintenance of Congress costs less than one-half of one per cent of the total ordinary national budget, but that is the case. As an item by itself the present expenditure on Congress is important enough to call for the most careful accounting and control and perhaps for a separate office of financial management. On the other hand it may be true that too little is now being expended on certain

Congressional activities to permit Congress to become as efficient as it needs to be in legislating for the nation.

CONSTITUTIONAL APPORTIONMENT OF MEMBERS

The great compromise in the convention of 1787 upon the issue of representation in Congress covered primarily the question of apportionment or how many members to each state. The methods of electing the members of the two houses were also dealt with briefly, but the provisions on this subject have been changed by constitutional amendment, statutes, and custom. Apportionment, districting, and methods of election are all very important in determining who shall be elected to Congress, the quality of its members, and the extent to which they will represent their states or districts, and the nation as a whole.

APPORTIONMENT AND ELECTION OF SENATORS

According to the national Constitution, each state is to have two Senators, and "no State, without its Consent, shall be deprived of its equal Suffrage in the Senate." [10] Whatever their population, area, or wealth, states are entirely equal in the Senate. When this so-called equality was established, Delaware (59,000 population) had less than one-twelfth the population of Virginia (747,000). In 1940 the discrepancy between the most and least populous states, New York and Nevada, was 122 to 1, while in area Texas exceeds Rhode Island 250 to 1. In the Senate today 12 Senators represent less than 2 million people, whereas 12 others represent over 50 million. Fourteen Senators from 7 states represent fewer people than the 2 Senators from such an average state as Iowa or Minnesota. These inequalities in the apportionment of Senators are likely to increase rather than decrease as the industrial states continue to outstrip the agricultural states in population growth. They reveal also the extent to which the Senators fall short of being truly representative of the nation in the sense of representing equal numbers of people.

For 125 years the Senators were elected from their respective states by the state legislatures. This was in accordance with the intention of the framers of the Constitution to have the Senate somewhat removed from direct popular control. But the wave of democratic ideas that swept the country during this period cut deeper and deeper into the control of the legislatures over Senate positions. Men were nominated for the United States Senate in various states by popular petitions, party conventions, and legally established preference primaries which the legislatures dared not ignore. In many cases men who were elected to state legislatures were pledged in advance to vote for a certain man for United States Senator. Great wealth also played a part in the Senatorial elections with the result that there were scandals over the illegal use

---

[10] Art. I, sec. 3, par. 1; Art. V, last sentence.

of money and deadlocks in the legislatures over Senatorial elections which prevented the legislatures from performing properly their legislative functions. Public opinion finally became so overwhelmingly against the system of legislative election of Senators, that Congress proposed and the states ratified (1913) the Seventeenth Amendment, for the direct election of Senators by the body of voters who choose Representatives. Over thirty years have passed under this plan without any serious proposals to change it.

The districts for the election of Senators are entire states. Each state has two Senators, but as a rule only one is elected at a time, so that in effect the state is for this purpose a "single-member district." Whenever by death or resignation there is an additional Senate vacancy from a state to be filled at the same election the ballots list one set of candidates for the regular or full-term position and a separate group for the short-term vacancy. In most of the states the governors are now permitted to fill temporary vacancies, but only until a special election can be held, or until the next regular election. Many Senators come in through such temporary appointments, but not all run for election thereafter.

Practically all the states provide for the nomination of Senate candidates through partisan direct primaries. The contests for party nomination for the Senate are among the most exciting in any state primary, and the final election contest frequently draws more votes and more publicity than the contest for the governorship.

In short, the Senators have been brought within the range of popular control in each state without having been made fully amenable to state or national party control. Many of them conduct their own campaigns in their own way, and offer views and policies that are contrary to those of the national party leaders. They are not all elected to office along with the President, and the national party has no control over their nominations. For these reasons, among others, they continue to be an unpredictable element in the conduct of national affairs.

APPORTIONMENT, DISTRICTING, AND ELECTION OF REPRESENTATIVES IN CONGRESS

Apportionment of the House of Representatives. Each state is guaranteed one member in the House of Representatives. The rule for the apportionment of all the other members of this House is stated in the Fourteenth Amendment as follows: "Representatives shall be apportioned among the several States according to their respective numbers, counting the whole number of persons in each State excluding Indians not taxed." [11] Prior to this amendment (adopted in 1868), Negroes in slavery had been counted as only three-fifths of one person each; since then all Negroes must be counted fully, and

[11] Amend. XIV, sec. 2.

the number of Indians not counted because not taxed is small and steadily decreasing.

It should be noted that it is not the number of *citizens*, nor the number of *voters* that is considered, but the total number of natural persons in the states, excepting untaxed Indians. Aliens are counted along with others. This situation cannot be lawfully changed except by constitutional amendment. On the other hand should any state abridge the right of adult citizens to vote "except for participation in rebellion or other crime," Congress may proportionately reduce that state's representation in the House of Representatives. This provision of the Fourteenth Amendment, designed to ensure Negroes the right to vote equally with whites in the southern states, has never been applied. It is today the settled sense of the country that this clause in the Fourteenth Amendment will not be enforced, because enforcement would probably result in more social losses than gains. The southern states continue, therefore, to have full representation in Congress, and other means must be found to ensure Negroes a fair right to vote.

The Census and Decennial Reapportionments. The Constitution further provides that a census shall be taken every tenth year, beginning in 1790, with the implication that a reapportionment of members shall follow each census.[12] Representation was so reapportioned after every census down to and including 1910, and the House was almost steadily increased in size from its original 65 to 435. By that time public opinion demanded that there be no further increases. But if no more members were to be added, and if the states of largely increased population were to get their due, some states of declining or stationary population would have to give up members and some Representatives would lose their seats. When a state is cut from ten to nine or four to three representatives, someone has to drop out. This aroused such opposition in Congress that the decade after the 1920 census passed without a reapportionment—the only case of its kind in the nation's history.

Apportionment Act of 1929. A long controversy ensued, both in and out of Congress, which ended in 1929 when Congress passed an act shifting the responsibility for reapportionment after the 1930 and later censuses to the President.[13] He is directed by the act to send to Congress following the 1930 census and each succeeding one, a statement showing the number of persons in each state to be counted for apportionment purposes, and the number of representatives to which each state would be entitled (a) according to the system of apportionment last used, (b) according to the system of major fractions, and (c) according to the method of equal proportions. If Congress took no action after receiving the President's message, the reapportionment was to be made according to the system last used. The system of calculation last used before 1930 was that of major fractions, so that in the reapportionment

---

[12] Art. I, sec. 2, par. 3.
[13] *Statutes at Large*, vol. 46, p. 26; *U. S. Code Annotated*, 1936 supplement, Title 2, ch. I, sec. 2; and amendatory act of April 25, 1940, 54 St. at L., 162.

following the 1930 census, and later after the 1940 census, methods (a) and (b) were the same. The differences between (b), major fractions, and (c), equal proportions, is a mathematical one not necessary to explain here.[14] Indeed the two methods would have produced the same results in 1930-31; and in 1940-41 the difference between them would have affected only one seat. This would have been transferred from Arkansas to Michigan by major fractions and would have remained with Arkansas under equal proportions. Congress thereupon enacted in 1941 that all future reapportionments shall be made by the method of equal proportions. The immediate result was to save one seat for Arkansas.[15] Following the 1930 census 27 seats in the House were shifted from state to state, but after the 1940 census only nine seats were transferred, mostly from the Northeast and Middle West to the South and Far West. The average population per member in all states has risen to over 301,000.

It is to be presumed that the present legislation on reapportionment of seats in the House will remain undisturbed for some time to come. Since it provides a just and almost automatic method to be used after each census, it will avoid much argument and bitterness in Congress. Complete justice requires, however, not only that the *apportionment to each state*, but also that the *districting for elections within it*, shall be fair.

Districting for Representatives in Congress. The Constitution provides that each Representative shall be a resident of the state from which he is elected, but says nothing about the districts from which members are to be elected. Prior to 1842 the states followed various practices in these elections, electing both from the state at large and by districts. In that year Congress enacted that all Representatives should be elected by single districts, and this is still the general requirement. This necessitates the division of all the more populous states into Congressional districts by acts of the state legislatures. Redistricting is supposed to follow each new apportionment. Where redistricting has been delayed, however, Congress has been willing to seat one or more Representatives from a state elected at large to complete a state's quota. There are ten such members in the 79th Congress (1945-46), not counting the single members from Delaware, Nevada, Vermont, and Wyoming.

From 1842 to 1872 Congress left it to the legislature of each state to divide the state into Congressional Representative districts composed of "contiguous territory" according to each legislature's own judgment. Then from 1872 down to 1901 it regularly provided in each decennial reapportionment act that the Representatives should be elected by districts composed of a contiguous territory, and containing as nearly as practicable an equal number of inhabitants. In 1901 and 1911 it went farther, providing that each district should consist of contiguous *and compact* territory. This provision placed a

[14] See E. V. Huntington, A Simple Explanation of the Method of Equal Proportions and of Two Conflicting Methods, Cambridge, Mass., 1928. See also Laurence F. Schmeckebier, Congressional Apportionment, espec. chs. II, III.
[15] Act of November 15, 1941, c. 470, sec. 1, 55 Stat. 761, Title 2 U. S. Code, sec. 2a.

legal responsibility on the state legislatures to provide for single-member Congressional districts, and at least a moral responsibility to be fair in defining their boundaries.

There was no way provided to enforce the rules about equal population and contiguous and compact territory, however, and Congress omitted these requirements from the reapportionment act of 1929. The Supreme Court has held, therefore, that since the last prior apportionment act, that of 1911, has been superseded, the state legislatures are now free to make the Congressional districts as they see fit.[16] It is not certain that they are required to make Congressional districts at all, but the practice of districting still prevails. In the more populous states (New York with 45 Representatives in Congress, Pennsylvania with 33 and so on down through the "average" state with nine to those with even fewer Representatives) there is much opportunity for differences of judgment as to how the districts shall be drawn upon the map.

In order to judge fairly as to how the districting system works for the election of Congressmen, we need to consider first the arguments for the adoption of the system.

Reasons for Single-Member Districts. Several reasons are usually put forward for the wide prevalence and popularity of this method of electing representatives. (1) In the first place the system is exceedingly simple for the voter. From among two or more candidates he needs to choose but one. (2) Secondly, the voter gets a strictly local representative, one who probably lives near him; one whom he may come to know; and one who is definitely *his* representative, whereas if there were two or three from the district he might not know to which one to turn. (3) There is an assured territorial distribution of representatives; not all will be bunched in one place, while other areas of the state go unrepresented. (4) For the candidate, too, it is simple. The area over which he must campaign is reduced to a minimum; the candidates against whom he must campaign are few; he can "size them up" and plan his campaign accordingly. (5) Party leaders also generally favor this method, since it simplifies their problems, too, and enables them to select candidates suitable to the district and to vary their campaign methods to meet local requirements. (6) Then, too, they can often devise ways to split the opposition in a particular district, and thus enable their own candidate to win by a plurality. (7) Finally, for the public at large, this method usually gives the majority of the voters a majority of members, although this result is not assured and, when it takes place, it is partly a result of gross local inequalities canceling each other.

Most of the advantages alleged in favor of the single-member district system have been borne out in practice, at least when the system is compared with possible alternatives. The system tends somewhat to over-emphasize the importance of local representation, and it encourages the idea that the Representative in Congress is to be a chore boy for individuals and groups in his

---

[16] Wood v. Broom (1932), 287 U. S. 1. For state maps of existing Congressional districts see the latest *Official Congressional Directory*.

district. This puts the emphasis in the wrong place and as the districts have become more populous it has resulted that some members have been overwhelmed with such work. On the other hand the voters have a right to know who represents them, and public education is already slowly changing the people's idea of the function of the Representative.

By way of contrast the election of members at large by the ordinary system of voting in any state that is entitled to three or more members would demand much more of the voter and in states that elect a dozen or more members would probably result in much blind voting or the acceptance of party slates and emblems without much individual judgment on candidates. Furthermore in a few cases where at-large election of members has been tried, as in Minnesota in 1932, it happened that all the successful candidates were bunched in one part of the state instead of being distributed according to population.[17]

The Question of Majority Rule. It is clear, however, that the single-member district system does not *guarantee* either majority rule or a fair minority representation. This is true for several reasons. *First*, to get a majority or a winning plurality in more than half the districts it is not necessary for a party to have a majority of the whole number of voters. Even if the district boundaries are fairly drawn to provide compact districts of contiguous territory, the voters may be so grouped that one party controls a majority of districts by small but safe margins while the other party or parties have their votes highly concentrated in a few districts. The mathematical basis for this is that 51 per cent of 51 per cent (a majority of majorities) is only a little over 26 per cent, but that is enough to control. Just suppose five Congressional districts in a state with an average of 100,000 voters in each. The result in votes and seats might be something like this if only two parties were involved:

	Dist. 1	Dist. 2	Dist. 3	Dist. 4	Dist. 5	Total Votes	Total Seats
Party A....	55,000	53,000	55,000	36,000	35,000	234,000	3
Party B....	45,000	47,000	45,000	64,000	65,000	266,000	2

Here a minority party, with less than 47 per cent of the votes, wins more seats than the majority party, with over 53 per cent. On the other hand the district boundaries might be so drawn that the 53-per-cent party could win all the seats.

If three or more parties are in the running the largest single party may have a still easier time in winning seats because the total opposition, even though considerably larger, will also be more split up.

[17] See R. V. Shumate, "Minnesota's Congressional Election at Large," *Am. Pol. Sci. Rev.*, vol. 27, pp. 58-63 (1933).

The mathematical principle that has just been illustrated is entirely neutral as between the contending political parties. It is not surprising, however, that political leaders learned very early to take advantage of the principle. They developed the practice that came in this country to be called "gerrymandering." This is nothing more than the arrangement of district boundaries in such a way as to give your own party the advantage over other parties in electing members of a legislative body. Knowing the relative voting strength of different parties in all the voting precincts, towns, and counties, you simply group these together in such ways as will assure your party of victory in a maximum number of districts. To achieve this result you may have to create some queer-shaped districts ("salamander," "horse-shoe," "shoe-string," "saddlebag," and so on). The term "gerrymander" came from the name of Elbridge Gerry, an early Massachusetts practitioner of the art, one of whose products looked like a salamander, and hence the word "gerrymander."

The party that dominates the state legislature may itself be a minority party that controls the state only because of prior state gerrymandering or because of constitutional rules that give each town or country equal representation without regard to population. Such a party will naturally be under great temptation to gerrymander the Congressional districts also in its own favor, but so will a true majority party that wants to perpetuate its own power.

Second. Although gerrymandering is entirely possible even where the districts are kept substantially equal in population, there are further possibilities when it is permissible to make districts of unequal population. If the state average for Congressional districts is 300,000 population, differentials of as much as 10 per cent each way (i.e., 270,000 to 330,000) are not uncommon at the time of redistricting. As population shifts occur in the state, even greater discrepancies appear. The growing cities of the northern states, in which the Democratic vote has been increasing, have suffered grave injustices in recent decades from rurally dominated Republican legislatures which have refused to make new districts on a strict population basis. Some of these states continue to elect one or more Congressmen at large because, although recent reapportionments have allowed an additional member or more to the state, the legislature has refused to allot the added members to the urban areas that are entitled to them. Some states have not redefined their Congressional district boundaries for a long time, so that already there are great differences in population among the districts.[18]

Third. Another factor that operates to prevent true majority rule and adequate minority representation under the single-member district system is the influence of great "landslide" votes for popular candidates for the Presidency. When such landslides take place enough extra votes are swung to the winning side in enough districts to permit many of the party's Congressional candidates to squeeze through on small pluralities or majorities. Thus in the

[18] See Census Bureau Release, July, 1945, entitled "Population of the United States by Congressional Districts," 2 pages.

1936 election President Roosevelt carried the country with 60.7 per cent of the popular vote, the Republicans receiving 36.4 per cent. Disregarding minor parties, the Democrats would on this basis have been entitled to 57 members in the United States Senate and 261 in the House. Instead the 75th Congress began in 1937 with 75 Democratic Senators and only 17 Republicans, while in the House there were 334 Democrats to 89 Republicans. Such sweeping majorities for victorious parties, and such gross underrepresentation of minorities are not desirable, since they prevent the minority party from performing effectively its function of opposition, yet such sweeps occur frequently where the single-member district system is used.

Generally in the off-year elections, i.e., those in which a President is not being chosen, the minority party recovers a little of the ground it lost under the "landslide" of the Presidential election. This backward swing cannot be counted on, however, to give truly proportionate representation. Generally speaking, also, the local inequalities favoring one party in one state do not balance or cancel out the inequalities that favor the other party elsewhere. Some corrective device is needed to ensure a more proportionate distribution of seats between majority and minority parties.

The Local Residence Rule. In the American mind the single-member district system is strongly associated with the local residence rule. The latter is the principle that only a person resident in the district can properly represent it in a legislative body. The elected member is to be not a representative of all the people, but only of that specific portion of them confined within the district boundaries. As far as Congress is concerned, Senators and Representatives are required by the Constitution to reside within the states they represent but not within any particular district of the state. It is only custom and tradition that make residence within his district necessary for the Representative in Congress, but the custom is almost unbroken. The consequences of this rule are numerous and important. A member, no matter how able, experienced, and valuable to the public at large, if defeated in his own district, is deprived of his chance to serve the public, temporarily or permanently. He cannot re-enter Congress through election from some other district, as is often done in England. There may be a sudden end to his legislative career. Other men of ability, seeing the uncertainty of legislative careers, are no doubt deterred in many instances from even attempting them.

Sensing this situation, many an elected Representative turns to the work of looking out for his own district. If he is shrewd, he lets no opportunity slip to do something for his constituents even though it be unwise and uneconomical for the public as a whole. The member cannot afford to neglect his district; he must get something for it or rival candidates will arise locally to charge him with neglect. "My worthy opponent has become a statesman. He has no time to give to the people back home." This is an accusation particularly hard for a Representative in Congress to meet, for he, even more than the Senator, is supposed to get favors for his district and his constituents: post office buildings, river and harbor improvements, emergency works and relief appropriations, jobs, and pensions. Those who are successful in these things are the ones who tend to survive politically. Only those members who have strong holds on their constituencies can afford to give largely of their time and energy to national affairs.

Summary. The present system of electing Representatives to Congress by single-member districts, although it has the general support of the nation, has revealed certain defects in practice. It does not guarantee either majority rule or adequate minority representation. It lends itself to the injustices of gerrymandering whereby minorities can sometimes perpetuate themselves in power and, conversely, majorities can deprive minorities of proportionate representation. It plays into the hands of those who emphasize the local residence tradition, encourages a narrow localism, and induces the Representatives to devote an excessive amount of time and attention to local as against national interests. As Congress has worked out a fair and nearly automatic system of reapportioning representation among the various states, so the call is now for some equally effective devices to assure a just districting of every state and some means of "raising the sights" of the members elected by districts from local to national issues.

Election of Representatives. As is the case with Senators, Representatives in Congress are ordinarily nominated in direct partisan primaries conducted in accordance with state laws by local election officials. The rules concerning candidacy vary somewhat but in general all that a person has to do to become a candidate is to file his name with the proper state or county officer and pay a small fee. One consequence of these laws is that the party leaders have far less control over the candidates than they did in the days of nomination by party conventions. To some extent this breaks down state control over Congressional delegations, but it does so without giving the national party any added control. There is nothing like the English system of party designation or approval of the candidates for the various districts. Is it surprising, then, that party discipline in Congress is very lax and that there are defections from the party line even on important issues?

It may be that the American system will prove, in the long run, to be the better one. It may, in fact, be necessitated by the great extent and the multiplicity of the interests of the country. At the same time it brings to both houses of Congress a rather varied array of talents and views, and makes very difficult the attainment of responsible party government. An able and popular President can do a great deal to keep down insurgency in his party, but even one as popular as Franklin Roosevelt had to face open revolt at times.

From among those who have been nominated the voters in each Congressional district make their choices at the regular November election in the even-numbered years. The elections are conducted by state and local authorities under state laws, but are carefully watched by the national authorities to discourage fraud and the violation of the national laws. Some prosecutions by the national government against state and local officials for frauds in Congressional elections take place after almost every biennial election.

Vacancies in the House are filled by special elections called by the governor of the state concerned in accordance with the national Constitution and laws.

HOW REPRESENTATIVE IS CONGRESS?

Summarizing a little of what has been said it appears that the Senate clearly over-represents the small states and thus falls short of representing the nation, but the House comes very close to representing states in accordance with their population. On the other hand through gerrymandering and the failure to redistrict, many states fail to accord equal Congressional representation to all parts of their population.

From the viewpoint of education and ability the Senators and Representatives in Congress average far higher than the populations they represent. In the light of this known fact it comes as a shock and surprise to find that various polls of public opinion have shown the members of Congress to lag far behind their constituents on such vital issues as international organization and wartime price controls. Why is this? Is it related to the fact that most of the members are lawyers (309 out of 531 in 1944), and therefore belong to a traditionally conservative profession? Or is it connected with the fact that the typical Congressman is well above average age, a man whose education dates back to about World War I or even earlier? While science, industry, medicine, social work, and the administrative branch of government have become "research minded" and bold in trying out new discoveries, very few members of Congress make any effective use of even their own Legislative Reference Service. Indeed when they come to Washington many of them have very little idea of what the national government is.

This is not to say that Congress has not done good work under able leadership, but it does raise the question whether Congress, composed as it now is, can itself provide the leadership of the nation. Its true function may be a very different one.

All these questions bring us to some other major topics. What is the role of Congress in the national government? How is it organized and how does it do its work? It may be that the difficulties lie largely in improper organization and procedures.

REFERENCES

Robert Luce, *Legislative Assemblies*, Boston and New York, 1924, chs. II-VI, X-XII.

——, *Legislative Principles*, Boston and New York, 1930, chs. IX-XII, XV-XVII.

Joseph P. Chamberlain, *Legislative Processes: National and State*, New York, 1936, ch. III.

Harvey Walker, *Law Making in the United States*, New York, 1934, ch. VIII.

W. F. Willoughby, *The Government of Modern States*, rev. and enl. ed., New York, 1936, chs. XVII, XIX.

John M. Mathews and Clarence A. Berdahl, *Documents and Readings in American Government: National and State*, rev. ed., New York, 1940, pp. 407-29, 694-702.

A. N. Christensen and E. M. Kirkpatrick, *The People, Politics, and the Politician: Readings in American Government*, New York, 1941, pp. 336-49, 368-76, 385-95.

L. F. Schmeckebier, *Congressional Apportionment*, Washington, 1941.

C. G. Hoag and G. H. Hallett, Jr., *Proportional Representation*, New York, 1926.

Geo. H. Haynes, *The Senate of the United States, Its History and Practice*, 2 vols., Boston, 1938.

Lindsay Rogers, *The American Senate*, New York, 1926.

CHAPTER 12

Congressional Organization and Procedure

THE CHANGING ROLE OF CONGRESS

In the first few years under the national Constitution Congress was busy creating executive departments, organizing the national judiciary, and in general giving shape to the new national government. President Washington had no large positive program of legislation to urge upon it, although his secretaries (especially Hamilton) laid certain major proposals directly before Congressional committees. In those early years Congress played a highly constructive role in the formation of public policy and administrative organization.

For many decades thereafter, while the national government followed a policy of relative inactivity and the Presidents usually did little more than head the administration, it was generally conceded that Congress not the executive had the responsibility for shaping national policy. The President was to carry out the laws, not to say what the laws should be. All the early textbooks on the Constitution made this clear, and both Congress and the President were usually inclined to accept it as good gospel. In fact, of course, each major party early agreed upon a general policy for the government to follow, and each President made definite recommendations for legislation in accordance with his party's policy, but by and large this left Congress a relatively free hand in the enactment of laws. Policies concerning the territories, the admission of new states, tariffs, and slavery, for example, were largely made by Congress.

In time there came a substantial shift in this respect. Presidents arose who assumed a more masterly tone and who accepted the responsibilities of both party and national leadership. Even more, as the tasks of government multiplied, as the number of administrative agencies became greater and their importance increased, and as the nation grew in population, in area, and in the interdependence of its parts, Congress became increasingly unable to cope alone with the nation's problems. It had its own problems of increasing numbers, the recurrent additions of poorly informed members, and the splitting up of its work among committees. It more and more lost touch with what the government was actually doing. Most individual members felt and many still feel a sense of frustration in the face of a great national administrative machine, which earlier Congresses had helped to create but which they found almost impossible to understand or to influence except in minor ways at a few peripheral points. Congress had come to be, as it were, excluded from the government and relegated to the role of an outside critic. On the other hand the President, with direct control over the major departments, and in position to receive the best available advice from the increasing numbers of permanent civil servants, as well as from the department heads, became more and more the center of national energy and direction. He alone was able to present national and co-ordinated plans for the general policy of the government. The major proposals for legislation simply had to come more and more from the administrative branch of the government rather than from the individual members or committees of Congress.

The true role of Congress today is, therefore, something quite different from what it was in the beginning but certainly it is not a less important role. Looking at what Congress does, and what in some respects it could do better, its functions appear to be somewhat as follows:

1. With respect to *policy* its primary role is *not to initiate, but to examine, criticize, modify,* and in extreme cases *even to veto policies* proposed by the administration. The President and the administrative agencies under him are in the best position to understand national needs and to express a national viewpoint. The President makes policy proposals to promote what he conceives to be the national welfare. But Congressmen represent more thoroughly all the particular sections and interests of the country. If a number of them representing a real majority of the people find any proposal by the President to be undesirable, then Congress should modify or even reject the proposal. This in fact is what Congress does on policy today. Most of the important policy recommendations come from the President or, with his approval, from the principal agencies of the government. For Congress and for the American people it is better that Congress keep an effective independent control and a genuine veto over new policy proposals than that it seek to regain the initiation of policy.

2. Having approved a proposal, Congress has the function of *enacting* it into *enforceable law.* Both the enactment and enforcement are covered in the same legislation and both call for most careful drafting. Faulty drafting of legislation, and loose and careless delegations of authority to the administration lead to defective administration and much public criticism of the government.

3. When Congress has enacted any law it at once becomes jointly responsible with the administration for its proper enforcement. In consequence of this, and as a result of its somewhat detached position, Congress has the

function of continuously *examining and criticizing the administration* and of *holding it to public account*. This censorial function is of the utmost importance. It is being exercised constantly, through regular committee hearings on requests for funds and for new legislation, through special investigating committees, through requests for reports, and through speeches by Congressmen, in Congress and out. This is a function for the majority party as well as for the minority, although the latter will make more political capital out of it.

4. Finally Congress and its individual members have the function of informing the people of what the government is doing, and informing the government of what the people need. This is a two-way function for every member. He needs to inform the Congress, the Administration and to some extent the whole nation about the needs and the views of his own state or district, but he also has the duty to inform his constituents in his state or district about national needs, policies, and administration. At this point he is often in a dilemma, for if he is an avowed critic of the administration, as many a minority member is bound to be, he cannot easily become the impartial reporter and informant. If when in the minority he overdoes his adverse criticism of the administration, his embarrassment may be considerable when his own party comes to power and has to carry out the same laws and in much the same way as the previous administration.

To the end that it may perform these functions adequately Congress needs (a) *a suitable organization and suitable procedures*; (b) *an adequate staff*, also properly organized; (c) *information about the nation*, its government and its problems, as few other groups need that information; (d) *facilities for reaching the public*, nationally as well as by states and districts, through every important medium of public information; and (e) *an objective, responsible, and national point of view*, so that it can see not only the needs of particular districts and states but the needs of a nation in a world of nations.

Like every organization whose functions are changing Congress finds itself today inadequately equipped to do what is expected of it. Its organization, rules of procedure, staff, and facilities were developed in earlier days when its role was a very different one. It has never fully overhauled its organization and methods. In recent years, however, many members have become convinced of the need for some drastic changes. Leaders of public opinion outside of Congress are even more insistent that something be done. The present arrangements will be set forth, and something will be said about proposed reforms in the pages that follow.

CONGRESSIONAL ORGANIZATION

The purpose of the organization of the legislative body is primarily to facilitate its business. But, since in democracies unanimity on any matter is seldom possible, the purpose may be defined more precisely as that of permitting the majority to have its way, while at the same time enabling the minority to perform its function of criticism. Wherever a so-called legislative body is found which does not permit the majority to act, the legislative function is temporarily paralyzed; and where the minority cannot be heard in criticism of what the majority is doing, one can suspect that a dictatorship rules the state.

Organization and Leadership. The majority itself must have organization if it is to do its work effectively and carry out its program. Such organization necessarily implies party or group leadership. The rules that define the organization must then be so framed as to permit not only the expression of individual members' views and minority protests, but also the presentation by the majority leaders of the measures that they deem necessary and the procuring of action upon them.

The importance of having leadership in legislative bodies cannot be emphasized too much. Unorganized individual action can be paralyzing to the body as a whole. Leadership may come from various sources such as: (a) from the executive branch of the government; (b) from the dominant party in the legislature, which may be opposed to the executive; (c) from some outstanding individual among the members, without regard to party; (d) from powerful interests organized in a lobby; (e) from leading newspapers that are creating a strong public opinion for some action. Whatever the final source from which the leadership comes, it must operate on and through the members of the legislature itself. Therefore it will be found that every legislature has an organization and a body of rules that facilitate the particular kind of leadership to which the nation in question is accustomed.

Rules of Organization and of Procedure. "Rules" and "organization" are closely related, but are not interchangeable terms. There are really two kinds of rules, those that define the legislative organization, create its offices, and confer powers upon them; and those that define the steps to be taken in the procedure on bills. These may be roughly distinguished as "organizational" and "procedural" rules, respectively.

Rules and Regulations of Parties. All the rules, whether organizational or procedural, may be further differentiated into those that are *official*, i.e., that have more or less the effect of law; and those that are *unofficial*, party-made, for the governance of the party's members in all partisan matters that arise. Technically, of course, only the official rules may be called rules of the legislative body, but it should not be forgotten that actually the caucus or conference of the dominant party, as well as the steering committee, the floor leader, and the party "whips," though not recognized in the official rules, are important parts of the working organization of Congress as they are of other legislatures.

Official Rules Governing Congress. The official rules governing the organization and procedure of Congress will be found in several places. *First*, there are a few highly important rules prescribed by the Constitution itself. These deal with presiding officers, sessions, adjournment, quorum, journals, votes, and the adoption of rules.[1] *Second*, there are a few statutes passed by previous Congresses that regulate the organization of each new House of Representatives, the compensation and expenses of members, the officers and employees of the two houses, their duties and their salaries, the Library of Congress, Congressional investigations, the calling of witnesses, contested elections in the House, and the office of legislative counsel.[2] *Third*, come the rules adopted by each house for itself. These deal primarily with procedure on bills and the committee system. *Fourth*, supplementing the special rules of each house there is Jefferson's Manual of Parliamentary Practice, formally adopted by each house as its guide, and an accumulation of rulings by the presiding officer and by the house itself, that serve as precedents and interpretations of the rules.[3]

Lack of Over-All Organization. Like other bicameral legislatures, Congress is without any over-all organization that can control both houses. Thus Congress sorely lacks the unity that the Presidential office possesses. Each house controls its own membership, organization, and procedure. It is necessary, however, for both to act favorably on all measures before they can go into effect. Consequently the rules of each house give some recognition to the other house, and a standardized procedure on bills has been worked out for both houses. Such matters as printing, the control of the capitol grounds and building, the library, and legislative reference and drafting services, are also of concern to both houses. Joint committees are therefore organized to handle them. Furthermore, joint sessions for hearing messages from the executive, for counting the electoral vote, and for ceremonial purposes, are provided for. When both houses pass the same bill, but in somewhat different form, there is need for what is known as a "conference committee." Such committees are temporary.

These official provisions for inter-chamber cooperation are altogether inadequate. Consequently when joint action is needed urgently and quickly the major party leaders of the two houses must get together unofficially and agree upon a program.

Presiding Officers. Each chamber has at its head an officer who presides over its deliberations. The Vice President of the United States, though elected independently of the Senate, is designated by the Constitution to preside over that body. On the other hand the House chooses its own Speaker who is thus the representative and leader of the majority party in that house.

Vice President as Presiding Officer of Senate. The Vice President, though he may succeed to the Presidency, would have had little to do had not the framers of the Constitution provided that he should be president of the Sen-

[1] U. S. Const., Art. I, sec. 2, par. 5; sec. 3, pars. 4, 5; secs. 5, 7.
[2] U. S. *Code Annotated*, Title 2, chs. II, III, IV, V, VI, VII, IX.
[3] For the rules of procedure see the House and Senate Manuals listed in the references at the end of the chapter.

ate. The Senate chooses its other officers, including a president pro tempore. The latter presides over the Senate in the absence of the Vice President and is generally a person of influence. While the Vice President is most commonly of the majority party in the Senate, he is not a Senator, his interests are not those of a Senator, he may vote only in case of a tie, and he is looked upon somewhat as an outsider. He has very few powers other than those of an impartial presiding officer. He does not appoint the important committees, he is not a member of any important committee, and his powers as a presiding officer are limited by the fact that debate under the Senate rules is singularly free.

Speaker of U. S. House of Representatives. History records very few important episodes connected with the work of the Vice President. The speakership of the House of Representatives presents quite a different picture. From the British House of Commons, and the speakership in the lower houses of the colonial and state legislatures, came the title and some of the traditions of the office.[4] In many cases the speakership had been the rallying point in the ultimately successful struggle for legislative freedom from and control over the executive.

The Speakership at Its Strongest. The Constitution simply provides that the House of Representatives shall choose "their speaker and other officers." In the nineteenth century, when Congress had far more to do with initiating policy than it now has, the Speaker held a position of tremendous importance, standing next to the President in power and in leadership. He had the power to appoint all the committees of the House, to recognize or refuse to recognize members who rose to speak, to rule on all points of order and thus to rule the opposition out of order, and to serve on the powerful committee on rules.[5] Majority party government of the House reached its highest point, and assumed its most dictatorial form, under a series of Republican Speakers from James G. Blaine (1869-75) through Thomas B. Reed and others to Joseph G. Cannon (1903-10). Thus, when opposition members tried to block business on the ground of "no quorum," by refusing to vote or answer to their names, although actually on the floor, Reed ruled that he would count those actually present whether they voted or not. Several Speakers also refused to entertain motions that they thought were offered for the purpose of delay and obstruction.

The Revolution of 1910-11. Continued Democratic opposition to such highhanded government by the chair, aided and abetted by the rising Progressive Republican opposition to Republican "Old Guardism," brought the fight against the Speaker's powers to a head against Cannon and "Cannonism" in 1910. At that time an adverse majority carried through the "Revolution of 1910," as a result of which the Speaker lost his membership in, and his right to appoint, the committee on rules, while the House gained the right to elect

[4] See M. P. Follett, *The Speaker of the House of Representatives*, pp. 1-26.
[5] Follett, *op. cit.*, chs. III-XI.

standing committees, and to recall from committees bills that committee leaders were attempting to bury by failure to report.[6]

Election of the Speaker. The Speaker of the House is legally elected by the members. In fact, each party holds its caucus in advance of the first session of the new Congress, and by majority vote agrees to support one of its older and more experienced members for the position. The vote in the House is merely a ratification of the decision of the majority party caucus.

Present Powers of the Speaker. The Speaker has a salary of $15,000 a year. He is assisted by a private secretary, a clerk, a parliamentarian, and an assistant parliamentarian. His principal powers at the present time are: (a) to enforce the rules of the House, and to make rulings in doubtful cases, subject to being overridden by the House; (b) to recognize or fail to recognize members who rise and ask permission to speak; (c) to appoint select and conference committees, subject to the approval of the House; (d) to designate the committee to which any bill shall be referred. While he is still a party man, he tends to be, far more than in the days of Cannon, an impartial presiding officer. He still has the power to prevent obstruction and delays by ruling dilatory motions out of order, by refusing to recognize members, and by counting members physically present as present for the purposes of ascertaining a quorum. As a party leader, quite apart from his official powers as Speaker, he has usually a considerable influence. He is frequently consulted by the President and by other party leaders in Congress. He and the majority floor leader together have a very firm hold upon the House.[7]

Other Officials and Employees. In both houses of Congress there is a considerable staff of other officials. The more important ones are nominated by the party caucuses on the advice of the party leaders, and are elected by the members of the house concerned. These include the clerk of the House and secretary of the Senate, sergeants at arms in both houses, reporters of proceedings, doorkeepers, postmasters, and others. Minor officials and employees are appointed by their immediate superiors, i.e., assistant clerks by the clerk, and so on, but it is well known that the members, particularly of the majority party, enjoy a certain amount of patronage in these positions. Congress has not seen fit to have the staffs of the two houses selected by examination under the Civil Service law.

The Party Caucus. In each house there are also the extra-legal organizations of the members of the two major parties. The meeting of all the members in good standing of a particular party in a legislative chamber is usually called the "caucus" of that party. The term caucus in this connection has come to mean a meeting under conditions in which the participants have agreed in advance to be bound by the decision of the majority of the group, or by some

---

[6] See Floyd M. Riddick, *Congressional Procedure*, ch. III; George Rothwell Brown, *The Leadership of Congress*, espec. chs. V-XI.

[7] See Roland Young, *This Is Congress*, ch. III; Floyd M. Riddick, *Congressional Procedure*, ch. III.

stipulated majority such as two-thirds. In a house of 100 members where the majority has only 51 members, 26 of them, or just one over a quarter of the entire membership, could conceivably make the important decisions if party lines hold firm. Such rule of the house by what is really a minority of the members through use of the caucus system, has been strongly condemned. Consequently not only the institution but the very name of the caucus has become unpopular, so that in some cases the term "conference" is used instead. The latter implies a mere meeting of the party members to discuss common problems, without binding each member to stand by the decisions made. Republicans in both houses of Congress seem to like the name "conference," but they actually caucus just as the Democrats do.

Democratic Caucus Rules. The Democrats in the House of Representatives have followed the rule that a two-thirds vote of those present and voting shall be necessary to bind the members to united action in the house,

> *Provided*, the said two-thirds vote is a majority of the full Democratic membership of the House; *And provided further*, That no member shall be bound upon questions involving the construction of the Constitution of the United States, or upon which he made contrary pledges to his constituents prior to his election or received contrary instructions by resolutions or platform from his nominating authority.[8]

This allows the member some leeway, but he must inform the caucus before it adjourns as to his intentions to vote in the House contrary to the caucus decision, so that other members will be warned of his intention.

What Is Done at Caucuses. There is, of course, a separate caucus organization for each party in each house, but the Senate makes even less use of the caucus than does the House. Meetings are held when the chamber is not in session, and may be called on the request of a certain number of members or by the chairman. Before the House starts its first session in the two-year term, a caucus is held by each party's members to agree on the choice of a candidate for Speaker, to make up a slate of nominees for other officers of the House, and to take preliminary action concerning committee appointments. The caucus elects its own chairman, its "steering committee," headed by the man who is to be "floor leader," and its quota of the members of the committee that is to make up the slate of committees for the House. Later it approves the slate of committee appointments, before the entire list is voted by the House. This is usually the most important caucus of the session. Other caucus meetings may be held from time to time to decide on the legislative program. As a rule, the more successful the party leaders are, the fewer are the caucuses that need to be held.

[8] For the Democratic Caucus rules of about 1927, see Mathews and Berdahl, *Documents and Readings in American Government*, rev. ed., pp. 433-34. See also Roland Young *op. cit.*, pp. 94-98.

Steering Committees and Floor Leaders. The "steering committee" is a small group of leading members designated by the caucus to direct the party's work in the House in accordance with caucus decisions and party policies. Each party has also its "whips" or members who are responsible for keeping party members in line and bringing them in for important roll calls.[9]

The Committee System. Both houses have developed elaborate systems of committees. Most important and most numerous are the *standing committees*. There are also at any time a number of temporary *select* or *special* committees that have been created to investigate some particular matter. Each of the standing committees is a more or less permanent body that is appointed to deal with an important field of legislation, and to which the house concerned can assign all the bills in that field.[10]

Committee Appointments in U. S. Senate. The United States Senate controls the appointment of its committees; the Vice President does not exercise this function. Since the Senate and its committees are continuing bodies, all that is needed at the beginning of a new Congress is to arrange to fill vacancies in committees resulting from changes in Senate membership. Each party through its caucus appoints a number of members to a committee on committees, a body that is not recognized by the rules. The Republican members of this committee arrange to fill the Republican vacancies and the Democrats to fill the Democratic vacancies on each committee. The dominant party determines how many members it shall have on each committee; it allows itself a safe majority and also designates the chairman.

Committee Appointments in House of Representatives. In the House, committees were appointed by the Speaker until 1911 when the House adopted practically the same system as the Senate. One difference is that House committees are made up entirely anew each time a new Congress begins. The older and more experienced members who have been re-elected are permitted to continue on the same committees as before, and there is much continuity of service. The House rules fix the size of each committee, the majority party decides how many members it will have on each, and it allots the rest to the opposition party or parties. Each party caucus elects its committee on committees, the Democrats using for this purpose the members elected by the caucus to serve on the ways and means committee, and then each committee makes up its list of members for each House committee. The majority party list designates which member shall be chairman according to rule of seniority. Following approval by the party caucuses, the lists thus prepared are combined and ratified by vote of the House.

Composition of Committees: Seniority. Whether the new method of election of committees by the House has produced any better results than when

[9] See Floyd M. Riddick, op. cit., ch. IV.

[10] On the committee system in general see Roland Young, op. cit., pp. 98-120, 243-47; Floyd M. Riddick, op. cit., chs. V, VII, VIII, and pp. 312-18; *The Reorganization of Congress* (a Report of the Committee on Congress of the American Political Science Association, 1945), pp. 29-48.

the Speaker appointed them is doubtful. Continuity of membership is the general rule; the member who is re-elected time and again to Congress may usually remain on the same committees indefinitely. Seniority in the length of continuous service on the committee also advances men up toward the chairmanship. If a member is reasonably regular in his support of the party, and continues as a member of Congress, he may ultimately become the chairman of his committee, but usually of only one important committee. There are objections to the rule of seniority; it sometimes puts at the head of committees men who are no longer vigorous and active, or who are not in sympathy with the majority of younger members, or who are not as able as other members. On the other hand, these men have the advantage of long experience, knowledge of the committee's work, knowledge of procedure, and acquaintance with other members; and the bickerings and bitterness that would result if younger and more able men were pushed ahead of them are avoided by the rule of seniority. Thus each committee is headed by an experienced man, and next to him stand a ranking majority member and a ranking minority member, also men of long experience.

Number and Size of Committees. The so-called "committees of Congress" are in most cases committees of the separate houses. Joint committees of the two houses are distinctly the exception. A recent (1945) enumeration reveals that there were then 47 standing committees in the House and 33 in the Senate, or 80 in all.[11] Many of these committees are of minor consequence but 15 in the House (2 in finance, 5 in public works, and 8 in general legislation) and 12 in the Senate are of considerable importance. Even the minor committees have staffs and expenses, however, and it is generally conceded now that both houses have far more committees than are either needed or desirable. With so many committees and a normal size per committee of around 18 or 19 members the average Representative has two committee positions and the average Senator has five or six. Most Senators are simply unable to attend all the meetings of the committees of which they are members. A few leaders in each committee carry the load of work and in many cases they make the decisions. Non-attending members often supply the leaders with "proxies" or authority to act in their behalf. In the House there has been frequent complaint by members that committee chairmen sometimes proceed in an arbitrary manner, at times even without holding committee meetings. Yet it is in committees rather than on the floor of either house that the important decisions on legislation are made. These many "little legislatures" have tremendous power.

Distribution of Functions among Committees. The division of work among the standing committees is not the same in the two houses. Obviously the lower house has subdivided the fields of legislation far more than the Senate has. Even major committees of similar or identical names in the two houses do not have the same jurisdiction. Neither does the division of work among

---

[11] *The Reorganization of Congress* (cited in footnote 10), pp. 29-33.

Congressional committees correspond with that among the major agencies of the administration. Thus a particular committee may handle matters that concern several departments of government, while each administrative department or agency in turn has to deal with several committees of the same house as well as with an additional committee or committees in the other house. This is confusing because the committees may hold different views on an agency's proposals; and it is time-consuming because the heads of government agencies have to appear before several committees about the same matter. There is a great deal of duplication as well as scattering of effort, and much waste of time and energy.

Proposals for Committee Reorganization. Responsible leaders in both houses who have recently given careful thought to the committee system as a whole are agreed that a reorganization of the committee system is needed, including a substantial reduction in the number of committees. The Committee on Congress of the American Political Science Association has also recommended a reduction in the numbers of committees down to about fifteen in each house through the elimination of the inactive ones and the consolidation of those with overlapping jurisdictions. This committee proposes also that there be "twin committees" of the two houses on each major field with jurisdictions corresponding in scope with the principal areas of public policy and administration, so that each major department and agency would be responsible to only one committee in each house and so that joint committee meetings could be held.[12] If each Senator and Representative were then a member of only one or two committees, greater expertness could be developed.

The Committee on Congress has also recommended that the chairman of standing committees be either chosen every two years by the Committee on Committees of the majority party or be limited to a term of six years as chairman, so as to give more emphasis to ability than to seniority in the selection of chairmen. It also proposes rules that will require committee chairmen to call committee meetings when desired by a majority, to report bills within ten days or let some other member report them, and to keep an adequate record of committee proceedings. These recommendations all look in the direction of more competent and responsible action by Congressional committees.

THE SESSIONS OF CONGRESS

The Constitution provides that Congress shall assemble "at least once every year." [13] Down to 1934 the annual session began on the first Monday in December, and more or less by accident a curious system developed of having a long and a short session in every two-year period. This resulted from the

---

[12] *The Reorganization of Congress* (cited in footnote 10), pp. 43, 79; see also Roland Young, *op. cit.*, pp. 243-47.

[13] Art. I, sec. 4, par. 2.

fact that the terms of President, Vice President, and members of Congress began and ended on March 4 of the odd-numbered years. Members newly elected in November of the even years could not take office until the next March 4, and consequently, the members of the old Congress continued in office, and held a short session from December of the even year until March 4 of the odd year—over three months after a new Congress had been elected. This practice continued for over 140 years, despite the obvious absurdity of having the older Congress, many of whose members had been defeated for re-election, continue to legislate after a new body had been elected. Unless a special session were called after March 4 in the odd years, the newly elected members of Congress would not actually participate in a session until thirteen months after they had been elected. The short session, later called the "lame duck" session, was usually ineffective for any important purpose other than the enactment of revenue and appropriation measures and non-controversial legislation. The long session, on the other hand, being without any legal terminating date short of a year, was the time for doing most of the important business of Congress for a whole two-year period, but it was handicapped by the fact that it ran on long into the even-numbered years in which the new elections were to take place, and when the members needed to return home for the campaign.

Present Rule for Sessions of Congress. These and other difficulties led to a movement that found leadership in Senator Norris of Nebraska for a change to two equal sessions in every two-year period. The so-called "lame duck" amendment that he proposed was submitted to the state legislatures for ratification in 1933, was ratified within the year, and went into effect in 1934.[14] Under this amendment, the terms of members of Congress begin on January 3, following their election in the preceding November, and the regular sessions, one each year, begin on the same date. Thus it is now possible to have two sessions of approximately equal length in each Congress, and they may last the entire year, if the members so order, from January 3 to January 3. For example, the last sessions of the 76th Congress lasted for 367 days—from January 3, 1940, to and including January 3, 1941—but there were many recesses, and only about 200 days were used for legislative business.

Degree of Continuity of Congress. Congress is not likely to adjourn often hereafter much short of June 1, and in the odd-numbered years it is more likely to extend its sessions well into the summer. Its work is thus never put away for very long. Because the national House of Representatives is completely renewed every second year, however, Congress divides its calendar into two-year periods, each beginning and ending on January 3 of an odd-numbered year. Each of these two-year bodies is called a Congress; the 79th serving during 1945 and 1946, the 80th during 1947 and 1948, and so on. A bill introduced in either house at the beginning of a Congress is potentially before it

---

[14] Amendment XX.

during the entire two years. If not acted on in that time it is dropped, but may be reintroduced in the next Congress.

Special Sessions of Congress. When the regular session adjourns in a stalemate, or with a great deal of business unfinished, or when emergencies arise after the session that call for legislative action, special sessions can be called. The old Congressional session arrangements resulted in the call of many special sessions of the Congress to meet after March 4, especially following Presidential elections. Up to 1934 there had been 47 special sessions of the Senate alone, and 40 special sessions of Congress as a whole. The President alone has power to summon special sessions of Congress.

> . . . he may, on extraordinary Occasions, convene both Houses, or either of them, and in Case of Disagreement between them, with Respect to the Time of Adjournment, he may adjourn them to such Time as he shall think proper; . . .[15]

Once a session is convened, Congress is in full control of the measures it will take up. The President may suggest, but cannot command or limit action. His power to adjourn sessions to a certain time when the houses disagree has never been used.

BEGINNING OF SESSIONS

Organizing a New Congress. At the beginning of a new Congress, the Senate, being always organized, proceeds immediately to its work under the Vice President or president pro tem. The credentials of the new and re-elected members are read, and the oath is delivered to them singly or in small groups. The Senate is then ready for business. In the House, the clerk of the previous Congress calls the members to order, reads the preliminary roll of members-elect, announces the presence of a quorum, and calls for the election of a speaker. The rival party caucus leaders make their nominations from the floor, the clerk appoints tellers, and the count is made. When the result is announced, the speaker-elect is conducted to the chair by the defeated candidate, and the felicitations take place. The members must then be sworn in, and the custom has developed of administering the oath to the entire group at once. Any member-elect whose election is contested is asked to stand aside. This being done, the rest of the members take the oath, and then the oath is administered separately to the disputed members. The House then elects the majority candidates for clerk, sergeant at arms, doorkeeper, postmaster, and chaplain, and they are sworn in. The rules of the previous session are also adopted, perhaps with some slight changes.

Presidential Messages. Ordinarily the houses meet in joint session within a day or two after January 3 to hear the President's annual message. This is a document that the chief executive has formulated with the advice of cabinet

[15] Art. II, sec. 3.

members and others, and that usually presents a program of legislation as well as the President's administrative policies for the next year or more.

PRESENTATION OF BILLS

Introduction of Bills. Important business begins with the introduction of bills for laws and resolutions. A bill is only a draft of a proposed law. Only members may introduce bills; the executive, not being a part of the legislature (strictly speaking), cannot himself introduce a bill in either house. Members may, as a rule, introduce any number of bills they choose, and they frequently introduce measures "by request" that they do not themselves approve. In Congress there is no time limit on the introduction of bills. A bill is introduced by merely dropping it in a box at the desk of the chief clerk or secretary of the chamber concerned. The clerk gives the bill a number, and each house runs its own series of numbers, so that a bill introduced in both houses will have both a senate and a house number.

Sources of Legislative Bills. With respect to source, bills may be classified as follows:

1. *Administration or Government Bills.* These originate with the administrative departments or chief executive, and come before Congress with the support of the executive.[16] The most important legislation originates in this way. Much of it relates to departmental powers, finances, organization, and programs of work. The leaders of the President's party in the two houses do their best to see that these measures are enacted.

2. *Committee Bills.* In a number of cases, a committee combines various proposals for legislation on the same general subject, and drafts a bill to take the place of the others and to accomplish much the same result.

3. *Special Interest Bills.* Many bills are introduced that have been drafted by lawyers and others outside the government on behalf of special interests—railroads, farmers, liquor interests, organized labor, and others of varying importance.

4. *Local Bills.* There are also many bills that are sponsored by the governments of particular counties, cities, or other local units. In Congress these bills usually ask government permission to bridge a navigable stream, or request Congress to transfer to the local government some local parcel of land that the national government owns.

5. *Private Bills.* Also very numerous, these bills usually aim to authorize the treasury to pay some claim of an individual against the government. They are uniformly entitled "a bill for the relief of —— ——" giving the name of the person to whom the money is to be paid.

[16] See Roland Young, *op. cit.*, pp. 55-62.

PROCEDURE ON BILLS[17]

First Reading and Reference to Committee. The bill is given its "first reading" by number and title only, and is then referred to a committee by the clerk or secretary, subject to control by the presiding officer and ultimately by the house concerned. This question of "reference" to a committee is an important one. Referred to one committee, say, on agriculture, the bill may be reported out for passage promptly and enthusiastically. Referred to another committee, say, the one on appropriations, it may receive a cold burial. The House of Representatives has a rule, that "No bill or joint resolution carrying appropriations shall be reported by any committee not having jurisdiction to report appropriations. . . ."[18] Thus in effect every bill that calls for an appropriation must be referred to the appropriations committee as well as to the subject-matter committee that is concerned.

Committee Work. In the course of a single session each important committee will have from dozens to hundreds of bills referred to it. If committees are conscientious they will scan them all and make some decision about each. Since the House and Senate usually meet at 12 noon, committee work must be done mostly in the mornings although other times can be arranged. There are regular schedules of committee meetings so that interested persons can attend, but it does not follow that every bill referred to a committee will come up for consideration. The chairman has considerable power over the committee's agenda and it is not unusual for a chairman to pocket certain bills that he does not like so that the other members and the proponents of these measures get no real hearing on them. In every session hundreds of bills are buried in committee or in the chairman's desk.

Committees exist in part to sift out good measures and to provide for quick disposal of trivial and undesirable bills, but it does not follow that bills should be condemned to death by the chairman alone and without a committee hearing, nor even that the committee should be free to sidetrack bills that many members of the appropriate chamber would like to have considered.

Rules on Discharge of Committees. Some device is obviously needed to get bills out of a reluctant or dilatory committee and back before the chamber as a whole. Such a device is the motion to discharge the committee from further consideration of a bill. The House of Representatives first adopted a discharge rule in 1910, as a part of the general movement for liberalizing the rules. This rule has been modified several times. Once as few as one-third of the members could petition to take a measure out of committee and bring it before the House. After several changes back and forth the number now required is 218, a majority of the House.[19] In that form it is difficult to operate.

---

[17] On Congressional procedure generally see Floyd M. Riddick, *op. cit.*; Roland Young, *op. cit.*, ch. IV; and the House and Senate Manuals.

[18] Rules of the House, XXI, sec. 4.

[19] Rules of the House, XXVII, sec. 4. See also Floyd M. Riddick, *op. cit.*, ch. XIII.

Of seventeen attempts to invoke the rule in one recent year, for example, only two succeeded. It is nevertheless, a wholesome rule to have. Even better might be a strictly enforced rule that every bill should be reported back within a certain number of days with a recommendation that it pass, or not pass, or with some other proposal for disposing of it.

Committee Hearings. The purposes of public hearings on bills are (1) to ascertain what interests are supporting a measure and how much public opinion there is behind it; (2) to ascertain the probable effect of the proposed law if enacted—effects not only on the sponsors and opponents, but on other groups in the community; (3) to have discussion of and suggested improvements in the detailed provisions of the bill. Committee hearings, properly conducted, can be of immense value to all concerned, and particularly to the public at large. Congress has had much success in getting the benefits of committee consideration of bills. Since a bill introduced early in the session may be before Congress for two years, there is usually ample time for committee hearings. Leading members of Congress, furthermore, give full time to their work, and some of the abler ones spend much of their working time during and even between sessions studying matters before their committees. They may obtain, also, the benefit of the assistance of specialists in the administrative departments at Washington; and they can call upon experts in all parts of the country for advice, and can even get them to come to committee meetings. Some committee reports on major bills have been very ably prepared.

Executive Session of Committee. When a committee has held its public hearings, it usually goes into executive session, i.e., it excludes all persons except the members and the clerk of the committee, and proceeds to discuss what to do about the bill, whether to support it, bury it, or report it unfavorably or without recommendation. Here the members speak more freely, and make their compromises without the public knowing just what they are. With these understandings reached, the chairman or other member is instructed to redraft the bill for report back to the legislature. In some cases, an entirely new bill may be needed.

Finally an approved bill is reported back to the Senate or House and is listed for consideration on the appropriate calendar, as noted below. With the bill may go a printed committee report. In any case the chairman or other designated member of the committee is responsible for the progress of the bill from that point on.

Readings of Bills. In each chamber it is required that a bill receive three "readings." Originally this meant what the word implies, but now that all bills reported out for adoption are printed and available to all members, the "reading" has become just a step in the procedure.

In the Senate a bill usually receives a first and second reading by title at the time of introduction; but if there is objection, the second reading may be postponed a day, and as a rule the three readings occur on separate days.

In the House, even the first reading by title is practically superseded by the practice of depositing bills with the clerk and having him print the list in the journal. The second reading, so-called, takes place when the bill is taken from its proper calendar (after the committee has reported it out), debated and amended, usually in Committee of the whole, before final passage, and the third reading takes place by title at the time of final passage or rejection.

Daily Order of Business. To facilitate and regularize its work, each house has a regular daily order of business beginning with prayer by the chaplain and going on through ten or more items of routine character until the major business for the day is reached, which is usually the discussion of bills from a certain calendar on second or third reading.

Calendars in House of Representatives. The rules provide for the classification of business with the general objective of giving first place to important measures. The House of Representatives has a complicated arrangement of calendars for this purpose. All business reported from any committee is to be placed on one of the following three calendars:

1. The "Union calendar"—"a Calendar of the Committee of the Whole House on the state of the Union, to which shall be referred bills raising revenue, general appropriation bills, and bills of a public character directly or indirectly appropriating money or property."

2. The "House calendar"—"to which shall be referred all bills of a public character not raising revenue nor directly or indirectly appropriating money or property."

3. The "Private Bill calendar"—"a Calendar of the Committee of the Whole House, to which shall be referred all bills of a private character." This calendar has priority on the first and third Tuesdays each month. In fact there are also two other calendars.

4. "Consent Calendar." The purpose of the primary classification for the three foregoing calendars is partly defeated by the fact that bills must be taken from each calendar, as a rule, in the order in which they appear. But this means that some important bills may be far behind unimportant ones, and that measures to which few if any members have objections often stand far down the list, while more controversial ones, that will take much time to debate, stand ahead. To overcome these obstacles to the despatch of business, a fourth calendar, called the "consent calendar," was created. On it is placed, at the request of any member, any bill to which there is little or no opposition and which can be quickly passed when the consent calendar is taken up.

5. In addition there is the "Calendar of Motions to Discharge Committees," usually very short, which has preference on the second and fourth Mondays of the month.

Selection of Important Bills for Passage. Besides the calendars the House has developed a set of rules that permit the majority party to cut through and around them to get at what is important. The principal device is that of permitting the Committee on Rules to report at any time a special rule that the House take up a certain bill at a certain time, for limited debate and passage. This committee, dominated by leaders of the majority party, usually follows the suggestions of the party caucus and steering committee. Certain other important committees, such as ways and means, and appropriations, have leave also to report at any time, although not to take up the time of the House for debate; and on Wednesdays, "calendar Wednesday," the committees are called according to a prearranged order, and are permitted to bring up any bills from the House or Union calendar for debate lasting not over two hours on any measure. If all the committees cannot be reached in the first session of the Congress, the House begins at the start of the second session with the next committee on the list. In addition it is possible to suspend the rules by a two-thirds vote, so that bills can be passed under suspension of the rules.

The Senate Calendar. The Senate has a much simpler arrangement. It has one general calendar, but uses also the terms "Calendar of General Orders" and "Calendar of Special Orders." At the end of the "Morning hour," the Vice President announces "Morning business is closed," whereupon any Senator may arise and ask unanimous consent that a certain bill on the calendar be taken up. If there is no objection, the bill is considered and may be at that time ordered engrossed and passed. This consideration of bills to which there is no objection usually ceases at 2 o'clock, and then the Senate takes up in order from the "Calendar of General Orders" bills to which there is objection. In this way, unopposed bills are being constantly eliminated from the calendar, and the more controversial bills at the head of the list are there to be taken up at any time. However, the Senate too needs short cuts through the rules, so it provides that by a two-thirds vote any bill may be made a "Special Order" at any time, and such bills are separately listed.

Committee of the Whole. In the House of Representatives, when bills are taken from the calendars for consideration on second reading, the House usually resolves itself into "committee of the whole." This means that the Speaker resigns the chair to some other member, 100 members constitute a quorum, yea and nay votes are omitted, and the rules of debate are somewhat relaxed. In this stage of procedure the bill may be considered clause by clause, amended, and then either recommended for passage or given an adverse vote. The committee then "rises," i.e., it reports to the whole House, with the Speaker back in the chair, what it recommends. The entire House then passes not on the proposed amendments, but usually on the bill as a whole as amended, and often without debate. In short, the bill is then on its third reading prior to final passage, and there is usually no opportunity for amendment, although debate may be permitted.

The Senate makes no use of the committee of the whole procedure for legislation although it does use it for the consideration of treaties. The advantages of this procedure are that the house concerned can carry on its work with only the more directly interested members present, without maintaining the constitutional quorum, without elaborate record votes, and with greater informality. The disadvantages are that record votes are not taken, and that under the procedure in the House, for example, the debate in committee of the whole may be all that is permitted, since the time limits apply to that form of procedure as well as to procedure in the House.

DEBATE AND PASSAGE OF BILLS

Debate on Final Passage. When the formality of a third reading has been completed, a bill is put on its final passage. In other words, there is a motion that it be passed. At this stage, there is further opportunity for debate, and obstructive tactics become most important. The methods of obstruction or filibustering are many: (1) presenting many dilatory motions, calls for a quorum, motions to adjourn, to take a recess, etc., debating each where possible, and asking for the yeas and nays on roll calls; (2) attempting to break a quorum by absence or refusal to answer to the roll call; (3) making long speeches that ramble over many fields, with the reading of documents and parts of books thrown in. In the Senate long speeches have been much used; Senator La Follette, the elder, once spoke for eighteen hours on a currency bill. In the House, before the present rules were put into forces, there was once a session lasting eight days and nights, during which "there were over 800 roll calls on motions to adjourn and to take a recess."

Freedom of Debate in Senate. Except in the increasingly frequent cases of unanimous agreement in advance to limit debate on a particular bill, the Senate puts no limit on the length of speeches, and permits a Senator to speak twice each legislative day, even though on the same bill. Thus a group of Senators, working in relays and yielding the floor only to each other, can keep the debate going on a long time. There is also considerable freedom to propose amendments, and this consumes much time when used. Furthermore, the Senate does not provide for the motion known as "the previous question" by which debate can be closed by majority vote in the House. Thus the Senate majority has found itself at times unable to override minorities, and it finally decided to adopt a rule permitting closure of debate. This took place under pressure from President Wilson early in 1917. The rule permits sixteen Senators to present a motion to close debate.[20] If the motion is adopted by two-thirds of those voting, the measure in question remains before the Senate until disposed of, no member may speak more than one hour on it, no new amendments may be presented without unanimous consent, and dilatory motions may be ruled out of order. This rule was invoked to force a vote on the Versailles Treaty and on adhesion to the Permanent Court of International Justice, but has been used very little, on the whole.

From the standpoint of accepted principles of majority rule and responsibility the present Senate rules that permit almost unlimited obstruction of

[20] Senate Standing Rules, XXII.

Senate action are indefensible. The Senate like the House exists under the Constitution to do the nation's business, not to allow it to go undone, and the Constitution grants to the Senate the same powers as the House has to see to it that majority rule prevails. Except in the few cases where the Constitution itself specifies a two-thirds vote, it implies the principle of majority rule. It provides that "a majority of each [house] shall constitute a Quorum to do Business" [21] and no Senate majority can hide indefinitely behind a rule that the Senate has itself made and that requires two-thirds of the members to consent before business can be done. It is time for someone to make an appeal from the Senate rules to the Constitution.

Rules of Debate in the House. In the House, most important bills are debated under strict time limitations. These result either from special rules, or from the general rules of the House. On a particular bill, for example, the House may rule that debate shall be limited to two hours or to some other fixed period on certain days. This time is divided between those who support and those who oppose the bill. When the time is up, the question is put on the passage of the bill. Amendments may be voted on first, usually without debate, and then the final vote is taken. The House permits also another method of closure, the previous question. When the majority members think that the debate has gone long enough, one of them arises, moves the previous question, and the chair states the motion: Shall the previous question now be put? If a majority approves, the vote is then taken on the bill. This practice is essentially in accord with sound parliamentary procedure wherever majority rule is recognized and wherever decisive action is considered to be more important than long drawn-out debate.

Majorities Required for Passage. Whether a bill has passed or not is determined by the particular constitutional voting requirement that prevails. In Congress a majority of the members must be present to constitute a "quorum," the minimum number for doing important business, and this means 218 in the House, and 49 in the Senate, assuming that there are no vacancies. If at least a quorum is present, the general rule is that a bill is passed if approved by a majority of those present and voting. Those not voting cannot be counted on either side. Thus, for example, if only 65 out of 96 Senators are present and voting, 33 is enough to pass a bill, though this is just a little over a third of the total membership. Similarly in the House. The Speaker of the House has and uses a vote like any other member. The Vice President in the Senate may vote only in case of a tie, and these occasions are rare.

The Constitution provides, however, that in a few exceptional cases a two-thirds vote is required. These cases include (a) the proposal of amendments to the Constitution, (b) the ratification of treaties by the Senate, (c) conviction by the Senate of persons impeached by the House, (d) the expulsion of a member by either house, and (e) the passage of an act over the President's veto. Most of these exceptions, it will be noted, are not ordinary cases of law

[21] Art. I, sec. 5, par. 1.

making. In each instance the interpretation of the two-thirds rule is the same: It means two-thirds of those present and voting, assuming at least a quorum to be present.

Methods of Voting. To determine whether a measure shall pass there are at least five different methods of voting: (a) viva voce, which is a simple call for ayes and noes; (b) a division, in which first the members for and then those against a bill rise in their places and are counted; (c) by tellers, in which two members appointed by the chair stand one on each side of the center aisle, and count the members who pass between them, the affirmative votes first, and then the negative; (d) by yeas and nays, or roll call; and (e) by ballot, which is rarely used.[22] The roll call is a time-wasting method but it has the advantage that it records votes in such a way that the citizen can know how his Senator and Representative voted. A number of state legislatures have installed electric voting devices which save a great deal of time. Partly to save time many measures are passed without roll call and hence without a full record. Each house decides which method to use in voting on any motion or bill, but one-fifth of the members present in either house have the constitutional right to demand a roll call to get the yeas and nays upon the record.

Engrossed and Enrolled Bills. When a bill has passed one house, it is "engrossed," that is, a perfect copy of it is printed under the direction of the engrossing committee and the clerk of that house. When it has passed both houses, it is "enrolled." This means that the committees on enrolled bills and the enrolling clerks of the two houses get together, compare their copies to see that they are identical, and have the final or enrolled copy printed and proofread for signature by the presiding officers of the two houses and by the chief executive.

Conference Committees. Should the houses pass bills of the same number, but in different form, that is, if the second house amends in some respect the bill passed by the first, the normal procedure is to appoint conference committees. Each house, under its rules, authorizes its presiding officer to appoint three or more members, representing both majority and minority members of the committee concerned with the bill, to meet a group of the same size from the other house in conference on the bill. As a rule, conferees are not supposed to strike from a bill any matter that both houses have agreed to, or to insert what is really new legislation, but conference committees have in practice a great deal of freedom. In many cases they fail to agree at first, and then must meet again, or give way to other conferees. Great power is exercised by conference committees, and as their work is largely unreported and not public, the conference committee has come under great condemnation. Senator Norris has put the conference committee down as one of the chief evils of the bicameral system. It, or something like it, is a necessity, however, as long as two chambers are retained. When the conferees agree, both houses usually

22 See Floyd M. Riddick, *op. cit.*, pp. 232-34.

adopt their report, readopt the bill in revised form, and send it to be enrolled.

A bill adopted by both houses is still not a law. Under the Constitution the bill must go to the President for his approval. This matter will be discussed in the next chapter.

Publication of Laws. All acts of legislation certified by the executive as having been made law, and those passed over his veto or permitted to become law by his failure to veto them, are sent to the Secretary of State, and are by him published in the manner provided by law, while the originals are kept in the archives. Publication takes place first in the form of separate "slip laws," and then in the form of bound volumes of *Statutes at Large.* Each law takes effect at the time therein stated, or when enacted, if no other time is stated.

THE CURRENT UNEASINESS ABOUT CONGRESS

No one can study Congress long and carefully without being deeply and favorably impressed with what it is, with what it has done, and with the genuine merit of much in its organization and procedures. Taken as a whole it is one of the most independent, powerful, and constructive legislatures in the world today. The body of legislation that it has enacted down through the decades has many admirable chapters and features. Its organization and its procedures continue, in general, to work effectively in the national interest.

Nevertheless there is a great deal of uneasiness in the American public mind about Congress and its future. This concern has crept into the membership of Congress itself. In the first session of the 78th Congress (1943) there were over forty resolutions introduced by various members for improvements in Congressional organization and procedures and for inquiries into its methods. Perhaps never in history have the members become as conscious of Congress as a whole or of its difficulties and problems as a co-ordinate branch of the national government. Evidently disturbed by the situation the 79th Congress appointed a Joint Committee on the Organization of Congress to investigate and report.

Some of the principal difficulties relate to the relationships between Congress and the executive branch of the government. These will be dealt with mainly in the next chapter. It appears, however, that one of the most disturbing facts for the thoughtful Congressman is the contrast between the unprogressiveness of Congress and the great strides forward that have been made by the executive branch and even by the judiciary. Reorganization, modernization, and the improvement of personnel and methods have been leading items on the agenda of the other two branches for a number of years. By contrast Congress seems to be clinging to outmoded ways or even slipping backward. It finds itself subjected, therefore, to an unusual amount of adverse criticism even from its friends. Some of the difficulties may be summarized as follows.

1. Unrepresentativeness. The United States has become a nation while Congress continues still, in considerable degree, to represent sections, special interests, pressure groups, and states. The President and the Supreme Court both hold definitely national views on most issues. Congress constantly yields to the pressures of particular producer groups and sections and must be almost whipped into line by the executive even on so elementary a national interest as the avoidance of wartime inflation. Since the Constitution fixes the basis of representation, Congress cannot be blamed for its relative unrepresentativeness, nor can the present situation easily be changed without constitutional amendment except by a more national viewpoint on the part of its members.

2. Qualities and Attitudes of Membership. The members of Congress on the average are better educated and abler by far than the average of the nation; and in the great majority of cases they are also high-minded, faithful and earnest public servants. At the same time Congress as a whole suffers by newspaper exploitation of the foibles, stupidities, and occasional outrageous statements and actions of a few members, and of the nepotism that it permits its members to practice and that a considerable number do practice. The standards of personnel and of official morality have gone up very considerably in the national administration and in the judiciary, but the evidence of any general and comparable rise in the standards of Congressional personnel is rather meager.

While the majority seem to be above the abuse of official power and position for personal and partisan motives, the House has in recent years appointed as chairman of a committee to investigate the Federal Communications Commission the very member against whom the commission had brought serious charges; has tolerated some very highhanded actions on the part of the chairman of its Committee on Un-American Activities; and has attempted in a wholly unconstitutional and unfair manner to oust without trial or hearing several national employees whose political views the majority did not like. These were actions that the intelligent public in general condemned and for which the House majority was directly responsible. In one sense these were rather minor matters in comparison with the many constructive things that Congress was doing, yet they reveal an attitude toward the responsibilities of high public office that is very disturbing.

3. Failure of Congress to Grasp Its True Role. At the beginning of this chapter there is a statement of what has obviously become the true role of Congress. There is a great deal of evidence, however, that Congress has not accepted that role or adjusted its attitude, organization and procedures to the performance of it. The facts are that the United States has become a great integrated nation with an extensive program of public services and some hundreds of thousands of public servants to perform its work. Congress itself has helped to bring about this situation and might well take pride in it. Instead, many of its members, in both houses and in both parties, carry on a querulous attack upon what they call "bureaucracy" and complain unceasingly that Congress has too little to say about public policies and administration. To many persons in the American public these complaints do not ring true. They believe that there is a great deal that Congress could do constructively to cooperate with, to control, and to improve the administration. In order to do this, however, Congress will need to set its own house in order and change both its attitude and some of its procedures.

4. Waste of Time and Energy on Petty Business. Individual members in both houses and Congress as a whole spend too much time on petty matters that are not proper functions of a great national legislature. A large amount of attention is devoted to (1) legislation for the District of Columbia and investigations of its local affairs; (2) the introduction and passage of thousands of private claims against the government, all of which could be handled far more expeditiously, economically, and fairly by the courts, by existing administrative agencies, or by some special tribunal set up for the purpose; and (3) the multifarious little chores that many members do in Washington for their constituents and friends—a type of work that many members even encourage their constituents to impose upon them. With respect to the private claim nuisance, including pensions, it should be noted that as long as Congress handles these matters through numerous special bills it also imposes added work upon the President to read all that pass, to sign those he approves, and to veto the others. It is beneath the true dignity of Congress to shift to the President the duty of saying "No" to unwarranted claims for individual pensions and other small payments.

5. Lack of Proper Organization. As previously noted, power and responsibility are badly split up and dissipated among many standing committees in both houses. The committees of the two houses meet separately even when they have to deal with the same governmental agencies and the same subjects of legislation. The jurisdictions of comparable House and Senate committees are not entirely the same even when their names are identical, and neither do their fields correspond closely with those of present administrative agencies. As a result both members of Congress and national administrators waste their time in attending various meetings that cover the same subject. There is no over-all organization of Congress that could bring greater order out of the present situation, but much could be done to simplify and regularize the committee arrangements by negotiation between the houses and by action within each house.

6. Improper Use of Personnel. Congress also does not make the best use of all its able personnel. While Committee chairmanships go by seniority, many able younger men have no important responsibilities.

7. Faulty Rules of Procedure. The House has made substantial improvements in its procedures in recent times, with the result that the majority can act, and the minority can always get an opportunity to be heard. In the Senate the situation is different. There it is possible for very small minorities to defeat the will of the majority whenever a minority is willing to work hard enough and to be sufficiently disagreeable. This is often justified as unlimited freedom of debate although it is nothing of the kind. It is not debate but simple obstructionism when a few members can hold the floor indefinitely, read irrelevant matter into the record, and prevent the Senate from proceeding with its business. The Senate has adequate constitutional power to correct this abuse.

8. **Lack of Expert Aids and Information.** Each committee has a small staff, each house has its Legislative Counsel, and Congress as a whole has the Legislative Reference Service as well as the Library of Congress. With all these possible sources of legislative assistance and information it is still true that Congress is inadequately provided with expert aids. When it is proposed that more be added, however, the observer comes up against the disquieting fact that many, if not most, of the members do not make any real use of such present facilities as the Legislative Reference Service. Are Congressmen too busy with their other activities to study the major problems before them, or are they unaware of the importance of better informing themselves? Why is it that the important committees of Congress have in only a few instances developed staffs of outstanding experts to aid them in their work?

9. **Lack of Communication Facilities.** Congress suffers generally from the manner in which it is treated by the press. In this respect the President has a tremendous advantage over it. It would seem to follow that Congress should develop more adequate facilities for telling the nation at large, and for enabling each member to tell his constituents, about the constructive work of Congress. How can this best be done? It is up to Congress to study the matter, to make some experiments with various media of communication, and then to go ahead with a comprehensive publicity program.

These nine criticisms of Congress are not those of only the author of this book. He has simply tried to summarize what many publicists and not a few members of Congress say and believe to be true. The criticisms do not go to the vitals of the Congressional system. Congressional government has not failed. It does fall short of what it might be at its potential best. A number of the suggested reforms can be made by Congress as a whole or by one of its houses. For the improvement of its membership and its representative character the nation as a whole is responsible.

REPORT OF JOINT COMMITTEE ON CONGRESS

On March 4, 1946, the special Joint Committee on the Organization of the Congress made its report.[23] It recommended in part as follows:

1. **Committee Structure and Operation.** (1) That the Senate standing committees be reduced from 33 to 16 and the House standing committees from 48 to 18, with clearer definition of their fields of work. (2) That the standing committees review the legislation and the operations of administrative agencies within their fields, instead of employing special committees. (3) That

[23] *Organization of the Congress.* 79th Congress, 2d Session, Senate Report, no. 1011.

committee hearings be regularized and that records thereof be kept. (4) That each committee be provided with an adequate expert staff, and that the expenditures on Legislative Counsel be increased.

2. Majority and Minority Policy Committees. (1) That each major party in each house establish a policy committee of seven with funds and staff. (2) That the House and Senate majority policy committees meet together to consult the Executive and set up a majority policy.

3. Research and Staff Facilities. (1) That the Legislative Reference Service be substantially enlarged. (2) That each House and Senate member be allowed to appoint at $8,000 a year an administrative assistant to handle his nonlegislative work. (3) That an Office of Congressional Personnel be established to set up a modern personnel system for managing Congress's service employees.

4. Strengthening Fiscal Controls. (1) That the Revenue and Appropriations Committees of the two houses jointly set a maximum for national government receipts and expenditures for the next fiscal year, recommend any necessary borrowing to meet expenditures, or else get Congress to provide for scaling down expenditures to stay within the agreed total. (2) That the Appropriations Committees receive additional staff. (3) That the Comptroller General make an annual "service audit" for Congress of each agency of government. (4) That unexpended appropriations be not extended, reappropriated or transferred, but terminated, and that all agency earnings be turned over to the Treasury. (5) That the practice of attaching legislation to appropriations be discontinued.

5. More Efficient Use of Congressional Time. (1) That Congress give up trying to govern the District of Columbia and delegate this function to the voters under a city charter. (2) That it give up passing private claims and pension bills and local bridge bills by delegating these duties to the courts and administrative agencies. (3) That it provide for a regular annual recess for members to visit their constituencies.

6. Registration of Organized Groups. (1) "That Congress enact legislation providing for the registration of organized groups and their agents who seek to influence legislation and that such registration include quarterly statements of expenditures made for this purpose."

7. Congressional Pay and Retirement. (1) That beginning with the 80th Congress (1947-48) the annual salary of all members be $15,000 instead of $10,000. (2) That members be permitted to join the Federal Retirement System on a contributory basis. (3) That the Vice President, Speaker and other officers of Senate and House also have their salaries substantially increased.

8. Other Recommendations include improvements in the chambers and caucus rooms of both houses, improved restaurant facilities, more adequate committee rooms, and changes in the *Congressional Record*.

Some of these recommendations are obviously important and others far less so. A number are certainly debatable while others will meet very little opposition. The Joint Committee avoided some very controversial issues, but dealt boldly with others. That much is wrong with Congress is now fairly established by a joint committee of its own members. What will the outcome be?

REFERENCES

Harvey Walker, *Law Making in the United States*, New York, 1934, chs. IX, X.

Joseph P. Chamberlain, *Legislative Processes: National and State*, New York, 1936, chs. V, VI.

W. F. Willoughby, *Principles of Legislative Organization and Administration*, Washington, D. C., 1934, chs. XX-XXII, XXXII-XXXIV.

George R. Brown, *The Leadership of Congress*, Indianapolis, 1922.

Paul DeWitt Hasbrouck, *Party Government in the House of Representatives*, New York, 1927.

Robert Luce, *Legislative Assemblies*, Boston and New York, 1924.

——, *Legislative Procedure*, Boston, 1922.

U. S. Congress, House of Representatives, *Constitution, Jefferson's Manual and Rules of the House of Representatives*, Washington, new ed. each Congress.

U. S. Congress, Senate, *Senate Manual, Containing the Standing Rules and Orders of the United States Senate*, Washington, new ed. each Congress.

U. S. 79th Congress, 1st Session, *Official Congressional Directory*, Washington, 1945 (corrected to February 2, 1945), and later editions.

American Political Science Review, annual articles on Sessions of Congress (various authors).

John D. Millett and Lindsay Rogers, "The Legislative Veto and the Reorganization Act of 1939," *Public Admin. Rev.*, vol. I, pp. 176-89 (1941).

American Political Science Association, Committee on Congress, Report of, entitled *The Reorganization of Congress*, Washington, 1945.

Floyd M. Riddick, *Congressional Procedure*, Boston, 1941.

Roland Young, *This Is Congress*, New York, 1943.

Congress, Special Joint Committee on the Organization of, *Symposium on Congress*, Washington, 1945.

——, *Hearings of*, Parts I-IV, 1945.

——, *First Progress Report*, 1945.

——, *Report*, entitled *Organization of the Congress*, March 4, 1946, 79th Congress, 2d Session, Senate Report, no. 1011.

John M. Mathews and Clarence A. Berdahl, *Documents and Readings in American Government: National and State*, rev. ed., New York, 1940, pp. 455-62.

A. N. Christensen and E. M. Kirkpatrick, *The People, Politics, and the Politician: Readings in American Government*, New York, 1941, pp. 396-402.

CHAPTER 13

Congress, the President, and the Separation of Powers

THE PRESIDENTIAL FORM OF GOVERNMENT

Representative democracies may be organized in a variety of ways but in modern times they tend to conform to one or the other of two principal types. One form, called the *presidential*, prevails in the national and state governments of the United States, and has been adopted to some extent, with important local variations, in certain Latin American republics. The principal rival system of organization, called the *cabinet* or *parliamentary* form, originated in England and spread thence to other countries in Europe such as France, Belgium and the Scandinavian countries, and also to the British self-governing dominions such as Canada and Australia.

Parliamentary Form Explained. In the parliamentary form there is ordinarily a titular or ceremonial head of the government (limited monarch or president) but the real powers of government are vested in a legislative body. This usually consists of two houses, of which one, the larger and everywhere directly elected one, is recognized as dominant. Following the election for this house, the leaders of the party (or group of parties) that won a majority of the seats in it, organize a "cabinet" of a small number of their own members which is almost automatically approved by the titular head of the government. Thereupon this cabinet becomes "the government." On the one hand the cabinet members keep their seats in the house, and debate, vote, and answer questions there. On the other hand individual cabinet members take charge of important government departments. The cabinet as a whole meets from time to time under its leader, the premier or prime minister, to decide questions of policy, and to formulate proposals to be submitted to the legislature. Thus the cabinet is both an administrative body and the leader in the legislative branch. The powers of government are unified in it, but it is directly under legislative control. Should its policies be rejected by the legislature, it must either (a) resign, and permit the organization of a new cabinet that has the support of the legislature, or (b) order a dissolution of the house and call for new elections, to test out what the voters wish the government's policy to be. Thus no cabinet (government) can constitutionally carry on for any length of time if it is out of harmony with the legislative branch or with the voters. Even if no dissolution takes place, elections normally occur according to law once in four or five years.

Essentials of Presidential Form. In contrast to the parliamentary form, the presidential is one in which the executive and legislative branches are separately elected. Each is responsible to the voters directly, but not responsible to or dependent upon the other branch, except in specific ways provided by the constitution. Terms of office are fixed by law and calendar, and it often happens that the executive and legislative are out of harmony, being controlled by rival parties. There is division of responsibility between the executive and the legislative branches, and frequent difficulty in getting harmonious action.[1]

Separation of Powers the Main Issue. The differences between presidential and parliamentary forms of government are many, but they revolve largely around the question of *separation* versus *unification* of the powers within a particular government such as the national. At the same time the participation of the voters is not the same under the two plans, and written constitutions and the power of the courts to review legislation are more in keeping with the presidential than with the parliamentary form.

THE SEPARATION OF POWERS

Origin of Idea. The theory of the separation of powers is one of ancient origin. Perhaps it arose as early as when the first man saw the danger to personal liberties in having one man or the same group of men given complete power to make laws, then to enforce them, and then to decide whether a violation has taken place and what the penalty shall be. This, in Jefferson's words, is "precisely the definition of despotic government." [2] Hence the purpose of the separation is to give protection to personal liberties and private property against government by arrangements within the governmental mechanism itself but without impairing the power of the government to act in the protection of public interests.

John Locke on Separation of Powers. The framers of the first constitutions of Virginia, Pennsylvania and Massachusetts, at least, and the men who for-

---

[1] For generalized comparisons of parliamentary and presidential government see H. L. McBain, *The Living Constitution*, New York, 1927, chs. IV, V; W. F. Willoughby, *The Government of Modern States*, rev. and enl. ed., New York, 1936, chs. XIV-XV; R. G. Gettell, *Political Science*, New York, 1933, ch. XIII; H. J. Laski, *The American Presidency*, New York, 1940; Don K. Price, "The Parliamentary and Presidential System," *Public Admin. Rev.*, vol. 3, pp. 317-34 (1943), with a reply by Harold Laski and a rejoinder by Don Price in *Public Admin. Rev.*, vol. 4, pp. 347-63 (1944).

[2] See footnote 5, below. Madison called it "the very definition of tyranny." *The Federalist*, no. 47.

mulated the national Constitution, were strongly in favor of the separation of powers, but were not in agreement as to how to make it effective. Their reading on the subject had been underscored by their experiences under the colonial governments. John Locke, a late seventeenth-century English writer, well known in the colonies, had argued that the powers of government should be "directed to no other end but the peace, safety, and public good of the people," and that therefore even the supreme legislative power "is not, nor can possibly be, absolutely arbitrary over the lives and fortunes of the people." Therefore, "in well-ordered commonwealths" there should be an executive branch of government separate from the legislative body to execute the laws, as well as another that he called "federative" to manage war and foreign affairs.[3] Locke's idea of "executive power" apparently included both the executive power as we know it in all internal affairs and the judicial power.

Montesquieu on the Separation of Powers. Montesquieu, a French scholar writing sixty years later than Locke, had a more clear-cut view of governmental powers. He wrote:

> When the legislative and executive powers are united in the same person, or in the same body of magistrates, there can be no liberty; . . .

> Again, there is no liberty, if the power of judging be not separated from the legislative and executive powers.[4]

He thus describes the typical three-fold separation that has since become familiar to Americans. Montesquieu made the mistake of thinking that the English constitution in 1748 embodied a true separation of powers, whereas the parliamentary or cabinet system of government with its unification of powers was already in existence; but his theory was widely accepted in America.

Before *The Federalist* appeared (1787-88), both John Adams and Thomas Jefferson had published strong expressions on the necessity for a separation of powers in the state governments.[5] Madison and Hamilton in *The Federalist* restated the arguments in relation to the new national constitution.[6] Evidently a rising sentiment was in favor of separation, and in time the doctrine came to prevail in both national and state governments.

Various Aspects of the Separation Doctrine. It will be noted that the term "powers" in the phrase "separation of powers" refers not to police power,

[3] *Two Treatises of Government*, Bk. II, chs. IX, XI, XIII.

[4] *The Spirit of Laws*, Bk. XI, ch. 6.

[5] John Adams, *Defence of the Constitutions of Government of the United States of America*, 1786-88, 3 vols.; Jefferson, *Notes on the State of Virginia*, 1782. See B. F. Wright, *A Source Book of American Political Theory*, pp. 151-73. Jefferson's remarks came in the course of a scorching criticism of the system of legislative supremacy that had been set up in Virginia. See ch. 2, pp. 21-22, above.

[6] *The Federalist*, nos. 47-51. Hamilton was somewhat inconsistent, however; he actually worked for such a fusion of the executive and legislative powers of the national government as might have created an American replica of British parliamentary government.

taxing power, and war power, for example, but to the three so-called "branches" or main departments of government, the legislative, executive, and judicial. As developed in practice the doctrine has various aspects. These are:

1. The separation of legislative, executive, and judicial branches of government considered as impersonal organizations. The theory assumes that the legislative, executive, and judicial processes or functions in government are wholly distinct so that they can be assigned to different branches.

2. The separation of personnel, so that as a rule no individual may serve at the same time in two or more distinct branches.

3. The use of checks and balances that permit each department, largely for its own protection, to check the work of the other two.

4. Rules against the delegation of powers, to prevent those persons who are in charge of one branch of government from turning their responsibilities and functions over to another branch.

5. Provisions whereby each branch may to some extent control the "housekeeping" in its own department, so as not to be unduly dependent on the other departments.

Checks and Balances Needed. It is not difficult to write out a formula of words for the separation of powers. The problem that was not solved at the outset was that of making the separation effective. The solution was later found to lie in large part in a system of "checks and balances." These two ideas, separation of powers and checks and balances, are usually associated in discussion, because they are really *opposing and compensating parts of the same governmental mechanism.* The one provides for separation, the other for interlocking, and both are needed. Suppose that a constitution simply said that "all legislative power is vested in the legislature, all executive power in the governor, and all judicial power in the courts." As the legislative or lawmaking *function* is certainly superior to the other two, the legislature would in ordinary times probably be able to dominate the other two branches, while in times of grave crisis the legislative *body* being large and unable to act quickly would probably transfer a great part of its legislative function and power to one or a few of its members or to the executive. In any case, however, the judiciary would have little power to resist the legislature, and in quiet times the executive would have little more unless he were to violate the constitution and seize dictatorial power.[7] This is what the American people learned under their first state constitutions. They had been so anxious to clip the wings of the governors and the Crown that while they set up paper provisions for a separation of powers, they in effect turned nearly all powers over to the legislatures.

---

[7] John Locke said that "there can be but one supreme power, which is the legislative, to which all the rest are and must be subordinate." *Two Treatises of Government,* Bk. II ch. XIII.

SEPARATION OF POWERS IN NATIONAL GOVERNMENT

The national Constitution provides for the separation of powers in the national government by four principal clauses:

> All legislative Powers herein granted shall be vested in a Congress of the United States. . . .
>
> The executive Power shall be vested in a President of the United States of America.
>
> The judicial Power of the United States, shall be vested in one supreme Court, and in such inferior courts as the Congress may from time to time ordain and establish.
>
> . . . and no Person holding any Office under the United States, shall be a Member of either House during his Continuance in Office.[8]

This series of provisions provides for a separation of the three great functions among three distinct branches, and also provides against any overlapping of personnel between Congress and the executive and between Congress and the courts.[9] Since a member of Congress may not serve as an executive officer, the English type of cabinet government is practically excluded. Similarly one cannot at the same time be a member of Congress to pass laws and a judge in the courts to apply them. There is no express provision, however, to prevent a person holding positions under the executive and judicial departments at the same time.

Checks and Balances in National Government. The clauses on the separation of powers give no idea of checks and balances. The latter are provided for by distinct provisions of the Constitution. In general they permit each department to invade the sphere of each of the others to an extent sufficient to enable each to check the others in order to protect itself. That is, the checks and balances represent a partial *mingling of powers* at points that are deemed important for self-protection, as indicated below.

Checks by Congress on Other Departments. 1. *Congress* alone may propose constitutional amendments and declare them to be in effect. These may seriously affect the other departments.

2. The House may impeach, and the Senate may try cases of impeachment of executive and judicial officers, and thus remove them from office.

3. Congress may by legislation, passed over the President's veto if necessary, establish, regulate, limit, or abolish inferior courts and executive establishments.

4. Congress controls the purse for all; it alone may levy taxes, make appropriations, and borrow money on the credit of the United States.

[8] U. S. Const., Art. I, sec. 1; Art. II, sec. 1; Art. III, sec. 1; and Art. I, sec. 6, respectively.

[9] On the right of members of Congress to serve on special treaty missions, see Mathews and Berdahl, *Documents and Readings in American Government*, New York, 1928, pp. 303-11.

5. The *Senate* has a limited control over the executive and the courts, through its power to reject the President's nominations for executive and judicial positions.

6. It may control the President's foreign policy to some extent through the rejection of proposed treaties.

7. The *Senate* and the *House* check each other in the passage of legislation, in making appropriations, and in proposing constitutional amendments.

Checks by President on Others. 8. The President may check both houses through his veto power, which can, however, be overridden by a two-thirds vote.

9. The President may also keep Congress in ignorance of important matters by refusing to transmit vital information in his possession.

10. The President also has a check on the courts through his power to appoint judges.

Checks by the Courts on Others. 11. Although the place of the courts in the general scheme of separation is to be considered later, it will give a more complete picture if we list here the checks that they have in the other departments. The Courts, in interpreting, construing, and applying the acts of Congress and the treaties of the United States, have a check on both Congress and the President.

12. The courts may also declare acts of Congress, and possibly even treaties, to be unconstitutional and void, thus preventing enforcement.

13. The courts also control executive and administrative action through entertaining suits and issuing court orders against public officers.

Many other specific but less important checks might be stated, but these are enough to illustrate the situation.

PRESIDENT AND CONGRESS

It is against this background of constitutional provisions for the separation of powers and checks and balances that we must consider the relations between Congress and the President. It would be unwise, however, to consider only the formal constitutional arrangements. Practice, custom, and personal human relations and reactions are in the long run very important.

Human Factors in Relations of Congress and President. Not many years ago, American writers gave a great deal of attention to the "chasm wide and deep" between the President and Congress. The impression was given that the executive was kept at arm's length or farther by Congress, and that the separation of powers prevented close communion and cooperation between the two. This view seems to have been based in part on the words of the Constitution and in part on certain passing controversies between particular Presidents and Congress rather than on a close study of general practice. The facts seem to be that public opinion, the party system, and the more personal relations of the executive with Congressmen produce a degree of cooperation not generally realized, and through methods not always fully understood. Men who have worked together in political campaigns, who have many friendly personal relations with each other, and who have common purposes in public service cannot be kept apart by words in a constitution. But the Constitution does enable an American President to carry on his work after a fashion even when he is angry and at odds with the majority and with the leaders of Congress.

For the government to be carried on successfully there is need for consideration and cooperation at both ends of the long stretch of Pennsylvania Avenue between Capitol Hill and the White House. Congress and the Presidency are differently constituted and have different functions to perform, but both are necessary to successful operation of the government.

President Represents the Nation; Congressmen Represent States and Districts. A President is elected once in four years. At the same time the entire membership of the House of Representatives is reconstituted for two years, but only one-third of the Senate is elected at that time. The President has received popular support in every state; hence he represents, in a sense, the whole nation. Each Senator and Representative is to some extent a party representative, but primarily he represents his state or district, certainly not the entire nation. Since regions, states, and districts have many competing interests, there is never the same unity of purpose in House or Senate as in the President's office. Even Congressmen of the same party may be strongly at odds on important measures. These internal differences in each house and between the houses of Congress frequently drive the members to find leadership elsewhere, and naturally they turn to the President.

Time and Circumstances Affect the President's Influence. If in his first term his party has a clear majority in both houses as is customary, the President is in a very strong position—strongest, of course, if his party has just turned out the opposition. Thus Franklin Roosevelt, taking office in 1933, was in much better position to wield influence than Mr. Hoover was in 1929 for the simple reason that before Mr. Hoover's administration his party had been in power for eight years already, and had filled the most important positions with Republicans whom he hardly wished or dared to turn out. Mr. Roosevelt, on the contrary, coming in as a Democrat after twelve years of Republican rule, had literally thousands of positions to fill with Democrats. As long as these places were available, Democratic Senators and Representatives naturally felt a need of working with the President in order that he in turn might recognize their claims to patronage. In his second term even the strongest of Presidents is somewhat less influential, partly because the available patronage is less, partly because the political leaders are already beginning to cast about for his successor. Franklin Roosevelt was something of an exception to this rule, but the rule probably still stands.

Prior to 1932 the off-year election, and especially the one in a President's second term, was likely to go against the party in power, so that the President faced for two years a House of Representatives, and sometimes even a Senate, in which the party majority had been greatly reduced or had even disappeared. Among recent Presidents, Mr. Taft, Mr. Wilson, Mr. Coolidge, and Mr. Hoover all experienced this situation. The resultant loss of prestige and influence to the President was a truly serious matter. This reveals, indeed, one of the most important defects in American constitutional arrangements. Congress and the President need to work together, and any provision that makes possible and even probable a stalemate between them is to be condemned. The simplest solution, as has been previously suggested, might be to have the House and also the Senate completely renewed at the same time and for the same term as the President.

Conditions Affecting Relations of President and Congress. Assuming that the same party dominates both houses and the Presidency, the working relations between President and Congress will depend upon many factors such as (a) the President's personality and qualities as a leader and executive, (b) the general condition of the country with respect to prosperity or depression, peace or war, (c) the weapons the President has at hand for maintaining discipline in his party, in and out of Congress, and (d) the strength and ambition for power of the party leaders in Congress.

Personal Qualities. The system of nomination and election in no sense insures the selection of an outstanding leader, and yet the "batting average" has been fairly high. Americans may well take pride in the high average quality of their Presidents. Every careful observer can see differences in effectiveness between Theodore Roosevelt and Taft, between Wilson and Harding, between Franklin Roosevelt and Hoover, Not all have been outstandingly successful. Still, the times and conditions had much to do with the comparative failure of some Presidents, and no absolute judgment can be made on their personal fitness for leadership.

Economic Conditions. Whoever is in office will get blamed for a depression that arrives in his term, even as he will be credited for winning a war while President. The members of Congress are naturally influenced in their actions toward the President by the standing that he has among their constituents whether it is the result of good luck or of ability. They dare not support a loser or a wholly unpopular figure, or turn against one who has achieved great popular success.

PRESIDENT AS LEGISLATIVE LEADER

Since the President is the only person in important office who campaigns over the whole country and is in a sense the choice of the nation, the people have in the course of time come to look to him for leadership in all matters of policy and legislation. The words of the Constitution confer on him executive power, and say that the legislative power is vested in the two houses of Congress. In fact, his leadership in legislative matters outweighs his other responsibilities nearly all the time. *The legislative power is actually vested in Congress and the President.* To exercise this legislative leadership, to get the proper cooperation from Congress, what powers and what instruments has he at hand?

Unity and Strength of President's Position. The President is responsible to Congress for neither his nomination nor his election. These he owes only to his party, the party convention, and the voters. His position is rooted solidly in popular favor. It is, furthermore, the most conspicuous and respected position in the country. What he says and does is always front page news even when the press is generally opposed to him; it nearly always has priority on the radio and the screen.

In addition, as already stated, his position has a unity not possessed by Congress. He no doubt has difficulty at times in making up his mind on important measures; he must consider carefully the various interests involved before reaching a decision. But his decision can be made in private, behind closed doors and in conference with a few trusted advisers. The people always know how torn and divided is Congress; so, too, do its members. The President by comparison seems to stand serenely at ease and confident, wholly united in purpose.

Expert Advice. Back of his decisions, also, is more command of expert advice than Congress has available to it. He can and does summon department heads and bureau chiefs, distinguished diplomats, professional men, captains of finance and industry, and the leaders of farmers' and laborers' organizations, not to mention the members of Congress themselves. The experts in government's employment have no choice but to give him their best advice and service.

Party Leadership. The party candidate for the Presidency becomes automatically the leader of his party. His success in being elected only welds the party more strongly behind him. The future success of the party, the very re-election of many members of Congress, depend upon the maintenance of a united front and an air of confidence and success. That is why party leaders in and out of Congress are slow to rise in opposition to what a President proposes. As for him, if he is not so self-willed and sure of his own wisdom that he fails to consult with party leaders, he will try to carry his Congressional supporters with him through frequent conferences with their leaders. His tact in doing this, his sympathy with the ambitions and views of party members in Congress, will go far toward solidifying his party behind him and his position as leader. He must know that there are times when members must be allowed their own head and the right to oppose party measures for sectional, local and personal reasons. To the extent that he fails to measure up to the standards of party leadership, to that extent he fails as a leader in legislation.

Personal Contacts Between the President and Congress. To make effective his leadership in Congress and to maintain close relations with it, every President in recent years has had the aid of a specially devised machinery. He has usually one or more assistants whose main function is to maintain contacts with the members of Congress and their committees, and to keep him informed of progress on bills as well as of the attitudes of members. His reports from these contact men sometimes result in meetings between the President himself and wavering members of Congress. The floor leaders of the party in both houses, the Vice President and the Speaker, and other outstanding party members in both houses, also confer often with the President to inform him of progress and difficulties. During sessions these conferences with the party legislative leaders usually take place once a week.

Patronage. In many instances the President has undoubtedly been able to wield some influence over Congress through a judicious use of his appointing power. There are probably very few cases in which a President says, even through an intermediary, to a member of Congress: "If you vote for this bill, your friend X will get the post he wants." Such bargains are in general too crude. "Understandings" may be reached, however, under the rule that one good turn deserves another, and historians could probably present many cases of strange coincidences between favorable votes on Presidential measures and appointments to government positions.

None of the foregoing means of Presidential influence over Congress and consultation with it in legislative matters is contrary to either the letter or the spirit of the Constitution. A number of the framers of the Constitution must have expected the President to become a leader in policy. This is revealed in part by several specific provisions of the Constitution.

Calling and Ending Sessions. While regular sessions are held annually, beginning now on January 3 and lasting as long as desired, the President and only the President may call special sessions.[10] He may summon both houses, or either house separately; there have been a number of special sessions of the Senate to consider appointments and treaties. He may also, in case of disagreement between the houses as to the time of adjournment, "adjourn them to such Time as he shall think proper." [11] This power has never been used.

No Power to Prorogue or Dissolve. In parliamentary countries that follow closely the British model, the cabinet with the approval of the titular head of the government may either "prorogue" parliament, i.e., bring its current session to an end, or both prorogue it and "dissolve" the elective chamber, i.e., end the session and require a new election of elective members. This power in the hands of colonial governors deeply incensed the colonial leaders. It was abolished in the United States at the time of the Revolution, and has not been reestablished in either the national or the state governments. Legislative bodies may carry on even though wholly out of sympathy with the executive.

[10] Art. II, sec. 3, and Amend. XX.
[11] Art. II, sec. 3.

This naturally enhances the independence of the legislative branch, and often makes the position of the executive very difficult.

Messages and Proposal of Measures. The President has the power and the duty to give Congress from time to time "Information of the State of the Union," and to "recommend to their Consideration such Measures as he shall judge necessary and expedient." [12] He is naturally the judge of how much information he shall give, and how frequently. It is customary for him to deliver a message at the beginning of each session of Congress, and also to send special messages or communications from time to time.

The first two Presidents delivered their messages orally. The first Democratic President, Jefferson, sent his messages in writing, and thus began a practice that lasted until another Democratic President, Wilson, in 1913 returned to oral presentation. Since then the practice has varied. When messages are delivered orally, the two houses assemble in one chamber and the presiding officers of both houses are on the rostrum with the President. President Coolidge was the first to have a radio hookup when delivering a message, and Franklin Roosevelt made extensive use of this device for addressing the people at the same time that he addressed Congress. Indeed to some extent he appealed directly to the people on legislative matters and thus built up a certain popular pressure that Congress could not easily resist.

Administration Bills in Congress. To "recommend . . . measures" is not exactly the same as to present fully formulated bills, but a practice has developed of having bills favored by the President and the departments drawn up in the department concerned, or in the Attorney General's office or Budget Bureau, for submission to the two houses through influential members of the party. Indeed, nearly all important legislation now originates in, or is approved by, the appropriate department. The times and the party situation in Congress and in the country, as well as the personality and leadership of the President, largely determine the result of the President's proposals. Presidents Wilson and Franklin Roosevelt had great success in their first terms; and in the war emergencies of 1917-18, and 1941-45 each was able to carry through practically his entire program. There is no assurance, however, that the President's proposals will be enacted by the legislative branch, but even a reluctant Congress approves a great deal of what he proposes. After all, the majority party and its leaders in both houses are obligated to maintain party unity. They cannot afford to flout their leader's considered program of legislation as a whole although they may reject or modify important items.

Executive Approval and Veto of Bills. The Constitution confers upon the President a sweeping power to approve or disapprove bills passed by Congress, as follows:

> Every Bill which shall have passed the House of Representatives
> and the Senate, shall, before it becomes a Law, be presented to the

[12] Art. II, sec. 3.

President of the United States; If he approve he shall sign it, but if not he shall return it, with his Objections to that House in which it shall have originated, who shall enter the Objections at large on their Journal, and proceed to reconsider it. If after such Reconsideration two thirds of that House shall agree to pass the Bill, it shall be sent, together with the Objections, to the other House, by which it shall likewise be reconsidered, and if approved by two thirds of that House, it shall become a Law. But in all such Cases the Votes of both Houses shall be determined by Yeas and Nays, and the Names of the Persons voting for and against the Bill shall be entered on the Journal of each House respectively. If any Bill shall not be returned by the President within ten Days (Sundays excepted) after it shall have been presented to him, the Same shall be a Law, in like Manner as if he had signed it, unless the Congress by their Adjournment prevent its Return, in which Case it shall not be a Law.

Every Order, Resolution, or Vote to which the Concurrence of the Senate and House of Representatives may be necessary (except on a question of Adjournment) shall be presented to the President of the United States; and before the Same shall take Effect, shall be approved by him, or being disapproved by him, shall be repassed by two thirds of the Senate and House of Representatives, according to the Rules and Limitations prescribed in the Case of a Bill.[13]

Acts of Congress Subject to Veto. In its enactments, Congress uses two different forms rather indiscriminately, the *Act*, and the *Joint Resolution*. Thus in any volume of *Public Laws* printed by Congress, many joint resolutions will be found scattered among a still larger number of acts. Many joint resolutions are more important than many acts, but all have the same legal force. Under the Constitution, both these types of enactments must be sent to the President for his approval. The same is true of the many *Private Acts* that fill the second large volume produced by the ordinary Congress. But in the latter volume there are also certain so-called *Concurrent Resolutions*. These are resolutions passed by one House, in which the other concurs, that relate primarily to the relations between the Houses in their own work: resolutions to appoint joint committees, to correct the enrollment of acts, to authorize the printing of documents, and to provide for adjournment. These concurrent resolutions do not go to the President, and neither do resolutions proposing amendments to the Constitution.

Because of long practice with the use of concurrent resolutions, a feeling seems to have grown up in some circles, inside Congress as well as outside, that by calling what it does a concurrent resolution Congress may take certain actions even of a substantive nature, i.e., actions that change the laws of the land, without submitting them to the President for his approval. This is not

[13] Art. I, sec. 7, pars. 2, 3.

what the Constitution says at all. With only one exception, and that on the question of adjournment, if the concurrence of both the Senate and House is necessary, the measure is required to go to the President for approval. Each house separately may adopt and enforce its own rules, discipline and expel its own members, and so on, and such actions do not require Presidential consent. But there is no case in which either house may change the substantive law alone, or make any appropriation; and if the concurrence of both houses is required for any measure except an adjournment or for a Constitutional Amendment, then that measure should be sent to the President for approval. Presidents may have been negligent in not insisting upon this from the beginning, but it is doubtful whether they have lost any power through long neglect, and even more doubtful whether they can sign away their constitutional powers to have measures submitted to them by approving bills that permit the two houses to do certain things by concurrent resolution. Congress may not enlarge its own constitutional powers by legislative act even with the President's approval.

It has been held, however, that constitutional amendments, which require a two-thirds vote, need not be submitted to the President for his approval.

Types of Executive Action on Bills. In a single Congress the President has to pass upon many hundreds of public acts, joint resolutions, and private acts. In the President's office any one of five things may happen to a bill.

During the session the President may either (1) sign the bill, and thus make it law, or (2) fail to either sign it or veto it, but hold it beyond the ten-day period, in which case it becomes law, or (3) fail to sign it, and return it to the House in which it originated with a statement of his reasons for objecting to it. The last is the direct or ordinary veto. *After the session* has ended, he may either (4) sign it within a ten-day period, and thus complete its enactment, or (5) fail to sign it, in which case it fails to become law by the so-called "pocket veto." For many years it was assumed that the fourth was an impossible case, constitutionally, since with Congress adjourned there was no house to which to return the bill as provided in the Constitution.[14] It was then the custom for the President to go to the capitol for some hours at the end of the session in order to sign bills as fast as they were rushed through, and to return them before Congress adjourned. Woodrow Wilson got a ruling from the Attorney General upholding his power to sign bills after adjournment. The Supreme Court has upheld this view, and every President now uses this power.[15] The advantage of this arrangement is that it gives the President sufficient time to give more careful consideration to the many bills that are passed in the closing days of the session.

Pocket Veto. Congress can do nothing immediately about a pocket veto. Bills that fail in that way cannot be revived until the next session, and then,

[14] W. H. Taft, *Our Chief Magistrate and His Powers*, pp. 23-24.
[15] See L. F. Schmeckebier, "Approval of Bills After Adjournment of Congress," *Am. Pol Sci. Rev.*, vol. 33, pp. 52-54 (1939).

if Congress insists upon passing them, they must be reenacted early enough in the session to make possible a direct veto, which can be overriden. The bill may be passed again in both houses, and if two-thirds of the members present and voting again approve it, it becomes a law without the President's signature. In these cases, then, the President has not only achieved a postponement and a reconsideration, but he has also forced another yea and nay vote, so that the members are put on record.

Nature of the Veto Power. The power of the President to disapprove legislation can be looked upon as having a twofold purpose: *first*, to enable the executive to prevent serious encroachments by Congress on his own powers; and *second*, to give him a strong voice in general legislative policy. It has been argued by some that this power was intended to be of limited scope, and that it should be exercised only when the President feels that an act passed by Congress is unconstitutional. Under this theory Congress would be wholly responsible for the *policy* of all legislation. This has not been the view of the majority of Presidents, and the growth of the President's leadership in legislation and in party matters makes this limited view of the veto power impracticable. The words of the Constitution support the broader view: "if he approve he shall sign it," but otherwise he shall state his "objections" and return the bill to Congress.

Exercise of the Veto Power.[16] Early Presidents made little use of the veto. With Jackson the Presidency took on a new phase. Jackson looked on himself as the leader in a great popular cause, whether against Congress, the courts, or the banks, and he vigorously asserted the independence of the executive department. His vetoes, though not numerous by present-day standards, struck a new and stronger note. President Johnson, faced by a hostile Congress, vetoed many acts but his successor, Grant, vetoed many more.

Presidential use of the veto power was evidently on the increase, and yet all the twenty-one Presidents before Cleveland vetoed only 202 acts, 117 by direct or regular vetoes and 85 by the pocket veto method. Cleveland, in his efforts to prevent the indiscriminate pensioning of men from the Union Army who could not qualify under the general laws vetoed 584 acts, or nearly three times as many as all his predecessors. His total is still the record for an eight-year period. Franklin Roosevelt in a little over twelve years vetoed 635 bills, 372 by regular vetoes and 263 by pocket vetoes. From the beginning of Cleveland's first term until Franklin Roosevelt's death early in 1945, eleven Presidents vetoed a total of 1,563 bills, 894 by regular vetoes and 669 by pocket vetoes. The grand totals down to President Truman are 1,011 direct or regular vetoes, 754 pocket vetoes, or 1,765 in all, a truly impressive total.

Of this total number only 59 measures were passed over direct vetoes. Fifteen of these overriding acts were passed in President Johnson's administra-

---

[16] Data on the use of the President's veto power were drawn from a table compiled by Professor George C. Robinson of Iowa State Teachers' College and certain additional information supplied by the Legislative Reference Service of the Library of Congress.

tion, nine in Franklin Roosevelt's. Vetoes of minor bills nearly always stand, but when a major measure is backed by important pressure groups the President is likely to be overridden. Such was the case with several soldiers' bonus measures after World War I, the Volstead Act when the Anti-Saloon League was strong, and the Philippine Independence Act, which was strongly supported by the "Agricultural Bloc."

Net Results of Veto Power. But what are the governmental results of the President's possession of the veto? Surely it strengthens his position as against Congress. Even though the opposing party controls Congress, the President's party usually has over one-third of one of the houses, and that is enough to uphold him on a straight party vote. Thus at such a time strongly partisan measures cannot be passed, and Congress is likely to be relatively inactive. For political purposes, however, such a Congress may pass bills that force the President to do the unpopular thing in vetoing them. Such vetoes may become campaign issues for the opposing party which on coming into power later, sometimes passes a measure previously vetoed.[17] Even a Congress controlled by the President's own party sometimes embarrasses him by passing a bill that they know he must veto, and then enough members of the party later switch their votes to uphold the veto. In many cases a vetoed bill is amended to meet the President's wishes and is then repassed and approved. Often a threat of veto is sufficient to force its proponents to make important modifications in a pending measure.

CONGRESSIONAL CHECKS UPON THE EXECUTIVE

On its own side Congress has certain powers of control over the executive. It alone of the three branches can propose constitutional amendments to the states; by two such amendments the method of electing the President, the beginning of his term, and the rules of succession to the office have been changed.[18] An attempt by amendment to limit his powers is not inconceivable. Congress also passes measures for establishing, regulating, and altering all divisions of the executive department, and such has been its jealousy of executive freedom that it has usually fixed the salaries, tenure of office, duties, and powers of officers and employees in considerable detail. Its control of the purse reinforces its legislative power, and is used to advance or hold back departments according to Congressional desire. Presidents might, theoretically, veto more acts than they do, but often they dare not for fear of losing the necessary appropriations.

The special powers of the Senate to reject or amend treaties and to disapprove the President's nominees for appointive office will be discussed later.[19]

[17] The Budget and Accounting Act, 1921, for example, was vetoed by President Wilson, and then repassed by Congress and signed by President Harding.

[18] Amendments XII, XX.

[19] See chs. 14, 23.

Power of Impeachment. The two houses may also remove from office a President or any of his important subordinates by a process called "impeachment." This may be defined as the power and method of ousting high officials from office by action of the legislature. It usually consists of two stages, the bringing of charges, which is the impeachment in the strict sense; and the trial of the case, with the resultant verdict, which if successful results in removal from office. The provisions for impeachment in the national Constitution read as follows:

> The President, Vice President, and all civil Officers of the United States, shall be removed from Office on Impeachment for, and Conviction of, Treason, Bribery, or other high Crimes and Misdemeanors. (Art. II, sec. 4.) The House of Representatives . . . shall have the sole power of Impeachment. (Art. I, sec. 2, par. 5.) The Senate shall have the sole Power to try all Impeachments. When sitting for that Purpose, they shall be on Oath or Affirmation. When the President of the United States is tried, the Chief Justice shall preside: And no Person shall be convicted without the Concurrence of two thirds of the Members present. Judgment in Cases of Impeachment shall not extend further than to removal from Office, and disqualification to hold and enjoy any Office of honor, Trust or Profit under the United States: but the Party convicted shall nevertheless be liable and subject to Indictment, Trial, Judgment and Punishment, according to Law. (Art. I, sec. 3, pars. 6, 7.)

Impeachment Procedure in Congress. When charges are reported to the House of Representatives against any person subject to impeachment, that body may on the motion of a member appoint a select committee to investigate the charges, or assign the task to some standing committee. After conducting its inquiry, such committee either formulates and votes a series of charges, or drops the matter. Sometimes the officer being investigated resigns at this stage, and nothing more can be done except through regular criminal prosecution by the proper authorities. If there is no resignation, the committee reports its charges to the House, which passes on them by ordinary majority vote, and if the charges are approved, in the form of articles of impeachment, a committee of managers is appointed by the House to prosecute the case before the Senate, and the latter body is notified. The Senate then votes to hear the charges, and later on a regular trial is held. At the end the Senate must vote, and a two-thirds vote of those present is necessary to convict.

Impeachments in Practice. While this power of impeachment is undoubtedly a necessary one for use in unusual cases, it is obviously a cumbersome and time-consuming method of achieving the desired result of removing officers who have been guilty of criminal conduct in office, or of conduct or official acts detrimental to the public welfare. The House has voted articles of impeachment only thirteen times, with only four convictions. Ten of these cases affected federal judges; one a President, Johnson; one a Secretary of War; and one a Senator (in which case expulsion from the Senate ended the matter). Only four persons, all judges, have been removed from office in this way. It appears, then, that as an emergency weapon, "a gun behind the door," the power of impeachment may have a little value, but that its usefulness for day-to-day control by Congress over the administration is very small.

Controls over Executive Functions. As far as the President's strictly executive work is concerned, and this includes also his powers as commander in chief of the army and navy, Congress can do very little to control his actions. The entire executive power is vested by the Constitution in the President. Influenced and guided as it is by the controlling principle that "the government must be carried on," Congress cannot avoid providing authority, money, and personnel for the essential public services. Having done this much—and in certain instances it has refused to appropriate money—it is relatively helpless to interfere in the execution of the laws and the administration of the services.

Control over Expenditures. It has been found in fact that even its control over the purse is not absolute. For over a century and a half it has attempted to enforce the rule that no money shall be expended from the national treasury except in the amounts and for the purposes stated in its appropriation acts. Up to now it has never succeeded in making this rule effective. Not only in cases of outright emergency but even in the normal conduct of their affairs executive agencies spend more than was appropriated, or vary the purposes of expenditure. When they have overspent their allotments, they come before Congress with requests for "deficiency appropriations" and Congress generally yields.[20]

Control over Administrative Powers and Procedures. Congress is also unable to supervise or control the day-to-day work of the many administrative officers and agencies that make up the executive branch under the President. The members of Congress have too much other work to do, or they lack the knowledge of what to look for, and even their committees are not so organized and staffed as to be able to keep in close touch with the operations of the administrative agencies.

When members of Congress think of these two irritating problems, the enforcement of restrictions on expenditures, and the continuous supervision of administration, the easiest solution seems to be to get someone else to do the work. The office of Comptroller General was set up to watch expenditures, and the United States courts have received varying powers of review over administrative rules, orders, and decisions. These have been partially effective, but they have not really enhanced the control of Congress itself over the executive branch. To delegate new powers to other agencies is not

[20] For a discussion of this topic see Lucius Wilmerding, Jr., *The Spending Power, A History of the Efforts of Congress to Control Expenditures*, New Haven, 1943.

an effective way to recover powers already delegated. If Congress really wants to exercise control its members and committees will have to do more of the work themselves.

The Power of Investigation. More effective than such new delegations is a power not expressly mentioned in the Constitution but long and rather successfully practiced—the power of Congressional investigation into the work of executive agencies. Congress has simply assumed the power to investigate the executive branch and all its works at any time. This power is so natural an incident to the legislative power that its existence can hardly be questioned. "We are of opinion," the Supreme Court has said, "that the power of inquiry—with process to enforce it—is an essential and appropriate auxiliary to the legislative function." [21] The term "investigation" is usually applied to the more formal inquiries made by one or both houses of Congress through select committees that are created by resolutions which define the scope of what is to be done. Such investigations may go into almost any subject affecting the legislature itself or any other branch of government or any proposed subject of legislation. The power includes the authority to compel witnesses to attend and to produce pertinent books and papers. The extent to which the power of investigation is used is shown by such facts as these: Between 1789 and 1928 Congress authorized about 330 investigations by committees. The increase in such investigations in recent decades is impressive; in Franklin Roosevelt's first four years the houses of Congress initiated 165 investigations, of which 85 were by their own committees and 80 by other agencies. [22]

Congressional Investigations. The House of Representatives has not made very great success of its investigating activities. This may be due to the short terms of the members, or to the strict party discipline that prevails in that House and that prevents even the most alert and vigorous of minorities from making effective demand for investigations, or to the lack of power of the House over such matters as appointments. Whatever the cause, investigations by the House, although more numerous, have been less important than those by the Senate. The latter body has in recent decades raised the investigating function and power to its highest point. The Senate has investigated almost every important evil and problem in American national life. Wall Street, the munitions industry, the oil scandals, aviation, banking, administrative reorganization, agriculture, Muscle Shoals, monopolies, and many other important matters have come under the scrutiny of Senate committees. President Truman, while serving as a Senator, made an enviable reputation for his committee's investigation of the national war effort. Newspapers have given extensive publicity to committee hearings, with much resultant education of the

[21] On Congressional investigations see McGrain v. Daugherty (1927), 273 U. S. 135.

[22] On Congressional investigations generally see Marshall E. Dimock, *Congressional Investigating Committees*, Baltimore, 1929; E. J. Eberling, *Congressional Investigations*, New York, 1940; M. N. McGeary, *The Development of Congressional Investigative Power*, New York, 1940.

public. Further, the executive has learned to fear the Senate and its investigations more than any other thing, and has perhaps been led to be more careful in the management of public affairs.[23] The explanation of the Senate's success in investigations will doubtless be found in the longer terms of the Senators, the continuity of the Senate and of its committees, the courage and independence of its members, its frequent successes in its struggles with the executive, its prestige, and the great news-value that attaches to its debates.[24]

Power to Compel Executive to Give Information. From the constitutional point of view, several questions arise respecting the powers of legislative investigating committees. The first, touching the separation of powers, is whether Congress can compel the President to deliver to an investigating committee any documents that the legislators may wish to see. The President has on a number of occasions refused to transmit documents to the Congress, even on direct request, on the ground that it was incompatible with the public interest to make the information public. The executive has, in short, as much freedom in his sphere as the legislature has in its.[25] There is no power in Congress or in the courts to compel him to divulge information.

Compulsion on Individuals to Testify. Another question concerns the extent to which private individuals may be compelled to testify before legislative investigating bodies. As to this, the investigation must be one within the general scope of the legislature and must relate to something that it can do, whether to legislate, or to impeach, or to pass on election returns, or to approve appointments.[26] Assuming that the questions asked are pertinent to a proper subject of legislative inquiry, the individual might still refuse in some cases to testify on the ground that he would be incriminating himself, and that self-incrimination cannot be compelled by a legislature any more than by a court.[27] Except for this defense, individuals are required to give testimony to legislative bodies and their committees. Congress has covered this matter by legislation that grants immunity to those who testify. Persons who refuse to give information and testimony when it is demanded by legislative committees can be punished for contempt. The committee itself cannot punish the individual, but must report to the chamber that appointed it and the latter may then order its sergeant at arms to arrest the individual and to bring him before the house, where, if he persists in his refusal, he may be sentenced directly for contempt.

The wide use of the power of legislative investigation has brought in its

[23] James A. Perkins, in his "Congressional Investigations of Matters of International Import," *Am. Pol. Sci. Rev.*, vol. 34, pp. 284-94 (1940), shows that investigations have little effect on the President's control of foreign relations.

[24] See L. Rogers, *The American Senate*, ch. VI; and Dimock, *op. cit.*, pp. 29-32.

[25] See Grover Cleveland, *The Independence of the Executive*, Princeton University Press, 1913, and his message to the Senate on March 1, 1886.

[26] The Supreme Court did not include the non-legislative functions in its discussion in McGrain v. Daugherty, footnote 21, above, but this seems to follow of necessity.

[27] See Cooley, *The Constitutional Limitations*, etc., 4th ed. (1878), p. 164, note 3.

wake a number of abuses.[28] United States Senators and Representatives have on occasion made an investigating committee a forum for political speeches, and have baited, ridiculed, and bulldozed witnesses. They have occasionally gone far outside the scope of the investigation with their questions, and they have investigated personal files, telegrams, and other records with apparent abandon. These abuses have aroused considerable opposition to all such investigations. Fortunately these are all abuses that can be controlled or eliminated by Congress itself without damage, and indeed with much benefit, to its power to investigate.

IMPROVING THE RELATIONS BETWEEN CONGRESS AND THE PRESIDENT

Toward the end of President Franklin Roosevelt's second term and from then until his death early in 1945, the relations between him and Congress grew increasingly strained. It looked as if they were headed for a period of embittered wrangling such as has occurred during several other periods of great tension in American history. A large section of his own party in Congress worked against some of his major policies, and, as he had been long in office, his Congressional relations suffered from an accumulation of grievances against him. This situation and the prospects of worse to come at a time when complete cooperation between Congress and the President seemed to be essential aroused once more an interest in institutional reforms that would improve legislative-executive relations. His unexpected death and Mr. Truman's accession to the Presidency changed the situation almost overnight. Mr. Truman had served long in the Senate and was highly acceptable to most members of Congress. His success in getting the cooperation of Congress in the first few months of his administration was almost phenomenal, but he also soon ran into strong opposition.

In the discussions before this sudden change in the situation some of the old proposals and a few new ones were brought forth. The oldest proposal and one that has had some distinguished proponents in the past was not urged strongly by any responsible leader in the recent discussions. This is simply the proposal that cabinet members be given seats in both houses with the right to speak but not to vote. Administration policies and measures could then be laid directly before Congress through chosen spokesmen, it is urged, whereas now even cabinet members usually get no closer to Congress than the meetings of its committees. Under the proposed plan, Congressmen could also ask questions of cabinet members as to executive policies, but without the President himself being there. The executive might even be given power to control some part of the time of the houses, so as to give priority in debates to administration measures.

[28] See Laird Bell, "Probes: Congress on the Warpath," *Atlantic Monthly*, vol. 160, pp. 23-31 (1937).

To carry out even these limited proposals would involve important changes in Congressional procedure. It is difficult to see what would be gained by them. When the same party controls both branches of the government, and the President has any power of leadership, there is now no real difficulty in getting party leaders in both houses to sponsor any bills proposed by the President, nor is there much difficulty in getting adequate time for such bills. Floor leaders and committees work loyally with such a President. But if his party lacks a majority in either house, Presidential spokesmen on the floor could do very little by taking up the time of the House. In fact, Congressmen generally would probably greatly prefer to have administration measures and policies explained and defended by their own colleagues than by cabinet members.

Representative Estes Kefauver of Tennessee proposed more recently that the House set aside a period of two hours once every week or two, to which cabinet members and other heads of agencies could be invited for questioning before the whole House. Presumably most of the questions would be formulated in advance.

Shortly after this proposal Secretary of State Cordell Hull, a former highly respected member of Congress, addressed the two houses in joint session upon his return from the famous Moscow Conference of the foreign secretaries of the "Big Three" (Great Britain, the United States, and the Union of Socialist Soviet Republics). His reception in Congress was very cordial, and many persons said that this type of meeting should be more frequent.

The war period brought several proposals for formal institutionalized arrangements to unite the two branches. One was for a foreign affairs advisory council to include leaders from the State department and from the foreign affairs committees of Congress. Another suggested a Joint Committee on War Problems, to represent both houses and both parties equally, which was to meet with the President and the heads of principal war agencies, to provide better information to Congress and more cordial relations between it and the executive.

These are some examples of the many proposals that were made. It is questionable whether any of the institutional changes proposed really hits the mark or would do much good. There should certainly be no objection to some experimentation in the search for new and more fruitful methods of contact between the two branches but to set up anything in a rigid form in advance would be unwise. Informal contacts and meetings of many kinds between legislative members and executive leaders are surely desirable. At the same time the integrity of the two major branches should not be compromised, and the institutions of party leadership and organization should be preserved and strengthened. The United States has under its Constitution certain strengths and advantages that are not inferior to those of any foreign system of government.

REFERENCES

John Locke, *Two Treatises of Government*, 1690, Bk. II, espec. chs. IX-XIII.

Montesquieu, *The Spirit of Laws*, 1748, Bk. XI, ch. 6.

Woodrow Wilson, *Congressional Government*, Boston, 1885.

——, *Constitutional Government in the United States*, New York, 1908.

H. L. McBain, *The Living Constitution*, New York, 1927, chs. IV, V.

W. E. Binkley, *The Powers of the President*, Garden City, 1937.

Pendleton Herring, *Presidential Leadership*, New York, 1940.

W. F. Willoughby, *The Government of Modern States*, rev. and enl. ed., New York, 1936, chs. XIV, XV.

C. G. Haines and B. M. Haines, *Principles and Problems of Government*, rev. ed., New York, 1926, Pt. III, ch. IV.

H. J. Laski, *The Dangers of Obedience*, New York, 1930, pp. 31-58.

——, *The American Presidency*, New York, 1940.

Don K. Price, "The Parliamentary and Presidential Systems," *Public Admin. Rev.*, vol. 3, pp. 317-34 (1943).

Howard White, "Executive Responsibility to Congress via Concurrent Resolution," *Am. Pol. Sci. Rev.*, vol. 36, pp. 895-900 (1942).

CHAPTER 14

The President and the Executive Power

Several aspects of the Presidency, including the general position of the office and its relation to internal legislative policy, have already been indicated. In this chapter the cluster of Presidential powers generally called "executive" will be considered, while control over foreign and military affairs will be discussed later. In dividing things up in this way for purposes of discussion the Presidency may seem to become a mere list of unrelated powers whereas in fact the office is a genuine unity filled by one live and active person.[1]

Origins. While many Americans in 1787 undoubtedly feared the creation of a powerful executive, the majority of the members of the Federal Convention, following such models as the governorship of New York and Massachusetts, and the prime ministry and the Crown in Great Britain, determined to create such an office for the national government. The Presidential office that they set forth in the Constitution was designed to vest in one person the whole executive power of the government. He was to stand on a plane of equality with the other two departments, and was not to owe his office to Congress or be checked by any "Council of Revision" or cabinet, although the Senate would pass upon major appointments and all treaties. He was, in fact, to be a sort of check upon the radicalism of legislative bodies, as that tendency had been revealed in the early state legislatures—a rallying point for conservatism and the rights of property.[2]

Theories of the Presidency. Of the various theories as to the nature of the office, three stand out distinctly: 1. The "Whig" theory was that the President should stay scrupulously within his legal powers, not attempt to be a leader in legislation, use his veto power only to prevent encroachments on his office and other unconstitutional acts, and simply enforce the laws as Congress passed them. He was to be firm, dignified, safe—a protector of prop-

[1] Compare C. C. Thach, Jr., *The Creation of the Presidency, 1775-1789*, p. ix.
[2] The author owes much at this point and later to W. E. Binkley, *The Powers of the President, Problems of American Democracy*, Garden City, 1937.

erty, not a tribune of the people or a proposer of innovations in government and business.

2. Andrew Jackson acted upon a contrary theory. He was willing to be the "tribune of the people," ready to appeal against Congress, the courts, and any or all vested interests in favor of popular rights and aspirations. Lincoln later disappointed many of his conservative followers by acting upon a somewhat Jacksonian view of his office. Theodore Roosevelt and Woodrow Wilson also accepted this theory with some modifications and put it into words. Theodore Roosevelt held that "every executive officer in high position was a steward of the people bound actively and affirmatively to do all he could for the people and not to content himself with the negative merit of keeping his talents undamaged in a napkin." [3] Woodrow Wilson looked upon the President as the "unifying force in our complex system, the leader both of his party and of the nation." [4] Franklin Roosevelt followed this line of thought more fully, perhaps, than any other President. This whole conception of the office, from the days of Jackson on, forced the more conservative interests to turn their devotion away from the Presidency and give it to Congress. The new "Whig" theory was that the legislative branch should dominate the government and should lead in matters of policy.

3. Recently a theory has been advanced that the President is a sort of business manager of a great public business corporation, "the center of energy, direction, and administrative management." [5] Here the emphasis is less on his political leadership, and more on his responsibility to keep a great administrative organization running efficiently. This theory properly calls attention to an aspect of the office that has become more important since the national government has assumed so many new and important services and business activities. Standing alone, however, the theory is inadequate as an expression of the multifarious types of things that Presidents have to do. The President's duties as commander in chief of the armed forces, as leader in foreign policy, and as head of a political party, for example, must also be given due weight. In short any theory of the office must be a very comprehensive one, one that is practically coextensive with all the interests of the nation and its government.

Whatever the theories of the Presidency may be, there are certain facts about the office and its powers that need to be marshaled if it is to be seen in its full and true proportions.

QUALIFICATIONS AND EMOLUMENTS

No person except a natural born Citizen, or a Citizen of the United States, at the time of the Adoption of this Constitution, shall

---

[3] Quoted by Taft, *Our Chief Magistrate and His Powers*, p. 143.
[4] *Constitutional Government in the United States*, pp. 57, 60.
[5] President's Committee on Administrative Management, Report of, January, 1937, p. 3.

be eligible to the Office of the President; neither shall any Person be eligible to that Office who shall not have attained to the Age of thirty-five Years, and been fourteen Years a Resident within the United States.[6]

Qualifications for Office. The clause requiring citizenship for eligibility has never been authoritatively expounded. What a "natural born citizen" may be is not fully defined. Does it include (a) a person born abroad of American parents, (b) a person born abroad, one of whose parents is American, (c) a person born in the United States of foreign-born and unnaturalized parents, or must the individual be born in this country of parents who are American citizens? As yet there has been no occasion for answering these questions. That women are eligible on the same basis as men cannot be doubted.

Age, Birthplace, and Ancestry. Up to the present time all the thirty-two different individuals who have served as President have exceeded the lower age limit of thirty-five by a considerable margin. Theodore Roosevelt, who was 42 when he succeeded McKinley at the latter's death, was the youngest incumbent of the office. Five others were also under 50 at the time of inauguration, and six were over 60, the oldest being William Henry Harrison, 68, who died in office. The other twenty were between 50 and 60.[7] Eight were natives of Virginia, seven of Ohio, four of New York, the two Adamses of Massachusetts, and the rest were scattered among nine other states, one or two to a state. Only two were born west of the Mississippi River. The names of all except Van Buren, the two Roosevelts, and Hoover are old English, Welsh, Scottish, and Scotch-Irish, and most Presidents have come from older American stock and not from families of recent immigration. In education, ability, and general attainments they have covered a wide range but the average has been very high and some Presidents have been among the most brilliant Americans of their age.

Emoluments. The Presidency carries at the present time a salary of $75,000 a year. This amount "shall neither be encreased nor diminished during the Period for which he shall have been elected, and he shall not receive within that Period any other Emolument from the United States, or any of them." [8] This provision prevents Congress from dominating the executive either by cutting off his salary or by granting him special sums beyond his salary.

OFFICIAL POWERS

President's Executive Power. The Constitution does not say that the President is "chief executive." That would imply that there are other executives, of lesser power, associated with him. Instead the phraseology is that "The executive Power shall be vested in a President of the United States of

---

[6] U. S. Const., Art. II, sec. 1, par. 5.
[7] See table in World Almanac, 1945, p. 438.
[8] U. S. Const., Art. II, sec. 1, par. 7.

America." [9] This "vesting clause" places the entire executive power of the United States government in the hands of one man. It does so by constitutional provision, beyond the power of Congress or the courts to take it away.

Case of *In re* Neagle. What is the nature of this thing called "the executive power"? Is it simply the power to enforce the laws passed by the legislative branch? If this be true, why was it necessary to add in the Constitution the clause: "he shall take care that the laws be faithfully executed, . . ."? Was it not recognized that the "executive power" is in itself a distinct power? In a leading case the President through the Attorney General assigned a federal deputy marshal to protect a federal judge who had been threatened with death by a litigant.[10] No act of Congress expressly authorized this. This deputy in fact killed the man when he again threatened the judge, and the deputy was tried for murder. The latter pleaded that he was acting under government orders, but the opposing attorneys argued that the President had no power to employ such special deputies. In upholding the power of the President to go farther than the law required or authorized, the Supreme Court asked whether the duty to see that the laws are executed is "limited to the enforcement of acts of Congress or of the treaties of the United States according to their *express terms*," or whether it includes "the rights, duties and obligations growing out of the Constitution itself, our international relations, and all the protection implied by the nature of the government under the Constitution?" In answer to its own question the court showed by examples how the duty is not strictly limited to the express words of statutes, and how the executive power and duty includes many things by implication.

The "executive power" in fact is something broader and more inclusive than the specific powers and duties listed for the President in later sections of the Constitution. It confers upon the President in the exercise of his powers a wide range of discretion. Not everything can be covered in detail in acts of Congress and treaties. There are unforeseen circumstances and emergencies. As to these the executive branch, the one branch of government that never takes a complete vacation, is empowered by the Constitution itself to act in the national interest, not in ways *contrary* to existing laws, but in ways not forbidden and as to things for which no provision has been made.

Implied Powers of the President. To put it in another way, the executive *is* the government in a very real sense. The courts and the legislature participate in exceedingly important ways, but they cannot take the place of the sleepless executive power which must be ready for every emergency. Consequently, the President, who is the executive, has *implied powers* in somewhat the same sense as Congress has. The power to formulate programs of action for carrying out the Constitution and the statutes and treaties, to organize the personnel that Congress authorizes, to direct their actions, to lay down rules of procedure, and to do related things needed to promote and protect public

[9] U. S. Const., Art. II, sec. 1, par. 1.
[10] *In re* Neagle (1890), 135 U. S. 1.

interests, are among the implied powers of the executive. Without them the executive power would be executive weakness, and the government would be paralyzed.

Limits on Executive Power. To say that "the executive power" as a totality is broader than the specific powers and duties granted to the President by the Constitution, is not to assert that the power is either unlimited or incapable of limitation. Quite the contrary. The Constitution itself shows how in the matter of appointments his power may be limited by law in the appointment of "inferior" officers.[11] Furthermore, Congress always has the power to make "necessary and proper" laws for carrying into execution the powers vested "in any department or officer" of the government. Under this power Congress may not take away the President's executive power, but it certainly may define more fully and clearly the limits of power conferred by statute on Presidential subordinates and the methods of exercising that power. But it is unlikely ever to cover everything by legislation; thus there will always be a considerable margin or fringe of implied executive power.

Appointing Power. At the center of the President's power as executive in internal affairs lies a solid core of powers expressly granted to him by the Constitution. The appointing power, for example, is stated thus:

> . . . and he shall nominate, and by and with the Advice and Consent of the Senate, shall appoint Ambassadors, other public Ministers and Consuls, Judges of the supreme Court, and all other Officers of the United States, whose Appointments are not herein otherwise provided for, and which shall be established by Law; but the Congress may by Law vest the Appointment of such inferior Officers, as they think proper, in the President alone, in the Courts of Law, or in the Heads of Departments.
>
> The President shall have power to fill up all Vacancies that may happen during the Recess of the Senate, by granting Commissions which shall expire at the End of their next Session.
>
> . . . and [he] shall Commission all the Officers of the United States.[12]

Nomination and appointment are two distinct steps in the appointing process. Legally the President has both powers, to nominate and to appoint, but the Senate is associated with him through "advice and consent" in the making of the appointments. In practice the advice and consent of the Senate follow nomination and precede appointment. Once the advice and consent of the Senate have been given, the President may make the appointment, and the Senate has no power to withdraw its consent, even though the members

---

[11] See the dissenting opinion of Justice Brandeis in the Myers case, cited in footnote 17 below, for numerous examples of Congressional acts limiting the President's powers. But were all those acts constitutional?

[12] U. S. Const., Art. II, sec. 2, pars. 2, 3; sec. 3.

have changed their minds; but the President, if he has changed his mind, may refuse to appoint even after the Senate has given its consent.

Political Considerations in Appointments. The actual process of making appointments is naturally colored and controlled by numerous political considerations. Senators and Representatives of the President's party expect to be consulted about important appointments in their own states or districts, or at least they expect the President not to appoint any person who is obnoxious to them.[13] The President, on the other hand, needs the advice of trusted leaders in the various states, and wants to make appointments that strengthen the party rather than harm it. Although the senior Senator from a state has first call on patronage, the President has some choice and he may be anxious to build up the strength of the Senator who is more loyal to him. Representatives in Congress receive consideration in the appointment of officers in their own districts. When the state is not represented in Congress by any Senator of the President's party, some Representative in Congress from the state, or some other party member will be primarily consulted. The latter may be the governor, a national committeeman, or some other fellow partisan.

Senatorial Courtesy. There is, in short, a whole series of customs and understandings concerning matters of patronage. Into the President's office pour hundreds of communications conveying recommendations concerning appointments. Telephone conversations and private memoranda are numerous. A large part of the time of the President's personal staff, and an undue amount of his own time, are taken up with patronage matters.[14] But to neglect these things is to run a very serious risk. What is more, any President who tries to put through an appointment in any state against the wishes of the Senators who represent it, often finds himself blocked by "senatorial courtesy." This phrase implies no courtesy of the Senators toward the President; quite the contrary. It means that the Senators will stand together in courtesy to each other and in protection of their privileges, and will refuse to approve nominations that are sufficiently displeasing to the Senator concerned.

Senatorial Scrutiny of Nominees. Senatorial scrutiny of nominees and their qualifications is usually brief. If the majority party Senators from the state concerned give proper assurances, little more inquiry is made. However, for the higher posts the Senate as a whole assumes more responsibility. Generally the President's nominees for department headships are accepted with little question; one important exception was that of Mr. C. B. Warren, nominated by President Coolidge to be Attorney General, and rejected by the Senate by a close vote. Nominees for the Supreme Court are generally scrutinized with considerable care, and a number have been rejected.

Vacancies and Recess Appointments. When a vacancy occurs, during the recess of the Senate, in any office subject to Presidential appointment with

13 See in general, Taft, *op. cit.*

14 Taft, *op. cit.*, pp. 59-66; F. W. Reeves and P. T. David, *Personnel Administration in the Federal Service*, pp. 2-3, 10, 13-14; also in President's Committee on Administrative Management, *Report with Special Studies*, 1937, pp. 68, 71-72.

Senate consent, the President has power to make appointments that are valid without Senate consent until the end of the next Senate session or until a successor is appointed. No such recess appointment is valid beyond the end of the session, but if the Senate fails to confirm the nomination, another recess appointment can be made. In a number of cases where the President and Senate could not agree, men have held offices by Presidential recess appointment for several years.

Inferior Officers. The appointment power over all offices "established by law" (and that, in general, would seem to be the only way in which they can be established) belongs to the President with the advice and consent of the Senate, unless Congress otherwise provides. Congress has no constitutional power to take appointments into its own hands, but may vest the appointment of "inferior officers" in one of the following: (a) the President alone, (b) the courts of law, and (c) the heads of departments. A full definition of what is an inferior officer has never been given. It may be assumed that all officers who are now by law appointable in one of the three ways mentioned are inferior, and that Supreme Court justices, ambassadors, and heads of departments are *not* inferior. Between these categories there are some thousands of ordinary and non-emergency positions of undetermined status that are filled by the President with Senate consent.

Numbers of Presidential Appointments. Despite the increased use of examinations for selecting personnel, the President has had an increasing burden in the making of appointments. In the 1940 session of Congress the President sent 17,732 nominations to the Senate, including over 10,000 in the military services, over 6,000 in the postal service, and more than 1,000 to the other civilian positions.[15] During the war years this number was greatly increased. The total for ten years through 1942 was over 100,000 nominations submitted. Naturally the President could not give personal attention to the great majority of these. It is a little hard to believe that many of them, such as first, second, and third class postmasters, and federal marshals, are not inferior officers whose appointment could be vested in the heads of departments. Indeed, all postmasters were appointed by the Postmaster General until 1836. Despite recent merit system laws, the President must still appoint, with Senate approval, many hundreds of persons whose appointments could be otherwise provided for. The reason is primarily that Senators, Representatives, and even some Presidents, and the party organizations that stand behind them, do not wish to give up all patronage, with all that it means in the way of rewarding party workers and building up the party organization. In a close election, this host of political appointees, spread all over the country, may be just the force needed to bring victory to the party.

Certain Senators have tried in recent years to have even more national officials and employees put in the class that requires Senatorial approval.[16]

---

[15] See Am. Pol. Sci. Rev., vol. 35, p. 301 (1941); also Reeves and David, op. cit., pp. 13-14
[16] See Arthur W. Macmahon, "Senatorial Confirmation," Pub. Admin. Rev., vol. 3, pp 281-96 (1943).

One proposal was that all officials and employees who are paid $4,500 a year or more should have their appointments approved by the Senate. Already the President's personal staff must give a great deal of attention to appointments in the national service, but if any such proposal were to be enacted the burden would become very much greater.

Removals by the President. The Constitution makes no provision on the subject of removals from office, except in the clause dealing with impeachments. The President is given the power to appoint, but nothing is said about the power to remove. In the very first Congress the question came up concerning the President's power to remove the Secretary of State, but it was agreed that this official was one of those high, confidential and political officers that the President could probably remove without express authority in the statutes, so that the law then enacted to create the office said nothing about removals. In time it came to be assumed that in the absence of any statutory provisions concerning removal, officers appointed by the President with the consent of the Senate could be removed by the President alone. In other words, a power to remove was *implied* from the President's power to appoint, or from this and his executive power combined.

Attempts to Limit Power of Removal. President Jackson removed so many officers, and so summarily, that the Senate began to protest, and a sharp controversy arose concerning the power. It seemed that the only way to check the President was to provide by law for Senate consent to removals. Thus the original idea of this sort of Senatorial check on removals was to protect supposedly meritorious men in office against partisan removals. Congress would not go this far, but in 1836 for the first time Congress enacted that postmasters should be appointed by the President by and with the consent of the Senate. After the Civil War the Republican Congress, in its struggle to wrest control of the government from President Johnson, passed, over his veto, the Tenure of Office Act (1867) under which the President could not remove, without Senate approval, any officer appointed by him with Senate consent—not even a department head, a member of his cabinet. President Johnson chose to disregard the act as unconstitutional, and was impeached, though not convicted on the impeachment charges. Later Presidents urged the repeal of the act, and in 1887 it was repealed.

The Myers Case. A similar act of 1876 relating to postmasters remained, however, and in 1920 President Wilson raised a new controversy by removing a postmaster of the city of Portland, Oregon, without getting the consent of the Senate as required by the act. When suit was brought in the Court of Claims for his salary, the constitutional question of the removal power was brought squarely before the Supreme Court on appeal.[17] The decision, in which six justices concurred, was that the President has the sole and exclusive power to remove "executive officers" appointed by him even where Senate consent is required for appointment, and that Congress has no power to

[17] Myers v. United States (1926), 272 U. S. 52.

restrict the President's authority by requiring the Senate's approval for such removals. The President's power was drawn, by implication, not merely from the power to appoint, but from the executive power and the duty to take care that the laws be faithfully executed. How could the President enforce law if disobedient or inefficient underlings could not be discharged?

Three justices of the Supreme Court, Brandeis, Holmes, and McReynolds, dissented against the majority decision, and there was considerable public criticism of it as leading to excessive power in the hands of the President. The minority justices particularly pointed out how the work of certain great boards and commissions like the Interstate Commerce Commission and the Federal Trade Commission could be disrupted and made subject to political control if the President had an illimitable power of removal. The Whig distrust of strong executives and confidence in legislative action were at the bottom of much in the dissent.

The Humphrey Case. Some years later a new case arose involving the removal of a member of the Federal Trade Commission.[18] William E. Humphrey had been reappointed to the Federal Trade Commission for a seven-year term in 1931, under a statute providing that members could be removed by the President only for inefficiency, neglect of duty, or malfeasance in office. President Roosevelt removed Humphrey from office on the grounds of differences in opinion as to policy, without alleging that he had been inefficient, neglectful, or a wrong-doer in office, and suit was filed for the balance of his salary. The question taken to the Supreme Court was whether the act restricting the President's power of removing members of the commission was constitutional. In this case the court unanimously upheld the act, and thus denied the President's power to remove Humphrey without legal cause. It held that the Federal Trade Commission's duties "are neither political nor executive, but predominantly quasi-judicial and quasi-legislative." The commission is, in fact, "wholly disconnected from the executive department," and "exercises no part of the executive power vested by the Constitution in the President."

Thus, to maintain the independence of such regulatory tribunals, the Supreme Court, which had written new constitutional law in the Myers case, found itself forced to write more new law in the Humphrey case. There is no word in the Constitution about "quasi-legislative and quasi-judicial" commissions or other similar bodies. The Constitution does not recognize any class of officers except legislative, executive, and judicial, the three separate and presumably distinct departments. This recognition by the court of certain separate or intermediate types of functions and powers may be more important in the long run than the limitation on the President's removal power.

Despite the unanimity of the court in this decision the author ventures to question the correctness of what was said, as quoted above. The President is vested with the entire executive power of the United States. It is he who is required to "take care that the laws be faithfully executed." In the agencies

18 Humphrey's Executor (Rathbun) v. United States (1935), 295 U. S. 602.

under him, and for which public opinion holds him responsible, there are almost innumerable cases of the exercise of powers just like those vested in the Federal Trade Commission. The words "quasi-judicial" and "quasi-legislative" are vague and almost indefinable, but if all the activities that can be characterized by these words are therefore "wholly disconnected with the executive department" then there is little or nothing left of the executive power. If the court had simply said that, as to agencies set up by Congress within the executive branch, Congress may use its discretion within limits as to the terms on which men shall be appointed and removed, its position would have been far more defensible. This was practically what Justice Holmes said in his dissent in the Myers case. What the court did say was that commissions like the Federal Trade Commission may be set up as permanent agencies not under the executive but in a new and dubious position as agencies "of the legislative or judicial departments" (which one is not stated), and may be empowered "to carry into effect legislative policies embodied in the statute," etc.—but that is simply another way of describing an executive function. If carrying into effect legislative policies is not executive, then almost nothing is.

Status of Comptroller General. The problem of the Presidential power to remove officers is also brought out by the office of the Comptroller General. This office was created by act of Congress in 1921, after Wilson had in 1920 vetoed a similar bill on the ground that it was unconstitutional. His reason for the veto was that the Comptroller General was to be given a fifteen-year term, and was not to be removable by the President at all, but only by joint resolution of Congress, after notice and hearing. The powers given to this officer were and are such that he can interfere with the work of the executive departments, and yet he is not responsible to the President. Clearly if Congress can vest more and more powers in such officers as the Comptroller General, and in such commissions as are described by the court as "quasi-legislative and quasi-judicial," great inroads can be made upon the powers of the President.[19]

Power of Direction and Control. In so far as the strictly executive departments are concerned, the President has a power of direction and control over them that is partly expressed and partly implied from his general executive power. The Constitution provides that "he may require the Opinion in writing, of the principal Officer in each of the executive Departments, upon any subject relating to the Duties of their respective Offices."[20] This provision was undoubtedly intended to make it the duty of the heads of departments to report to the President. While it is true that some departments, such as the Treasury, are expressly required by statute to make formal reports also to Congress, the real responsibility of department heads for all matters of

[19] See President's Committee on Administrative Management, *Report with Special Studies,* pp. 219-228.

[20] U. S. Const., Art. II, sec. 2, par. 1.

policy is to the President. Each department head has, of course, a personal legal responsibility under the statutes; he may not violate the law. But the political responsibility for all that the departments do is that of the President alone.

Cabinet Is Without Powers. This lack of any political responsibility on the part of the department heads leads to the curious impotence and irresponsibility of that organ that is called the cabinet. The public generally seems to think that this body consists of the ten department heads. Actually it has no fixed composition at all, since it has never been set up by either an Act of Congress or a Presidential order. It consists of those high officers and personal advisers whom the President chooses to invite. During the attacks upon the "personal government" of President Franklin Roosevelt there was much talk about "restoring cabinet government." A more egregious blunder, or studied distortion of the facts about the American system of government, it would be hard to find. The United States has never had "cabinet government."

The Convention of 1787 decided against the creation of a special council to advise and control the President in executive matters. Under Washington there were at first but three recognized departments, namely, foreign affairs, treasury, and war, with the Attorney General's office as a possible fourth. Washington consulted with the heads of these departments separately, and he began also to call the four together. In a few years these informal meetings of the department heads with the President came to have the name "cabinet" attached to them in popular discussions, and the word has continued without any express legislation to provide for such an organization.[21] Indeed to this day the cabinet has no legal existence, powers, or responsibility as a body. It has never acquired anything more than an advisory capacity. It meets at regular hours, several times a week as a rule, and also on special call according to the President's convenience. There is, naturally, no published record of its deliberations. It issues no orders, no proclamations, not even announcements. Its discussions help, no doubt, in the co-ordination of work between and among departments, but even for this purpose it is sometimes less important than special war councils and emergency councils set up at times of great national stress or activity. It is only one part of the extensive machinery of consultation that the Presidents have set up to assist them in their duties.

Other Powers. Also not mentioned in the Constitution is the so-called "ordinance-making power" of the President. This extensive and important power is discussed later in Chapter 19.

In connection with his executive duty to see that the laws are enforced, the President has also the power to use the army, navy, and the militia (national guard) of the states.[22] This results from the fact that he is commander in chief of the armed forces by constitutional provision. Congress has by law

---

[21] On the history of the cabinet see Learned, *The President's Cabinet*, espec. chs. II-VI; McLaughlin, *A Constitutional History of the United States*, ch. XVII.

[22] U. S. Const., Art. II, sec. 2, par. 1; Art. IV, sec. 4.

put some limitations on his use of the forces, but the final discretion with respect to when and how they shall be used to enforce law and to prevent domestic disturbance rests with him.

Pardons, Reprieves, and Amnesty. Closely related to the executive power is, also, the power conferred on the President by the Constitution "to Grant Reprieves and Pardons for Offenses against the United States, except in Cases of Impeachment." [23] This power is his to use alone and as he sees fit. In practice he gets most of his information and advice on pardon matters from the Attorney General's department, in which there is a director of prisons, a pardon attorney, and a parole board, to look after different phases of the penal problem. A *pardon* is a grant to an individual offender or to named offenders of release from the punishment that has been imposed on them. It may be complete or conditional. It may be issued even before conviction, but usually it is given after a criminal has served at least part of his sentence. The power to grant pardons conditionally includes also the power to reduce the penalty, or to commute a sentence, as when a death penalty is commuted into a sentence of life imprisonment. A reprieve is a postponement of the execution of a sentence, as in the case where a death penalty has been imposed, and the time for carrying it out is postponed.

The President has also what is known as the power of *amnesty*. This is the power to order that a whole class of persons subject to trial for a certain type of crime, or who have been convicted thereof, shall be released from the consequences of their acts. It was used during and after the Civil War, for example, with respect to those who had opposed the government with arms. Something similar to this took place also when, upon the repeal of the Eighteenth Amendment, the President ordered that all further prosecutions for violation of the prohibition laws be stopped.

It goes without saying, of course, that the President may not pardon offenders against state and local laws. That power is reserved to state and local officials. The restriction preventing him from pardoning in cases of impeachment was wisely designed to prevent a President from restoring to office one of his partisans who has been impeached and removed by Congress.

Even so brief a consideration of the executive powers of the President suggests the tremendous amount of work that, with the growth of population and governmental activity, has been imposed by the Constitution and laws upon one man. In addition, the laws have failed to relieve him of a very considerable amount of detailed and routine work, such as the signing of hundreds of commissions and other documents. Congress could authorize someone else to sign many things for him, but citizens want the President's own signature, even though it is inscribed by him by use of a machine that permits him to sign a number of documents at once. On top of all this he must spend some time each day in meeting people who feel they must be able

[23] U. S. Const., Art. II, sec. 2, par. 1.

to say that they have met the President, and other long hours in answering correspondence.

Effect of War on President's Powers. It is frequently said that in the course of United States history the President's powers have grown at the expense of Congress, and also that his powers have grown most rapidly in times of war and other crises. It is certainly true that Presidents today have a much more active role in the nation's government than certain earlier Presidents had, and also that the affairs of government are far more numerous and perhaps more complicated than they used to be. In a purely constitutional sense it is very questionable, however, whether the President's powers have grown at all. From the beginning in 1788 the office of the President has been endowed with the entire executive power of the national government, the whole power of commander in chief of the armed forces, and a number of other specific powers. These express powers have not been changed, added to, or subtracted from, since the Constitution was adopted.

Wars, crises, and other emergencies do not add to these powers in the constitutional sense, but they do give occasion for more numerous and more important exercises of power. Furthermore, in times of crisis like the recent war, Congress perforce delegates more authority to the President for the duration of the war (not for longer) and leaves more to executive action than it would in times of peace and quiet. Thus, when the emergency ends, the relative positions of President and Congress are substantially restored in the practical sense, and as far as the written Constitution is concerned those positions never were changed.

World War II and the defense period that preceded the United States entry into it, provided many examples of important Presidential actions that would not have taken place in time of peace.[24] The declarations of the several defense emergencies, the deal for air bases in exchange for over-age destroyers, the warning to Congress to pass anti-inflation legislation or the President would act within the range of his powers, the seizure of industries and commercial establishments to avert or to end strikes, and the authorization to develop the atomic bomb at tremendous cost, are some outstanding examples. These do not represent additions to the President's constitutional powers but new modes of exercising powers that already existed. Latent powers merely became active. More than anything else the war revealed to the people of the United States that the executive head of a great nation that is active in war and in international leadership must make decisions of tremendous importance and do so quickly at times.

It is a happy circumstance that the framers of the Constitution made the powers of the President adequate to the needs of the executive office of a great nation. In three grave periods of national crisis, 1861, 1917, and 1941, the nation has been so fortunate, also, as to have in the office of President

---

[24] See Louis William Koenig, *The Presidency and the Crisis, Powers of the Office from the Invasion of Poland to Pearl Harbor*, New York, 1944.

a man of outstanding ability, of great devotion to duty, and with a sense of responsibility to the Constitution and to the people. This has made it possible for the nation to wage war vigorously and successfully without danger of dictatorship.

The President's Personal Staff. For the handling of the great amount of work that comes to his office, the President has a considerable personal staff in "the White House office" including three private secretaries, a personal secretary, a group of administrative assistants, and an executive clerk. Much of the routine correspondence is handled for the President by this staff, but the amount that is left for him to do is still prodigious. The difficulty is, of course, that he is not only the titular and "ornamental" head of the administration, comparable to the king in Great Britain, but also the active, working head, comparable to the prime minister, and that in addition his cabinet members do not share the responsibilities of government with him as is the case in the parliamentary system. Thus concentration of duties and responsibilities has been carried almost to the breaking point.

Divisions of Executive Office. Full recognition of this situation was first evidenced in the 1937 plans for administrative reorganization of the national government. In the next few years, these plans were largely carried out.[25] The Executive Office of the President was reorganized in 1939 and 1940 by attaching directly to the President the Bureau of the Budget and the National Resources Planning Board, and by establishing a group of new units, each under an administrative assistant to deal with personnel management, the issuance of government reports, and emergency management. When the war broke out in Europe and spread over the world, the President of the United States had, for the first time in history, a group of staff aides and supporting agencies adequate to the needs of his office.[26] Further changes were made in the organization of the Executive Office even during the war, but the essentials were already provided before Pearl Harbor.

REFERENCES

Charles C. Thach, Jr., *The Creation of the Presidency, 1775-1789: A Study in Constitutional History*, Baltimore, 1922.

William H. Taft, *Our Chief Magistrate and His Powers*, New York, 1916.

——, *The Presidency*, New York, 1916.

James Hart, *The Ordinance Making Powers of the President of the United States*, Baltimore, 1925.

Woodrow Wilson, *Constitutional Government in the United States*, New York, 1908, ch. III.

Edward S. Corwin, *The President's Removal Power Under the Constitution*, New York, 1927.

[25] See "The Executive Office of the President: A Symposium," *Pub. Admin. Rev.*, vol. 1, pp. 101-40 (1941).

[26] Louis Brownlow, in *Pub. Admin. Rev.*, vol. 1, p. 105 (1941).

Norman J. Small, *Some Presidential Interpretations of the Presidency*, Baltimore, 1932.

National Archives of the United States, *Federal Register*. Publication began March 14, 1936.

Howard L. McBain, *The Living Constitution*, New York, 1927, ch. IV.

U. S. President's Committee on Administrative Management, *Report with Special Studies*, Washington, 1937.

C. G. Haines and M. E. Dimock (eds.), *Essays on the Law and Practice of Governmental Administration*, Baltimore, 1935, pp. 47-93.

W. E. Binkley, *The Powers of the President*, New York, 1937.

Pendleton Herring, *Presidential Leadership*, New York, 1940.

H. J. Laski, *The American Presidency*, New York, 1940.

Edward S. Corwin, *The Presidency, Office and Powers*, New York, 1940.

J. M. Mathews, *The American Constitutional System*, 2nd ed., New York, 1940, chs. X, XII.

Clarence A. Berdahl, *War Powers of the Executive in the United States*, Urbana, 1921.

Robert S. Rankin, *Readings in American Government*, New York, 1939, pp. 137-50.

John M. Mathews and Clarence A. Berdahl, *Documents and Readings in American Government: National and State*, rev. ed., New York, 1940, pp. 246-98.

A. N. Christensen and E. M. Kirkpatrick, *The People, Politics, and the Politician: Readings in American Government*, New York, 1941, pp. 355-66, 435-44.

Louis William Koenig, *The Presidency and the Crisis, Powers of the Office from the Invasion of Poland to Pearl Harbor*, New York, 1944.

L. Vaughn Howard and Hugh A. Bone, *Current American Government*, New York, 1943.

Arthur W. Macmahon, "Senatorial Confirmation," *Pub. Admin. Rev.*, vol. 3, pp. 281-96 (1943).

CHAPTER 15

The National Administrative Organization

No one can begin to comprehend the present national government of the United States without spending some days in the capital. Washington is a city of over 660,000 inhabitants. In its suburbs live probably 300,000 more. This metropolis of approximately a million people is not noted for its manufacturing and commerce; it is, as it was intended to be, almost entirely a political and administrative center for the nation's government. At first the visitor goes to see the White House, the Capitol, the Supreme Court Building, the Library of Congress, the memorials and museums. Soon it dawns upon him, however, that these are only the most noted and most publicized buildings. Up and down some of the main avenues are immense government office buildings, one after another. They are quite unlike modern city skyscrapers. Their rather heavy, classic pillared design becomes somewhat tiresome when it is seen so often repeated. What is most impressive about the buildings is their tremendous size and the great areas they cover. The buildings of the Departments of Agriculture, Commerce, and Interior in the District are noteworthy in this respect, but those of the Navy, Social Security Board and others are also very large. Soon the visitor learns, however, that some of the offices he wants to visit are not in these great central buildings at all. Many are scattered around Washington in less pretentious quarters. Others are outside the District like the giant Army headquarters, The Pentagon, across the Potomac in Virginia, and the group of Census Bureau buildings in Suitland, Maryland. Even before World War II the crowding in Washington was very great. To avoid the congestion the administration of the social security numbers and accounts was set up in Baltimore. When the war came other huge units were simply moved to other cities, the Patent Office largely to Richmond, Virginia, for example, the Farm Credit Administration to Kansas City, Missouri, and the Rural Electrification Administration to St. Louis.

All this is only a partial sketch of the tremendous facilities that are required for the many services of the present-day national government. The civilian field services that operate throughout the nation and in many foreign places account for over three-fourths of the national government's personnel. They occupy buildings and use other facilities in hundreds of cities and villages and in rural and forest areas.

This chapter will deal with the organization of the civilian administrative agencies of the national government. It will not cover Congress, the court system, or the armed forces. Those marginal agencies that the Supreme Court has designated as "quasi-legislative" and "quasi-judicial" will be considered as parts of the administrative branch. It appears that Congress, which created these agencies, also generally takes this view of their position in the government.

The administrative organization of any active government, business, or association constantly changes, to meet new conditions and to satisfy new needs. Before considering this dynamic aspect of the administrative organization of the national government, let us first take a snapshot of it as it was late in 1945, and name some of its principal parts. At that time the agencies of government could be classified roughly as follows: [1]

1. **Over-all or "Topside" Agencies.** This group includes first those connected directly with the President. These are designated as belonging to the Executive Office of the President, and the most important are (a) the White House office, (b) the Bureau of the Budget, (c) the Liaison Office for Personnel Management, and (d) the Office of Emergency Management. The first three are active in assisting the President on political, executive, and financial matters, and on appointments. The fourth, the Office of Emergency Management, was useful in the early days of the war in facilitating the work of the many new war agencies but has recently waned in importance. Two other important agencies that belong in this over-all group are (e) the Civil Service Commission, and (f) the General Accounting Office under the Comptroller General. The Civil Service Commission is fairly close to the President, although not a part of his executive office, but the General Accounting Office, which exercises a comprehensive auditing function over national receipts and expenditures, is set up to be quite independent.

Toward the end of the war there was created, also, an Office of War Mobilization which, by an act of Congress, became the Office of War Mobilization and Reconversion under a director whose position is practically that of an Assistant President, and whose powers include that of co-ordinating the activities of all national agencies. This office is something distinctly new in American government.

2. **Ten Regular Departments.** In the public mind the ten regular departments stand out as the most typical and most important agencies of national administration. Actually a number of them were somewhat overshadowed

---

[1] The best source for current information on the administrative organization and functions of the national government is the *United States Government Manual,* a substantial volume that is issued now once or twice a year.

during World War II when so much was being done by special wartime agencies; and for many years now, both in peace and in war, there have been a number of other agencies similar to the departments in organization and also of great importance. The departments are distinctive in being designated as departments, in their greater age, and in the fact that each has been set up by act of Congress as a continuing administrative agency.

Listed in the order of their creation the ten departments are: State, Treasury, War, Justice, Post Office, Navy, Interior, Agriculture, Commerce, and Labor. The heads of departments are entitled Secretary in all cases except two. These two are the Attorney General, who heads Justice, and the Postmaster General. The salaries of all department heads are uniformly $15,000 a year and their terms expire with that of the President.

Each department consists of an overhead staff and a number of bureaus or units of similar rank under other titles, and these in turn may be divided up into divisions or other subordinate units. Some of the bureaus are so distinctive in their functions and traditions that they operate themselves without much guidance from the department head.

3. Miscellaneous Ordinary Operating Agencies. First under this heading may be placed four major units that are similar to departments in everything except name. These are the Veterans' Administration (rehabilitation, medical care and hospitalization, and pensions for veterans), the Federal Security Agency (social security program, public health service, and Office of Education), the Federal Works Agency (public buildings, public roads, and other works), and the Federal Loan Agency (Reconstruction Finance Corporation, and government loans to industry, commerce, and public agencies).

Under this heading belong also the Tennessee Valley Authority (TVA), the United States Maritime Commission (construction and operation of the merchant fleet), the National Housing Agency (public housing, and loans to private housing ventures), various research agencies, the units that plan, construct, and operate the public facilities of the District of Columbia and administer its government, the American Battle Monuments Commission, and other agencies too numerous to list. These many units of administration, together with the next group, are sometimes called the "independent agencies" because they are not attached to any department.

4. National Regulatory Boards and Commissions. When the national government wishes to regulate some branch or aspect of the nation's economy, while leaving ownership and operation in private hands, it usually sets up a plural body called a board or commission, and charges its members with a joint responsibility for administering the law. The most outstanding of these agencies are the Interstate Commerce Commission (railroads and other means of transportation), the Federal Reserve Board (banking operations and monetary controls), Federal Deposit Insurance Corporation (bank examination and insurance of deposits), Federal Trade Commission (preventing unfair competition and monopolization), Federal Communications Commission (radio, telegraph, telephone), Federal Power Commission (dams and power developments in navigable waters, interstate transmission of electricity and natural gas), United States Tariff Commission, National Labor Relations Board, National Mediation Board (labor disputes on railroads and other transportation systems), and Railroad Retirement Board (pensions for retiring railroad workers). It should be added that other government agencies not here listed also have important regulatory functions over commerce and industry (e.g., Department of Agriculture over grain, cotton, and cattle exchanges).

5. Emergency Agencies for War and Reconversion. Had this book been written in wartime several chapters would have been needed to describe the more important wartime agencies of the national government and the controls that they exercised over the entire national economy. All civilians will remember the rationing of certain civilian goods (meats and fats, sugar, canned goods, shoes, gasoline, and fuel oil) and some will recall with satisfaction the price and rent controls that prevented uncontrolled inflation. This program of activities was largely entrusted to OPA (Office of Price Administration). Industrialists will remember also the War Production Board with its controls over metals, lumber, paper, and other scarce materials, and the National War Labor Board whose function it was to prevent wartime strikes and to maintain the wages of labor without letting them get so high as to threaten inflation.

WARTIME EMERGENCY ADMINISTRATIVE AGENCIES, 1945

Manpower and Labor
War Manpower Commission (WMC)
Selective Service System (SSS)
National War Labor Board (NWLB)
Committee on Fair Employment Practices (CFEP)

Economic Controls and Production
Office of Economic Stabilization (OES)
War Production Board (WPB)
Office of Price Administration (War Price and Ration Boards) (OPA)
Smaller War Plants Corporation (SWPC)
Petroleum Administration for War (PAW)
War Contracts Price Adjustment Board (WCPAB)
Defense Plant Corporation
Rubber Reserve Company
Metals Reserve Company

Transportation
Office of Defense Transportation (ODT)
War Shipping Administration (WSA)

Communications and Information
Office of War Information (OWI)
Office of Censorship (OC)
Board of War Communications (BWC)

Civilian Welfare
Office of Civilian Defense (OCD)

Research
Office of Scientific Research and Development (OSRD)
Office of Strategic Services (OSS)

Foreign Affairs
Office of Co-ordinator of Inter-American Affairs (OCIAA)
Foreign Economic Administration (FEA)
Office of Alien Property Custodian (OAPC)
President's War Relief Control Board (PWRCB)

Every important aspect of the American economy was regulated during the wartime period, and it took the efforts of all the regular government agencies and of many others, created for the emergency, to accomplish the task. It is unnecessary here to describe the many emergency administrative units, or to discuss the reasons for them and the tasks that they performed. The foregoing listing of them by name and alphabetical designation, although not complete, may serve to emphasize this wartime aspect of national administration.

As previously indicated the list does not include every wartime emergency agency, but only the leading ones and a few examples of the smaller ones as they stood when the fighting ended in 1945. At that time some reconversion legislation had already been enacted and the Office of War Mobilization and Reconversion was already giving most of its attention to reconversion. There was a separate office for disposing of surplus war supplies and properties. The problems of demobilization, of getting industry and agriculture reconverted to civilian production, of ensuring high levels of employment and public services, confronted all parts of the national administration.

New administrative units, and the reorganization of older ones, will undoubtedly be needed from time to time during this crucial transition period. In fact acute national emergencies like great depressions and great wars seem to call for unusual activity in the reorganization of the national administration. Recent experience has revealed that administrative agencies that were created to meet one crisis have not all been liquidated before another emergency has arisen to demand the creation of still newer agencies. The ten years from 1946 on are likely to be such a period of transition.

6. **International Administrative Agencies.** From the end of World War II and as far as we can see into the future, the United States must be prepared to participate actively in international affairs. It was already cooperating vigorously with its wartime allies, separately or as a group, through various "joint boards" and "combined boards" while the war was in progress. In no other way could the total might of the allies have been brought to bear upon the enemy countries. As the United Nations gains members and increases in strength, more American participation in international administration will result. This means that in any survey of the administrative organization of this nation, its part in international agencies must be recognized. At least at its outer edges national administration becomes international.

The official *United States Government Manuals* in recent years have taken cognizance of this new fact. A recent issue of this manual [2] reveals several main types of international agencies in which the United States participates. First are the joint and combined boards in which the United States joined with Canada, or the United Kingdom (Great Britain), or both, on war production, shipping, and similar joint efforts. These were wartime and strictly limited organizations, and may be expected to disappear. Second are the several United Nations organizations for relief and rehabilitation, war information, and food and agriculture. These have many nations as members and presumably have somewhat longer time objectives. They will undoubtedly be in-

[2] First Edition of 1945, pp. 162-84, 204-16.

creased in number in due course by the addition of new United Nations administrative agencies in such fields as public health, narcotics control, and financial and security matters. Third, the State Department listed in 1945 over seventy different international organizations of which the United States is a member or in the work of which it participates. These all preceded the establishment of the United Nations. Some like the International Labor Office were connected with the League of Nations but others had a more independent status. Many in the list of over seventy were for scientific and cultural purposes, while others had more specific governmental and administrative possibilities. Some were Pan-American in scope, some world-wide, and others were limited to only two nations, such as the International Fisheries Commission (United States and Canada).

The foregoing conspectus of the national administrative organization of the United States inevitably conveys to the reader a number of impressions such as those of immensity, complexity, confusion, and lack of symmetry. How can so elaborate an array of administrative mechanisms be kept under public control? How can they be co-ordinated in policy and prevented from overlapping upon each other in their daily work? Is there any way in which the whole scheme could be simplified and systematized? These questions lead to a consideration of some continuing questions in American administration.

Development of Power to Organize Administration. Under the Articles of Confederation the Congress stood alone in its attempts to provide an over-all government for the thirteen states. There was no executive head to assist it, and no array of administrative agencies to carry on the war, to raise, spend, and account for public money, or to do the many other things that fall upon a central government. It struggled to administer the common affairs of the Confederation through committees of its own members. It even attempted to carry on foreign affairs in this way. The results were not satisfactory, and in the end several of the committees appointed non-members of Congress as secretaries to do their work for them. These paid officials foreshadowed the "secretaries" who head most of the executive departments of the national government today.[3]

In the Federal Convention of 1787 it was agreed that the new national government should have an executive branch separate from the legislative, that the executive branch should be headed by one man, and that the executive and administrative work of the government should be organized in departments under his direction and control. Proposals to designate certain departments in the Constitution were rejected. What the Constitution says directly on this subject of departments is rather limited. The President "may require the Opinion in writing, of the principal Officer in each of the executive Departments, upon any subject relating to the Duties of their respective Offices" and Congress may delegate to "the heads of departments" the power

[3] See Lloyd M. Short, *The Development of National Administrative Organization in the United States*, ch. II.

to appoint "inferior officers." The President's control over department heads is implied also in his power to appoint, by and with the advice and consent of the Senate "all . . . Officers of the United States, whose Appointments are not herein otherwise provided for, and which shall be established by Law." [4]

Congressional Creation of Administrative Agencies. These clauses, coupled with the general power of Congress to make all laws which shall be "necessary and proper for carrying into Execution the foregoing Powers, and all other Powers vested by this Constitution in the Government of the United States, or in any Department or Officer thereof," [5] have been construed in practice as authorizing Congress, subject to the usual executive veto, to establish, alter, combine, or abolish any and all departments and agencies in the executive branch. Since no particular executive department is frozen into the Constitution, Congress has power to alter the entire administrative organization or any part of it from time to time to meet new requirements. The question whether Congress may create administrative agencies to carry out laws without placing such agencies clearly under the President and in the executive branch is not clearly settled.[6]

Every Congress since the Constitution was established has passed laws to organize or reorganize agencies in the executive branch. In the early years Congress itself took the lead in this matter and even now, although recent Presidents have made most of the recommendations for administrative changes, Congress uses its own judgment on many questions of administrative organization, up to the point of going directly counter to the President's wishes. Congress is, therefore, very largely responsible for the present organization of the administrative branch.

Down to about 1880 the national government was relatively inactive, and Congress kept practically the entire administration within the range of seven departments, one quasi-department (Agriculture), and one independent unit (the Smithsonian Institution).[7] Since that time the situation has changed immeasurably, and the inefficacy of Congressional methods of control over the administrative organization has become increasingly clear.

Recommendations for administrative changes come to Congress from the President, from the departments, from its own members, from pressure groups. Different House and Senate committees handle these measures, according to the field or function that is concerned, and each committee works more or less by itself according to its own ideas. It must be admitted that there are not many principles of organization that every experienced administrator would accept; and a certain amount of experimenting is unavoidable. Never-

[4] U. S. Const., Art. II, sec. 2.
[5] U. S. Const., Art. I, sec. 8, par. 18.
[6] See ch. 14, above, pp. 237-39.
[7] See Lewis Meriam and Lawrence F. Schmeckebier, *Reorganization of the National Government*, ch. VIII; Lloyd M. Short, *op. cit.*, chs. X-XVIII.

theless there is little to justify the welter of organizations that Congress has authorized upon the basis of its committees' recommendations. Such words as "board," "commission," "bureau," "division," "agency," "authority," and "administration" are applied to different units without any common standards of meaning. Boards or commissions are used where a single head would be preferable. The size of commissions varies, terms are long or short, staggered or not staggered, without any evident reasons. Congress yields to pressure to create new units for new functions when some existing agency could well handle the new work. When defects in organization are called to its attention, it sometimes fails to correct them either because of pride in its own creations, or from fear or jealousy of the President, or because the pressure groups directly concerned oppose a change. Thus the advantages that should flow from complete control by Congress over the administrative organization are not fully realized.

As in other matters Congress not only lacks the inside knowledge and experience of administration that is needed, but it tends always to work at particular problems instead of keeping in mind the entire administration. Its efforts necessarily result, therefore, in a multiplicity of agencies, variety, duplication, and confusion. This is not an assertion that its work on administrative organization has all been bad nor is it a claim that any other branch of the government would create a perfect result. There is a strong tendency, however, for Congress when working alone to bungle in matters of administrative organization, to fail to see the woods for the trees, and to produce a confusing total result that Congress itself certainly never planned.

Presidents as Reorganizers of Administration. The obvious question then arises whether the executive branch could do a better job.[8] Standing at the head of the administration, the President sees every day the problems of co-ordination. He is compelled to take an over-all view and to think of fitting the various parts of the organization into their proper places so that the best results can be obtained. While Congress deals almost entirely with particular cases, the President must also work for integration of the entire administrative mechanism. He has at hand the Bureau of the Budget and other agencies to advise him on problems of organization as seen from the topside of the administration, and can also hear from those at lower levels. If he is at all interested in the success of his administration, he will in most cases be anxious to improve the administrative mechanism; and he will do so, if duly authorized, upon the best available advice.

It is an interesting fact that the leading Presidents from Theodore Roosevelt to Truman have repeatedly urged the reorganization of the administration, to increase its efficiency and to produce greater economy. The story of their

[8] See President's Committee on Administrative Management, Report of, 1937, espec. ch. V; Peyton Hurt, "Who Should Reorganize the National Administration," Am. Pol. Sci. Rev., vol. 26, pp. 1082-98 (1932).

several proposals and of what happened to them is too long to recount here.[9] In both World Wars Congress authorized the President to transfer functions among agencies, and to create, abolish and combine agencies, as needed for the better prosecution of the war. This legislation made possible a number of quick and important changes by the President on the suggestion of his administrative advisers, without waiting for action by Congress. The changes made by Presidents Wilson, Franklin Roosevelt, and Truman under these authorizations were primarily for war purposes and did not greatly alter the administration of ordinary civil affairs. In each case the power granted to the President expired with the end of the war.

President Hoover made an earnest effort to obtain power from Congress to reorganize and consolidate the administration in his term and almost succeeded. At the last moment Congress postponed action until the beginning of Franklin Roosevelt's administration. Then for two years President Roosevelt had broad statutory powers of administrative reorganization, but other problems were then too pressing to make possible any systematic reorganization. President Roosevelt had not pushed the New Deal very far, however, before he came up against the same problem as his predecessors, and in a more acute form. During 1936 a special Committee on Administrative Management appointed by him carried on a study of certain phases of the problem, while several committees of Congress also held hearings and conducted studies. In January, 1937, reporting to Congress the findings of his own committee,[10] the President said:

> Now that we are out of the trough of the depression, the time has come to set our house in order. The administrative management of the Government needs overhauling. We are confronted not alone by new activities, some of them temporary in character, but also by the growth of the work of the Government matching the growth of the Nation over more than a generation.
>
> Except for the enactment of the Budget and Accounting Act of 1921, no extensive change in management has occurred since 1913, when the Department of Labor was established. The executive structure of the Government is sadly out of date. I am not the first President to report to the Congress that antiquated machinery stands in the way of effective administration and of adequate control by the Congress. Theodore Roosevelt, William H. Taft, Woodrow Wilson, and Herbert Hoover made repeated but not wholly successful efforts to deal with the problem. Committees of the Congress have also rendered distinguished service to the Nation through their efforts

---

[9] See Meriam and Schmeckebier, *op. cit.*, chs. VIII-XII; *Report of President's Committee on Administrative Management*; W. F. Willoughby, *The Reorganization of the Administrative Branch of the National Government*, 1923.

[10] Message of January 12, 1937, transmitting to Congress the *Report* of the President's Committee on Administrative Management.

from time to time to point the way to improvement of governmental management and organization.

The Committee on Administrative Management points out that no enterprise can operate effectively if set up as is the Government today. There are over 100 separate departments, boards, commissions, corporations, authorities, agencies, and activities through which the work of the Government is being carried on. Neither the President nor the Congress can exercise effective supervision and direction over such a chaos of establishments, nor can overlapping, duplication, and contradictory policies be avoided.

The Committee has not spared me; they say, what has been common knowledge for 20 years, that the President cannot adequately handle his responsibilities; that he is overworked; that it is humanly impossible, under the system which we have, for him fully to carry out his constitutional duty as Chief Executive, because he is overwhelmed with minor details and needless contacts arising directly from the bad organization and equipment of the Government. I can testify to this. With my predecessors who have said the same thing over and over again, I plead guilty.

This statement included a candid summary of the difficulties, and was accompanied by some very specific recommendations for changes. These called for legislation authorizing six "administrative assistants" for the President, reorganizing the Civil Service Commission, the Bureau of the Budget, and the General Accounting Office (Comptroller General), creating two new departments (Social Welfare and Public Works), and integrating the administrative work of many independent agencies with the executive departments. To carry out the desired reorganizations it was proposed to delegate the necessary authority to the President. The proposals for reorganizing the judiciary (the so-called "court-packing" proposals) having been submitted by the President at about the same time, a terrific controversy arose in Congress and the press over the alleged plans to make the President a "dictator." In reality the opposition was made up largely of numerous small groups having diverse interests in preventing certain changes, aided and abetted by the leaders of the opposition party.[11] The result was a major defeat for the President's proposals in 1938, but in 1939, when the fury had partly abated, a substantial part of the reorganization proposals was enacted.

The Reorganization Act of 1939 authorized the President, subject to certain exceptions, to present "plans" of reorganization to Congress up to January, 1941. If not rejected by both houses any such plan was to become effective within 60 days after its submission to Congress. The President submitted five such plans during 1939 and 1940 which, taken all together, effected a sub-

[11] Lindsay Rogers, "Reorganization: Post Mortem Notes," *Pol. Sci. Quar.*, vol. 53, pp. 161-72 (1938); Meriam and Schmeckebier, *op. cit.*, ch. XI.

stantial simplification and integration of the national administrative mechanism, and in no case did both houses of Congress reject any proposed plan. Thus they all went into effect, but this would not have been the case if both houses had had to approve. Here is something new in American legislative procedure—a sort of legislation by the President and a veto by Congress if both houses can agree to veto.[12] With such a safeguard or veto introduced Congress could safely grant to the President a continuing power of reorganization. Executive "plans" or orders thus approved, or not disapproved, by the legislative branch, provide as valid a legal basis as any statute.

President Truman had been only a few weeks in office in 1945 before he requested Congress to grant him broad powers of administrative reorganization.[13] He was looking forward to the postwar reconversion period and had in mind the need for overhauling the administrative machinery that had grown so greatly and had assumed so many new functions since the beginning of active defense measures in 1940.

Reorganization Act of 1945. In response to the President's request, and after careful consideration, Congress passed the "Reorganization Act of 1945."[14] This law is similar to that of 1939. It authorizes the President to submit reorganization plans to Congress up to April 1, 1948, and sets forth the procedure whereby the two houses may by concurrent resolution prevent any plan from going into effect. Any plan not disapproved by Congress within sixty days after submission, during which time Congress has been in session, goes into effect of its own force. No reorganization plan may abolish an entire department, or take away all its functions, or create a new department or secretary of a department, or authorize any new governmental function, or continue any agency or function beyond the period set for it by law. The Interstate Commerce Commission, Federal Trade Commission, Securities and Exchange Commission, National Mediation Board, National Railroad Adjustment Board, and Railroad Retirement Board, may not be reorganized by any plan of the President, although functions may be transferred to them, and practically the same protection is thrown around the civil functions of the Army Corps of Engineers. The law contains, also, other restrictions on the President's power to reorganize the administration. For example, in defining the agencies that may be reorganized the act says that "Such term does not include the Comptroller General of the United States or the General Accounting Office, which are a part of the legislative branch of the Government." On any careful analysis of functions the last clause would be very hard to defend.

Despite these restrictions in the legislation, President Truman possesses a very broad power of administrative reorganization. The Bureau of the

---

[12] John D. Millett and Lindsay Rogers, "The Legislative Veto and the Reorganization Act of 1939," *Pub. Admin. Rev.*, vol. 1, pp. 176-89 (1941).

[13] Messages of May 24, 1945, and September 6, 1945.

[14] Act of December 20, 1945; Public Law 263, 79th Congress, ch. 582, First Session.

Budget will probably serve as his principal adviser in carrying out the purposes of the law. It has contact with the work of all national administrative agencies and has on its staff a number of specialists in administrative organization and management.[15]

Administrative Reorganization: The Task and the Aims. The goals of administrative reorganization can be stated briefly: a more natural and logical grouping of functions; fewer agencies (instead of a hundred or more) for the President to try to supervise; elimination of overlapping activities among agencies; clear lines of responsibility everywhere in the administration; sufficient simplification of work for all agencies so that they can more easily and freely perform the work expected of them; and adequate means for co-ordinating work among all agencies so that they can jointly meet emergencies successfully. If these objectives can be attained greater efficiency and economy in the work of government should be achieved.

Field Organization. Whenever the task of simplifying and systematizing the administrative organization is undertaken, more attention will need to be paid to the field services. Not only departments but bureaus and even divisions of bureaus in departments have used their own judgment about organizing their field staffs and activities. As a result there are over one hundred different schemes of field organization in the national administration.[16] Their field headquarters are scattered out among hundreds of communities without much relation to each other, their district boundaries do not coincide with each other, their officials rent space in different buildings in the same community instead of being grouped together, and even in instances where their functions impinge on those of other national agencies in the same area, they do not always have contacts with the others. Thorough investigation would probably reveal numerous economies and many improvements in service that could be effected through the better application of known principles of proper field organization. Among other things, a far closer co-ordination of their work with that of state and local agencies could undoubtedly be achieved.

REFERENCES

Lloyd M. Short, *The Development of National Administrative Organization in the United States*, Baltimore, 1923.

W. F. Willoughby, *Principles of Public Administration, with Special Reference to the National and State Governments of the United States*, Washington, 1927, chs. III-XIII.

[15] See Harold D. Smith, *The Management of Your Government*, New York, 1945, especially ch. V; Norman M. Pearson, "The Budget Bureau: From Routine Business to General Staff," *Pub. Admin. Rev.*, vol. 3, pp. 126-49 (1943).

[16] National Resources Committee, *Regional Factors in National Planning*, pp. 2-9, 71-82, 155-70, and maps that follow; J. W. Fesler, "Federal Administrative Regions," *Am. Pol. Sci. Rev.*, vol. 30, pp. 257-68 (1936); Earl Latham, "Executive Management and the Federal Field Service," *Pub. Admin. Rev.*, vol. 5, pp. 16-27 (1945).

Harvey Walker, *Public Administration*, New York, 1935, chs. II-IV.

John M. Pfiffner, *Public Administration*, New York, 1935, chs. II-IV.

United States Government, *United States Government Manual*, Washington, D. C. One or more issues each year.

United States, President's Committee on Administrative Management, *Report of the Committee, with Studies of Administrative Management in the Federal Government*, Washington, 1937.

Luther Gulick and L. Urwick, *Papers on the Science of Administration*, New York, 1937, espec. papers I-III.

Schuyler Wallace, *Federal Departmentalization*, New York, 1941.

Lewis Meriam and Lawrence F. Schmeckebier. *Reorganization of the National Government*, Washington, 1939.

Public Administration Review, 1941 ff.

Louis Brownlow, "Reconversion of the Federal Administrative Machinery from War to Peace," *Pub. Admin. Rev.*, vol. 4, pp. 309-26 (1944).

Fritz Morstein Marx (ed.) and others, "The American Road from War to Peace: A Symposium," *Am. Pol. Sci. Rev.*, vol. 38, pp. 1114-91 (1944), espec. pp. 1179-91, Arthur W. Macmahon, "The Future Organizational Pattern of the Executive Branch."

Harold D. Smith, *The Management of Your Government*, New York, 1945.

CHAPTER 16

The National Civil Service

Nations that have been touched by the wand of modern education, science, and industry are all governmentally active. They employ many persons because they endeavor to meet the public demand for a host of public services. Upon the zeal, the efficiency, the honesty and the ideals of their numerous civil servants depends in no small measure the welfare of the people.

If the United States government was slow at first to engage in a program of modern social and economic services, it soon made up for a belated start. In 1816, after the national government had been a going concern for over twenty-five years it had only 6,300 civil servants in all, throughout the nation. About the year 1881 the number first reached 100,000, and sixty years later, just before the United States was drawn into World War II, the figures passed the one million mark. Wartime expansion carried the number to over three million. While population increased fifteen fold between 1816 and 1940, the number of regular civilian employees of the national government increased ten times as fast, or 150 fold.[1]

Constitutional Basis for National Civil Service. The Constitution covers the problem of civilian employment by the national government in the article on the executive. Reference is there made to the President's appointing power and to certain offices and officers. One clause reads that "the Congress may by Law vest the Appointment of such inferior Officers, as they think proper, in the President alone, in the Courts of Law, or in the Heads of Departments." [2] This reference, and the power conferred on Congress "to make all laws which shall be necessary and proper for carrying into Execution the foregoing Powers, and all other Powers vested by this Constitution in the Government of the United States, or in any Department or Officer thereof," [3] obviously confer on Congress the power to create all such offices and employ-

[1] See *Statistical Abstract of the United States*, 1941 ed., p. 168; 1943 ed., p. 165.
[2] Art. II, sec. 2, par. 2.
[3] Art. I, sec. 8, par. 18.

ments, and to employ such persons to fill them, as it deems necessary. Offices are ordinarily created by express act of Congress, but the thousands of less important employment positions call for little more than the appropriation of funds and the authorization to governmental agencies to employ such persons thereunder as they need, subject to the general laws.

Early Civil Service Policies. The first Congress, meeting in 1789, did not have to face the difficulties of creating a complete civil service system. The national government began with practically no going functions and no staff, although some were taken over from the previous agencies under the Articles of Confederation. Congress proceeded to establish a few departments and to authorize the appointment of officers and employees to staff them, but it laid down no elaborate rules on recruitment. It fell to President Washington, therefore, to set the personnel standards. He made it clear that "fitness of character" was the first qualification to be considered. The men appointed were to be respectable persons, "known in public life," and such as "would give dignity and lustre to our National Character." [4] He declined to appoint any of his own relations, or men who were unduly indolent or too much given to drink. Washington recognized local residence as an important requirement for officers who were to be stationed in various localities, and, after the struggle between the Federalist and Republican parties became notorious and bitter, he refused to appoint to any office of consequence any person "whose political tenets are adverse to the measures which the general government are pursuing; for this, in my opinion, would be a sort of political Suicide." [5]

President John Adams leaned even more heavily toward the appointment of Federalists, so that when Jefferson became President a swing in the other party's direction was to be expected. Jefferson removed a number of Federalists from office, because deaths and resignations were creating too few vacancies, and the pressure upon him to find posts for Republicans was very great. He even made a few appointments for the private benefit of friends, but in general, after he had in large part corrected the balance between Federalists and Republicans in the service he followed a moderate policy. He had previously declared that he would "return with joy to the state of things, when the only questions concerning a candidate shall be, is he honest? Is he capable? Is he faithful to the Constitution?" [6]

The United States Senators were already in Jefferson's day reaching out to control the nominations to national offices. Toward this Jefferson's reaction was positive and clear. He refused to send to the Senate the letters of recommendation that he had received concerning men whom he nominated. "Nomination to office is an executive function. To give it to the legislature . . . swerves the members from correctness, by temptations to intrigue for

---

[4] Quoted from Leonard D. White, "Public Administration Under the Federalists," *Boston Univ. Law Rev.*, vol. 24, pp. 144-86, at pp. 182-83 (1944).

[5] *Ibid.*, p. 184.

[6] Leonard D. White, *Introduction to the Study of Public Administration*, rev. ed., p. 278. See also Lynton K. Caldwell, *The Administrative Theories of Hamilton and Jefferson*, ch. 12.

office themselves, and to a corrupt barter of votes; and destroys responsibility by dividing it among a multitude." Years later he deplored the passage by Congress of the four-year tenure of office act (1820) because of the "intrigue and corruption" that would result from throwing every appointment before the Senate for approval every four years.[7]

Jefferson's successors down to the days of Jackson followed a fairly "correct" policy in appointments, but the spoils system had, in the meantime, developed a firm foothold in state and local governments, and many party leaders and even more party followers insisted upon having it. With Jackson the spoils system definitely entered the national civil service. He removed numerous officials in order to replace them with men of his party and with personal friends. Careful examination of the qualifications of the appointees would have been impossible even if it had been attempted. There was no agency of government to conduct examinations or to inquire into character and credentials. Jackson himself presented a bold argument against permanence in office and he claimed to be benefiting the country and the democratic system of government by his extensive removals of incumbents. Education, training, and experience weighed very lightly in his scales. "The duties of all public officers are, or at least admit of being made, so plain and simple that men of intelligence may readily qualify themselves for their performance; and I can not but believe that more is lost by the long continuance of men in office than is generally to be gained by their experience."[8]

The principle that to the political victors belong the spoils of office introduced by Jackson remained to control and hamper the national administration for a long time. It has never been fully rooted out, in fact, and it continues to find many supporters in Congress and in party councils. The four-year tenure law that applies to numerous presidential appointments is one of its principal anchors. Every new incumbent in the office of President even today is bedeviled by some of the "four-year locusts" who come to Washington in hope of appointments or get influential friends there to try to obtain appointments for them. Proportionately the numbers are now much smaller than in past years, and there are also more arrangements for protecting the Presidents from their importunities. Nevertheless, as long as there is any considerable element of the spoils system left in the national service, that service will suffer in morale.

The Battle Against the Spoils System. The fifty years following the beginning of Jackson's administration, say, from 1829 to 1880, constitute an era of almost complete dominance of the spoils system in national government. There were halfhearted gestures toward reform in 1853 and 1871, but Congress gave little support to these efforts and nothing important came out of them. Individuals and small groups first carried on the propaganda against

[7] Caldwell, op. cit., pp. 192-93.
[8] First message to Congress (1829); Richardson, Messages and Papers of the Presidents, vol. 2, pp. 448-49; White, op. cit., p. 280.

the spoils system. In 1877 there was organized the New York Civil Service Reform League which expanded to become the National Civil Service Reform League in 1881.[9] In that year President Garfield was assassinated by a disgruntled office seeker and Congress was galvanized into action. In 1883 Congress passed the Pendleton Act, the first important national civil service reform measure. It covered only 14,000 out of over 100,000 national employees of that day, but it authorized the President to extend the act to cover other groups by executive order. Grover Cleveland, coming to the Presidency in 1885, extended the coverage of the act very considerably. President Theodore Roosevelt and Woodrow Wilson, in particular, made further extensions of the act. Thus the movement against the spoils system went forward.

Between World War I and World War II some further progress was made in extending the merit system. Then came the great depression and the hurried creation by the national government of new social services and the new governmental agencies required to administer them. In the haste to get things done there appeared to be a danger of a return to the spoils system. Congress created several new agencies whose employees were to be outside the merit system. Public reaction to this threat was surprisingly prompt. In 1935 a National Commission of Inquiry on Public Service Personnel advocated a career service, based on merit, for all public service personnel.[10] The President's Committee on Administrative Management recommended in 1937 the extension of the merit system "upward, outward, and downward" throughout the national administration.[11] Congress and the President responded to the new demand with appropriate legislative and executive actions. The Ramspeck Act of November 26, 1940, authorized the President "to cover into the classified civil service" nearly all positions in the national service not previously covered "notwithstanding any provisions of law to the contrary." [12] A little before this another act of Congress had extended the merit principle to first, second, and third class postmasters, but had retained Senate approval for all such appointments. The President followed in 1941 with a series of executive orders that are reported to have raised to about 95 per cent of the total the number of positions in the national administration that are covered by the civil service laws. Wartime shortages of manpower made necessary from 1941 to 1945 some temporary deviations from the high standard thus established, but did not destroy the substantial gains that had been made.

The remaining proponents of the system of spoils and patronage in public employment are rather well known. They include certain machine politicians and party workers who cannot get public employment on the basis of merit

[9] See the works of Carl R. Fish, William D. Foulke, and Frank M. Stewart cited in the references at the end of this chapter.

[10] Better Government Personnel, Report of the Commission of Inquiry on Public Service Personnel, New York, 1935, pp. 3-9.

[11] Administrative Management in the Government of the United States, Report of the President's Committee on Administrative Management, Washington, 1937, pp. 7-14.

[12] Statutes at Large, vol. 54, p. 1211, ch. 919.

alone, or who feel that they need to have jobs to distribute to retain the support of other party workers; and scattered businessmen and other individuals who fear the results of government becoming highly efficient. In general these elements are in retreat, but they frequently win rear guard victories.

Polls of public opinion reveal that the great majority of citizens believe in the merit system of selecting and retaining public employees. Just how far the system should be extended still remains a question for practical judgment. To have effective party government and to enable the victorious majority to achieve a change in public policy when desired, the winning party must be able to fill at least the principal policy-making offices of the government with loyal party leaders. The number of such positions needs to be kept small if the merit system is to be effective.

The Shift to Public Personnel Management. The Pendleton Act of 1883 was fashioned primarily as a weapon to use against the spoils system. For many years after it was enacted, much of the effort of the Civil Service Commission, which was set up under the act, was devoted to fighting off the spoilsmen and to establishing the principle that appointments should be made on the basis of merit, not influence or party loyalty.

A more positive approach to the personnel problem of government was needed. It began to appear some time after 1900. New developments in the study of psychology, personnel management, and public administration induced students and administrators with vision to think less of eliminating spoils and more of improving the civil service constructively through better methods of testing, rating and selection, through education, and training, and through building up morale. This trend coincided with the general shift of government policy from laissez faire to a philosophy of government as a positive and active instrument to improve social conditions. As a result the political drive for "civil service reform" was supplemented by the new emphasis of the experts on scientific "public personnel administration." It is not enough just to keep out the unfit and unworthy. Government needs to seek out actively the most competent persons who are available for public employment, and to create such conditions in public employment as will call forth the best efforts of those who are appointed.

New developments along these lines took place not on the political battlefield but partly inside the civil service and partly in the universities and the professional societies that were encouraging studies that dealt with personnel and management. The advances in this field have been so many and important that an entirely new field of study and service has been opened up, the field of public personnel management. The techniques in this new discipline cannot be discussed here.[13] Instead we will try to consider briefly the essential

[13] On this subject see *Public Personnel Review* (quarterly since 1940); William E. Mosher and J. Donald Kingsley, *Public Personnel Administration*, rev. ed., 1941; Leonard D. White, *op. cit.*, Part IV, chs. 18-29.

problems of government that arise in connection with the nation's civil service system.

THE PRESENT LAW AND ITS ADMINISTRATION

Civil Service Act and Rules. The Pendleton Act of 1883, "an act to regulate and improve the civil service of the United States," as modified by various subsequent statutes, is still the basic law of the national civil service. Under Section 2 of this brief statute the President is authorized to promulgate "suitable rules" for carrying the act into effect. The Civil Service Commission aids him in the preparation of rules. At the present time the rules are far more extensive than the act, and the interpretations of the rules are even longer. This entire code, which is published from time to time by the Commission, is now so comprehensive and technical that very few persons can claim to be masters of it. It appears that all administration tends to develop in this way, from the first simple proposal into a complicated and specialized code of rights and procedures.

The Civil Service Commission and Staff. The act sets up a body of three commissioners, one of whom is usually a woman and "not more than two of whom shall be adherents of the same party," who are appointed by the President with the advice and consent of the Senate. There is no fixed term of office; of the present members two have already served for over twelve years and one for more than six years. Each receives what is a very common top salary in national administrative agencies, $10,000 a year.

Under the Commission there are a chief examiner and other officers and employees, numbering some 7,500 in early 1943, but increased somewhat more during the later war years. The Commission has not established an over-all director of its work; the act does not clearly provide that it should. As a result the three members themselves play a considerable direct role in the operations of the agency. Many things have to be approved by the commission as a whole that might better be delegated to one responsible officer.

The Commission's staff is not located entirely in Washington; about half the total number is divided among thirteen regional offices, each of which serves one of the major regions of the nation.

The Work of the Commission. With the aid of its staff the Commission is responsible for a few major and many minor activities.

1. *Classification of Positions.* Before examinations can be prepared or pay scales and promotional ladders be devised and recommended to Congress, it is necessary to have a job description of each position and a classification of positions into which each one can be placed. The Commission itself has never been able to classify most of the positions outside the national capital; the classification of these must be left to the agencies concerned. Even for those in Washington and its immediate vicinity the Commission's work is always incomplete because jobs are changing nearly all the time. When new duties

are added or old ones taken away, and when new combinations of work are arranged, new job analyses and classifications have to be made.

2. *Examinations and Recruitment.* The civil service act provides for "open, competitive examinations for testing the fitness of applicants for the public service now classified or to be classified hereunder. Such examinations shall be practical in their character, and so far as may be shall relate to those matters which will fairly test the relative capacity and fitness of the persons examined to discharge the duties of the service into which they seek to be appointed." This statutory requirement of open, competitive, and practical examinations is not absolute; in certain cases there can be non-competitive examinations, and in other instances examinations may be reduced to no more than the approval of credentials, or be postponed or even waived. During World War II in particular the Commission was forced to adopt a variety of expedients in order to try to fill the ranks.

Ordinarily, however, the open competitive type of examination is the one used. The number of persons examined is simply astounding. Tens of thousands will take a single examination. That is why post offices and other federal buildings throughout the land have to be used for this phase of the work. For each person who is examined there has to be a great deal of paper work— "red tape" some persons call it, but very important just the same. The individual has to make out his application, which has to be checked and approved to see that it complies with the law and that the individual is eligible. A considerable volume of correspondence may ensue over a single application. Then after the examination has been written the papers have to be scored and ranked, and later the lists of eligibles must be compiled. At this stage the added points given under veterans' preference laws must be considered and all pertinent provisions of law must be observed.

During most of its history the Civil Service Commission has been able to announce and to offer examinations with reasonable assurance that enough qualified persons will apply to fill up the necessary eligible registers. World War II with its extraordinary demands for manpower in the armed forces and in defense industries presented the Commission with a radically different situation. It became necessary for it to engage in a very vigorous campaign of recruitment. The demands for civilian help in the military branches coupled with unusually high turnover in all government employment made this effort to recruit personnel a first claim upon the time of the Commission and its staff. In fiscal year 1943 nearly 2,700,000 persons were placed in government employment, a truly impressive number. If the demands for help in industry and agriculture continue high, it remains to be seen whether the Commission will not have to keep up an active recruiting program.

3. *Checks on Appointments.* When vacancies occur in government agencies the commission is required to submit to the appointing officers the names of the three top eligibles for each vacancy. Before appointments can be approved for certain key positions the commission must also investigate the character,

loyalty and experience of the individual to determine his suitability for the position. In so far as possible it must also enforce the rule that appointments shall be distributed among the states in proportion to their population.

The civil service rules provide that neither in examinations nor in appointments are there to be any discriminations against anyone on the basis of political or religious beliefs. Under the rule that requires the names of three eligibles to be submitted it is, of course, impossible to prevent some such discriminations from taking place. The requirement of Senate approval for postmaster appointments also leaves the door open to some extent for party affiliations to be considered. Because this is known to be so, the competition for these positions is not as keen as it might be. The Civil Service Commission has strongly recommended that the requirement of Senate approval for these positions be eliminated.

4. *Regulation of Promotions, Transfers, Demotions, Suspensions, and Dismissals.* Under each of these headings the Commission has important functions. During World War II, when it was hard to get and to keep suitable employees, many agencies promoted or upgraded numerous persons as a means of holding their services, and many transfers also took place. All these the Commission had to approve.

Persons appointed under the merit system are given indefinite tenure, that is to say, during good behavior and satisfactory service. This lays the basis for a career service, but it raises also the question as to how to remove inefficient, dissolute, or disloyal persons whose presence in the service is an obstacle to good administration. The heads of agencies need some disciplinary authority— to demote, suspend, or even to dismiss. The rule on removals from the service is as follows:

> No person in the classified civil service of the United States shall be removed therefrom except for such cause as will promote the efficiency of said service and for reasons given in writing, and the person whose removal is sought shall have notice of the same and of any charges preferred against him, and be furnished with a copy thereof, and also be allowed a reasonable time for personally answering the same in writing; . . . but no examination of witnesses nor any trial or hearing shall be required except in the discretion of the officer making the removal. . . .[14]

It is definitely stipulated, however, that removals may not be made for political or religious reasons, and the Civil Service Commission has power to investigate removals when the person removed offers to prove that the reasons were political or religious.

5. *Prevention of Partisan Activity.* One of the great evils that developed under the spoils system was the excessive political activity of those appointed to public positions. Some appointees did very little work except for the party.

[14] Civil Service Act and Rules, Rule XII, sec. 1.

They were also expected to pay considerable amounts from their salaries into the party treasury, or into the hands of those whose influence got them their appointments. It was said, and in some cases proved, that appointments to postmasterships went to the highest bidder. The right of the party organization to assess public servants for the purposes of the party was accepted as a matter of course. Hence it was one of the purposes of civil service reform laws to put an end to political assessments. The civil service act forbids any other person from making such solicitation in any federal building or place used for the purposes of the national government.[15] Violators are guilty of a gross misdemeanor, and are subject to a fine of not over $5,000, imprisonment for not over three years, or both. The first Hatch Act (1939) extended similar protections to workers on relief projects.[16]

It is a most important question of public policy as to how far those who are in the public service on permanent tenure shall be permitted to engage in political activities. On the one hand they are an intelligent and high-minded group, who have a real contribution to make to the discussion of public questions and to the solution of specific problems. On the other hand if any of them engage in work for one party, and that party is defeated, the officers elected by the other party cannot have complete confidence in the willingness of such officers and employees to perform their duties faithfully under their direction. For many years the rule of the national civil service has been that persons in the competitive classified service, "while retaining the right to vote as they please and to express privately their opinions on all political subjects, shall take no active part in political management or in political campaigns." [17] The first Hatch Act extended this rule to cover the unclassified service as well, and the second Hatch Act (1940) made the rule applicable to state and local employees whose principal employment is in connection with any activity financed in whole or in part by federal grants or loans.[18] The Civil Service Commission annually passes on a number of cases of political activity, and where violation of the regulations is proved it metes out various penalties up to and including recommended dismissal from the service. Dismissal is mandatory in the case of employees of the national government but not so in the case of state and local employees who are paid from national funds. The Commission has recommended a change in the law to permit it to vary the penalty for national employees in accordance with the gravity of the offense.

6. *Unionization of Civil Servants and Employer-Employee Relations.* The question of unionization and union activities among civil servants is closely related to that of political activity. There have been unions of employees of the national government for many years and it is now possible to assess more accurately their true role in public administration.

[15] United States Civil Service Act, secs. 11, 12.
[16] 76th Cong., 1st Sess., Public No. 252; *U. S. Code*, Title 18, sec. 61.
[17] United States Civil Service Act, secs. 1, 2.
[18] 76th Cong., 3rd Sess., Public No. 753; *U. S. Code*, Title 18, sec. 61.

National government agencies like private corporations have in many instances grown so large that the employee has lost, or never has had, a feeling of close personal contact with his superiors. He enters the service in most instances through the rather impersonal process of written application and examination, and becomes a part of a large staff in which he sometimes feels that he is only a number and a name on the payroll. Because he is only one of thousands he is in a very poor position to do anything about his working conditions or remuneration. The union supplies him to some extent with the contacts and the spokesmen that he needs. At the same time he gets some feeling that he is part of the labor movement as a whole, and that other unions will be interested in his welfare.

The primary objectives of the unions are to improve wages, hours, and working conditions. Actually the unionized civil servants, with their rights as individuals under the civil service laws added to their political rights and their economic power achieved through unionization, may easily gain power and influence far exceeding those of other workers. Many persons have great fears of this possibility becoming an actuality. They picture the organized civil servants as standing over the government with a club, threatening strikes and disorder if they do not get what they want. There can be no doubt that, improperly led, unions of civil servants could cause a great deal of trouble, but at the same time there is another side to this picture. The civil servants have the best of reasons for favoring an efficient public service. They will themselves suffer if they force the government into extravagance through their wage and hours demands. They cannot in the long run afford to tolerate inefficient employees in the public service, for that will react upon them and upon their standing with the public at large. In short, with moderate and intelligent leadership, unions of public employees may become a force really favorable to the public welfare. Up to now the unions of civil servants in the national government have given little cause for alarm, and they have been very helpful, and at the same time persistent, in working for better pay scales and working conditions.

Fully recognizing the role that unions now play in government as well as in private employment the Civil Service Commission late in 1942 set up a Labor-Management Advisory Committee to assist it in meeting its wartime responsibilities in maintaining the national civil service at full strength and efficiency. On this committee were placed two representatives of the AF of L, two of the CIO, two of the National Federation of Federal Employees, and six representatives of management.

Some such machinery for consultation with unions and management may well become a permanent part of the national government's organization for personnel management and employer-employee relations. The Commission realizes that one of its main responsibilities has come to be the promotion of good morale and high standards of service among the nation's civil servants. The original plan for a civil service law said nothing about this and indeed the law has very little to do with it even now. It is simply a fact that the main problems of employer-employee relations and of sound personnel management have to be faced in the nation's service and that leadership in this field falls largely upon the Civil Service Commission. A democratic society with adequate instruments for popular control over the administration of its government should be able to work out satisfactory methods of employer-employee relations in its own service. The civil servant like every other citizen is a human being and a person whose rights and just claims to recognition must be accepted.

7. *Remuneration.* Many persons in private business feel that civil servants are overpaid. This may be said truthfully of many who have obtained their employment through the spoils system, and whose duties are small while their compensation may be considerable. It can hardly be said of those who have come in through examination. The latter are, in fact, not highly paid.

During the year 1938, the last year prior to the war for which the figures are available, the standard rates of pay for a 40-hour week in the national government's service were as follows: [19]

		Cumulative
Under $1,200 a year	13.3% of all employees	13.3%
$1,200 to $1,499 a year	18.7% " " "	32.0%
1,500 to 1,799 " "	14.1% " " "	46.1%
1,800 to 1,999 " "	10.8% " " "	56.9%
2,000 to 2,199 " "	20.6% " " "	77.5%
2,200 to 2,599 " "	9.1% " " "	86.6%
2,600 to 3,199 " "	6.9% " " "	93.5%
3,200 to 3,799 " "	3.1% " " "	96.6%
3,800 to 5,599 " "	2.7% " " "	99.3%
5,600 and over " "	0.7% " " "	100.0%

The basic rates of pay remained unchanged up to almost the end of the fighting in the Pacific in 1945. Undoubtedly by that time the distribution of employees in the various pay brackets had been changed by the promotion of many persons to higher brackets and the upgrading of many positions. Furthermore during most of the period of active hostilities there was an addition of about 15 per cent to the basic rates to cover the increased cost of living for those who did not work overtime, and for others there was overtime pay for working a 48-hour week which added about 20 per cent for employees in this category. On July 1, 1945, by Act of Congress, a new basic scale of pay was established, which raised pay as much as 20 per cent in the most poorly paid positions down to about 9 per cent in the best paid. At the same time, except in the war agencies, most of the overtime was eliminated. The 1938 median pay for all government officers and employees was $1,871 a year, or $156 a month. Today the median base pay (including the postal employees increase of 1946) must be about $2,400, or $200 a month.

[19] *Statistical Abstract of the United States,* 1941, p. 172; ibid., 1943, p. 165.

These rates are fairly good in the median and lower pay brackets when compared with the wages and salaries paid by state and local governments and by private industry. In the more responsible positions, however, the situation is far from good. Congress set a maximum of $10,000 a year under the 1945 pay bill, but most of the top positions pay far less than that. The national government undoubtedly gets into its higher positions many persons of outstanding ability, but it gets them not because they could not earn more elsewhere but because they prefer national public employment to any other.

The Civil Service Commission prepared much of the information and made the recommendation for the 1945 upward adjustment of civil service salaries. Its stated objective in all its work is to make the national government "the most progressive employer in the nation." If this goal is to be attained, the Commission and the government as a whole need to give much more attention to the problems in their higher administrative and research positions. The competition from private employers, and especially from the great corporations, is very keen.

Already the Commission has set a goal that is far beyond the mere formal requirements of the law. It has been looking into, and doing something about, such matters as assuring the veterans of their full legal rights under recent legislation, making better utilization of manpower in all branches of the administration, promoting programs for the in-service training of national employees, experimenting with new types of examinations that might tend to draw more of the best brains of the country into the national service, providing adequate rewards and incentives for outstanding achievement, improving the civil service retirement system, which it administers, and in general trying to raise civil service morale and efficiency.

Other Agencies Concerned with Personnel Administration. The Civil Service Commission is not the only agency that is concerned with improving the personnel practices of the national government. Among others the Bureau of the Budget and the President's Liaison Office for Personnel Management have important personnel functions. The United States Employees' Compensation Commission administers the laws that provide compensation for injuries and deaths incurred by the nation's civil employees in the course of their duties.

The Council of Personnel Administration is an interdepartmental committee that is composed of the personnel officers of the many government agencies that have established such positions, together with representatives of the Budget Bureau and Civil Service Commission. This council suggests another phase of personnel administration in the national government. The larger departments and agencies have been compelled to establish their own personnel offices to help recruit the types of personnel they need, and to deal with all the personnel problems within the agency. Each has its own needs, its own special conditions of work. They cannot rely entirely upon the Civil Service Commission either to recruit the personnel they want or to provide for the morale and efficiency of their employees. And yet there are enough common elements in the personnel problems of all agencies so that a clearing house of ideas and information is desirable. The Council of Personnel Administration supplies this need in large part, and the over-all personnel agencies of the government mentioned above cooperate closely with it.

PROPOSALS FOR FURTHER ADVANCES IN PERSONNEL ADMINISTRATION

Both the great depression of the 1930s with its spate of new problems and new agencies to deal with them, and World War II with its terrific manpower demands and shortages, put very severe strains upon the personnel agencies of the national government and especially upon the Civil Service Commission. Despite the valor and the sincerity of its efforts, the Commission, and the highly concentrated system of personnel administration that it represents, drew a great deal of adverse comment. The critics pointed out that the Commission was too clumsy and too slow to cope adequately with great emergencies. It was too deeply involved in a round of traditional, law-enforcing duties to be able to see and to grapple with its larger responsibilities as the main personnel agency of a great nation.

According to another line of argument the national government has become entirely too big to have its personnel management so completely vested in one agency. That agency succeeds fairly well in the administration of large-scale examinations for the relatively simple and standardized, low-paid positions, but fails to a considerable extent in meeting the needs for the many specialized, professional and higher-level administrative positions.

The proposals for improvement are various. One is to abolish the three-member bipartisan commission, with its semi-independent status, and to set up in place thereof a single civil service administrator as a direct and responsible aide of the President in all personnel matters. This plan includes also a Civil Service Board of seven members to advise the administrator and to discuss all questions of policy with him, but not to control him. One of the Board's main functions would be "to act as watchdog of the merit system and to represent the public interest in the improvement of personnel administration." [20]

Another proposal is to delegate to the major agencies of the national government a great deal more control over the selection and management of their own personnel. Some persons would give each major agency practically the same freedom as TVA has in the handling of its entire personnel problem. This would leave the Civil Service Commission or some similar agency to set over-all standards for personnel, to supervise all other agencies of the govern-

---

[20] *Report of the President's Committee on Administrative Management*, 1937, pp. 10-11; and see also Floyd W. Reeves and Paul T. David, *Personnel Administration in the Federal Service*, 1937; and Floyd W. Reeves, "Civil Service as Usual," *Pub. Admin. Rev.*, vol. 4, pp. 327-40 (1944).

ment in their handling of personnel matters, to do research, and to lead and stimulate all government agencies toward the attainment of better personnel practices. Most personnel work would then be done in the major departments and agencies, and the Civil Service Commission could get along with a relatively small staff. It is interesting to note that not only the President but the Commission itself strongly recommends that each principal agency of national administration employ a chief personnel officer, showing that it realizes the importance of having much personnel work done by the departments and agencies for themselves.

Still another suggestion is that the Commission should delegate more of its work to its regional directors, especially for the recruitment of personnel to serve in regional and field offices. World War II forced the Commission to do this in very large measure, and no doubt some of the delegated functions will be left in the regional offices when the reconversion to peace has been completed.

All these and various similar suggestions say in effect that the nation must raise its sights a great deal if it is to achieve better results in recruiting and in managing its public service personnel. The proposals should be directed, however, more to public opinion and to Congress than to the Commission. It has shown over the years a commendable desire to bring about improvements. Recent Presidents also have gone along willingly with proposals to improve the government's personnel practices, but Congress holds back and is very reluctant to make any organic change. It looks upon the present law and rules and upon the Commission itself as desirable checks not only upon the spoils politicians but even more upon the President himself. The question of further changes turns largely upon the relations between Congress and the President. (*Note.* On February 4, 1946, after these pages had been written, President Truman issued Executive Order No. 9691 (vol. 11 *Federal Register,* p. 1381). By this order he directed the Civil Service Commission to do the following things among others: (1) To resume as rapidly as possible the announcement of open competitive examinations for classified positions and the establishment of eligible registers so as to replace temporary employees by persons having permanent tenure. (2) To "establish U. S. Civil Service Boards of Examiners in the field service" and to utilize these boards to fill positions in the field. (3) To establish in Washington, D. C., in consultation with the departments and agencies concerned, "U. S. Civil Service Committees of Expert Examiners" to assist in recruiting scientific, professional, and technical personnel. The Civil Service Commission is to retain supervision over these boards and committees of examiners, but it seems to be intended that much of the work of recruiting shall be done in the departments in Washington and in the regional offices for the field service.)

REFERENCES

Carl R. Fish, *The Civil Service and the Patronage*, New York, 1905.

Frank M. Stewart, *The National Civil Service Reform League: History, Activities, and Problems*, Austin, Texas, 1929.

William Dudley Foulke, *Fighting the Spoilsmen: Reminiscences of the Civil Service Reform Movement*, New York, 1919.

Commission of Inquiry on Public Service Personnel, *Better Government Personnel*, New York, 1935.

——, *Problems of the American Public Service*, New York, 1935, including Carl J. Friedrich, "Responsible Government Service under the American Constitution"; William C. Beyer, "Municipal Civil Service in the United States"; Sterling D. Spero, "Employer and Employee in the Public Service"; John F. Miller, "Veteran Preference in the Public Service"; George A. Graham, "Personnel Practices in Business and Governmental Organizations."

W. E. Mosher and D. J. Kingsley, *Public Personnel Administration*, rev. ed., New York, 1941.

President's Committee on Administrative Management, *Report with Special Studies*, . . . Number 1, "Personnel Administration in the Federal Service," by Floyd W. Reeves and Paul T. David.

Leonard D. White, *Introduction to the Study of Public Administration*, rev. ed., New York, 1939, espec. chs. IX-XVII.

W. F. Willoughby, *Principles of Public Administration*, Washington, 1927, espec. chs. XVIII-XXIX.

Harvey Walker, *Public Administration in the United States*, New York, 1937, ch. V.

John M. Pfiffner, *Public Administration*, New York, 1935, chs. VIII-XII.

Herman Feldman, *A Personnel Program for the Federal Civil Service*, 71st Congress, 3d Session, House Doc. No. 773, Washington, 1931.

National Civil Service Reform League, *The Civil Service in Modern Government, A Study of the Merit System*, New York, 1937.

United States Civil Service Commission, annual reports of.

——, *Civil Service Act and Rules: Statutes, Executive Orders and Regulations*, etc., Revised from time to time. Washington.

Proceedings of The Civil Service Assembly of the United States and Canada, annual.

Good Government, bimonthly, published by the National Civil Service League.

News Letter, monthly, of the Civil Service Assembly, Chicago.

Public Personnel Review, quarterly, 1940 ff., Civil Service Assembly, Chicago.

Morris B. Lambie (ed.), *Training for the Public Service: A Report and Recommendations*, Chicago, 1935.

——, (ed.), *University Training for the National Service*, Minneapolis, 1932.

Leonard D. White, *Government Career Service*, Chicago, 1935.

Lewis Meriam, *Public Service and Special Training*, Chicago, 1936.

Commission of Inquiry on Public Service Personnel, *A Bibliography of Civil Service and Personnel Administration*, by Sarah Greer, New York, 1935.

President's Committee on Civil Service Improvement, *Report* of, 77th Congress, 1st Session, House Doc. No. 118 (1941).

Floyd W. Reeves, "Civil Service as Usual," *Pub. Admin. Rev.*, vol. 4, pp. 327-40 (1944).

Lewis Meriam, *Public Personnel Problems from the Standpoint of the Operating Officer*, Washington, 1938.

John Fischer, "Let's Go Back to the Spoils System," *Harper's Magazine*, vol. 1145, pp. 362-368 (October, 1945).

Ismar Baruch, "The Federal Employees Pay Act of 1945," *Public Personnel Review*, vol. 6, pp. 201-12 (1945).

Robert S. Rankin, *Readings in American Government*, New York, 1939, pp. 165-81.

John Mathews and Clarence A. Berdahl, *Documents and Readings in American Government*, rev. ed., New York, 1940, pp. 376-406.

A. N. Christensen and E. M. Kirkpatrick, *The People, Politics, and the Politician: Readings in American Government*, New York, 1941, pp. 468-79, 497-531.

CHAPTER 17

The National Judiciary

Before the Constitution. In the colonial period of American history, the English colonies were concerned with two sets of courts. These were their own courts, of which each colony had a different system, and the higher courts, located across the Atlantic in England, some of which had appellate power over the courts in all the colonies. During the Revolution, state courts in each state took the place of the former colonial courts, but the Articles of Confederation failed to provide a general system of courts for the Confederation as a whole. This lack of an over-all court system was in Hamilton's judgment the crowning defect of the whole system of government under the Articles.

Forming the National Court System. That the need for a national judiciary was widely felt is shown by the fact that all four plans that were presented to the Convention of 1787 for the improvement of the Articles or for a new constitution made some provision for a supreme court of the United States. They left the creation of the inferior national courts up to Congress. Apparently the framers were especially concerned about two things, *first*, that there should be a uniform, nation-wide interpretation of the national Constitution, laws, and treaties; and *second*, that interstate disputes, controversies between citizens of different states, and cases between citizens and foreigners, should be so handled that the possible bias of the state courts against out-of-state parties might be prevented from resulting in injustice. Both these ideas were incorporated in the new Constitution.

Building upon the work of the Convention, the first Congress enacted the famous Judiciary Act of 1789. This act established and provided for the organization of the Supreme Court, three circuit courts, and thirteen district courts, and defined their respective jurisdictions. Thus, after an interval of about fifteen years in which there had been no judicial organization of general scope over the thirteen states, the national court system of the United States came into existence.

Dual Court System Today. In each of the forty-eight states there are today two systems of courts. Each state has its own scheme of courts organized under the state constitution and statutes. This extends from the justice of the peace and municipal courts upwards to and including the state supreme court. Superimposed upon this, and also reaching into every state and territory and extending throughout the United States and its dependencies, is the system of national or federal courts. Of nation-wide and general significance today are the Supreme Court of the United States, the Circuit Courts of Appeals, and the District Courts. Between the national and state courts there are numerous close relations and a considerable overlapping of jurisdiction. This double system of courts is one of the complications that most persons in the United States seem to accept as a necessary concomitant of federalism. The judicial arrangements in other federal systems are substantially different, however, and so extensive a duplication of courts is not everywhere considered necessary to federal government.

ORGANIZATION OF THE FEDERAL COURTS

The Constitution makes the following specific provision for the organization of the courts of the United States:

> The judicial Power of the United States, shall be vested in one supreme Court, and in such inferior Courts as the Congress may from time to time ordain and establish. The Judges, both of the supreme and inferior Courts, shall hold their Offices during good Behaviour, and shall, at stated Times, receive for their Services a Compensation which shall not be diminished during their Continuance in Office." [1]

It is more than likely that, if this clause had been omitted from the Constitution, Congress would nevertheless have had ample power to create courts under its authority to pass whatever laws are necessary and proper for carrying into effect the Constitution. In that case, however, the restrictions stated as to the tenure and compensation of judges might also have been omitted. As it is, these restrictions are applicable whenever Congress acts under the authority granted by this section. Congress recognized these restrictions when it passed the Judiciary Act of 1789, and has continued to recognize them with respect to the nation-wide three-level system of courts of general jurisdiction, which consists now of the Supreme Court, Circuit Courts of Appeals, and District Courts.

The express power to create courts that was conferred upon Congress by the section just quoted calls to mind an important fact. Congress and the office of President were definitely established by the Constitution itself. On the other hand the Supreme Court was not clearly established and certainly was not organized by the Constitution. That document made no provision

[1] Art. III, sec. 1.

as to the number of justices, or their salaries, or the terms or sessions of the Court. All these matters were left for Congress to regulate, and its power over the Court in these and other matters is a continuing one. The Court's existence is thus dependent, in a sense, upon the good will of Congress.

All the other courts of the United States, being not even named in the Constitution, depend entirely on Congress for their existence. As it created them so it may alter them at will, and even abolish them as it did in the case of the circuit courts when it set up the Circuit Courts of Appeals. When altering or abolishing any court set up under the section quoted above, however, Congress must observe the constitutional rules concerning the tenure of judges during good behavior and their right to undiminished compensation during such tenure.

Constitutional versus Legislative Courts. In its various efforts to develop a system of courts adequate to the needs of the nation, the territories, and the District of Columbia, Congress has not always relied upon the general section on the judiciary that is quoted above. It has other powers that it may utilize. When establishing courts for the territories and the District of Columbia, and courts for deciding cases in special fields such as taxation, patents, and commerce, Congress falls back upon the distinctive constitutional powers that correspond with these subjects, and upon the "necessary and proper" clause that supplements these powers. By doing this it avoids the obligation to provide for tenure during good behavior, for example; it can set the tenure of the judges in the courts created under these powers at any number of years that it chooses. It is equally free to reduce the compensation of such judges if it so chooses.

In addition to the courts of the District of Columbia and the territories, there are today in this category of special and local courts the Court of Claims, the Court of Customs and Patent Appeals, the Customs Court, and the Tax Court. The Supreme Court calls these courts "legislative courts," to distinguish them from the so-called "constitutional courts" (Supreme Court, Circuit Courts of Appeals, and District Courts). It holds also that the two classes of courts differ in still other ways. For example the constitutional courts are recognized as being strictly judicial, and Congress is held to be without power to impose any non-judicial functions upon them. This is not true of legislative courts. The Supreme Court has stated this distinction between constitutional and legislative courts in part as follows: [2]

> While Article III of the Constitution declares, in section 1, that the judicial power of the United States shall be vested in one Supreme Court and in such inferior courts as the Congress may from time to time ordain and establish, and prescribes, in section 2, that this power shall extend to cases and controversies of certain enumer-

---

[2] *Ex parte* Bakelite Corporation (1929), 279 U. S. 438. See also *Columbia Law Rev.*, vol. 34, pp. 344-56 (1934).

ated classes, it long has been settled that Article III does not express the full authority of Congress to create courts, and that other articles invest Congress with powers in the exertion of which it may create inferior courts and clothe them with functions deemed essential or helpful in carrying those powers into execution. But there is a difference between the two classes of courts. Those established under the specific power given in section 2 of Article III are called Constitutional courts. They share in the exercise of the judicial power defined in that section, can be invested with no other jurisdiction, and have judges who hold office during good behavior, with no power in Congress to provide otherwise. On the other hand, those created by Congress in the exertion of other powers are called legislative courts. Their functions always are directed to the execution of one or more of such powers and are prescribed by Congress independently of section 2 of Article III; and their judges hold for such term as Congress prescribes, whether it be a fixed period of years or during good behavior.

The several "constitutional courts" of the United States will now be briefly described.[3]

The Supreme Court of the United States. This distinguished body, the highest court within the judicial system of the United States, was established by law in 1789 with a chief justice and five associate justices. Today there are eight associate justices and a chief justice. The salaries are $20,500 annually for the chief justice and $20,000 for each associate justice. The Court always sits as one body, *en banc* as the lawyers say, but individual judges sometimes act upon and sign certain papers with respect to litigation before the Court, especially when the Court is not in session. There is an annual "term" or session of the Court; it begins on the first Monday in October and ends usually in June. Sessions are held in the Supreme Court building, a beautiful structure near the Library of Congress on Capitol Hill.

Six members constitute a quorum, and decisions are rendered by a majority of the justices who participate in trying a case. Frequently one or more justices announce themselves to be disqualified from participating in a case because in their earlier practice as lawyers or service as judges they have already had a part in the same litigation.

Only attorneys qualified to practice before it present cases to the Court. They do so on the basis of printed briefs, but oral arguments are also heard. Consultation among the justices results in a general agreement among them as to how each case shall be decided. Then the chief justice assigns to one member of the Court the duty of writing the decision. When this in turn has been

[3] For more details on the history and organization of the United States courts see Roscoe Pound, *Organization of Courts*, Boston, 1940; C. N. Callender, *American Courts: Their Organization and Procedure*, New York, 1927; Evan A. Evans, "History of the Federal Judicial System," *Sup. Ct. Rep. Advance Sheets*, vol. 60, XVII-XXIV (1940).

examined and corrected by the other justices, and all concurring and dissenting opinions have been written, the Court on some following Monday announces its decision. In this manner something like a thousand cases a year are disposed of, many without formal opinions. Nowadays it usually requires three stout volumes of *United States Reports* to publish the decisions of a single year's term of the Court.[4]

The Circuit Courts of Appeals. These courts were created in 1891 and are now 11 in number, one for the District of Columbia and one each for the ten judicial circuits into which the rest of the country is divided. The first circuit consists of Maine, New Hampshire, Massachusetts, Rhode Island and Puerto Rico; the second includes Vermont, Connecticut, and New York; and so on. One justice of the Supreme Court is assigned to each circuit, but his connection with it is very slight; the judicial work in each Circuit Court of Appeals is done by the regular circuit judges. There are from three to seven such judges for each circuit. A court in action normally consists of three judges but two constitute a quorum for the conduct of judicial business .Thus in several circuits two Circuit Courts of Appeals can be sitting at one time with a full complement of regular judges. In case of need a district judge can be summoned to fill the bench of a circuit court.

The Circuit Courts of Appeals exist primarily to relieve the Supreme Court of a large amount of work. Their work is entirely appellate, and their decisions are final in many cases. They take appeals not only from the District Courts but also from several of the principal administrative tribunals of the nation such as the Interstate Commerce Commission, Federal Trade Commission, Federal Reserve Board, and National Labor Relations Board.

The District Courts of the United States. These courts were established by the Judiciary Act of 1789. Their jurisdiction was at first restricted to relatively unimportant cases, while the important ones were tried in the Circuit Courts, which also tried appeals from the District Courts. The Circuit Courts, which were abolished in 1911, consisted originally of two justices of the Supreme Court and a district judge each. This plan of dividing the trial of new cases between the one-judge District Courts and the three-judge Circuit Courts did not work satisfactorily. The Supreme Court justices grumbled against it from the beginning and in time their own duties became so arduous that they could not perform adequately their Circuit Court functions. Congress was slow to improve the situation; it tried several halfway measures, but not until 1911 did it abolish the separate Circuit Courts.

By legislation enacted in that year the District Courts for the first time acquired their present status and importance. They are today the principal courts of original jurisdiction for the nation, both for cases arising under the national Constitution, statutes, and treaties, and for cases based on "diversity of citizenship" (to be explained later). "Original jurisdiction" means the

[4] See Felix Frankfurter and James M. Landis, *The Business of the Supreme Court*, 1927, for a thorough analysis of the court's activities and methods.

power and the duty to try and to decide cases in the first instance, while "appellate jurisdiction" is the power to take cases on appeal from lower courts. The District Courts stand in the front line, taking on new cases as they arise. They handle about one hundred thousand cases a year, of which about 95 per cent are settled without any appeal.

The number of judicial districts is now over 90. In each there is at least one District Judge but many districts have more. Each judge holds his own court except in certain rare cases in which legislation by Congress requires three judges to sit. The salary of the district judge is $10,000 a year.

In each judicial district there are also the following officers: a United States District Attorney, a United States Marshal, a Clerk of the District Court, and a United States Commissioner. The latter is appointed by the District Judges to perform a variety of minor judicial duties comparable to those of a justice of the peace under the state governments.[5] The clerk and his deputies are also appointed by the district judges.

JUDICIAL PERSONNEL

The Appointment of Judges. The judge is the central figure in any court. Upon his character, training, ability, tact, and firmness depend the success of the court and its standing among the people.

Under the Constitution the justices of the Supreme Court are required to be appointed by the President by and with the advice and consent of the Senate.[6] There is no such requirement for the appointment of the judges of the other United States courts, but the practice is the same. It follows that partisan, political, and personal considerations enter into the appointment of United States judges, from the Supreme Court justices down. To some extent this is unavoidable and much can be said for a President's refusing to appoint as judges men whose political views are diametrically opposed to his own. The courts to some extent influence if they do not actually decide the policies of the government, and recalcitrant judges can do much to obstruct and hamper the administration of laws.

More serious than the attempts of Presidents to find, for judicial positions, lawyers who accept the general policy of the administration, have been the frequently successful efforts of party leaders, Senators, and Representatives in Congress, to obtain judicial appointments for faithful party workers or personal supporters without sufficient regard for their ability, training, and temperament. Recent Presidents, with the aid of their own secretaries and the Justice Department, have done much to sift out and reject the least acceptable nominees for judicial posts, but there is a limit to what can be achieved in this way. It is evident that positions as District Judge are frequently a reward

[5] See Norman J. Griffin, "United States Commissioners," *Jour. of Amer. Judic. Soc.*, vol. 29, pp. 58-59 (1945).
[6] Art. II, sec. 2, par. 2.

for party service, and that ex-Representatives and ex-Senators too often receive appointments to the bench. As a result the general standards of judicial appointments are not nearly as good as they might be, and it is not the result of mere chance that ten out of thirteen impeachments brought by the House of Representatives and all the convictions by the Senate have involved United States judges. The personnel of the Supreme Court and of the Circuit Courts of Appeals has in recent decades reached very high levels of character, training, and ability, but a great deal remains to be done in the District Courts.

To overcome this major difficulty it has been suggested that United States judges below the level of the Supreme Court might be appointed by the Chief Justice of the Supreme Court, with or without the approval of the Associate Justices.[7] The Constitution speaks of the courts below the Supreme Court as "inferior courts" and it also provides that "the Congress may by Law vest the Appointment of such Inferior Officers, as they think proper, . . . in the Courts of law. . . ." If the judges of inferior courts are inferior officers, or if the discretion vested in Congress is broad enough to declare them to be so, then presumably Congress may vest the appointment of such judges in the Supreme Court.

Tenure, Salaries and Retirement of Judges. As previously noted the Constitution guarantees the tenure of the judges of the Constitutional courts during good behavior, and also assures them of undiminished compensation during their continuance in office.[8] The grand objective of this provision is to establish the independence of the courts despite any efforts that Congress or the President might make to dominate them. This objective has been achieved in substantial measure. Once in office the judges of the constitutional courts are not beholden to anyone for their positions or salaries. The importance of this independence of the judges for the preservation of personal and property rights can hardly be overestimated.

As officers of the United States judges are subject to impeachment,[9] but no other method of removing them has been established. It would appear that the retirement of judges upon reaching a certain age is beyond the present power of Congress to compel as long as their behavior continues to be good. The liberal allowances that have been established for United States judges who retire voluntarily have not induced many early resignations. The average age of judges at the time of their appointment is over 50 years, and in 1937, when President Franklin Roosevelt made his famous proposal for court reorganization, some thirty United States judges were over 70 years old. These judges would have completed their formal education about 1890 and could easily have become out of touch and out of sympathy with the then recent changes in government, as President Roosevelt insisted that many were.

[7] See Burke Shartel, "Federal Judges—Appointment, Supervision, and Removal—Some Possibilities Under the Constitution," Mich. Law Rev., vol. 28, pp. 485-529, 723-38, 870-909 (1930).

[8] Art. III, sec. 1. See footnote 1, above, and corresponding text.

[9] Art. II, sec. 4; Art. I, sec. 2, par. 5; Art. I, sec. 3, pars. 6, 7.

Congress has as yet done nothing to work out a constitutional amendment or any other plan for the systematic retirement of elderly United States judges. It is evident, however, that when inadequate attention is given to the appointment of the best persons as judges, guarantees of tenure during "good behavior" and the lack of any means for early retirement combine to encumber the bench (especially in the District Courts) with elderly persons some of whom were from the beginning without great ability or industry, and at least a few of whom display low standards of judicial deportment.

If the Supreme Court were given the power to appoint the district judges, it might also be given some authority (by constitutional amendment if necessary) to supervise, discipline, and even remove corrupt, negligent, and inefficient judges. There could not be the same objection to the Supreme Court disciplining and removing judges as to the President or Congress doing so. In fact the national judiciary as a whole might become more responsible and more independent if the Supreme Court had such power.

THE LEGAL SYSTEM OF THE UNITED STATES

Before the jurisdiction of the United States courts can be understood it is necessary to grasp the essentials of the system of laws. Because both the nation and the states are sources of law, there are some complications in a federal system that can be unraveled only by careful analysis.

Written Law. The law in general is that body of rules applicable in the community that the courts and administrative agencies will interpret and apply to legal controversies. It is roughly divisible into written and unwritten law. In the written law are included written constitutions, statutes and resolutions of lawmaking bodies, treaties, administrative rules and regulations, and local ordinances and bylaws. Some of these come from the nation, some from the states, and some from local authorities. They vary in their degree of authority and in the extent of the territory they cover. Those laws that come from higher levels of authority usually prevail over those from lower levels, but this will vary with the circumstances. Except for occasional contradictions the written laws of national, state, and local governments are complementary and interdependent.

In any single case before the courts several laws coming from different sources may be involved. A municipal licensing ordinance may regulate the rights of aliens that are also regulated by treaty, or a national statute or administrative regulation may cover some aspect of railroad operation that is also dealt with in a state statute or regulation. Thus any court either state or national, in which a case arises, may have to decide questions of both national and state written law.

Unwritten or Common Law. Back through the centuries the courts have been making decisions in particular cases upon the rights and duties of the parties involved. Out of these decisions, many of which did not depend upon any written law at all, has developed the so-called "unwritten law." This consists of the many rules and principles that the courts will follow in later cases. The principle of standing by former decisions as precedents in later cases is called *stare decisis*. The courts naturally want to keep in harmony with the older law when handling the new cases that continue to arise. When old rules no longer fit the present facts, of course, the rule of *stare decisis* must be broken.

This whole body of court-made or "decisional" law is sometimes called the "common law" but it actually includes more than the old common law. For example the decisions of the United States courts that interpret the national Constitution, statutes, and treaties have developed into a very considerable body of decisional law, with many guiding rules and principles, but these are not usually called a part of the common law.

Common Law in the States. Until about the eighteenth century the English colonists in America had gone forward developing their own separate legal systems, but as commerce increased and the colonists found it desirable to have the same law and to assert the same economic and political rights as Englishmen, the English law was taken over more and more, and lawyers trained at the Inns of Court at London became more numerous and more important in America. The "free system of English laws" was considered the birthright of every American. When the separation from England came, the colonies had so fully accepted the English system of laws that it became necessary for the new states to continue to operate under it. Virginia promptly declared that the common law of England was to be the rule of decision in its courts. New York made similar provision in its first constitution (1777), and other states necessarily followed suit. Even the states admitted later to the Union have provisions in their laws making the common law a part of their law. An exception is Louisiana, where the French or "civil law" is also important.

Through this "reception" of the common law by the states, every court that finds that the written law and the decisions in that state do not fully cover or provide for some new contingency, may fall back for a guiding rule upon the English court decisions, the English statutes of general application, the colonial decisions and statutes of general nature, and the various branches of law that were attached to the English common law.

The Constitution of the United States mentions the common law in connection with jury trial in civil cases, and it uses so many terms of common law origin that the federal courts, too, do in fact follow the common law on many points. Referring to the Seventh Amendment the Supreme Court has said that "Beyond all question, the common law here alluded to is not the common law of any individual state (for it probably differs in all), but it is the common law of England, the grand reservoir of all our jurisprudence." [10]

[10] Slocum v. N. Y. Life Ins. Co. (1913), 228 U. S. 364, quoting a lower federal court in U. S. v. Wonson (1812), I Gall. 5, 20, Fed. Case no. 16, 750.

There has been no formal enactment by Congress directing the federal courts to follow the rules of the common law. Instead, ever since 1789 there has been a section of the federal statutes providing that "the laws of the several states, except where the Constitution, treaties, or statutes of the United States otherwise require or provide, shall be regarded as rules of decision in trials at common law, in the courts of the United States, in cases where they apply." [11] In compliance with this statute the federal courts follow the local state court decisions as to the common law rules of that state, and also follow the state courts in their interpretation of the state constitution and statutes.

No Federal Common Law. From 1842 to 1938 the national courts followed a different rule with respect to one part of a state's common law. They declined to follow state court rulings in general commercial matters where a uniform rule of interpretation throughout the United States seemed to be more desirable.[12] It thus happened that the United States courts and the state courts sometimes followed different rules on the same subject within the same state. For example, is a railroad liable to pay damages to one who is injured by a train when he is trespassing on the railroad right of way? The Pennsylvania rule said no, and the United States courts said yes. The Supreme Court finally reversed its own early ruling on this point and held that "Except in matters governed by the Federal Constitution or by acts of Congress, the law to be applied in any case is the law of the state. . . . There is no federal general common law." [13] This rule makes for uniformity of substantive law in each state, and prevents litigants from getting different decisions by going into federal rather than state courts. On the other hand it checks to some extent the development of a uniform commercial law throughout the United States. It is still possible, however, to build up a more uniform law of commerce throughout the Union by national legislation under the commerce power, by uniform state laws, and other means.

The present situation is, therefore, that the United States courts have the right to interpret the national Constitution, statutes, and treaties, and the state courts must follow their decisions thereon, but the United States courts must follow the state court decisions on all common law questions in the particular state as well as on the state's constitution and statutes. Therefore, the judges of both systems of courts must know the law of the nation and also of the particular state in which they hold court. By their numerous decisions in which they deal with the law of both levels of government they constantly link the two more closely together into a single system of legal rules and principles.

Law and Equity Distinguished. The Constitution distinguishes between "law" and "equity." These are two broad classes of law that differ from each

[11] *U. S. Code of Laws*, Title 28, ch. 18, sec. 725.
[12] Swift v. Tyson (1842), 16 Peters (U. S.) I.
[13] Erie Railroad Co. v. Tompkins (1938), 304 U. S. 64; Ruhlin v. N. Y. Life Ins. Co. (1938), 304 U. S. 202.

other in the procedures that they lay down and in the results that they can produce. When the common law of England several centuries ago had developed to a certain point it was very rigid both in its procedures and in its remedies for wrongs. Thereupon the kings created chancery or equity courts to do justice in cases where the law courts were incapable of giving relief. Equity was looked upon as something extraordinary, to be used only in cases where the common law could not help. Some of the equity writs or court orders, like injunction, are still considered as extraordinary, but in fact equity is now just another body of law with its own procedural rules. In the nation's legal system, as well as in most of the states, law and equity have been woven together in a general code of procedure. The national courts utilize both procedures. When sitting as a court of equity a United States District Court operates without a jury, and it is able through the writ of injunction to prevent certain wrongs from being done. In common law proceedings juries are general, and as a rule the common law provides for remedies (e.g., damages) after a wrong has been done.

Civil and Criminal Law Distinguished. The Constitution distinguishes also between "criminal" and "civil" law. *Criminal law* is that branch of law in which offenses against the public peace, dignity, and order are defined. Murder, robbery, and treason are examples of such offenses. Lesser offenses, called misdemeanors, are also criminal in a general sense. In all these cases the government concerned has the accused person arrested and brought to court, where he is prosecuted for the offense. The result of such a trial is either acquittal or conviction, and if conviction, then punishment is supposed to follow, although a pardon may prevent this. *Civil law* in this connection is the branch of law that relates to suits between one person and another (considering the government or a corporation as a person just as much as any individual). There is a plaintiff who brings the suit, and a defendant. The case may relate to a contract, to a tort, to the title to real estate, to the relations of husband, wife, and children, or to any one of many other matters. If the plaintiff wins, the result is a "judgment" in a law case, a "decree" in an equity case, and the loser must satisfy the order rendered by paying money damages or in some other way specified. There is no necessary stigma attached, as in criminal cases, nor is there any punishment in the true sense.

There is a national code of criminal law, which defines offenses against the nation and their punishment, and each state also has its own criminal law. Again these several codes are complementary but cover different offenses. Robbery in general is an offense defined by state law, whereas robbery of the mails or of a national bank is an offense against the nation.

Admiralty and Maritime Law. The "admiralty and maritime" cases referred to in the Constitution are cases arising on the high seas or other navigable waters, concerning vessels, shippers, seamen, and others. Matters concerning piracy and the capture of prizes in time of war also come under this heading.

International Law and the National Courts. The Constitution practically adopts the "law of nations," or international law, as a part of the national system of laws for the federal courts to interpret and apply.[14] This is a rather extensive body of rules drawn from treaties, international practice, and other sources, and relating to governments and individuals and their relations in times of peace, in war, and in what is called neutrality.

JURISDICTION OF THE NATIONAL COURTS

The foregoing paragraphs present some ideas as to the legal system of the United States and as to the major bodies and classes of law that the Constitution mentions. With this exposition in mind the reader can more easily grasp the scope of the jurisdiction of the national courts.

Jurisdiction Defined. A court may hear and decide cases (i.e., speak or pronounce the law) only within the limits of its jurisdiction. Where there is a dual system of courts, national and state, as in the United States, the definition of a court's jurisdiction is a necessary first step to understanding what the court does. No court in the United States may handle absolutely every type of case.

Jurisdiction is definable in terms of (a) *subject-matter of the cases* (e.g., divorce, murder, treason, traffic violation, taxation, property ownership), (b) *persons involved* (e.g., states, foreign corporations, local citizens, aliens, citizens of other states) and (c) *geographical or territorial extent* (How far can a court reach in accepting cases for trial?). In short the jurisdiction of a court means over what subject matters, over what persons, and within what territorial limits a court may exercise its powers.

What the court can do about a case after it has claimed jurisdiction is another matter. This question touches its *powers* rather than its jurisdiction. In general courts are restricted to issuing orders to the parties in a case. They cannot actually *enforce* these orders, as a rule, but must leave that to the executive branch of the government. As Hamilton said in *The Federalist*, the courts are the weakest branch of the government; they have neither purse nor sword.[15]

Jurisdictional Boundaries. The broad lines for the division of jurisdiction between national and state courts are laid down in the Constitution. It is the underlying theory that for every legal wrong there is a remedy and a court that can prescribe the remedy, although there are some exceptions. The Constitution defines the general outlines and the utmost scope of the jurisdiction of the United States courts, leaving it to Congress within these limits to define more precisely the exact jurisdiction of each court. Only one type of jurisdiction is expressly granted by the Constitution to a court, and that is the original jurisdiction of the Supreme Court. The appellate jurisdiction of the Supreme

[14] Art. I, sec. 8, par. 10.
[15] *The Federalist*, no. 78.

Court, and the entire jurisdiction of all other United States courts, are subject to definition and regulation by Congress.

It should be borne in mind, too, that a grant of jurisdiction to a national court by the Constitution or by Congress does not necessarily exclude the state courts from exercising jurisdiction over such cases as well. In the nature of things, only the Supreme Court can exercise jurisdiction in suits between two states. In other instances the courts have decided, or Congress has enacted, that certain kinds of jurisdiction shall be exercised exclusively by the national courts. By statute, all cases involving crimes and offenses against the United States laws, admiralty and maritime cases, cases of prizes taken during war, patent, copyright, and bankruptcy cases, suits between states, and cases involving foreign ambassadors, ministers, or consuls go exclusively to the national courts with a few minor exceptions.[16]

Jurisdiction of Federal Courts. The provisions of the Constitution concerning the *judicial power of the United States* fall into three groups: (1) the cases in which the national courts may have jurisdiction because of the *subject matter or nature of the law or controversy involved*; (2) the cases in which they may have jurisdiction because of *the parties involved*; and (3) the cases that come partly under both heads. Arranged in this way they read:

> The judicial Power shall extend (1) to all Cases, in Law and Equity, arising under this Constitution, the Laws of the United States, and the Treaties made, or which shall be made, under their Authority; . . . to all Cases of maritime and admiralty Jurisdiction; . . . (2) to all Cases affecting Ambassadors, other public Ministers and Consuls; . . . to Controversies to which the United States shall be a Party; to Controversies between two or more States; between a State and Citizens of another State; between Citizens of different States, . . . and between a State, or the Citizens thereof, and foreign States, Citizens, or Subjects, . . . and (3) between Citizens of the same State claiming Lands under Grants of different States, . . .[17]

By way of exception, under the Eleventh Amendment suits begun by private persons against states cannot be entertained in the United States courts.

Original and Appellate Jurisdiction. The Constitution makes a further distinction between "original" and "appellate" jurisdiction. Original jurisdiction is the right of a court to take cognizance of a case in the first instance, at the point where it begins. Appellate jurisdiction is the right to review and redecide cases that have already been decided in another court. The same court may, of course, have original jurisdiction in some cases, and appellate jurisdiction in others. The Supreme Court illustrates this point. Its principal work is appellate, but the Constitution grants it also original jurisdiction "in all cases affecting Ambassadors, other public Ministers and Consuls, and those in

---

[16] *U. S. Code of Laws*, Title 28, ch. 10, sec. 371.
[17] U. S. Const., Art. III, sec. 2, par. I, slightly rearranged.

which a State shall be a Party." This is an express and limited grant, and the Supreme Court itself has ruled that Congress has no power to confer additional original jurisdiction on the Court.[18]

Appellate Jurisdiction of Supreme Court. In all cases within the broad range of the national judicial power in which it does not have original jurisdiction, "the supreme Court shall have appellate Jurisdiction, both as to Law and Fact, with such Exceptions, and under such Regulations as the Congress shall make." [19] With the tremendous growth of national judicial business, it would be a sheer impossibility for the Supreme Court to hear all the appeals that are brought up from lower courts. The Circuit Courts of Appeals were created to carry a large share of this burden but even this relief was not enough. The Supreme Court was for a long time very much overcrowded and far behind in the handling of cases. Later changes in the law have limited the duty of the Supreme Court to the handling of appeals in constitutional questions, and in the interpretation of federal statutes and treaties, but have left it free to call up other cases from lower courts by writ of certiorari where it is not expressly obligated to hear an appeal.[20] Direct appeals come up to it from the highest state courts when the latter have upheld a state law or action against a claim that it violated the Constitution, and the court may by the writ called "certiorari" order the record of a state case laid before it where any "federal question," that is, a question under the Constitution, statutes or treaties of the United States, has been passed upon in the state court. This enables the Supreme Court to control the interpretation of the national Constitution, statutes, and treaties by the state courts and produce that uniformity of interpretation that the framers had in mind. The "highest court of a state in which a decision in a suit could be had" from which appeal may be taken is not necessarily the state supreme court. One of the "white primary" cases from Texas was appealed directly from a local justice court in that state to the Supreme Court, for the reason that no appeal to the state supreme court was possible.[21] Appeals are also taken from the United States district courts, the Court of Claims, and other courts of the national system, on questions involving constitutionality and on the final interpretation of United States statutes and treaties.

Appellate Jurisdiction of Circuit Courts of Appeal. While the Supreme Court controls the review of all questions involving constitutional questions, the Circuit Courts of Appeals have jurisdiction to review the decisions of the district courts in practically all other cases, both in law and equity, and this power of review extends also to the decisions of the territorial district courts as well as to the orders of the Federal Trade Commission, Interstate Commerce Commission, the Federal Reserve Board, and the National Labor Relations Board.

18 Marbury v. Madison (1803), I Cranch (U. S.) 137.
19 U. S. Const., Art. III, sec. 2, par. 2.
20 U. S. Code of Laws, Title 28, ch. 9, secs. 344, 345.
21 Grovey v. Townsend (1935), 295 U. S. 45.

Original Jurisdiction of United States District Courts. The jurisdiction of the district courts is all original jurisdiction, but of two kinds:

1. *Cases Under National Laws.* All cases of crimes and misdemeanors against national laws and treaties, all admiralty and maritime cases, all cases under the patent laws, copyright laws, bankruptcy laws, all suits brought by the United States, and so on, are tried in the first instance in the United States district courts. The famous section in which this jurisdiction is set forth cannot be fully analyzed here, but there has been little criticism of the law for assigning these cases to the national courts.[22] It seems only logical that a United States court should handle cases concerning the national government and arising under its own laws.

2. *"Diversity of Citizenship" Cases.* The other part of the jurisdiction of the district courts, that which is dependent on the character of the parties concerned, and particularly the portion that arises merely because there is "diversity of citizenship" between the parties, has been much more frequently criticized. Where a matter in controversy exceeds the sum or value of $3,000, exclusive of interest and court costs, and the suit is between citizens of different states, or between citizens of a state and foreign states, citizens, or subjects, the United States district court has jurisdiction. If a similar suit, let us say on a building contract, involves two citizens of the same state, it must be tried in a state court, whereas foreigners and citizens of other states may bring their suits in the national district courts. One result of this rule is that corporations, which are held to be citizens of the state in which they incorporate, are frequently able to escape the jurisdiction of the state courts in the states where they are doing business. Many corporators deliberately form their corporations in states other than those in which they expect to operate. Thus every time they are involved in any important case, they can apply to the United States district court and ignore the state courts. One of the outstanding abuses of this privilege arose in the cases of public utility corporations doing business in a state, but holding charters from other states. Time and again when a state rate-making body attempted to regulate their rates, these utility corporations went at once to a United States district court for an injunction, and thus tied the hands of the state authorities. Congress recognized the evil, and it first tried the expedient of having such cases handled only by a special panel of three district judges, but this did not greatly change the situation. Finally in 1934 and 1937 Congress enacted laws to the effect that where the state acts provide an adequate remedy in state courts in cases involving taxation, rate regulation and similar subjects, the United States district courts may not take jurisdiction merely because of diversity of citizenship.[23] It is now up to the states to provide adequate legal remedies at home. If they do so, all such rate and tax cases will be handled by the state court

[22] *U. S. Code of Laws*, Title 28, ch. 2, sec. 41.

[23] Act of May 14, 1934, ch. 283, 48 *Stat. at Large*, 775; act of August 21, 1937, ch. 726, 50 *Stat. at Large*, 738.

system, up to its supreme court, and will go from that court to the Supreme Court of the United States only where a constitutional question is involved.

Removal of Cases from State to National Courts. Since the jurisdiction of the United States courts is not in all cases exclusive, and since mistakes are often made by lawyers and judges, it frequently happens that cases are begun in state courts that could have, or should have, been brought to the United States district courts first. To prevent any possible injustice in such cases, Congress has provided for the removal of such cases, particularly on the application of the defendant, to the national district court before the trial in the state court has been completed. Criminal trials of national officers for things done in the course of their duties, and civil cases where there is diversity of citizenship, are illustrations of cases that may be thus removed to the United States courts.

PROCEDURE IN THE UNITED STATES COURTS

The Importance of Procedure. Certain parts of the law are described as *substantive* because they deal with such concrete rights as those of property and personal liberty. Other parts are *procedural*. They define how courts and administrative agencies must proceed when they act upon substantive rights, and how individuals may proceed to protect themselves. It might appear that substantive rights are of greater importance than procedural, but in fact the two go together. It is only through established fair and orderly procedures that rights can receive any protection at all. Although it seems like a mere procedure, jury trial in criminal cases is one of the most solid of bulwarks against the invasion of a man's right to life and liberty.

Sources of Procedural Rules. In the Constitution itself will be found a few of the more important procedural rights, such as guarantees of jury trial in both civil and criminal cases, and prohibitions against such practices as unreasonable searches and seizures, compulsory self-incrimination, bills of attainder, and ex post facto laws. In addition to these the statutes passed by Congress from the very first have made some requirements governing judicial procedure. Always the courts have been compelled to make some rules of procedure as they have gone along, and now the tendency is for Congress to delegate the making of rules of procedure to the Supreme Court.

Some years ago a distinguished law teacher made the assertion that the legislative branch of government (Congress or the state legislature) "exceeds its constitutional power when it attempts to impose upon the judiciary any rules for the dispatch of the judiciary's duties; and that therefore all legislatively declared rules for procedure, civil or criminal, in the courts, are void, except such as are expressly stated in the Constitution." [24] This astounding doctrine rested upon an interpretation of the separation of powers doctrine,

[24] The late Dean Wigmore of the Northwestern University Law School. See *Jour. of Amer. Judic. Soc.*, vol. 20, pp. 159-60 (1936); *ibid.*, vol. 24, pp. 70-71 (1940).

to wit, that since the courts may not tell the legislature how it shall proceed, neither may the legislature lay down rules for court procedure. In short the judicial power vested in the courts was held to include the entire power to make rules of procedure for the courts. Had this doctrine been put into effect it would have wiped out hundreds of pages of national and state legislation that regulate court procedure.

This whole doctrine is open to criticism from many viewpoints. If it were true, then, by parallel reasoning, Congress would have no power to regulate the procedure of the executive branch either, a truly shocking conclusion. There are in fact no words of the Constitution that support the general theory of the argument, but there are several important powers conferred upon Congress including those to "ordain and establish" inferior courts and to pass "necessary and proper" laws, that uphold the power long exercised by Congress to regulate court procedure.[25] It may be pointed out also that the distinction between substance and procedure is not always easy to make. If then a procedural rule made by the courts were to conflict with a substantive rule made by Congress, the courts would become judges in their own cause in deciding which to observe. The long established and accepted practice of Congressional control over judicial procedure, and the political advantages in having only one instead of two sources of legislation, argue strongly for a continuance of Congressional supremacy in this field.

The Conformity Act, and Confusion. As in other cases, however, Congress did not use its power to the full extent of its possibilities. After a period of uncertainty and experimentation, Congress in 1872 enacted the Conformity Act under which the United States courts were required to conform their procedures generally to the state law in the states in which they sat. Thus all the local vagaries and idiosyncrasies of state court procedures crept into the national courts. Furthermore Congress was not at its best when it attempted to legislate, as it did from time to time, on particular points in procedure. The total result was a somewhat chaotic and confusing situation in United States court procedure.

Rule-Making by the Supreme Court. Delegation of rule-making authority to the courts themselves seemed to be the sensible way out. It was clear that in any case the courts had to make numerous decisions concerning their own procedure as new situations arose. To extend and to regularize this practice, and to center responsibility for it in one place, Congress began over a century ago to confer some powers of rule-making upon the Supreme Court. Rules for procedure in particular branches of law were thus established. This tendency came to a climax in 1934 and later years, when Congress delegated to the Supreme Court the authority to make procedural rules for the United States courts, first in civil and later in criminal cases, such rules to become effective

---

· [25] See Charles H. Beardsley in *Jour. of Amer. Judic. Soc.*, vol. 24, pp. 115-17 (1940); *ibid.*, pp. 101-02; Silas A. Harris, "The Rule-Making Power," Amer. Bar Ass'n, *Judic. Admin. Monographs*, Series A, no. 1.

when laid before Congress and not disapproved by it. Thus Congress retained its position as the source of rule-making power, and the Supreme Court became its principal agent to do the work. This was a happy combination of amateur control with expert service. In 1937 the Supreme Court adopted a new code of uniform Federal Rules of Civil Procedure which became effective in 1938. Under these rules the main procedural distinctions between law and equity were wiped out. A similar code for criminal procedure was completed in 1944 and put into effect in 1945.

As a result of these changes the United States courts now have nation-wide, uniform rules of procedure in practically all civil and criminal cases. This is a great stride forward for national unity. In addition the new rules are not only simpler and more effective, but also more flexible and adaptable to changing situations, because the Supreme Court is in position to keep them up-to-date. But is it not about time for some organization to protest against this violation of the separation of powers through the imposition of legislative functions upon the Supreme Court? In making general rules of procedure it is not deciding cases or controversies; it is not even waiting for business to come to it but going out to make written rules of general future application.

The important rules of judicial procedure that affect the life, liberty, and property of individuals, such things as grand jury indictments, jury trial, the right of counsel, and due process in general, will be treated in chapter 20 on Civil Rights and the National Government. Before closing this chapter, however, one other important development in the United States courts needs to be mentioned.

ADMINISTRATIVE UNIFICATION OF UNITED STATES COURTS

For well over a century Congress worked spasmodically to improve the United States court system but did little or nothing to pull the courts together into a single administrative organization or to set up over-all advisory bodies. Each district court, circuit court, circuit court of appeals, and the Supreme Court, went its own way. There was no general or corporate responsibility on the part of the judges to see that the work of the national courts was done well or even done at all. Great differences prevailed in judicial methods, standards, and results among the different districts. One district could be so far ahead on its docket that the judge had much time for golf and fishing, while in a neighboring district the judge was bogged down in work.

In 1922 Congress authorized the establishment of an annual Judicial Conference of Senior Circuit Judges in Washington to be headed by the Chief Justice of the Supreme Court. The act "provided an executive head in each circuit, required standardized statistical reporting, and afforded responsible consideration of all problems at the annual meeting, with representation also of the department of justice." [26] Conferences were established also for the district and circuit judges and other leading lawyers in each of the circuits. This completed the machinery for responsible and regular consultation among the judges and lawyers interested in the federal courts.

Congress was persuaded also to create in 1939 the Administrative Office of the United States Courts. The director of this office is appointed by and responsible to the Judicial Conference of Senior Circuit Judges. Prior to this the Department of Justice had looked after the budget requests and certain business affairs of the United States courts. Under the new arrangements the United States judges became jointly responsible for budgeting and business management in the national courts, gained direct access to Congress for these purposes, and acquired a central secretariat in the Administrative Office to aid and represent them.[27] The secretariat manages the business affairs of the courts, collects, reports and keeps up-to-date the statistics on the status of the judicial business in the district courts and circuit courts of appeal, and serves the Judicial Conference in every feasible way to promote the efficiency of the courts. The results have already far more than justified the creation of the new office.

Today the United States courts are more fully than ever an integrated national system, jointly responsible for judicial efficiency, and autonomous as never before. Their experience and their best brains can now be pooled for the consideration and elimination of difficulties as they arise, and the services of their judges can be applied wherever needed to keep the courts as a whole abreast of their work. While the executive branch of government has faced formidable opposition in Congress to its attempts to modernize and integrate its organization and methods, and while Congress has done little or nothing to modernize itself, the courts have in a quiet but effective way accomplished for themselves a very thorough overhauling and integration.

REFERENCES

C. N. Callender, *American Courts: Their Organization and Procedure*, New York, 1927.

W. F. Willoughby, *Principles of Judicial Administration*, Washington, 1929.

Charles Evans Hughes, *The Supreme Court of the United States*, New York, 1928.

Felix Frankfurter, "Distribution of Judicial Power between United States and State Courts," *Cornell Law Quarterly*, vol. XIII, pp. 499-530 (1928).

Felix Frankfurter and J. M. Landis, *The Business of the Supreme Court: A Study in the Federal Judicial System*, New York, 1927.

J. M. Mathews, *The American Constitutional System*, New York, 2nd ed., 1940, chs. XIII-XV.

[26] Jour. of Amer. Judic. Soc., vol. 24, p. 108 (1940).
[27] Jour. of Amer. Judic. Soc., vol. 26, pp. 7-10 (1942).

Code of Laws of the United States, Title 28.

Journal of the American Judicature Society. (A mine of information on court reform.)

U. S. *Supreme Court Reports.*

U. S. Senate, Committee on the Judiciary, 75th Congress, 1st sess., *Hearings before . . . on S. 1392, Reorganization of the Federal Judiciary,* Washington, 1937.

Roscoe Pound, *Organization of Courts,* Boston, 1940.

United States Government Manual.

Comm. on Pub. Admin., *Research in Judicial Administration,* An Outline of Suggested Research Topics, Washington, 1942.

Charles Pergler, "Trial of Good Behavior of Federal Judges," *Va. Law Rev.,* vol. 29, pp. 876-80 (1943).

G. W. C. Ross, " 'Good Behavior' of Federal Judges," *Univ. of K. C. Law Rev.,* vol. 12, pp. 119-27 (1944).

Lewis W. Morse, "Federal Judicial Conferences and Councils: Their Creation and Reports," *Cornell Law Quarterly,* vol. 27, pp. 347-63 (1942).

Henry P. Chandler, "The Place of the Administrative Office in the Federal Court System," *Cornell Law Quarterly,* vol. 27, pp. 364-73 (1942).

John Parker, "The Integration of the Federal Judiciary," *Harvard Law Review,* vol. 56, pp. 563-75 (1943).

L. I. Perrigo, "The Federal Judiciary: An Analysis of Proposed Revisions," *Minn. Law Review,* vol. 21, pp. 481-511 (1937).

Administrative Office of the United States Courts, *Annual Reports,* 1940 ff.

John Mathews and Clarence A. Berdahl, *Documents and Readings in American Government: National and State,* rev. ed., New York, 1940, pp. 484-90, 785-811.

A. N. Christensen and E. M. Kirkpatrick, *The People, Politics, and the Politician: Readings in American Government,* New York, 1941, pp. 592-618.

CHAPTER 18

Judicial Review of Legislative Actions

THE COURTS AND THE SEPARATION OF POWERS

In addition to their ordinary work in deciding cases the courts of the United States exercise to a unique degree another important power, namely, that of passing upon the constitutionality of the acts of the legislative and executive branches. This function is usually designated as "judicial review." It is exercised to some extent by all courts in the United States but it reaches its highest point in the Supreme Court of the United States.

Position of Courts in System of Government. John Locke apparently looked upon the courts that decide cases as only a part of the executive in internal affairs.[1] An able American authority has reached a similar conclusion as to the true nature of the judicial function.[2] The prevalent American view is very different. Both the state and national courts are provided for by separate constitutional provisions; the separation of powers doctrine emphasizes this separateness; and the courts generally insist that they are a distinct third branch of government. Indeed the independence of the judiciary from the other departments, and its equality with others (if not superiority to them) is an important article of faith with many lawyers and other citizens.

Nature of Judicial Function. The judicial function, i.e., the function of the courts or the judiciary, is to decide cases of legal controversy between man and man, or between men and government. The function of deciding private civil cases, as where A sues B for injuries caused by an automobile accident, is one great phase of the courts' work. Another is that of deciding an increasing number of cases in which the government, or some governmental official, is involved, such as law enforcement and tax collection cases. Here the work of the courts appears as but one step in the process of government. The legislature enacts a tax law, for example; the executive branch proceeds to enforce

---

[1] See ch. 13, above.
[2] F. J. Goodnow, *Politics and Administration*, New York, 1900, espec. pp. 1-22, 72-93.

it; controversies arise, men evade the tax, or dispute the amount or the validity of the tax; and then the courts are called upon to decide as between taxpayer and tax collector.

Judicial Function in Relation to Others. Thus in testing the claims and rights of individuals and corporations in countless cases, the courts consider the meaning of legislative acts, and the validity of the actions of the officers who try to enforce them. In short they pass upon the work of both the other major branches of the government. Their decisions may usually be appealed to courts above them, to the supreme court of the state in state cases, and to the Supreme Court of the United States in federal or national cases. These highest court decisions are in a legal sense "final" as to the facts before the courts in the case, but are hardly final in any other sense. They can be effectively enforced only by the executive branch, which in some cases refuses to enforce them; and they may be so distasteful that legislative action to correct them is quickly begun. Thus the decisions of the courts represent a step in a governmental process that is like a link in a continuous chain, interlocked with legislative and executive actions.

Nature of Judicial Decisions. The more important decisions of the courts are recorded, and in the case of the higher courts are published for the benefit of judges, lawyers, and the public. Technically, of course, the "decision" is only the statement of what is actually decided; for example, that B must pay A for the automobile injury, or that the taxpayer owes the government only $1,000 instead of the $1,500 asked by the collector. As printed, however, the case or decision includes a statement of the facts and of the reasons given by the judge for his decisions on the several points involved. This reasoning or rationalization of the decision is more properly called "opinion," and frequently includes statements (*dicta*) that have little or no relevancy to the actual decision. If some of the judges disagree with the majority, their "dissenting" or "concurring" opinions are also usually published—a dissent where there is disagreement as to what the decision should have been, a concurring opinion where they agree on the decision but differ on the reasons for it.

Nature of "Constitutional Law." Thus a constantly increasing body of judicial decisions and opinions is being accumulated, and from this mass of materials the teachers in law schools select important cases for law students to study. In this way various subjects of study are developed—"contracts," "property," and "constitutional law," for example. In the latter subject what is studied is not primarily the texts of national and state constitutions, but the decisions and opinions of the judges. These law students in turn become lawyers, legislators, and judges, and go on building up this body of "constitutional law" which grows like a series of protuberances from the original slender stalk of the written Constitution. Whole volumes can now be produced based on court decisions and opinions relating to such short phrases in the Constitution as "due process of law" or "commerce . . . among the several states." The judge-made "law" far outbulks the "Constitution." As former Chief Justice Hughes once said: "We are under a Constitution, but the Constitution is what the judges say it is." This statement by the former Chief Justice is of very doubtful validity, but at any rate the judges go on saying what the Constitution is at very considerable length.

Influence of Court Decisions. The popular theory that the courts in rendering their decisions do not *make* law but only *declare* it as they find it has already been considered, and the conclusion was reached that they actually make law.[3] Another theory is that the decision settles only the case before the court. Technically this is true, but actually it is not. Like a stone thrown in quiet water, an important court decision sends the waves of its influence in every direction—and the influence in this case lasts much longer. A United States Supreme Court decision may actually set aside the law of only one state, but forty-seven other states and several territories are deterred from passing or enforcing similar acts. The rule that is laid down becomes a binding rule of judge-made law until overruled or by-passed.

Conflicts Between Written Laws. When a statute or an administrative regulation, or any other type of enacted or written law, is put before the court in a case, it must decide (a) what the law means, and (b) how it applies to the case before it. It is in most cases impossible to make a statute so clear on every point that it does not call for explanation or interpretation. Now in the United States there are several varieties of written law, including constitutions and statutes (both national and state), treaties, administrative regulations, and local ordinances. In any single case the lawyers may quote provisions from two or more of these classes of written laws. A city ordinance seems to authorize one thing, but the state law provides differently, and the state constitution may have a general clause bearing on the subject. If they conflict, which is to prevail in the case before the court? What is to happen to the other provisions? *And who is to decide these questions?*

The English courts began centuries ago to overrule municipal ordinances when they went counter to the common law (i.e., established court decisions), statutes of the realm, or to "reason"; and when colonies were established across the seas, the courts sometimes exercised the same right as to the statutes passed by the colonial assemblies. These were considered subordinate bodies and were treated accordingly. The statutes enacted by "the King in parliament," however, were not declared invalid. There was no higher written law with which they could be compared, or with which they could conflict. There was some talk among lawyers and judges that the common law was a body of higher law, and in the seventeenth century the famous Justice Coke made the following broad statement:

> It appears in our books, that in many cases, the common law will control Acts of Parliament, and sometimes adjudge them to be utterly

---

[3] See ch. 4, above, pp. 45-47.

> void: for when an Act of Parliament is against common right and
> reason, or repugnant, or impossible to be performed, the common law
> will control it, and adjudge such Act to be void.[4]

This voiding of acts of Parliament by the judiciary was, in fact, never carried
out directly. Instead the courts contented themselves with such interpretations
of statutes as would make them harmonize as fully as possible with the common law. And this is what the British courts do to this day.

Written Constitutions and Judicial Review of Legislation. In the United
States, however, there appeared those documents that are called "written constitutions," both state and national. Though the first state constitutions were
not essentially different from other statutes, in a short time they came to be
drawn up by special constitutional conventions and adopted either by, or in
the name of, the people. Thus written constitutions came to be looked upon
as higher than ordinary statutes, and the question arose whether the courts,
in deciding cases in the regular course of procedure, had the power to set
aside a statute when, in their judgment, it conflicted with the written constitution. This power the courts soon assumed, and they have exercised it now
for over a hundred years. It is this power that gives the courts a position over
against the legislative and executive branches quite different from the position
of courts in most other countries. In the separation of powers, the courts form
the third side of the triangle.

Judicial Review in the Supreme Court. The Supreme Court of the United
States, standing at the head of the entire judicial system, is spoken of as the
"balance wheel" of the Constitution. Its power seems impressive enough to
justify the phrases "judicial supremacy," "government by judiciary," and
"judicial oligarchy." This is largely because at each session this court passes
on the constitutionality of a number of acts of Congress and state legislatures,
and of important executive and administrative bodies. Some of them it upholds, or fails to declare invalid—whereupon the newspapers say it "validates"
them, which is absurd since they are no more valid afterwards than they were
before the court's action. Others it declares to be in violation of the Constitution, and these it refuses to consider as having legal force. In short it has become largely a tribunal for deciding constitutional questions, and thus is exercising a function not usually considered as a judicial function at all. This
function of the "judicial review" of legislation to test its constitutionality is,
no doubt, a higher political service than simply deciding cases between man
and man, but certainly it is a very different one. It is largely an American contribution to the art of government, and it calls for careful study.

[4] Dr. Bonham's case, 8 Rep. 118. See McLaughlin, *A Constitutional History of the United
States*, New York, 1935, p. 28; Haines, *The American Doctrine of Judicial Supremacy*,
Berkeley, 1932, p. 33.

ORIGIN OF POWER OF JUDICIAL REVIEW

Colonial Precedents. Colonial legislation, it will be recalled, was subject to (a) the executive veto by the royal governor, (b) disallowance by the Crown (aided by the Privy Council and Board of Trade), after it had gone into effect, and (c) disallowance in a later judicial procedure after it had passed through the first two screenings, but was found in some later case before the courts to be contrary to English law. This subsequent check was perhaps least known to the colonies, but the lawyers were not wholly unaware of it.[5]

Precedents in the States, 1776-87. When the colonies became states, and the legislatures assumed complete control in their respective states for the first few years, even to appointing judges, judicial review had no place in the system of state government. A little later, when constitutions began to be considered supreme law, the doctrine of judicial review of state legislation began to emerge. In 1786 in Rhode Island an act that required merchants to accept the state's paper money as legal tender for goods, and empowered courts to punish those refusing to do so without a jury trial, was said in the opinion of the supreme court justices to be "repugnant and unconstitutional"—not as violating any words of the Rhode Island constitution, which was still the old charter, but as against natural rights and ancient liberties.[6] This opinion of the judges was mere *dictum*; in fact for other reasons they threw out the case of the butcher who refused to give good meat for poor paper money. Nevertheless there was a tremendous outcry among paper money advocates against this action of the courts, and an attempt was made to oust all the justices. These and other evidences in the same period showed that lawyers and other conservative upholders of property rights were thinking of the courts as checks upon those legislatures that might move to the popular side in legislating on property matters, but there was no widespread or generally accepted doctrine of judicial review of legislation in this period.

The Constitutional Convention of 1787. In creating a stronger union with a national legislature for national purposes, the federal convention of 1787 faced the problem of how to keep state legislation from encroaching on national powers. There was also some feeling that legislation passed by the proposed Congress should be "revised" by someone, although at first the executive was not suggested for this purpose. The Virginia Plan covered both matters by proposing to empower Congress "to negative all laws passed by the several States, contravening in the opinion of the National Legislature the articles of Union; and to call forth the force of the Union against any member of the Union failing in its duty under the articles thereof," and by adding

[5] An important case was that of Winthrop v. Lechmere (1728), a Privy Council judicial decision invalidating a Connecticut statute concerning inheritances.

[6] Case of Trevett v. Weeden. See Haines, *The American Doctrine of Judicial Supremacy*, Berkeley, 1932, pp. 105-12; Hockett, *The Constitutional History of the United States*, 1776-1826, pp. 176-77.

"that the Executive and a convenient number of the National Judiciary, ought to compose a Council of revision with authority to examine every act of the National Legislature before it shall operate, and every act of a particular state Legislature before a Negative thereon shall be final; and that the dissent of the said Council shall amount to a rejection, unless the Act of the National Legislature be passed again, or that of a particular Legislature be again negatived by . . . the members of each branch." [7]

New Jersey Plan. The proposal for review of state legislation by Congress and the Council of Revision was quite obviously a partial return to the old royal disallowance of colonial legislation, although the grounds for disallowance were narrowed down to the question of conflict between the state act and the federal Constitution. That the proposed method was clumsy, and that the states would be almost certain to resist by force the first attempts to use the national veto, became clear in the convention's discussions. As an alternative there was the New Jersey Plan [8] which proposed that the acts of Congress "made by virtue and in pursuance" of its powers under the articles of Union, and "all treaties made and ratified under the authority of the United States, shall be the supreme law of the respective States, and that the Judiciary of the several States shall be bound thereby in their decisions, any thing in the respective laws of the Individual States to the contrary notwithstanding." Coupled with this, as in the Virginia Plan, was a proposal for a United States Supreme Court as a court of last resort in all appeals affecting national rights. Here was provided a *judicial* machinery and method for keeping state laws in line with the national Constitution.

Supreme Law of Land Idea. As to national legislation, the proposed council of revision idea was rejected, and the President was endowed with a veto, similar to that of the Massachusetts governor, which could be overruled by a two-thirds vote of Congress. The subject of a separate judicial check on national legislation that was contrary to the Constitution was also discussed briefly and by a few men. It appears that a few favored the idea, a few opposed, and the rest were silent. No formal proposal to authorize judicial review of acts of Congress was made; hence there is no clear expression of the sense of the convention. The power was neither provided for nor prohibited. If the courts were to have the power, it would have to arise from implication.[9]

In the Campaign for Ratification. In the state conventions called to ratify the Constitution, voices were again raised for and against the power of judicial review over Congressional acts, but now the voices seemed to be more in favor. It began to be recognized that the judicial branch, both to preserve its own freedom against encroachments by Congress and to secure the enforcement of other rights in the Constitution, might resort to the power of review. Alex-

[7] See Commager, *Documents of American History*, pp. 134-35.

[8] Commager, *op. cit.*, p. 137.

[9] See Haines, *op. cit.*, pp. 126-35; Bates, *The Story of the Supreme Court*, Indianapolis, 1936, pp. 26-29; Beard, *The Supreme Court and the Constitution*, New York, 1912, pp. 15-67.

ander Hamilton in *The Federalist* strongly supported the power, and argued that it was a point of excellence in the Constitution that it proposed to establish a strong, independent judiciary to protect the Constitution of the people against their chosen legislators.[10] There was some inconsistency between his arguments. In No. 33 he argued "that the National Government, like any other, must judge, in the first instance, of the proper exercise of its powers," and that if it overstepped its power and became tyrannical "the people" must and would act to correct it. In No. 78 he reasoned "that the courts were designed to be an intermediate body between the people and the Legislature, in order, among other things, to keep the latter within the limits assigned to their authority." At a time when lawyers and judges were extremely unpopular, it was a little humorous not to say audacious of Hamilton to argue that a body of lawyers, the Supreme Court, whom the people could in no way control, should be the people's defenders against legislators who came at least partly from the choice of the voters.

The Judiciary Act of 1789. The first Congress under the Constitution showed that it clearly expected courts, even state courts, to hold acts of Congress and treaties invalid, and it gave the Supreme Court of the United States definite authority to hear appeals in all cases in which the highest state courts had upheld state laws against national, or had denied some right claimed by an individual under national laws or treaties.[11]

CASES OF JUDICIAL REVIEW AFTER 1789

Beginnings of National Judicial Review. It was not long before the United States courts began in fact to exercise the power so casually and vaguely placed in their hands. The state legislatures were still engaged in depriving British subjects of property rights, in contravention of the treaty of peace, and in making laws to ease the burdens of the debtor class. Consequently some individuals, seeking a remedy against state laws that they could not find in the state courts, began to appear in the national courts for relief. The United States circuit courts found early occasion to declare several state acts unconstitutional on the ground that they impaired the obligation of contracts or treaty rights.[12]

State Courts Pass on State Laws. Meanwhile also the state courts were developing the practice of declaring state acts invalid, and were showing increasing confidence in their power to do so.[13] At first they were somewhat uncertain of the grounds on which such power rested, but more and more they accepted Hamilton's views that a constitution is a higher law, that it emanates directly from the people, that the legislature is under the constitution and is unfitted to decide the limits on its own powers, and that therefore the courts

---

[10] *The Federalist*, espec. nos. 33, 78, 81.
[11] Haines, *op. cit.*, pp. 144-47.
[12] Haines, *op. cit.*, 178-89, and footnote 20, p. 181; Bates, *op. cit.*, pp. 50, 53.
[13] See Haines, *op. cit.*, pp. 148-70; Boudin, *Government by Judiciary*, vol. I, pp. 51-72.

have a duty to stand between the legislature and "the people"—meaning, of course, between the legislature and the individual litigants and minorities who come to court for protection. The state supreme courts felt constrained to uphold the state constitution as against state statutes. Only later did state judges sometimes hold state acts invalid because they conflicted with the national constitution, laws and treaties.

National Courts Pass on Acts of Congress. Very soon, too, the United States courts faced the question whether certain acts of Congress itself were valid and enforceable. Judges were at the time fighting back against a wave of unpopularity that was leading legislators to impose additional duties on them without giving them extra pay. Several Virginia acts were held invalid on this ground by the state judges; members of the Supreme Court grumbled at being required to serve as circuit judges, a duty that some of them considered unconstitutional; but when another act of Congress assigned to them the duty of investigating disabled soldiers' pension claims, and to fix the amounts to be allowed, subject to review by the Secretary of War and finally by Congress, the revolt of the judges was immediate.[14] In several federal circuits they held that this was an unconstitutional attempt to impose a nonjudicial duty upon the judicial branch, in violation of the independence of the judges and their right and duty to perform only judicial functions. Presently other cases came before the federal courts in which lawyers argued that certain acts of Congress were unconstitutional, but the judges after considering them upheld them as valid. In these cases one judge after another made statements asserting the right of the courts, and of the courts alone, to pass on the validity under the Constitution of legislative acts—whether passed by Congress or by a state legislature.[15] Clearly the groundwork was being laid for a Supreme Court decision holding an act of Congress unconstitutional. Such a decision came in 1803.

Supreme Court Refuses to Give Advisory Opinion. Before this, however, one other incident showed the direction of judicial thinking. The French Revolution and the wars in Europe created grave problems of enforcing neutrality in the United States. The legal powers of the government not being clear, Washington had Hamilton draw up a series of legal questions that he forwarded to the Supreme Court with a request for answers. The Court declined, holding that, since there was no legal controversy or case before it, the matter fell outside its jurisdiction. In short it refused to give advisory opinions, or to be drawn into the problems of the other departments.[16] The precedent thus established in refusing to give advisory opinions has not been broken. In a number of states, however, under specific constitutional provisions, advisory opinions are regularly given by the courts to the legislature and the executive.

[14] Hayburn's Case (1792), 2 Dallas 410.
[15] Haines, *op. cit.*, pp. 175-79, 183, 191-93.
[16] Warren, *The Supreme Court in United States History*, 1926 ed., vol. I, pp. 105-11; Orth and Cushman, *American National Government*, p. 502.

Marbury v. Madison, 1803. The Federalists under Adams, defeated in the election of 1800 by Jefferson's Republican party, sought to perpetuate their hold on the government in at least the judicial branch. After the election they passed an act to reorganize and enlarge the judiciary, and appointed a number of Federalists to the new positions. In the shuffle, Marshall was appointed chief justice, but as retiring Secretary of State under Adams he failed to deliver the commissions to all the new judicial appointees. When Jefferson became President on March 4, 1801, he instructed Madison, his Secretary of State, to refuse to deliver the remaining commissions. One William Marbury, appointed justice of the peace in the District of Columbia, thereupon brought action along with others directly in the Supreme Court for a mandamus, i.e., for a court order, to compel Madison to deliver his commission.[17] This procedure was apparently authorized by the Judiciary Act of 1789.

The Republicans in Congress, supporting Jefferson against Marshall and the Federalists, proceeded to repeal the judiciary acts of 1801, and then postponed the Supreme Court's session for a year. When the Court met again in 1803 the Marbury case was still before it, but Marbury's commission, even if delivered to him, would be of little value, since his designated term was already nearly up. Nevertheless the Court went through with the case. It faced two questions: *First*, had it the jurisdiction to decide the case? If not, nothing more needed to be said. Otherwise it had a *second* question, that is, whether Marbury was entitled to his commission or whether Madison had the right to withhold it. The Court took these questions in reverse order. *First* it held that Marbury had a legal right to his commission, but *second* that it, the Supreme Court, had no jurisdiction to force Madison to deliver it! In deciding the latter point it held part of an act of Congress unconstitutional.

The clause held invalid was a provision of the Judiciary Act of 1789, which was enacted by the first Congress and approved by President Washington and which had been in effect for fourteen years. It provided that in an original proceeding, i.e., a case not coming up on appeal from a lower court, the Supreme Court should have power to "issue writs of mandamus . . . to . . . persons holding office under the authority of the United States." The Constitution itself provided as follows:

> In all Cases affecting Ambassadors, other public Ministers and Consuls, and those in which a State shall be a Party, the supreme Court shall have original Jurisdiction. In all the other Cases before mentioned, the supreme Court shall have appellate jurisdiction, both as to Law and Fact, with such Exceptions, and under such Regulations as the Congress shall make.[18]

Putting the statutory and the constitutional provisions on original jurisdiction alongside each other, the Supreme Court decided that Congress had

---

[17] Marbury v. Madison (1803), I Cranch 137.
[18] Art. III, sec. 2, par. 2.

attempted to impose on the Court a duty and a burden of work in connection with original cases that was not warranted by the Constitution; in short, that on this point the statute was unconstitutional. In the circumstances, what should and could the Court do? If it could not enforce both the Constitution and the statute, which should it elect to enforce? On these points the decision was so cogent, clear, and emphatic that its reasoning has never been improved upon. The Court must enforce the Constitution; the statute must be ignored. Consequently the Court did not have the power to issue the mandamus requested.

Considering the rules and practice of the Supreme Court in recent decades it is very doubtful whether the Court would today decide the Marbury case as the Court did decide it in 1803. (1) Marshall reasoned as if the Judiciary Act of 1789 attempted to expand the original jurisdiction of the Supreme Court. Modern legal research points out that the clause in question did nothing of the kind. Properly construed it gave the Court the *power* to issue writs of mandamus to officers of the United States only in cases that were already properly within the *jurisdiction* of the Court. So construed the statute could have been sustained and the Court could have refused to try the Marbury case because it was not within its jurisdiction. (2) Even if erroneously construed as an attempt to enlarge the original jurisdiction of the Supreme Court, the clause in question might still have been upheld. The Constitution says that "the Supreme Court shall have original jurisdiction" in certain stated cases. Marshall read this as if it said "in the following cases *and no others.*" It could just as well have been read as saying that *"in at least the following cases"* the Supreme Court shall have original jurisdiction, leaving it to Congress to enlarge this jurisdiction by "necessary and proper" laws within the broad limits of Article III of the Constitution. Such was apparently the view of the Supreme Court before Marshall became chief justice.[19] It is hard to escape the conclusion that Marshall and the other Federalist justices were seeking an opportunity to assert the independence and the power of the Supreme Court in the face of Republican dominance over Congress and the Presidency. In denying their own power to issue the writ of mandamus in this case they found the opportunity to assert a far greater power, one that has been very hotly debated many times since then but never relinquished by the courts.

Was the Power of Review Usurped? Since the time of this decision there have been repeated charges against the Court that it illegally grasped or usurped the power to declare acts of Congress unconstitutional, a power not given to it and not intended for it. The Court's misfortune was that it did not have a better case than Marbury v. Madison in which to assert the power; sooner or later a better case for the purpose would have arisen; but this does not mean that the power was illegally usurped. That the power was not

[19] See J. A. C. Grant, "Marbury v. Madison Today," Am. *Pol. Sci. Rev.*, vol. 23, pp. 673-81 (1929).

expressly granted to the courts by the Constitution is clear enough, but the more careful historians of the subject are agreed that the framers of the Constitution, although not in perfect agreement on the issue, understood the doctrine of judicial review, and that the words they inserted in the Constitution were probably intended to endow the courts with the disputed power. In fact by combining (a) the idea of a written constitution emanating from "the people," and superior to the government, (b) the doctrine of limited powers vested in the government, (c) an analysis of the nature of the judicial function, and (d) the words of the Constitution itself, as Marshall did in Marbury *v.* Madison, a very strong logical framework for upholding the power can be made out. The pertinent provisions of the Constitution may be summarized as follows, with italics to show the important words:

Pertinent Constitutional Provisions. Preamble. "We *the People of the United States* . . . do ordain and establish this Constitution. . . ." Whatever the reason of the framers for saying "We the people" the words seem to make the Constitution an expression of popular sovereignty.

Art. VI, par. 2. "This Constitution, and the Laws of the United States *which shall be made in pursuance thereof;* and all Treaties made, or which shall be made, under the Authority of the United States, shall be *the supreme Law of the Land* . . ." Statutes are not supreme law unless made in pursuance of the Constitution.

Art. VI, par. 3. Senators, Representatives, state legislators, "and all *executive and judicial Officers,* both of the United States and of the several States, shall be *bound by Oath or Affirmation,* to support this Constitution . . ."

Art. I, sec. 1. "All legislative Powers *herein granted* shall be vested in a Congress of the United States. . . ." Congress has no powers that are not granted to it by the Constitution.

Art. III, sec. 1. "The *judicial Power* of the United States, shall be *vested in one supreme Court,* and in such inferior Courts as the Congress may from time to time ordain and establish."

Art. III, sec. 2. "The judicial Power shall *extend to all Cases* . . . *arising under this Constitution, the Laws of the United States,* and Treaties made, or which shall be made, under their Authority. . . ." Thus the courts may pass on legal questions under the Constitution.

Amendment X. "The powers not delegated to the United States by the Constitution, nor prohibited by it to the States, are reserved to the States respectively, or to the people."

Thus from the words of the Constitution, Marshall was able to deduce that in a case properly before them, the courts, in the exercise of their judicial function, are in duty bound to enforce only those statutes passed by Congress that are in harmony with the Constitution. The Constitution is unqualifiedly supreme; the statutes are supreme only if they conform to the Constitution. Whatever may be the duties and powers of the other departments, the Court's duty is to uphold the Constitution, and this duty it cannot avoid without violating the oath taken by the judges.

Counter-Arguments. An argument often made in reply to this is that Congress and the President are equally bound by oath to support the Constitution, and that the courts should accept their actions as being in honest compliance with it. The answer to this is that the courts have their own responsibility, irrespective of what the other departments do. They are a separate, independent, and equal branch of the government. Thus only can the Constitution and the separation of powers that it provides be made effective.

If the contention that the courts have no power to set aside acts of Congress because it is not expressly stated in the Constitution is sound, then it is almost equally true that they have no power to set aside acts of state legislatures. Neither power is expressly provided for in the Constitution, although the national supremacy clause of the Constitution (Article VI, section 2) provides a firmer foundation for the refusal to apply state acts that conflict with the United States Constitution, statutes and treaties.

THE PRACTICE OF JUDICIAL REVIEW

Since the establishment of the independence of the United States, hundreds of statutes and administrative regulations, national, state, and local, have been tested for constitutionality by the courts. The Supreme Court of the United States has come to be looked upon by many persons as a body that is devoted primarily to this function. In the course of its experiences this court has developed a rather elaborate code of rules and practices for dealing with constitutional cases. It has put many limitations upon itself, and these have been adopted in turn by other courts, both state and national, although perfect uniformity of practice is hardly to be expected. What are the major rules and limitations in this field?

What Cases and What Courts. Judicial controversies or cases arise in every type of court from that of the untrained justice of the peace up through the various levels of state and federal courts to the Supreme Court of the United States. Each court has by law or constitution a definite jurisdiction, meaning the totality of the types of cases it may legally hear and decide. Even a justice of the peace acting within his jurisdiction may declare a statute pleaded before him to be unconstitutional, and refuse to give it effect. Acts of legislation newly enacted are often tested in a number of courts at about the same time. In order to protect the interests of their clients, lawyers try to raise the question of constitutionality if there is even the slightest ground for it. Sometimes in the same year different courts give opposite decisions on the same act: some hold it constitutional, others hold it unconstitutional. Confusion prevails temporarily, and an appeal to the highest available court becomes necessary to get an authoritative ruling. On all federal questions the highest court is the Supreme Court of the United States; on questions under the state constitution, it is usually the state supreme court. But federal constitutional questions can be raised against almost any state or local act—even the zoning ordinance of a city, for example—since all that is necessary is to allege a repugnancy between the state or local act and any part of the national Constitution, statutes or treaties; and such questions can be settled finally only in the Supreme Court of the United States. On the other hand, an act of Congress can be effectively attacked only for alleged violation of the United States Constitution.

Delays in Judicial Review. Where courts insist that they cannot pass on the constitutionality of an act unless a real case is before them, long periods often elapse during which an act is enforced before a decision on constitutionality is rendered. In Marbury v. Madison it was fourteen years, in the Myers case over fifty years.[20] The more common lapse of one or two years is also very important when large interests are involved. Earlier decisions would certainly be of great advantage to citizens and government. How can they be achieved? Decisions, or at least opinions, on the constitutionality of statutes might conceivably be given:

1. Before the statute is passed. This would be an advisory opinion.
2. Immediately after the enactment of the statute, but before the law had been put into force and been violated by someone. For this purpose (a) the declaratory judgment procedure is possible, and (b) an injunction, mandamus, or other writ is also sometimes available.
3. After the act has been put into effect, possibly at great expense.

Advisory Opinions. In its constitution of 1780, Massachusetts authorized both houses of the legislature or the executive to request, and required the state supreme judicial court to give, advisory opinions "upon important questions of law and upon solemn occasions." [21] Before important new laws are passed, the court is often called upon to give opinions on the constitutional questions involved. These "Opinions of the Justices" have a great deal of influence. Proposed legislation may be modified or dropped when the justices believe it would be unconstitutional. As precedents, these opinions are technically not as binding as decisions in actual cases; but they do not appear to be overruled any more frequently, and they do head off considerable litigation that might later arise. For this and other reasons, the Massachusetts supreme court renders fewer decisions of unconstitutionality than most comparable state supreme courts. A number of other state supreme courts are also authorized to render advisory opinions, and there is little evidence to show that the exercise of this power drags the courts too much into current political contro-

[20] Marbury v. Madison (1803), I Cranch 137, an act of 1789 held invalid in 1803; Myers v. United States (1926), 272 U. S. 52, an act of 1876 ruled unconstitutional in 1926.
[21] Const. of Mass., Pt. II, ch. III, art. 2.

versies.[22] On the other hand the Supreme Court of the United States has refused to render advisory opinions on constitutional questions. It insists that it cannot act except upon the presentation to it of a definite legal case or controversy, one in which actual rights are involved.[23]

Injunction or Mandamus to Test Constitutionality. When suing for an *injunction* or similar writ to prevent the enforcement of a law or administrative order the plaintiff must show that irreparable injury would result if he were to obey it. A public utility can show this when ordered to reduce a rate, or a large business corporation when confronted by a new labor regulation, but in many cases the individual cannot get an injunction. He must, for example, often pay a disputed tax and then sue for recovery. The remedy by injunction is, in other words, an "extraordinary" one, and is not always available. Much the same is true of *mandamus*. When an officer refuses to carry out a law that the citizen wants executed, the latter may ask the court to mandamus (command) the officer to do his duty, while the officer contends that the act is unconstitutional.

Declaratory Judgments. For the purpose of getting quicker action in important cases still another procedure, known as the *declaratory judgment*, has been devised.[24] Under it parties can bring actions in the courts to determine their legal rights before one has, for example, actually broken his contract, or refused to pay a tax. There must be a real situation, of course, such as an enacted tax law under which collector A is insisting that citizen B ought to pay a certain amount, and B insists that he is not obliged to do so. Under the declaratory judgment procedure the citizen and the collector simply agree on the facts, lay them before the court promptly, and get an early decision. The court then declares the rights of the parties but does not order either to do anything.

Congress and the majority of the states have now passed acts to establish this court procedure, many of the latter having adopted the Uniform Declaratory Judgments Act. The Supreme Court has recognized the validity of the state acts, and has by inference upheld that which was enacted by Congress.[25] In fact the United States statute on this subject has been used but little, the state acts only a little more. Lawyers and judges trained in the ways of the

[22] In Maine, New Hampshire, Rhode Island, and Colorado, as well as in Massachusetts, the state constitution permits either the legislature or the governor to ask for advisory opinions, while in Florida and South Dakota only the governor may make the request. In a few other states the supreme courts render advisory opinions without express constitutional authority. See A. R. Ellingwood, *Departmental Cooperation in State Government*, New York, 1918; Felix Frankfurter, "A Note on Advisory Opinions," *Harvard Law Review*, vol. 37, pp. 1002-09 (1924).

[23] See Muskrat v. United States (1911), 219 U. S. 346.

[24] See E. M. Borchard, *Declaratory Judgments*, Cleveland, 1934; also his short article in *Ency. of Soc. Sciences*, vol. 5, pp. 51-52.

[25] Nashville, C. & St. L. Ry. v. Wallace (1933), 288 U. S. 249; Field, *A Selection of Cases and Authorities on Constitutional Law*, 2nd ed., Chicago, 1936, pp. 33-37, and 37 n. See also Alabama State Federation of Labor v. McAdory (1945), 325 U. S. 450, 65 S. Ct. 1384, and CIO v. McAdory (1945), 325 U. S. 472, 65 S. Ct. 1395.

common law are slow to take up new ideas. Even so the new procedure has more than justified its enactment.

Actual Controversies Generally Necessary. To bring any question of constitutionality before the federal courts and the courts of the many states in which advisory opinions will not be given by the courts, an actual legal case or controversy is necessary. Except where declaratory judgments are authorized, the case must be one of which the courts not only can take jurisdiction but in which they can issue a positive order to one or more of the parties to do or refrain from doing something. This is a limitation that the courts have laid upon themselves, and that they insist is necessary in order (a) to keep them strictly judicial in their functions, (b) to prevent them from becoming entangled in political controversies, and (c) to give them the proper presentation of facts and arguments by attorneys to enable them to make sound decisions.

Political Questions. The courts insist, therefore, that their function is a strictly judicial one, and that it is nonpolitical. The legislature and the executive are the political departments according to this view of the Constitution. For this reason the Supreme Court says that it will not deal with political questions such as the recognition of a foreign government by the executive or of the existence of a "republican form of government" in a state.[26] The President has the right to recognize or to refuse to recognize a foreign government; he must also decide on sending troops into a state to enforce law; Congress may seat such members as it chooses from such states as it believes properly organized. In each such case the courts will consider the official actions of the other departments as binding on it. Even the adoption·or non-adoption of a United States constitutional amendment is held to be a political question.[27]

Court Not to Pass on Policy or Motives. For much the same reasons the judges say that they will not pass upon either the policy of an act or the motives behind it. Whether they think it good or bad in its effects, or whether the legislature acts honestly and with constitutional motives, or dishonestly and with other motives, the courts should not inquire. Their duty is simply to pass upon the legality, i.e., constitutionality, of what was done. Hence they should not condemn legislation because it violates their notions of sound economics, or natural right, or ancient usage, or proper morals.

This is what the courts say, but in the judgment of many competent authorities, they have failed to observe this wholesome restriction. Many acts have been declared unconstitutional not because they violated any words of the Constitution, but because they did not square with the economic or the political theories of the judges. Thus their theories concerning "due process of

---

[26] Field, "The Doctrine of Political Questions in Federal Courts," *Minn. Law Review*, vol. 8, pp. 485-513 (1924); and such cases as Luther v. Borden (1849), 7 Howard (U. S.) I, and Oetjen v. Central Leather Co. (1918), 246 U. S. 237.

[27] Coleman v. Miller (1939), 307 U. S. 433.

law," "dual federalism," the "right of contract," and, more recently, freedom of speech, press and religion, have been the basis for upsetting many statutes. In fact the courts have looked even into the motives of legislation. The income tax, minimum wage acts, child labor legislation, and regulatory laws of many kinds were in the past invalidated in these ways; and it was these decisions more than any others that brought criticism upon the Court.

One of the most friendly critics the Court has ever had describes the Supreme Court as "this extraordinary politico-juridical tribunal," and says of it:

> The Supreme Court is not only a court of justice, but in a qualified sense a *continuous constitutional convention*. It continues the work of the Convention of 1787 by adapting through interpretation the great charter of government, and thus its duties become political, in the highest sense of that word, as well as judicial.[28]

Reasonable Doubt and 5-4 Decisions. Even when proper legal questions are presented, say the judges, if there is any reasonable doubt whether the legislation being contested is valid, the Court must, out of the respect they owe to co-ordinate departments, uphold it and enforce it. Only in the clear case where there is no doubt that it is unconstitutional should it be so declared. To use the Court's own words: "Within the field where men of reason may reasonably differ, the legislature must have its way." [29] This or the equivalent the courts have said many times in their decisions but from the public viewpoint they have not always followed this rule. Each judge has felt justified in applying it in a purely subjective way; if he personally has no doubts it makes no difference how many disagree with him or how competent they are. The public viewpoint is more objective. When an outsider sees five judges in a case on one side and four on the other, or even six and three, and when he sees the same court reversing its earlier five-to-four or six-to-three decisions, he is entitled to hold that there *was* doubt about the constitutionality of the statute in the first place, and that under the rule the act should have been upheld.

Separability of Clauses. Where an act consists of a number of sections, and only one is held unconstitutional, the rest of the act is usually upheld if it is a complete act without the obnoxious clause. Such was the situation in Marbury *v.* Madison, and such has often been the case since. It has thus become a settled rule to consider whether the act is separable, and to act accordingly.

Interpretation of Acts. In many cases the courts are able to avoid declaring acts of legislation unconstitutional by giving them such construction and interpretation as will "square them" with the constitution. Justice Holmes once said that "the rule is settled that as between two possible interpretations of a statute, by one of which it would be unconstitutional and by the other valid,

[28] James M. Beck, *The Constitution of the United States*, p. 221.
[29] Williams *v.* Mayor and City Council of Baltimore (1933), 289 U. S. 36, 42.

our plain duty is to adopt that which will save the Act." [30] Particular things done under the statute may then be held invalid, while the legislation itself is at least nominally sustained. There are cases, however, in which "interpretation" is almost as serious as a flat declaration of unconstitutionality. When the Supreme Court held in the Sugar Trust case [31] in 1895 that the Sherman Anti-Trust Act could not be applied to a monopoly that was primarily engaged in manufacturing, not commerce, it effectively pulled the teeth of an act at a time when it might have been used to head off some of the many "trusts" then being formed. In fact, the act never fully recover from this early blow, and it is only within the past few years that the Court has in effect reversed the holding in the earlier case.[32]

Brandeis on the Avoidance of Constitutional Questions. For many years Associate Justices Holmes and Brandeis were the great dissenters against Supreme Court decisions that overruled state and national legislation. Both lived to see at least the beginning of the Court's subsequent reversal of position. Holmes' attitude was essentially one of great deference to legislative bodies. Brandeis seemed more inclined to build up a court policy of avoiding constitutional questions whenever possible. In a famous concurring opinion in a case upholding the constitutionality of TVA, he brought together a whole series of statements by the Court itself concerning the avoidance of constitutional issues.[33] His main points may be abbreviated as follows:

> 1. The Court will not pass upon the constitutionality of legislation in a friendly, nonadversary proceeding, declining because to decide such questions "is legitimate only in the last resort, and as a necessity in the determination of a real, earnest, and vital controversy between individuals."
>
> 2. The Court will not "anticipate a question of constitutional law in advance of the necessity of deciding it."
>
> 3. The Court will not "formulate a rule of constitutional law broader than is required by the precise facts to which it is to be applied."
>
> 4. The Court will not pass upon a constitutional question although properly presented by the record, if there is also present some other ground upon which the case may be disposed of.
>
> 5. The Court will not pass upon the validity of a statute upon complaint of one who fails to show that he is injured by its operation.
>
> 6. The Court will not pass upon the constitutionality of a statute at the instance of one who has availed himself of its benefits.
>
> 7. "When the validity of an act of the Congress is drawn in question, and even if a serious doubt of constitutionality is raised, it is a

---

[30] Blodgett v. Holden (1927-28), 275 U. S. 142, 148.
[31] United States v. E. C. Knight Co. (1895), 156 U. S. 1.
[32] NLRB cases (1937), 301 U. S. 1, 49, 58, 103, 142.
[33] Ashwander v. Tennessee Valley Authority (1936), 297 U. S. 288, at pp. 346-48.

cardinal principle that this Court will first ascertain whether a construction of the statute is fairly possible by which the question may
be avoided."

Even though the Court does not follow all these rules and all the other
doctrines of self-limitation to the letter, it is clear that it now exercises far
more restraint and caution in upsetting national and state acts than it ever
did before. It has in effect been retreating for many decades to a more restricted position, but a far more defensible one.

SCOPE AND RESULTS OF JUDICIAL VETOES

Effect of Decisions Upholding Laws. As a result of the mere existence of
the power of review, every legislative act is left in some doubt until a court
passes upon it, because the American people are so accustomed to attacks
upon legislation through the courts that no law seems quite a law until the
courts, like an extra branch of the legislature, have passed upon it. When the
Supreme Court cannot avoid a decision upon the constitutionality of an act
it can reach either a favorable or an unfavorable conclusion. Granted that
the court decision is favorable, what good does the decision do? It does not
make the act more valid, or improve it as a piece of legislation. It supplies
certain reasons why the law can be considered constitutional, but these could
as well have been written out by legislative committees and government attorneys. The Supreme Court gets much credit among lawyers and scholars for
"preserving and developing" the Constitution, but in each case the legislature
possesses and has already acted upon the powers that the Court later merely
explains in its opinions. It is Congress and the President who really help to
develop the Constitution.

Effect of Declaring an Act Unconstitutional. As to acts that are declared
unconstitutional by the courts, it is necessary to consider, *first*, the immediate
legal effect of the decision and, *second*, the long-run social, economic, or political consequences of the adverse decision. According to strict theory, an act
that is declared unconstitutional is utterly void, from the very beginning, as
if it had never been a law at all. In many cases this theory will not stand up.
Officers have been elected and have served under the unconstitutional acts;
taxes have been collected and are in the government treasury; men have served
time in prison because of them, and that time can never be recovered. What
would the reader do as judge about the millions of dollars in the United
States treasury after the AAA decision declared that the money had been
collected under an unconstitutional tax from milling companies and others,
who had in fact passed most of the tax along to the consumer? Would he
order the treasury of the United States to return the whole tax to those who
nominally paid it? He probably would not, and neither did the courts. The
judges have developed a whole body of law concerning the effect to be given

to unconstitutional statutes.[34] Officers appointed under them may be "de facto"—not strictly legal—or "de jure," mind you, but still such that they must be recognized for many purposes. The taxes are in the treasury, and the legislature may pass proper laws to compel claimants to prove their complete title to them before getting them out again. And so on through a veritable maze of other qualifications and exceptions.

It is true that a Supreme Court decision declaring an act unconstitutional usually prevents its future operation. Frequently, however, a persistent legislature proceeds to find some other way to achieve the result hoped for from the original act; and occasionally a stubborn executive refuses to enforce an obnoxious decision, holding himself equal to the courts in the right to construe the Constitution. The courts are in one sense the weakest of the three branches of government. The effectiveness of their decisions depends almost entirely on the people's respect for law, and the cooperation of the executive branch in accepting and enforcing the decisions.

Numbers of Acts Held Unconstitutional. As to the social and other consequences of judicial vetoes of legislation, defenders of judicial review as an institution make a point of the fact that relatively few acts of Congress have been declared unconstitutional. The first case after Marbury v. Madison (1803) came fifty-four years later when, in the Dred Scott case (1857), the Missouri Compromise Act of 1820 was held unconstitutional, thirty-seven years after it was passed. Since the Civil War, however, the Supreme Court has been more active and more assertive of its powers. Thereafter by decades the numbers of acts or parts of acts declared invalid are as follows: 1865-69, 4; 1870-79, 9; 1880-89, 5; 1890-99, 5; 1900-09, 9; 1910-19, 7; 1920-29, 17.[35] A compilation made for the Senate Judiciary Committee covering the 1933, 1934, and 1935 terms of court, and the 1936 term to March, 1937, showed 13 acts of Congress and 53 state acts held invalid.[36] In this short period, when New Deal legislation was under attack, about four acts of Congress and over a dozen state acts, on the average, were held unconstitutional each year, whereas before the Civil War the Supreme Court ruled invalid only two acts of Congress in seventy years, and a proportionately small number of state acts.[37] What was once thought of as a rare and exceptional use of power became in the early 1930's the regular and most important function of the Supreme Court.

Court Reversal Since 1937. By 1937 the high point in the exercise of the judicial veto had been reached, and in that year occurred what amounted to a revolution in the Supreme Court.[38] The sweeping Roosevelt victory of 1936 was soon followed by the President's proposal to revamp the federal courts

---

[34] See O. P. Field, *The Effect of an Unconstitutional Statute*, Minneapolis, 1935.

[35] This tabulation is based on Appendix I of Haines, op. cit., pp. 541-66.

[36] *Hearings Before the Committee on the Judiciary*, United States Senate, 75th Cong., 1st Sess., on S. 1392, Washington, 1937, pp. 1189-99, 1520-36.

[37] B. F. Moore, *The Supreme Court and Unconstitutional Legislation*, New York, 1913, Appendix II, pp. 131-32.

[38] E. S. Corwin, *Constitutional Revolution, Ltd.*, Claremont, Calif., 1941.

by adding a new judge for each one who failed to retire within six months after reaching the age of seventy. A tremendous clamor arose against this proposal to "pack" the courts but at the same time it was recognized that the New Deal leaders and supporters were not going to submit passively to wholesale judicial defeat of their measures. What caused the change is not fully known, but suddenly two members of the Supreme Court shifted from one side to the other, and on several important New Deal cases there were five votes to uphold them against four in opposition. A very substantial reversal of court doctrines on a number of important points began. This occurred without the change of a single member, but when within the years 1937-40 five Supreme Court vacancies occurred through deaths and resignations, and the President was able to appoint five new members to the Court, the revolution was complete. Since 1937-38 not one important act of Congress and very few state acts have been held unconstitutional.

In view of this substantial change of position, and the great concern of the present Court to uphold all national and state legislation, it may seem ungracious to analyze the results of the past work of the courts in vetoing legislation, and unnecessary to consider judicial review as any longer an important factor in the American form of government. This would be too sweeping a conclusion. The political powers of the courts, that is the powers of judicial review and veto, still exist, and may be brought into action at any time.

Policing Function of Supreme Court. The Supreme Court of the United States acts as a sort of judicial policeman, patrolling three sets of boundaries defined by the Constitution and by its own decisions. The results of its decisions declaring acts of legislation unconstitutional may be considered with respect to these three boundaries: (a) between the nation and the states, (b) between the three branches of the national government, legislative, executive, and judicial; and (c) between all government on one side (national, state, and local), and individuals on the other.

Supreme Court as Arbiter Between Nation and State. As patrolman of the boundary between state and national powers, the Supreme Court has had a very checkered career. Up to the Civil War it made no decision declaring any act of Congress invalid as an invasion of state powers. During most of this period it was a nationalizing influence, upholding the nation's powers and declaring invalid any state laws that interfered therewith. Since the Civil War it has, if anything, tended a little the other way, but when its decisions upholding state rights against national action are examined some curious facts appear. *First*, until recently the states as such were almost never represented in the litigation. They were not the ones protesting against the national legislation. *Second*, the actual parties were usually private individuals or business corporations. They were the ones who argued for state rights. *Third*, the basis of the suits was nearly always a question of property rights. National legislation was attacked and held invalid as an invasion of state rights, when in fact the parties involved were individuals and corporations trying to avoid taxes and government regulation of their businesses. Thus the state rights argument in these cases concealed entirely different motives, and became a means of protecting property interests against interference by the national government.

It is strange, after all, that the Supreme Court should be looked upon as a protector of state rights. In no sense does it represent the states, and the record of its rulings as umpire between nation and states shows that it nearly always takes the national side in a direct controversy over this issue.[39] Congress, on the other hand, represents states in both houses. Members of Congress can be elected only from states. If state rights are being invaded, they will be the first to hear it, not the courts. In fact Congress has been far more friendly to state rights than has the Supreme Court. The Court has been one of the bulwarks against state encroachments on national powers; but since 1937 the Court has tended to uphold state as well as national legislation.

Supreme Court and Separation of Powers. The Court has held very few statutes invalid as violations of the constitutional separation of powers. It has protected itself from attempts by Congress to impose nonjudicial duties upon it, and it has invalidated a few attempts by Congress to delegate its own legislative powers to the executive. On the whole its decisions in this field have been few and moderate, and several recent decisions against the delegation of legislative powers to executive and administrative bodies are likely soon to be overruled. Its decisions have not seriously affected informal cooperation between departments.

Supreme Court and Individual Rights. To pass judgment in a paragraph on the Court's work in upholding the bill of rights against encroachments by government would be absurd. The Court has ardent defenders, and it has sharp critics. The latter point to the earlier whittling away of the rights of free speech, press and assembly, in World War I and after, and to numerous other invasions of personal rights in connection with prohibition, immigration, and tariff law, often with the direct approval of the courts.[40] The former argue that without the Court, conditions would have been even worse for personal rights.

Down to about 1930 it was hard to decide between these two views and even now the record is not absolutely clear and incontrovertible. On the whole, however, since the decision in Near v. State of Minnesota [41] in 1931, the Court has turned strongly toward the upholding of freedom of speech, press, assemblage and religion, as will be shown in chapter 20, below. The majority of the justices have become convinced that the First Amendment, which guarantees these rights against national interference, can also be applied against the states, and that these rights are more important to uphold than any others

[39] O. P. Field, "State versus Nation, and the Supreme Court," in *Amer. Pol. Sci. Rev.*, vol. 28, pp. 233-45 (1934).

[40] See for example Zechariah Chafee, *Freedom of Speech*, New York, 1920; H. L. McBain, *Prohibition: Legal and Illegal*, New York, 1938; E. S. Bates, *This Land of Liberty*, New York, 1930.

[41] Near v. State of Minnesota ex rel Olson (1931), 283 U. S. 697.

because of their close connection with the operation of democratic government.

The Court and the Rights of Property. For several generations down to about 1937 the courts generally and the Supreme Court in particular placed great stress upon the protection of property rights and the related right of freedom of contract. Indeed the principal burden of the complaint against the Supreme Court during that period was its protection and expansion of the rights of private property and contract, at the expense of other human rights and in the face of a rapidly changing economic situation that has called for more and more governmental regulation of business, property, and employment relations. The Progressive attack upon the Court under Theodore Roosevelt and the Democratic or New Deal attack under Franklin Roosevelt were both centered in this proposition. Some of the most cherished measures of the New Deal were either upheld by a bare majority of the Court, or were declared unconstitutional. Until the shift in the Court's position began in 1937, the whole program of social and economic legislation, both state and national, that went under the name of the New Deal, seemed endangered by adverse Supreme Court decisions.

Decisions Invalidating Social and Economic Legislation. The chief failure of the Supreme Court has undoubtedly been in its handling of social and economic legislation. Whenever the Court has ventured to annul an act of Congress of wide social and economic significance, it has not only aroused tremendous public protest, but it has frequently been overruled, or has been forced later to reverse its decisions. Beginning with the historic Dred Scott decision of 1857 when it ruled against the power of Congress to prohibit slavery in the territories, the Supreme Court made a series of dubious decisions denying the power of Congress (a) to make paper money legal tender (overruled by the Court itself), (b) to levy an income tax (overruled by Sixteenth Amendment), (c) to establish minimum wages in the District of Columbia, (d) to prohibit interstate shipment of goods made by child labor and (e) to regulate manufacturing under the interstate commerce clause (all now substantially overruled). The anti-New Deal cases up to 1937 need not be listed here because its recent about-face has undone already most of the adverse decisions of 1934-36. With or without realizing it the judges in both federal and state courts developed a strongly laissez-faire or anti-government attitude that led them to invalidate numerous state and national legislative acts that were designed to ameliorate social conditions and to bring business under stricter regulation. No doubt some of the legislation was unwise, but experience has shown the legislatures to have been more nearly right on the whole than the courts were in determining the need for legislation. Most of the decisions holding such acts unconstitutional, furthermore, were not based on express words of constitutions, but on court-devised theories and rules of interpreting them.

In this connection mention should be made also of court review of the acts of the administrative bodies that were set up to carry out social and economic legislation. Frequently the attack in the courts was not upon the statute passed by Congress or by a state legislature, but upon the actions of the administrative agency that acted under the law. The resulting frustration of a public policy was in many instances the same as if the law itself had been ruled out. This topic will be discussed in the next chapter.

Court Review of Treaties. Treaties also fall under review by the Supreme Court, but no treaty has yet been held unconstitutional. Treaties must be made "under the Authority of the United States," and when so made they are a part of the "supreme Law of the Land," but the Constitution does not say that they must be "in pursuance of" the Constitution. Hence the treaty power seems broader than the power of Congress to pass legislation; it extends "to all proper subjects of negotiation between our government and other nations." [42]

PROPOSED REFORMS

Should the Power of Judicial Review Be Abolished? A course of reasoning can be presented to show that the Supreme Court should not have the power to declare acts of Congress unconstitutional. If the Court had no such power the lines of responsibility in government would be much more direct and clear-cut than they are now. Congress and the President would have entire legal and political responsibility for national policy, including the upholding of the Constitution itself, as the state legislatures and governors would in the states. Both houses of Congress being elected from the states, the members would not be likely rashly to invade the field of state rights, although a some-what more extensive use of national powers might be expected. Legislators and executives, being under oath to support the Constitution just as much as judges are, would not lightly trample on constitutional rights. Being in fact largely lawyers, they would certainly debate constitutional questions gravely, as they always do, before taking any important new action. The checks on government action would then be political, not judicial; the government could not go any farther or faster than public opinion permitted, but it could go that fast.

The late Justice Oliver Wendell Holmes once said, "I do not think the United States would come to an end if we lost our power to declare an act of Congress void. I do think the Union would be imperiled if we could not make that declaration as to the laws of the several states." [43]

Less Drastic Proposals. Most Americans would not go as far as to abolish this power of the courts, however; instead they put forward various schemes of court reform. Of these the most important are: (1) Easier amendment of constitutions, so that unsatisfactory court decisions can be overruled more speedily by constitutional amendment. (2) The requirement of an extraordinary majority in the Court (6 to 3, or 7 to 2) to overrule an act of legislation

[42] U. S. Const., Art. VI, par. 2; Asakura v. Seattle (1924), 265 U. S. 332.
[43] Address delivered in 1913; quoted in McBain, *The Living Constitution*, p. 247.

in state or nation. (3) The right of the legislative body to repass an act held invalid, thereby giving it validity. This has been favored by the American Federation of Labor, and was once half-heartedly approved by Chief Justice Marshall. (4) Various constitutional amendments (a) enlarging the powers of Congress, (b) defining such terms as "due process of law," and (c) limiting the power of the courts to declare acts invalid. President Roosevelt's proposals of 1937 as to the federal courts were far less drastic than any of these. He proposed merely to overcome the temporary adverse majority in the Supreme Court by adding new justices for each one over the retirement age who failed to retire. This was viewed as "packing the Court" and aroused opposition enough to defeat it.

At the present time there are persons who deplore the liberal tendencies of the Supreme Court justices and hope for the return of the day when the Court will again do battle against legislative innovations that increase taxes, restrict the rights of business and property, and enlarge the scope of social legislation. In general, however, the public is either indifferent to what the Court does or well content with its present policies. Attacks upon the judicial power of review over legislation are fewer than they have been for many decades.

REFERENCES

C. G. Haines, *The American Doctrine of Judicial Supremacy*, 2nd ed., Berkeley, 1932.

Chas. Warren, *The Supreme Court in United States History*, rev. ed., Boston, 1932.

——, *Congress, the Constitution, and the Supreme Court*, Boston, 1925.

E. S. Corwin, *The Doctrine of Judicial Review*, Princeton, 1914.

C. A. Beard, *The Supreme Court and the Constitution*, New York, 1912.

L. B. Boudin, *Government by Judiciary*, 2 vols., New York, 1932.

E. S. Bates, *The Story of the Supreme Court*, Indianapolis, 1936.

O. P. Field, *The Effect of an Unconstitutional Statute*, Minneapolis, 1935.

J. M. Beck, *The Constitution of the United States*, New York, 1922.

D. J. Ettrude, *Power of Congress to Nullify Supreme Court Decisions*, New York, 1924.

Felix Frankfurter and J. M. Landis, *The Business of the Supreme Court*, New York, 1927.

C. E. Hughes, *The Supreme Court of the United States*, New York, 1928.

R. E. Cushman, "The Supreme Court and the Constitution," *Public Affairs Pamphlets*, No. 7, Washington, 1936.

H. W. Edgerton, "The Incidence of Judicial Control over Congress," *Cornell Law Quarterly*, vol. 22, pp. 299-348, 1937.

O. P. Field, "The Doctrine of Political Questions in Federal Courts," *Minn. Law Review*, vol. 8, pp. 485-513, 1924.

C. G. Haines, "Judicial Review of Acts of Congress and the Need for Constitutional Reform," *Yale Law Journal*, 1936, vol. 45.

L. I. Perrigo, "The Federal Judiciary: An Analysis of Proposed Revisions," *Minn. Law Review*, vol. 21, pp. 481-511, 1937.

W. Y. Elliott, *The Need for Constitutional Reform*, New York, 1935, chs. VII, VIII.

E. S. Corwin, *Court over Constitution*, Princeton, 1938.

——, *Constitutional Revolution, Ltd.*, Claremont, Calif., 1941.

Cortez A. M. Ewing, *The Judges of the Supreme Court, 1789-1937, A Study of Their Qualifications*, Minneapolis, 1938.

Robert S. Rankin, *Readings in American Government*, New York, 1939, pp. 223-46.

A. N. Christensen and E. M. Kirkpatrick, *The People, Politics, and the Politician: Readings in American Government*, New York, 1941, pp. 562-591.

Robert K. Carr, *The Supreme Court and Judicial Review*, New York, 1942.

Library of Congress, *Provisions of Federal Law Held Unconstitutional by the Supreme Court of the United States*, Washington, 1936.

CHAPTER 19

Administrative Powers

As we have already noted, the written Constitution of the United States mentions administrative departments only very briefly.[1] It creates no such departments or agencies, and consequently it confers no powers upon them. The only powers that it does confer are designated as legislative, executive, and judicial, and these it delegates respectively to Congress, the President, and the courts of the United States. Nevertheless in order to achieve their designated purposes the administrative agencies of the national government do receive and exercise powers. What is the nature of these powers? How are they conferred upon the administrative agencies? How are they exercised and with what consequences to the people? How are they controlled in the public interest? These questions are unavoidable in any discussion of modern public administration. They lie close to the center of what is called "bureaucracy."

A rapid, widespread, and significant revolution has taken place in United States government. During its first hundred years Congress enacted very little social and economic legislation of the types that we know today. Outside of the Post Office, the Land Office (for the disposal of the public domain), and the collection of taxes and customs, it provided for very few administrative services or schemes of public regulation.[2] Such laws as it enacted were mostly of the type that did not call for public administrators to enforce them. For example under the patent laws every holder of a patent had to protect his rights against infringement by others through private suit in the courts. Similarly a man who received a grant of public lands from the government had to protect it himself, through lawyers and courts, against those who might try to "jump his claim." Even the Sherman Anti-Trust Act (1890) and later

---

[1] See ch. 15.

[2] See U. S. Attorney General, Committee on Administrative Procedure, Report of, under the title of *Administrative Procedure in Government Agencies*, pp. 7-9 for the mention of a few other early examples.

statutes have included provisions for enforcement of the law by private parties through the courts.

A century after the framing of the Constitution, Congress passed the important Interstate Commerce Act, 1887, a law that established a new pattern of national governmental action. This act set up a new agency, the Interstate Commerce Commission, and charged it with the responsibility for regulating railroad rates and services in the public interest. Much of what the law called for had to be done by the Commission itself, by administrative action. This was an important milestone on the road toward the development of the United States into a modern, active, public service state. Other laws of similar nature followed, for the regulation by national action of foods and drugs in interstate commerce, the telephone, telegraph, and radio, trucks and buses, stocks, bonds, and stock exchanges, grain, cotton, and cattle exchanges, natural gas, electric power, and oil pipe lines. To these examples of national regulatory activities should be added other services in which regulation is less important, such as the improvement of rivers and harbors, the parcel post and postal savings systems, old age and survivors insurance, and other nation-wide functions. In all these services private rights are frequently if not continuously involved, and the powers of the national administrative agencies are important. For each service the nation needs a considerable staff of officers and employees, scattered throughout the land, and what they do in the performance of their functions affects the personal and property rights and the employments and businesses of people everywhere.

Classes of Executive and Administrative Powers. The powers now vested in national executive and administrative agencies are of great range and variety. They may be classified as follows:

1. The *ordinary executive powers* to carry out and enforce laws enacted by Congress, treaties, and administrative rules and regulations that have the force of law; to arrest violators and to prosecute them before the courts; to operate governmental agencies and services; to construct and maintain public facilities; to employ and control personnel; to acquire and use lands, buildings, equipment, and supplies; and to raise and spend money according to law. Some of this work is described by the courts as "ministerial," because it involves little discretion; but there is generally a great deal of room for choice and discretion also. For example the FBI agent who apprehends an alleged violator of a national law must exercise his very best judgment upon the facts before he proceeds to make the arrest.

2. The *power to issue rules and regulations,* often called quasi-legislative or sublegislative, is possessed by many national agencies. Such rules and regulations may relate to the internal organization and procedures of the agency concerned, or to the rights of the public and of individuals outside the government, or to both at the same time. The effects of such regulations may be any one or more of the following: (a) to interpret the law with respect to particular cases, as the Customs Service might do in ruling that some new

type of goods falls in a particular class for tariff purposes; (b) to fill in the details of the law, as the National Park Service might do in making regulations for law and order in the parks; or (c) to change the law, when authorized by Congress to do so, as the President may do, in effect, when he lowers the tariffs on certain imports by agreement with a foreign nation under the Trade Agreements Act. The last type of regulation is unusual; it is also of very limited application, and the President does not have a general power of dispensing with the laws.

In any of these cases valid regulations have for most purposes the effect of law, and can be enforced by penalties against those who violate them.

3. *Powers to license and control business* belong to many agencies of government. To refuse a license, or to revoke one, is to bring a business to an end. Short of this, different agencies may stipulate the conditions for carrying on an enterprise, and keep close supervision over it. This is particularly true in the fields of transportation, public utilities, and radio broadcasting where the regulatory agencies have power to fix rates, to set standards of service, to regulate accounting and business practices, and even to decide on issues of stocks and bonds.

4. *Powers to investigate and prosecute, on their own initiative,* are also possessed by many governmental authorities. As to businesses and other matters under their control, they may send in investigators, call for the submission of books and papers, and hold hearings to get at any facts they deem important. On the basis of their findings they may revoke licenses, issue new regulations, order rate reductions, or even authorize prosecutions.

5. To executive and administrative agencies is sometimes granted also the *power to determine certain facts* on the basis of which laws and regulations are to take effect. For example, the President and the Tariff Commission may, upon finding certain facts, increase or decrease the tariffs on specified classes of imports from particular countries.

6. The *quasi-judicial powers* previously mentioned include the hearing of formal complaints filed by any individual or corporation or by the regulatory body itself, against any regulated concern, for alleged violations of laws and regulations, and the right to decide such cases and to impose penalties or grant the relief prayed for. The Interstate Commerce Commission, for example, hears many formal cases of alleged discrimination and overcharges in railroad rates and service, while the Federal Trade Commission decides cases of alleged "unfair competition."

In the foregoing examples of administrative powers we have refrained from mentioning any of the drastic powers that Congress conferred upon special wartime agencies to ration goods, fix prices, control allocations of available goods and to penalize violators directly. Even the ordinary peacetime powers of national administrative bodies are very far-reaching. No one who believes in the preservation of personal and property rights can view lightly these powers of executive and administrative agencies. It would be very shortsighted of the people in their effort to protect private rights, to watch closely the legislation enacted by Congress and the decisions being rendered by the courts, and to neglect to observe the activities of some hundred or more national administrative agencies that also make rules that are binding on the people and decide cases that involve their rights. Such agencies are unquestionably needed, but they must be watched and controlled.

The Delegation of Administrative Powers. Aside from the Presidential office itself, every executive and administrative agency of the national government has received its primary powers from an act of Congress. Some of the very first agencies created by Congress in the days of President Washington were endowed by Congress with powers to decide questions concerning customs payments and trade with the Indians, and the President himself was authorized to make "rules and regulations" on these and other matters.[3] These actions of Congress are generally called "delegations of power" to the President and to the administrative agencies concerned. Congress has seen fit, and in fact has found it necessary, to continue to make such delegations. Every new function of the national government has been covered by legislation that makes new grants of authority, whether to new agencies or to already existing ones.

Very few informed persons today question the need for delegations of power to executive and administrative agencies. The continuous and almost overwhelming rise of new demands upon the government make it impossible for the top agencies, Congress, the President, and the higher courts, to do all the work that is expected of the government. Delegation to other agencies is unavoidable, but the reasons for this vary somewhat according to the nature of the powers delegated.

Powers of a legislative nature (to make "rules and regulations" for the administration of a function) must be delegated to others by Congress because it does not have the time, the expertness, the flexibility, or the speed of action needed for deciding from day to day and in emergencies how a law shall be carried out.[4] There are too many other demands upon it, it needs to give more attention to general policy rather than to details, and its members cannot be experts in all fields if in any. The agencies set up to deal with particular functions, on the other hand, can gain the experience and develop the expertness needed for effective regulation in their respective fields.

Powers of a judicial nature (to decide controversies between parties over their respective rights under the law) are also necessary for successful administration. These may be delegated by Congress to the regular United States courts, but increasingly in recent years they are delegated to administrative agencies instead. The reasons for this choice are also connected with questions of expertness and volume of work. The district and circuit judges of the United States may be well trained on matters of ordinary common and statute law,

[3] Report of Attorney General's Committee, pp. 97-98. (See note 2, p. 319.)
[4] *Ibid.*, pp. 98-100, espec. footnote 17, p. 98.

such things as the law schools teach and as the older courts handled, but they cannot become experts in all branches of social and economic legislation (railroad regulation, labor relations, stock exchanges, and so on). Furthermore the volume of the new work to be done is very great, and the courts would need many times the present number of judges if they were to be responsible for it all. Then, too, there are important benefits to the public in having the same agencies that handle the rule-making and executive functions in a certain field exercise also the function of deciding disputes under their particular branches of law, provided the work of such agencies can be reviewed by others. In this way all the rules in a new field of regulation can be worked out in the first instance by those who are given special responsibility for its administration. The Interstate Commerce Commission is a well-known example of an agency that has received judicial, legislative, and executive powers over a particular field—railroad regulation—and which, through its increasing expertness in the field, has become accepted by both the public and the industry concerned.

The preceding paragraphs have reference to delegations of power by Congress, which is the source of the great majority of delegations of power to administrative agencies in the national government. But the President, as the national executive and as commander in chief, also is unable to exercise all the powers of his office without help, and that means delegations of power. The ultimate responsibility for all executive actions belongs to him; even Congress has no authority to delegate executive powers to anyone else. Under his constitutional powers as the national executive the President issues rules, regulations, orders, and proclamations from time to time in which he orders various agencies under his charge to perform certain duties and to follow certain procedures. We have seen in the case of *In re* Neagle (involving the deputy marshal who killed a man while protecting a federal judge, under orders from the President and without authority from Congress) that the Supreme Court will uphold such delegations of power by the President.[5]

Mixture versus Separation of Powers. We have already seen that the framers of the national Constitution were believers in a separation of powers and were careful to provide for it, although they modified it by checks and balances.[6] In recent decades many leading citizens, including some outstanding lawyers, have expressed great alarm over the fact that, while the Constitution assured a separation of powers at the top of the government (between Congress, the President, and the courts), at a level just below Congress and the President there are numerous agencies in which legislative, executive and judicial powers are inseparably mixed. The very same administrative agency that makes important rules in a particular field, like the regulation of railroads, may investigate to see whether the rules are observed, prosecute persons for

---

[5] *In re* Neagle (1890), 135 U. S. 1; see ch. 14, p. 233, above.
[6] See ch. 13, p. 212, above.

nonobedience, and itself sit as a court to hold them guilty and impose penalties upon them. This is held by the alarmists to be a very shocking departure from the Constitution. It is called by such names as "The New Despotism" and "Bureaucracy Triumphant." [7]

Official commissions in the United States and in Great Britain have looked into this question, and so have committees of the American Bar Association and the Lawyers' Guild. These inquiries have uncovered a great mass of information, and have emphasized the importance of this development in modern government, but the conclusions as to what needs to be done differ greatly. The official commissions in the United States and the Lawyers' Guild committee reveal little or no alarm, but the Special Committee on Administrative Law of the American Bar Association has recommended some far-reaching new legislation to correct what are supposed to be serious evils. [8]

In brief the Bar Association committee proposes a "back to the courts" movement for the decision of all important questions of personal and property rights that are now entrusted to administrative bodies. As to the delegation of rule-making or sublegislative powers to administrative agencies the committee conceded in 1935 that "a rigid application of the separation-of-powers doctrine is neither possible nor desirable. A wide latitude must be allowed to Congress." [9] Nevertheless its bill before Congress in 1939 proposed certain restrictions on administrative rule-making and authorized "any person affected" by a rule to take the question of a rule's validity to the courts within 30 days after publication.

On the exercise of judicial powers by administrative tribunals the Bar Association's committee was far more severe. It argued that "the prosecutor-judge combination should, so far as possible, be done away with (1) by segregating the judicial functions now exercised by administrative agencies and placing them in an independent tribunal and (2) where that is not feasible, by providing for review of the facts (as well as the law) by an independent tribunal." [10] Its bill before Congress in 1939 was so worded as to carry out fully the second of these proposals. Had the bill been enacted, the courts would have had imposed upon them the duty of making a substantially complete review of the facts in any administrative case where the disappointed party made an appeal. Such a review the courts have generally declined to make under most present statutes. If the courts are ever required to take over this

[7] See among others two English authors, Lord Hewart, *The New Despotism*, and Carleton Kemp Allen, *Bureaucracy Triumphant*, whose writings reveal that the problem is not peculiar to the United States, and the American writer, James M. Beck, *Our Wonderland of Bureaucracy*. Roscoe Pound, former dean of the Harvard Law School, has recently taken a similar position, as have various speakers before meetings of bar associations.

[8] The American Bar Association bill on the subject of administrative rules and procedures has appeared in several recent sessions of Congress. See for example H.R. 4236 and S. 915 of the First Session of the 76th Congress, 1939.

[9] American Bar Association, *Report of the Special Committee on Administrative Law* (1935), p. 260. Later reports of this committee showed little change on this point.

[10] *Op. cit.*, p. 225.

function the expense and the delays in administrative proceedings are likely to cause serious obstruction in much administrative business.

Other suggestions have been made for taking the judicial functions of administrative agencies out of their hands. One is to divide each administrative agency into two parts, the one to handle all the agency's work other than judicial, the other a wholly independent judicial body.[11] Another proposal is to set up an over-all "administrative court" in Washington to hear in the first instance or on review all cases involving parties and their rights that now go to administrative agencies.[12]

The various proposals for depriving administrative bodies of their judicial powers go upon the assumption that there is a strong tendency for administrative authorities to abuse their quasi-judicial powers, or that there is inadequate provision for appeal from their decisions. When a private individual, a corporation, or an officer of the tribunal itself complains against anyone before an administrative tribunal like the ICC or the NLRB, there is certainly a chance that the tribunal will be biased and that it will not do absolute justice in its decision. When a citizen importing goods contests the valuation put upon his goods by an appraiser, the Customs Court may be too much inclined to uphold the appraiser. In short there can be miscarriage of justice in administrative tribunals, but there is no evidence to show that there is even a strong trend toward injustice in such tribunals any more than there is in the ordinary courts.

It is certainly true, however, that where a number of administrative bodies, as in the national government, act upon similar matters, they do not always follow the same rules or reach the same conclusions. In order to bring about better standards and more uniformity in administrative adjudication in the national government it has recently been proposed that an "office of federal administrative procedure" be established to give continuous study to the problem.[13] It is generally agreed that absolute uniformity is neither possible nor desirable.

Judicial Review of Administrative Action. Furthermore there is already in the national government very extensive provision for judicial review of administrative and executive actions. Wherever substantial personal rights are involved in a real controversy between parties, the courts generally have jurisdiction to hear and decide finally the issues involved. Wherever this is not true, no one should object to legislation to make it true. To supplement this review, there is also unquestioned need for a competent person or unit to conduct hearings within each administrative agency, and a procedure that allows due notice and hearing to the persons involved. These are matters to be

[11] See President's Committee on Administrative Management, *Report, with Special Studies*, pp. 207-43.

[12] See Blachly and Oatman, *Federal Regulatory Action and Control*, pp. 264-66, 349-56.

[13] *Administrative Procedure in Government Agencies*, cited in footnote 2, above, pp. 123-26, 191-202.

worked out for each administrative agency in accordance with its peculiar problems.

To citizens interested in protecting their own rights against executive officers and administrative agencies, the courts stand primarily as the authorities that have the power to issue writs of *injunction* and *prohibition* against officials who are about to violate private rights, writs of *mandamus* to compel officers to perform their duties, and writs of *habeas corpus* to release a person from custody at least long enough to permit his case to be heard by the judges.[14] In many cases the procedure is a simple appeal to the courts from administrative action.

It should be noted, however, that some of the "great writs" are not available against the highest officers of the government. The President cannot be either enjoined by the courts from doing what he considers his executive duty, nor be commanded by them to do what somebody else thinks he should do. The high degree of immunity from interference by the courts that is enjoyed by the President is not shared by other executive officers or by boards and commissions. Thus the work of regulatory bodies is constantly being delayed, obstructed, and even set aside by action of the courts at the behest of interested individuals and corporations. In many cases the statutes make the decision of the administrative authority final as to the "facts" in the case, reserving only questions of "law" to be tested in the courts. In practice the line between these two is not clear, but the Supreme Court has insisted in recent years more and more strongly that the national courts shall accept in good faith all findings of fact by administrative agencies that are supported by substantial evidence and not try to reweigh the evidence. In a dissent in an important decision in 1936[15] Justice Brandeis stated a rule that is now practically the rule of the Court. The issue turned upon a so-called "constitutional fact," the alleged confiscation of the property of a stockyards company by a government order reducing its rates of charge. Justice Brandeis wrote as follows:

> Like the lower court, I think no good reason exists for making special exception of issues of fact bearing upon a constitutional right. The inexorable safeguard which the due process clause assures is not that a court may examine whether the findings as to value or income are correct, but [1] that the trier of the facts shall be an impartial tribunal; [2] that no finding shall be made except upon due notice and opportunity to be heard; [3] that the procedure at the hearing shall be consistent with the essentials of a fair trial; and [4] that it shall be conducted in such a way that there will be opportunity for a court to determine whether the applicable rules of law and procedure were observed. [Numbers in brackets supplied.]

[14] For summary statements about these and related "writs of court" see James Hart, *An Introduction to Administrative Law, with Selected Cases*, pp. 437-516.

[15] St. Joseph Stock Yards Co. v. United States (1936), 298 U. S. 38.

Executive and Legislative Controls over Administrative Procedure. Even if the courts were to assume a more active role than they now do in supervising the work of administrative agencies, it would be a mistake to think of the courts as alone responsible for protecting the people against abuses by administrators. Within the executive branch as a whole, and within each agency, there are means of control in the public interest over administrative activity. Furthermore, with his nation-wide public responsibility, any President is likely to be very sensitive to abuses by administrators that are brought to his attention.

Congress, also, with its continuing responsibility for criticism of the administrative branch, is always ready to call attention to administrative abuses. Minority party members are especially alert to find cases in which the administration has gone wrong. And even though the Supreme Court says that certain agencies like the Federal Trade Commission are not a part of the executive branch and no part of the President's responsibility, members of Congress and other public leaders will not hesitate to charge the President with failure if any regulatory body abuses its powers.

Between them, Congress and the President have done much in recent years to eliminate administrative malpractices and to raise the quality of service being rendered. For example, all administrative rules and regulations must now clear through the Budget Bureau and be checked for conformity to standards and must be published in the *Federal Register*, a relatively new official publication for all administrative and executive actions. Every questionnaire that is to be sent out by any agency to get information from the public must also be checked and approved in the Budget Bureau. This restriction upon the investigative powers of the administration has already resulted in considerable saving to the government and to thousands of individuals and corporations.

On the judicial side, many important agencies of government have now set up adequate and impartial boards of appeals right within their own staff, to make sure that no one will have his case before the agency decided upon the basis of a snap judgment. The procedures set up to ensure due notice and hearing are becoming, if anything, too involved and cumbersome.

Private Recourse Against the National Government. When all has been done that can reasonably be expected along these lines to check and control the actions of administrative agencies, there will still be occasional cases of abuse of power and other cases of unsatisfactory work due to human failure and various other causes. Administrative agencies will fail to live up to their contracts with corporations and citizens, will seize property for public use without adequate compensation, will collect more taxes from some corporations and individuals than they are obliged to pay, or will cause injury to persons through a variety of accidental causes. The numbers of such cases in the course of the year for the national government have never been computed. They must run into the tens of thousands annually. What provision has the national government made for making amends or restoring property or paying damages in such cases?

This topic is also closely related to that of civil rights and their enforcement, and will be discussed in connection with that subject in chapter 21.

REFERENCES

Frederick F. Blachly and Miriam E. Oatman, *Administrative Legislation and Adjudication*, Washington, 1934.

U. S. Attorney General, Committee on Administrative Procedure, Report of, entitled *Administrative Procedure in Government Agencies*, Senate Doc. No. 8, 77th Cong., 1st Sess., Washington, 1941.

Charles G. Haines, "The Adaptation of Administrative Law and Procedure to Constitutional Theories and Principles," *Am. Pol. Sci. Rev.*, vol. 34, pp. 1-30 (1940).

John Dickinson, *Administrative Justice and the Supremacy of Law in the United States*, Cambridge, 1927.

Ernst Freund, *Administrative Powers over Persons and Property*, A Comparative Survey, Chicago, 1928.

President's Committee on Administrative Management, *Report of the Committee, with Studies of Administrative Management in the Federal Government*, Washington, 1937, especially the studies by James Hart, "The Exercise of Rule-Making Power," Edwin E. Witte, "The Preparation of Proposed Legislative Measures by Administrative Departments," and Robert E. Cushman, "The Problem of the Independent Regulatory Commissions." (Brief title: *Report, with Special Studies*.)

American Bar Association, *Report* to, of the Special Committee on Administrative Law, 1935.

United States Senate, Select Committee to Investigate the Executive Agencies of the Government, *Report* to, etc., No. 10, "On the Government Activities in the Regulation of Private Business Enterprises," prepared by the Brookings Institution, 75th Cong., 1st Sess., Senate Committee Print, Washington, 1937.

James Hart, *The Ordinance Making Powers of the President of the United States*, Baltimore, 1925.

——, *An Introduction to Administrative Law, with Selected Cases*, New York, 1940.

James M. Beck, *Our Wonderland of Bureaucracy*, New York, 1932.

Charles G. Haines and Marshall E. Dimock, *Essays on the Law and Practice of Government Administration*, Baltimore, 1935, especially Part II, Part III, pp. 127-73, and Part IV, pp. 269-321.

Leonard D. White, *Introduction to the Study of Public Administration*, rev. ed., New York, 1939, chs. XXXIII-XXXVII.

James M. Landis, *The Administrative Process*, New Haven, 1938.

Robert E. Cushman, *The Independent Regulatory Commissions*, New York, 1941.

Joseph P. Chamberlain, *et al.*, *The Judicial Function in Federal Administrative Agencies*, New York, 1942.

CHAPTER 20

Civil Rights and the National Government

AMERICAN BACKGROUNDS

Prior to the Constitution. The English colonists in America claimed that they were entitled to all the traditional legal rights of Englishmen. These had never been written down in any systematic form. Some of them went all the way back to Magna Carta (1215) and even beyond. They covered rights of personal liberty, freedom of speech, press, and religion, and procedural rights such as that of jury trial. All were subject to modification by acts of Parliament, which was for Englishmen the highest source of law.

Failing to make good their claims to all the rights of Englishmen, leading colonists fell back upon the theory of natural rights. In other words they contended that they possessed inherent rights as men, rights that were even higher than and prior to their civil rights as Englishmen. The Declaration of Independence asserted the claims of the colonists to both natural rights and the civil rights of Englishmen. Logically the two types of claims do not readily mix, but the combination of the two proved to have a powerful emotional appeal.

Several of the state constitutions that were drawn up in this period contained bills or declarations of rights. Outstanding examples were those of Virginia and Massachusetts. These set a pattern for other states and in time all the state constitutions came to contain similar statements of rights. Their effectiveness was at first very limited. Wartime necessities, between 1776 and 1783, led to extreme measures in some states, and the state legislatures were practically unchecked by either the executive or the courts in those early years. It was understandable, therefore, that the framers of the early state constitutions should decide to include bills of rights in the state fundamental laws to protect the people against legislative oppression.

The National Constitution. The Convention of 1787 rejected almost without debate a proposal to include a bill of rights in the Constitution of the

United States. It was argued later in *The Federalist* that the national government's powers would be so limited that there was no reason to fear any encroachment upon personal liberties from that source. Hamilton pointed out, indeed, that the proposed Constitution already contained several important limitations upon the powers of the national government and that these were guarantees of personal rights. In addition he argued that to place a separate bill of rights in the national Constitution might by implication extend the nation's powers beyond what was intended. Why, then, forbid what had not been authorized? [1] The opposition was not convinced by these arguments. The Constitution was adopted with the understanding that a bill of rights would soon be added. This agreement was carried out in 1791 when ten amendments proposed by Congress were ratified by enough states to put them into effect.

The National Bill of Rights. The first ten amendments to the Constitution are ordinarily spoken of as the national bill of rights. In fact the passages of the original Constitution mentioned by Hamilton, and the three amendments adopted at the time of the Civil War (the Thirteenth, Fourteenth, and Fifteenth), are also of tremendous importance to civil liberties. The entire national bill of rights would consist, therefore, of all the civil rights provisions of the Constitution, and not of just the first ten amendments.

Alien and Sedition Laws. Prior to the Civil War the most serious invasion of civil rights by Congress was the enactment of the Alien and Sedition Laws of 1798.[2] One act permitted the President to order the deportation of men whom he considered to be dangerous alien radicals; the other authorized the criminal prosecution of all persons who published false and malicious writings against the government or against Congress or the President with bad intent. Numerous deportations and punishments took place under these statutes. These occurrences proved at least that Congress was not above encroaching on civil liberties, and that even the existence of the First Amendment and its provisions against Congressional interference with the freedoms of speech and press is no absolute guarantee of these rights.

Civil War and Three New Amendments. The Supreme Court did not have occasion to pass upon the constitutionality of these acts, but they were vigorously opposed by Jefferson and the Republicans. After these acts had expired (1801) there was very little invasion of civil liberties by the national government until the Civil War when Lincoln suspended the writ of habeas corpus in certain areas without waiting for the approval of Congress.

Then followed the adoption of the three "Civil War Amendments" to the Constitution, the Thirteenth, Fourteenth and Fifteenth. These were intended primarily to abolish slavery and to establish the civil and political rights of the Negroes, but the Fourteenth Amendment had a much broader scope and purpose. It established a new national standard of citizenship, and forbade

[1] *The Federalist*, No. 84.
[2] Acts of June 25 and July 14, 1798; 1 *Stat.* 570, 596.

the states to deprive *any person* (not just citizens or the ex-slaves) of life, liberty, or property without due process of law, or to deny to any person within its jurisdiction the equal protection of the laws. Indeed it went beyond even these measures by providing for protecting "the privileges or immunities of citizens of the United States" against abridgment by the states. This attempt to provide for a distinct category of privileges and immunities for the nation's citizens (as distinct from those of the citizens of the states) was potentially very important.

Supreme Court Upsets Nationalizing Trends. At this point in the trend toward the nationalization of civil liberties the Supreme Court stepped in to restore the balance in favor of state rights. In two path-breaking decisions [3] in 1873 and 1883 the Court practically destroyed any significance that the "privileges or immunities" clause of the Fourteenth Amendment might have had, and closed the door upon attempts by Congress to make direct enactments that define and provide for the enforcement of civil liberties.

"Due Process" and Property Rights. In the meantime, however, the possibilities in the "due process" clause of the Fourteenth Amendment had begun to receive judicial attention. This clause, as previously noted, forbids any state to "deprive any person of life, liberty, or property, without due process of law." The first important cases under this clause concerned property rights rather than life or liberty, and they involved corporations perhaps even more than natural persons. Nevertheless the decisions in these cases started a new trend, and one that was important for civil liberties. The Supreme Court (not Congress) stepped forth as the protector of rights against state encroachments in a great number of instances. It was at this stage, and mainly under the due process clause, that the Supreme Court acquired its reputation as a destroyer of social legislation. It invalidated many state acts on the ground that they deprived persons of property without due process of law.

The Emphasis Shifts to Personal Rights. Following World War I the Court experienced a change in basic philosophy. During and just after that war both Congress and the state legislatures, and the law-enforcing agencies of both the nation and the states, were guilty of numerous serious invasions of the freedom of speech and press and other personal liberties. The judges began then to see the great importance in a democratic society of these rights of free thought and expression. In the interwar period several state acts that impaired the freedoms of speech and press were declared unconstitutional as violations of the "liberty" guaranteed by the Fourteenth Amendment. Freedom of speech, press, and religion (First Amendment) was held to be included in "liberty" in the Fourteenth Amendment. After 1937 the number of these decisions increased and the frontiers of personal freedom were thus pushed forward very noticeably. In the meantime the Court's solicitude about property rights had suffered some decline.

[3] Slaughter-House Cases (1873), 16 Wall. 36; Civil Rights Cases (1883), 109 U. S. 3.

The Nation as Protector of Civil Liberties. The present position is, then, that the national government, as represented by the judicial branch rather than by Congress, has become to a large extent the protector of civil liberties against state encroachment. The Department of Justice has also become active in protecting civil liberties against both state and individual action. During World War II the states in effect relinquished to the national authorities the entire responsibility for the suppression and punishment of treason, sedition, and obstruction of the war effort. This trend seems to be practically the opposite of what the opponents of the Constitution in 1787-88 had expected. They had trust in the state governments but were fearful of national activity in the field.

But, though the enforcement and protection of civil liberties have become increasingly a national function, it does not follow that the national government has a spotless record. Let us next examine, then, what civil liberties are supposed to be guaranteed in the United States, and the role of the national government in protecting them. The account will be limited to the provisions of the national Constitution and the judicial decisions, legislation, and practices that throw light on them. In each state constitution there is also a bill of rights. These parallel the national constitutional provisions on most major points but they also contain additional provisions that apply only in the states concerned.

THE NATIONAL GOVERNMENT AND CIVIL RIGHTS TODAY

The National Bill of Rights. In a comprehensive sense the national bill of rights includes all or parts of the following provisions of the Constitution:

Art. I, sec. 9—Prohibitions against the national government on such subjects as habeas corpus, bills of attainder, and ex post facto laws.

Art. I, sec. 10—Prohibitions against the states with respect to bills of attainder, ex post facto laws, and the obligation of contracts.

Art. III, secs. 2, 3—Provisions governing the national judiciary in such matters as jury trial in criminal cases and the trial and punishment of treason.

Art. IV, sec. 2—The so-called "comity clause" which provides that "The Citizens of each State shall be entitled to all Privileges and Immunities of Citizens in the several States."

Amendments I to VIII, inclusive—Provide guarantees against national infringement of such *substantive* rights as freedom of religion, speech, press, and assembly, the right to bear arms, freedom from unreasonable searches and seizures, and "life, liberty and property"; and *procedural* guarantees for litigants in United States courts, in both civil and criminal cases, covering grand juries, jury trial, right to counsel, etc., and "due process of law" in general.

Amendments IX and X—General reservations of unspecified rights and powers to individuals and to the states against national action.

Amendment XIII—Prohibiting slavery and involuntary servitude.

Amendment XIV—Establishing national citizenship, guaranteeing "the privileges and immunities of citizens of the United States" against state interference, and forbidding the states to "deprive any person of life, liberty, or property, without due process of law" or to "deny any person within its jurisdiction the equal protection of the laws."

Amendment XV—Forbidding both national and state governments from setting suffrage requirements that discriminate against United States citizens "on account of race, color, or previous condition of servitude."

Amendment XIX—Making an identical prohibition against discriminations in voting "on account of sex."

Whom Does the Bill of Rights Protect? There is some confusion on this point because of the use of different words. The Constitution provides that "the citizens of each State" are entitled to certain privileges; that the right of "the people" to bear arms is not to be infringed by Congress; that "no person" shall be deprived of life, liberty, or property, without due process of law; and that the states may not impair the privileges and immunities of "citizens of the United States." Citizens, people, and persons—what do these different words mean?

Corporations as Persons. In the language of the law, "persons" is a broader term than "citizens" and more definite than "the people." It includes not only natural persons or human beings, but also so-called "artificial persons" such as corporations. Each corporation has a legal personality separate from that of its members, and is a distinct person at law. The Fifth Amendment, which forbids Congress, and the Fourteenth, which forbids any state, to "deprive any person of life, liberty, or property, without due process of law," showed the importance of the use of the term "person." A corporation may not have any "life" or "liberty" in the ordinary sense, but it is a person and it has property. The property rights of private corporations are protected, therefore, in practically the same way as the property owned by individuals.[4] On the other hand a local government corporation like a county or city is a mere agent of the state that creates it. What it owns it owns, not as a separate person, but on behalf of the state; hence the state is not prevented by the Fourteenth Amendment from taking the so-called property of local governments.[5] However, the national government could not take the property of a city any more than it could take private property or the state's property without due process. And "due process" in the case of taking of land and other things for public use under eminent domain always includes the duty to pay compensation.

Non-Citizens as Persons. Among natural persons, there are (a) aliens, (b) those who owe allegiance and are nationals but are not citizens, like the Fili-

---

[4] C. K. Burdick, *The Law of the American Constitution*, pp. 514-15; Covington Turnpike Co. v. Sandford (1896), 164 U. S. 578; Hugh E. Willis, "Corporations and the United States Constitution," in *University of Cincinnati Law Rev.*, vol. VIII, pp. 1-31 (1934).

[5] City of Trenton v. State of New Jersey (1923), 262 U. S. 182.

pinos, and (c) citizens, as well as some stateless persons. Where the Constitution protects the rights of "persons" it presumably includes all these. It is only where it uses some other term, such as "citizens," that the constitutional protection is more limited. Thus in fact non-citizens receive constitutional protection of their rights under a Constitution which is not theirs and from a government to which they owe only qualified allegiance. Some of the most important clauses in the national bill of rights thus give protection broadly to all "persons."

Rights Peculiar to Citizens. The previous discussion of the "comity clause" of the Constitution revealed that each state does give certain special privileges, mainly political, social, and educational, to its own citizens, whereas another group of rights, largely concerned with economic matters and protection, must be conceded by each state to citizens of all states.[6] By the Fourteenth Amendment the states are also forbidden to "make or enforce any law which shall abridge the privileges and immunities of citizens of the United States." This language implies that there is a special category of rights or "privileges and immunities" belonging peculiarly to United States citizens as such. In fact the Supreme Court has taken a narrow view of this part of the Fourteenth Amendment. In the Slaughter-House Cases,[7] previously mentioned, in which residents of Louisiana opposed a state act that gave a monopoly of the slaughtering business in New Orleans to one company, the Court held that the right to engage in an ordinary lawful business like that of slaughtering is not a privilege or immunity of citizens of the United States as such. It is instead one of the privileges that is controllable by each state according to its own policy.

Privileges and Immunities of United States Citizens. In this decision the Court tried to distinguish between the privileges of national and state citizenship. It was not intended by those who framed and adopted the Fourteenth Amendment, the Court said, "to transfer the security and protection of all the civil rights . . . from the states to the federal government." Among the privileges and immunities of national citizenship that are protected against state interference the Court mentioned the following examples: (1) the right of access to the seat of government, the courts, the subtreasuries, land offices, and other agencies of the national government, to transact necessary business; (2) the right to the protection of the national government while on the high seas or abroad; (3) the right to assemble peaceably and to petition for redress of grievances; (4) the privilege of the writ of habeas corpus; (5) the right to use the navigable waters of the United States wherever they may penetrate the territory of the several states; (6) the right to become a citizen of any State in the Union by a *bona fide* residence therein; (7) the right of expatriation; (8) the right to exercise the privilege (where it is possessed) of voting for members of Congress and Presidential electors without interference by public offi-

[6] See ch. 6, above; U. S. Const., Art. IV, sec. 2.
[7] (1873), 16 Wall. 36.

cials or others; (9) the right to enter the country and to prove citizenship where the right is questioned; and (10) the right of free migration from place to place within the United States.

All these privileges were actually set forth or clearly implied in the Constitution, statutes, or treaties of the United States prior to the Fourteenth Amendment, and they were already protected from state interference by the "supremacy clause" in Article VI of the Constitution. In effect, therefore, the Supreme Court ruled that the privileges or immunities clause of the Fourteenth Amendment adds nothing to the Constitution. This clause was just another way of saying what already was the law.[8] Congress itself was not convinced that the Fourteenth Amendment did not confer additional powers upon it. In 1875 it passed the Civil Rights Act which provided for equal treatment of all persons, without regard to race or color, in public conveyances, inns, theaters and other public places. When the question of the constitutionality of this act came before the Supreme Court, that tribunal ruled in 1883 that the Fourteenth Amendment privileges-or-immunities clause is a prohibition only against the states and not against individuals, such as innkeepers, and that it confers no power on Congress to regulate civil liberties directly.[9] Congress may act only to prevent abuses by the states, not to regulate the conduct of individuals. Subsequent efforts by litigants in the courts to read new content into the privileges or immunities clause have resulted in practically no net change.[10]

What the Supreme Court has done to make the Fourteenth Amendment privileges-or-immunities clause a dead letter has also had the effect of preventing a tremendous change in the federal system. This is one important instance in which the Court has had a marked retarding influence upon the development of nationalism. Those who drafted and put through the Fourteenth Amendment undoubtedly intended to establish national control in the civil rights field as a means of protecting Negroes, but this plan the Court has effectively vetoed up to this time.

We have now considered the various clauses of persons who are supposed to be protected in their civil rights. The next question is

Against Whom Does the Bill of Rights Give Protection? The possible violators of private rights are (1) the national, (2) the state, and (3) the local governments, and (4) private persons, including corporations.

1. *Protections Against National Government.* Some provisions of the national Constitution protect persons only against the national government. Thus the provisions in Article I, sec. IX, in Article III, and in the first eight

---

[8] See D. O. McGovney, "Privileges or Immunities Clause, Fourteenth Amendment," *Iowa Law Bulletin*, vol. 4, p. 219 (1918); reprinted in Association of American Law Schools, *Selected Essays on Constitutional Law*, Book 2, pp. 402-24.

[9] Civil Rights Cases (1883), 109 U. S. 3.

[10] See Colgate v. Harvey (1935), 296 U. S. 404, overruled by Madden v. Kentucky (1940), 309 U. S. 83; Hague v. CIO (1939), 307 U. S. 496; and the dissent of four justices in Edwards v. California (1941), 314 U. S. 160.

amendments in and of themselves give no protection against the states or against individuals. Some of these provisions are so worded that on first reading they seem to protect persons against both national and state governments. Thus Amendment V closes with the words "nor shall private property be taken for public use without just compensation." In an early case an individual whose wharf had been made almost valueless by some changes in its harbor made by the city of Baltimore sought in court to obtain damages from the city under the provision of Amendment V just quoted. He had been denied damages under the state laws and constitution. In the Supreme Court of the United States Chief Justice Marshall held that "the provision in the Fifth Amendment . . . is intended solely as a limitation on the exercise of power by the government of the United States, and is not applicable to the legislation of the states." [11] The Court made it clear, too, that all the first ten amendments were adopted as limitations on the national government alone, and the Court has at no time extended them beyond this. It is, therefore, one of the first rules for students of American government to learn that the first ten amendments *as such* limit the national government alone, and not the states. An interesting recent development will, however, be noted below.

2. *Limitations on State Governments.* The national Constitution includes some provisions, however, that expressly limit the powers of the states. Such are the restrictions in Article I, section 10, including the noteworthy contract clause: "No State shall . . . pass any . . . Law impairing the Obligation of Contracts. . . ." The Civil War Amendments (XIII, XIV, and XV) and the Woman Suffrage Amendment (XIX) are also limitations primarily on the states.

The state *governments* are further limited by the bills of rights in their respective state constitutions. These apply only to the states in question, and have no effect on the national government. The individual seeking protection against state action has, therefore, both certain provisions in the national Constitution and in the state bill of rights to support him. Both state and national courts are legally bound to uphold the provisions of the United States Constitution, and the rulings of the Supreme Court bind all judges in the enforcement of rights based thereon. State constitutions are in a different position. The final interpretation in each case is given by the state supreme court, and the national courts follow that interpretation whenever they are called on to enforce a state provision.

There is, however, a great deal of duplication of provisions between the national and state constitutions. There is, for example, a "due process clause" limiting the national government (Fifth Amendment), another in the national Constitution limiting the state governments (Fourteenth Amendment), and in almost every state constitution a similar provision limiting the particular state government. The same is true to some extent of other fundamental provisions. In these cases, because of the great respect shown by state supreme

[11] Barron v. Baltimore (1833), 7 Peters 243.

courts for the opinions of the Supreme Court of the United States, there is a marked tendency for the state courts to follow the national courts in their construction and interpretation of constitutional rights. As a result there is a fairly uniform interpretation throughout the country of the basic civil rights.

3. *Limitations on Local Governments.* Local governments within a state are agents of the state, created by it for better government in different parts of the state's area. The state is the responsible superior. Therefore in all cases where the United States Constitution forbids the states to do things, local governments are equally forbidden. A state may not do indirectly through its local governments what it is forbidden by the Constitution to do directly. Thus a local unit may not take property or liberty from persons without due process any more than the state may.

4. *Limitations on Private Persons.* Bills of rights are inserted in constitutions in order to protect private rights against invasion by the government—national, or state and local. There are a few cases, however, in which the provisions are broader than this, in which they actually protect individuals against other individuals as well as against government. Take for example the Thirteenth Amendment to the Constitution: "Neither slavery nor involuntary servitude, except as a punishment for crime whereof the party shall have been duly convicted, shall exist within the United States, or any place subject to their jurisdiction." Here is language broad enough to prohibit private acts of enslavement as well as those sanctioned by acts of government. Under its power to pass legislation to enforce this Amendment, Congress has enacted and the Department of Justice has long enforced an antipeonage statute. This legislation has been upheld by the Supreme Court.

Substantive and Procedural Rights Distinguished. Before proceeding to the analysis of the principal civil rights a major distinction needs to be made. Such rights as freedom of speech, press, and religion, and the right to acquire and use land and other valuable things (property rights) are called "substantive," whereas guarantees of jury trial, and the right of counsel in criminal cases, are called "procedural." The trial of a newspaper editor for seditious utterances would involve a substantive right (freedom of the press) but might also raise procedural questions such as the right to a jury trial of the case.

The Fifth and Fourteenth Amendments present interesting examples of the fusion of substantive and procedural rights. Their "due process" clauses provide that neither Congress (Fifth Amendment) nor the states (Fourteenth Amendment) shall "deprive any person of life, liberty, or property [substantive rights] without due process of law" [procedural right]. The terms that they use to designate the principal substantive rights—life, liberty, and property—may be taken as the basis for the following classification.

SUBSTANTIVE RIGHTS

1. *Life*

The most fundamental of all human rights is the right to live. In its two due process clauses quoted above, the Constitution guarantees every person's right to life against both the national and state governments. By the same clauses the right is qualified; it is not an absolute or unlimited right. Life may be taken by due process of law, as is illustrated by the death penalty for such crimes as murder and treason. Governments are also empowered to impose duties upon their citizens that may put them in danger of death, as they do when they draft men for military service. Such action also is not a deprivation of life without due process. What is meant by due process in criminal cases will be considered hereafter.

2. *Liberty of the Person*

Freedom from Bodily Restraint. The term "liberty" as used in the Fifth and Fourteenth Amendments is very broad, and difficult to define. There is persuasive evidence to support the assertion that it originally meant only freedom of the body or freedom from bodily restraint.[12] The free man (*liber homo*) of old English law was one who was not bound as a serf to serve one lord or bound to labor on one piece of land. He was free to move about without any restraint beyond that which the law put upon all citizens. Even this very limited but basic concept of liberty was not always accepted in practice, however; a number of states whose constitutions guaranteed liberty also tolerated slavery. This apparent contradiction was rationalized by saying that the slave was not truly a person.

Thirteenth Amendment. When the time came, therefore, to abolish human slavery in the United States a national constitutional amendment was adopted for the purpose. By this, the Thirteenth Amendment, it is provided that "neither slavery nor involuntary servitude, except as a punishment for crime whereof the party shall have been duly convicted, shall exist within the United States, or any place subject to their jurisdiction." "Slavery" as used in this amendment is a relationship in which one human being is the owner of another, and as such has an almost unlimited control over and property right in the other. The latter is called a slave. He is bought and sold as a chattel, and has only very limited legal rights or standing in the courts. "Involuntary servitude" as used in the amendment covers such a status as "peonage," or the enforced labor of one person for another to pay off a debt.

Congress under its power to enforce the Thirteenth Amendment "by appropriate legislation" has enacted a statute against peonage. This statute has

---

[12] On this point see Charles E. Shattuck, "The True Meaning of the Term 'Liberty' in those Clauses in the Federal and State Constitutions which Protect 'Life, Liberty, and Property,'" *Harvard Law Review*, Book 4, p. 365 (1891); reprinted in Association of American Law Schools, *Selected Essays on Constitutional Law*, vol. 2, pp. 185-208.

been fully sustained by the Supreme Court and has been applied by the courts in a number of cases—against state laws and also against private violations.[13] In general it has been held that to keep one man working for another under a threat of punishment either by law or by individual action is involuntary servitude.

On the other hand, compulsory military service and compulsory service on the roads are not forbidden, and by parallel reasoning jury service, posse service, and other duties of a civil nature are still enforceable by the proper government upon the individual. As the Supreme Court said concerning the Thirteenth Amendment in a road labor case:

> It introduced no novel doctrine with respect of services always treated as exceptional, and certainly was not intended to interdict enforcement of those duties which individuals owe to the State, such as services in the army, militia, on the jury, etc. The great purpose in view was liberty under the protection of effective government, not the destruction of the latter by depriving it of essential powers. . . .[14]

Imprisonment and compulsory labor as punishments for crimes and misdemeanors are also permitted. Apparently, also, the Thirteenth Amendment does not itself forbid imprisonment for debt, but most of the state constitutions cover this expressly.

Inviolability of the Body. Questions have come up as to the right of the government to compel vaccination and to sterilize those deemed unfit to reproduce their kind. In both cases there is a violation of bodily integrity. There is strong medical evidence to support both vaccination and sterilization as being effective in achieving their purposes, and both have been sustained by the Supreme Court as authorized infringements of personal liberty under the Fourteenth Amendment.[15]

Cruel and unusual punishments are forbidden to the national government by Amendment VIII, but the Constitution makes no similar express prohibition against the states. This question is usually considered as primarily procedural, but any maiming of the body seriously impairs one's basic right to bodily integrity.

Freedom of Movement and Residence. The right to choose one's place of residence and to move about freely anywhere within the country is essential to genuine liberty of the body. It was clearly implied in the comity clause of the Constitution: "The Citizens of each State shall be entitled to all Privileges and Immunities of Citizens in the several States," [16] and was conceded to be one of the "privileges or immunities of citizens of the United States" in the

---

[13] Bailey v. Alabama (1911), 219 U. S. 219; Taylor v. Georgia (1942), 315 U. S. 25; Pollock v. Williams (1944), 322 U. S. 4.

[14] Butler v. Perry (1916), 240 U. S. 328.

[15] Jacobson v. Massachusetts (1905), 197 U. S. 11 (vaccination); Buck v. Bell (1927), 274 U. S. 200 (sterilization).

[16] Art. IV, sec. 2, par. 1.

Slaughter-House Cases. Nevertheless when the California law that forbade any person to assist a pauper to enter the state was declared unconstitutional the Supreme Court gave as its main reason the interference with interstate commerce. Four justices disagreed vigorously with this reasoning and held that freedom to move from state to state is a privilege or immunity of national citizenship.[17] The compulsory removal of American-born citizens of Japanese descent from the entire Pacific coastal area as a measure of military precaution in 1942, and the restrictions placed upon their freedom of travel and residence constituted one of the most serious invasions of this personal liberty that has yet taken place. The Supreme Court sustained the validity of the action on the grounds of "pressing public necessity," but the justices were clearly troubled by what had been done, and three justices thought that it was unconstitutional.[18] Segregation ordinances that attempt to restrict Negroes to certain places of residence in cities have generally been held unconstitutional, but usually for the reason that such measures unduly invade property rights.[19]

3. Freedom of Worship, Thought, and Expression

The First Amendment. When drafting a bill of rights to attach to the Constitution, the early leaders of Congress placed the freedom of the human mind and spirit at the head of the list. In the First Amendment they provided that

> Congress shall make no law respecting an establishment of religion, or prohibiting the free exercise thereof; or abridging the freedom of speech, or of the press; or the right of the people peaceably to assemble, and to petition the Government for a redress of grievances.

It will be noted that in this single sentence a number of important freedoms are run together: religion, speech, press, assembly, and petition. These rights are in fact very closely related to each other. They are all necessary to freedom of thought, belief, and expression. Freedom of religion, for example, cannot be fully attained without freedom of speech, press, and assembly.

The Fourteenth Amendment Annexes the First. The Fifth Amendment, drafted and adopted along with the First, forbade Congress to deprive any person of liberty without due process of law. Had the term "liberty" been interpreted at that time as including the freedoms listed in the First Amendment it would have been mere repetition, or, conversely, the First Amendment itself could as well have been omitted. Evidently no one thought that there was any duplication. Nevertheless lawyers soon began to make assertions that

---

[17] Edwards v. California (1941), 314 U. S. 160. See also Williams v. Fears (1900), 179 U. S. 270.

[18] Korematsu v. U. S. (1944), 323 U. S. 214; Ex parte Mitsuye Endo (1944), 323 U. S. 283; Eugene V. Rostow, "Our Worst Wartime Mistake," Harper's Magazine, vol. 191, pp. 193-201 (1943); Robert E. Cushman, "Some Constitutional Problems of Civil Liberty," Boston University Law Review, vol. 23, pp. 335-78 (1943).

[19] Buchanan v. Worley (1917), 245 U. S. 60; Robert E. Cushman, loc. cit., footnote 18, above.

indicated a belief that the liberty guaranteed by the Fifth Amendment included such rights as free speech and free press.

When the Fourteenth Amendment was adopted (1868) the question arose once more. Lawyers tried to persuade the courts that the due process clause of the Fourteenth Amendment by its protection of liberty forbade the states to deprive any person of freedom of speech, press, or religion. Time and again the Supreme Court of the United States rejected this contention.[20] Nevertheless the pressure for a change of views persisted. As already indicated, during and just after World War I it became very clear that not only the national government but many states were making deep inroads into the ordinary civil rights of Americans. Leading lawyers and judges became greatly perturbed by this trend. At this juncture, therefore, it seemed as fitting a time as it ever would be for the Supreme Court to reverse its old position and to interpose the warning voice of the courts against those states that were undermining civil liberties. The reversal came in the decision that involved a person who was charged with violating the New York state law against criminal anarchy. To justify its own jurisdiction in this case the Court said that "For present purposes we may and do assume that freedom of speech and of the press— which are protected by the First Amendment from abridgement by Congress —are among the fundamental personal rights and 'liberties' protected by the due process clause of the Fourteenth Amendment from impairment by the states." [21] By other decisions the freedoms of religion and of assembly have also been assimilated to the Fourteenth Amendment due process clause, and have thus been made enforcible by national action against the states.

But if the Fourteenth Amendment can thus take over the First Amendment, why should it not also take over all the rest of the civil rights, substantive and procedural, that are stated in the first ten amendments? Some of the framers of the Fourteenth Amendment evidently had this objective in mind,[22] but the text of the amendment does not specifically provide for it, and the Supreme Court has rejected the idea.[23] The recently aroused interest of the justices in upholding the democratic process in American government has led them to single out the First Amendment with its substantive guarantees of free speech, press, religion, and assembly, as most important for the national government not only to observe but also to enforce against the states. Without these freedoms, it is held, democracy would fail and with democracy would go liberty.

As a result of this great change in views the Supreme Court has to some

---

[20] See Charles Warren, "The New 'Liberty' under the Fourteenth Amendment," *Harvard Law Review*, vol. 39, pp. 431-65; reprinted in Association of American Law Schools, *Selected Essays on Constitutional Law*, Book 2, pp. 237-66.

[21] Gitlow v. New York (1925), 268 U. S. 652, 666.

[22] See Horace E. Flack, *The Adoption of the Fourteenth Amendment* (1908), ch. 2, espec. pp. 57-59, 91-94.

[23] See Charles Warren, *loc. cit.*, footnote 20, above; and dissent by Justice Frankfurter in Malinski v. New York (1945), 324 U. S. 401.

extent made amends for its earlier emasculation of the privileges-or-immunities clause of the Fourteenth Amendment. The whole new trend has been described as "nationalizing the bill of rights." It has not, it seems, extended the power of Congress to legislate on civil rights, but instead has placed it in the power of the United States courts to control state legislative excesses in the field of civil liberties. Many cases of state and local interference with the freedoms of speech, press, religion, and assembly have been brought to the Supreme Court in recent years. The sect known as Jehovah's Witnesses has been responsible for much of the litigation, but trade unions and other groups as well as individuals have had considerable shares in it. The frontiers of civil liberties have thus been measurably advanced.[24]

Freedom of Religion. Congress and the states are now equally forbidden to make any laws "respecting an establishment of religion, or prohibiting the free exercise thereof." On the negative side it is generally agreed that freedom of religion does not justify acts of licentiousness and public disturbance. To these limitations the Supreme Court has recently added that freedom of religion does not provide a defense for using the mails to defraud, or for sending children into the streets to spread religious propaganda by selling religious tracts contrary to the child labor laws.[25] On the other hand it is unconstitutional to require religious groups to obtain licenses before engaging in their propaganda, to forbid them from going peaceably from door to door with their message, to impose a tax upon their sale of religious literature, or to require children in the public schools to salute the flag contrary to their religious beliefs.[26]

Freedom of Speech and Press. The First and Fourteenth Amendments also forbid the passage of laws "abridging the freedom of speech, or of the press." No act of Congress has ever been declared unconstitutional under this provision, but the Alien and Sedition Laws of 1798, mentioned near the beginning of this chapter, would very probably be held invalid if on the books today.

No further legislation of this type followed for over a century. When the United States entered World War I, Congress promptly passed an Espionage Act. It provided among other things that

> whoever, when the United States is at war, shall wilfully utter, print, write, or publish any disloyal, profane, scurrilous, or abusive language about the form of government of the United States, or the Consti-

[24] See for example Zechariah Chafee, Jr., *Free Speech in the United States*, Cambridge, Mass., 1942; Osmund K. Fraenkel, *Our Civil Liberties*, New York, 1944; Edward F. Waite, "The Debt of Constitutional Law to Jehovah's Witnesses," *Minn. Law Review*, vol. 28, pp. 209-46 (1944).

[25] U. S. v. Ballard (1944), 322 U. S. 78; Prince v. Massachusetts (1944), 321 U. S. 158. See also Chaplinsky v. New Hampshire (1942), 315 U. S. 568.

[26] Cantwell v. Connecticut (1940), 310 U. S. 296; Largent v. Texas (1943), 318 U. S. 418; Martin v. City of Struthers (1943), 319 U. S. 141; Murdock v. Pennsylvania (1943), 319 U. S. 105; Follett v. Town of McCormick (1944), 321 U. S. 573; West Virginia State Board of Education v. Barnette (1943), 319 U. S. 624.

tution . . . or the military or naval forces . . . or the flag . . . or
the uniform . . . and whoever shall wilfully advocate, teach, defend,
or suggest the doing of any of the acts or things in this section enumerated, . . . shall be punished by a fine of not more than $10,000,
or imprisonment for not more than twenty years, or both. . . .[27]

Prosecutions for wartime violations of this act continued long after the
actual fighting had ended, and many persons were fined or imprisoned. The
Supreme Court sustained the act as within the powers of Congress, but the
justices disagreed on the interpretation of it. One group of them, generally
described as the liberals on the Court, thought that the act should be applied
only when the words spoken or printed "so imminently threaten immediate
interference with the lawful and pressing purposes of the law that an immediate check is required to save the country." [28] This doctrine, sometimes called
that of "clear and present danger," was not accepted by the majority of the
justices. The opinion is now widely held that this act, as it was then enforced,
invades the right of free press and free speech guaranteed by the First Amendment.

The legislation just described is still in effect. In addition Congress in 1940
enacted a statute, applicable in times of peace as well as in times of war, which
makes it unlawful "to knowingly or wilfully advocate, abet, advise, or teach
the duty, necessity, desirability, or propriety of overthrowing or destroying
any government in the United States by force or violence, . . ." to print,
publish, or circulate any matter to the same effect, or to organize or assist in
organizing any group for the purpose.[29] This act resulted in several trials and
convictions in federal district courts, but the Supreme Court has not yet
passed upon its constitutionality.

State and Local Impairments of Free Speech and Press. During World War
I and later years the states also passed and enforced a variety of laws designated
as "antisedition" or "anticriminal-syndicalism" laws having much the same
character as the federal act. Some of them were sustained by the Supreme
Court of the United States, and a number are still in force.[30] Later decisions
of the Supreme Court indicate, however, that judicial opinion is swinging
against such statutes. In the case of Near v. Minnesota (1931) a state statute
permitting the supression by injunction of any "malicious, scandalous and
defamatory newspaper, magazine or other periodical," on the ground that
such a publication is a public nuisance, was held unconstitutional as violating
the "liberty" guaranteed to the individual by the Fourteenth Amendment.[31]
Similarly a California act that made it a crime to display a red flag "as a

[27] Act of June 15, 1917, ch. 30, Title 1, § 3; 40 Stat. at Large, 219; U.S.C.A., Title 50,
33; See Chafee, op. cit., Part I, and Appendix II.
[28] Schenck v. U. S. (1919), 249 U. S. 47; Abrams v. U. S. (1919), 250 U. S. 616.
[29] 54 Stat. at Large, 640, ch. 439; U.S.C.A., Title 18, §§ 9-13.
[30] See Chafee, op. cit., Parts II, III, IV, and Appendix III.
[31] 283 U. S. 697.

sign, symbol or emblem of opposition to organized government" was held unconstitutional under the Fourteenth Amendment.[32] Finally in 1937 the Court by a 5 to 4 vote practically adopted the "clear and present danger" rule to invalidate an old Georgia statute that was being employed against an organizer for the Communist Party.[33] The majority of the justices held that to secure a conviction it is not enough for the prosecution to show a "dangerous tendency" in speeches and printed matter. If every utterance that has a dangerous tendency may be forbidden there would be an end to a great deal of wholesome free discussion.

Since that decision there have been many more cases in the Supreme Court on state and local violations of free speech and free press. The religious freedom cases in most instances also dealt with and sustained the rights of free speech and free press. A decision in 1936 condemned a special tax by Louisiana upon newspapers of large circulation.[34] Later cases upheld the rights of free speech and press in connection with the distribution of handbills and other literature in the streets, peaceful picketing, and trade union organization meetings.[35] At the same time freedom of speech and press do not justify violence in connection with picketing, or forbid legislation that prohibits the distribution of commercial handbills and advertising in the streets.[36]

Harry Bridges, the widely known West Coast labor leader, was a party in two Supreme Court cases, in one of which the Court held that adverse criticism of the courts in speeches and editorials outside the courts is not punishable as contempt unless a clear and present danger is created.[37] In the other case the Supreme Court held, among other things, that freedom of speech and of press is granted also to aliens residing in the United States.[38]

Freedom of Assembly and Petition. By the First Amendment, Congress is forbidden to pass any act abridging "the right of the people peaceably to assemble, and to petition the government for a redress of grievances." This right, or pair of rights, is again not unlimited. One reads frequently of groups being refused police permits for the holding of meetings, and of meetings being dispersed by the authorities. To maintain peace and order in cities, it is almost necessary to have some system of notice and permits for meetings and parades, so that adequate police protection can be provided in cases where disorder may result. There is, also, in many cities a lack of public spaces for

[32] Stromberg v. California (1931), 283 U. S. 359.

[33] Herndon v. Lowry (1937), 301 U. S. 242. See also Taylor v. Mississippi (1943), 319 U. S. 583.

[34] Grosjean v. American Press Co. (1936), 297 U. S. 233.

[35] Lovell v. City of Griffin (1938), 303 U. S. 444; Schneider v. New Jersey (1939), 308 U. S. 147; Thornhill v. Alabama (1940), 310 U. S. 88; Carlson v. California (1940), 310 U. S. 106; Carpenters and Joiners Union v. Ritter's Cafe (1942), 315 U. S. 722; Bakery and Pastry and Drivers, etc., v. Wohl (1942), 315 U. S. 769; Cafeteria Employees Union v. Angelos (1943), 320 U. S. 293; Thomas v. Collins (1945), 323 U. S. 516.

[36] Hotel and Restaurant Employees' International Alliance v. Wisconsin Employment Relations Board (1942), 315 U. S. 437; Valentine v. Chrestensen (1942), 316 U. S. 52.

[37] Bridges v. California (1941), 314 U. S. 252.

[38] Bridges v. Wixon (1945), 326 U. S. 135.

such meetings, and it is obvious that the authorities cannot permit the streets to be packed with people so that traffic cannot move. No doubt there are also many cases in which overzealous or arbitrary-minded officials forbid the meetings of radical groups merely because they do not like their doctrines. Such a case, it appears, was that of Frank Hague, Mayor of Jersey City, versus the CIO.[39] A city ordinance forbade the leasing without permit from the chief of police of any hall in the city for a meeting at which obstruction to the United States government might be advocated. In practice not only CIO unions but all left-wing organizations were denied permits. Freedom of speech and of assembly were thus both involved. The ordinance was held invalid by 5 to 2 (two not voting). Of the five justices, three held the ordinance to be a violation of the liberty and due process clause, whereas two asserted that the privileges and immunities of United States citizens include the right of free assembly.

Freedom of Association. Freedom of assembly implies the right of people to get together for short periods to discuss and act upon matters that concern them and then to disperse. In most fields of human endeavor, however, what people need is a continuing association with a more or less permanent organization of officers and committees. We see every day that democratic society relies upon such associations for numerous semipublic services, and that it encourages far more than it discourages them. Churches, cooperatives, businesses, corporations, trade unions, and professional societies are important examples. It is, indeed, one of the glories of advanced democratic peoples that they have so much public spirit that a multiplicity of associations is needed to channel it into useful public services. No one seems to doubt, either, that there is a very extensive constitutional right of free association although the bills of rights do not expressly establish it.

On the other hand, an unlimited right of free association might be dangerous to the state and to society. It might give rise to criminal conspiracies and to insidious pressure groups seeking to rule the nation for purely selfish purposes. The nature and extent of the right of association and the powers of government to regulate associations are therefore important subjects for future public investigation and action.

Right to Bear Arms. It is sometimes said that the American people have a constitutional right of revolution whenever they dislike their government. This is doubtful. The Declaration of Independence asserts, indeed, "That whenever any Form of Government becomes destructive of these ends [life, liberty, and pursuit of happiness], it is the Right of the People to alter or to abolish it, . . ." but the Declaration is not a part of the Constitution. If the people have the "right" of revolution it is a right superior to the Constitution and not a part of it. Therefore it must be discussed in terms of ethics rather than law.

This may help to explain what is meant by the "right to bear arms." The

[39] Hague v. CIO (1939), 307 U. S. 496.

Constitution contains a provision on this subject, and so do a number of the state constitutions. The latter are in some cases so worded that they help to throw light on the meaning of this right. The right is conceded only for the purposes of defense for the individual, his family and the state or nation. It is not a right to bear arms against the state or the people. Hence the state and the nation have the power to limit the right to bear arms in order to achieve the desired purposes. It follows that laws against the carrying of concealed weapons, and against the possession of certain types of weapons used by criminals, such as sawed-off shotguns, and laws requiring the registration of weapons, are not unconstitutional.

Other "Liberty" Rights. Other rights stated in the national Constitution give further meaning to the concept of liberty. The quartering of troops in private homes in peacetime without the owners' consent is forbidden to Congress by the Third Amendment. The prohibition against unreasonable searches and seizures in the Fourth Amendment is a similar guarantee of the inviolability of the home, as well as of places of business.

Equality Before the Law. Equality before the law for all citizens is a right never fully achieved, but implied in many provisions and directly stated in some. The prohibition in the national Constitution against the granting of titles of nobility by either national or state governments is one that tends to promote legal equality among men. More important for practical and legal purposes are two other provisions of the Constitution: the "comity clause," previously discussed,[40] and the "equal protection" clause of the Fourteenth Amendment. "No state shall . . . deny to any person within its jurisdiction the equal protection of the laws."

Equal Protection Clause. The "equal protection clause" relates to all "persons," not merely to citizens. Its protection is available, for example, to corporations, to alien individuals, and to stateless persons. In general this clause forbids arbitrary or unreasonable discrimination by state laws between persons in the same general situation. A state legislature may enact one law for men and another for women, one law for railroads and another for local drayage companies, and so on, provided always that the basis of the classification is a reasonable one, founded on substantial differences. But some legislative classifications are held to be arbitrary, such as one forbidding Negroes to rent or buy homes in certain areas of cities, or one permitting only white persons to serve on juries. The prohibition runs against the states; there is no comparable express restriction upon the national government, although the "due-process clause" of the Fifth Amendment has somewhat the same effect.

4. Economic Rights

The Declaration of Independence speaks of life, liberty, and "the pursuit of happiness." The Fifth and Fourteenth Amendments, and most of the state constitutions, put "property" in place of the pursuit of happiness, in the

---

[40] See ch. 6, above.

clauses requiring due process of law. Property is undoubtedly one of the most important of the economic rights open to citizens and other persons under the American constitutional system.

Property. "Property" is the legal right of a person to possess, own, control, and use such valuable things as land, buildings, automobiles, stocks, bonds, money and mortgages, in fact anything that has value.[41] A person may acquire property rights through gift, inheritance, purchase, and other legal methods, but until he acquires something, he has no actual right of property. The right of property is basic to an individualistic society. It is defined by laws, and is protected by courts, police, and executive officers generally. No government, national, state, or local, may take property rights from persons, either individuals or corporations, without due process of law.

As already seen, property may be taken from individuals for public use through taxation without compensation to the person taxed, and through eminent domain if compensation is paid. It may be regulated, also, in many different ways, but there have been cases in which attempted regulations such as price fixing have been held by the courts to be unconstitutional "deprivations" of property without due process of law.[42]

Contract Rights. The impairment of contract rights by the early state legislatures, with resultant insecurity and losses to business, was one of the important motives for the creation of a strong national government. In Article I, sec. X, the Constitution forbids the states to pass any "law impairing the obligation of contracts." It is a curious fact of some importance that there is no similar provision in the Constitution forbidding the national government to impair the obligation of contracts, although it is forbidden to take property without due process.[43]

Contracts with the Government. Two classes of contracts are important here. First are the contracts between a government (national, state, or local) and some individual or corporation. Such contracts are numerous: for paving highways, building schools or battleships, supplying typewriters, or lending money to the government on its bonds or promises to repay. These contracts once made are supposed to be as binding on the government as if it were a private person, but there is always the problem of enforcing payment. A local government may be sued like anyone else, and no state has the power to free its local units from their just debts. But private persons may not sue either a state or the national government without its own consent. The contractual duty to pay may be complete, but the method of enforcing payment is incomplete and faulty. Thus many states have in fact repudiated some of their debts and failed to live up to their contracts, and the United States courts have

[41] See ch. 8, above.

[42] Tyson & Brother v. Banton (1927), 273 U. S. 418; Ribnik v. McBride (1928), 277 U. S. 350. The latter decision was overruled in Olsen v. Nebraska (1941), 313 U. S. 236. See also Nebbia v. New York (1934), 291 U. S. 502.

[43] On the United States contract clause in general, see B. F. Wright, Jr., *The Contract Clause of the Constitution*, 1938.

usually been unable to do anything about it. The national government, too, has sometimes failed to observe its obligations. In World War II the national government "renegotiated" many of its large munitions contracts in order to scale down its own obligations. The right to do this was expressly reserved by law, but the other parties were in many cases very disappointed with the resultant payments.

Private Contracts. Second, and far more numerous, are private contracts—between man and man, between individuals and corporations, or between two corporations. Business in general is most secure when lawful contracts are fully enforceable in the courts, and when neither Congress nor the legislature of the state has any power to interfere. But frequently business conditions are such that the legislative body feels it must do something for large bodies of persons under contracts, whether debtors or creditors. To illustrate this point, at the time of the depression tens of thousands of American farmers and home owners were under contracts in the form of mortgages to pay large amounts of interest and principal for money previously borrowed, and for which they had pledged their farms or homes. Meanwhile their incomes had gone down tremendously or had been wiped out entirely through unemployment. They clamored at the doors of Congress and state legislatures for such relief as would save their farms and homes. A number of state legislatures thereupon passed so-called "mortgage moratorium" laws, to postpone the required payments and to prevent for a time the foreclosure of the mortgages and the seizure of the property to pay the mortgage holder. In an important decision the Supreme Court admitted that the state mortgage moratorium laws impaired the obligation of contracts to some extent, but held that in such emergencies the protection given by the contract clause of the Constitution cannot be as complete as in more normal times. This "emergency" doctrine is clearly an exception. The general rule is that "if the contract, when made, was valid by the laws of the State as then expounded by all departments of the government, and administered in its courts of justice, its validity and obligation cannot be impaired by any subsequent action of legislation, or decision of its courts altering the construction of the law." [44]

The Making of Contracts in General. What has been said above relates to contracts previously made; they may not be impaired by later state action. What about the power to make contracts generally for the future? This is nowhere specifically mentioned in the national or state constitutions. In general, state legislatures may regulate this right, and may forbid contracts that are against public policy, such as gambling contracts, contracts for immoral conduct, and contracts for child labor. At the same time the courts have read into the rights of "liberty and property" the right of the individual or other person to make lawful contracts for personal labor and services and for the buying and selling of things generally. In the right of liberty is included,

[44] Home Building and Loan Association v. Blaisdell (1934), 290 U. S. 398. See also East New York Savings Bank v. Hahn (1945), 325 U. S. —, 66 S. Ct. 69.

then, the right to work and to engage in lawful businesses of any kind. In each of these cases there is the right to make contracts and to have them enforced— contracts between worker and employer, between the businessman and his customers. The right of property also includes usually the right to sell or dispose of one's property to others who want to buy, and the right of the buyers to buy. Nevertheless it is unwise to be dogmatic about this supposed right of contract. Lawyers and judges in the late nineteenth and early twentieth centuries tended to exaggerate this right, and they succeeded in delaying un- duly long the types of social legislation that were required by the times.

The Right to a Job. The suggestion about the right of a man to contract to dispose of his own labor raises another question: Is there a constitutional right to a job? Public policy seems to be moving in this direction. It empha- sizes economic security and full employment, with the government standing in the background and ready to supply the jobs if other means fail. This whole problem is a very complicated one.[45] If the time ever comes when job-security for everyone is guaranteed by law, then the form and the functions of the national government will already have undergone very great changes.

5. *Political Rights*

For various reasons political rights, or rights of participation in political and governmental processes, are not usually stated in formal bills of rights, and hence are not discussed under that heading. In a democracy this is a strange thing, for surely they are as important as any other body of rights that the people possess. A people needs only to pass under dictatorship to realize how much it has lost in giving up certain political rights. These rights, most of which are discussed elsewhere,[46] are simply listed here for comparison with other constitutional rights.

Citizenship. The right of citizenship in the United States, and in particular states, is guaranteed by the Fourteenth Amendment.

Political Power. Nearly all the state constitutions contain a clause near the beginning of the bill of rights that declares that "All political power is inherent in the people." The clause usually goes on to assert the right of the people to alter the government "whenever the public good may require." This is not the right of any individual; it could not be enforced in favor of anyone by a court. It is rather a general assertion of popular sovereignty, and of the duty of the government to serve the interests of the people as further defined in the constitution.

Suffrage. The state constitutions, supplemented by the national, guarantee to certain classes of persons the right to vote in public elections, national, state, and local. Any person having the requisite qualifications can have his right to vote enforced by judicial orders.

[45] See Henry R. Bernhardt, "The Right to a Job," *Cornell Law Quarterly*, vol. 30, pp. 292-317 (1945).
[46] See chs. 6, 7.

Election to Office. The national Constitution defines the qualifications a person must have to be elected President, Vice President, United States Senator, or Representative in Congress. The state constitutions lay down the fundamental requirements for eligibility to state or local elective office, which are generally very liberal. Any person who has the constitutional qualifications is entitled to be elected to office. This right too can be enforced by the proper courts against any who would attempt to deny it.

In the preceding pages the reader will have gained some conception of the cardinal rights of free men as they have developed in the United States. In addition he may have sensed in some degree the increasingly important role of the national government in the protection of those rights. One more group of questions remains to be discussed. When any civil right is threatened or has already been invaded by an act of government, how can the individual protect himself or how can he get redress? This brings us to another chapter.

REFERENCES

Henry Rottschaefer, *Handbook of American Constitutional Law*, St. Paul, 1939, ch. 19.

Association of American Law Schools (ed.), *Selected Essays on Constitutional Law*, Book 2, "Limitations on Governmental Power," Chicago, 1938.

American Bar Association, Bill of Rights Committee, *The Bill of Rights Review*, New York, 1940-42.

Osmond K. Fraenkel, *Our Civil Liberties*, New York, 1941.

American Civil Liberties Union, various publications.

Zechariah Chafee, Jr., *Free Speech in the United States*, Cambridge, Mass., 1942.

Carl L. Becker and others, *Safeguarding Civil Liberty Today*, Ithaca, 1945.

Edith M. Phelps (ed.), *Civil Liberty* (The Reference Shelf, vol. IV, no. 9), New York, 1927.

A. N. Christensen and E. M. Kirkpatrick, *The People, Politics, and the Politician*, New York, 1941, ch. 7.

Benjamin F. Wright, Jr., *The Contract Clause of the Constitution*, Cambridge, Mass., 1938.

Robert E. Cushman, *Our Constitutional Freedoms, Civil Liberties, An American Heritage*, Pamphlet, New York, 1944.

Edward F. Waite, "The Debt of Constitutional Law to Jehovah's Witnesses," *Minnesota Law Review*, vol. 28, pp. 209-46 (1944).

CHAPTER 21

Procedural Rights and the Redress of Public Wrongs

1. THE RIGHT TO JUDICIAL TRIALS

Equality of Procedural Rights. All persons who have a standing before the courts have approximately the same procedural rights. Citizens as such have no special advantage over non-citizens in this respect. Corporations have much the same rights as individual men and women, but since corporations are not often indicted or tried for crimes, their main interest is in civil procedure, while individual men and women are concerned with their rights in both criminal and civil cases.

Right to Judicial Trials. In practically all criminal cases, and in all the important civil cases known to the common law, the individual or corporation is entitled to a trial in a regular judicial court, or at least to a review by a court on questions of law. This is one of the personal rights that is so general and pervasive that it usually goes unexpressed. There are, also, a number of exceptions to it in modern times, particularly in the field of administrative justice, as we saw in chapter 19, but these exceptions only serve to emphasize the importance of the central principle. This is the principle of the separation of powers, to wit, that those who make the law and those who enforce the law shall ordinarily be distinct and separate from each other and also from those who interpret the law and apply it to the facts in particular cases. A few important exceptions need to be noticed.

Trials by Congress. Each House of Congress may punish its own members for neglect of duty or disorderly behavior, and, with the concurrence of two thirds, expel a member. The House of Representatives may also bring charges of impeachment against executive officers and judges in the national service, which the Senate may try. Convictions in impeachment cases require a vote of two thirds of the Senators present, and the punishment extends only to "removal from office, and disqualification to hold and enjoy any office of honor, trust or profit under the United States." In these express provisions the Constitution circumscribes very closely the power of Congress to try persons and to impose punishment.[1]

One other power of Congress to impose penalties has been implied from the Constitution. Whenever either house or a committee authorized by it seeks information that it needs for the performance of its constitutional duties, the house in question may punish for contempt any person who willfully withholds or refuses to give testimony.[2] The recalcitrant witness can be put in jail or be fined, or both, for his contempt.

Bills of Attainder Forbidden. The British Parliament, being both a high court and a legislative body, for centuries exercised the power to pass acts called *bills of attainder*, inflicting punishment on individuals without a separate judicial trial. As Parliament became more and more a legislative body, its power to pass bills of attainder came under severe public criticism. In the United States bills of attainder are expressly forbidden by the Constitution. Except as already indicated, neither Congress nor any state legislature may set itself up as a court to impose punishments on anyone through bills of attainder.[3]

Ex Post Facto Laws. Identical provisions of the Constitution also forbid both Congress and the state legislatures to pass *ex post facto* laws.[4] Such a law has been defined by the courts as one having a retroactive effect *in criminal matters* which either (a) makes some action a crime that was not a crime when committed, or (b) increases the punishment for a crime after its commission, or (c) "which, in relation to the offence, or its consequences, alters the situation of a party to his disadvantage," i.e., makes it easier to convict him, etc.[5] The legislature may change the legal penalties from time to time, but may increase them only as to crimes committed after the law is passed.

Retroactive Laws in Civil Cases. Retroactive laws covering civil cases are not entirely forbidden. In many instances they are necessary to correct defects in public elections, public bond issues, corporation charters, and many other matters. However it would violate the principles of due process for the legislature to attempt to overrule or set aside a decision already made by a court in a civil case, or to order a new trial, or to make a retroactive law that impairs the obligation of pre-existing contracts. In these cases the legislature would be stepping out of its true role as a legislator for the future and into the role of a court deciding particular cases.

Military Trials and Habeas Corpus. In times of war or great internal disorder the ordinary courts may find it difficult and in some areas even impos-

---

[1] Art. I, sec. 5, pars. 1, 2; sec. 2, par. 5; sec. 3, par. 6.

[2] McGrain v. Daugherty (1927), 273 U. S. 135; Jurney v. MacCracken (1935), 294 U. S. 125.

[3] Art. I, sec. 9, par. 3; sec. 10, par. 1. And neither may a state constitution impose a penalty without a judicial trial. Cummings v. Missouri (1867), 4 Wall 277.

[4] Art. I, sec. 9, par. 3; sec. 10, par. 1.

[5] Calder v. Bull (1798), 3 Dallas (U. S.) 386; U. S. v. Hall (1809), 2 Wash. C. C. 366, Fed. Cas. No. 15, 285.

sible to operate. What happens then to the right of persons to have their cases tried in the regular judicial courts? Is the President or the local commander of the United States military forces empowered under such conditions to take command of the area, to set up military courts, and to try and punish civilians through military agencies? The provision of the Constitution that is designed to prohibit or at least to regulate this practice contains a restriction on the powers of Congress that reads as follows:

"The privilege of the Writ of Habeas Corpus shall not be suspended, unless when in Cases of Rebellion or Invasion the public Safety may require it." [6]

The writ of *habeas corpus* is an order issued by an ordinary civil court to any official who has arrested a person or is holding him in custody, to deliver him to the court for a hearing to determine whether he is being lawfully detained. If he is being legally held the court will order him returned to jail or released on reasonable bail until he can be tried; if he is being held unlawfully, the court must order him released at once. A sheriff or other officer who refuses to recognize such an order is guilty of contempt of court, and can be punished; but in the face of military usurpation the civil courts are exceedingly weak.

Doctrine of Military Supremacy Rejected. Theoretically the President may not suspend the writ of *habeas corpus* at all, but President Lincoln during the Civil War used the military forces to arrest men who opposed the government's military policies in a zone stretching some distance from the actual war area. In the case of *Ex parte* Milligan,[7] a private citizen residing some distance from the scene of military operations, was arrested by army officers in 1864, taken before a military court, tried for inciting insurrection and for acts of treason, convicted, and sentenced to hang. His sentence was later commuted to life imprisonment, and his attorneys asked the United States court in Indiana for a writ of *habeas corpus*, to have him brought in for regular judicial hearing. The Supreme Court, finally ruling on the case, repudiated the doctrine of military supremacy under the conditions given. The regular courts were in operation. There were laws under which Milligan could have been tried, and he had a right to be brought before the proper courts and to be tried in the usual legal way. Otherwise, "republican government is a failure, and there is an end of liberty regulated by law." The Court said also that "The Constitution of the United States is a law for rulers and people, equally in war and in peace, and covers with the shield of its protection all classes of men, at all times, and under all circumstances. No doctrine involving more pernicious consequences was ever invented by the wit of man than that any of its provisions can be suspended during any of the great exigencies of government."

This does not mean that the writ of *habeas corpus* may never be suspended, but rather that the suspension must be strictly in conformity with the Consti-

[6] Art. I, sec. 9, par. 2.
[7] (1866), 4 Wall. 2.

tution. When war actually prevails in an area, and the civil courts simply cannot function, the military branch may govern until normal conditions have been restored, and no longer. At all times, of course, the military trial of military personnel, including enemy soldiers, spies, and saboteurs in war-time, is beyond the reach of the civil courts, and *habeas corpus* does not apply.[8]

In World War II, as we noticed in the preceding chapter, the action of the military authorities in removing all persons of Japanese ancestry from their Pacific Coast homes to inland relocation centers was a serious invasion of their rights although it was justified by the authorities and the courts on the ground of military necessity. At the same time this procedure did not suspend the operation of the courts or their power to issue writs of *habeas corpus* to release citizens of Japanese ancestry from the custody of the War Relocation Authority.[9]

The discussion to this point shows, then, that neither Congress, nor the military authorities under executive control, can legally take the place of the ordinary courts in the trial of cases except in specified and exceptional instances. The individual is entitled to "the law of the land," the due course of law, in all cases involving his liberties.

Given his right, then, to hearing or trial in the regular courts, the individual finds that he is there entitled by the Constitution to certain established procedural rights. We will consider first the procedural requirements in criminal cases.

2. PROCEDURE IN CRIMINAL CASES

A crime is an offense against the public as represented by the national, state, or local government. Crimes and their appropriate penalties are defined in the statutes and in the common law or decisions of the courts. Strictly speaking, crimes are only the more serious public offenses. The lesser offenses are usually called misdemeanors, but in a broad sense the term crime includes them also. When one is accused of a crime or misdemeanor, he is brought to trial by a public prosecutor, national, state, or local, who represents the public. The result is a verdict of guilty, or not guilty, and if guilty, a penalty is supposed to follow.

Requirements for National and State Courts Differ. The Constitution states a number of very specific procedural requirements for criminal trials in the United States courts. For the states, however (and this includes the state courts), it merely requires in the Fourteenth Amendment that they shall not deprive any person of life, liberty, or property without due process of law, or deny to any person within its jurisdiction the equal protection of the laws. What is the "due process" that is required of the states in the conduct of criminal cases?

[8] *Ex parte* Quirin (1942), 317 U. S. 1.
[9] *Ex parte* Mitsuye Endo (1944), 323 U. S. 283, 65 S. Ct. 208.

An easy answer to this question would be that the states are required to observe the same procedural rules in criminal cases in the state courts as the Constitution requires to be observed in the national courts. Since the substantive requirements of the First Amendment have been applied to the states by the Supreme Court's interpretation of the Fourteenth Amendment, why should not the procedural requirements of the rest of the Bill of Rights be equally applicable against the states, as necessary for due process? This simple way of determining the meaning of due process in state criminal cases would have made for uniformity of national and state requirements and would have greatly simplified the work of the Supreme Court in defining due process in state cases. At the same time, however, it would have seriously restricted state experimentation with new methods of procedure, and would have prevented the states from adapting their procedures to their peculiar needs and desires.

The Supreme Court, therefore, rejected this convenient and easy way of defining due process of law for state criminal cases. This policy left the states free to develop their own procedures in criminal as well as civil cases provided they observed "those canons of decency and fairness which express the notions of justice of the English-speaking peoples even toward those charged with the most heinous offenses." [10] With this point in mind let us examine the procedural requirements of the Constitution as they apply to national and state criminal cases.

Warrants, Searches, Seizures. Before a trial for crime there must be a surrender or arrest of the accused person and a gathering of evidence. At this point the Constitution gives a certain amount of protection to individuals. The Fourth Amendment to the Constitution provides as follows:

> The right of the people to be secure in their persons, houses, papers and effects, against unreasonable searches and seizures, shall not be violated, and no Warrants shall issue, but upon probable cause, supported by Oath or affirmation, and particularly describing the place to be searched, and the persons or things to be seized.

Warrants for searches, seizures, and arrests are orders issued to the police by judges or other officers of the courts. This procedure provides a preliminary check upon the zeal of the police. It may not be a serious check, since the "probable cause" may be based upon mere hearsay, but judicial officers have it in their power, at least, to exercise some restraint upon the officers. General warrants, such as authorize wide search throughout the county or city, are forbidden. A man's house is his haven of refuge, and it is the purpose of these constitutional provisions to give some protection to it. There are many exceptions to this rule, of course, but the protection is still an important one, and the national courts by refusing, as they now generally do, to accept in evidence papers and articles taken by the police without warrant, often by

[10] See concurring opinion of Justice Frankfurter in Malinski v. New York 1945), 324 U. S. 401. See also Buchalter v. New York (1943), 319 U. S. 427.

outright theft, and evidence procured by "wire tapping," are making the right more effective.[11] Congress has prohibited wire tapping by agents of the national government, but this does not prohibit the use of a detectaphone against a wall to overhear a conversation in the adjoining room, or prohibit the use of intercepted telephone messages against parties who had no part in the conversation. The statute protects only the direct parties to the conversation.[12]

The issue that is involved in these cases is a very important one. Police officers and public prosecutors have in many cases taken a "fight the devil with fire" position. They have argued that, since criminals are able to use for their purposes every new technological development (speedy automobiles and airplanes, swift and secret means of communication), the public authorities are handicapped if they are not able to use all available countermeasures such as wire tapping and the purchase of stolen evidence. Justice Holmes put the discussion on a higher plane in his dissent in an earlier decision on wire tapping:

> It is desirable that criminals should be detected, and to that end that all available evidence should be used. It is also desirable that the government should not itself foster and pay for crimes, when they are the means by which the evidence is to be obtained. If it pays its officers for having got evidence by crime I do not see why it may not as well pay them for getting it in the same way, and I can attach no importance to protestations of disapproval if it knowingly accepts and pays and announces that in future it will pay for the fruits. We have to choose, and for my part I think it a less evil that some criminals should escape than that the government should play an ignoble part.[13]

Congress and the Supreme Court have not taken a position as advanced as that suggested by this dissent, but the Court does insist upon a higher standard for the national government under Amendments IV and V than it does for the states under the Fourteenth Amendment.[14] Due process for the states, as was said before, does not require that they conform in full to all the specific procedural requirements of Amendments II to VIII. This point is again illustrated in the next topic.

Indictment in Criminal Cases. The Fifth Amendment provides that "No person shall be held to answer for a capital, or otherwise infamous crime, unless on a presentment or indictment of a Grand Jury, except in cases arising in the land or naval forces, or in the Militia, when in actual service in time

[11] See McBain, *Prohibition, Legal and Illegal*, for an analysis of this problem. On wire tapping see Nardone v. U. S. (1937), 302 U. S. 379; *ibid.* (1939), 308 U. S. 338.

[12] Goldman v. U. S. (1942), 316 U. S. 129; Goldstein v. U. S. (1942), 316 U. S. 114, interpreting Communications Act of 1934, 3(a), 501, 605, 47 U. S. Code, 153 (a), 501, 605.

[13] Olmstead v. U. S. (1928), 277 U. S. 438, at p. 470.

[14] See People v. Defore (1926), 242 N. Y. 13; McNabb v. U. S. (1943), 318 U. S. 332; Palko v. Connecticut (1937), 302 U. S. 319.

of War or public danger." A capital crime is one that may be punished by death; an infamous crime one that may be punished by imprisonment at hard labor for a term exceeding one year. A federal grand jury "is a group of citizens summoned by a United States District Court at regular intervals or on special occasions to inquire into crimes alleged to have been committed within the court's jurisdiction, and to prepare indictments or presentments, that is, formal charges, against those believed to be guilty. In the United States District Courts the grand jury consists of from sixteen to twenty-three persons. In the state courts it is usually somewhat smaller, the smallest being the "one-man grand juries" in Michigan and a few other states.

Great store has been placed by the grand jury procedure as a community check upon unpopular prosecutions. Although the United States District Attorney drafts the indictments, the grand jury must vote to approve them before they become effective, and it may even draft its own charges (presentments) which have the same effect. The main point is that the United States district attorney may not proceed by "information" (i.e., presentation of charges by the prosecuting attorney without a grand jury) in any capital or infamous crime case. Procedure by information is permissible in the United States courts, however, when authorized by statute in less important criminal cases, and the recently adopted Rules of Criminal Procedure for the District Courts of the United States permit the accused to waive indictment in any noncapital case.

The due process clause of the Fourteenth Amendment does not require the states to use the grand jury for bringing persons to trial in criminal cases, not even in capital cases. In the leading decision on this subject [15] the Supreme Court ruled that, although indictment by a grand jury prior to trial in criminal cases has become accepted as due process through long usage, other suitable methods are not forbidden by the Fourteenth Amendment due process clause. In fact many states make extensive use of the procedure by "information" and reserve indictment by a grand jury for only the most serious offenses. It is the general opinion of jurists that procedure by information is more prompt, economical, and efficient, and no less just, than procedure by indictment through a grand jury.

Right to Bail. Pending trial, appeal, or commitment to prison, a person may be released on bail in the discretion of the judge. Amendment VIII, binding on the national government, provides that "Excessive bail shall not be required." This apparently does not require that bail must be allowed in all cases. The judge may consider the seriousness of the crime and the danger that an accused person may "jump bail," and so may refuse to allow bail at all.

Trial by Jury. The most distinctive and valued procedural requirement in criminal cases in the United States is the right to jury trial. With respect to trials in the national courts Amendment VI provides that "In all criminal prosecutions, the accused shall enjoy the right to a speedy and public trial,

[15] Hurtado v. California (1884), 110 U. S. 516.

by an impartial jury of the State and district wherein the crime shall have been committed, which district shall have been previously ascertained by law, and to be informed of the nature and cause of the accusation." Here are a number of guarantees to the individual who is being tried for crime in a national court —a speedy trial, a public trial, a trial in his home state and district—but the heart of it all is a jury trial. The jury represents the views of the local community, and through it there comes the check of public opinion upon the laws and upon the procedure of the courts. In the United States courts, and also generally in the states, the jury in criminal trials must consist of twelve men, or men and women, and its verdict for conviction must be unanimous, otherwise no conviction is obtained. These trial juries, both federal and state, are frequently called "petit" or *petty juries* to distinguish them from the grand jury.

Exceptions to Right of Jury Trial. In the federal courts and in many of the states, the accused person may waive his right to a jury trial.[16] There are also some cases of a criminal nature in which the right does not exist. These are, in general, the minor offenses, of which there are a number under acts of Congress, and many more under state laws and city ordinances.

Knowledge as to Charges. It is a part of due process in both federal and state courts that the accused shall be apprised of the charges against him. This means in practice that he and his attorney must see the indictment for some time before the trial in order to be able to prepare their defense. It is important, too, that laws defining crimes should be clear and definite, so that the individual need not be in any doubt as to what the offense is.[17]

Self-Incrimination. One accused of crime, even before formal indictment, has the right to refuse to testify in court. He may not be compelled to testify in any way so as to incriminate himself nor may his personal papers be seized and brought into court to be used against him. Men have at times even refused to testify before other bodies such as legislative committees, on the ground that what they say might later be used as a basis for criminal charges. This seems to be stretching very far an important constitutional protection. In practice this right often benefits the man in high position more than a poorer person, for the police at times subject the latter to a "third-degree" inquisition in which, under pain, duress, and fear, they wring from him a confession, whereas a man higher placed is seldom so treated. The Supreme Court has been especially severe in its condemnation of all "confessions" that have been obtained by violence, force, and fear, in both national and state criminal cases.[18] These lectures from the high bench do some good, without doubt, but a substantial reduction in third-degree methods will probably have

---

[16] Adams v. U. S. (1942), 317 U. S. 269, 605.

[17] Lanzetta v. New Jersey (1939), 306 U. S. 451 (anti-gangster law); but see Minnesota v. Probate Court (1940), 309 U. S. 270 (psychopathic personality case).

[18] See Chambers v. Florida (1940), 309 U. S. 227; Hysler v. Florida (1942), 315 U. S. 411; ibid., 316 U. S. 642; Ward v. Texas (1942), 316 U. S. 547; Ashcraft v. Tennessee (1944), 322 U. S. 143; Malinski v. New York (1945), 324 U. S. 401.

to wait upon a very considerable improvement in the personnel of police forces.

Of course the accused person may testify voluntarily, and, if he does so, he can be cross-examined the same as any other witness. The privilege of not testifying is one that he must claim, for otherwise his voluntary testimony will be construed as a waiver of his right.[19] And it is not a violation of the rule against self-incrimination for the United States to use against an accused person the testimony that he gave voluntarily in a state court case.[20]

Witnesses and Counsel. The Constitution further guarantees to the accused that in the federal courts he shall have the rights "to be confronted with the witnesses against him; to have compulsory process for obtaining witnesses in his favor; and to have the assistance of counsel for his defense." These guarantees mark a considerable advance over earlier practices. Except that he must usually pay his own witnesses' expenses, and that the lawyer who is assigned to him by the court is not often one of the best, he is placed in a position fairly equal to that of the prosecution, to wage his own defense. There is evidence to indicate that the right to have counsel originally meant not that the public was obligated to employ a lawyer to defend a person, but only that he was entitled to have a lawyer to defend him if he could obtain one himself. The Supreme Court now holds that the Sixth Amendment requires that impecunious defendants in the United States courts are entitled to have counsel at public expense, but it has declined to say that they are entitled to counsel at state expense in every criminal case in a state court.[21] And the right to counsel may also be waived by a competent accused person [22] (although there is a saying in the profession that even a lawyer who serves as his own attorney has a fool for a client).

Double Jeopardy. One of the clauses in the national bill of rights that is most difficult to explain is the provision in Amendment V that reads: "nor shall any person be subject for the same offense to be twice put in jeopardy of life or limb." The purpose of this guarantee is to prevent the government, which is as a rule the more powerful party, from using its power to carry prosecution to the extreme where it becomes persecution, and to wear out the accused person and use up his resources by repeated trials. Once a person has been indicted and put on trial he has been put in jeopardy and he has a right to have the case carried through to its conclusion. Of course, there are proper reasons for the judge to postpone a case—the illness of a juror or the prosecutor, or the obvious spiriting-away by the defense of a key witness for the prosecution, for example. If the jury is unable to agree there can be a retrial, but once an acquittal is obtained, the book is closed, except for proper appeals

[19] U. S. v. Monia (1943), 317 U. S. 424.
[20] Feldman v. U. S. (1944), 322 U. S. 487.
[21] Betts v. Brady (1942), 316 U. S. 455. See also Glasser v. U. S. (1942), 315 U. S. 60; White v. Ragen (1945), 324 U. S. 760; Rice v. Olson (1945), 324 U. S. 786.
[22] Adams v. U. S. (1942), 317 U. S. 269, 605.

to higher courts.[23] There can never be legally a second trial for the same offense. On the other hand, a single act may be several offenses—one against a federal law, one against a state law, and possibly a third against some local ordinance. Hence it is not putting a man "twice in jeopardy" for each to proceed separately against him.[24] This is a complication that is most noticeable in a federal system of government. In addition, however, different steps in the same course of action may be separate offenses against the law of the national or state government alone, such as, for example, possessing, transporting, and selling narcotics without a license, so that each step may be separately punished.[25] Furthermore, the action that subjects an offender to criminal prosecution may also open the door to civil suit against him for damages. This piling up of penalties against offenders for the same acts is rather irrational, and the whole problem needs to be carefully reconsidered.

Equal Protection in Criminal Cases. The Fourteenth Amendment requires the states not only to provide due process of law but also to give equal protection of the laws. A deliberate state policy of excluding Negroes from juries has been condemned by the Supreme Court as denying equal protection.[26] Similarly a "habitual offender" act that provided for the sexual sterilization of persons already twice convicted of chicken stealing but did not do the same for embezzlers was held to be unequal and unconstitutional.[27]

Procedure in Treason Cases. World War II brought to the Supreme Court its first opportunity to review a conviction for treason against the United States. The constitutional requirement for conviction in treason cases (Article III, sec. 3) is that "No Person shall be convicted of Treason unless on the Testimony of two Witnesses to the same overt Act, or on Confession in open Court." The case of Cramer v. United States was a close one; the Supreme Court divided 5 to 4 in deciding it; but the majority held that the government had failed to present direct and clear evidence by two witnesses to the same overt act of treason.[28]

3. PROCEDURE IN CIVIL CASES

A civil case is one of suit by one person against another—Smith *versus* Jones, or Gray *versus* the City of New York. The grounds on which civil suits may be brought (breach of contract, tort, etc.) are defined in the statutes and in the accumulated decisions of the courts. In a civil action there is no charge of crime or misdemeanor, and no penalty will result to either party. Instead there will usually be a judgment requiring a payment of money or some other

---

[23] Palko v. Connecticut (1937), 302 U. S. 319, where the state appealed from a verdict of second degree murder and on retrial convicted Palko of first degree murder.
[24] U. S. v. Lanza (1922), 260 U. S. 377.
[25] See Harvard Law Review, vol. 45, p. 535 (1932).
[26] Hill v. Texas (1942), 316 U. S. 400.
[27] Skinner v. Oklahoma (1942), 316 U. S. 535.
[28] Cramer v. United States (1945), 325 U. S. 1.

valuable thing. The public is not a party, except as it may be suing someone, or may be sued by someone, as in the case of Gray *versus* the City of New York for injuries suffered by Gray when struck by a city work truck.

One of the most important constitutional rights of litigants in civil cases is that of jury trial. The Seventh Amendment to the Constitution provides for it in explicit language, as follows:

> In suits at common law, where the value in controversy shall exceed twenty dollars, the right of trial by jury shall be preserved, and no fact tried by a jury, shall be otherwise reexamined, in any Court of the United States, than according to the rules of the common law.

This right of jury trial is rather limited. (1) Suits at common law are indeed numerous, but there are also many suits in equity and additional ones based on statutes, and in these no jury trial is required by the Constitution. (2) The right "shall be preserved" as it was before 1788; it is not expanded by this section. (3) In fact the federal courts have very few suits at common law in which the amount in controversy is as small as indicated. (4) The right to a jury in civil cases may be waived by the parties and it frequently is. Thus, in short, this guarantee is not of the greatest importance, and the people might well have left it to Congress to define due process in civil cases.

As a matter of fact under the Fifth and Fourteenth Amendment requirements of due process of law the Supreme Court has evolved some guiding principles of due process in civil cases for both national and state governments that are broader and more fundamental than the express requirement of jury trial. These principles are, in general, that the parties must have due notice and hearing, that the tribunal to try cases must be impartial and must have jurisdiction over each case that it handles, that the parties shall have substantially equal opportunity to present their facts and arguments, and that the proceedings must conform to the prescriptions of the statutes, the rules of court, and the general essentials of a fair trial. If these requirements are met, then the rights of all persons are adequately protected in civil cases.

4. THE REDRESS OF PUBLIC WRONGS

Invasions of Individual Liberties by Government. Notwithstanding the imposing array of substantive and procedural rights previously described, there are thousands of invasions of these rights by officers and employees of government every year. These wrongs and injuries to the individual emanate from all units of government, national, state, and local, and from all departments and divisions. Legislative bodies frequently pass acts that directly invade personal rights, especially through police power regulations and tax laws. The courts often render wrong decisions, through the ignorance of judges and juries, or because under the pressure of an inflamed public opinion, or even from dishonesty. Men are sent to prison and fined who are in no way guilty, and in civil suits the wrong party often wins. Most numerous of the invasions of rights occur, however, in the executive branch and in the numerous law-enforcing and administrative services under it. There are false arrests, illegal deportations, improper exclusions of children from school, damaging collisions between public trucks and private automobiles, and a thousand other types of invasion of personal rights.

How Can Redress Be Obtained? To the individual sufferer in each such instance one question stands out as most important: What recourse, what remedies, has he to obtain restitution of the rights or possessions taken from him, or to obtain money damages if restitution is impossible? He desires to know the means by which the injury can be proved and redress can be obtained, for otherwise the right has little value. The ideal outcome in most of these cases is clear. Every person injured without fault of his own by any act or negligence of governmental officers and employees should obtain redress to the full amount of his loss or injury. Governments are created to "establish justice," and one should have as much remedy for wrongs done by government as for those done by individuals, or even more. This idea is stated in many state constitutions in language somewhat as follows:

> Every person ought to find a certain remedy in the laws for all injuries and wrongs which he may receive in his person, property or reputation; he ought to obtain, by law, right and justice, freely and without being obliged to purchase it, completely and without denial, promptly and without delay.[29]

The Law on This Subject. The law relating to the government's liability and the remedies available to the individual is found mainly in judicial decisions. The statutes on the subject are not numerous, and they cover only a small part of the subject. Hence it is that the student cannot go to the statutes to find a systematic statement of the government's suability and liability. He must piece together (a) judicial decisions, (b) statutes, and (c) actual practices, as best he can. In general there is *no constitutional* provision that either ensures or denies the individual the right to redress when his rights are violated. It follows that the courts and the legislatures are almost entirely responsible for the law as it exists. Legislatures have it in their power to make practically all necessary changes.

Threatened Invasions of Rights. Individuals may learn of threats to their rights before the actual occurrence thereof. If the threat is in the form of a bill in Congress, state legislature, or local body, individuals and groups can apply to their representatives and try to get it defeated. Great vigilance is needed here, since this is one of the front-line trenches in the defense of rights.

Injunction. If the legislation has already been enacted, but not yet enforced, it is possible for the individual to apply to the proper courts through his attorneys for an *injunction* to prevent the officers designated in the law from

[29] Illinois Const., Art. I, sec. 19.

carrying it out. The court will sometimes issue a temporary order to forbid the enforcement of the act until a judicial test of it can be had. If the complaining individual can then show that he will suffer irreparable injury if the act is enforced, that he has no other effective remedy against it, and that the act is clearly unconstitutional, the temporary injunction may be made permanent. The term injunction means a court order forbidding certain parties to do particular things that are specified in the order that would cause irreparable damage to certain others.[30] A person who violates such a court order is punishable personally by fine or imprisonment for "contempt of court."

The writ of injunction may be used to prohibit not only threatened invasions of rights, but also the continuance of wrongs already begun. Two other writs or court orders are also available in certain cases, namely *habeas corpus* and *mandamus*. These and the writ of injunction are often called the "Great Writs."

Mandamus. In cases where a public officer is clearly obliged to perform some duty for an individual under certain conditions, and refuses to act even after the individual has complied with these conditions, the person wronged may in many cases receive from the proper court an order called a "mandamus" in which the officer is commanded to do his duty or be held guilty of contempt of court. Thus, suppose an election official refuses to let a man vote who has fully complied with the law, or a local governing body refuses to renew a restaurant license after the owner has complied with all the legal requirements. In the first case perhaps the election official does not like the color or the politics of the voter; in the second the local authorities may want to try to enforce the "closed shop" on all restaurants, while the owner wishes to employ nonunion labor. Such arbitrary or capricious reasons for refusing to perform a clear legal duty are unlawful, and the court's mandate or mandamus will compel the officials to do what is right.

The writ of mandamus may not be used against the President of the United States, and is usually not issued against a governor. Likewise it is not available to compel Congress or a state legislature to act. It is very commonly used, however, against national, state and local administrative officers, from the heads of national departments down to the officials of towns and villages.

Habeas corpus was mentioned in the preceding chapter. It is one of the most important forms of court orders for the enforcement of personal liberties by releasing individuals from prison or police custody when they are being illegally detained. The writ can be sued for by the person concerned or by others on his behalf, and if granted by the court it is an order to the custodian to deliver the person who is being detained to the court for a determination of his right to freedom. Many important questions of substantive and procedural rights have been decided in connection with *habeas corpus* proceedings.

[30] See Bouvier's *Law Dictionary*, Rawle's Third Rev., vol. I, pp. 1569 ff.; James Hart, *An Introduction to Administrative Law With Selected Cases*, pp. 458-67.

Suits for Damages. By the use of one of the three writs mentioned above, the court may forbid illegal actions, and require the performance of certain legal duties. In all cases a specific action is commanded, but there is no payment of damages for injuries or losses already suffered. For such redress the normal procedure is for the individual through his attorneys to make a claim for damages, and if payment is not forthcoming to file a suit for damages in the proper court. The claim and suit might theoretically be against either the offending officers or employees as individuals, or against the governmental unit as a whole—the United States, or the particular state or local unit. Consider first the right of the individual to sue the governmental unit itself.

Nonsuability of United States. One person can sue another successfully only when the court in which he files his suit has power to command the other party either to appear to answer the complaint or suffer the consequences, such as loss of property. Under the Constitution the judicial power of the national courts extends "to Controversies to which the United States shall be a Party." [31] It does not follow that anyone who has a claim against the United States can hail the national government into court to answer him. On the contrary, the courts have said that the United States may not be sued without its own consent.[32] The courts being only an arm of the government cannot command it to be present. Not even one of the states may sue the United States in the federal courts without its consent,[33] and of course no state court has jurisdiction over a suit against the United States.

States Not Suable by Individuals Without Consent. The judicial power of the United States extends also "to Controversies between two or more States; —between a State and Citizens of another State . . . and between a State, or the Citizens thereof, and foreign States, Citizens or Subjects." [34] In the early case of Chisholm v. Georgia (1793) a citizen of North Carolina sued the State of Georgia for damages for property seized by the state during the Revolution.[35] Although the state denied the jurisdiction of the Supreme Court to hear the case, the latter, claiming it had jurisdiction, entered judgment against the state. This was at least a misinterpretation of the prevailing public sentiment. An amendment to the federal Constitution (the Eleventh) was promptly proposed by Congress and adopted by the states. It reads as follows:

> The Judicial power of the United States shall not be construed to extend to any suit in law or equity, commenced or prosecuted against one of the United States by Citizens of another State, or by Citizens or Subjects of any Foreign State.

[31] Art. III, sec. 2.
[32] U. S. v. Lee (1882), 106 U. S. 196; U. S. ex rel. Goldberg v. Daniels (1913), 231 U. S. 218; U. S. v. Michel (1931), 282 U. S. 656.
[33] Kansas v. U. S. (1906), 204 U. S. 331.
[34] U. S. Const., Art. III, sec. 2.
[35] 2 Dallas (U. S.) 419.

Now, suits against a state by any of its own citizens had never been within the scope of the national courts, and the state courts early adopted the rule that as arms of the state they could not entertain suits against the state to which the legislature did not consent. Thus today the individual may not sue either the United States or his own state or any other state, in any court, state or national, without the consent of the government being sued. When the proper officers of the national or state government lack adequate power to pay claims presented to them, or refuse to do so, and when the government in addition does not consent to being sued, there is practically only one way in which a claimant can get relief, and that is to have a friendly member in the legislative body introduce a private claim bill, and to get it passed like an ordinary law. Such an act usually authorizes the payment of an amount stipulated in full settlement of the claim.

Court of Claims. Congress handled practically all contested claims against the national government in this manner until 1855, when it created the Court of Claims. As later strengthened this court has jurisdiction over all suits for sums claimed against the government on the basis of "any contract, express or implied," as well as certain other suits that are covered by special laws. Thus the national government permits itself to be sued in these cases, and practically agrees in advance to pay the judgments rendered. The United States district courts may also entertain suits on contracts for not over $10,000 against the United States. Governmental contracts include among others those for the purchase of land and goods, for personal services, and for the borrowing of money. Once such contracts have been made and performance has begun, the other parties have become vested with property rights. In making the government suable on contracts, therefore, Congress has given a special protection to property rights.

The national government has made other provisions for judicial settlement of cases involving money and property rights. There is a special Customs Court for cases of alleged overcharges in import duties, a Court of Customs and Patent Appeals, and also a Tax Court for claimants who insist their taxes should be lower. Congress annually appropriates millions of dollars for tax refunds, many of which are awarded by these courts.

Pension Claims. Two important classes of claims are definitely excluded from the jurisdiction of the Court of Claims, namely, (a) pension claims and (b) tort claims. While there are general laws under which pension claims may be filed and awarded, there are also hundreds of claims presented to Congress every year to allow pensions to men whose services or injuries do not come within the terms of the general laws. Such pensions require special legislation.

Tort Claims. Tort claims are quite different. A tort is "a private or civil wrong or injury . . . a wrong independent of contract." [36] Some violations of private rights are so serious to the public at large as well as to the individual sufferer that by law they are declared to be "crimes" or "misdemeanors." But

---

[36] See Bouvier's *Law Dictionary*, Rawle's Third Rev., vol. II, pp. 3285 ff.

there are many wrongs, injuries, and violations of private rights, not declared by law to be criminal. Such are injuries resulting from collisions on the highways, from the sale of impure foods or infected milk, from trespass on or destruction of property, and many others. These are torts. In these cases there is no contract between the parties; they may not have seen each other before. Neither are there the elements of a crime. More commonly there is merely carelessness or negligence, but injury results to life, limb, or property, and if the case is between private parties there is usually ample ground for suit and recovery of damages.

National Government and Torts. When the government or one of its officers or employees commits the wrong and a private person suffers, the case is somewhat different. A national postal truck runs over a boy or damages a private automobile; a government food inspector destroys valuable goods while making an inspection; and so on. These are torts, or in the nature of torts. Such cases the Court of Claims may not handle. It is necessary for the injured person or his heirs to get Congress to pass a private bill before restitution or damages can be had. These cases are not as numerous as pension claims, nor is there any organization like a veterans' society to reward or punish Congressmen for their handling of such claims. There is much less political advantage to Congressmen in handling these tort cases and yet Congress has not seen fit to turn them over to a court to decide according to law. Each one is referred to one of the Congressional Committees on Claims, and there decided according to no publicly known or consistent standard. Little or no record of the committees' decisions is ever made public. Congress usually adopts what the committees propose.

Thus the volume of "Private Acts" issued after each session of Congress records hundreds of special pensions granted by Congress, giving the name of each pensioner and the amount to be paid, and also numerous payments to satisfy private tort claims. Each of these acts provides "for the relief of" one or more persons named therein by authorizing the payment of definite sums of money like $1,000, $311.70, $61.15, and so on, in full settlement of the claim against the government. Many of these are personal injury cases resulting from collisions with government vehicles, but they are of great variety.

The best that can be said of this method of settlement is that perhaps a crude sort of justice is finally done; but it is done belatedly at considerable cost, and with a clumsy and expensive instrument—the Congress. How many cases are never settled it is impossible to say, but surely the certainty that compensation will finally be granted cannot be high. The United States district courts if authorized to do so could provide a more speedy, certain, and inexpensive settlement of such cases.

Congress has made one small move toward relieving itself of this burden. Every executive department is authorized by law to settle claims of less than $1,000 where the injury is to property and not to the person, and where the owner of the property agrees that the settlement is to be final.[37] This type of claim can be settled directly, without recourse to the courts. But again property rights are placed ahead of personal. If one's automobile is damaged by a mail truck to the extent of $1,000 or less, the post office department may settle the claim, but if a pedestrian is run over by the same truck and suffers bodily injuries that cost him heavily for hospitals and doctors, or if he is unlawfully arrested or detained by government officials, only a private bill passed by Congress will avail, as a rule, to give him compensation.

REFERENCES

E. M. Borchard, "Government Liability in Tort," a series of articles in *Yale Law Journal*, vol. XXXIV, pp. 1-45, 129-43, 229-58; vol. XXXVI, pp. 1-41, 757-807, 1039-1100; *Columbia Law Review*, vol. XXVIII, pp. 577-617, 734-75.

——, *Convicting the Innocent: Errors of Criminal Justice*, New Haven, 1932.

Duke University Law School, *Law and Contemporary Problems*, Spring, 1942, "Governmental Tort Liability."

J. M. Mathews, *The American Constitutional System*, 2nd ed., New York, 1940, 23-31.

Edward G. Jennings, "Tort Liability of Administrative Officers," *Minn. Law Rev.*, vol. 21, pp. 229-62 (1937).

Leon T. David, *The Tort Liability of Public Officers*, Chicago, 1940.

James Hart, *An Introduction to Administrative Law with Selected Cases*, New York, 1940, Part V.

See also References at end of Chapter 20, above.

[37] Act of Dec. 28, 1922, 42 *Statutes at Large* 1066; *U. S. Code Annotated*, Title 31, ch. 6, sec. 215.

CHAPTER 22

The United States and International Relations

A recent magazine article depicted a supposedly normal businessman who "rarely has time to ponder the world outside Indianapolis." There must be many others, perhaps millions like him—businessmen, farmers, workmen and assorted other citizens, both men and women. There is no class that has a monopoly on limited horizons. Many such persons even get into Congress and other high official circles.

Fortunately there are other equally normal men and women—and an increasing number of them—who are intensely aware of the world beyond their doorsteps. New recruits are always welcome to this group. A famous one was Wendell Willkie who, after failing to attain the Presidency, took an extended trip abroad, learned that this is *One World*, told his fellow citizens about his great discovery in a very persuasive book, and became a leader in the movement for effective international cooperation.

It is customary to say that the world has changed, that it has shrunk in size due to the speeding up of transportation and communications. This change, it is added, brings us in effect closer to our neighbors in other nations and makes international relations more important to us. There is considerable truth in this view but it can easily be overemphasized. To those who established the independence and the Union of the United States nearly two hundred years ago, what Wendell Willkie learned would not have been startling. They knew it perfectly well in their own time, even though it took much longer then to cross the Atlantic. The real change in our time is the "collapse of space" through technological change, with a corresponding expansion of our mental horizons. There has been an awakening of large sections of the public in the United States to the importance of international policy. Many persons are learning that what happens in other parts of the world is not really "foreign" to us, and that the surest way to get into international trouble is to pursue a policy of indifference to world affairs. Wartime discoveries in

369

new methods of destroying people and places, including the atomic bomb, give solemn warning to all.

If geography alone ensured security and the ability to live in isolation from other nations, the United States would seem to be the most fortunate of nations. Without rivals to the north or the south, it is separated by broad oceans from the nearest great states to the east and the west. It has a large population and tremendous industrial and agricultural resources. In spite of these fortunate circumstances the United States has from the first been in close contact with, and often in danger from, the great states of Western Europe. More recently it has been threatened also from the Far East.

NATIONAL CONTROL OF EXTERNAL AFFAIRS

Struggling for independence 170 years ago, and much weaker then than it is today, the nation allied itself to one European nation and sought aid from others. Later it attempted a policy of neutrality and isolation, but time and again found itself endangered if not directly embroiled in the struggles of great powers. All its major pronouncements of international policy—Washington's neutrality proclamation, the Monroe Doctrine in its several forms, the Open Door in China, the demands for freedom of the seas, and various others —represent reactions to critical situations elsewhere in the world, in which American interests were seriously involved. International relations, in short, are not a matter of free choice for any nation, but mainly a problem of necessary adaptation to conditions that arise. The Japanese attack on Pearl Harbor gave sharp emphasis to this point.

Early Central Control over External Affairs. In the War for Independence the thirteen states stood together as one against the common enemy and in their dealings with other nations. The Continental Congress controlled the international relations of the United States even before the Articles of Confederation were adopted. In this important respect the several states were never really separate or independent of each other. By mutual consent if not by sheer necessity there was national, not state, control in this field.

Under the Articles of Confederation (1777-88) this control by Congress was definitely confirmed in writing by all the states, and was made exclusive. The pertinent clauses of the Articles were as follows:

> The United States in Congress assembled, shall have the sole and exclusive right and power of determining on peace and war, except in cases mentioned in the sixth article [self-defense by a state in case of actual invasion by an enemy]—of sending and receiving ambassadors—entering into treaties and alliances, [with a proviso to protect state control over tariff rates, imports, and exports]—of establishing rules for deciding in all cases, what captures on land or water shall be legal, . . . of granting letters of marque and reprisal in times of

peace—appointing courts for the trial of piracies and felonies committed on the high seas. . . . Art. IX.

No state without the consent of the United States in Congress assembled, shall send any embassy to, or receive any embassy from, or enter into any conference, agreement, alliance or treaty with any king, prince, or state; . . .

No two or more states shall enter into any treaty, confederation or alliance whatever between them, without the consent of the United States in Congress assembled. . . . Art. VI.

These and other specifications in the Articles make it clear that the United States was considered by the people as one nation for all important purposes of international relations, peace and war. France, Holland, and later other nations accepted this situation and dealt only with the representatives of the nation as a whole. Thus the field of external affairs was one in which the confederacy or union had some real authority, and in which central control existed from the outset.

Organization for Foreign Affairs Under the Articles. Lacking a national executive the new nation had no choice but to entrust foreign affairs to Congress. In 1777 that body organized the Committee of Foreign Affairs, consisting of five members, whose duty it was to conduct correspondence with American representatives and friends abroad. This committee method of handling foreign affairs did not prove satisfactory. A special committee in 1780 criticized "the fluctuation, the delay, and indecision to which the present mode of managing our foreign affairs must be exposed," and recommended that there be a department of foreign affairs, headed by a secretary. In 1781 Robert R. Livingston was appointed the first American secretary of foreign affairs,[1] but the Committee continued for purposes of policy, and to supervise the work of the secretary.

Provisions of the Constitution. The framers of the national Constitution had through experience become deeply concerned that there be a correct organization for all international dealings by the United States. The Committee of Detail of the Federal Convention first proposed that the Senate have the power to make treaties and to appoint ambassadors, but Madison, who had served in Congress, was opposed to this, and he urged that the President should have the power. Madison's suggestion was adopted, but the consent of the Senate was required for the making of treaties. The sections of the Constitution that bear directly on the problems of foreign affairs read as follows:

[The President] shall have Power, by and with the Advice and Consent of the Senate, to make Treaties, provided two-thirds of the Senators present concur; and he shall nominate, and, by and with the

[1] Short, *The Development of National Administrative Organization in the United States,* pp. 46-47, 55-61.

Advice and Consent of the Senate, shall appoint Ambassadors, other public Ministers and Consuls . . .

[The President] shall receive Ambassadors and other public Ministers . . .

No state shall enter into any Treaty, Alliance, or Confederation . . .

No state shall, without the Consent of Congress, . . . enter into any Agreement or Compact with another State, or with a foreign Power, or engage in War, unless actually invaded, or in such imminent Danger as will not admit of delay.

This Constitution, and the Laws of the United States which shall be made in Pursuance thereof; and all Treaties made, or which shall be made, under the Authority of the United States, shall be the Supreme Law of the land . . .[2]

While the power over external relations is not completely covered by these provisions, certain general lines are clearly laid down. (1) The states as such have no direct part in the conduct of foreign relations. (2) The national government is given exclusive control over external affairs. (3) In the national government, the President has the initiative, but he is checked by the Senate's participation both in the ratification of treaties and in the approval of appointments to the principal posts in the foreign service.

The States and Foreign Affairs. Because the American system of government is federal, it is necessary to consider more fully the position of the states with respect to the control of foreign affairs. "Treaties" by the states with foreign powers are expressly forbidden, but lesser "agreements and compacts" are possible if Congress gives its consent. One such agreement, between New York and Canada respecting a bridge over the Niagara River, may be given as an example. And where the interests of particular states are deeply involved in some negotiation between the United States and either Canada or Mexico, it is not uncommon for the national government to utilize representatives of the border states as assistants and advisers in drawing up the treaties. Such was the case when the boundary of Maine was in dispute a century ago, and also more recently when the water-power rights of New York were involved in a proposed treaty with Canada for a deep-sea waterway. The states as such are not parties to the treaty, but are consulted before it is concluded. It is also possible for treaties to authorize border states to take action in certain extradition cases without going through the State Department in Washington. This has been done in a treaty with Mexico.

The division of powers between the national government and the states, under which the states can exercise independently many powers that affect foreigners, occasionally leads to difficulties for the national government.[3] For

[2] U. S. Const., Art. II, sec. 2, par. 2; sec. 3; Art. I, sec. 10, pars. 1, 3; Art. VI, par. 2.
[3] See H. W. Stoke, *The Foreign Relations of the Federal State*, Baltimore, 1931.

example, laws are passed by the states restricting the property rights of aliens ineligible to become citizens, such as the Japanese, or there is discrimination, open or concealed, against foreigners who try to go into local businesses. Sometimes aliens are attacked by mobs, whereupon their home countries demand that the offenders be punished, but the courts in the state concerned, using the jury system, may find it difficult to convict. In such cases the treaty rights of foreigners in this country may be seriously invaded. The foreign government has a right to hold the national government of the United States responsible because the nation alone is internationally recognized. The nation has no right under international law to plead lack of power to enforce its own treaties and its constitutional powers are now admitted to be adequate for the enforcement of all its treaty obligations without regard to any state objections. Congress is in fact very reluctant to interfere with or to apply compulsion to the states in such matters, but it certainly does not lack the power to carry out its treaty obligations.

Labor Treaties, the ILO, and State Rights. The point just made may be illustrated from the field of labor. For some years the United States has been a member of the International Labor Organization. This body draws up projects for treaties to improve the conditions of labor throughout the world. It is believed that only by international agreement can some of the evils of long hours and poor working conditions be eliminated; and that until some of these evils can be at least reduced it will be impossible to put an end to competitive underbidding and tariff wars among the nations. It happens, however, that in certain federally organized nations like Canada and the United States the member states or provinces and not the national governments pass most of the labor legislation. Is it necessary, then, to submit such a treaty to each member state or province in the federation in order to procure the legislation needed to carry out the labor treaty? The highest court for Canada has ruled in effect that this is necessary in that country. The opposite opinion prevails in the United States.

Treaty Legislation. This difference of views turns upon two related questions: the scope of the treaty-making power, and the right of the central government to enact "treaty legislation." 1. The Constitution puts no express limits on the treaty-making power of the United States. That power is supposed to be ample for every international need. Consequently the so-called "reserved powers" of the states do not limit the treaty-making power.[4] Treaties need not, therefore, be limited to the list of subjects set forth in the Constitution on which Congress may legislate.

2. Once a treaty has been made under the authority of the United States, Congress has the power to enact the necessary "treaty legislation," which may be defined as legislation to put a treaty into effect. This is true no matter what the subject matter of the treaty. Here again the specific items of Congressional power in the Constitution are not controlling because Congress is

[4] Missouri v. Holland (1920), 252 U. S. 416; U. S. v. Belmont (1937), 301 U. S. 324.

authorized to pass *all* laws that are necessary or proper to carry into execution any and every power vested by the Constitution in the national government or in any department or officer thereof.

The Chaco Arms Embargo Case. One of the most interesting explanations of the nation's power in foreign affairs appears in a Supreme Court decision of 1936. The case involved the prosecution by the government of an exporting company for conspiring to sell machine guns to Bolivia at a time when the President, under a power delegated to him by Congress, had proclaimed an embargo against such shipments.[5] The act of Congress provided "That if the President finds that the prohibition of the sale of arms and munitions of war in the United States to those countries now engaged in armed conflict in the Chaco may contribute to the reestablishment of peace between those countries," he should, after certain consultations, make proclamations to that effect, and then such sales were to be unlawful. A severe penalty was provided by Congress for violations of the act. The defendants contended that this act made an unconstitutional delegation of legislative power to the President. It gave him unlimited power to make the proclamation or not to make it as he saw fit.

External and Internal Powers Distinguished. The Court's opinion as to the nature of the power over external affairs is so significant that a substantial quotation from it is necessary. Stressing the difference between powers over external and internal affairs, the Court said:

> The two classes of powers are different, both in respect of their origin and their nature. The broad statement that the federal government can exercise no powers except those specifically enumerated in the Constitution, and such implied powers as are necessary and proper to carry into effect the enumerated powers, is categorically true only in respect of our internal affairs. In that field, the primary purpose of the Constitution was to carve from the general mass of legislative powers *then possessed by the states* such portions as it was thought desirable to vest in the federal government, leaving those not included in the enumeration still in the states. . . . That this doctrine applies only to powers which the states had, is self-evident. And since the states severally never possessed international powers, such powers could not have been carved from the mass of state powers but obviously were transmitted to the United States from some other source. . . .
>
> As a result of the separation from Great Britain by colonies, acting as a unit, the powers of external sovereignty passed from the Crown not to the colonies severally, but to the colonies in their collective and corporate capacity as the United States of America. Even before the Declaration, the colonies were a unit in foreign affairs, acting

[5] U. S. *v.* Curtiss Wright Export Corporation (1936), 299 U. S. 304.

through a common agency—namely the Continental Congress, composed of delegates from the thirteen colonies. . . . Sovereignty is never held in suspense. When, therefore, the external sovereignty of Great Britain in respect of the colonies ceased, it immediately passed to the Union. . . .

It results that the investment of the federal government with the powers of external sovereignty did not depend upon the affirmative grants of the Constitution. The powers to declare and wage war, to conclude peace, to make treaties, to maintain diplomatic relations with other sovereignties, if they had never been mentioned in the Constitution, would have vested in the federal government as necessary concomitants of nationality.

Much might be said both in support and in refutation of this doctrine, but there it stands, authoritatively stated. If it be true, the power over external affairs *does not depend on the Constitution.* The latter document may define the manner in which and the officers by whom it shall be exercised on behalf of the nation, but such clauses could not set aside the dominant fact that the full power must continue to exist, and that it belongs to the nation as a unit, not to the states.[6]

Overlapping of Powers. The doctrine as stated seems also to imply that there is a sharp and clear line between the external and the internal powers of government, but the decision itself shows that the line cannot be drawn. Here certain corporations and individuals were to be punished within the country for acts they had done entirely within the country but in violation of the nation's laws on external affairs. To make effective the external powers, internal powers of every type may have to be brought into use, and since the external powers are dominant and sovereign, the internal powers must bend to external necessities. Thus, for example, the internal powers are divided between the nation and the states, but can the states stand up against the exercise of the national external powers when a conflict comes? In general, this is impossible. The reserved powers of the states to control property relations, for example, bend before the treaty power, the war power, and the other external powers of the national government.

Scope of the Nation's External Power. A power that inheres in the nation because it is a nation; a power that is not granted by the Constitution but merely allocated in its totality to the national government rather than to the states, is very hard to limit by any words of the Constitution. Many citizens of the United States who are unprepared for the active role that the nation must play hereafter in international affairs look to the Constitution as a shield against international commitments. They are likely to find it a

[6] The author of this decision was Associate Justice George Sutherland. Some years earlier he had delivered a series of lectures at Columbia University in which his ideas had been more fully expounded. See George Sutherland, *Constitutional Power and World Affairs*, New York, 1919.

Maginot Line. This nation like every other one must do what is necessary internationally for its own self-preservation. Becoming a member of the United Nations is only an important first step. Whenever the world is ready for world federation, and whenever United States membership in a world federation becomes necessary to save the American people from destruction by other nations, or wise from the viewpoint of national policy, the power of the nation to enter such a federation even at the expense of its so-called "sovereignty" will be found to be ample.[7] The existence of a written Constitution, or of reserved powers in the states, is not a limitation upon the nation's power in external affairs.

THE PRESIDENT AND THE CONTROL OF EXTERNAL RELATIONS

Delegation of Powers to President. The decision quoted above also considered the delegation to the President of the power to proclaim embargoes. It is shown that under the Constitution the national power in external affairs is vested in fewer hands than is the case with the internal powers. "In this vast external realm, with its important, complicated, delicate and manifold problems, the President alone has the power to speak or listen as a representative of the nation. He *makes* treaties with the advice and consent of the Senate; but he alone negotiates. Into the field of negotiation the Senate cannot intrude; and Congress itself is powerless to invade it. As Marshall said in his great argument of March 7, 1800, in the House of Representatives, 'The President is the sole organ of the nation in its external relations, and its sole representative with foreign nations.' " The Court then proceeds to show how, in external affairs, where inside knowledge, secrecy, despatch, and unity of purpose are often necessary, it is best to "accord to the President a degree of discretion and freedom from statutory restriction which would not be admissible were domestic affairs alone involved. Moreover he, not Congress, has the better opportunity of knowing the conditions that prevail in foreign countries, and especially is this true in time of war. He has his confidential sources of information. He has his agents in the form of diplomatic, consular and other officials." In short, the delegation of power in this particular "neutrality" law was wholly justifiable since it accorded with the President's already extensive constitutional power in external affairs.

The broad power over external affairs having been stated, it is desirable to consider next the specific elements of this power and the methods of exercising it.

1. *The Power of Recognition.* In order that there may be foreign relations at all, various foreign powers, their governments, and their territorial limits must be recognized. The "power of recognition" is in fact provided for in the

[7] See Edward S. Corwin, *The Constitution and World Organization*, Princeton University Press, 1944.

Constitution but not in those words. Recognition is usually given through the simple device of receiving ambassadors or other public ministers who are sent to establish relations with the country to which they are sent. In this way new states are given recognition, and also new governments in old states. This power to receive foreign ambassadors and ministers is conferred by the Constitution on the President alone. Neither the Senate nor Congress as a whole has any control over it.

The power to recognize includes of necessity the power to refuse to recognize, and also to terminate recognition. Representatives of foreign governments who are sent here may have to live as private citizens for lack of being recognized, and in the meantime their governments go unrecognized. Such was the case with USSR between 1917 and 1933, and such has often been the case with revolutionary governments in Latin America as well as in Europe. In similar ways, or by refusing to send consuls, the President may refuse to recognize territorial conquests, such as those of Japan in Manchuria and of Italy in Ethiopia during the 1930s. There is a danger in the use of this power, for governments whose claims go unrecognized will have grounds for animosity toward us. The dangers that come from a premature recognition of a rebel government can also be easily understood.

The President's recognition or nonrecognition of a new government is binding on the courts and on Congress, as well as on the people of the United States. It may seriously affect property rights and other interests.[8] No other branch of the government can legally go behind what the President has done, or question his reasons. Because of the important issues involved, the President has on occasion admitted the desirability of having the advice of Congress, but he has never yielded to that body the power to make the recognition.

Dismissal and Recall of Diplomats. When the policy of a government that the United States has recognized causes offense, or when the representative of any recognized country commits acts that are unbecoming a diplomat, the President has the power also (a) to ask the foreign government that the representative be recalled, or (b) to dismiss him and send him home, and (c) to recall the American representative in that country. In its extreme form this is known as breaking off diplomatic relations, and it is a very serious step, since it may lead to other incidents and ultimately to war.

2. *Control of Communications with Foreign Powers.* The control of official communications with foreign powers is one of the important elements in the control of external relations. The laws of the United States forbid private individuals to undertake diplomatic negotiations with foreign powers, and the houses of Congress are also without means of beginning such negotiations. They have "neither eyes to see nor ears to hear" the agents of other nations. By law and by custom the President's office has complete control in this field, although the Department of State as the President's agency handles most communications, both oral and written, and most of the less important ones

[8] U. S. v. Belmont (1937), 301 U. S. 324.

are never seen by him. The chief sources of communications dealing with foreign affairs are (a) the many American foreign service officers scattered throughout the world, (b) foreign ambassadors, ministers, and consuls in the United States, and (c) the departments of foreign affairs of other nations.

3. *Power to Appoint and Control Foreign Service Officers.* The President's complete control of all official diplomatic communications results from his power to appoint ambassadors, other public ministers, and consuls, as well as the Secretary of State and the principal subordinates in the State Department, and from his executive powers of control over those whom he appoints, including the power to remove them. It is true that the Senate must give its consent to the President's appointments to all regular positions in the service, but this gives it no control over the individuals so appointed. Furthermore, almost from the beginning of the national government the President has exercised the power to appoint special commissions to negotiate treaties with other countries, and special agents to go abroad to seek out information and to make contacts important to the President, and to do these things without Senate approval. Indeed, in some cases the Senate does not know that the President has such confidential agents abroad, or who they are. Since they hold no public offices, they do not require regular appointments.

4. *The Making of Treaties.* In the making of treaties there are certain initial stages for which the Constitution does not provide. Someone has to decide that a certain kind of treaty with certain countries would be desirable. It may be the State Department that first gets the idea, but it is the President who must give the approval for going ahead, and any ideas that he has on the subject must be carried out by the department unless the President can be convinced that he is making a mistake. Approaches must next be made by the Secretary of State to ambassadors and ministers of the foreign countries resident in Washington, or by American representatives abroad to the foreign offices there. In none of these matters does Congress have any part. Individual members, or the committees on foreign relations, may approach the President to start negotiations looking toward some kind of treaty, but they cannot set the ball rolling. These statements run counter to the interpretation sometimes put on the words "advice and consent of the Senate" in the clause on treaty making, but ever since Washington's unfortunate experience there have been few if any formal attempts on the part of Presidents to get the Senate's advice in advance. If he is wise he talks the matter over confidentially with party leaders and the members of the Senate Committee on Foreign Relations, but he may go ahead even without doing this.

Preliminary Negotiations. Preliminary negotiations may go on in Washington or in foreign capitals. These negotiations are confidential and secret. At the time of World War I there was much criticism here and abroad of this kind of "secret diplomacy," and especially of the "secret treaties" that certain countries had with each other. President Wilson in the Fourteen Points stressed the need of "open covenants, openly arrived at," but he found at

Versailles that treaties cannot be negotiated in a combined newspaper room and telegraph office with any prospect of success. Under conditions of complete publicity, compromises and concessions on the part of the different countries represented are almost impossible.

Submission to the Senate. If the negotiators can agree, a treaty is drawn up, signed, and transmitted to the governments concerned. In the American system, the President then submits the measure with a letter of explanation to the Senate. A leading authority insists that the action of the Senate in passing upon treaties is part of the negotiation, and not part of the ratification.[9] His reason for this is that the Senate has power to propose amendments or reservations to the document, and that when this is done it is necessary for the President to submit the amendments or reservations to the other nations for their further consideration. Thus negotiations have not really ended. This probably places too much emphasis on the technical step called "ratification" which, in a strict sense, is an action of the President alone after the Senate has approved a treaty. On the other hand, the Senate does not meet the representatives of the other nation, and thus can hardly be said to have any part in the negotiation.

Secret and Open Sessions. The Senate's procedure on treaties is to submit them first to the Committee on Foreign Relations, and to await its report before taking further action. Then the Senate usually goes into executive session where the measure is debated, and amendments or reservations may be offered. It was once the uniform custom of the Senate in its consideration of treaties to meet in secret executive session. By executive session is meant, of course, a session in which executive rather than legislative business is taken up. Treaties have been placed in the class of executive business, despite the fact that they become laws when ratified. Most persons think of all executive sessions as secret, but the Senate, in its historic struggle over the approval of the Versailles Treaty, decided to hold open executive sessions, and such sessions can be ordered at any time now when a treaty is being considered. Unless there is a special vote for open sessions, the proceedings are held in secret, the galleries are cleared, and every member and officer present is enjoined by the rules to maintain secrecy about what is done until the Senate by its own vote removes the injunction. The punishment for violating the pledge of secrecy may be expulsion in the case of a member, dismissal and punishment for contempt in the case of a clerk or other officer.

The actual treaty veto of the Senate will be considered a little farther along.

Final Steps on Treaties. If a treaty comes out of the Senate approved with proposed amendments or reservations, the President may submit the proposed changes to the other powers involved, and if they agree to them, he may proceed to the next steps in the process. Otherwise he may recall the treaty at any time, and the Senate has no power of its own to revive a treaty that has gone back to him. Assuming that it has approved a treaty without amendment,

[9] J. M. Mathews, *American Foreign Relations*, p. 398.

or that the other powers have accepted the proposed amendments, the next steps toward making it effective are three: ratification of the treaty by the President; exchange of ratifications with the other powers concerned, assuming that they have also ratified; and proclamation of the treaty by the President. This proclamation is published separately while the treaty itself, as approved, is printed in the volume of private acts at the end of the session of Congress.

Contents of Treaties. A brief perusal of the index of a leading collection of American treaties shows the following subjects dealt with among others: arbitration of international disputes; claims of one country or its citizens against another; commerce and navigation; consular arrangements between countries; copyrights, trade-marks, and patents; estates and wills of persons who die abroad; extradition of criminals; naturalization of aliens; neutral rights in time of war; peace and amity treaties; and property rights and rights of trade.

In addition there is a series of multilateral treaties (involving many nations), also called "international acts," relating to the Red Cross, weights and measures, health matters, suppression of the opium trade, submarine cables, railroads, the white slave traffic, the laws of war, and many other things.

Treaties and Laws. In their legal effect these treaties are laws. This is especially true of treaties that are "self-executing," i.e., that require no act of Congress to put them into effect, but the relationship between treaties and laws passed by Congress is not always clear. According to the Constitution every law passed by Congress "in pursuance" of the Constitution is a supreme law of the land, and every treaty made "under the authority of the United States" is a supreme law. Which prevails in case of conflict? Since they are of equal validity, as a rule the self-executing treaty or the law that was last made prevails over the other. Thus, if a law enacted by Congress on the subject of foreign commerce covers ground previously regulated by treaties, the courts in this country must enforce the law, not the treaties. The foreign countries may seek redress from the treaty-making power of the United States, since the treaty is still morally binding, but nothing can be done about it unless Congress is willing to back down and change the law.

Legislation to Carry Out Treaties. If a treaty cannot be made effective without enforcing legislation or appropriations enacted by Congress, the latter is in a sense morally bound to enact the legislation, but legally it is entirely free to refuse to do so. Usually there is sufficient harmony between the executive and the Congress so that the needed legislation is enacted. When state legislation is needed, uniform state action can hardly be expected, but, as we have seen, Congress may enact what the English courts have called "treaty legislation," i.e., legislation based upon the treaty, and to carry it into effect.

The Two-Thirds Vote on Treaties. Votes upon treaty amendments and reservations and upon other motions connected with treaty are by ordinary majority; only the final vote requires the two-thirds vote, and this is two-thirds of those present and voting (assuming a quorum to be present), and not two-thirds of the entire membership.

The one-third-plus-one of the Senators required to defeat a treaty, or to force obnoxious amendments upon the President and upon the Senate majority, may represent far less than a third of the people. The seventeen states smallest in population have fewer inhabitants than the single state of New York, yet these seventeen states, with less than ten per cent of the national population, have enough Senators to defeat a treaty. The vote against adhering to the World Court was cast by a group of Senators representing far less than a third of the population. The danger of minority control over treaties, to which James Wilson pointed in the Federal Convention when he proposed that treaties be adopted by a majority vote, has in fact come to pass. There has in consequence been considerable discussion of a proposed change in the Constitution to establish majority rule, or to have treaties ratified by a simple majority vote of both houses. No amendment proposed to this end has been pushed with enough vigor to promise early success,[10] but other developments of recent years suggest the conclusion that such an amendment may not be required. It is sufficiently clear, however, that if the United States had only the ordinary treaty-making process on which to rely in making agreements with other nations, its position would be an unhappy one. The treaty veto of one-third-plus-one of the Senators tips the scales heavily in favor of American isolationism.

Conflicts Between Senate and President over Treaties. Senators fundamentally represent their districts, which are states, and the classes and groups predominant in those districts. There are very few who are able to rise entirely above their local interests in considering matters of foreign affairs, as the Presidents must. Consequently all Presidents in recent generations, Republicans and Democrats alike, have been defeated on important treaty proposals by combinations of opposing Senators, sufficient to make up the one-third-plus-one necessary to reject a treaty, or at least sufficient by their threat of rejection to force the adoption of stultifying amendments and reservations. Proposals for improved arbitration treaties, for adherence to the World Court, and for membership in the League of Nations, as well as less important treaties, met the same fate at the hands of the Senators—defeat! A number of motives undoubtedly played a part in these rejections of treaties. For political reasons, that is, to hold in line the voters in their own states, many Senators found it necessary to be thoroughly nationalistic, against all "truckling to foreign potentates," while others were personally and by conviction "isolationist" in extreme degree. Numerous reservations proposed to treaties showed a purpose to force the President to come to the Senate for approval in every possible case of a foreign commitment. The opposition of the Senators arose in

---

[10] See D. F. Fleming, *The Treaty Veto of the American Senate*; R. J. Dangerfield, *In Defense of the Senate*; Lindsay Rogers, *The American Senate*, Chs. I-III; Kenneth Colegrove, *The American Senate and World Peace.*

part from their determination to preserve and to increase the power of the Senate *vis-à-vis* the President.

Recent Change of Senate Attitude. Even before World War II there was evidence of a change in the attitude of the Senators. It was a Senate with a Republican majority that defeated the League of Nations covenant after World War I and that held an isolationist viewpoint throughout the 1920s. The return to power of the Democratic party in the early 1930s brought a partial change in attitude. Furthermore the Senate leaders in the fight against the League began to drop out and some of the younger men who replaced them, untinged by anti-Wilsonism, urged the Senate to adopt a constructive program of international cooperation. The continuous pounding of certain leading newspapers against Senate isolationism, and the obvious shift in public opinion in favor of more international cooperation, also had some effect. It became increasingly clear that the Senate was in bad repute for its myopic isolationism, and that it could begin to regain public favor only by a change of attitude.

The shock and disillusionment of World War II finally produced the long-awaited reversal. Spurred on by similar action in the House, the Senate passed a strong resolution favoring full participation by the United States in an international organization to prevent war. Later the Senate passed by large majorities various measures for bringing the United States into the United Nations organization and for other international purposes. This temporary change of attitude may become permanent, but of this there is no certainty as yet. Political attitudes are as changeable as the weather. In the meantime it must not be forgotten that the treaty veto power of the Senate still stands, and that it is a power that can be exercised by far less than a majority of the Senators.

5. *International Agreements by Joint Resolutions.* One factor in the recent change of Senate attitude was the realization that treaties do not constitute the only method for effecting international agreements. Students of the Constitution and of international law had been aware of this for some decades but it dawned upon the majority in Congress only within the last few years.[11] With a President then in the White House who was willing to use his constitutional powers to the utmost to procure international agreements to prevent wars, the Senators suddenly realized that the right to approve treaties does not give them a monopoly in the control of American international agreements. There are, in fact, two important alternatives to the treaty-making power.

One of these is the joint resolution of Congress which can be adopted by a simple majority in each house and then be approved by the President, or, conversely, can be adopted by Congress to ratify something that the President

[11] One book that probably had great influence was Wallace McClure's *International Executive Agreements*, New York, 1941, which bears the significant subtitle: "Democratic Procedure Under the Constitution of the United States."

has already done. Two formerly independent states, Texas and Hawaii, were annexed to the United States by joint resolution; the war with Germany was thus terminated in 1921; and there are many other examples of this procedure. The Supreme Court has fully sustained this method of international action by the United States, and it is now primarily a question of convenience or policy with the President whether he will use the treaty method or the joint resolution method. Whichever is used, the resulting agreement becomes a part of the supreme law of the land.

6. *Simple Executive Agreements under Statutory Powers.* An important variation of the foregoing method is found in two recent acts of Congress. Under the "reciprocal trade agreements" act of 1934 and the "lend-lease" act of 1941 Congress gave advance approval in statute form for certain types of agreements to be made by the President with foreign countries. These delegations of power to the President in external affairs are similar to many others that Congress has made to authorize rule making by the President in internal affairs. The difference is that the two acts mentioned call for actual agreements to be made by the President with foreign powers and then to be put into effect by him. Such executive agreements acquire practically the same status as treaties, although not subsequently approved by either the Senate or Congress as a whole. The delegation of power in the Chaco arms embargo case previously discussed was somewhat different.[12] Under that act the President was authorized, upon finding certain facts, to declare and enforce an arms embargo. The act did not call for an agreement with any other country although it dealt with a matter of international concern.

7. *Simple Executive Agreements Under Constitutional Powers.* In his capacity as the nation's executive or as commander in chief or both the President has broad powers that are conferred upon him by the Constitution. In addition he has specific powers to see that the laws are enforced, to receive foreign ambassadors (and hence to recognize foreign governments), and to do certain other things. These powers cannot be taken from him by Congress, although within limits Congress may regulate his exercise of them. Under these powers, and without clear statutory authority, Presidents frequently make and carry out agreements with foreign powers without even asking the Senate or Congress to approve.

It used to be thought that such executive agreements standing by themselves could not be enforced in the courts because they did not have the status of laws. The Supreme Court has decided otherwise. For example, in the case of United States *v.* Belmont, previously mentioned,[13] an exchange of diplomatic correspondence between the USSR and the United States had culminated in an executive agreement by which the United States received the right to certain funds that had been deposited in New York with Belmont by a Russian corporation which the Soviet government had liquidated and whose

---

12 See footnote 5, above.
13 See footnote 8, above.

property it had claimed. By this executive agreement, which was not submitted to Congress or to the Senate for approval, the President recognized the Soviet government, recognized also (as far as this country was concerned) the validity of all its acts from the commencement of its existence, and gained for the United States government all the property and assets of the USSR situated in the United States. This "international compact" the Supreme Court fully sustained. "Governmental power over external affairs is not distributed, but is vested exclusively in the national government. And in respect of what was done here, the Executive had authority to speak as the sole organ of that government. The assignment and the agreements in connection therewith did not, as in the case of treaties, as that term is used in the treaty making clause of the Constitution (Article II, sec. 2), require the advice and consent of the Senate."

It appears, therefore, that not only those executive agreements that have the approval of majorities in both houses of Congress, but also, within their proper sphere, those made by the President alone under his constitutional powers, have the same legal force as treaties. Furthermore, as international activity has increased, executive agreements of all kinds have outstripped in numbers the treaties of the United States. This trend is comparable to that in internal affairs, in which the number of administrative rules and regulations has gained upon and even outrun the number of statutes passed by Congress. Speed and decisiveness being at a premium in these times, it is difficult to see how this tendency toward more complete executive dominance in external affairs can even be checked, and even more difficult to believe that it can be reversed.

8. *Declarations of Foreign Policy.* As "the sole organ of the nation in its external relations" the President exercises the right to announce new phases of foreign policy from time to time, and to give warnings both to foreign powers and to American citizens as to what the policy will be, without consulting the Senate or Congress as a whole, and without negotiating with other powers. The history of American foreign relations since the days of Washington is replete with declarations of policy by the Presidents. The first great announcement of policy made by a President on his own initiative was Washington's proclamation of neutrality in 1793, when France was locked in struggle with Great Britain and various continental powers. Thirty years later came the declaration of the Monroe Doctrine, and at other times throughout our history there have been declarations such as that of the Open Door in China, Wilson's Fourteen Points, Franklin Roosevelt's Good Neighbor Policy toward the nations of the two Americas, and his joint announcement with Prime Minister Churchill of the Atlantic Charter. Many more examples could be given. Of course a policy once announced is not unchangeable. The Monroe Doctrine with Monroe and John Quincy Adams meant one thing, but with Grover Cleveland it was something different, and so with Theodore Roosevelt, with Wilson, and with Franklin Roosevelt.

To back up his position as national spokesman in foreign policy, the President has also his powers as the executive in all internal affairs, and as commander in chief of all the armed forces. Considering the freedom with which the latter powers can at times be used, foreign powers need to weigh his announcements with the utmost care. There are, however, certain potential dangers in the exercise of this power. The President can by no means be sure that the country, and particularly Congress or the Senate, will follow him in his declarations of policy. In addition, one-sided declarations of policy may arouse strong resentment in the nation or nations to whom they are addressed. An agreement based upon negotiations with the powers concerned is always more acceptable.

The houses of Congress have also, at times, attempted to assume the role of spokesman on American foreign policy. Various resolutions have been directed, for example, at British policy in Ireland, India, and Palestine. Twisting the British lion's tale is an old pastime in Congress, and in consequence its resolutions of this character are heavily discounted even before they are adopted. The best rules for a responsible legislative body are not to exacerbate international relations and not to adopt resolutions on subjects over which it has no power or about which it does not intend to do anything. In any case, although Congressional resolutions are some evidence of public opinion, or at least of pressure group activity, they do not always express the policy of the government.

It should be pointed out, too, that if present steps toward international organization are substantially successful, there will be less occasion in the future for unilateral declarations of foreign policy even by the Presidents. Under the charter of the UN, for example, and through it and its affiliated organs, many if not most of the important international questions will be settled by joint action of the nations. When important questions are to be decided in international conference, it is unfortunate for any nation to be committed in advance to adopt a definite line of policy. Wise Presidents will be inclined, therefore, to keep silence on major issues until an international understanding has been reached.

DEPARTMENT OF STATE AND FOREIGN SERVICE

Presidents Need Advice and Assistance. No President could handle the multifarious duties that are imposed upon him by the Constitution and laws, and at the same time be fully informed about all aspects of the nation's external relations. Even if he had great knowledge, he would still need a great deal of aid in carrying out the country's policies. A few Presidents have almost set aside their Secretaries of State in order to deal with the major international questions themselves, but it cannot be said that these attempts have been highly successful. In short every President must rely heavily on the accumulated knowledge and experience of those officers and agencies of government that have been provided by Congress to operate in the field concerned. The policy of the government at any time is to a large extent determined and controlled by such officers and agencies. In the management of external relations the Department of State with its central staff in Washington and its numerous agents in the foreign service abroad constitutes the primary reliance of every President; but in recent years a number of other agencies have also become important.

Secretaries of State. The Department of State, first called the Department of Foreign Affairs, was the first executive department to be established by the new national government in 1789. It is therefore generally accorded first place in the ranking of departments, and the Secretary of State follows the Vice President in the succession to the Presidency. What is more, this office has attracted to it more distinguished American statesmen than any other department headship or similar office, in this respect rivaling the Presidency itself and surpassing the position of Chief Justice of the Supreme Court. John Jay carried over from the Confederation, and then when he became Chief Justice, Jefferson became the first regularly appointed Secretary. Later holders of the office, to name but some of them, have included John Marshall, James Madison, James Monroe, John Quincy Adams, Henry Clay, Daniel Webster, John C. Calhoun, William H. Seward, Hamilton Fish, James G. Blaine, John Hay, Elihu Root, William J. Bryan, Charles E. Hughes, and Cordell Hull.

Departmental Organization and Staff. Since the beginning of World War II the Department of State has undergone several reorganizations and a very considerable expansion. At the beginning of 1941 the total personnel of the department in Washington, D. C., was only 1,264. This gave the department the dubious honor of being the smallest as well as the oldest of the departments in the national capital, smaller even than the then much-shrunken Department of Labor. With all the foreign service officers and employees added, it was still next to the smallest among the departments. The diminutive size of its staff and its need for drastic war-time reorganization can both be explained against the background of American isolationism and the very limited range of functions that had been entrusted to the department. Looking after the nation's external relations—under a policy of inactivity in this field—did not seem to call for a large, dynamic department. "Our international relations consisted mainly of negotiating treaties, maintaining our neutral rights, and protecting our citizens abroad." [14] Since there was so little to do, and so few people to do it with, the department's organization had been permitted to develop by minor accretions and adjustments without any careful planning of the organization as a whole. When World War II suddenly plunged the nation into the arena of world-wide international activities—military, economic, social, diplomatic, cultural—and the role of world leadership could no longer be

---

[14] Walter H. C. Laves and Francis O. Wilcox, "Organizing the Government for Participation in World Affairs," in *Amer. Pol. Sci. Rev.*, vol. 38, p. 914.

avoided, the department had to expand, reorganize, and come to life, all at the same time.

As a result of its latest reorganization the department had in 1945, in addition to the Secretary, an Under Secretary, six Assistant Secretaries, a Legal Adviser, and a group of important "special assistants" to the Secretary. Under each Assistant Secretary was a group of "offices," some of which were organized for particular world regions (Europe, Far East, Near East and Africa, American Republics) and others for broad functions such as Special Political Affairs (international organization, security and dependent areas), International Trade Policy, Financial and Development Policy, Transportation and Communications, and so on. The "offices" in turn consisted of "divisions." A "Secretary's Staff Committee" for planning long-range foreign policy, and a "Co-ordinating Committee" for interoffice relations helped to unify the department's policies and its administration.

A published list of the officers and employees of the department in Washington early in 1945 [15] included over 4,000 names, or over three times the number at the beginning of 1941. Substantial further growth seems almost inevitable.

In the early part of World War II there was a rapid growth of agencies to deal with external affairs outside the State Department. The army and the navy found themselves unavoidably involved in negotiations abroad. The Combined Chiefs of Staff in Washington, the Lend-Lease Administration, the Board of Economic Warfare, the Office of War Information, and various others either included representatives of other countries in their membership, or had contacts with other nations. Attempts were made to give the State Department the power to co-ordinate their work in Washington, and to require all the agencies' representatives abroad to clear through the resident United States ambassador or minister in order to co-ordinate their work in the field. The speed and volume of work were simply too great to make this always possible and there were cases of different agencies of the United States in the same country doing contradictory things.

It is now entirely clear that the State Department, as it was constituted before the war, would never have been able to handle even the present United States external relations. For the future there must either be a considerable further enlargement of the personnel and expansion of the functions of the State Department and of the foreign service, or else a number of separate agencies will have to operate in the foreign field with some kind of co-ordinating mechanism among them.

Another change will result from the rise of various international policy-making bodies and administrations. Formerly the Department of State and the foreign service dealt mainly with one nation at a time. In the future more of the external relations of all countries will be planned and administered by

[15] *Organization of the Department of State*, April 1, 1945, U. S. Government Printing Office, 1945.

international agencies. Multilateral action will replace bilateral. The emphasis will have to shift somewhat from the ambassador or minister accredited to one country to the new type of agent who represents the nation in some international body. How much of a change this will be remains to be seen.

The Foreign Service. Located mainly outside the United States and scattered out among the capitals and the larger commercial cities of the world are the several thousand foreign service officers and employees who are supposed to look out for United States interests abroad.

The Constitution itself requires the appointment of "Ambassadors, other public Ministers and Consuls" by the President with the advice and consent of the Senate. Following a high standard of appointments begun by Washington and continued by several later Presidents, the spoils system entered the foreign service about a century ago and continued to dominate it until about 1906. During most of this period there was a distinction between the consular and the diplomatic divisions. Consuls are, of course, primarily commercial agents of the government that appoints them. They are charged with obtaining commercial information, looking after the interests of shippers, shipowners, and seamen, and giving such protection and assistance as they can to travelers abroad. Diplomatic officers, on the other hand, are accredited to the government to which they are sent, and are charged with political functions, the promotion of friendly relations, and the negotiation of treaties and other agreements. According to old usages, diplomatic officers carry long and distinguished titles, such as "ambassadors extraordinary and ministers plenipotentiary," but for practical purposes they may be grouped according to rank as follows: Ambassadors, with salaries of $17,500, who are ordinarily sent to about fifteen leading countries; Ministers, whose salaries are $12,000 or $10,000, according to the posts they hold, and who are sent to the smaller countries; Ministers Resident, in the smallest countries; and Charges d'Affaires, who are temporary substitutes.

Reforms in the Service. After a long period of neglect and the continued prevalence of the spoils system in appointments, Theodore Roosevelt in 1906 by executive order put the consular service on a merit basis, and Taft followed a few years later with an order putting much of the diplomatic service on the same footing. These were the beginnings of a career service system, but they left much to be desired. There was insufficient security, since any President could change the regulations, and there was too sharp a differentiation between the consular and diplomatic branches. Then, too, salaries were very low compared to the requirements on the foreign service officers; and housing conditions were very bad, since the government owned practically no buildings abroad. Agitation for still further improvement continued, with the result that in 1924 was passed the Rogers act for the further reorganization of the service. This act created a single, unified foreign service out of what were once two separate branches; established the title "foreign service officer" which covers "all counselors of embassy or legation, diplomatic secretaries, consuls general, consuls, and vice consuls of career," provided for the selection of such foreign service officers by examination; and established various classes of such officers, ranging from beginners with a salary of $2,500 to those of the first class, with salaries of $9,000 to $10,000. It is under this act and various additional laws and executive orders that the foreign service has definitely become a career in recent decades. Certain posts of ambassadorial and ministerial rank are still filled by appointment from outside the service—the appointment usually of wealthy men, since indeed no others can as a rule afford to accept ambassadorships. Nevertheless, a number of ministers are now career men.

This is not the place to go into details concerning examinations, promotions, and other matters in which college students are often interested. The Department of State publishes a special bulletin [16] that is available to those who have thoughts of applying for the examinations. A word of caution may, however, be given. It is the writer's experience that each year there come up to the colleges and universities many young people, both men and women, who have romantic and unduly exaggerated ideas about the foreign service. There is a pull to it that draws the imagination, just as is frequently the case with distant fields, while opportunities that lie close about us are overlooked. In fact the annual number of appointments in the foreign service in the past was rather small; in some years there were practically none, and seldom would the number reach 100 positions of interest to college graduates. As a rule thousands applied for the examinations, and only a relatively small number passed both the written and the oral parts. Even of those who passed by no means all could be appointed. In the years ahead the service will undoubtedly need more recruits. Embassies, ministries, and consulates that had to be closed during the war are being reopened, and the staffs of others will be increased. This will bring new opportunities for those who have the capacity and who earnestly seek appointment. The intention here is not to discourage applicants but to help them to see the probabilities in a clear light. The service is an important and a distinguished one, one to which the ablest students may well aspire. It is by no means a sinecure, however, but rather a challenge to the best efforts of the most outstanding. It offers a call to hard work in the public service, sometimes in rather disagreeable places, rather than an opportunity to travel abroad at the government's expense.

FROM ISOLATION TO INTERNATIONAL COLLABORATION

This is not the place, either, for a résumé of the foreign policy of the United States. It is necessary to point out, however, that the major change in policy that is now taking place is likely to have profound effects upon the organization and the work of the national government. The change from attempted

[16] See *The American Foreign Service*, a pamphlet published by the Department of State and revised from time to time.

isolation to international collaboration is one that has been too long delayed, and is, therefore, the harder to make.

For a generation or more prior to World War II the nation had the uneasy conscience of one who means to do well but whose pretensions and whose deeds were largely contradictory. It desired a large volume of foreign trade, especially exports, but for a long time kept its tariffs and other restrictions on imports so high as to hamper the trade it desired. It wanted to stand by itself, free from all international responsibilities, yet expected all the benefits of international trade, communications, and security. It somehow expected that its own good intentions, its lack of any desire to conquer territory, should be a sufficient reason for other nations to give it their trade and their confidence, to heed its remonstrances to them when they did something it did not like, and to leave it alone otherwise to do as it pleased. It wished for peace but would not take the constructive steps necessary to ensure it, and in fact followed policies that led to war.

At last the nation and its leaders seem to have awakened. They have begun to realize that a nation's policies must be judged not by its own good intentions, or lack of bad ones, but by the necessary consequence of those policies. They have come to understand that the United States cannot get the benefit of international order without making rational and responsible efforts and substantial sacrifices to that end. They seem to see now that there are no foreign nations but only international neighbors; that there are not two worlds, that of the United States and that of all foreigners, but only one world.

At the end of World War I the nation rejected membership in the League of Nations, refused to accept any responsibility for peace and security in Europe, and proceeded to pursue policies that helped to bring economic ruin, despair, and militaristic dictatorships to countries that had tried to become democracies. Since the end of hostilities in World War II the nation's policy has been, up to now, almost the opposite. The Senate was almost unanimous in approving the Charter of the United Nations. Furthermore, Congress as a whole has followed the President's recommendations in providing appropriations for international relief work, in authorizing further tariff reductions under the Reciprocal Trade Agreements Act, and in approving the International Monetary Fund and the Bank for Reconstruction and Development. These are tremendous steps forward and yet they are only the beginnings.

The consequences and the obligations arising from the new commitments must not be ignored. International pressures and activities have repercussions within each nation. New functions and new ways of performing old functions necessarily result in changes in organization. Many questions that were once domestic or national will in the future be settled by international action. The international administration of functions will increase and will penetrate into the nations themselves. Already the nation is a member not only of the general United Nations organization but also of other, more specialized international agencies. It stands internationally close to the position in which the thirteen original United States stood with respect to each other under the Articles of Confederation. Its war powers and its peace powers have been deeply affected by the international commitments that it has made. Its new international relationships must inevitably affect its entire system of government. Not only the work of the State Department, but also that of the War and Navy departments, and the very balance of power between Congress and the President, must be different in the years ahead from what they were in the immediate past.

REFERENCES

John M. Mathews, *American Foreign Relations: Conduct and Policies*, rev. ed., New York, 1938.

Edward S. Corwin, *The President's Control of Foreign Relations*, Princeton, 1917.

——, *The President: Office and Powers*, 2nd ed., rev., New York, 1941.

——, *The Constitution and World Organization*, Princeton, 1944.

Quincy Wright, *The Control of American Foreign Relations*, New York, 1922.

Graham H. Stuart, *American Diplomatic and Consular Practice*, New York, 1936.

Wallace McClure, *International Executive Agreements*, New York, 1941.

Kenneth Colegrove, *The American Senate and World Peace*, New York, 1944.

Denna F. Fleming, *The United States and the World Court,* Garden City, New York, 1945.

——, *The Treaty Veto of the American Senate*, New York, 1930.

George Sutherland, *Constitutional Power and World Affairs*, New York, 1919.

Walter H. C. Laves and Francis O. Wilcox, "The Reorganization of the Department of State," *Amer. Pol. Sci. Rev.*, vol. 38, pp. 289-309 (1944).

—— ——, "Organizing the Government for Participation in World Affairs," *Amer. Pol. Sci. Rev.*, vol. 38, pp. 913-30 (1944).

—— ——, "The State Department Continues Its Reorganization," *Amer. Pol. Sci. Rev.*, vol. 39, pp. 309-17 (1945).

Charter of the United Nations, 1945.

Harold W. Stoke, *The Foreign Relations of the Federal State*, Baltimore, 1931.

Samuel B. Crandall, *Treaties: Their Making and Enforcement*, 2nd ed., Washington, 1916.

Royden J. Dangerfield, *In Defense of the Senate: A Study in Treaty Making*, Norman, Oklahoma, 1933.

William S. Holt, *Treaties Defeated by the Senate: A Study of the Struggle Between President and Senate over the Conduct of Foreign Relations*, Baltimore, 1933.

William M. Malloy (Comp.), *Treaties, Conventions, International Acts, Protocols and Agreements Between the United States of America and Other Powers*, 1776-1909, 2 vols., 61st Cong., 2nd Sess., Senate Doc. No. 357, Washington, 1910.

Hunter Miller, *Treaties and Other International Acts of the U. S. of America,* Washington, 1931 ff., 7 vols. to date.

Samuel Flagg Bemis, *A Diplomatic History of the United States,* New York, 1936.

James W. Garner, *American Foreign Policies,* New York, 1928.

Benjamin H. Williams, *American Diplomacy, Policies and Practice,* New York, 1936.

Frank H. Simonds, *American Foreign Policy in the Post-War Years,* Baltimore, 1935.

Robert S. Rankin, *Readings in American Government,* New York, 1939.

John M. Mathews and Clarence A. Berdahl, *Documents and Readings in American Government: National and State,* rev. ed., New York, 1940, pp. 585-91, 594-611, 614-27.

A. N. Christensen and E. M. Kirkpatrick, *The People, Politics, and the Politician: Readings in American Government,* New York, 1941, pp. 690-703.

CHAPTER 23

National Defense and War Powers

CONSTITUTIONAL POWERS: NATIONAL AND STATE

Early Views and Experiences. Those citizens of the thirteen English colonies in America who took up the struggle for independence were in general suspicious of a strong executive and of a standing army. For defense they favored the use of the militia, which consisted of all able-bodied male citizens of suitable age. Intensive special training was not considered necessary, and even strict military discipline was not thought highly important. In those days many men wanted no higher government than that of the colony to control military affairs. When the war for independence began, however, they accepted as a necessity a national military force under a single commander in chief, Gen. George Washington, appointed by and responsible to Congress.

In the Articles of Confederation the thirteen states purported to grant to Congress the full power to conduct wars. In fact, however, all the money that was required and the troops themselves had to be supplied by the states on requisitions by Congress. Furthermore, the states retained considerable control over the troops that they supplied, even to the appointment of officers up to the rank of colonel. Although a few states loyally supplied the men and money requested by Congress, others did little or nothing. As a result of shortages in men and supplies General Washington's position was at times well nigh hopeless. Out of this experience he and his young aide, Alexander Hamilton, learned the great importance to the nation of having a strong, unified military organization. In the Federal Convention of 1787 their ideas bore fruit despite some opposition:

National Constitutional Provisions. As the Constitution came from the hands of the framers it contained the following provisions pertinent to the national defense:

> The Congress shall have Power To lay and collect Taxes . . .
> to . . . provide for the common Defence . . .

To declare War, grant Letters of Marque and Reprisal, and make Rules concerning Captures on Land and Water;

To raise and support Armies, but no Appropriation of Money to that Use shall be for a longer Term than two Years;

To provide and maintain a Navy;

To make Rules for the Government and Regulation of the land and naval Forces;

To provide for calling forth the Militia to execute the Laws of the Union, suppress Insurrections and repel Invasions;

To provide for organizing, arming, and disciplining the Militia, and for governing such Part of them as may be employed in the Service of the United States, reserving to the States respectively, the Appointment of the Officers, and the Authority of training the Militia according to the discipline prescribed by Congress; . . .[1]

The United States shall guarantee to every State in this Union a Republican Form of Government, and shall protect each of them against Invasion; and on Application of the Legislature, or of the Executive (when the Legislature cannot be convened) against domestic Violence.[2]

These clauses authorize Congress itself to provide for the army, navy, and militia, and for the taxes and regulations required for them. How great an advance they represent over the corresponding provisions in the Articles of Confederation is evident on very slight study.

President as Commander in Chief. But the Constitution goes beyond the Articles also in the centering of responsibility and power for the conduct of war, and in its provisions giving protection to the people against the abuse of the strong military power that it authorizes. The most important clause on the first of these points is as follows:

The President shall be Commander in Chief of the Army and Navy of the United States, and of the Militia of the several States, when called into the actual Service of the United States; . . .[3]

The President's appointing power, his authority to demand the opinion in writing of the heads of all executive departments, and his right to "commission all officers of the United States" must also be given weight in this connection. No doubt the public confidence that General Washington had inspired and the expectation that he would be the first President had much to do with making these provisions acceptable to the people.

Limitations on War Power. The provisions that give the people special protection against the abuses of military power, and that ensure to some extent

[1] U. S. Const., Art. I, sec. 8.
[2] U. S. Const., Art. IV, sec. 4.
[3] U. S. Const., Art. II, sec. 2.

the preservation of the state militia, are to be found partly in one section of the original Constitution and in the first few amendments:

> The privilege of the Writ of habeas corpus shall not be suspended, unless when in Cases of Rebellion or Invasion the public Safety may require it. . . .
>
> Treason against the United States, shall consist only in levying War against them, or in adhering to their Enemies, giving them Aid and Comfort. No Person shall be convicted of Treason unless on the Testimony of two Witnesses to the same overt Act, or on confession in open court. . . .
>
> A well regulated Militia, being necessary to the security of a free State, the right of the people to keep and bear Arms, shall not be infringed.
>
> No Soldier shall, in time of peace, be quartered in any house, without the consent of the Owner, nor in time of war, but in a manner to be prescribed by law.
>
> No person shall be held to answer for a capital, or otherwise infamous crime, unless on a presentment of indictment of a Grand Jury, except in cases arising in the land or naval forces, or in the Militia, when in actual service in time of War or public danger; . . .[4]

Limitations on State War Powers. The foregoing provisions are limitations on the powers of Congress and the national government. For protections against the state governments the individual may look to both the state and national constitution and laws. The national Constitution provides that "No State shall, without the Consent of Congress, . . . keep Troops, or Ships of War in time of Peace, . . . or engage in War, unless actually invaded, or in such imminent Danger as will not admit of delay."[5] For years the national government has made even such limited defense activities by the states unnecessary by posting regular army units near the only borders that might be crossed by an enemy. Thus in effect the war powers of the national government are exclusive, and the states have no part in them except with respect to the militia.

Nevertheless, the state constitutions, assuming a greater military power and activity on the part of the states than has actually been provided for, contain a number of clauses on military affairs. These may be summarized as follows: Every state constitution except that of New York provides that "the military shall, in all cases, and at all times, be in strict subordination to the civil power," or words to that effect. Some of the constitutions state the need for having a "well regulated militia," and all make some provisions for militia organization. The governor is declared to be commander in chief of the militia except when it is called into actual service of the United States, and

---

[4] U. S. Const., Art I, sec. 9; Art. III, sec. 3; Amendments II, III, V.
[5] U. S. Const., Art. I, sec. 10, par. 3.

he is allowed to appoint the adjutant general or active head of the militia, and various classes of other officers.

The state constitutions also contain provisions protecting personal liberties against infractions by the military. Thus there are provisions against the quartering of soldiers in private homes, and protecting the right of citizens to bear arms. Most important, perhaps, are the provisions concerning martial law, and the suspension of the writ of habeas corpus. On the latter point, most of the state constitutions say that the privilege of the writ of habeas corpus is not to be suspended "except when, in case of rebellion or invasion, public safety requires it." Who may suspend it in such cases is not usually stated, but some provide that it may be done only by the legislature.

Supremacy of Civil over Military Power. In the national Constitution, as in that of New York, there is no provision that the civil authorities shall be supreme over the military. The civil authorities are, of course, the legislature, the civilian executive and administrative officers, and the courts. The supremacy of the national civil authorities over the military is nonetheless achieved in other ways. The President himself—the commander in chief—is a civilian officer and the voters can insist if they will that he shall always have a civilian background as well. On several occasions the voters have chosen military heroes as Presidents, but of those elected only Washington was outstanding in both military and civil achievement.

Congress maintains its supremacy through the provisions authorizing it to make regulations for the land and naval forces, giving it full power over all appropriations of money, and forbidding appropriations for the army to run for more than two years. The supremacy of the ordinary courts is somewhat assured by the prohibitions against suspending the right to the writ of habeas corpus, since by the use of that writ the courts can ordinarily command military officers to bring those whom they have arrested into court for trial.[6] It may be noted in addition that civilian supremacy is further assured by the almost unbroken practice of appointing civilians rather than admirals and generals to be secretaries of the navy and of war.

Military Powers at Home in Time of Peace. When the nation is not at war, what power has the President to use the armed forces to suppress domestic violence and to assist in the enforcement of ordinary law? Upon the request of a state legislature, or of a governor when the legislature is not in session, he may send troops into any state to assist the civil authorities in putting down disorder. May he in such cases establish martial law, which has the effect of placing the civilian population under the military authorities, and thus in effect suspend the writ of habeas corpus and the operation of the ordinary courts? To this the Supreme Court has said No. Only Congress may suspend the writ in such cases. If the ordinary courts are capable of functioning they may issue the writ of habeas corpus.

When there is domestic disturbance, but no call comes from a state legis-

[6] *Ex parte Mitsuye Endo* (1944), 323 U. S. 283.

lature or governor for troops, the President himself make take note of the situation and send in troops to see that the national laws are enforced. President Cleveland did this in the Pullman strike in Chicago when he found that the carriage of the mails was being obstructed by strikers.[7] This use of the troops to enforce the ordinary federal laws is unusual, yet it seems that Cleveland was acting within his constitutional powers.

Power to Use Military Force Abroad in Time of Peace. When Congress at the end of 1945 debated the measure for making effective the United States' participation in the United Nations organization, great concern was expressed by a few members over the power of the President to use military forces abroad in the absence of a declaration of war by Congress. The correct rule seems to be that the President, both as the nation's executive head and as commander in chief, has the power and the duty to use the nation's military power to protect the best interests of the country, both at home and abroad. From the early years of the republic the Presidents used the navy and the marine corps, and sometimes units of the army, as a police force, to undertake "measures short of war," such as protecting American ships, men, and interests wherever their safety was threatened. Over a hundred years ago the American navy fought the pirates of Tripoli and Algiers and forcefully resisted French seizure of American vessels without a declaration of war. Later there were many naval actions in the Caribbean and Central American area. Japan was opened to American trade, and the Boxer rebellion in China (with its threat to American officials and civilians there) was resisted by force of arms. In these and many other cases no declaration of war was ever made. A declaration of war in any of these cases might have been a misfortune. The actions involved were limited in scope and of a protective nature, like the use of a police force, and were held down to a small scale partly because there was no declaration of war. In each case it was the President who was responsible, because it was under his constitutional authority that the action was taken.

The power of the President is, of course, limited by the forces that are available to him. It is at this point that Congress' power of control is revealed, because only Congress can decide the size and composition of the armed forces. Under the law passed in 1945 to make effective the United States' part in the United Nations organization this limitation upon the President is made clear. The United States, like every other participating nation, is to negotiate a special agreement with the Security Council as to the military forces and equipment to be made available to the Council, and the President is not to assign any more contingents to the Council than the agreement authorizes. This still leaves him as free as before, however, to use his powers as commander in chief and as the nation's executive to defend the nation's interests with all its armed forces.

Declaration of War. It is true, of course, that whenever in the past the President ordered the nation's military forces to protect American rights he

[7] Grover Cleveland, *Presidential Problems*, ch. II.

ran the risk of involving the nation in war. The action taken was, in all but a few instances, unilateral, i.e., it was an action of the United States alone to enforce American claims of right. In every such instance the other party to the dispute must have been somewhat tempted to resort to war in resisting the force that was applied. Resistance took place in a number of instances, but in very few cases was there a formally declared war.

The Constitution confers upon Congress, not upon the President, the power to declare war. There can be no formal declaration of war except by Congress. Does it follow that there cannot be war without Congressional approval? Not at all. The United States cannot control what other powers will do; if they declare war or attack without a declaration, there is a state of war. The unprovoked Pearl Harbor attack is only the latest example. In a number of important instances of actual warfare (the naval war with France, 1789-1800, the first and second Barbary wars, and the hostilities with Mexico, 1914-17) Congress did not recognize that a state of war existed.[8]

In five other conflicts (War of 1812, Mexican War of 1846-48, Spanish-American War, 1898, and World Wars I and II) the President recommended and Congress enacted resolutions recognizing the existence of a state of war. Congress has never declared war on its own initiative. This is another interesting example of the development of executive leadership in the formation of national policy. The importance of having a Congressional check upon the President in the making of war cannot easily be overestimated. At the same time good sense supports the idea that Congress should never declare war unless advised so to do by the nation's executive and commander in chief. He is certainly in the best position to know whether and when war is the only recourse for the nation.

Civil War Not Declared. The Civil War, or War between the States, was a unique occurrence. Without calling Congress into session President Lincoln instituted a number of warlike measures, including a naval blockade, against the southern states. In upholding the legality of the blockade in the famous "Prize Cases" the Supreme Court said:

> By the Constitution, Congress alone has the power to declare a national or foreign war. It cannot declare war against a State, or any number of States, by virtue of any clause in the Constitution. The Constitution confers on the President the whole executive power. He is bound to take care that the laws be faithfully executed. He is commander-in-chief of the army and navy of the United States, and of the militia of the several states when called into the actual service of the United States. He has no power to initiate or declare a war against a foreign nation or a domestic state. But by the Acts of Congress of February 28th, 1795, and 3rd of March, 1807, he is

[8] James Grafton Rogers, *World Policing and the Constitution*, World Peace Foundation, Boston, 1945, pp. 45-55.

authorized to call out the militia and use the military and naval forces of the United States in case of invasion by foreign nations, and to suppress insurrection against the government of a state or of the United States.

If a war be made by invasion of a foreign nation, the President is not only authorized but bound to resist force by force. He does not initiate the war, but is bound to accept the challenge without waiting for any special legislative authority. And whether the hostile party be a foreign invader, or states organized in rebellion, it is none the less a war, although the declaration of it be *"unilateral."* [9]

Scope of the National War Powers. Near the beginning of this chapter are printed the important specific powers relating to war that are granted to the national government by the United States Constitution. Read as separate items these do not seem to be very sweeping. It is only through the study of legislative and executive practice, the decisions of the Supreme Court, and the writings of constitutional lawyers and publicists, that the full stretch and reach of these powers can be visualized. They go far beyond the powers of military action that have been discussed above.

Many writers use the term "war power" or "war powers." The Constitution does not sanction this term but it is an appropriate one for denoting the totality of the powers available to the national government for defense and war purposes. In this sense not only the specific clauses previously mentioned but also every other power available to the nation—the commerce power, the postal power, and every other—may be adapted and utilized for war purposes. The list would include, also, the so-called "implied powers."

If the evidences from the Civil War and from World War I and World War II are any indication of the scope of these war powers within the country, the nation may under these powers tax to the very limit of the people's ability to pay; borrow almost without stint; conscript the services of all citizens and of others who owe any allegiance to the nation; take any land, buildings, equipment, machinery, patents, and goods that it needs, paying such compensation as its officers and courts deem just; suppress any business considered not useful to the war effort (e.g., liquor traffic, gold mining) and encourage others; shut off imports and forbid exports; ration goods and regulate prices and rents; restrict travel and transportation; apply security censorship in order to keep information from the enemy; and do all the other things needed in the judgment of the government to make the war effort a success. Externally the nation may acquire military bases, ships and supplies; engage in propaganda and espionage services; and do many other things to bring the full weight of the nation's military might to bear upon the enemy. What the military authorities in the field may do to destroy the enemy or to break his will to fight is a question that goes far beyond the constitutional issues that

[9] (1863), 2 Black 635.

we have in mind here. It does not follow that there are no limits upon the powers of the government. The essential civil liberties, as we have already noted, continue in time of war as well as in peace.[10] War brings greater tensions and more breaches of rights but it does not wipe out civil rights.

War Powers Not Confined to Wartime. Many persons seem to think that the war powers are confined to the period of actual hostilities after a formal declaration of war. Again the question is a broader one than that discussed above of the power of the President to use the existing army, navy, and militia in time of peace to repel invasion or to suppress domestic disorder. To illustrate the breadth of the question: May Congress provide for compulsory military service in time of peace? May it continue wartime rent and price regulations and the rationing of goods when the war is over? As we have already seen, the Constitution itself does not use the term "war power" or "war powers." The specific clauses of the Constitution, e.g., "to raise and support armies," and "to provide and maintain a navy," are not limited to wartime. It would indeed be absurd to say that the nation could not prepare for war until after war has begun. Congress and the President have wisely acted upon the assumption that the war powers exist at all times. The Supreme Court has lent support to this interpretation. In a decision following World War I the court upheld the "War-Time Prohibition Act" which was passed by Congress after the Armistice of November 11, 1918, was not to go into effect until June 30, 1919, and was to run not only until the legal end of the war but also thereafter until the termination of demobilization.[11] The Court quoted with approval the following statement from an earlier decision:

> The war power is not limited to victories in the field and the dispersion of the insurgent forces. It carries with it inherently the power to guard against the immediate renewal of the conflict, and to remedy the evils which have arisen from its rise and progress.[12]

It must be said, however, that the Court has not been entirely consistent. During and just after World War I national and state laws that provided for rent control were upheld as justified by the housing emergency.[13] Later, however, the Court declared that a law which depends upon an emergency will cease to have effect when the emergency ends, and that the Court must be the judge of these facts.[14] Here the judges gave weight not to the continuing powers involved but to the changing circumstances. This is a very dubious practice for the courts when they are deciding questions of constitutionality.

The Power to End War. The end of actual hostilities usually comes before the legal termination of the war. Congressional legislation for war purposes

---

[10] See ch. 20.

[11] Hamilton v. Kentucky Distilleries & Warehouse Co. (1919), 251 U. S. 146.

[12] Stewart v. Kahn (1871), 11 Wall. 493, 507.

[13] Block v. Hirsh (1921), 256 U. S. 135; Marcus Brown Holding Co. v. Feldman (1921), 256 U. S. 170; Levy Leasing Co. v. Siegel (1921), 258 U. S. 242.

[14] Chastleton Corporation v. Sinclair (1924), 264 U. S. 543.

usually contains clauses by which the laws will expire at the end of the war or a certain number of months thereafter if not earlier repealed. Such clauses refer to the legal end of the war, not to the cessation of fighting. The Constitution does not say how war may be legally terminated. If Congress may declare war it may presumably end a war, also. It did this in 1921 when a joint resolution approved by the President terminated World War I. The joint resolution procedure had become necessary because the President and the Senate had been unable to agree upon a treaty with Germany to end the war and the negotiation of a new treaty seemed to be impractical. Historically the treaty process has been the more common method.

It is not improbable that the President himself may terminate a war either by executive agreement with the other powers concerned or by a proclamation saying that, the objectives of the war having been achieved, and the wartime laws having been carried out, the war is declared at an end. This suggestion may be more academic than practical, however, since it is hard to conceive a situation in which Congress would not approve a President's recommendation that it terminate the war itself. Furthermore, under the arrangements for international security that are now taking shape, unilateral action by any nation in declaring or ending a war is less likely to occur and will be of little significance if it does take place.

Respective War Powers of President and Congress. President Lincoln and his advisers made extreme claims for the almost complete dominance of the President in the conduct of the Civil War.[15] The combination in the President's office of the executive power and the powers of commander in chief was considered sufficient to justify the President in declining to call Congress into session while the President alone began to raise troops and authorize the borrowing of money, ordered a blockade of the southern states, and took other actions. Later he also suspended the writ of habeas corpus and proclaimed the freedom of the slaves without benefit of Congressional authorization. In short the claims of power made by him and for him were that he could "in an emergency do things on military grounds which can not constitutionally be done by Congress."[16] The President's powers in wartime were held to be "without limit, because, if defending, the means of defence may be nearly illimitable, or, if acting offensively, his resources must be proportionate to the end in view—to conquer peace."[17]

These extreme claims to executive power do not stand up under examination. The war powers of the nation are nearly without limit, but the division of those powers between the President and Congress is as set forth in the Constitution. Congress is empowered not only to declare war and to raise men and money, but also to enact all the laws under which the war is to be

[15] Edward S. Corwin, *The President: Office and Powers*, pp. 155-66, and notes, pp. 382-86; William Whiting, *War Powers Under the Constitution*; J. G. Randall, *Constitutional Problems Under Lincoln*.

[16] Corwin, *op. cit.*, p. 382.

[17] Corwin, *op. cit.*, p. 163.

conducted. It is true that the tempo and the urgency of a great war are such that a slow-moving Congress cannot do everything in detail. It is necessary for it to delegate wide discretion to the President under "war powers" legislation. This was done in both World Wars, and in this way the essentials of constitutional government were retained without impairment of executive efficiency.

NATIONAL DEFENSE ORGANIZATION

In the several versions of his plan for a national constitution in 1787 Alexander Hamilton spoke of only three administrative departments, "finance, war, and foreign affairs." Evidently he had in mind a single department of war for the nation's defense. Other members of the Convention mentioned also a department of navy or admiralty. The convention itself approved separate clauses in the list of powers to be granted to Congress, one "to raise and support Armies" and the other "to provide and maintain a Navy." This wording did not require but it gave some support to the traditional idea of having separate departments for the land and sea forces. Nevertheless Hamilton's idea was carried out in 1789 when Congress created a single Department of War. In 1798 Congress established a separate Department of Navy, to which it transferred several functions previously handled by the War Department. Since that time the two departments have continued as separate agencies.

The War Department is headed by the Secretary of War, who is the second ranking member of the cabinet. He is responsible for administering the War Department and through it for organizing, training, and maintaining the army, for planning military expenditures, for procuring defense supplies, and for many other things connected with creating and using an efficient defense machine. The department under him is responsible, also, for rivers and harbors work, certain large flood control and power projects, the Panama Canal, the United States Military Academy at West Point, and other semimilitary or civilian functions. He is aided by an Under Secretary of War, an Assistant Secretary of War, an Assistant Secretary of War for Air, numerous other civilian assistants, and, on the military side, the Chief of Staff and supporting military advisers.

Army Staff and Line Organization. The National Defense Acts of 1916 and 1920 substantially reorganized and expanded the work of the War Department.[18] The latter act established a General Staff, consisting of selected army officers who had passed through various types of special training, and headed by the Chief of Staff, who is also chief military adviser to the Secretary of War. The Staff is responsible for research, for thinking, and for planning with respect to all matters of national defense, and it is also responsible for seeing to it that the plans approved by the Secretary of War (who, of course, consults the President) are carried out by the line organization. In the Staff there

---

[18] See John Dickinson, *The Building of an Army*, 1922.

are various divisions, each of which is charged with some branch of the work, such as personnel, military intelligence, organization and training, supply, and war plans. It must be understood that the Staff agencies do not do the work, but only plan the work, supervise it, and see that it is done. The Chief of Staff is the highest ranking officer in the army. All orders issue from him, so that there is unity of command within the army.

The line organization of the army underwent a substantial change in World War II. Among the new factors that had to be faced were the world-wide nature of the struggle and the correspondingly acute problem of supply, the tremendous scale of the forces involved, and the decision to make air power a major part of the army. Early in 1942, under authority of the President, the Secretary of War announced the grouping of all army forces within the United States under three heads: the Army Ground Forces, the Army Air Forces, and the Army Service Forces, each under a commanding general. The Army Service Forces became responsible for practically all the supply services, while the Air and Ground Forces, although unequal in size, were made administratively equal to each other. It was with this "streamlined" organization that the Army met the problems of the greatest and most desperate war ever faced by the nation.

Peacetime Organization of the Armed Forces. Under the terms of the National Defense Act, the fighting forces of the nation, other than the Navy and Marines, were divided before the recent war into three principal parts:

1. *The Regular Army.* The Regular Army is "the permanent military establishment, which is maintained both in peace and war." It consisted of the regular army officers who give full time to their service, and of a varying number of enlisted men and noncommissioned officers who were enlisted on a voluntary basis for periods of one to three years, at the option of the soldier, with reenlistment for periods of three years. Appropriation acts from time to time fixed the maximum size of the regular force of enlisted men, but the National Defense Act authorized up to 280,000 men, including the Philippine Scouts.

2. *National Guard and Militia Distinguished.* The National Guard constituted a second element in the available military forces. It may be defined roughly as the equipped, organized, and trained portion of the militia. The first section of the national law on the subject of the army provides that "all able-bodied male citizens and declarants between 18 and 45 years of age shall constitute the national forces, and shall be liable to perform military duty." [19] The state constitutions and statutes use much the same language in defining the militia of the states, so that the militia as a whole may be considered to include all such able-bodied men. Obviously, in the absence of compulsory, universal military service the militia as a whole is an unorganized, untrained mass of men. Usually, however, when people say "militia" they mean the

---

[19] U. S. *Code of Laws,* Title 10, ch. I, sec. 1.

National Guard. Enlistment in the Guard is voluntary, the amount of drill that is required in the course of the year is ordinarily not great, and usually only a few Guard officers and men give full time to their duties. The pay of the guardsmen is correspondingly small, and their military equipment is not nearly as elaborate and costly as that of the Regular Army. Each state provides for its own guard units and armories, and appoints its own adjutant general and other officers, but the pay of the Guard comes from the national government, the units are trained and drilled in conformity with the national regulations and to some extent by officers of the Regular Army, and a bureau of the War Department, the National Guard Bureau, supervises the training and equipment. The Guard is, furthermore, subject to call into the national service by the President in times of emergency, and by authorization of Congress the Guard was called to national duty late in 1940. At that time the guardsmen numbered about 210,000.

3. Reserves. The Reserve Forces constituted a third element in the army organization. The law provides for the commissioning of former army officers, national guard officers, graduates of reserve officers' training corps such as those that are in operation in a number of colleges and universities, and others, as officers in the Reserve Corps. These numbered about 120,000 in 1940 when many of them began to be called to service with various units.

The postwar pattern of the army organization has not yet been determined. The proposal to continue compulsory service and training in times of peace must first be decided as a matter of policy. If the nation decides against the compulsory plan, then the prewar pattern of organization is likely to be the basis for the postwar plan. It should be noted, however, that in both World Wars compulsory selective service was the method used for recruiting most of the ground forces.

Selective Service in World War II. In September, 1940, Congress for the first time in United States history enacted a peacetime military conscription law, the Selective Training and Service Act of 1940. Under it over 16 million men between 21 and 35 were registered that year. Later the draft age was lowered from 21 to 18, and men of over 35 were also registered. Late in 1940 the War Department began to call its first contingents. Inductions were speeded up after Pearl Harbor. Before the war ended the nation had enrolled and trained its greatest army of all time, mostly under Selective Service.

Articles of War and Courts-Martial. The Regular Army at all times, and the other units when called into active service, are governed by a special body of military law set forth in the statutes under the title of "Articles of War." These have been enacted by Congress in pursuance of its power to "make rules for the government and regulation of the land and naval forces." There are 121 of these "articles" or sections, dealing with the conduct and discipline of the troops, and providing punishments for fraudulent enlistment, desertion, absence without leave, disrespect toward superiors, insubordination, assault, mutiny, and various other offenses. The articles also provide for courts-martial, composed of officers who are to try offenders, and lay down a code of procedure for trials and appeals.

Department of Navy. The Department of the Navy was established as a separate department of national administration in 1798. It is headed by a Secretary of the Navy who has under him an Under Secretary of the Navy, an Assistant Secretary of the Navy, an Assistant Secretary of the Navy for Air, and a large number of office and division heads for shore establishments, engineering, civilian personnel, procurement, and other functions. For the operating functions there is a Chief of Naval Operations who is Commander in Chief (under the Secretary and the President) of the United States Fleet, while for all naval personnel, supplies, ships, ordnance, and related purposes there is a group of bureaus under separate chiefs.

It will be noted that, as in the case of the Army, the air force in the Navy has been given its own Assistant Secretary. The Marine Corps is an important element in the naval organization, and during the recent war the Coast Guard was also a part of the navy.

Separate women's organizations, WAC's and WAVE's, were parts of the army and navy, respectively, during World War II.

Co-ordination of Army and Navy. Numerous devices have been tried in recent decades to induce a natural and fruitful cooperation of army and navy, in the attempt to make them pull together as one team. The statutory Council of National Defense, which was set up in 1916, and of which both Secretaries are members, represents one such effort. There are also several joint army-navy boards, for aeronautics, for munitions, for welfare and recreation, and for general cooperation. Early in World War II President Roosevelt, as commander in chief also organized the Joint Chiefs of Staff for the comprehensive planning and co-ordination of all military operations. An admiral was the President's chief of staff. There were three other members: the chief of staff of the army, the chief of naval operations of the navy, and the commanding general of the Army Air Forces. In particular fields of operation, also, one officer was made head of all military elements—an admiral in one area, a general in another. The final success of the nation's military efforts was attributable in large part to the co-ordinated action of all available forces.

Why Not a Single Department? If co-ordination is so important in times of war, would it not be highly beneficial at all times? Both the late President Roosevelt and President Truman have recommended unification, or at least a much more effective method of co-ordination for the two departments. It stands out now very clearly that the debacle and defeat at Pearl Harbor were largely attributable to the failure of the Army and Navy to work closely together. The petty squabbles between the two, their competition for arms, munitions, and appropriations, their maintenance of duplicating army and navy posts, and numerous other evidences of wastefulness and inefficiency are also chargeable in part to their separateness and their jealousies.

In the era that lies ahead other considerations argue strongly for greater unification in the nation's defenses. The atomic bomb and other means of offense and defense call for a thorough reconsideration of the nation's entire war and defense policy. It is a single, complicated problem, and not several separate ones. Furthermore, the Security Council of the United Nations Organization will expect each nation to supply forces for a single united effort, not separate army and navy units that are unco-ordinated and uncooperative. And finally, the President, as commander in chief, as the officer responsible for the entire defense of the nation, and a man who must carry a terrific burden of other responsibilities, needs to have an integrated defense organization to advise him and to act for him in every national crisis. He should not have to make so many important decisions himself.

But while unification of the defense agencies is being discussed, the role of the State Department must not be neglected. There have been instances of War, Navy, and State Departments not pulling together in important external affairs.

What the new pattern of organization for external policy and defense will be cannot be predicted now. There has been a considerable "battle of the blueprints" before a Congressional committee, and more is yet to be said on the major issues. Some of the principal pieces in the puzzle that must be put together into a single working pattern are: Congress and its appropriate committees, the President, the Departments of State, War, and Navy, the land forces, the sea forces, and the air forces, the atomic bomb and further scientific advances in the art of war, the United Nations organization and the Security Council, conscription or voluntary military service, public opinion, and the capacity of a large democratic population to adopt and carry through a sane consistent policy of national defense.

REFERENCES

Clarence A. Berdahl, *War Powers of the Executive in the United States*, Urbana, Illinois, 1920.

James G. Randall, *Constitutional Problems Under Lincoln*, New York, 1926.

Grover Cleveland, *Presidential Problems*, New York, 1904, ch. II, "The Government in the Chicago Strike of 1894."

John Dickinson, *The Building of an Army*, New York, 1922.

U. S. *Code of Laws*, Titles 5 (Executive Departments), 10 (Army) and 34 (Navy).

U. S. Secretary of War, *Annual Reports*.

U. S. Secretary of the Navy, *Annual Reports*.

U. S. *Government Manual*, First Ed. of 1945 and later editions.

U. S. War Department, A *Manual for Courts-Martial*, U. S. Army, Washington, D. C., 1927.

U. S. War Department, *The Work of the War Department of the United States*, Washington, D. C., 1924.

Pendleton Herring, *The Impact of War*, New York, 1941.

Basic Military Training: A Textbook for the R.O.T.C. Basic Course, 10th ed., Washington, D. C., 1931.

The R.O.T.C. Manual: Infantry, 14th ed., vol. IV, Washington, D. C., 1931.

Robert P. Erdman (ed.), *Reserve Officers' Manual: United States Navy*, Washington, D. C., 1932.

Lloyd M. Short, *The Development of National Administrative Organization in the United States*, Baltimore, 1923, chs. II, III, V, VII.

W. F. Willoughby, *The Reorganization of the Administrative Branch of the National Government*, Baltimore, 1923, ch. VIII.

Harold S. Quigley (ed.), *Peace or War? A Conference at the University of Minnesota*, April 7-9, 1937, Minneapolis, 1937.

Charles A. Beard, *The Navy: Defense or Portent?*, New York, 1932.

Silas B. McKinley, *Democracy and Military Power*, New York, 1934.

Carl Brent Swisher, "The Control of War Preparations in the United States," *Am. Pol. Sci. Rev.*, vol. 34, pp. 1085-1103 (1940).

Edward S. Corwin, *The President: Office and Powers*, New York, 1940.

James Grafton Rogers, *World Policing and the Constitution*, Boston, World Peace Foundation, 1945.

Somervell, Brehon, and others, *Administrative Management in the Army Service Forces*, Public Administration Service, Chicago, 1944.

Forrestal, James, and others, *The Navy: A Study in Administration*, Public Administration Service, Chicago, 1946.

CHAPTER 24

Territories, Special Districts, and Dependencies

TERRITORIES AND OTHER DEPENDENCIES

In the course of less than two centuries, the American people have passed through all the stages from separate colonial dependency to that of a strong imperial power. First there were the 13 English colonies in America, then 13 revolting colonies that became states, then the union of these states into the United States, and finally the rise of the United States to the position of a world power with colonies and dependencies under its own control. The people of the United States in their brief history have seen the colonial problem first as colonists and later as the acquirers and rulers of colonies. The next stage may well be that of cooperation with other nations in the administration of colonies through the Trusteeship Council of the United Nations organization (UN). This arrangement may be especially suitable for the supervision of islands in the Pacific from which the Japanese were driven in World War II.

The history of American acquisition of territories may be sketched as follows: First came the continental expansion with the annexation of contiguous lands only, until the Pacific Coast had been reached and the north and south extension of American territory was from 1,000 to 1,500 miles. The large acquisitions that made possible this great expansion began with the Treaty of Peace of 1783, and ended with the Gadsden Purchase of 1853, which established the southern boundary of Arizona and New Mexico. Next came the noncontiguous annexations on the continent of North America, including the purchase of Alaska from Russia in 1867, and the acquisition of the Panama Canal Zone from the recently established Republic of Panama in 1904. The Canal Zone is a strip of land from sea to sea, only ten miles wide with ports at each end, and a total area of about 550 square miles. Alaska is a thousand times as large—586,000 square miles. Then there were the acquisitions of the island possessions, from the Philippines in the Far East to Puerto Rico and the Virgin Islands in the Caribbean Sea. These, taken in chronological order, are Hawaii in 1898; the Philippines and Puerto Rico following the war with Spain in 1899; Guam in 1899; American Samoa in 1900; and the Virgin Islands by purchase from Denmark in 1917. To these must be added some scattered small islands here and there of no great importance. Of the insular possessions, the Philippines are largest (114,000 square miles in all); Hawaii with 6,400 square miles, and Puerto Rico with 3,435, are next in size. Guam, Samoa, and the Virgin Islands are very small; together they would not equal an average American county. Their importance is military or naval, as far as the United States is concerned. The status of the recently acquired air and naval bases in the Atlantic from Iceland and Greenland south, and that of the islands conquered from Japan in the Pacific, is yet to be decided.

The total area of the continental United States is over 3,000,000 square miles, that of the outlying possessions is over 700,000, mostly in Alaska and the Philippines (the latter to be independent in 1946). In population (1940) the continental United States outranked all the possessions by 132,000,000 to 19,000,000. Most of the latter figure was made up by the population of the Philippines (over 16,000,000) and Puerto Rico (1,869,000). Hawaii had 423,000 and Alaska about 73,000 inhabitants.

The Western Lands. Before the framing of the national Constitution the only territorial problem was that of the lands west of the Alleghenies, to which different states still had somewhat conflicting claims. The Articles of Confederation did not directly provide for the government of this western territory. The Maryland legislature refused to ratify the Articles until reasonable assurances had been given that the western land claims of the several states would be turned over to Congress. The purpose behind this insistence was not only to avoid territorial disputes later, but even more to prevent the states with western lands from growing to a size out of all proportion to states like Maryland.

Congress resolved in 1780 that any such lands as might be "ceded or relinquished to the United States, by any particular state," should be "disposed of for the common benefit of the United States, and be settled and formed into distinct republican states, which shall become members of the federal union. . . ." [1] This resolution set the policy to be followed in later years. Despite the deficiencies of the Articles there seems to have been no serious question as to the power of Congress to acquire lands, govern them, and erect them later into states. Neither did the negotiators of the Treaty of Peace seem to have any doubt as to the power of the United States to acquire by treaty as much land as they could get the British to cede.

Plans for Territorial Government and Statehood. The Congress of the Confederation in its closing days provided regulations for the settlement and government of the western lands. In the resolution of 1780 the general policy of giving ultimate statehood to settlements in the West was foreshadowed. In

[1] See Commager, *Documents of American History*, pp. 119-20.

1784 Congress adopted another resolution, drafted by Jefferson, providing a scheme for territorial and later state governments in the area. In 1787 Congress adopted the famous Ordinance of 1787, or Northwest Ordinance, applicable to the territory north of the Ohio and east of the Mississippi River.[2] This provided an initial and temporary form of government for the area under a governor, a secretary, and judges appointed by Congress, to be followed, "so soon as there shall be five thousand free male inhabitants of full age in the district," by a more fully organized territorial government with an elective legislative body; and the latter in turn was to give way when states should be formed and admitted to the Union.

The Constitution and National Territories. Before the provisions of the Northwest Ordinance were carried out, the new Constitution of the United States had been adopted. It was thus left to the national government under the Constitution to work out more fully the territorial policy. The Constitution provided that "The Congress shall have Power to dispose of and make all needful Rules and Regulations respecting the Territory or other Property belonging to the United States; and nothing in this Constitution shall be so construed as to Prejudice any Claims of the United States, or of any particular State."[3]

Jefferson and Acquisition of Louisiana. Despite the fact that by the Treaty of Peace of 1783 the United States had acquired territory extending to the Mississippi, under Articles of Confederation that made no provision for the acquisition of territory, on the first occasion when the question of acquiring territory and incorporating it into the United States arose under the Constitution, doubts were raised as to the power of the nation to do so. The occasion arose in 1803 when Napoleon offered to sell the Louisiana territory to the United States at what now seems like a ridiculously low price, $15,000,000. Jefferson was President. He recognized that the people would strongly favor the purchase, and that it would solve certain troublesome questions concerning the opening up and defense of the western country. Nevertheless he had grave doubts as to the power to make the purchase, and he wanted a constitutional amendment adopted to make it legal. His actions were more practical. With the approval of Congress, the purchase was promptly made. Under later Presidents, acquisitions have been made without question.

National Power over External Affairs. If a source for the power be needed, the doctrine previously discussed as to the power of the United States in external affairs should suffice. This power, the Supreme Court has said in substance, depends not on the Constitution but upon the status of the United States as a sovereign power among the nations. Twenty-five years after the Louisiana purchase, Marshall stated that "The Constitution confers absolutely on the government of the Union the powers of making war and of making

---

[2] See Commager, *op. cit.*, pp. 121-23, 128-32, for these two documents.
[3] U. S. Const., Art. IV, sec. 3, par. 2.

treaties; consequently, that government possesses the power of acquiring territory, either by conquest or by treaty." [4] But in international law territory may also be acquired by discovery and occupation. Did Marshall mean to say that only by war or treaty could the United States acquire territory? Probably not, and certainly Congress has not acted upon that assumption, for in the Guano Island act passed in 1856 it provided a means whereby, if an American citizen discovers and occupies such an island not claimed by any other government, it may "at the discretion of the President, be considered as appertaining to the United States." [5] It goes without argument that the power to acquire territory is wholly national, and cannot be exercised by the states.

Power to Govern Territories. The power to govern territories is also exclusively national. The express constitutional provision on this subject gives Congress the authority to provide for territorial government, but this relates mainly to the more or less final and permanent arrangements that can be established and carried out peacefully. Before this power can be exercised the President as commander in chief has the authority to govern conquered territory temporarily, and as general executive of the government he probably has power to govern temporarily any ceded territory, or any territory discovered and occupied in the name of the United States.

Status of Territories. A more difficult question arises concerning the legal status of territory. It appears that conquered territory, prior to annexation, or territory that is merely occupied by American forces, is not a part of the United States in any constitutional sense, although internationally it must be recognized by other powers as belonging to the United States. During the period of occupation the United States tariff laws still apply against occupied territory, since the latter is still in a constitutional sense foreign territory. When annexation takes place, does it make the territory really a *part of* the United States, or does it merely cause it to *belong to* the United States? The Constitution was established "*for* the United States" but not necessarily, in all its parts, for territories that merely belong to the United States. As long as the United States possessed only such contiguous territory on the continent as was clearly destined for statehood, the territory was considered to be really a part of the United States, and the entire Constitution was held to apply to it. But if territories are annexed that are remote, and are populated by a wholly different people, so that they are not likely to become states, there is less reason why the whole Constitution should apply to them.

Incorporated and Unincorporated Territory. In the treaty of 1803 by which the United States acquired Louisiana, the following words were used:

> The inhabitants of the ceded territory shall be incorporated in the Union of the United States, and admitted as soon as possible, accord-

[4] American Insurance Co. v. Canter (1828), 1 Peters (U. S.) 511.
[5] U. S. Code of Laws, Title 48, ch. 8, sec. 1411.

ing to the principles of the Federal Constitution, to the enjoyment of all the rights, advantages, and immunities of citizens of the United States; . . .[6]

This idea of a people being "incorporated" into or made part of the body of the United States gave the courts a clue when questions arose a century later concerning the annexation of Puerto Rico, the Philippines, and other territories. The courts found that a distinction can be made, broadly, between *incorporated* and *unincorporated* territories, and that the treaties of acquisition and the acts of Congress provided the clues as to whether a particular territory belonged in one or the other category. If a territory is incorporated, all parts of the Constitution and all the laws and treaties of the United States apply fully to it. If it is not incorporated, Congress may decide which parts of the Constitution, and which laws and treaties, shall apply. When a territory is incorporated, its people can ship goods into the United States without paying duty, they can migrate to the continental United States without being stopped by immigration laws, and they stand in practically every other way, except that of representation in Congress and the right to vote, on the same footing as the people in the states. Citizenship is also usually conferred on them, but the conferment of citizenship upon part or all of its people does not prove that a territory has been incorporated.

Alaska and Hawaii as Incorporated Territories. The two territories that are today definitely incorporated into the United States are Alaska and Hawaii. As to both of them Congress has enacted, though in slightly different words, that "the Constitution of the United States, and all the laws thereof which are not locally inapplicable, shall have the same force and effect within the said territory as elsewhere in the United States."[7] The comparable provision as to Puerto Rico omits mention of the Constitution and has a somewhat different expression concerning the laws, whereas the laws governing the Philippines (up to 1934) and other possessions make it clear that only a part of the laws of the United States apply to them. In the acts governing Puerto Rico and the Philippines, there are special bills of rights, in which grand jury proceedings and the right of jury trial are omitted, among others, whereas the federal bill of rights applies fully to Alaska and Hawaii.

Government of the Organized Territories. The territories of Alaska, Hawaii, Puerto Rico, and the Virgin Islands have more or less fully organized governments in which the people of the territory play some part. The written constitution of each of the aforementioned organized territories consists of the acts of Congress that provide for its government. These include the basic "organic law" of the territory and subsequent laws as well.[8] These are subject

---

[6] See Commager, op. cit., pp. 190-91.

[7] U. S. Code of Laws, Title 48, sec. 23, 495.

[8] See generally U. S. Code of Laws, Title 48, ch. 2, Alaska; ch. 3, Hawaii; ch. 4, Puerto Rico; ch. 5, the Philippine Islands; ch. 7, the Virgin Islands. The Philippines will be discussed later.

to change only by Congress. In the two incorporated territories (Alaska and Hawaii), and also in Puerto Rico and the Virgin Islands, there are appointed governors, elected legislative bodies, and appointed judges, and the main elements of a system of separation of powers and checks and balances.

Territorial Governors. The executive organization in the organized territories reflects most fully the differences between the incorporated and unincorporated territories. All governors are appointed by the President with the consent of the Senate. The governors of Alaska and Hawaii are appointed for definite four-year terms. They have the veto power over the acts of the legislature, including the item-veto on appropriations, but their vetoes may be overridden by a two-thirds vote, and acts so passed are law. It is true that Congress reserves the right to annul any act of any territorial legislature, but in Hawaii and Alaska there is almost complete legislative autonomy under the Constitution and the acts of Congress. In addition, the governor of Hawaii must be a local resident at the time of appointment. In the unincorporated territories, on the other hand, the governor is appointed to serve during the pleasure of the President, and his veto power is such that any measure passed over his veto which he still thinks should not become law he may submit to the President with his reasons, and if the President backs him up, the measure cannot become law. The governor is both the chief representative of the United States in the territory and the executive for the enforcement of territorial laws. It is rather interesting to note that in most of the territories the governor is given the power, on his own initiative, to declare martial law, to suspend the writ of habeas corpus, and to use the military forces to suppress insurrection or other serious disorder, but that he must notify the President as to what he has done and abide by his decision if the latter overrules him.

Territorial Legislatures. There are locally elected legislative bodies in all the organized territories, and these are bicameral in all except the Virgin Islands. The latter are divided into two "municipalities," each of which has its "municipal council" with powers of local ordinance making. The council in one consists of nine elected members, and in the other of seven, and these two are called together at least once each year by the governor to act as the legislature for the islands as a whole. In the other territories the size of the legislative bodies corresponds roughly to the population to be governed: Alaska with the smallest population has 8 and 16 members in the two houses, while Puerto Rico, most populous of the four, has 19 and 39, respectively. Note that the bicameral arrangement has been applied in the territories in imitation of that in the states. The right to vote for members is given generally to those adult male residents who do not owe allegiance to any country other than the United States, and who have resided in the territory for a year. There are no property tests or other special qualifications. Elections are biennial. Sessions are also biennial in most cases, and, as in the states, are generally limited in length. Pay is on the per diem basis.

Legislative Powers of Territories. The legislative power is stated in the laws governing the particular territory. In general the power to legislate is stated in broad terms: it "shall extend to all rightful subjects of legislation not inconsistent with the Constitution and laws of the United States; . . ." (Alaska, Hawaii); or "All local legislative powers in Puerto Rico . . . shall be vested in a legislature. . . ." [9] It must be understood, however, that the legislation by Congress controls that of the territories, and that this legislation is very extensive in some cases, notably in the case of Alaska. Furthermore, in most instances there is a provision that the laws enacted must be laid before Congress, which reserves the right to repeal them by legislation of its own.

Financial Powers. Congress has seen fit, also, to limit the territories in financial matters. They are authorized to borrow money, and to authorize municipalities within their limits to do so also, but the amounts of indebtedness are limited in the organic acts to a certain percentage of the taxable valuation. Furthermore, the territorial legislatures are not permitted to cut off the appropriations for the executive department, the courts, and the ordinary governmental services. The laws provide that in case of failure of the territorial legislature to make appropriations, the executive branch may continue to spend at the rates set in the previous appropriation act. If the legislatures attempt to make any extraordinary appropriations, the governor may exercise his item-veto, as noted above. The territorial organic acts also provide usually for the office of auditor, and give the auditor rather extensive powers to investigate expenditures, and to disallow such as he considers excessive or illegal. This officer, like the governor, is usually appointed by the President with the consent of the Senate.

Delegates to Congress and Resident Commissioners. The incorporated territories, Alaska and Hawaii, are permitted to elect, by popular vote, one Delegate each to sit in the lower house of Congress and there to participate in the proceedings but not to vote. The similar representatives from the unincorporated territories, Puerto Rico and the Philippines, are called Resident Commissioners, and they are also permitted to have seats and to speak in the House of Representatives.

Territorial Courts. Each territory has a judicial system to perform the functions of both state and federal courts. In Alaska these have been combined into one court system. In Hawaii and Puerto Rico there are two systems, the territorial courts properly so-called, and the federal district court. The judges of the higher courts in the territories are appointed by the President with the advice and consent of the United States Senate.

The So-called Unorganized Territories. The Canal Zone, Guam, Samoa, and lesser islands and areas are governed in a manner quite different from that which prevails in the organized territories. By authority of Congress, the Canal Zone is governed by the President through a governor and other officers appointed by the President with the consent of the Senate. There is no elected or representative body. In practice an army officer is made governor,

[9] U. S. Code of Laws, Title 48, secs. 77, 562, 811; and see also sec. 821.

and the War Department thus keeps supervision of the area. The islands of Guam and Samoa fall similarly under the Department of the Navy, and are governed by naval officers stationed there. These are sometimes said to have "Presidential government" as distinct from "Congressional government" in the organized territories.

Protectorates. For reasons of national defense and the maintenance of peace and order in the Caribbean Sea, the national government has assumed certain limited powers of protection over Cuba, Haiti, and Santo Domingo. These are in no sense territories of the United States, but rather protectorates. They have their own standing in international affairs as independent powers, but for certain purposes accept American protection and occasional or limited intervention in their affairs.

Central Supervision of Territories. Through administrative reorganizations effected since 1939, three departments in Washington now have important powers with respect to territories and dependencies. The Department of the Interior through its Division of Territories and Island Possessions has chief responsibility for supervising the administration of the four territories organized under acts of Congress, while the Navy Department through its Office of Island Governments is concerned with places like Guam and Samoa whose populations are very small and whose interest to the American government is primarily strategic or defensive, and the War Department has a similar responsibility for the Panama Canal Zone and for like reasons. The new air and navy bases also fall under the War and Navy Departments for supervision.

Philippine Independence Act. In the case of the Philippines, independence is already authorized and is on the way to being achieved. By acts passed in 1933 and 1934, after years of agitation and a number of adverse reports, Congress authorized the Philippines to take steps that would lead to their independence. The first of these, forced through Congress and passed over President Hoover's veto, was rejected by the Filipinos. Although the act offered independence, its real motivation was entirely different. Large amounts of Filipino products such as cocoanut oil and sugar had been coming into this country to be sold in competition with products raised here. Farming interests, seeking to make the tariff effective, and trying to cut off all importations of foreign farm products as completely as possible, were the real instigators of the legislation, and they attached clauses to the independence act that were bound to hurt Philippine trade seriously even during the ten-year transition period. When the Filipinos rejected this first act, another was passed in almost the same terms, but this was accepted.[10]

In conformity with the provisions of this act, a constitutional convention was elected by the Philippine voters, and a constitution was drawn up which was then submitted to and approved by President Roosevelt. The Filipino voters gave the constitution their approval, an election was then held to

[10] Act of March 24, 1934, *Statutes at Large*, vol. 48, p. 456.

choose the first officers of the new government, and on November 14, 1935, the President signed in Washington a proclamation establishing the freedom of the Philippines, while at the same time in Manila the first President of the Philippine Republic took his oath of office.

Ten-Year Period of Partial Independence. Under the terms of the act authorizing independence, the sovereignty of the United States is to be withdrawn, July 4, 1946, a little over ten years after the establishment of the republican government. During this period the Filipinos continued to owe allegiance to the United States, and their officers took oaths recognizing American sovereignty. The United States continued to control Philippine foreign relations; and all acts creating new government loans, or affecting the currency, coinage, imports, exports, and immigration, as well as all amendments to the Philippine constitution, were to be submitted to the President for his approval. Also during this ten-year period the United States government might intervene to preserve the government and to protect life and property. Immigration from the Philippines to the United States practically ceased, since a quota of only 50 a year was established by the Independence Act, while trade was throttled to a very considerable extent by provisions of the act imposing import duties on sugar, cocoanut oil, and cordage and fibers, and by additional clauses requiring that export duties be levied by the Philippines on goods that were admitted into the United States free of duty. The funds obtained from these export taxes were to be used to retire the Philippine debt.

Pending the establishment of complete independence in 1946, the President appointed a United States High Commissioner who was to represent the United States and see to it that the provisions of the Independence Act are observed. The Philippines sent in return a Resident Commissioner to the United States, who was entitled to a seat in the House of Representatives with the right to speak but not to vote. He was to be recognized by all departments of the national government as the official representative of the Philippine government.

The short-lived Japanese conquest of the Philippines (1942-45) wrought great destruction in the islands and set back the development of complete self-government by the people. The legal status from the United States viewpoint did not change, however, and Congress reasserted its intention to promote the full independence of the Philippines. At the same time it reserved the right to establish defense bases there. In the meantime (1945-46) an American high commissioner was installed until independence was established. In April, 1946, the people of the Philippines elected a new President and Congress, and by the time this book is published complete independence and self-government should have been achieved.

SPECIAL JURISDICTIONS WITHIN THE UNITED STATES

Up to this point certain areas outside the United States proper over which the national government has control have been considered. Within the country, too, there are certain areas and people over which the national government has rather special powers. These are (a) the Indians, (b) certain purchased and ceded areas, and (c) the District of Columbia. Over all these there is direct government by the nation as a whole.

Early Policy Toward Indians. The British theory about the Indian lands was that by discovery, occupation, and conquest the land in these parts of America belonged to the British Crown. The native population had certain special rights of occupancy and possession, but not the legal title to the land. To make room for English settlers, the Indians could be driven back, but it was best to make treaties with them and thus extinguish their rights to the land. Thus began the policy of making treaties with the Indian tribes and of considering them as separate treaty-making powers. Unfortunately for their sake, the Indians were not so organized governmentally that they could properly make or enforce treaties. Another difficulty arose early in the negotiations because the British government did not keep centralized control of Indian affairs. Each colony had its own relations with the Indians, to a certain extent, and there was no uniformity of policy. As a result of this experience, the British government proclaimed in 1763 that trade with the Indians was to be open only to those who procured a license from the Crown, and that all other matters of Indian relations were also to be controlled by the Crown.[11] This policy of a centralized control of Indian affairs was one that was destined to continue.

Under the Articles of Confederation, Congress received the "sole and exclusive right and power of . . . regulating the trade and managing all affairs with the Indians, not members of any of the states, provided that the legislative right of any state within its own limits be not infringed or violated."[12] Congress was thus in a position to make treaties with the Indain tribes in the West just as it made treaties with European powers to the east. In the Constitutional Convention, Madison proposed that the new Congress should have power "to regulate affairs with the Indians as well within as without the limits of the United States." The provision actually adopted says merely that "The Congress shall have Power . . . to regulate Commerce . . . with the Indian tribes; . . ."[13] This provision is a part of the general commerce clause. What does it mean?

National Policy as to Indian Trade. Congress early adopted the method of direct trade by the government with the Indians. This was to eliminate the evils of private trading, with its bad effects on Indian relations, resulting from

[11] See Commager, op. cit., pp. 47-50.
[12] Articles of Confederation, Art. IX, par. 4.
[13] U. S. Const., Art. I, sec. 8, par. 3.

cheating, the sale of liquor and firearms, and all the other concomitants of private trade for profit between the clever "civilized" person and the more ignorant and simple-minded barbarian that the Indian then was. The office set up to control all trade with the Indians broke down under the pressure of private trading interests and was abolished. Later the Bureau of Indian Affairs was established, but without much more success. The westward-moving settlers wanted the Indians pushed farther to the west while the fur traders preferred to keep out the white settlers in order to keep alive the fur trade. In this clash of interests the settlers won, while the Indians steadily lost. All the time treaties were being made by the President and Senate with one tribe and then another to clear off Indian claims to the lands, and to assure them of secure reservations further west; but these treaties could not be kept on either side. In desperation the Indian often saw but one thing to do, and that was to fight back. As a result there was an almost continuous succession of wars with the Indians, with the federal troops usually victorious. The number of Indians constantly dwindled—from an estimated 3,000,000 at one time to a low figure of around 300,000. War, disease, liquor, and forced changes in the mode of life all took their toll of the Indians. In recent years numbers have increased again, so that in 1940 the Office of Indian Affairs reported 361,000 Indians under its jurisdiction.

Guardianship over Indians. When the Indians ceased to be a menace to the spread of the white settlers, a feeling arose that they had been treated rather shabbily and that it was incumbent on the American nation to accord to them some measure of justice, and to make it possible for the Indians to adjust themselves to the civilization that had grown up all around them. A theory had been developing in the law that the national government was the guardian of the Indians, and that it had a special and exclusive responsibility for protecting them from further violations of their rights. Even before the Civil War legislation had been enacted dealing with crimes by the Indians and giving them the protection of the federal courts. In 1871 Congress passed a law providing that no further treaties should be made with the Indians, but that treaties previously made and ratified should not be affected by this decision. Thereafter Congress enacted more and more legislation to give protection to the Indians and to carry out the idea that the national government was their guardian. Under this policy most Indians were drawn together into special areas called "reservations," and legislation was passed forbidding the sale of liquor to them and regulating all trade and intercourse with them. Indian agents, appointed by the national government and under the supervision of the Office of Indian Affairs in the Department of the Interior were assigned to these reservations to enforce the new policy. Schools were set up for the Indian children. From the sales of Indian lands and the timber, oil, and other products found on them, trust funds were established under the government, from which annuities are paid to the members of the tribes concerned. The lands on the reservations are held by the government in trust for the Indians, and severe penalties are provided for those who are caught trespassing upon these lands or taking timber and other valuable things from them. The Indians are not allowed to dispose of the reservations, but in some cases in recent decades the government has made individual allotments to families that seemed prepared to go forward on their own initiative and ability, to make a living as farmers or in other ways. Thus some reservations have been in fact broken up. Nevertheless, in 1930 there were separate Indian reservations of more than 100 square miles total area in 14 states, and the total area of all reservations was about 80,000 square miles in 1935. Today there are 21 states with over 1,000 Indians each, the largest populations being in Oklahoma (103,000), Arizona (50,000), New Mexico (37,000), South Dakota (28,000) and California (23,000). Since the passage of the Indian Reorganization Act in 1934, the Indian tribes have become largely self-governing in internal affairs and have taken an active part in the economic and social advancement of their people.

Exclusive National Power over Indians. Thus at the present time the government is engaged in a large-scale program of supervising, educating, regulating, and administering the economic affairs of over 360,000 Indians on a total land area that would make a large state. Where they so desire and where they show the capacity to do so, the Indian tribes are permitted to retain their own organization and to enforce their own laws on the reservations to a considerable extent. Over them stands, however, the national government which, within the areas of the reservations, has almost exclusive powers of government. The sale of liquor is forbidden, whatever may be the law of the surrounding state. Crimes on the reservation are regulated by national and not by state law. The regulation of trade on the reservations and the provision of such services as education, poor relief, health, and public works are handled by the national government's officials. Indeed, the states do not want the burden of supporting and caring for the Indians.

Source of This Power. From what source does the national government get this power to control completely and exclusively the affairs of the Indians? The Constitution speaks only of "commerce" with the Indians, and "commerce" is sometimes given a rather limited meaning. In its consideration of the question the Supreme Court has upheld the power but it has not been able to give a wholly consistent explanation of its conclusions. (1) The section concerning commerce with the Indians is clearly not enough. (2) The fact that the Indian tribes had been considered from the first as nations, "domestic, dependent nations," with whom treaties could be made, and that these treaties needed to be enforced and could be enforced only by additional national legislation, has also been suggested. As in the case of external affairs, the power of the national government with respect to the Indians might be said, therefore, not to depend on the words of the Constitution, but on the necessities of the case after a whole web of treaty relations had been woven about the Indians.

The power of the general government over these remnants of a race once powerful, now weak and diminished in numbers, is necessary to their protection, as well as to the safety of those among whom they dwell. It must exist in that government, because it never has existed anywhere else, because the theatre of its exercise is within the geographical limits of the United States, because it has never been denied, and because it alone can enforce its laws on all the tribes.[14]

(3) In the same decision this power is also placed on the basis of "wardship," the national government being the guardian.

These Indian tribes *are* the wards of the nation. They are communities *dependent* on the United States; dependent largely for their daily food. Dependent for their political rights. They owe no allegiance to the states, and receive from them no protection. Because of the local ill feeling, the people of the states where they are found are often their deadliest enemies. From their very weakness and helplessness, so largely due to the course of dealing of the federal government with them and the treaties in which it has been promised, there arises the duty of protection, and with it the power.[15]

Purchased and Ceded Areas in States. The national Congress also has power "To exercise exclusive Legislation in all Cases whatsoever, . . . over all Places purchased by the Consent of the Legislature of the State in which the Same shall be, for the Erection of Forts, Magazines, Arsenals, dock-Yards, and other needful Buildings; . . ."[16] This is an express authority that is of considerable importance. Not only purchased areas, but also lands reserved by the nation for forts and other functions from the original public domain fall under exclusive national control. The law that is to prevail in these areas, of which there are now hundreds, is only such as Congress enacts, or as it adopts from the laws of the surrounding state. Crimes that occur in such areas are triable only in the federal courts, and actions concerning real estate therein are likewise assigned to the federal courts. The states are usually permitted to send in officers of their courts to serve legal processes or papers, in order that the federal areas may not become sanctuaries for criminals, and they may now tax private property within such places, but even these rights are subject to Congressional control. The central idea is that the power of Congress over these areas is exclusive, and the states may not tax or exercise police power or eminent domain in such places without express Congressional consent.

How many of these areas there are, or how extensive, it would be hard to say. Several years ago it was pointed out that the national government main-

[14] U. S. v. Kagama (1886), 118 U. S. 375.
[15] U. S. v. Kagama (1886), 118 U. S. 375. Cf. U. S. v. Sandoval (1913), 231 U. S. 28.
[16] U. S. Const., Art. I, sec. 8, par. 17.

tains military or naval stations in every state but one, and that it has many other properties such as prisons, power sites, the United States military and naval academies, hospitals, asylums, and other institutions.[17] The recent war production program greatly increased the numbers of such places. On these ceded areas reside many thousands of civilians, as well as the official personnel, and in several places the national government has itself been compelled to provide for institutions of local government, as at Norris and Boulder Dams.

THE DISTRICT OF COLUMBIA

The National Capital. The most important of all these ceded places within the states is the seat of the national government, the District of Columbia. On this the Constitution provides that Congress shall have power "To exercise exclusive Legislation in all Cases whatsoever, over such district (not exceeding ten Miles square) as may, by Cession of particular States and the acceptance of Congress, become the Seat of the Government of the United States. . . ." [18] The site selected by Washington lies on the Potomac River at the head of navigation. The original cessions were made by Maryland and Virginia, and the area was at that time a square with its four corners turned to the points of the compass. Then the city was laid out on the Maryland side of the river, and the principal growth began there, so that the area on the Virginia side of the river seemed to be unnecessary, and was returned to Virginia, leaving an area of about 64 square miles. Within this area the population had increased to 663,000 by 1940, and it is today probably well beyond that mark.

The importance of having the national capital under the exclusive control of the national government, and not subject to any state, can hardly be questioned. Furthermore, a capital that is somewhat removed from the greatest cities of the country, the centers of wealth and population, is less likely to be swayed by waves of temporary opinion and more easy to defend against uprisings such as those that have originated in great cities like Paris.

Legal Status. The district is not a state in the Union, although it has a body of laws such as every state has relating to property rights, marriage and divorce, civil and ciriminal law, and business matters. Congress has treated it as a state for some purposes, but not for others, and it has no representation in Congress. It is not a county, although again the ordinary county functions with respect to courts, land registration, tax collection, and law enforcement have to be carried on within it. It is not merely a city, either, although it is declared to be a municipal corporation, and it has all the problems of a city with respect to streets, water supply, parks, and other urban services. In short, it is a peculiar entity, that is *functionally* a state, a county, and a city, all

[17] *Yale Law Journal*, vol. 37, p. 796; Field, *A Selection of Cases and Authorities on Constitutional Law*, 1st ed., 1930, pp. 552-58.
[18] U. S. Const., Art. I, sec. 8, par. 17.

rolled into one, while *legally* it is a mere creature of the national government, and closely intermeshed with its various branches.

Congress Legislates for the District. From the beginning Congress has enacted the controlling legislation for the district, but between 1801 and 1878 the people of the district had some powers of self-government under various forms of organization. Extravagance and other difficulties led Congress to wipe out local self-government, and since 1878 the people have been without the vote even in local matters.

Congress today passes laws for the district such as a state legislature would pass for a state, and also passes some statutes that are little more than local ordinances, such as a city council would enact. There are special committees in both houses for district business. Codes of the laws enacted for the district have been compiled unofficially, but the *Statutes at Large* are still the most authoritative place in which to find them. Congressional legislation for the district is, of course, subject to veto by the President like other legislation. The same holds true of the District of Columbia appropriation bills, also enacted by Congress.

Administrative Organization. Actual administration is carried on mainly by three commissioners, appointed by the President with the consent of the Senate, and a number of other officers and boards similarly appointed. The work is divided among these commissioners roughly in this way: One deals with finances, law, poor relief, and general business matters; another handles police, fire, health, and various other services; while the third one is primarily responsible for engineering matters and public works, such as streets, water distribution, school buildings, and so on. There are also certain more or less independent boards, such as those for schools, public libraries, city planning, zoning, and other ordinary municipal activities, as well as some that suggest state government, such as a public utilities commission and various boards of examiners for professions and vocations. In addition a number of things are done for the district by regular agencies of the national government. There is also a separate court system of the district, headed by the Court of Appeals, below which is the Supreme Court of the District, while at the bottom are the usual local courts: a police court, a municipal court, and a juvenile court.

Lack of Local Popular Control. Over this system of local authorities, the people resident in the district have no direct legal or political control. They have in fact no votes at all, since they may not vote for members of Congress, Presidential electors, or local officers. This is a cause of very considerable complaint among the more vocal elements, but Congress shows no disposition to do anything about it.

The demand for self-government in local affairs, and for some representation in Congress, is very strong in the District of Columbia, while the cry for statehood comes insistently from Hawaii and is heard also in Alaska. To the writer it seems that there would be a real gain all around if the people of the District of Columbia were given some power to participate in their own government. On the other hand, Alaska certainly has too small a population for immediate statehood, while Hawaii's population is both remote and much smaller than that of the average state today. It would seem that the needs of these three, the District of Columbia, Hawaii, and Alaska, probably call for a status intermediate between that of statehood and complete territorial dependency. By a new constitutional amendment, and subject to the continuing control of Congress, they might be given not only powers of local self-government but also definite representation in either or both houses of Congress.

REFERENCES

United States Code Annotated, Title 48 (Territories and Insular Possessions), and Title 25 (Indians).

J. M. Mathews, *The American Constitutional System*, rev. ed., New York, 1940, ch. XX.

Hawaii Bureau of Governmental Research, *Our Territorial Government*, Honolulu, T. H., 1937.

Robert M. C. Littler, *The Governance of Hawaii: A Study in Territorial Administration*, Stanford, Calif., 1929.

George W. Spicer, *The Constitutional Status and Government of Alaska*, Baltimore, 1927.

Maximo M. Kalaw, *Philippine Government Under the Jones Law: An Account of Contemporary Philippine Government and Politics*, Manila, 1927.

Victor S. Clark (ed.), *Porto Rico and Its Problems*, Washington, 1930.

Lewis Meriam and Associates, *The Problem of Indian Administration*, Baltimore, 1928.

The Indian Rights Association, *Annual Reports*.

Laurence F. Schmeckebier, *The District of Columbia: Its Government and Administration*, Baltimore, 1928.

—— and W. F. Willoughby, *The Government and Administration of the District of Columbia: Suggestions for Change*, Washintgon, D. C., 1929.

Fiscal Relations between the United States and the District of Columbia, Report of an Independent Study, etc., Washington, D. C. Government Printing Office, 1937.

U. S. Secretary of the Interior, *Annual Reports*.

Grayson L. Kirk, *Philippine Independence*, New York, 1936.

Robert S. Rankin, *Readings in American Government*, New York, 1939, pp. 369-84.

John M. Mathews and Clarence A. Berdahl, *Documents and Readings in American Government: National and State*, rev. ed., New York, 1940, pp. 628-70.

CHAPTER 25

National Taxes, Revenues, and Borrowing

THE NATION'S POWER TO TAX

Origin of the Taxing Power. During the colonial period of American development the "King in parliament" claimed the entire power of taxation over England and also over the commerce of the colonies. At the same time the elected assemblies in the several colonies in America exercised the power of taxation locally. Friction developed at the points where these two taxing powers overlapped, and one of the issues in the war for independence was that of "no taxation without representation." This slogan advertised colonial resistance to any taxation of the colonies by Parliament.

During the struggle for independence the revolutionary state legislatures acted upon the assumption that they, as representatives of the people, had the full power to levy any and every kind of tax. They taxed property, sales, imports, exports, and other transactions in addition to levying poll taxes. Their representatives in the Continental Congress when drawing up the Articles of Confederation refused to grant any taxing power to the Congress. This decision could be justified to some extent by the argument that Congress was not a proper taxing body. It was not representative of the people as such but only of the states in their corporate capacity. Its members were chosen by and dependent upon the state legislatures. Congress could requisition funds from the states, but the state legislatures alone represented the people and had the power to levy taxes. The defects in this financial arrangement from the nation's viewpoint were recognized by the outstanding leaders of the times. Lacking the power to tax and being thus without ability to protect the nation's credit, the Congress under the Articles grew progressively weaker and more frustrated.

The Constitution on the Taxing Power of Congress. The framers of the national Constitution were in the main strongly in favor of giving a substantial taxing power to the national government that they helped to create, as the following provisions of the Constitution reveal:

The Congress shall have Power To lay and collect Taxes, Duties, Imposts and Excises, to pay the Debts and provide for the common Defence and general Welfare of the United States; but all Duties, Imposts and Excises shall be uniform throughout the United States. . . . Representatives and direct Taxes shall be apportioned among the several States . . . according to their respective Numbers. . . . No capitation, or other direct, Tax shall be laid unless in Proportion to the Census or Enumeration herein before directed to be taken. No Tax or Duty shall be laid on Articles exported from any State.[1]

Export Taxes Forbidden. These are the principal original clauses of the Constitution that deal with taxation. On the basis of them, what things may Congress tax? One tax only is expressly forbidden, and that is a tax on exports. The southern states were in 1787 the great exporters: tobacco, indigo, and rice were some of their principal products. They did not want these exports to be taxed for the benefit of the United States as a whole and to the detriment of their own commerce. In applying this prohibition the Supreme Court has tried to make exports as such really free from taxes, but it has ruled that the *incomes* of exporting firms are subject to nondiscriminatory taxation along with other incomes.

Implied Prohibition Against Taxes on States. In the early decision of McCulloch v. Maryland [2] the Supreme Court held that a state has no power to levy a tax on the instrumentalities of the national government, at least not without its consent. The obverse of this case came up after the Civil War. In the case of Collector v. Day,[3] where a state official objected to paying a national income tax levied against his state salary, the Supreme Court upheld him, saying that the "unimpaired existence" of the states is as important as the equally unimpaired existence of the national government, and that, although there is no express clause prohibiting national taxes on state instrumentalities and operations, such a prohibition "rests upon necessary implication." Later a case arose in which a state operating a liquor dispensary system objected to paying the federal tax.[4] But suppose a number of states owned and operated distilleries; if they all escaped taxation, would not this undermine the whole national tax? When the Supreme Court had to face this question, it qualified its first rule by saying that the tax exemption of state instrumentalities applied only to their necessary governmental functions, and not to any business enterprises into which a state may enter. This distinction between the purely governmental and the business or proprietary functions of state government was naturally hard to apply.

The Taxation of Incomes. Such was the status of constitutional law on the taxing power of the national government when another and more serious

[1] U. S. Const., Art. I, sec. 8, par. 1; sec. 2, par. 3; sec. 9, pars. 4, 5.
[2] (1819), 4 Wheaton 316.
[3] (1870), 11 Wallace 113.
[4] South Carolina v. U. S. (1905), 199 U. S. 437.

question arose. It concerned the power of Congress to enact an income tax law.

The original Constitution adopted a distinction that was then generally accepted by economists between "direct" and "indirect" taxes. Direct taxes, said the Constitution, were to be apportioned among the states according to population, as determined by the census. Other taxes were to be levied uniformly throughout the United States, that is, at the same rate everywhere without regard to the number of people. But what is a direct, and what an indirect, tax? Neither then nor now can an unequivocal answer be given. The income tax presents a case in point. First levied by the national government during the Civil War at uniform rates throughout the country, it was then sustained by the courts, apparently on the theory that it was an indirect tax.[5] This tax was repealed, but in 1894 Congress enacted another income tax law, and this time the Court, by a five to four vote, held that an income tax is a direct tax, like a property tax, and that it must be apportioned among the states according to population.[6] Since this would have involved making a different scale of rates in every state, and would have imposed the heaviest burdens upon the people in the poorer states, the tax was allowed to expire. Thus for nearly twenty years there was another restriction on the nation's taxing power. After years of agitation, Congress proposed and the state legislatures approved the Sixteenth Amendment (1913), which was designed to permit a uniform national income tax law to be enacted. The amendment reads as follows:

> The Congress shall have power to lay and collect taxes on incomes, from whatever source derived, without apportionment among the several States, and without regard to any census or enumeration.

This amendment does not say whether an income tax is direct or indirect; it avoids that question, and expressly authorizes the levy of income taxes without apportionment. An income tax was immediately enacted by Congress, and it has been a principal source of national government revenue since World War I.

"From Whatever Source Derived." But the wording of the amendment raised a new question. The phrase "from whatever source derived" seemed to say that such a decision as that in Collector v. Day was overruled. Whatever the source of income, thought some, it now became taxable. When this question later came before the Supreme Court,[7] it held that the amendment does not enlarge the power of Congress to levy taxes, but simply changes the basis for making the levy, by permitting a uniform instead of an apportioned income tax. Under this interpretation the national government was still sup-

[5] Springer v. U. S. (1880), 102 U. S. 586.
[6] Pollock v. Farmers' Loan and Trust Co. (1895), 157 U. S. 429, 158 U. S. 601.
[7] Brushaber v. Union Pacific R. R. Co. (1916), 240 U. S. 1; Evans v. Gore (1920), 253 U. S. 245.

posed to be forbidden to levy an income tax on the salaries of state and local officers, for example, and on the income from state and municipal bonds.

Later there came new light upon this question. During the depression of the 1930s both national and state governments were in desperate need of revenues. While other citizens in the states that had income tax laws paid both national and state income taxes, state and local officers and employees paid no national income tax, and national officers and employees resident in the states paid no state income tax. These inequities were widely condemned. When the national government proceeded to tax the salary of a New York State officer, the Supreme Court of the United States sustained its power to do so.[8] Such a tax upon the income of the officer, the receiver of the salary, was held not to be a tax upon the state government as such. It might be true that the state would in the long run have to pay somewhat higher salaries to its officers and employees because of the new national tax burden, but this was held to be an unavoidable incident of having two governments, national and state, operating over the same territory. State officers get benefits from the national government and should contribute to its support. So long as the tax was not discriminatory, the Court thought that it was constitutional.

Thereupon New York State proceeded to tax as income the salary of a national officer in New York, and the Supreme Court upheld this tax also.[9] In this way the decision in Collector v. Day was overruled and the door was opened to nondiscriminatory income taxes by the nation upon state and local officers' salaries and by the states upon the salaries of locally resident officers of the national government. Congress and the state legislatures promptly took advantage of the new powers. Another barrier to a complete national taxing power had fallen.

Only one important type of income still remains exempt from the national income tax. This is the income derived by bondholders from interest on state and municipal bonds. It is strongly contended by leading state and local officials that it would be unconstitutional for Congress to tax this bond income. Such a conclusion seems hardly to be warranted today. Every argument used in upholding the power of Congress to tax the salaries of state and local officers and employees would apply to the taxation of the interest on state and municipal bonds. It remains for Congress to enact the necessary legislation to put this view to the test.

Wide Sweep of National Taxing Power. With the exceptions noted above as to taxes on exports and direct taxes on state and local governmental instrumentalities, everything else that is within reach by Congress—businesses, incomes, property, inheritances, sales, admissions to theaters and sporting events, and all other taxable things and events—is today taxable by Congress. Its power to tax, the Supreme Court has said, "is exhaustive and embraces every conceivable power of taxation." Congress may make its own rules about taxation

[8] Helvering v. Gerhardt (1938), 304 U. S. 405.
[9] Graves v. New York ex rel. O'Keefe (1939), 306 U. S. 466.

for national purposes without regard to any state laws. Furthermore there is no constitutional limit on the *amount or rate* of taxation. If incomes or imports may be taxed 5 per cent, they may be taxed 10 or 50 or 75 or more per cent. Congress alone may determine how high a tax shall be. In the case of imports the tax may exceed the original cost or the value-before-tax of the thing imported. Thus the tax may be high enough to be prohibitive.

Other provisions of the Constitution and doctrines of the Supreme Court lend support to the broad taxing powers of Congress. Various provisions of the Constitution put restrictions upon the taxing powers of the states, and the supremacy clause has the effect of making national taxes a prior lien where national and state governments have taxed the same thing or person. The Supreme Court has been liberal in upholding state and local taxes in recent decades, but almost never at the expense of the power of Congress.

At various times the Supreme Court has inquired into the purpose of national taxes, and has held at least two taxes to be unconstitutional because they encroached upon the states.[10] These holdings were contrary to the Court's own declaration in other decisions that the purposes of Congress in enacting tax laws are not for the Court to scrutinize.[11] The taxing power may be used, therefore, not merely to raise a revenue, but also to assist in regulating or even to suppress certain activities. A national tax upon state bank notes put an end to their circulation, while the taxes upon dealing in narcotics and upon the sale of oleomargarine have definite regulatory and restrictive purposes.

Should the National Taxing Power Be Limited? It is difficult to believe that the framers of the Constitution had any forewarning of the tremendous expansion of national taxation that has in fact taken place. They thought in modest terms, in figures of a few millions rather than tens of billions. However, the bold and imaginative Alexander Hamilton in his argument for the adoption of the Constitution stated most cogently the case for an unlimited power of taxation in the national government: [12]

> Money is, with propriety, considered as the vital principle of the body politic; as that which sustains its life and motion, and enables it to perform its most essential functions. A complete power, therefore, to procure a regular and adequate supply of it, as far as the resources of the community will permit, may be regarded as an indispensable ingredient in every constitution. . . . Every *power* ought to be in proportion to its *object*. . . . Who can pretend that commercial imposts are, or would be, alone equal to the present and future exigencies of the Union? . . . Its future necessities admit not of calculation or limitation; and upon the principle, more than once

---

[10] Bailey v. Drexel Furniture Co. (1922), 259 U. S. 20; U. S. v. Butler (1936), 297 U. S. 1.

[11] McCray v. U. S. (1904), 195 U. S. 586.

[12] The Federalist, nos. 30-36.

adverted to, the power of making provision for them as they arise ought to be equally unconfined. . . .

Constitutions of civil government are not to be framed upon a calculation of existing exigencies, but upon a combination of these with the probable exigencies of ages, according to the natural and tried course of human affairs. Nothing, therefore, can be more fallacious than to infer the extent of any power, proper to be lodged in the national government, from an estimate of its immediate necessities. There ought to be a *capacity* to provide for future contingencies as they may happen; and as these are illimitable in their nature, it is impossible safely to limit that capacity.

The history of the United States has proved again and again the truth and the prophetic wisdom of Hamilton's words. The nation has surmounted one crisis after another, rushing in a single decade from the depths of the Great Depression with its unemployment to the tremendously intense effort of World War II with its peaks of employment, productivity, and destructiveness. Had it not been for its almost unlimited powers of taxing and borrowing it is hard to see how the nation could have survived these crises and maintained its credit and its institutions.

It happens, however, that at the very time of the last two great ordeals of the nation, certain citizens were urging upon the nation a constitutional amendment that was designed to limit national income and inheritance taxes to not over 25 per cent.[13] A number of state legislatures were persuaded into approving the proposal, which was solemnly laid before Congress as a major remedy for the nation's ills. The good sense of the nation prevailed, and the proposal went into the graveyard of bad bills; but the nation's leaders need to be ever watchful against such quack remedies.

THE NATION'S TAX LAWS AND REVENUES

The Old Revenue System. Congress has modified and expanded the nation's tax laws from time to time to meet all changes in needs and conditions. Prior to 1913 the national government operated under what might be called the old revenue system. The government establishment was relatively small and so was the annual expenditure. Miscellaneous revenues, such as those from the sale of public lands, were considerable. During many years in the nineteenth century the treasury showed substantial annual surpluses, and once, in 1837, there was a distribution of the surplus among the states.

As late as 1912 the total national budget was less than $700,000,000. The revenue was raised as follows: $311,000,000 from import duties; $293,000,000 from excise taxes, mostly on liquor and tobacco; and the rest (about 10 per cent) from minor taxes, land sales, and miscellaneous receipts. Could anything

[13] Tax Institute, *Should There Be a Constitutional Amendment Limiting Federal Income, Estate, and Gift Taxes?* Forum Pamphlet Three, New York, 1944.

have been simpler? In retrospect the financial situation of the national government now seems to have been very satisfactory—but not so. Expenses even then were increasing. Tariff reductions were being strongly urged. A national highway system was badly needed. The government needed more revenue!

The Income Tax and the New Revenue System. Since 1913 there has been almost a revolution in the nation's financing. Increased civil expenses during the first Wilson administration were followed by the tremendous revenue demands of World War I. The first billion-dollar national budget (1917), including a great increase of expenditure for national defense, was followed by the unprecedented expenditures of World War I, $31 billion in two years. Revenues fell far behind. The income tax amendment had been adopted and put into effect, however, and the new tax quickly became the mainstay of the national revenue system. Wartime needs spawned new taxes also, and increased the rates of older taxes. Inheritance and estate taxes, sales and stamp taxes, corporation and admissions taxes brought in substantial sums, but income and profits taxes were far out ahead. However, the Eighteenth Amendment and the prohibition law reduced the revenue from liquor taxes to a negligible amount.

While manful efforts were made throughout the 1920s to reduce national government expenditures, the lowest total (1927) was just under $3,500 million, or about five times the 1912 total. During this period, however, taxes were substantially reduced from their wartime levels and the budget was balanced from 1920 to 1930. A high level of production and employment made it relatively easy to achieve this goal.

The Great Depression's Fiscal Problems. As the deflation and depression gathered headway, and employment dropped to a very low level, tax revenues fell and substantial deficits were incurred. For two years before Franklin Roosevelt took office the government had large deficits, and in all his twelve years in office there was no single year with a surplus. Nevertheless revenues were considerably increased in spite of depression conditions. Income tax rates were increased; prohibition was repealed and liquor began to produce large revenues again; payroll taxes for unemployment compensation and old-age insurance were introduced; tobacco, inheritance, sales and other taxes tended upwards. By 1938 the deficit had been greatly reduced—and then came the war in Europe! The United States began almost at once to increase its expenditures on national defense—and to increase its deficits again. Revenues in 1939 had risen to well over $5 billion, but expenditures were $3.5 billion more than that.

World War II Financing. Congress was slow to apply new rates of taxation in wartime, but when it did act it raised the national revenues to heights never dreamed before. Tax collections in 1942 (fiscal) exceeded $13 billion, in 1943 approached $23 billion, in 1944 passed $40 billion, and in 1945 were nearly $45 billion. Rates on personal incomes, corporation incomes, excess profits, liquor, tobacco, admissions, and so on, had never been so high. Unfortunately, wartime expenditures had to be much higher. At the peak in 1945, tax revenues were just about half the expenditures. Deficits and debts reached almost astronomical figures.

New Features of the Revenue System. The new revenue system of the past generation has certain well defined characteristics.

1. There have been tremendous increases in the national government's revenues, from less than $1 billion annually before World War I to nearly $45 billion in 1945. Even the estimates for 1947 call for receipts of over $31 billion and expenditures of $35 billion.

2. Despite great increases in revenue there has not been one year of balanced budget since 1930. Deficits have been piled on deficits until the national debt stands at about $275 billion.

3. Income taxes both individual and corporate (and in wartime the closely related excess profits taxes) have gone way out in front as revenue producers. Customs duties and even liquor and tobacco taxes, which once supplied 90 per cent of the national government's revenue, have fallen far behind.

4. Since about 1915 a new group of taxes on inheritances, estates, gifts, gasoline, payrolls, admissions, sales, manufactures, and legal documents (to name some of the more important ones) have been added to the list of national taxes and have become producers of substantial revenues.

5. The tax system as a whole, instead of being the relatively simple and stable thing that it was for many years prior to 1913, has become very complicated and has been more or less in flux for the entire period. Congress has been playing by ear and has changed the tax tune time and time again.

TAX LEGISLATION AND ADMINISTRATION

The Enactment of Tax Laws. Taxes may be established only by law. National taxes are authorized by Congress in the form of either acts or joint resolutions. The Constitution provides that "All Bills for Raising revenue shall originate in the House of Representatives; but the Senate may propose or concur with Amendments as on other Bills." [14] This gives the House and its Ways and Means Committee priority in the consideration of new tax programs and measures. Nevertheless the Senate has made full use of its power to "propose or concur with Amendments," and has in most cases, after the House passage of an important tariff or other tax bill, assumed the right to take it apart and reconstruct it, or even to insert an entirely different measure drawn by its powerful Finance Committee. Broadly speaking, there is no class of measures before Congress that arouses as much public interest and as earnest lobbying and wirepulling as do tariff, taxation, and revenue bills.

Taxes of Fixed and Changing Rates. Tax laws are, in general, of two kinds: those that provide standing rates of taxation and that are little changed from year to year, and those that are subject to an annual or at least a frequent

[14] U. S. Const., Art. I, sec. 7, par. 1.

change in rates. The revenues that taxes of the former type bring in each year vary with the ups and downs of the business, privilege, or activity taxed. Inheritance taxes, for example, yield much or little, according to the number and value of estates probated during the year. The tariff produces more or less, according to the amount and value of imports. The yields of these taxes can be only roughly estimated in advance, yet estimates must be made in order to determine how much needs to be raised from other sources.

Every government needs one or more important taxes of the second type, the rates of which can be changed from year to year in order to bring in more or less revenue, and to enable the government to balance its budget if possible. Great Britain uses the income tax as the principal flexible tax for budget-balancing purposes, shifting the rates up or down according to expected needs. Congress has not worked as hard to get an exact balance of the budget each year, and has not developed the practice of changing income tax rates annually.

National Tax-Collecting Agencies. The principal agencies of the national government for the administration of tax laws are the following: [15]

1. Department of the Treasury
   (a) Bureau of Internal Revenue
   (b) Bureau of Customs
2. United States Customs Court
3. Court of Customs and Patent Appeals
4. The Tax Court of the United States
5. Court of Claims.

The Bureau of Internal Revenue is headed by a Commissioner of Internal Revenue, and the work under him is subdivided among an Income Tax Unit, an Alcohol Tax Unit, and a Miscellaneous Tax Unit, with various supporting agencies. The regular staff includes many thousand officers and employees, of whom four-fifths are in the field service, scattered among the various local offices in the states and territories. This, the largest tax-collecting organization in the United States, is responsible for the collection of all the internal taxes of the national government. The Bureau of the Customs is also under a commissioner. It also has a large staff of officers and employees, of whom about 80 per cent are in the field service, stationed in the various "ports of entry" where dutiable goods are brought in and appraised for payment of duties, and where the money is actually paid.

In both bureaus the bulk of the work is done by a permanent staff whose members have been selected and appointed under the merit system. Bureau heads, the chief customs officers at the principal ports, and the chief internal revenue officers in each state, however, are noncareer men, appointed from the dominant party by the President with the advice and consent of the Senate.

---

[15] See *U. S. Government Manual,* recent editions, for details and for current changes.

Whatever political advantage this may give the majority party, it certainly is not conducive to better tax administration or to economical service.

Appeals in Tax Cases. Decisions on tax matters—assessments, classification of imported goods, amounts of tax to be paid—are made in the first instance by the field officers, and ultimately by the heads of the bureaus at Washington. From such decisions there can be appeals. In the case of the tariff, the first appeal is to the Customs Court. This court consists of 9 judges in all, holding office during good behavior, and receiving salaries of $10,000 a year. If either the importer or the government is not satisfied with the decision of this court, an appeal may be taken to the Court of Customs and Patent Appeals. This court has 5 judges in all, serving during good behavior, and receiving $12,500 in annual salary. Its decisions are practically final. For internal revenue matters there is the Tax Court of the United States. This is also a sort of administrative court. It is composed of 16 judges, appointed for overlapping terms of 12 years each, and paid $10,000 a year. The income-taxpayer, for example, can appeal from decisions of the Bureau of Internal Revenue to this court in tax refund and deficiency cases and get a decision as to how much tax he must pay or to what refund he is entitled. Appeals can be taken from this court to the Circuit Courts of Appeals, and may ultimately reach the Supreme Court.

Tax Law-Enforcing Agencies. The collection agencies and the courts that administer the national tax laws are supported by a number of other agencies, mostly in the Treasury Department. Among the important functions to be performed is that of detecting and arresting violators of the tax laws. This function, in its various phases, is assigned to the Coast Guard and the Customs Agency Service, both being concerned with smuggling, while the latter also investigates cases of undervaluation and false invoicing; to the Intelligence Unit, and the enforcement division of the Alcohol Tax Unit, both in the Internal Revenue Bureau, concerned with evasions and violations of the alcohol tax laws; to the Bureau of Narcotics; and to other agencies in the Treasury Department. The Federal Bureau of Investigation in the Department of Justice also concerns itself with income-tax evaders. Thus there is a complicated set of law-enforcing agencies connected with tax law administration. Where the laws have been knowingly and deliberately violated, conviction will result in imprisonment, or fine, or both. Where the case is only one of mistake or oversight, it is customary to recover the unpaid tax with penalties in the form of interest.

Local Depositories. Since taxes are collected in all important centers throughout the country, it is convenient to have them deposited to the credit of the government in the various local depositories of government funds that have been approved by the Treasury Department. These include the Federal Reserve Banks, Federal Land Banks, approved national banks, and certain others, including some abroad. The depositories are responsible for the safe keeping of the funds, and for transferring them on call, or for checking them out, as the case may be.

CONFLICTING AND DUPLICATING TAXES

The inability of the national government to get along with the older revenues alone—the customs and the excises on tobacco and liquor—and the corresponding inability of the state governments to rely upon the property tax as a chief revenue source, led both national and state governments to search out new taxes, new sources of revenue. The inevitable result was that as each looked out for its own new sources without considering the other, there came to be a number of conflicting and duplicating taxes—on incomes, gasoline, liquor, tobacco, and other subjects of taxation. There is considerable duplication, too, between state and local tax authorities, although this does not seem as serious, since the state legislature can make the necessary regulations to avoid the most serious effects of such duplication.

Possible Remedies for Conflicting Taxation. In recent years, both Congress and the state legislatures have begun to give serious consideration to the problem of conflicting taxation, and it is likely that in the future some changes will be made that will result in a more integrated and in some respects simpler tax system.[16] The following are some of the things that can be done.

1. The national government alone might collect certain taxes, with state consent, and return to each state a fixed proportion of the tax raised within that state. This would be an easy solution for the state, but would tie its hands to some extent.

2. The national government might provide in its tax law for high, uniform rates of taxation, but permit taxpayers a credit of the amount of tax paid to the state under a complementary law, as a means of reducing their federal tax. In effect this is the situation in inheritance taxation, where a credit of up to 80 per cent of the national tax is allowed for the payment of the state tax. One cannot today move from one state to another in hope of escaping inheritance taxation, since the national rates are the same everywhere, and any state that has no inheritance tax law is simply losing a certain amount of revenue without relieving its taxpayers at all.

3. There can, alternatively, be cooperative federal and state consideration of tax problems, with mutual give and take in the enactment of tax schedules, and this may even be accompanied by cooperative administration of the laws, so as to reduce somewhat the expense of administration. This could be done, for example, in the case of income taxation.

4. Another solution might be to have a separation of sources, so that the national government would tax only certain things, the states certain others. This is of doubtful wisdom. It has been tried in state and local governments

---

[16] See *Conflicting Taxation* and *Federal, State, and Local Government Fiscal Relations*, cited in references.

to some extent, but has not been a signal success, although some states continue it to this day.

5. If the national government continues to expand its taxation at the expense of the states, increased federal aid to the states may be necessary.

THE PROBLEM OF TAX EXEMPTION

The increased needs of national, state, and local governments for revenue have raised anew the problem of tax exemption. The total amounts of tax-exempt property and tax-exempt income are staggering, and there are many taxpayers who feel that their own burdens would be lightened considerably if most or all exemptions were eliminated. Among others, there are the following large blocks or aggregates of property and income that are now partly or wholly tax exempt.

1. Land and buildings of the national government, exempt from all state and local taxation.

2. Lands and buildings of the states exempt from local taxation, and considerable amounts of land and improvements owned by some local governments within the areas of other local units, and also exempt.

3. Churches, privately owned schools, and charitable institutions with combined values probably running into the billions of dollars for the whole United States, are exempt as a rule from state and local taxes. Some private schools also own great endowments, and even own rented buildings here and there, which are tax exempt.

4. The billions of dollars invested in national government bonds are exempt from taxation as property by any government in the United States, and the income from them is also exempt.

5. State and local government bonds are also exempt from taxation by the national government, and usually are exempt also from state and local taxation within the state in which they are issued. While the federal bonds outstanding amount to over $270 billion, state and local bonds exceed $18 billion.

What would happen if attempts were made to tax the bonds issued hereafter by national, state, and local governments? No doubt there would have to be some increase in the rates of interest paid, partly or wholly offsetting the gain from taxation. Taxation by the national government of state and local salaries and by state and local government of national government salaries has already begun without seriously upsetting central-local relations. How much revenue is being obtained is not yet certain, but it is probably not a large part of the total income tax, either state or national. A great number of state and local employees, and of national employees, too, receive salaries or wages so low that, if married, they are exempt under present income tax laws.

THE POWER TO BORROW

Taxing and Borrowing Powers. The power to tax and the power to borrow on the public credit are closely interrelated. The Congress under the Articles of Confederation proved this point to the hilt. For a short time it was able to borrow from foreign nations and from private individuals, but almost as soon as it became known that it could not tax and could not get the states to honor its requisitions, its credit was lost. Hamilton drove the point home time and again in his argument in *The Federalist*. People who lend money expect repayment. To limit the power to tax is to limit the power to repay loans, and hence to limit the borrowing power. Therefore sound public credit depends upon the government's having ample power to tax.

Constitutional Provisions on the Borrowing Power. Those masters of the practice of public affairs, the framers of the United States Constitution, were thoroughly familiar with the principles of public credit. They tied the taxing and borrowing powers closely together in the powers granted to Congress: [17]

> The Congress shall have Power To lay and collect Taxes . . . to pay the Debts . . . of the United States;
> To borrow money on the credit of the United States; . . .

The borrowing power thus conferred is limited by only one thing, "the credit of the United States." As long as that credit remains good, there can be borrowing without limit. It is up to Congress to see to it that the nation's credit remains unimpaired. This can be done only by raising enough revenue to ensure the payment of the debts that the nation incurs. The limit, in short, is economic rather than constitutional or legal. Within the economic limit of the nation's credit, it is for Congress to say how much may be borrowed, at what rate of interest, for what periods of time, and on what other conditions.

Revolutionary War and Civil War Debts. Two other provisions of the national Constitution relate to the national debt. One of these, which had only a passing importance, guaranteed that "All Debts contracted and Engagements entered into, before the Adoption of this Constitution," should be as valid under the new government as under the old.[18] This was in a sense merely the acceptance of the rule that a new government must assume the debts of the old government that served the same people, but it was a positive and voluntary acceptance of the debts of the Confederation. It was the recognition of an honest debt.

After the Civil War, questions arose concerning the great war debt incurred by the national government and the debts incurred by the Confederacy and the southern states in prosecuting the war from their side. By the Fourteenth Amendment, which went into effect in 1868, it was provided that

[17] U. S. Const., Art. I, sec. 8, pars. 1, 2.
[18] U. S. Const., Art. VI, par. 1.

The validity of the public debt of the United States, authorized by law, including debts incurred for payment of pensions and bounties for services in suppressing insurrection or rebellion, shall not be questioned. But neither the United States nor any State shall assume or pay any debt or obligation incurred in aid of insurrection or rebellion against the United States, or any claim for the loss or emancipation of any slave; but all such debts, obligations, and claims shall be held illegal and void.[19]

Thus the national debt was secured against legal attack, while the Confederate war debts were repudiated, and payment of them was forbidden. This did not impair the nation's credit but rather tended to strengthen it, as well as to discourage other attempts at secession.

Greenbacks. The constitutional provisions discussed above relate to open and direct borrowing. But there are other provisions that have some bearing upon questions of national debt and credit. Congress has, for example, the powers to "coin Money" and to "regulate the Value thereof." [20]

During the Civil War the government issued considerable quantities of paper money known as "greenbacks" to pay for goods and services. These were notes or promises of the national government to pay money, but in addition the law provided that they should be "legal tender" in the payment of private debts, although the government itself would not accept them for some purposes. A person to whom these notes were offered in payment of a debt had to accept them as money, or he might lose all that he had coming. Considerable amounts of these notes were thus forced into circulation, creating in effect a concealed loan from the public. When the question first came before the Supreme Court as to the power of Congress to make its notes or promises to pay legal tender, the Court held by a close vote that Congress had no such power, that it was not a power that could be implied under the "necessary and proper" clause. Soon after this there came a change in the Court's membership, and in a new case the power of Congress was upheld.[21]

Bills of Credit and Greenbacks. It is interesting to note that the greenbacks thus made legal tender were practically the same as the "bills of credit" that the Constitution forbids the states to issue. They had had a long and sorrowful history beginning with issues by Massachusetts Bay Colony in 1690. Most of the colonies and the succeeding states had issued them, and in a number of places they had depreciated to a point where they were worth practically nothing. The Continental Congress also issued them, under an express power to do so, and it had the same experience. They went down in value until the phrase "not worth a Continental" became a term to express utter worthlessness. Over $400,000,000 in such paper promises to pay were issued

---

[19] Sec. 4.
[20] U. S. Const., Art. I, sec. 8, par. 5.
[21] Knox v. Lee (1871), 12 Wallace 457; also Legal Tender cases (1884), 110 U. S. 421.

by the Congress and the states during the Revolution, and thus in effect loans on a large scale were extracted from the people. They circulated for a time, growing less and less valuable, until they finally stopped circulating. When it was proposed in the Federal Convention to give Congress the power to issue bills of credit, the idea was voted down, and the provision that came out was simply that for direct and open borrowing.[22] Nevertheless the power evidently exists by implication in the power to coin and to "regulate the value" of money.

This implied power of Congress has given rise to one movement after another for the government to pay its obligations in this way, and thus to force into circulation a larger amount of money. The Greenback Party represented one of these movements, arising mainly in Middle Western depressed agricultural sections. The argument is very plausible. When the government needs money, why should it go to moneylenders and pay interest for what it gets? Why not simply print "treasury notes" or other promises to pay, use them to pay off those to whom the government owes money, make them legal tender so that others have to accept them, and thus at the same time increase the amount of money in circulation and stimulate prices and business? The immediately felt need for more money in circulation blinds many to the inflationary dangers to themselves as well as to the government's credit in such measures.

Voluntary and Involuntary Loans. The lending of money to the government under ordinary borrowing methods is voluntary. The individual who has money to lend can use it to buy government bonds if he wishes, but he does not have to do it. At times, however, public opinion puts upon the individual a great deal of pressure to subscribe to government loans. Such was certainly the case with the borrowings of the national government during World Wars I and II, although legally all lending was voluntary. Furthermore the machinery probably exists in the present banking system under the Federal Reserve Board for making bank loans to the government almost compulsory.

Unilateral Changes in Obligations of Bonds. As a rule, it is understood that the obligation of government bonds cannot be changed by the government without the consent of the bondholder. Such is the case with private business contracts, where both parties must agree to any changes in the terms of a contract. In public borrowing, however, the national government is more powerful than any private moneylender, and in at least one case it has refused, for reasons of public policy and general welfare, to live up to its bonds. The government used to issue bonds payable in gold, and large amounts of these were outstanding when in 1933 Congress took the nation off the gold standard, and later reduced the legal gold content of the dollar. When the holder of a Liberty Bond asked for payment in gold at the standard in effect

[22] See Madison's Notes of August 16th; *Documents Illustrative of the Formation of the Union of the American States*, pp. 556-57.

when the bond was issued, the Supreme Court faced the question as to the power of the national government to alter its obligations. In its decision it said:

> The Constitution gives to the Congress the power to borrow money on the credit of the United States, an unqualified power, a power vital to the government, upon which in an extremity its very life may depend. The binding quality of the promise of the United States is of the essence of the credit which is so pledged. Having this power to authorize the issue of definite obligations for the payment of money borrowed, the Congress has not been vested with authority to alter or destroy these obligations. The fact that the United States may not be sued without its consent is a matter of procedure which does not affect the legal and binding character of its contracts. While the Congress is under no duty to provide remedies through the courts, the contractual obligation still exists, and, despite infirmities of procedure, remains binding upon the conscience of the sovereign.[23]

This undoubtedly expressed the correct moral and legal principle. But the claimant, knowing that he could not get gold from the government, wanted $1.69 in paper money for each $1 of the face value of the bond, because the gold content of the dollar had been depreciated that much. Did he get it? No. His only method was to sue in the Court of Claims, and in order to collect damages for breach of contract, he had to prove that there had been damages. This he could not do, since the actual purchasing power of money had not depreciated by that time to any considerable extent. In fact all forms of money available to him had been stabilized and made equal in value, dollar for dollar. Thus he won a moral victory, but no damages. Even if the Court of Claims should at a later time allow damages in such cases, Congress could refuse to appropriate the money to pay the claims. Subsequent legislation put an end to the right even to sue on this ground in the Court of Claims.

BORROWING PRACTICES

Borrowing by National Government. Under standing legislation, the Treasury Department of the United States has the power to borrow from time to time as funds are needed, and in times of war and special emergencies additional borrowing powers are enacted by Congress. The rate of interest and the time period of loans are determined by the Secretary of the Treasury after consultation with leading financiers. When money is needed quickly, treasury notes or certificates running for short periods are sold through the Federal Reserve System, leading banks, and dealers in securities. Longer-term bonds are issued later from time to time as needed to take up the short-term notes, and also to refund bond issues that are coming due, when that is necessary.

[23] Perry v. United States (1935), 294 U. S. 330.

Sometimes the bonds are "callable" by the Treasury after a certain length of time, and where this is the case savings are sometimes made by calling in bonds that carry a high rate of interest and issuing instead of them bonds with a lower rate. There has been a considerable amount of saving in interest charges in this way since 1932. When tremendous quantities of money need to be raised quickly, as during World Wars I and II, resort is had to public sale throughout the United States, and advertising campaigns are conducted to dispose of all the bonds.

Repayment of National Loans. Under Congressional authorization the Treasury Department also makes regular provision for paying the interest on bonds and for meeting the payments on issues that are falling due. Payments are made regularly and according to law from the revenues into the sinking fund for the retirement of bonds. When in the period following World War I the annual revenue of the government was ample for all requirements, and more, the surplus revenue was used to a considerable extent to buy up outstanding bonds and to retire them. The outstanding debt was thus reduced by more than $10 billion before the depression brought a slump in revenue that not only put an end to this further reduction but made new borrowing necessary. It has always been the policy of the national government to reduce its debt whenever possible, but it is always hard to carry out a decision to reduce expenditures and to increase taxes sufficiently to bring this about. It is held by many economists, moreover, that a very rapid reduction of the public debt is unduly disturbing to the business world. On the other hand it increases public confidence in the government and its credit to have the government make regular efforts to reduce the public debt.

This is not the place for a discussion of the economic implications of the present national debt. As everyone should know, the debt is now at its all-time peak, at about $275 billion. This amounts to nearly $2,000 for every man, woman, and child in the nation's population. The interest rate is low, under 2 per cent on the average, but even at that the annual interest charge is about $5 billion or nearly $40 per capita per year. This interest charge alone is more than 5 times the total national budget in the years before World War I. Even so it is by no means unbearable. The bonds are practically all held within the country, and nearly every family has some government bonds on which it receives interest payments from the government.

REFERENCES

Harold M. Groves, *Financing Government*, New York, 1939; rev. ed., 1945.
Roswell Magill, *The Impact of Federal Taxes*, New York, 1943.
Sidney Ratner, *American Taxation: Its History as a Social Force in Democracy*, New York, 1942.
Roy G. and Gladys C. Blakey, *The Federal Income Tax*, New York, 1940.

Lewis H. Kimmel and Associates, *Postwar Fiscal Requirements, Federal, State, and Local*, Washington, 1945.

Harold M. Groves, *Production, Jobs and Taxes*, New York, 1944.

Tax Institute, *Financing the War*, A Symposium, Philadelphia, 1942.

National Tax Association, *The Bulletin* of, monthly, October-June.

——, *Proceedings* of, annual.

Taxes: The Tax Magazine, monthly, Commerce Clearing House, Chicago.

Henry Rottschaefer, *Handbook of American Constitutional Law*, St. Paul, 1939, ch. 7, "Federal Taxing and Other Fiscal Powers."

Federal, State, and Local Government Fiscal Relations, Senate Document no. 69, 78th Congress, 1st Sess. (1943).

U. S. Treasury Department, *Annual Reports*.

U. S. Treasury, Commissioner of Internal Revenue, *Annual Reports*.

U. S. Department of Commerce, Bureau of the Census, *Statistical Abstract of the United States*, annual.

Interstate Commission on Conflicting Taxation, *Conflicting Taxation*, Chicago, 1935.

United States Government Manual.

The Twentieth Century Fund, *Facing the Tax Problem*, New York, 1937.

Tax Institute, *Tax Policy*, monthly, Philadelphia.

Robert S. Rankin, *Readings in American Government*, New York, 1939, pp. 251-60, 489-507.

John M. Mathews and Clarence A. Berdahl, *Documents and Readings in American Government: National and State*, rev. ed., New York, 1940, pp. 519-52.

A. N. Christensen and E. M. Kirkpatrick, *The People, Politics, and the Politician: Readings in American Government*, New York, 1941, pp. 634-54.

CHAPTER 26

The National Budget and Expenditures

•

The Importance of Public Budgets. In recent years the annual Budget of the United States has become a large quarto volume of over a thousand pages replete with financial tables, footnotes, and textual explanations. Even the experts find it "hard reading" and the average citizen, if he ever saw a copy, would be appalled by its magnitude and its wealth of detail. It is, nevertheless, the most important annual document of the executive branch of the government and next to the annual volume of statutes the most important for the legislative branch as well. Leaders in government wonder now how the nation got along for over a century without a genuine annual budget and without a budget system.

Many years ago William E. Gladstone, several times Prime Minister of England, said that "Budgets are not merely affairs of arithmetic, but in a thousand ways go to the root of the prosperity of individuals, the relation of classes, and the strength of kingdoms." If this were true in Gladstone's day in England, how much more true it is in the United States today! As compared with the present, governments in Gladstone's day taxed little, spent little, and did little. His was a period of relative *laissez faire* in government, whereas the present is a time of extensive public activity and of profound public concern with the major public services. Is there today any part of the social and economic life of the American people that is not deeply affected by what the government does? And if we contemplate a future in which government, agriculture, industry and labor cooperate to ensure full employment and high levels of income and production, is not the national budget bound to assume even more importance than ever?

The Power of Congress to Make Appropriations. Coming down to practical details, what does the national Constitution provide as to budgets, expenditures, and appropriations? In express words it says very little on these subjects. The term budget does not appear at all although it was known and used abroad

442

in the eighteenth century. On the other hand the word "appropriation" appears in two passages in connection with the powers of Congress.

> No Money shall be drawn from the Treasury, but in Conse-
> quence of Appropriations made by Law; and a regular Statement
> and Account of the Receipts and Expenditures of all public Money
> shall be published from time to time, [and] The Congress shall have
> Power . . . To raise and support Armies; but no Appropriation of
> Money to that Use shall be for a Longer term than two Years.[1]

The term "appropriation" as used in these two provisions means a legal authorization by Congress for expenditure from the national treasury. In both clauses it is assumed that money has been raised and is in the treasury, but both make it clear that no money in the treasury may be taken out for expenditure without the authorization of Congress. This is one of the most effective controls in the hands of the legislative branch. It is a major part of the power of the purse. Neither the executive nor the courts may authorize any money to be spent without the permission of Congress.

The Spending Power. A recent book entitled *The Spending Power*[2] uses this term as equivalent to the power to make expenditures from funds appropriated by Congress. It might better have used the title *The Executive Power to Expend Appropriated Funds* because "the spending power" has been long used in constitutional law with a different meaning. It refers to the constitutional power of Congress to authorize expenditures for various functions or services. The general issue involved in the spending power is this: What are the functions or services for which Congress may constitutionally appropriate money? This is a broader and deeper question than that of the power of the executive to expend funds under appropriations lawfully made by Congress.

There are no express words like "the spending power" in the Constitution. The idea of such a power is drawn by implication from the taxing power. A government does not tax merely to tax, or even to raise revenue. Taxing or having a revenue is not an end in itself. Money is raised by governments in order that it may be put to some use; in short, in order that it may be spent upon lawful and useful public services.

What is the range of things, functions, or services for which the national government may raise and spend money? The words of the Constitution (Article I, section 8) are not without some vagueness and ambiguity: "The Congress shall have Power To lay and collect Taxes, . . . to pay the Debts and provide for the common Defence and general Welfare of the United States; . . ." In this grant of powers it is now generally agreed that the last phrases, "to pay the Debts," etc., are not independent grants of power, but rather statements of the purposes for which taxes may be raised and spent.

---

[1] U. S. Const., Art. I, sec. 9, par. 7; sec. 8, par. 12.
[2] Lucius Wilmerding, Jr., *The Spending Power: A History of the Efforts of Congress to Control Expenditures*, New Haven, 1943.

The "general Welfare" phrase in this context does not, for example, authorize Congress to pass any laws that it pleases for the general welfare, but indicates rather that taxes may be raised and spent for the general welfare. The other two authorized purposes of national taxing and spending, "to pay the Debts and provide for the common Defence" are fairly definite and understandable. But what is this thing called the "general Welfare" for which Congress may raise and spend money? Does this phrase throw the door wide open to national spending for any and every purpose that may strike the fancy of Congress? This is a crucial question in any broad consideration of national budget making, taxing and spending.

National Spending for the General Welfare. There have been two principal views on the range or scope of the power of Congress to increase the list of services for which national revenues may be spent in the promotion of the general welfare. These views may be called the Hamiltonian and the Madisonian. The Supreme Court in 1936 explained them and chose between them in the following language: [3]

> The Congress is expressly empowered to lay taxes to provide for the general welfare. Funds in the Treasury as a result of taxation may be expended only through appropriation. . . . They can never accomplish the objects for which they were collected, unless the power to appropriate is as broad as the power to tax. The necessary implication from the terms of the grant is that the public funds may be appropriated "to provide for the general welfare of the United States." These words cannot be meaningless, else they would not have been used. . . .
>
> Since the foundation of the nation, sharp differences of opinion have persisted as to the true interpretation of the phrase [general welfare]. Madison asserted it amounted to no more than a reference to the other powers enumerated in the subsequent clauses of the same section; that, as the United States is a government of limited and enumerated powers, the grant of power to tax and spend for the general national welfare must be confined to the enumerated legislative fields committed to the Congress. In this view the phrase is mere tautology, for taxation and appropriation are or may be necessary incidents of the exercise of any of the enumerated legislative powers. Hamilton, on the other hand, maintained the clause confers a power separate and distinct from those later enumerated, is not restricted in meaning by the grant of them, and Congress consequently has a substantive power to tax and to appropriate, limited only by the requirement that it shall be exercised to provide for the general welfare of the United States. . . . Mr. Justice Story, in his Commentaries, espouses the Hamiltonian position. We shall not

[3] U. S. v. Butler (1936), 297 U. S. 1.

review the writings of public men and commentators or discuss the legislative practice. Study of all these leads us to conclude that the reading advocated by Mr. Justice Story is the correct one.

Examples of Purposes of National Expenditure. This broad view of the taxing and spending power is, in fact, the one that has guided Congress for many decades. The specific powers granted to Congress in the Constitution include none of the following subjects, and yet Congress has authorized expenditures for them all and for many more, too—agriculture, education, public health, social security, public and private housing, national parks, the welfare of women, children, war veterans and workers in industry, safety in factories and mines, general scientific research, and numerous aids to state and local governments. Eliminate these purposes of expenditure from the national government's list and you push the government back over a century.

A Future Full Employment Budget. The broad scope of the nation's power to spend for the general welfare carries important implications for the future. Even though its ordinary lawmaking powers are somewhat limited, Congress is able through its taxing and spending powers to launch the national government into many fields of public service. The doctrine of *laissez faire* cannot be found enshrined in a constitution that permits unlimited expenditures for the general welfare. Having so strongly implied and so long practiced a power to spend for a wide variety of public purposes, Congress may be able to imply other powers from this one, such as, for example, the power to take land by condemnation for public housing purposes,[4] and to regulate institutions and facilities that have been set up through the spending power. How else can the power to spend for the public welfare be made effective?

From all this it follows that Congress probably has ample power to budget in the future to maintain full employment by any program of taxing and spending, of public works, and of aids to agriculture, labor, industry, and state and local government, that it sees fit to adopt. A "full employment budget" for the nation may be economically and administratively hard to manage and to make successful, but the attempt to provide it would not be unconstitutional. In addition the Supreme Court has by various decisions made it almost impossible for the citizen or taxpayer and even for a state to contest in the courts the validity of any particular expenditure authorized by Congress.[5]

Authorization of Services versus Appropriations. Congress has a number of functions in connection with taxes, budgets, and expenditures. The authorization of every new purpose of expenditure is, for example, within the power of Congress. Sometimes these authorizations are on a comprehensive scale, like a public roads program or a social security system. At other times they are minor expansions in some going service, like empowering the Census Bureau

[4] Kohl v. U. S. (1875), 91 U. S. 367; City of Cleveland v. U. S. (1945), 323 U. S. 329.
[5] Massachusetts v. Mellon and Frothingham v. Mellon (1923), 262 U. S. 447.

to undertake some new enumeration, or establishing a new national monument. It is certainly true that under stress of war or in the struggle to end unemployment, administrative agencies sometimes go beyond what Congress has authorized and start new services themselves. These are frowned upon in Congress, but that body has found it to be very hard to prevent these unauthorized extensions of the national services.[6]

In the original act authorizing a service there may also be an appropriation of money for it. Let us say that a board or commission is created by Congress for a new purpose, or that a new type of aid to farmers is authorized, to be administered by an established agency. The difference between the authorization of the service and the appropriation for it is usually recognized in these cases by sending the bill in each house first to the subject matter committee and second to the appropriations committee. A service may be a good thing in itself, but the question of how much to spend upon it must be weighed in the light of the available resources and the other legitimate demands for funds. Furthermore the authorization of a service or agency needs to be made only once, as in establishing the Census or the Interstate Commerce Commission, but the question of appropriations comes up every year thereafter. The distinction between service-authorization and appropriations for the service is clear enough, therefore; but it sometimes happens that a change of wording in an appropriation act serves also as the authorization of a new service, without any other action by Congress.

Early Lack of Budget System. The American people had the good fortune, or misfortune, during most of the nineteenth century to have ample natural resources, great energy, and self-confidence, coupled with a certain contempt for politics and administration. Public functions were so few and inexpensive, and the public revenues so ample, that the government, and especially the national government, faced at times the problem of what to do with the surplus, not what to do about meeting a deficit. As a result, there was much laxity and carelessness in the handling of public finances. One evidence of this was the failure to develop a definite budget system, and to bring the annual revenues and expenditures into regular balance.[7]

Appropriation Bills in Congress. The early practices of Congress in the handling of appropriations were better than some that developed later. In the decades before the Civil War it was the custom to have one committee in each house handle both revenue and appropriation bills, a practice that centered the responsibility and made possible a regular consideration of the problem of budget balancing. In 1865 the House, which initiated both bills as a rule, separated the committee into two, one for revenue (ways and means), the other for appropriations. This did not satisfy some elements in the House who wanted more liberal appropriations for certain services, and

[6] Lucius Wilmerding, op. cit. See footnote 2, above.
[7] See H. J. Ford, The Cost of Our National Government: A Study in Political Pathology; W. F. Willoughby, The Problem of a National Budget, Washington, 1918.

twenty years later the House had eight different committees dealing with appropriation bills, with no common machinery for bringing their proposals into harmony. Some were economical to the point of stinginess, while others proposed expenditures with great liberality.

Several other abuses also developed. Certain departments, backed up by friendly appropriations committees, developed the practice of spending more than was appropriated, and then when Congress met again, before the fiscal year was up, department officials came in with requests for "deficiency appropriations," which were usually allowed. The members of Congress, recognizing the fact that the President was unlikely to veto appropriation bills, developed the practice of attaching thereto legislation that was otherwise distasteful to the President, in the form of added sections or "riders" to appropriation bills. This prevented vetoes and clear-cut votes on the riders themselves. After the end of the 1945 session President Truman pocket-vetoed a bill to cancel certain appropriations to which Congress had attached a rider to return the Employment Service to the states within ninety days. His memorandum of explanation made emphatic protest against legislation by riders on appropriation bills.

Executive Leadership Lacking. During the entire period down to World War I, it was not expected that the President would assume responsibility for financial proposals, and there was no provision for giving the executive any help to enable him to make a study of budget problems each year. It was assumed, apparently, that the planning of revenues and expenditures was entirely a matter for Congress. There was nothing in those days comparable to an "executive budget." The nearest thing to it was a compilation of requests from the departments and independent agencies, brought together by the Secretary of the Treasury, and presented to the members of Congress as a "Book of Estimates." The estimates dealt only with proposed expenditures, and even these had not been studied and harmonized by any central authority.

Budget Reform Movement. The movement to establish definite budget systems in national, state, and local governments in the United States developed after 1900. It came as a part of the general progressive movement for making government more systematic and efficient. Students like Professors Charles A. Beard, Frederick A. Cleveland, and W. F. Willoughby joined hands with practical politicians and administrators in promoting it. Presently a number of cities and states had established budget systems by law or charter, and in 1920-21 the movement reached the national government. Tremendous wartime expenditures and revenues (the first "billion dollar budgets"), and the feeling that there had been much waste in the conduct of the war, helped to advance the cause. A Republican Congress in 1920 enacted a Budget and Accounting Act which President Wilson vetoed on the ground that the provisions in it for the Comptroller General were unconstitutional. Re-enacted in 1921, and signed by President Harding, the act is still in effect.[8]

[8] See U. S. *Code of Laws*, Title 31, ch. 1.

President's Responsibility for Annual Budget. Through the Budget and Accounting Act Congress fully recognizes the need for Presidential leadership in budget making. "The President shall transmit to Congress on the first day of each regular session the budget. . . ." In the act are also set forth the types of data concerning past, current, and future revenues, expenditures, balances and debts that he is to include in the budget document for the information of Congress. The estimates of the financial needs of Congress itself and of the Supreme Court are to be included in the budget without revision, but with the aid of the Bureau of the Budget he is expected to revise and harmonize all the other requests for funds. The budget that he submits is to be a comprehensive and unified one, a complete financial program, covering revenues, expenditures, and borrowing operations.

The logic of centering in the President the responsibility for comprehensive financial planning for the government is hardly questioned today. As the leader of the majority party in Congress as well as in the country, and as head of the executive establishment, he is able to obtain a comprehensive, balanced, and close-up view of all the government's financial needs. In the light of the party's commitments and its policies, and of the government's needs and resources, he is in the very best position to plan the financial program of the entire government. His plan, as embodied in the budget, and as later modified and approved by Congress, becomes the all-inclusive work program of the national government for the ensuing year. It is a work program stated in terms of money available, and it thus brings means and ends into close relationship.

The Bureau of the Budget. Created by the Budget and Accounting Act of 1921, the Bureau of the Budget is today part of the Executive Office of the President. It is headed by a Director and an Assistant Director appointed by the President without Senate approval. It is organized in a series of divisions under assistant directors or chiefs, the more important ones being responsible respectively for Estimates, Administrative Management, Legislative Reference, Fiscal studies, Statistical Standards, and Field Service. The Estimates Division has most to do with the preparation of the expenditure estimates, which make up the greater part of the annual budgets. But the Bureau has other important functions, also, under the act of 1921 and under legislation of later date.

The Bureau as Management Agency for the President.[9] The act of 1921 authorized the Bureau, when directed by the President, to make organizational and management studies of departments and establishments with a view to recommending measures for administrative improvement to the President and Congress. This authorization is the legal basis for the work of the Division of Administrative Management, which is continuously engaged in studying the organization and procedures of administrative agencies, and in making recommendations for improvement. To prevent conflicts in legislative proposals and administrative regulations among executive departments and agencies, the President has ordered that all such proposals be cleared through and

[9] Harold D. Smith, *The Management of Your Government*, ch. V.

harmonized in the Budget Bureau. This function in the Bureau devolves upon the Legislative Reference Division. In like manner all government statistical work and new projects for fact-gathering and the issuance of government questionnaires are routed through the Statistical Division of the Bureau. A Division of Field Service checks up on the co-ordination and efficiency of administrative services in the field, away from Washington, where so much of the work of the national government is done. More recent laws and executive orders have imposed upon the Bureau important examining and control functions over the government-owned corporations, government publications, the government information service, and other important administrative activities.

Until 1939 there had been very little development of this side of the Bureau's work. The change came at that time with the adoption of the President's plan of reorganization for the Executive Office of the President and the appointment of a new Director of the Budget. Since that time the Bureau has expanded its services steadily until it has become for most management purposes the chief support of the President. The reorganization of the administration for conversion to peace and to carry out the purposes of the Reorganization Act of 1945 will come largely as the result of the studies and recommendations of the Bureau of the Budget.

Looked at from another angle the Bureau is the central planning agency of the government. It does not plan the objectives that are to be attained or the broad policies of government. These are worked out at a higher level, by the major party, the President, and the majority leaders in Congress. But when policy has been agreed upon, the planning of how the work shall be done and how it can best be co-ordinated with all the rest of the work of government devolves largely upon the Bureau in its capacity as management adviser to the President.

Preparing the Budget. The fiscal year of the national government begins on July 1 and ends on the following June 30. Even before the current fiscal year has ended, the Bureau is looking ahead to the fiscal year that is to begin more than twelve months hence. By June Congress will have passed most of the appropriations and other financial measures for the year beginning on July 1, but the Budget Bureau is then already setting in motion the machinery for making a budget for the next following year.

Standard forms and instructions are sent out by the Bureau in June to all the departments and to all other agencies of government. Each department and agency has its own budget officer and procedure. These departmental budget officers compile the requests of all bureaus and divisions in the department and, under the guidance of the department head, formulate a comprehensive budget plan for the year to come. These departmental and agency requests then go to the Budget Bureau.

In the Bureau the Estimates Division has an examiner and assistants for each major division of the national administration. These officers have been busy throughout the year studying the needs of the division of the administration for which they are responsible so that they are already familiar with its personnel, organization, services, and needs, and with the acts of Congress under which it operates. In the late summer or early fall, or as soon as the agency estimates are in, they begin to study the requests and to hold conferences with the budget officers of the agency. More formal hearings are also held, in which the higher officials of the Budget Bureau participate to some extent. In the course of these proceedings estimates are further revised and additional information is compiled. By late fall the examiners present their recommendations to the Director of the Budget.

Up to this point the account has mentioned only the estimates of expenditure. In the meantime the Fiscal Division has been making studies of revenues, revenue prospects, and general economic trends as they affect the budget and the fiscal outlook for the government. The income side of the budget thus receives its share of attention.

Upon the data and recommendations laid before him the Director of the Bureau makes his own tentative decisions and then confers with the President at some length to inform him as to the budget outlook and to obtain his agreement upon the major items and upon the budget as a whole. All the work plans of all branches of the administration will thus have been brought together into a single document. This is edited by the Fiscal Division and printed in one large book under the title of *The Budget of the United States Government for the Fiscal Year Ending June* 30, 19—, and is submitted to Congress early in January with an explanatory message from the President.

Budget Procedure in Congress. The next steps in the budget process take place in the committees of Congress. To conform to the budget procedure, the houses of Congress have now each just one committee on appropriations. The House committee, consisting of 35 members, has entire authority over appropriations measures in the House. In the Senate "all general appropriation bills shall be referred to the Committee on Appropriations." This committee consists of 24 members, but provision is made for adding three members of each of several other important committees (Agriculture and Forestry, Post Office, Military Affairs, Naval Affairs, Foreign Relations, etc.) to the Appropriations Committee, *ex officio*, when appropriations concerning their special fields are being considered. As a result of these changes, Congress now has four principal committees on financial matters: two for revenue and two for appropriations. It is through the consultations of the chairmen of these committees with each other and with the Secretary of the Treasury and the Director of the Budget that some co-ordination of revenues and appropriations is achieved.

The Budget and Accounting Act forbids heads of departments and other officers to present directly to Congress any proposals for appropriations not included in the budget proposals. This does not, however, prevent the presence of such officials at the hearings held by the appropriations committees. At such hearings, and they are of great importance, the appropriate examiners from the Bureau of the Budget, the budget officer of the department, the head of the department, bureau heads and others with special knowledge of needs and requests, are usually present. Each department is taken in its turn, and as the House appropriations committee, which acts first, goes through page after page of the budget proposals, some reductions are usually made. On the basis of the figures thus arrived at, appropriations bills are prepared and enacted as laws. Of these bills there are some ten to a dozen or fifteen each session, including emergency and deficiency appropriations. They generally go into considerable detail, listing the exact salaries of many important officers (department and bureau heads, ambassadors, ministers, etc.), the amounts allowed for the contingent expenses of each agency (stationery, furniture, files, automobile service, etc.), the amounts for printing and binding, and so on, and they fill many pages in the statutes. Additional changes in the amounts appropriated are often made in the House and Senate and in the conference committees of the two houses.

Lump Sum or Itemized Appropriations? Whether appropriations passed by Congress should be itemized and detailed or should be in gross amounts or "lump sums" for each agency or subdivision has been much debated. When budgets have to be prepared so long before they are to take effect, and are to run for an entire year after, they naturally become out-of-date in many particulars before they terminate. Administrators would like to have more freedom than they usually have to adjust their budgets as they go along. On the other hand accounting officers and members of Congress who are suspicious of administrators prefer to have detailed itemization of appropriations. What happens in fact is that when Congress meets in annual session in January it must then or soon after face a number of requests for deficiency appropriations. The experience of the first six months of the fiscal year, July 1-December 31, has already revealed maladjustments between appropriations and needs. Congress has been, on the whole, rather lenient about overspending and generous in providing for deficiencies in appropriations.

In times of great emergency, like wars and severe depressions, Congress has no way of avoiding lump sum appropriations. Even the administrators who are in daily contact with the work to be done simply cannot predict even from month to month what the needs will be. The best protection for the public in such cases is to have certain statutory standards for controlling expenditures and alert committees of Congress to investigate every allegation of serious abuse of authority.

Budget Accounting. When the appropriation acts have been passed, and the new fiscal year is about to begin, the administrative controls over expenditure also begin. Accounts must be set up for each department and spending agency, on which are entered the amounts that are to be available during the year for each bureau, division or activity. Several dangers at once occur. Will the spending agency, like a person on an allowance, spend most of its money in the first part of the year, and then have to come back for a "deficiency" appropriation before the year is out? Will it be certain to expend its money for only the authorized purposes? May it not decide to start new projects that the legislature never contemplated? In the absence of proper controls over expenditure these things have happened many times. To put some checks upon expenditure, the national Budget and Accounting Act gave certain powers to the Bureau of the Budget and still more to the Comptroller General and the General Accounting Office, while the Treasury Department also has some powers of control over what is done with the money. The Director of the Budget is authorized to apportion to each spending agency a certain amount of its appropriation for each month of the year, and he gets monthly reports as to the rate of expenditure, to see whether the agencies are keeping within their apportionments.

Also at the beginning of the year, the Treasury Department issues to each spending agency an appropriation warrant, approved by the Comptroller General, advising the agency as to the amount of money available from appropriations for its expenditure. Thereupon the administrative agencies can proceed to incur obligations against the amount in conformity with law. Since the national government is a tremendous and far-flung administrative organization, issuing millions of checks and paying a multitude of claims each year, it is necessary to have disbursing officers for each major agency and at many points throughout the country. To these officers are advanced funds, not cash but credits at their local depository, against which they may draw for the payment of salaries, transportation charges, and other claims. The Comptroller General must approve these advances, which are made by the Treasury.

Accounting Control. Soon actual expenditures have to be made. Payrolls have come in, and purchases have been made. The disbursing officers pay most routine and regular claims on their own responsibility, in conformity with the rules and the accounts kept in the department concerned. In doubtful cases, claims are sent to the General Accounting Office, where the Comptroller General may have to pass on the matter himself. The line between the clear and the doubtful cases is not an easy one. Disbursing officers frequently find that they have paid illegal or improper claims, and thus they become personally liable to make up the amount. They must then try to get the money back from the person who received it, or as a last resort they may try to get Congress to make an appropriation to make it up. They are all under bond, so that in the meantime the bonding company may have been compelled to make good the amount involved.

Comptroller General of the United States. It is the Comptroller General, and the General Accounting Office under him, that have final say as to the validity of expenditures, short of any possible appeal to the courts against his rulings. This officer is appointed for a term of 15 years by the President with the approval of the Senate, and may be removed only by joint resolution of Congress or by impeachment. He heads probably the largest accounting and auditing organization in the world, consisting of thousands of regular officers and employees, including lawyers and highly skilled accountants and investigators in considerable numbers, not to mention numerous temporary employees. To this agency has been assigned by law the final power to settle accounts and to audit the books of all branches of the government. In the exercise of his functions the first Comptroller General (1921-36) handed down a very important series of decisions concerning expenditures by the administrative agencies.[10] Many expenditures were disallowed before they were made, and many others after they had been made. His decisions touched upon almost every administrative problem of the government: the hiring of personnel, the purchasing of goods, salaries, wages, pensions, travel allowances, and many other things.

Controversy over Comptroller General's Status. A sharp controversy concerning this office arose several years ago. On the one hand it was argued that the Comptroller General had been responsible to no one, not even to Congress; that his decisions had been arbitrary, technical, and often meddling; that great delay had been caused in many cases by the necessity of resorting to him for decisions; that he had failed to establish a comprehensive system of central accounting; and that he had even failed to make annual reports or constructive suggestions as to the improvement of accounting and administrative methods. Those who held this view thought that the control of current finances should be vested in the President, who is responsible for administration, and should be exercised by him through the Treasury Department, as it was down to 1921 without any serious charge of corruption or inefficiency. The Comptroller General would then become an Auditor General, with the power and the duty to audit accounts after they have been settled, and to report to Congress for its information as to expenditures and the progress of administration. On the other hand, there were those who felt that the strong outside check on current expenditure policies exercised by the Comptroller General should be continued.[11]

The result of this controversy was apparently to stiffen the resistance of Congress to any change. The Reorganization Act of 1939 forbade the President to tamper with the General Accounting Office or the Comptroller General. After having waited several years to fill the vacancy that occurred in 1936, in the hope that Congress might modify the law, President Roosevelt finally yielded in 1939 and appointed a successor to the first Comptroller General. Time has not brought any change in the position of Congress. In the Reorganization Act of 1945 it has asserted that the General Accounting Office

---

[10] See *Decisions of the Comptroller General of the United States.*

[11] For the controversy over this office see especially A. E. Buck, "Financial Control and Accountability" and Harvey C. Mansfield, "The General Accounting Office" in the President's Committee on Administrative Management, *Report with Special Studies,* pp. 135-68 and 169-202; "Financial Administration of the Federal Government," being report no. 5 prepared by the Brookings Institution for the Select Comm. to Investigate the Executive Agencies of the Government, etc., 75th Cong., 1st Sess., Senate Comm. Print; Daniel T. Selko, *The Federal Financial System,* The Brookings Institution, 1940, and Harvey Mansfield, *The Comptroller General,* New Haven, 1939. See also Lucius Wilmerding, *op. cit.,* note 2, above, espec. chs. 12, 13.

and the Comptroller General are parts of the legislative branch of government (a most astounding proposition!) and has again denied the President any power to reorganize the office.

In the meantime, as was earlier predicted, Congress has clearly been lulled into a state of feeling that all is well as long as the General Accounting Office stands.[12] It still has no real audit of national expenditures, and no adequate analysis either by its own committees or by the Comptroller General of the course of national expenditures.

REFERENCES

A. E. Buck, *The Budget in Governments of Today*, New York, 1934.

Henry Jones Ford, *The Cost of Our National Government: A Study in Political Pathology*, New York, 1910.

Harvey Mansfield, *The Comptroller General*, New Haven, 1939.

Daniel T. Selko, *The Federal Financial System*, Washington, 1940.

E. F. Bartelt, *Accounting Procedures of the United States Government*, Chicago, 1940.

Harold D. Smith, *The Management of Your Government*, New York, 1945.

Lucius Wilmerding, Jr., *The Spending Power: A History of the Efforts of Congress to Control Expenditures*, New Haven, 1943.

Edward S. Corwin, *The Twilight of the Supreme Court*, New Haven, 1934, ch. 4, "The Breakdown of Constitutional Limitations—the Spending Power."

President's Committee on Administrative Management, *Report with Special Studies*.

W. F. Willoughby, *The Problem of a National Budget*, Washington, 1918.

John M. Mathews and Clarence A. Berdahl, *Documents and Readings in American Government: National and State*, rev. ed., New York, 1940, pp. 552-70.

A. N. Christensen and E. M. Kirkpatrick, *The People, Politics, and the Politician: Readings in American Government*, New York, 1941, pp. 655-75.

[12] Lucius Wilmerding, Jr., op. cit., note 2 above, chs. 12, 13.

CHAPTER 27

Money, Banking, and Insurance

MONEY

Money serves as a measure of the price or monetary valuation put on things and services; it serves as currency or a medium of exchange; it is something that may be saved against a rainy day as well as a measure of savings; and it has other uses. Money serves its various uses best when there is a uniform system of it over wide areas, when it is divided into easily calculable units, like dollars, dimes, and cents, and when its value is kept approximately stable.

Power of Congress over the Currency. During the Revolution and the post-Revolutionary period, Congress had a monetary system, but a number of states had their own legal tender laws, under which other things than money could be used to pay debts. Gold and silver were scarce, and soon disappeared from circulation because of hoarding, while issues of paper money and other forms of legal tender were used in the financing of trade. As inflation progressed, i.e., as more money was issued, the prices of goods went up, money became less and less valuable, and so still more of it had to be printed. Interstate trade was particularly hampered, but local business was also handicapped. To avoid such conditions in the future, those who framed the Constitution decided to authorize the national government to establish a sound, uniform monetary system for the whole United States. The Constitution they drew up provides as follows:

> The Congress shall have Power . . . To coin Money, regulate the Value thereof, and of foreign Coin, and . . . To provide for the Punishment of counterfeiting the Securities and current Coin of the United States. . . .
>
> No State shall . . . coin Money; emit Bills of Credit; make any Thing but gold and silver Coin a Tender in Payment of Debts; . . .[1]

[1] U. S. Const., Art. I, sec. 8, pars. 5, 6; sec. 10, par. 1.

Here the power so fully granted to Congress is made exclusive by an equally sweeping prohibition against the states. The old state legal tender laws that made paper money and commodities available for the payment of debts were invalidated and made illegal for the future. Furthermore, state issues of "bills of credit" or simple promises to pay were forbidden.

Coinage and Legal Tender. The power to coin money and regulate the value thereof has been used by Congress to provide for the coinage of gold, silver and other coins, and the printing of paper money. Congress has determined the amount in weight of gold and of silver to go into the dollar, and has later changed the amounts so established. Two fundamental constitutional questions have been raised and settled concerning this power. (1) Has Congress the power to make paper bills, so-called "greenbacks," that are mere promises to pay, and are not backed up by either gold or silver, "legal tender" in the payment of debts? To make anything legal tender is to make it legally obligatory on individuals to accept the thing in payment of debts. The Constitution does not expressly provide for this power, but the Supreme Court, after first deciding against it, has ruled that Congress has this power by implication.[2] (2) Does the power of Congress over the currency extend so far as to authorize it to withdraw all gold from circulation, thus preventing persons who have agreed to pay in gold from so doing, and impairing the obligation of private contracts? To put it another way, are gold and silver commodities in which individuals have the right to trade freely, or may the government take over all available stocks of these precious metals, and thus force individuals to settle their contracts not by paying gold or silver, but by using the paper money issued by the government? To this question also the Supreme Court has answered affirmatively.[3]

Gold and Silver Money. In establishing a monetary system in 1792, Congress introduced the decimal system which is far simpler to calculate than the English system of pounds, shillings, and pence. This has never been changed, but the metallic basis for money has several times been altered. At first both gold and silver were coined at the then-prevailing market ratio, and thus there was no preference given to one over the other. But the market value of silver declined, while the number of grains in the silver and gold dollars (371.25 and 24.75, respectively, or 15 to 1) were fixed by law and did not change. Consequently, with the decline in the market value of bullion silver it became easier to pay debts in silver, at the 15 to 1 ratio, and so the silver dollar came to prevail. Gold went out of circulation as a result of hoarding. Later Congress reduced the number of grains of gold required to make a gold dollar to a point where it was easier to pay debts in gold than in silver, and then gold coinage prevailed for a time, while silver coins (now worth more as bullion than as

[2] The Legal Tender Cases—Hepburn v. Griswold (1870), 8 Wallace (U. S.) 603; Knox v. Lee (1871), 12 Wallace (U. S.) 457; Juillard v. Greenman (1884), 110 U. S. 421.

[3] Norman v. Baltimore and Ohio Railroad Co. (1935), 294 U. S. 240; Nortz v. U. S. (1935), 294 U. S. 317; Perry v. U. S. (1935), 294 U. S. 330.

coins) went off the market. During the Civil War and for some time after it, both gold and silver were largely withdrawn from circulation, because the "greenback" paper money issued by the government to finance the war was made legal tender, and as the greenbacks fell below the market rate for gold and silver, men paid in paper rather than in metallic money.

The Gold Standard. In 1900, following the successive defeats in Presidential elections of the "greenbackers" and those favoring the free coinage of silver at the ratio of 16 to 1, Congress definitely established the "gold standard" as the basis for the currency of the United States. This meant that, although there were silver dollars and certificates or bills outstanding, anyone could go to the Treasury of the United States or to a bank with any kind of lawful money and get gold for it if he so desired. Furthermore, there was free commerce in gold, and anyone could accumulate or hoard all the gold he could legally acquire. The government and the banks kept a reserve of gold presumably sufficient to back up all other money.

During the depression that began in 1929-30 and grew steadily worse despite attempts of the government to check it, people who had money in the banks became panic-stricken and began to go to the banks to get their money out. Many took it in gold. The bank reserves of money were depleted, still further endangering the deposits of those who had not withdrawn theirs. On March 6, 1933, President Roosevelt, two days after taking office, closed all the banks under authority of an old act of Congress. A few days later the banks were partly reopened, but gold payments were restricted and gold exports from the United States were forbidden. Congress had in the meantime empowered the President to draw in all gold coin, gold bullion, and gold certificates outstanding, and to forbid further hoarding. Another act authorized him to reduce the gold content of the dollar by not more than 50 nor less than 40 per cent. Finally, on June 5, 1933, Congress by joint resolution in effect abrogated all "gold clauses" in existing public and private contracts and securities by providing that

> All coins and currencies of the United States (including Federal Reserve notes and circulating notes of Federal Reserve banks and national banking associations) heretofore or hereafter coined or issued, shall be legal tender for all debts, public and private, public charges, taxes, duties, and dues, . . .

Present Parity of All U. S. Money. This put all currencies on a par with each other. The gold content of the dollar was reduced by the President to about 59 per cent of what it had been, ostensibly to put it on the same basis as the deflated currencies of foreign countries, but free trading in gold was at an end. The government went into the market offering to pay $35 (in paper money) for an ounce of gold, a price above its nominal coinage value even at the new rate, and all gold produced in the country, or imported into it, went to the Treasury. The coinage of gold ceased; the gold was melted into bars and put away. Thereafter the only kinds of money that circulated freely were (a) government paper money (silver certificates and treasury notes), (b) the note issues of the Federal Reserve banks and affiliated banks, (c) silver dollars, halves, quarters, and dimes, and (d) token coins (nickels and pennies) in other metals than silver. Gold can be obtained today from the treasury only by special permit, and for scientific and mechanical purposes, not for coinage. A generation is growing up that may never see gold coins, at least in this country, and it may wonder why there was once so much attachment to the gold standard.

The Currency and the Price Level. The provision for the reduction of the gold content of the dollar was attached to an act for agricultural relief. The thought was that by reducing the gold content of the dollar money could be sufficiently cheapened to assist the farmers by raising the prices they received for agricultural products. Thus an attempt was made to solve the problem of low farm prices through adjustments in the currency and coinage system of the nation. The danger in this method is very great. If one dose helps the patient, and it frequently does, why not more and stronger doses later? Why not large issues of paper money? That way lies demoralization of government finances and the destruction of the incomes of those classes that live on annuities, pensions, small investments, or fixed salaries. One of the most desirable qualities in any system of currency is stability, or steady purchasing power, and this may be destroyed by frequent tinkering with money.

Present Stocks of Bullion, Coins, and Currency. All gold coin and bullion in the United States, except such as belongs to foreign governments and is here for safekeeping, is now the property of the government. A large part of it is kept in the new bullion depository at Fort Knox, Kentucky. This depository and the several mints of the United States are under the Bureau of the Mint in the Department of the Treasury. The mints coin all silver and token coins, and melt gold and silver into bars of appropriate weight to be stored as bullion. The paper money of the United States and of the Federal Reserve banks, as well as all government securities, stamps, and checks, are printed by the Bureau of Engraving and Printing, also in the Treasury Department.

THE CONTROL OF BANKING

Early State and National Banks. The state legislatures began before the end of the Revolution to authorize the organization of banks. In 1791 the Congress under the new Constitution created, on Hamilton's recommendation, the First Bank of the United States which received a charter for 20 years. This bank was owned by private capitalists who put up its funds, but it was to serve primarily as the fiscal agent of the national government. It had a head office at Philadelphia, and branch offices in cities from Boston to New Orleans. When its charter expired in 1811, it was not renewed, as there was considerable opposition to such a central bank. The difficulties of the national government in financing the War of 1812 resulted in a change of policy, and in 1816 the Second Bank of the United States was established, also for 20 years.

Power to Incorporate Banks. It was this second bank that Maryland attempted to tax, with the result that the Supreme Court was called upon to decide the momentous question of whether the Congress had the power to incorporate banks to serve as instrumentalities of the government. Banks can serve, obviously, as depositories of taxes and other public funds, as agents for the sale of public bonds and the payment of the principal and interest thereon, and as disbursing offices for the payment of salaries, wages, pensions, and other claims against the government. Considering these facts and the powers of the government to tax, to borrow, and to spend, the Supreme Court reached the conclusion that the national government has the implied or "resultant" power to create banks and other similar instrumentalities to help carry on its acknowledged functions despite the fact that there is no provision in the national constitution directly on banking.[4] The Court decided also that the states may not tax such instrumentalities without the consent of Congress.

The power of Congress to establish national banks has not been pushed to the point of establishing an exclusively national system of banking. From the beginning the states have exercised the power to incorporate and to regulate state banks. It has been argued with good reason that Congress with its superior powers over interstate and foreign commerce could legally exclude state banks from the field of commercial banking,[5] but Congress has never even seriously considered such action. As a result the nation has two different series of banks, national and state, although there are many connections between the two.

National and State Banks, 1863-1913. The period from 1836 to the Civil War was an exceptional one when there were no national banks. Then in the Civil War the national government found it necessary to employ a private banker, Jay Cooke, to help sell the bonds needed to finance military operations, and out of this experience grew the national banking system. Under the national banking acts passed in 1863 and 1864, Congress authorized the organization of national banks.

Since 1863 the United States has had both national and state banks. Although some states enforced strict requirements on state banks as to the amount of reserves, the total capital required to commence operations, examination of accounts and assets, and other factors, the national banks were on the whole much better regulated and managed. The difficulties in this dual system were many, however, and bank failures were much more frequent than they should have been. Indeed, the United States has led the world in bank failures. It was too easy, especially under the state laws, to get bank charters. Little money and practically no banking experience were required.

---

[4] McCulloch v. Maryland (1819), 4 Wheaton 316.
[5] See Charles W. Collins, *The Constitutional Power of Congress to Enforce a Single System of Commercial Banking*, pamphlet, Washington, 1931.

In many states the supervision of banks was not sufficiently strict to be effective. It was impossible, also, to increase the supply of money when it was needed by trade, and to decrease it when the demand for loans fell off. The transfer of funds between banks was also more difficult than it should have been, with the result that the funds were not always in the banks where and when they were needed.

The Federal Reserve System. To overcome these and other defects in the American banking system, Congress in 1913 created the Federal Reserve System. For the purposes of this system the country is divided into 12 Federal Reserve districts, in each of which there is a Federal Reserve bank. The national banks in each district were required initially to use 6 per cent of their capital and surplus to acquire shares in the stock of the district Reserve bank; approved state banks in the district are required to subscribe to a proportionate extent when they join the system. Each district Reserve bank is managed by a board of 9 directors, of whom 3 represent the member banks, 3 others (also elected by these banks) represent agriculture, commerce, and industry in the district, and the remaining 3, appointed by the Federal Reserve Board, are other residents of the district who are not engaged in banking. Thus each Reserve bank is locally owned and locally managed. The Board of Governors of the Federal Reserve System has its offices in Washington. It is composed of 7 members appointed for 12-year terms by the President with the consent of the Senate. This board has general control over all the Reserve banks.

Functions of Reserve Banks. The Reserve bank in each district is the "bankers' bank" for all the member banks, and it also has close connections with other Reserve banks. Each Reserve bank serves its own member banks by lending them money on proper security, receiving their deposits of reserve balances, transferring funds, and serving as a clearing house and collecting agency for them. It serves the national government as a depository and fiscal agent. It issues Federal Reserve notes to expand the volume of money in circulation, and is supposed to contract this volume when the demand falls off. Up to 1934 the Reserve banks had no direct business connections with any but the member banks, but in that year Congress conferred power on them to make loans, in exceptional circumstances, to establish industries and businesses in the district. Thus each Reserve bank is at the center of the banking network of its area, and each is in turn part of a larger network in the Federal Reserve System.

The Board of Governors. This board has power to regulate the rate of interest charged by the Reserve banks, to change the reserve requirements for member banks, to control the lending by member banks for stock market operations, to admit new banks to the Reserve System in any district, and to examine the books and assets of all Reserve banks and member banks. As fiscal agency for the national government, the board and the so-called "open market committee" have power to instruct and compel Reserve banks and member banks to buy and sell government bonds as needed, to maintain the government's credit and to accommodate business. With all its tremendous powers, the Board of Governors is a human institution, subject to human errors. It has been charged that the board could have avoided much of the unwise speculation in stocks and the lending to foreign borrowers that led up to the stock market crash of 1929, with its resultant bank failures and the extreme deflation of agricultural prices. The board is no doubt influenced like other agencies by the spirit of the times, and the party that is in power.

Insurance of Bank Deposits. One outcome of the collapse of the banking system in 1932-33, and of the subsequent effort of Congress to reconstruct and improve the system, was the establishment of a national system of insurance for bank deposits. The idea of guaranteeing depositors in state banks had long been agitated. Beginning in 1907, a number of states in a tier from North Dakota to Texas, together with Mississippi and Washington, introduced systems of guaranty of bank deposits. The method was to assess each state bank a percentage of its daily deposits, and turn the fund so accumulated over to a state board to use to bolster up weak banks and to pay depositors in banks that failed. Naturally the stronger state banks resented the system of assessing them to insure their weaker brothers, and some of them became national banks to avoid the assessments, leaving largely the smaller and weaker banks in the state systems. As the states that tried the system were mainly agricultural states, where crop failures for a few years would be disastrous, and where the banks at best were not of the strongest, the guaranty system was not tried out under the best circumstances. During the good years up to about 1920 all went fairly well, but in the postwar deflation one after another of the state guaranty funds was found inadequate and had to be given up.

The FDIC. Under the Banking Act of 1933, and subsequent amendments to it, Congress authorized the creation of the Federal Deposit Insurance Corporation. This corporation is managed by a board of three members consisting of the Comptroller of the Currency, ex officio, and two other members appointed by the President with Senate consent for 6-year terms. The government subscribed $150,000,000 and the Federal Reserve banks $139,000,000 to its capital stock. In addition the corporation may issue bonds if necessary. All banks in the Federal Reserve System, and such other banks as are admitted by the board, are members of the deposit insurance system. Each one is assessed annually one-twelfth of 1 per cent of its average daily deposits, for the purposes of the insurance fund. All individual deposits in insured banks up to $5,000 are insured in full. Deposits above that amount for any one account are insured on a descending scale, so that amounts of over $50,000 are insured only 50 per cent. The board has power to examine all insured state banks that are not part of the Federal Reserve System, and to examine other banks with the approval of the Comptroller of the Currency or the Federal Reserve Board. It is also authorized to admit new banks to the insurance system, to exclude banks for cause, to prohibit or limit the payment of interest by insured state banks within certain limits, and to control various actions by insured banks that might make them less safe. Well over 90 per cent of the commercial banks in the United States are within the insurance system, and far more than 90 per cent of all depositors are insured. Whenever an insured bank fails or is in danger of failing, the FDIC takes over its assets and affairs and pays off the insured depositors.

Tendencies Toward Further Centralization. Many persons thought in the bank crisis of 1933 that the national government should nationalize the entire banking system. They assumed that a completely unified system was desirable. There was a good deal of centralization at that time, and more has taken place since then, especially through the operations of the Federal Reserve System and the deposit insurance scheme. Though much reduced since 1920, the number of state commercial banks is still over 9,000, of which over 7,500 are not in the Federal Reserve System. Also under state charters are about 550 mutual savings banks, including some very large ones. All told, the state banks are still a very important element in the nation's banking arrangements.

THE GOVERNMENT AS A MONEYLENDER

Agricultural Credit. Not content with the opportunities for borrowing offered to them by the banks, life insurance companies, and other private corporations and individuals, the agricultural population began long ago to demand that the government itself lend money to farmers, or provide special facilities for the financing of farm buying and farming operations.

The first important law designed to meet this demand was the Federal Farm Loan Act of 1916, which set up the Federal Land Banks. This was followed in 1923 by the creation of the Intermediate Credit Banks, and in 1929 by the organization of the Federal Farm Board. In 1933 Congress reorganized and extended still further the system of agricultural credit and integrated it under the present Farm Credit Administration (FCA), which is now in the Department of Agriculture. This agency, with its headquarters in Washington, consists of a governor, two deputy governors, and various commissioners in charge of different branches of the work, all appointed by the President with Senate consent. In Washington alone the FCA has over 3,000 employees and an operating budget of nearly $10,000,000 annually.

Federal Farm Loan Districts and Banks. For loan purposes the country is divided into 12 regions, in each of which one city serves as the center for the local organization. Moreover, the district organization is now highly integrated to correspond with the national organization centered at Washington so that all agricultural credit needs can be met. The principal banks to be found in each district are as follows: (1) A *Federal land bank*, with its related national farm loan associations consisting of farmers in the various communities in the district who wish to borrow from the banks. (2) A *Federal intermediate credit bank*, with its "production credit associations," livestock loan associations, and other affiliates. (3) A *production credit corporation* and its clients, the production credit associations, composed of farmers or ranchers. (4) A *bank for cooperatives*, providing credit for the farmers' cooperative associations. Other agencies such as units of the Emergency Crop and Feed Loan Section, the Regional Agricultural Credit Corporations, and the Federal Credit Union System are also under the FCA.

Unification of Farm Credit Facilities. Beginning with various agencies for different farm credit purposes, the national government soon unified them under the present FCA. Within each district also there is unification of services and agencies through using the same officers as a board of directors (Farm Credit Board) for each of the principal farm credit agencies in the district, while this board in turn has one general agent as its executive and coordinator of services. Funds for lending are borrowed through the Federal Farm Mortgage Corporation, whose bonds in turn are guaranteed by the national government.

Government Loans to Business. For the national government, loans to farmers were only the beginning of government lending activities. The War Finance Corporation (of 1917-18), whose affairs are still not entirely closed, made some wartime loans for military production purposes. Congress enacted in 1932 the law creating the Reconstruction Finance Corporation (RFC) with a large capital subscribed by the government, which had the power, among others, of making loans to banks, railroads, and other businesses and industries to help tide them over the emergency caused by the depression. These were to be "lifesaving" loans. In 1933 this corporation, with changed powers and purposes, bolstered up many banks by putting money into them, in return for which it received their preferred stocks to an equal amount. This was an emergency measure, and the banks are buying back their stocks and thus retiring their loans from the government. Much of the money lent to railroads and industries will also be repaid. During World War II the RFC received new powers to aid in producing and acquiring essential war materials and in constructing works essential for defense.

Loans to Home Owners and Builders. The depression emergency called for other lending activities on the part of the national government. The Public Works Administration (PWA), also supplied with government funds, made numerous and important loans to states and municipalities for the purpose of aiding them in construction projects that would put men back to work. This took the government into the fields of housing, public utilities, and other activities of local governments. In the same general program it was provided also that home ownership, home building, and housing repairs should be encouraged. There was created, therefore, in 1934, a Federal Housing Administration for a number of related purposes. Some of the less expensive ones were the provision of small loans for home modernization, and aid to building and loan associations and federal savings and loan associations. The largest single activity in housing loans was that of refinancing mortgages on homes that the owners were likely to lose on account of mortgage foreclosures during the worst of the depression. This was handled by the Home Owners' Loan Corporation (HOLC) which lent out over $3 billion of government funds in a 2-year period. It stopped lending in June, 1936, and is now in liquidation.

Federal Loan Agency. As in the case of agricultural credit, the multiplication of national government lending agencies soon called for some integration to prevent unwise and contradictory loan policies and the waste of public funds. This was achieved in 1939 when the Federal Loan Agency was created to supervise and co-ordinate the work of practically all national lending agencies not concerned primarily with agriculture. It has under its control the RFC mentioned above, the Federal Home Loan Bank Board, the Federal Housing Administration, the Export-Import Bank of Washington, the Disaster Loan Corporation, the Electric Home and Farm Authority, and others of a civilian nature; and during World War II it had also a group of defense and war agencies—to provide a rubber reserve, metals reserve, defense plants, defense supplies, and defense homes: Although not called a department, the Federal Loan Agency is organized like one, under a single administrative head. The breadth of its powers to lend public money suggests that the government as banker and moneylender "has arrived."

CONTROL OF SECURITY ISSUES AND EXCHANGES

Dangers of Fraud in Stock Sales. The financing of many small and most large-scale private businesses is carried on in whole or in part through the sale of stocks, bonds, and other evidences of ownership. The stockholders are usually the true owners of the business, while the bondholders have claims against the property similar in nature to mortgages. Millions of Americans are owners of stocks and bonds, mostly on a small scale, and there are other millions who have hopes of investing and who are therefore prospective buyers. The field for the unscrupulous issuer and for the man selling stocks of dubious value is simply immense. No one knows how much is lost by investors in companies that are either very doubtful or positively fraudulent. The usual estimates of such losses run into hundreds of millions each year.

Difficulties in Checking Frauds. The extreme laxity of American corporation laws, and the ease with which companies organized in one state can slip into another to do business, make it difficult to prevent stock frauds through state corporation laws. A uniform, compulsory federal incorporation act may be the ultimate solution for preventing such frauds. The common law remedies of the investor against the one who practices fraud upon him are ineffective, because so many stock promoters are here today and gone tomorrow, and even when caught are found to have transferred their money to others or to have lost it in gambles of their own. Criminal prosecutions are effective only in putting a few of this ilk "out of circulation." It is not surprising, therefore, that the states began to seek other controls over issues and sales of stocks. Kansas, in 1911, enacted the first "blue sky law," or law to regulate the issue and sale of stocks within its limits. Today all states seem to have at least some minimum regulations.

State Securities Commissioners. Most of the state laws set up a state department or office for the licensing and control of issues and sales of securities. As a rule there is one chief officer rather than a board at the head of this office. Legislation requires either that no stocks may be issued or sold in the state without being registered with this office, or that all dealers and salesmen of stocks shall be licensed, or both. The latter provision makes it possible to bring criminal action against all salesmen who fail to obtain licenses. Control over the issues of stocks varies considerably. In some states simple registration and filing of the prospectus are all that seem to be required. In others the securities commissioner of the state has the right to investigate the company, at the latter's expense, and to refuse it the right to sell the stock, or to put stringent limits on the amount to be sold, the price, and the advertising statements to be used. The permission given by the state office for the sale of the stock is not a public guarantee that the stock is good, but only that it is not an outright fraud. As in the purchase of the more reputable, seasoned stocks listed on the stock exchanges, the investor takes his own risks.

Failure of States to Check Sales of Fraudulent Stocks. The difficulty faced by the small staffs of officers employed by the state securities commissioners in attempting to learn about all cases of fraudulent sales, the frequent changes in their personnel, lack of experience, and the changing policies of these offices, coupled with the ability of the stock promoters to slip into and out of the state and to use the mails in their selling schemes, operate to reduce the effectiveness of state blue sky legislation. It is even debated whether fraudulent stock sales have been reduced at all by the attempts to enforce such laws. The efforts of the more than 40 states that have really tried to put an end to stock frauds are nullified in large part by their lack of control over interstate dealings, and by the fact that a few states make no serious effort to cooperate. Some progress is being made, however, through the National Association of Securities Commissioners, working in cooperation with legitimate investment bankers and the national government's Securities and Exchange Commission.

National Legislation. The national government has for years attempted to enforce its own laws against the use of the mails to defraud. In many cases, but frequently too late to save the investors' money, the postal inspectors have arrested and obtained the conviction of those who sold fake stocks by mail and those who used the mails in other ways to get the unwary to send them money. In 1933 Congress enacted a law to control the issue and sale of securities through interstate commerce and the mail. The next year it created the Securities and Exchange Commission (SEC). This commission consists of 5 members appointed by the President with Senate consent. Terms of office are 5 years, and so arranged that one new member can be appointed each year.

Not more than 3 members are to be of one political party. Its powers and duties are as follows:

1. *Control of Security Issues by SEC.* All issues of stocks, bonds, and similar securities that are to be offered to the public to be sold in interstate commerce or through the mails must be registered with the commission before they may be sold. The commission has the power to compel the issuers to fill out standard forms giving a "full and fair" statement of the material facts regarding the stocks and bonds to be sold. The commission then has 20 days before the registration becomes effective in which to examine the statements. If it refuses to accept the registration on the ground that a fraud is being committed, the securities may not legally be sold. One of the principal divisions of SEC gives full time to examining and registering proposed new issues.

2. *Control over Stock Exchanges and Dealers.* The regulation of stock exchanges is a separate matter. Although stock exchanges perform a useful function, on the whole, many practices by individuals and groups operating in the exchanges have resulted in fraud on the investor. Sales on excessively small margins, "pools" and "matched orders" designed to give an artificial stimulus to the price of certain stocks, and many other practices have been successful in attracting the ignorant investor into unwise buying, with resultant loss to himself and gain to the manipulators. The commission requires the registration of exchanges and of dealers in stocks, and regulates the conduct of business on the exchanges and in the local offices of stockbrokers, in the public interest, while the Federal Reserve Board has power to set the minimum amount of "margin" or down payment that the stock buyer must make, as well as to control borrowing for the purposes of floating and selling stocks. To limit stock speculation and thus to limit inflation, the Board in 1946 required that securities sold on the exchanges be paid for in full in cash.

3. *Control of Investment Companies and Advisers.* In 1939 and 1940 Congress enacted new laws imposing on SEC the duty of regulating investment companies and investment advisers, and of protecting the rights of investors in bonds and other trust "indentures."

4. *Control over Public Utility Holding Companies.* The commission's powers over public utility holding companies, established by act of Congress in 1935, are designed to prevent a number of abuses such as overinflation through the acquisition of scattered and unrelated plants and businesses, purchase of operating companies at excessive prices, milking of operating companies for the benefit of the holding companies, and various practices of deception to the injury of investors. Some of the larger holding companies have already been deflated and streamlined.

BANKRUPTCY

Purposes of Bankruptcy Laws. When any person, whether workman, farmer, businessman, or large corporation, has assets that are too small to pay outstanding debts or obligations, there is need of some legal method for giving the creditors a fair and proportionate part of the assets, and of relieving the debtor from further legal obligation to attempt to pay. The workman's case is not the most important, financially, but every year thousands of workmen and farmers go through bankruptcy proceedings. The largest number of cases consists of small merchants, but in times of severe depression even giant corporations are involved.

State versus National Power over Bankruptcy. During the Revolution and the Post-Revolutionary period, with each state fixing its own rules on bankruptcy, the tendency seemed to be to favor the debtor. The merchant in the adjoining state who had sold goods across the line was fair game for all who wanted to avoid their legal debts. To prevent such interstate injustices, the Constitution authorized Congress to establish "uniform Laws on the subject of Bankruptcies throughout the United States." From almost every point of view, uniform, national legislation on bankruptcy is to be preferred over many diverse and conflicting state laws. On three different occasions in American history, 1801-03, 1841-43, and 1867-78, before the passage of the present act (1898) there were national bankruptcy laws in effect, but in each case the return of better times led to the repeal of the act. During the intervals between these acts, state laws filled the gaps, and even while the national laws were or are in force, state laws are available to cover matters not covered in the national bankruptcy code. In addition to general national and state bankruptcy legislation there are national and state acts covering particular businesses like banks and railroads.

Bankruptcy Proceedings. Proceedings under the general bankruptcy law are begun in the federal district courts, and are carried up to the circuit courts of appeal and in rare cases to the Supreme Court. They may be begun by the debtor, who finds that his assets will not cover his debts and proceeds voluntarily to get court action; or they may be initiated by the creditors, under certain conditions, and in this case the proceedings are called involuntary. Creditors may take such action whenever a debtor who is not meeting his obligations has concealed some part of his assets, or has turned some of his assets over to certain creditors, or has made an assignment of his assets to his creditors, or has admitted his inability to pay his debts. In such cases the courts will take jurisdiction and will appoint a referee in bankruptcy to handle the assets and business of the debtor. All the various claims against the estate are assembled, while at the same time all the assets are appraised and totaled. There are hearings for the creditors, and they are allowed to appoint a trustee to look after their interests. In the end, the assets are sold and the creditors are paid their proportionate shares, and the insolvent person is given a discharge which is equivalent to a legal wiping out of his debts. In certain cases the proceedings take the form of a "receivership" in equity, the aim in these instances being to preserve the business as a going concern, to reorganize it if possible, to scale down its debts, and perhaps to sell it as a complete unit.

Railroads and public utilities are frequently handled in this way, but under separate legislation.

The New Deal and the Bankruptcy Laws. The severe drop in business during the years 1931-34 threatened bankruptcy to many concerns that were inherently sound. As a result there were several acts passed by Congress in 1933 and 1934 to permit the reorganization of certain corporations and to authorize compositions with their creditors, in order to avoid bankruptcy. The RFC was given power also to make the necessary loans to stave off bankruptcy for banks, railroads, and industries wherever possible. Other acts were passed to enable farmers with heavily mortgaged farms to continue to live on and to operate their farms upon payment of certain rents fixed as reasonable by the courts, and to permit municipal corporations also to compromise with their creditors. Several of the first acts were held unconstitutional, including the first Frazier-Lemke act for the benefit of farmers, and the act for municipal bankruptcies, but later laws were sustained and are still being used to clear up old debt situations.

THE REGULATION OF INSURANCE

Extent and Importance of Insurance. The insurance business has grown to be one of the largest and most important in American society. Insurance is now available against almost every type of risk and uncertainty known to man, such as sickness, accidents, fire losses, burglary, crop losses, embezzlement, industrial accidents and disease, automobile damages and lawsuits, and unemployment, while life insurance policies in effect alone amount to about $150 billion. Life insurance has become one of the most important ways of saving on the part of most people, while all insurance has the effect of spreading risks over a considerable number of persons, each of whom pays a little now (called a premium) in order to be assured of the payment of a much larger sum later in case accident, robbery, or fire loss comes to him.

State Control. Naturally this business is of tremendous public importance. To give the buyer of insurance some guarantee that his premium payments will be well handled and safely invested, and that he will not be defrauded or caused to suffer loss by the dishonesty or the ignorance or carelessness of the insurer, it has been necessary to develop extensive codes of legislation, large bodies of judicial decisions, and powerful administrative agencies to keep supervision over those who offer to sell the various types of insurance.

Congress has never entered seriously upon the task of regulating the insurance business. The states were the first to undertake such work, and they have continued to occupy most of the field. In 1869 the Supreme Court, in upholding a Virginia statute for the regulation of insurance companies, said that "issuing a policy of insurance is not a transaction of commerce." [6] This limited utterance became the basis for broader dicta such as these: that "contracts of

[6] Paul v. Virginia (1869), 8 Wall. 168, 183.

insurance are not commerce at all, neither state nor interstate," [7] and that "the business of insurance is not commerce." [8] These statements assured the states and the insurance companies that Congress had no power to enter this field of regulation.

In none of these cases, however, was any act of Congress before the Court for consideration. Finally, in 1944, the question of the power of Congress was raised directly. A group of fire insurance companies in the southeastern states were charged under the Sherman Anti-Trust Law with monopolistic practices, including rate-fixing, and boycotting and coercing their few competitors. The constitutional question was whether the insurance business is commerce, since the Sherman Act was passed under the commerce power of Congress. After considering the nature, incidents, and effects of the insurance business the court majority ruled very definitely that insurance is commerce and subject to regulation in its interstate phases by the national government.[9] The majority also ruled that the Sherman Act covered the types of monopolistic practices that were alleged in this case.

This decision aroused a tremendous furore. The states petitioned for a rehearing of the case; the rehearing was granted, but the Supreme Court did not change its ruling. Resort was had also to Congress. That body did not amend the Sherman Act to exempt insurance companies, but it did allow the companies a respite during which they could set their house in order and thus escape prosecution. The net result is that state supervision continues practically unimpaired, but the threat of possible future action by Congress hangs over the state insurance commissions and the insurance companies.

REFERENCES

Charles C. Rohlfing, and others, *Business and Government*, 4th ed., Chicago, 1941.

Gerald O. and L. G. Dykstra, *Selected Cases on Government and Business*, Chicago, 1937.

Thomas J. Anderson, *Federal and State Control of Banking*, New York, 1934.

Edwin W. Kemmerer, *The ABC of the Federal Reserve System*, Princeton, N. J., 1922.

Brookings Institution, *Report to the Select Committee of the U. S. Senate to Investigate the Executive Agencies of the Government*, . . . no. 1, Report on Government Financial Agencies, Washington, 1937.

Harold D. Koontz, *Government Control of Business*, Boston, 1941.

Emanuel Stein, *Government and the Investor*, New York, 1941.

Merle Fainsod and Lincoln Gordon, *Government and the American Economy*, New York, 1941.

[7] New York Life Insurance Company v. Deer Lodge County (1913), 231 U. S. 495, 503, 504, 510.

[8] Hooper v. California (1895), 155 U. S. 648, 654, 655.

[9] U. S. v. South-Eastern Underwriters Association (1944), 322 U. S. 533.

Temporary National Economic Committee, *Final Report and Recommendations*, Senate Doc. no. 35, 77th Cong., 1st sess.; also its *Hearings* series, and *Monographs* series.

United States Government Manual.

Board of Governors, Federal Reserve System, *The Federal Reserve System—Its Purposes and Functions*, Washington, 1939.

A. N. Christensen and E. M. Kirkpatrick, *The People, Politics, and the Politician: Readings in American Government*, New York, 1941, pp. 737-77.

CHAPTER 28

Commerce and Industry

THE ECONOMIC ROLE OF GOVERNMENT

Politics and economics, or government and business, are inseparable activities in any organized community or state. In a communist state they are practically indistinguishable. In an individualistic society the two activities are more clearly definable because they are in different hands. The economic activities are conducted and controlled primarily by the owners and workers. Each individual must make his own way and his own choices in such matters as making a living and acquiring property. The government—and this is true of the national government of the United States—determines and tries to enforce the rules of business so that there will be adequate production and fair distribution. In the main it encourages, protects, and regulates, but does not try to operate business. Depression conditions and wartime needs bring a very considerable increase in the economic activities of government. Recent thinking on the part of many leaders and various actions of Congress and the President point also to a greatly increased and more positive economic role for government in the future. There are plans for a public guaranty of full employment, under which government will stand by in readiness to fill the gap when general employment declines. In the meantime, however, the economic functions of the national government are more limited but still highly important.

Regulation and Promotion of Business. It is impossible to draw a sharp line between governmental activities that promote and those that regulate business. So-called regulations that prohibit or restrict one type of business activity are generally only parts of a broad scheme, the aim of which is to increase the total volume of business and employment. Thus the purposes of regulatory laws and promotional measures may be listed together as follows: (1) To prevent downright stealing, fraud, and cheating in business transactions. (2) To ensure the buyer of reasonably good quality, honest measure, and low prices. (3) To protect the people's health, safety, and morals insofar as these may be adversely affected by business and industrial activities. (4) To promote business convenience through a uniform currency, standard weights and measures, better transportation, and numerous other devices. (5) To promote national economic independence and protect home industries from undue foreign competition. (6) Through these and other methods to increase the total volume of business and employment, raise the American standard of living, and promote the "general welfare."

THE POWER TO REGULATE BUSINESS

Regulation of Early American Commerce. The general commerce of the English colonies in America was regulated by Parliament. The regulations aimed in part to make the colonies serve as producers of raw materials for the factories in England, and to prevent the colonists from competing with the English manufacturers. At the same time there was a considerable amount of local regulation of business in each colony by the colonial assembly, as well as a little in the cities like New York. When independence was declared, Congress assumed the right to make commercial treaties with foreign countries, but in the Articles of Confederation the states expressly reserved the right to tax imports.[1] Congress also had powers with respect to coinage, the fixing of standards of weights and measures, regulating trade with the Indians, and providing for a postal system among the states, but these powers were exceedingly limited, and Congress had no power to enforce its regulations. In general the states regulated business according to the English common law, of which more hereafter.

The Constitution and the Commerce Power. The makers of the Constitution aimed to make the United States a single economic unit, with complete freedom of trade internally, so that the market for every business would be as wide as the country. Not only the so-called "commerce clause" of the Constitution, but many others vest powers in Congress that tend in the same direction. The clauses on money, on patents and copyrights, on weights and measures, on the post office, on bankruptcy, and on taxation, all buttress the commerce clause, which reads:

> The Congress shall have Power . . . To regulate Commerce with foreign Nations, and among the several States, and with the Indian Tribes.[2]

Congressional regulation of commerce was rather meager before the Civil War, and it was not until 1879 that any act passed by Congress to regulate commerce was held to be beyond its powers.[3] Between that time and the pres-

---

[1] Articles of Confederation, Art. IX, par. 1.
[2] U. S. Const., Art. I, sec. 8, par. 3.
[3] The Trade Mark Cases (1879), 100 U. S. 82.

ent, commercial regulations have increased greatly, and yet not more than a half dozen other acts of Congress have been held invalid as beyond the commerce power. The practical and judicial interpretation of this power is important enough to warrant careful analysis.

1. *Powers of Congress over Foreign Commerce.* The commerce clause is clearly divisible into three parts, each relating to a different branch of commerce: (a) that with foreign nations; (b) that with the Indian tribes; and (c) that among the states. The first of these, the power over foreign commerce, must be read in conjunction with the Court's attitude concerning the complete and exclusive power of the national government over all matters connected with external affairs.[4] Congress has regulated foreign commerce in almost every respect. It has passed acts governing navigation, shipping and the safety of ships, pilotage, the employment and compensation of seamen, and many other details for ships in foreign commerce. It has shut off commerce completely with certain foreign powers, it has forbidden some kinds of commerce, permitted other kinds to come in free, and put heavy tariffs on still other kinds of goods. Not one of its acts in this field has ever been held invalid. Its power over foreign commerce is evidently complete and exclusive, and if any state regulations as to ports and harbors are permitted to stand, it is only because they control local matters that Congress has not itself intended to regulate.

2. *Commerce with the Indians.* The power to regulate commerce with the Indian tribes is also completely in the hands of Congress.[5]

3. *Interstate Commerce Power.* The power to control commerce "among the several states" presents a different situation. The Tenth Amendment reserves to the states or to the people all powers not granted by the Constitution to the national government, or denied by it to the states. This provision introduced an element of confusion into the meaning of the commerce clause, a confusion that has only recently begun to be eliminated. Because the states always have regulated many aspects of industry and commerce, and because Congress has at no time attempted to regulate everything in the field, there has been a vast zone for possible overlapping and conflict between state and national regulations. In cases where actual dispute has arisen the courts have scrutinized closely the words of the clause that grants to Congress the power to regulate interstate commerce. They have asked: What is *commerce?* What is *interstate* commerce, or commerce "among the states"? What is *regulation?*

Growth of Law of Interstate Commerce. What is essentially a political question, as to which of two bodies shall exercise a certain power, a question on which there was originally no law whatever, has become a complicated constitutional question, the complications being largely the result of Supreme Court decisions. The Court has not been able to follow throughout its history

[4] See ch. 22.
[5] See ch. 24.

a clear and consistent line of reasoning and decision.[6] In the earliest decades it was constructive and nationalistic; later it took a sharp swing toward upholding state rights in matters of commercial regulation; and still later it began to apply the Fourteenth Amendment to invalidate state regulations also, so that the law became considerably confused. The ones who benefited from this confusion were naturally those commercial interests who desired no regulation by either the states or the nation.

The Nature of Commerce. Gibbons v. Ogden, the leading case on what is commerce, involved the validity of an exclusive franchise given by the state of New York to Robert Livingston and Robert Fulton to operate steamboats in New York waters.[7] Ogden was operating such a boat for Fulton and Livingston, while Gibbons, the other party to the suit, was operating over the same route between New York and New Jersey under a license from the United States government. In a suit by Ogden to prevent Gibbons from competing with him, the Supreme Court of the United States had to decide on the rights of the two parties, and this meant that it had to settle the relative powers of the states and of the national government over interstate commerce. Chief Justice Marshall wrote as follows:

> The subject to be regulated is commerce; and . . . to ascertain the extent of the power, it becomes necessary to settle the meaning of the word. The counsel for the appellee would limit it to traffic, to buying and selling, or to the interchange of commodities, and do not admit that it comprehends navigation. This would restrict a general term, applicable to many objects, to one of its significations. Commerce, undoubtedly, is traffic, but it is something more; it is intercourse. It describes the commercial intercourse between nations, and parts of nations, in all its branches, and is regulated by prescribing rules for carrying on that intercourse.

The Supreme Court did not continue, however, to hold this broad view of commerce. As noted in the preceding chapter, insurance was considered for a time as not constituting a part of commerce.[8] Similarly agriculture, fisheries, mining, and manufacturing were held not to be included under the commerce power. "Commerce succeeds to manufacture, and is not a part of it." Since commerce is "intercourse for the purposes of trade," the Court said at one time, "plainly, the incidents leading up to and culminating in the mining of coal do not constitute such intercourse." [9]

[6] See Edward S. Corwin, *The Commerce Power versus State Rights*, Princeton, 1936; Joseph E. Kallenbach, *Federal Cooperation with the States Under the Commerce Clause*, Ann Arbor, 1942; F. D. G. Ribble, *State and National Power over Commerce*, New York, 1937.

[7] Gibbons v. Ogden (1824), 9 Wheaton 1.

[8] See ch. 27, and decision in Paul v. Virginia (1869), 8 Wallace 168.

[9] See Kidd v. Pearson (1888), 128 U. S. 1; U. S. v. E. C. Knight Co. (1895), 156 U. S. 1; Carter v. Carter Coal Co. (1936), 298 U. S. 238.

The decisions in which these statements were made have all been overruled in recent years. During the great depression of the 1930s Congress and the President found it necessary to adopt a substantial program of new legislation to revive and to regulate American commerce, industry, and labor. After some preliminary resistance the Supreme Court fell into line, and upheld what had been done. The national commerce power was thus extended in new directions and to points far beyond what had been reached before.

Concept of Commerce Power Today. In the background of the Court's position today lies a change of attitude—from an uncompromising belief in *laissez faire* to a recognition of the need for greater control by government over the economic processes. The thinking of the judges on the specific subject of the national commerce power has been influenced by a number of factors and ideas such as the following:

1. It is impossible to draw a precise line between commerce and noncommerce. For example, in the Minnesota open-pit iron mines the scoop shovels with one single sweep dig the ore out of the ground and start it on its journey by depositing it in the cars that are to carry it to the Great Lakes ports. At what point in this single, unified movement of the scoop shovel does mining cease and commerce begin?

2. When Congress wishes to regulate commerce it must in practice regulate the instrumentalities by which commerce is carried on. Modern corporations, which are some of the chief instrumentalities of commerce, engage in a great variety of activities in many states and between them. How can Congress separate these various activities which are so intertwined and interdependent in order to regulate some and exempt others? How can it regulate the instrumentalities themselves if it cannot make its regulations impinge upon those activities of the instrumentalities that are most important to the resultant commerce?

> When industries organize themselves on a national scale, making their relation to interstate commerce the dominant factor in their activities, how can it be maintained that their industrial labor relations constitute a forbidden field into which Congress may not enter when it is necessary to protect interstate commerce from the paralyzing consequences of industrial war? We have often said that interstate commerce itself is a practical conception.[10]

3. The supposed conflict between the power of Congress over commerce and the reserved powers of the states can be resolved by giving proper emphasis to the supremacy clause of the Constitution. The acts of Congress made in pursuance of the Constitution are the supreme law of the land. To protect and promote commerce Congress may need to regulate many things that do not seem in themselves to be commerce but that seriously *affect* commerce.

[10] N.L.R.B. *v.* Jones & Laughlin Steel Corporation (1937), 301 U. S. 1.

How else can a supreme power maintain its supremacy? Thus the commerce power includes the power to regulate the conditions that affect commerce.

The Relationship Between Interstate and Intrastate Commerce. By what principles, then, may the state and national governments determine their respective powers over commerce? In the case of Gibbons v. Ogden, the attorneys on one side argued as if the power of the national government to regulate commerce could operate only at the state line, and not within the state, or in short that commerce is interstate only at the instant and at the point where it crosses state lines. This was of course absurd, and had to be overruled. Commerce is interstate, or among the states, from the time the transaction begins in one state continuously until it terminates in another. It is interstate, also, even though the beginning and the end of the transaction are in the same state, if in its course the shipment or the communication crosses a state line. It is a part of interstate commerce also if it is an intrastate activity that links up with interstate commerce.

Validity of State Regulations That Affect Interstate Commerce. It is sometimes said that the power of Congress over interstate commerce is exclusive, that the states have no share in it. Another saying is that if Congress has neglected to regulate some phase of interstate commerce "the silence of Congress" must be construed to mean that that phase of commerce shall be wholly free from regulation. Various attempts by the states to enforce regulations in such instances have been held unconstitutional. On the other hand state regulations of local aspects of commerce, to protect the health, morals, safety, and welfare of the people, have generally been upheld. This entire subject needs greater clarification than it has received. Many regulations of a local nature, made by state and local governments, actually affect interstate commerce. Some do so only indirectly, such as regulations requiring railroads to maintain watchmen at important traffic crossings, which add to the expense of operating railroads and have some effect on interstate rates. Others do so more directly, as a regulation of the state of Washington, recently upheld by the Supreme Court, by which the state required state inspection of certain motor-driven tugboats that were not regulated by act of Congress.[11] The state was in this case filling in a void in the national laws, and it was admittedly making a direct regulation of interstate and foreign commerce. In like manner, state and local taxes on interstate carriers and on interstate business are not necessarily invalid. If they do not place excessive or discriminatory burdens on such commerce, they will be sustained.[12] Had any other conclusion been reached, the states would have lost the power to tax railroads, telegraph and express lines, goods carried in interstate commerce, and many other things.

Original Package Doctrine. One rule for determining at what point interstate and foreign commerce ends is the "original package" doctrine. (1) Goods

[11] Kelly v. State of Washington ex rel. Foss Co. (1937), 302 U. S. 1. See also S. C. State Highway Department v. Barnwell Bros. (1938), 303 U. S. 177.
[12] McGoldrick v. Berwind-White Coal Mining Co. (1940), 309 U. S. 33.

imported from a foreign country on which the import duties have been paid are not subject to state taxation until the original packages have been broken and the goods have been taken out for sale. They may then be taxed and regulated like other goods, but without discrimination.[13] (2) Goods produced in one state and shipped into another may be taxed like other similar goods, without discrimination, even though in the original package, but are not fully subject to regulations as to sale and use until the original package has been broken.

State Control of Liquor Business. In the days before the Eighteenth Amendment there was a great deal of difficulty over this doctrine, owing to the fact that states attempting to prohibit the liquor traffic found that liquor was being shipped in from other states. Congress thereupon passed various acts modifying the original package doctrine, which is entirely a court-made rule, in order to give the "dry" states more control over liquor so shipped. When the Eighteenth Amendment was in effect there was no such problem, since all transportation of liquor for beverage purposes was forbidden. The Twenty-first Amendment repealed the Eighteenth Amendment and made the following provision:

> The transportation or importation into any State, Territory, or possession of the United States for delivery or use therein of intoxicating liquors, in violation of the laws thereof, is hereby prohibited.

Under this rule the Supreme Court has said that the states have complete regulatory control over the liquor business in every respect, including the shipment of liquor into or out of the state.[14]

Supremacy of National Regulations. In regulating railroads and other interstate carriers, and particularly in regulating their rates, Congress faces the problem that the same transportation companies also carry goods between points in the same state. In the same freight car there may be both interstate and intrastate shipments. It is next to impossible for the railroads to operate under two different systems of rates in such cases. Furthermore, the income of the roads might be seriously impaired by excessively low rates within states, so that they could not operate successfully and efficiently. The courts have found it necessary, therefore, to invalidate systems of state rates that are lower than the interstate rates. Thus interstate regulations are held to prevail over state laws. The result is that the *instrumentalities of interstate commerce*—waterways, railroads, express companies, pipe lines, telegraph lines—tend to come completely under national regulation, to the exclusion of all but minor state regulations.

Power to Regulate and to Prohibit. The power to regulate foreign commerce includes not only the power to make and enforce laws that regulate such commerce as to safety, labor conditions, rates, and service, but also the

---

[13] See Hooven and Allison Co. v. Evatt (1945), 324 U. S. 652.
[14] Ziffrin, Inc., v. Reeves (1939), 308 U. S. 132.

power to prohibit such commerce in whole or in part. Likewise commerce with the Indians may be strictly controlled through licensing systems and even prohibited. When applied to interstate commerce, does the power to regulate include the power to prohibit? [15] It is clear that goods that are in themselves harmful may be forbidden in interstate commerce, and so too may goods that are not in themselves harmful but which, by the law of the state into which they are to go, are forbidden to be sold there. Such is the purport of the decision upholding the law forbidding the shipment into any state of prison-made goods, where the state law forbids them to be sold.[16] In one of the child labor cases, the Supreme Court held that Congress lacks the power to forbid the interstate shipment of goods that are in themselves not harmful, and that the receiving state permits to be sold.[17] Recent decisions of the Supreme Court indicate that this rule is no longer followed, and that Congress may prohibit any commerce under its power to regulate.[18]

TRUSTS, MONOPOLIES, AND RESTRAINTS OF TRADE

Business Regulation at Common Law. In adopting the common law of England, the states took over a system of business regulation and an attitude toward business that remain in large part to this day. The common law intended that business should be free, that a citizen should be entitled to enter upon any lawful business, to employ land and laborers, and to sell his products without unnecessary burdens. Restraints or restrictions existed but they were the exception, not the rule. There had to be special legislation or grants from the Crown to justify monopolies. The basic common law of business regulated (a) property, and how it may be acquired and sold and rented, (b) contracts as to labor, services, and sales, (c) business organization, and (d) special branches such as those relating to insurance, banking, and common carriers. A part of this fundamental body of business law has entered into the federal statutes and decisions, too, but the general laws of business organization and procedures are state laws, and they are very largely of common law origin.

Monopolies. It is the common law rule that trade shall be free, except as it is regulated by public authorities in the public interest. Nearly half the states tried to put this rule beyond legislative control by inserting it in the state constitution. Thus Maryland provides that "monopolies are odious, contrary to the spirit of a free government and the principles of commerce, and ought not to be suffered." [19] A monopoly is in a position not only to charge excessive prices for its goods and services, but also to operate as a restraint on trade. The common law provided remedies whereby the injured individual

---

[15] See Edward S. Corwin, *The Commerce Power versus State Rights*, Princeton, 1936.
[16] Kentucky Whip and Collar Co. v. Illinois Central Railroad Co. (1937), 299 U. S. 334.
[17] Hammer v. Dagenhart (1918), 247 U. S. 251.
[18] U. S. v. Darby Lumber Co. (1941), 312 U. S. 100.
[19] Maryland Constitution, Declaration of Rights, sec. 41.

could sue in the civil courts for redress, but there was little or no state enforcement of the rule. Even at common law there were exceptional cases where monopolies were permitted. This was particularly true of such public facilities as ferries, plank roads, and bridges. Usually private capital could not be attracted to build such facilities without assurance that there would be no competition. Later came such public utilities as water, gas, electricity, street railways, and telephones, and again monopolies had to be permitted.

Incorporation of Business Companies. The states also began early to charter corporations for the conduct of business. A corporation has the advantage of great flexibility in size, since its capital and membership can grow almost without limit, and it also has advantages in the limited liability usually granted in the franchise, and in the possibility of highly concentrated control. A corporation with hundreds of millions in capital investment and tens of thousands of stockholders, can be managed by a small board of directors and a general manager. At first each corporation received a special charter from the state, and no corporation was entitled to existence except for some good public purpose. The idea soon spread, however, that every group that so desires has a "natural right" to this form of organization. As the demand for charters increased the states enacted general incorporation laws under which the incorporators could organize with no more formality than that of depositing a certificate of incorporation with the secretary of state and paying a small fee.

Corporations Operate in Many States. In the period of industrial growth after the Civil War came the great flowering of business corporations. Nearly every important business was incorporated. Congress incorporated some banks and railroads, but states like Delaware, New Jersey, New York, and others lying near the great centers of capital did most of the chartering. Once organized in any state, a corporation would enter other states to do business. It is true that there is no constitutional right on the part of a corporation to establish offices and factories and do a local business except in its own state,[20] but most states were so anxious to promote local business that as a rule nothing was required of foreign corporations, i.e., corporations chartered in other states, except simple registration in the states where they desired to operate, and the payment of moderate license taxes.

Trust and Holding Companies. Then came the great financiers and the captains of industry who began the work of combining or merging smaller corporations into bigger ones, to form so-called "trusts," which are a special form of supercorporation holding the stocks and assets of other corporations, and "holding companies," a later type. The latter replaced most of the trusts and became especially common in the field of public utilities. The number and importance of these great corporate enterprises are almost beyond belief. In 1933 200 great corporations held one-fifth of the national wealth, or about

---

[20] Atlantic Refining Co. *v.* Commonwealth of Virginia (1937), 302 U. S. 22.

50 per cent of the industrial wealth.[21] A number of these corporations had each over a billion dollars in assets.

Cutthroat Competition Destroys Competition. The common law rules against ruthless competition were inadequate. When some of the large corporations began to rise to power, they found it possible either to buy out their small competitors or to force them out of business by underselling them. The great combination could thus pick off one small competitor after another, while making its profits in the areas where competition was already crushed. Thus the lack of rules against unfair competition resulted in the creation of monopoly conditions in many lines of business. Competition does not enforce itself in the sense of guaranteeing that competition will always be possible. Even without a monopolistic franchise, a great oil company or steel company may be in the position of having a virtual monopoly, leaving the public more or less dependent on its mercy. Farmers protested strongly against alleged monopolies in farm machinery, while city dwellers were more conscious of monopoly conditions in the sugar and tobacco industries and others that affected the consumer.

By chartering corporations so freely the states helped to create powerful instrumentalities of business, with great aggregations of capital, that the individual states soon were unable to control. The common law against monopolies was reinforced by statutes in many states, but the giant, sprawling corporations operated in many states and were effectually beyond the power of any state. That is why men turned to the national government for relief.

The Sherman Anti-Trust Act, 1890. In 1890 Congress moved into the field of antimonopoly legislation by enacting the Sherman Anti-Trust Act. The essence of this act, given below, is little more than a national re-enactment of the common law rule, with added penalties.

> Sec. 1. Every contract, combination in the form of trust or otherwise, or conspiracy, in restraint of trade or commerce among the several states, or with foreign nations, is hereby declared to be illegal. Every person who shall make any such contract or engage in any such combination or conspiracy, shall be deemed guilty of a misdemeanor, . . . (Fine up to $5,000, imprisonment up to one year, or both.)
>
> Sec. 2. Every person who shall monopolize, or attempt to monopolize, or combine or conspire with any other person or persons, to monopolize any part of the trade or commerce among the several states, or with foreign nations, shall be deemed guilty of a misdemeanor, . . . (Same penalties.) [22]

Early Cases Under Anti-Trust Law. This act put the burden on the government to prosecute monopolies. There were a few successful early prosecutions

[21] National Resources Committee, *The Structure of the American Economy* (1939), Pt. 1; Berle and Means, *The Modern Corporation and Private Property*, p. 27.

[22] U. S. *Code of Laws*, Title 15, ch. 1, secs. 1, 2.

under the act in matters of somewhat local concern, but in 1895, in the so-called Sugar Trust case, the Supreme Court held that the act was not applicable to manufacturing, and that the sugar trust was engaged primarily in manufacturing and only incidentally in interstate commerce.[23] This gave the act something of a body blow. In the same year a labor union was successfully enjoined from interfering with interstate commerce, and some years later the Sherman Act was held to apply as against labor unions which by strikes and boycotts interfere with such commerce. In short, instead of giving the expected results, the act was found to be a new weapon against labor.

The "Rule of Reason" Applied. During the administrations of Theodore Roosevelt and Taft, there were further prosecutions under the act, and then came the 1911 decisions in the Standard Oil and Tobacco company cases.[24] In these the Supreme Court more fully considered the Sherman Act, and the common law meaning of what the act was trying to do, and decided that the law was aimed only at "undue restraint" of trade, and that it was left "to be determined by the light of reason . . . in every given case whether any particular act or contract" was contrary to the law. Naturally this left it to the courts to have the last say as to what is reasonable in given circumstances. The Standard Oil Company was indeed ordered to be dissolved, as was the American Tobacco Company as then organized, but the public was left with the impression that no one was going to be punished under the law, and that the teeth of the act had been drawn.

Clayton Act, 1914. The Democratic party, coming into power in 1913 under President Wilson, tried a new tack. The Clayton Act, passed in 1914, forbade (in interstate commerce) various kinds of price discrimination by sellers against buyers, and also prohibited price-fixing agreements; it provided that "labor, agricultural, or horticultural organizations" should not be "held or construed to be illegal combinations or conspiracies in restraint of trade, under the antitrust laws"; and it forbade any corporation engaged in interstate commerce from acquiring such stock control in any other corporation as would "substantially lessen competition" between the several corporations involved.[25]

Federal Trade Commission, 1914-   . This act was accompanied by another that created the Federal Trade Commission.[26] The commission consists of five members appointed by the President with the consent of the Senate. The terms of the members are seven years, and not more than three of the five members are to be of the same political party. The commission has from the first been empowered to enforce various provisions of the Clayton Act, as well as to prevent "unfair competition" in interstate commerce. Later laws empowered it to prevent certain price discriminations (aimed at chain stores), and unfair and deceptive acts in the food, drug, and cosmetics businesses, and

[23] U. S. v. E. C. Knight Co. (1895), 156 U. S. 1.
[24] Standard Oil Co. of N. J. v. U. S. (1911), 221 U. S. 1; U. S. v. American Tobacco Co (1911), 221 U. S. 106.
[25] U. S. *Code of Laws*, Title 15, ch. 1, sec. 13.
[26] *Ibid.*, Title 15, ch. 2, sec. 41.

to enforce the law on honest labeling of wool products. Another of its functions is to make studies and investigations with respect to the conduct of interstate commerce, and to keep Congress and the public informed.

Complaints by business concerns against other concerns are made to the commission by the hundreds every year. In many cases nothing more is done beyond a preliminary examination; the complaint is found to be without serious merit, or it alleges some violation over which the commission has no control. Other cases are investigated further, and are settled by "stipulation," both the parties agreeing to a statement of the facts and to a settlement. These stipulations are published without the names of the parties, so that no one gets any harmful publicity. Only a small per cent of the cases go so far as to require a formal trial by the commission and the issuance of a "cease and desist" order. These orders are like court decisions; each commands certain named parties to desist from the specified unfair trade practices. Appeals from them may be taken to the Circuit Court of Appeals.

Difficulties of the Commission. The commission has been, and to some extent is still, handicapped in a number of ways. (1) During its first years it endeavored to enforce the laws vigorously, but the courts frequently upset its decisions. (2) The commission was supposed to be the judge as to the facts in the case, but in a number of cases the courts presumed even to overrule the commission on questions of fact. (3) Reductions in appropriations and staff handicapped the commission to a considerable extent at one stage. (4) When the Republican party came back into power in 1921, substantial changes were made in the board's membership, and an entirely new policy was adopted over the protest of the minority. President Coolidge in particular made it a point to select only such commissioners as would deal gently with business. In short, the commission has in its membership reflected the changing politics and policies of the great parties. (5) Actual terms of service on the commission have been short, so that a strong, permanent membership, a judicial yet public-minded attitude, and a stable policy were not easily attained. In recent years, however, the Commission has won increasing support from public opinion, Congress, the President, and the Courts. It is now one of the most firmly established regulatory commissions in the national government.

What Is Unfair Competition? (6) Great difficulty has arisen out of the fact that the laws do not clearly lay down the rules as to what is "unfair competition" or what is likely to "lessen competition." The courts in construing such phrases in the laws have limited the powers of the commission considerably. (a) The commission may order the cessation of such activities only as are unfair; (b) the unfairness must be among competitors, and not the unfairness of a dealer to his customers; (c) the practices complained of must be in interstate commerce; and (d) the commission's orders must be strictly in the public interest. When the commission merely forbade business practices that were already illegal at common law, i.e., as to which the courts found some precedents in judicial decisions, the commission's orders were usually sustained, but when it forbade practices of a novel kind, the decisions usually went against it, until very recent years.

Trade Practice Conferences. One outgrowth of the period of Republican domination of the Federal Trade Commission was the series of so-called "trade practice conferences." These meetings of representative leaders in various industrial fields were designed to get the various businesses in each field to agree on codes of elementary business ethics. If agreement were possible, the code would be drawn up, adopted, and distributed throughout the industry. This was a sort of beginning of industrial self-government.

Trade Associations and Restraints of Trade. Long before this there had been a considerable growth of "trade associations" in particular lines of business. Manufacturers, lumber dealers, grocers, druggists, and many others had their national associations, and many of these had offices in Washington where they maintained lobbyists. The trade practice conferences stimulated the movement, and it came to be more and more respectable to have such trade associations. Unfortunately, the line between a trade association and a combination in restraint of trade is not always clear. If the members of such an association agree, openly or secretly, not to cut prices below a certain point, there is an illegal price-fixing agreement, a restraint of trade.

The Depression and Regulation. When the depression grew worse after 1930, business practices that were not at all necessary in good times became rather common. Price wars developed that were ruinous. In desperation some businesses, fearing bankruptcy, went beyond anything previously known in competitive methods to keep themselves going. From the business world came various plans to stop such ruinous competition, to rebuild the morale of business, and to start a movement to restore and stabilize business through the trade associations. In at least one plan membership in the associations was to be compulsory, each association was to have the power to fix minimum selling prices, there was to be uniform cost accounting, codes of fair competition were to be binding on all the members, and labor was to be guaranteed a minimum wage and a minimum amount of work each year.

NRA and Codes of Fair Competition. In 1933 some of these ideas became the basis for the National Industrial Recovery Act. In essence this act provided for the adoption of a code of fair competition within each branch of industry and commerce, to include the protection of labor and the stabilization of the industry. When approved by the President each code was to have the force of law, and violators of it could be punished. The National Recovery Administration (NRA) was then set up, and for over a year there was the most feverish activity in almost every branch of industry and trade to draw up these codes. Every train brought more representatives of industry to Washington to participate in conferences preliminary to the approval of particular codes. In the codes approved minimum wages were set, child labor was ruled out, and provisions were made to enforce the very rules of fair competition that the Federal Trade Commission had been stressing. In addition, to help industry get on its feet, there were provisions against price cutting. Necessarily prices rose very soon in most lines to cover the new costs occasioned by higher wages and other requirements. At the fringe in every industry and trade were dissenters, men who said that the small businessman was going to be squeezed out, that only the large one could meet the conditions of the code and survive. Nevertheless, the codes were approved in considerable numbers. They went into effect, and enforcement began. Then came the Supreme Court decision in the "sick chicken" case, and the whole NRA, which indeed was already losing its popularity, was declared unconstitutional.[27]

At this writing the national government has returned at least in part to a policy of enforcing the antitrust laws. The trade associations carry on in many lines of industry and trade, but without legally compulsory power. In a case recently decided a number of oil companies were convicted of price fixing, although they contended that the thing they had been doing was the very thing they were encouraged to do under NRA. Attention is being turned, also, toward international monopolies (cartels) and toward monopolies that are built upon patents. Various investigations made during World War II disclosed some very unsavory and hurtful restraints on trade that resulted from combinations between American and foreign producers. Wartime munitions contracts of necessity favored the largest corporations, and efforts are now being made by the government to encourage the re-establishment of numerous small competitive industries.

Chain Store Regulations. The drive against monopolies and in defense of the small business has turned also in recent years against the chain stores that are now so important in groceries, drugs, dry goods, and general merchandise. The states began the attack upon them by requiring that drugstores be locally owned by licensed pharmacists (invalidated) and by imposing especially high, progressive taxes upon them. Thus a number of states now have laws taxing chain stores, in addition to regular property taxes, so much for (let us say) the second to the fifth store in the chain, then a larger amount for the sixth to the tenth store, and so on up the scale. Some of these laws have been upheld by the courts, others not, depending upon the reasonableness of the classifications made. This still did not suffice to satisfy the small merchants, so that some states then passed acts, paralleled by an act of Congress, forbidding price discriminations to be made by manufacturers and wholesalers in favor of any businesses. The national (Robinson-Patman) act applies to interstate commerce, and state laws to intrastate trade. In the former it is forbidden "to discriminate in price between different purchasers of commodities of like grade and quality . . . where the effect of such discrimination may be substantially to lessen competition . . ." provided that differential prices may be charged where they are due to differences in cost of manufacture, sale, or delivery, resulting from the different methods of manufacture or sale, or the different

[27] Schechter Poultry Corporation v. U. S. (1935), 294 U. S. 495.

quantities made or sold. Thus there can still be price differences where the facts justify them.

GENERAL BUSINESS REGULATION AND PROMOTION

Other Agencies Regulating Business. The whole policy of the government with respect to the regulation of business is not tied up with the antitrust laws and the Federal Trade Commission, nor do all the powers of the national government stem from the commerce clause. The Department of Agriculture, to take an important example, is empowered to enforce a number of laws concerning processors and dealers in farm products. Grain exchanges, packers, and stockyards, for example, come under its control so far as their business practices, services, and charges are concerned. Other departments, too, have some regulatory functions over trade. In fact, one of the present difficulties is that the same industry may be regulated by two different agencies as to different phases of its business.

Local Business Regulation. Where national and state regulations of business are designed to promote the health, the morals, the safety, and the general convenience and welfare of the people, they supplement many municipal regulations that have the same objectives. These local regulations deal, necessarily, with local businesses, such as the local grocer, butcher, restaurant keeper, and hotel, but some of them have their effects beyond the city limits and even outside the state. Such are the regulations forbidding the sale of milk that has not come from inspected, tuberculosis-free herds of cattle, and that has not been produced under sanitary conditions. In most places pasteurization ordinances have taken the place of the older type regulations, but even these have their effects on the farmers' costs and income.

In the field of health, national, state, and local regulations cover the inspection of foods and drugs made and sold to the public. There is national inspection of food and drug production under the Federal Security Agency, state inspection under state departments of agriculture and other agencies, and municipal inspection under city health departments. In the field of morals, federal regulations forbid the interstate transportation of women for immoral purposes, and the mailing of prize fight films and obscene literature. State and local laws regulate the conduct of hotels, dance halls, liquor dealers, and theaters, among other things. Safety is covered by national regulations with respect to railroads, ships, airplanes, and other interstate carriers, while state and local laws cover a host of businesses and activities, with requirements for safety against fire hazards (fire escapes, steam boilers, electric wiring, proper building), against accidents in industry and against traffic accidents.

Special Fields of Regulation. Certain types of business are regulated almost entirely by state and local governments. *Mining* is directly regulated by the states in which it takes place. There is a Bureau of Mines in the United States Department of the Interior, also, but this bureau is without coercive power over mine operators. It studies the causes of mine accidents, gives instruction in safety methods and rescue work, and also studies the economic problems of the mining industry. State regulations of mines deal mainly with the safety of the workers, and the protection of the rights of landowners whose land may be undermined by mining operations. *Manufacturing* as such is also regulated mainly by the states, and here again the primary purpose of regulation is safety for the workers. The *construction industry* is regulated very largely by the municipalities within which most of the larger buildings are erected. The regulations adopted cover the location of the buildings, different types of buildings being assigned by zoning ordinances to different parts of the city; the height and bulk of buildings, so as to prevent overshadowing and the excessive shutting out of air and sunlight; and the safety of the building structure. Buildings that are to be used for housing come under especially strict rules. In all cases, inspection is made of structural strength, electric wiring, fire safety, and other features. The national government through the Bureau of Standards has done a great deal to improve the standards of building through its tests of various types of materials, and through the National Housing Agency and its subsidiaries has done much to raise home building standards.

Every regulation of business is in a sense a service and an aid to business. In the following pages are outlined a few governmental activities in which the service motive is probably the outstanding one. These services have become primarily national because business itself has become national.

Weights and Measures. Congress has the power "to fix the Standard of Weights and Measures." [28] Presumably when it has fixed the standard in any particular case, that standard will prevail and will practically prevent any state from having a different standard. In fact, however, Congress has not made full use of this power. It has fixed the standards for apple barrels, vegetable and fruit baskets, sheet iron and steel, electrical measurements, and time zones, for example, but has left far more to be done by executive order under specific legislation. In general it has followed the English measurements that prevailed before the English introduced their own reforms. What is more, Congress has not set up any national bureau with the police authority and the funds to enforce the standards that have been set. As a result, the actual enforcement of weights and measures laws is left to the state and local governments, and the states also have passed laws to fix the standards in matters not covered by national regulations. Thus there is no completely uniform system.

One thing important the national government has done, and that is to create and maintain the Bureau of Standards in the Department of Commerce. This remarkable bureau not only keeps the standard units of measurement for the United States, but also carries on important researches designed to test materials, to increase the accuracy of measurements, and to do a thou-

[28] U. S. Const., Art. I, sec. 8, par. 5.

sand other things important in business and science. The bureau sends out a
constant stream of reports on its various tests, and its handbooks of standards
are accepted as authoritative.

Patents and Copyrights. Congress has the power also "To promote the
Progress of Science and useful Arts, by securing for limited Times to Authors
and Inventors the exclusive Right to their respective Writings and Discoveries." [29] This clause establishes the power of Congress to issue patents covering inventions and scientific discoveries, and copyrights covering books, plays,
songs, pictures, and other products. A patent is, of course, a legal right or
license attested by a legal document giving the owner the exclusive right to
reproduce the thing patented. A copyright similarly gives an exclusive right
of reproduction. These are legally established, and are recognized exceptions
to the common law rule against monopolies. They are justified as a means
of rewarding the one who has labored to produce the original invention or
writing, and as a means of encouraging further efforts on the part of inventors
and authors. To prevent perpetual monopolies, the exclusive rights are given
for only a limited time. For patents the term in the United States is 17 years,
for copyrights 28 years. Copyrights are renewable under some conditions for
another 28-year period.

Issuance of Patents. New mechanical devices and manufacturing processes
may be patented if they are sufficiently distinct and novel. To avoid excessive
litigation over questions of infringement of patent rights, Congress has established the Patent Office, a bureau of the Department of Commerce, and has
made it the duty of this office to investigate all applications for new patents
and to make an initial decision before a patent is issued. From the decisions
of the patent examiners, appeals go first to the Board of Appeals within the
Patent Office, and may then be taken to the Court of Customs and Patent
Appeals, or to a United States district court. Ultimately a number of patent
cases reach the Supreme Court. Necessarily the Patent Office employs a considerable number of chemists, physicists, engineers, lawyers, and other specialists. The number of new patents issued each year is about 50,000.

The owner must protect his patent rights by civil suits against those who
infringe them; the government does not do this for him. This puts a considerable burden on the patentee. If he is a man of small means, and the violator
a wealthy corporation, his means may be exhausted by litigation. It is frequently possible, therefore, for powerful interests to force individuals to sell
them patent rights for less than they are worth. Some industries are more or
less dominated by "patent pools"—single corporations, or groups of corporations in combination that control all the important patents in the industry.

Issuance of Copyrights. Copyrights are issued by the Copyright Office of the
Library of Congress. This is a much simpler process than that of issuing patents. There is no investigation. The author or publisher simply sends two
copies of the book or other publication to the Copyright Office with a certifi-

[29] U. S. Const., Art. I, sec. 8, par. 8.

cate giving certain information concerning it, and a $2 registration fee. The copyright is then effective immediately. If in fact the new publication is an infringement of the copyright of some other author, the matter may be determined by a suit in court, and the violator of the original copyright may recover damages from the one who has plagiarized his work.

Fifty years ago there was established an International Copyright Union. Works copyrighted in the nations that belong to this union are automatically copyrighted in all the other nations that belong to it for the lifetime of the author and for fifty years thereafter. The United States has not joined this union; consequently the copyrighting of a book abroad is no protection to it here except in those cases where by treaty or executive agreement the United States has made special arrangements with a particular foreign country. A book published abroad in English may be given a four months' privilege in this country, but full copyright will not be given to it unless it is set up and printed in this country.

Trade-marks and Names. Trade-marks, trade names, and distinctive labels and designs, so important in the advertising of a business, are not expressly mentioned in the Constitution. Congress has, nevertheless, passed legislation permitting the registration of trade-marks used in foreign and interstate commerce, and it is recognized to be an illegal and unfair practice for others to duplicate or simulate such a trade-mark. The states have in most cases also provided for the registration of trade-marks and trade names, so that the local businessman can be protected against the unfair competitor. In the national government, registration of a picture, drawing, or design is made in the Copyright Office, but marks that are to be used for advertising must also be registered in the Patent Office. Enforcement of the right to use a trade-mark or trade name is by civil suit.

Protection Against Foreign Competition. Protection of the domestic producer against foreign competition is covered by an extensive and complicated group of laws and regulations. Besides the regular tariff laws enacted by Congress, there are acts to protect the home market from the "dumping" here of foreign-made goods that are to be sold below cost, and from the operation of foreign monopolies in American markets. Conversely, American monopolies that are intended to sell goods abroad are permitted by the law. The Tariff Commission is a body consisting of six members appointed by the President with the consent of the Senate, whose duty it is to study the operation of tariff laws and trade policies, and to recommend to the President changes in the tariff needed to equalize the cost of production here and in other countries. The President may either ignore the commission's recommendations, or he may increase or decrease rates, within certain limits, upon the commission's recommendation. The commission is also an adviser to the President and State Department under the act authorizing reciprocal trade agreements.

Other Services and Subsidies. Services by the national government that involve little or no regulation of business are very numerous. A few may be particularly mentioned. The postal rates on books, magazines, and newspapers are deliberately set at a figure below the cost of providing the service. This amounts to a subsidy. Direct subsidies are given to ocean-going vessels and to airplane operators for carrying the mails, for the purpose of developing and maintaining the merchant marine and the aviation industry. Foreign trade is promoted through an extensive trade information service centering in the Departments of Commerce, State, and Agriculture. Consuls, commercial attachés, and agricultural experts are located throughout the world for this purpose. In times of emergency, the government makes direct loans to business, as discussed in the preceding chapter, through the RFC.

Wartime Aids and Regulations. No attempt will be made here to review the numerous interventions by government into economic processes during World War II. These were so sweeping as to amount almost to a complete regimentation of the nation's economy. Many of the controls have already been dropped, but others are being continued in the effort to prevent inflation and to provide for a just allocation of available products until full supply has been achieved. Although the conversion of the nation's economy to a peacetime basis is the task primarily of private industrialists and businessmen, the national government provides a great deal of aid and guidance.

REFERENCES

Dexter M. Keezer and Stacy May, *The Public Control of Business*, New York, 1930.

Ford P. Hall, *Government and Business*, 2nd ed., New York, 1939.

Charles C. Rohlfing, and others, *Business and Government*, 4th ed., Chicago, 1941.

Benjamin E. Lippincott (ed.), *Government Control of the Economic Order*, Minneapolis, 1935.

John M. Clark, *Social Control of Business*, 2nd ed., New York, 1939.

Gerald O. and L. G. Dykstra, *Selected Cases on Government and Business*, Chicago, 1937.

Edward S. Corwin, *The Commerce Power versus States Rights*, Princeton, 1936.

Harold D. Koontz, *Government Control of Business*, Boston, 1941.

Adolf A. Berle, Jr., and Gardiner C. Means, *The Modern Corporation and Private Property*, New York, 1933.

Thomas C. Blaisdell, Jr., *The Federal Trade Commission*, New York, 1932.

National Industrial Conference Board, *Mergers and the Law*, New York, 1929.

——, *Mergers in Industry: A Study of Certain Economic Aspects of Industrial Consolidation*, New York, 1929.

U. S. Federal Trade Commission, *Decisions, Findings, Orders, and Stipulations*, annual, Washington.

E. Pendleton Herring, *Public Administration and the Public Interest*, New York, 1936, chs. VII, VIII, XVIII, XIX.

Harlan Fiske Stone, *Public Control of Business; Selected Opinions*, edited by Alfred Lief, New York, 1940.

C. J. Friedrich and Edward S. Mason, *Public Policy*, 1940, chs. II-V, X; *ibid.*, 1941, Part II, ch. I; Cambridge, 1940, 1941.

Merle Fainsod and Lincoln Gordon, *Government and the American Economy*, New York, 1941, espec. chs. 4, 8, 13-16.

Temporary National Economic Committee, *Final Report and Recommendations* (Senate Doc. no. 35, 77th Congress, 1st sess.), 1941.

——, *Hearings*, parts 1-31.

——, *Monographs*, nos. 1-43.

National Resources Committee, *The Structure of the American Economy*.

Arthur G. Coons (ed.), *Government Expansion in the Economic Sphere, The Annals*, vol. 206, Philadelphia, 1939.

Leverett S. Lyon and others, *Government and Economic Life*, 2 vols., Washington, 1939.

Walton H. Hamilton and Douglass Adair, *The Power to Govern*, New York, 1937.

John M. Mathews and Clarence A. Berdahl, *Documents and Readings in American Government: National and State*, rev. ed., New York, 1940, pp. 571-84, 838-50.

A. N. Christensen and E. M. Kirkpatrick, *The People, Politics, and the Politician: Readings in American Government*, New York, 1941, pp. 778-807.

CHAPTER 29

Transportation, Communication, and Utilities

For purposes of defense, industry, agriculture, commerce, and recreation, every modern people needs an adequate system of transportation, communication, and utilities. Such a system is one test of a nation's civilization and standard of living. Unlike the older nations of Europe, the American people were able to build some of their transportation facilities in advance of settlement; the railroads and river steamers carried the settlers into the West, and the governments of nation and state had much to do with promoting both settlement and transportation.

National Constitutional Provisions. At the time of the Federal Convention none of the modern means of travel and communication had been devised. Sailing ships plied the coastal waters, and horses and oxen carried men and goods overland. The framers of the Constitution readily agreed to make the national government responsible for "Post Offices and post Roads," but a proposal that Congress have the power also "to provide for cutting canals where deemed necessary" was rejected. Another proposal, to permit the states with the consent of Congress to collect "duties of tonnage . . . for improving their harbors and keeping up lights" was amended to read, "No State shall, without the Consent of Congress, lay any duty of Tonnage," and in this form was placed in the Constitution.[1]

These examples of specific provisions in the Constitution do not even remotely suggest the amplitude of the national government's powers to provide and regulate transportation and communication facilities. To find the full sweep of those powers one must combine the resources of the commerce power, the war powers, the postal power, the taxing and spending powers, the power over territories, and the power in foreign affairs, and interpret all these in the light of long practice and a very favorable line of Supreme Court decisions. It is doubtful whether there is anything of importance that the

[1] U. S. Const., Art. I, sec. 10, par. 3.

nation may not do toward providing, maintaining, and regulating a complete nation-wide system of transportation and communication facilities.

Governmental Aids for Transportation. Congress early began to improve harbors, build lighthouses, and regulate coastal shipping, but its first venture in promoting inland transportation, the building of the famous Cumberland Road (1806-25), was only partially successful and aroused a controversy over national powers that now seems almost incredible. As a result Congress discontinued the construction of highways, and kept hands off in the building of canals and railroads from the 1830s on. It was the state and local governments that gave aid to these ventures. By 1840 the East was joined with the Middle West by canals, roads, and railroads; and steamships were using the Mississippi and Ohio river systems and the Great Lakes. The demand for transport facilities continued to grow as more settlers moved in to develop the West, and in 1850 Congress made its first grant of public lands for railroad building. Thereafter each new state admitted to the union expected a grant of lands from Congress to promote the building of railroads, wagon roads, and other internal improvements, and many grants were made directly to railroad corporations. All told, 140 million acres of public lands were granted for railroad building, while state and local governments also gave aid in cash and credit.

State Railroad Regulation. No sooner had the railroads become important in economic life than complaints began to arise concerning their rates and services. The railroad companies had a sort of monopoly position in internal transportation. They charged what seemed excessive rates, gave rebates and special considerations to favored industries, and benefited or seriously injured whole cities by favoring some and penalizing others with respect to rates and service. In the 1850s, long before the problem had become national, Rhode Island and Connecticut began to regulate railroads, and in 1869 Massachusetts set up the first railroad commission. Soon the farmers of the Middle West, sorely tried by low prices and high transportation costs, organized the Granger movement, and persuaded their states in the 1870s and later to establish state commissions to regulate railroads and grain elevators. This aroused the railroads to fight back. In politics since the beginning of the land grants, they now organized their lobbies and moved upon the legislatures and the railroad commissions everywhere to prevent railroad regulation from impairing their investments and profits. Congress in the meantime did practically nothing toward regulating railroads generally.

Supreme Court Decisions on Regulation. It was not long before the railroads and grain elevator owners contested in the courts the power of the states to regulate their rates and services. The Fourteenth Amendment to the United States Constitution, adopted in 1868, just a few years before the passage of the Granger railroad regulation laws, forbade the states to deprive any person of property without due process of law. The Supreme Court at first refused to construe this clause as a prohibition against railroad rate regulation, and also held that, although the state regulations to some extent affected inter-state commerce, they were valid as long as Congress had not adopted any conflicting legislation on the subject. In the case of Munn v. Illinois (1876) the Court upheld the state rate-making power with respect to grain elevators.[2] Ten years later the court reversed itself in part, holding that states are without power to regulate the rates charged for hauling goods in interstate commerce, even though the haul in question is entirely within the state.[3] Since many of the goods carried on all railroads are in interstate commerce, this put great obstacles in the way of any state regulation of railroad rates.

Interstate Commerce Commission. The answer to this decision of the Supreme Court was the passage by Congress in 1887 of the act creating the Interstate Commerce Commission (ICC). This act laid the foundation for the regulatory responsibilities of the national government in the field of economic enterprise. The commission's powers were at first very limited, and subsequent court decisions put further restrictions on them, until by 1900 the commission seemed to have very little worth-while work to do. Then followed a series of acts beginning in 1906 that strengthened the commission and expanded the scope of its work, until today it exercises a very effective control over not only the railroads but also other transportation facilities, in both interstate and foreign commerce.

Renewed Interest in Highways. While the struggle for government control over the railroads was going on, new instrumentalities for transportation were appearing. The national government had begun to improve rivers and other inland waterways on a considerable scale. Indeed, the annual "pork barrel" bill for the improvement of rivers and harbors and for the construction of public buildings became something of a national scandal. About 1900 auto-mobiles appeared, and by 1914 over a half million of them were operating on the roads and streets. The demand for better highways grew more and more insistent. Farmers had previously been urging better "farm to market" roads, and the states had begun in a small way to respond to the new demand. The "dark age" in American road building, which began about 1820, was soon to come to an end. New Jersey in 1891 had already established a state highway department, and other states had followed suit. This was not enough. After 1900 the question of federal aid for road building was raised again and again in Congress. Farmers, automobile owners and builders, the postal authorities, and other interests, joined forces in a drive on Congress that resulted in 1916 in the passage of a federal-aid road act that provided for $75 million to be allocated to the states over a 5-year period for a start on a national high-way system.

Truck, Bus, and Air Lines. The improvement of the highways was continu-ously outstripped by the increase in the number of registered motor vehicles.

[2] 94 U. S. 113.
[3] Wabash, St. L., and P. R. R. Co. v. Illinois (1886), 118 U. S. 557.

There were at no time enough good roads to satisfy all the demands. Then came the motor buses for passengers, and the truck lines for hauling freight over the highways. These presented serious competition for the railroads and raised new problems of traffic and rate regulation. The states first tried their hands at regulating, but finally Congress had to assume a part of the work of regulation of interstate trucks and buses. Overlapping this development came the airplane, with a subsequent drive for government aid in fostering the service, followed in turn by the necessity for government regulation.

This outline of transportation developments leaves out of account the expansion through the years of the postal system, the rise of the rural free delivery, and the parcel post service, the coming of competing instrumentalities of communication such as the telegraph, then the telephone, and more recently the radio. All these have come to require regulation and coordination with other instrumentalities.

What the total investment in these facilities may be is quite unknown. No money value can be placed upon the public highway and street system. Railroads alone have an estimated value or investment of about $26 billion. All other transportation agencies must have a value approaching that of the railroads. Private ownership under public regulation is the rule except for the highways, the waterways, and the postal system.

RAILROAD REGULATION

State Regulation of Railroads. Both state and national governments exercise some measure of control over railroads. Local governments have little to do with them at present, although they have some power to provide for local safety measures at crossings and in stations and offices. Most of the states exercise their powers through the commissions that regulate public utilities generally. Their powers extend to the establishment of intrastate rates for the various railroad services (freight, passenger, express, etc.), the hearing of complaints concerning unreasonable or discriminatory rates, the establishment of service requirements, schedules, local stations and facilities, health and safety requirements, grades and crossings, new lines and track abandonment, and even matters of finance. In all cases the intent is to regulate intrastate matters primarily, but of course many regulations and decisions have some bearing on interstate commerce. Recently many states have authorized their commissions to cooperate with the Interstate Commerce Commission in the joint handling of cases, and to appear before that body in cases where questions of state concern are considered. State regulation over purely intrastate lines, street railways, and interurban bus and electric lines is practically complete.

Powers of Interstate Commerce Commission. The Interstate Commerce Commission, established originally as a body of 5 members, was later increased to 11. The members receive salaries of $12,000 a year, and are appointed by the President with the consent of the Senate. Of all the boards and commissions of the national government engaged in regulatory work, this commission has the longest history and has acquired the greatest power. Its powers have been increased since 1906 by successive acts, so that they now cover nearly all phases of railroad administration and policy. The establishment of new lines and the abandonment of old ones, stock and bond issues, health and safety requirements, the supply and interchange of cars, uniform accounting and reporting, train schedules and service, and the determination of rates, all fall within its powers. It has additional duties in connection with the making of a complete valuation of all the railroad facilities of the country, the establishment of rates for air mail, the regulation of interstate bus and truck lines, the making of certain joint rail-and-water rates, the supervision of railroad holding companies and railroad reorganizations, and the regulation of water transportation. It must annually decide hundreds of cases involving complaints by shippers against carriers, and by carriers against each other, and must see that the laws against illegal rebates, false weighing and invoicing, and acceptance of illegal concessions are enforced. Its recent annual reports fully bear out the impression gained from a study of the laws that this is a very busy if not overworked commission.

Railroad Difficulties and Government Operation in World War I. Even before World War I the railroads were getting into financial difficulties. Financial manipulation had resulted in the looting of certain railroad treasuries for the purpose of expansions and for profits to promoters. There had also been an overdevelopment of railroads, especially in the sparsely settled parts of the country, where traffic was normally light. Some roads were in receivership because of inability to meet their obligations, and others were not keeping their rolling stock or roadbeds in satisfactory condition. When the war in Europe increased the demand for American goods, the railroads of the East could not handle all the traffic, and had to declare embargoes against accepting further shipments. When the United States entered the war, the administration, with Congressional authority, took over the railroads and operated them for the duration of the war as a branch of the government. This was an act dictated by necessity, and the debate will probably never end as to whether governmental operation was a success or a failure. Certainly it was very expensive.

Transportation Act of 1920. At the end of the war, the roads were returned to private operation, and Congress passed the Transportation Act of 1920 which fully recognized for the first time the need for protecting the railroads and their investors. The roads were in effect considered as a single system of transportation, and the law guaranteed them minimum earnings by spreading the surplus earnings of the prosperous roads to weaker roads through a revolving fund in the United States Treasury. The "recapture" of the excess earnings of some roads in order to build up this fund was sustained by the Supreme Court as a constitutional exercise of the power of Congress to regulate interstate commerce. In fact, however, the recapture provision proved unworkable because of difficulties in determining excess earnings and in recapturing them for the use of other roads, and it was repealed in 1933. Other clauses of the 1920 law authorized the Interstate Commerce Commission to fix minimum as well as maximum rates, to do this upon its own initiative and, where several roads carry goods or passengers together, to allocate to each participating road its share of the total revenue. The plan was to give the commission the power needed to adjust the income of each road in such a way as to enable it to perform its part in an orderly, integrated transportation system for the whole country.

Railroads in the Doldrums. The events of the following years prevented this legislation from accomplishing its objectives. The improvement of highways and of automobiles and the rise of bus and truck lines cut down railway earnings very seriously. The railroads tried to meet the increasing competition by cutting rates, but when the volume of traffic did not greatly increase, the net result was a further decline in earnings. The railroads with their great capital investments succeeded in buying up a number of bus lines, but were in no position to compete successfully with all the newer transportation facilities. They reduced costs steadily after 1920, but not enough to make up for the increased losses in earnings.

New Deal Measures to Help the Railroads. The depression reduced freight and passenger revenues once more and took a very heavy toll of the railroads. Many roads were forced into receivership or into attempts to reorganize. Congressional aid was again invoked. The Reconstruction Finance Corporation, established by Congress in 1932, was empowered to lend money to them at reasonably low rates to tide them over to better times. Up to 1933, governmental policy was designed to help the railroads through the depression by shifting the burden of readjustment at least partly to labor and the consumer of railway service. This policy was modified when Congress passed the Emergency Railroad Transportation Act of 1933 authorizing the Interstate Commerce Commission to regulate holding companies in the railroad field, to bring about consolidations of railroads where they are needed to improve transportation or eliminate wasteful competition, and to fix rates according to a new formula designed to give the roads the revenue they need to provide adequate, economical transportation service. It further provided for a temporary Coordinator of Transportation who was empowered to study the entire American transportation problem and to make proposals for strengthening and improving it.

The Railway Labor Act of 1934 provided for more explicit recognition of the right of employees to organize and to bargain collectively. The first Railroad Retirement Act (1934) was declared unconstitutional,[4] but a substitute measure was promptly enacted and put into effect. In 1938 a railroad unemployment insurance act was also passed. The Transportation Act of 1940 contains some new provisions designed to help railroads. The lending powers

---

[4] Railroad Retirement Board v. Alton R. R. Co. (1935), 295 U. S. 330.

of the RFC were liberalized; railroads were given greater freedom to pursue their own consolidation plans; the government's 50 per cent discount for transportation over land grant roads was repealed; the filing of claims by shippers against the railroads was expedited; and the ICC was authorized to fix minimum and maximum joint rail-and-water rates.

World War II brought no important permanent changes in the nation's railroad laws or policies. Private operation was retained, and a special wartime agency, the Office of Defense Transportation (ODT), exercised full authority to coordinate and to expand the services of all transportation facilities within the nation. As ODT passes away with the war emergency, the ICC reoccupies the field as the most important regulator of all internal transportation services.

BUS AND TRUCK REGULATION

Unregulated Truck and Bus Competition. Even the most farsighted automobile manufacturers and state highway officials in the early years of the automobile industry did not foresee the tremendous development that was soon to take place in the commercial transportation of passengers and goods upon the highways. Trucks and buses were first used only for local purposes, but even when they began to operate over longer routes the states did not begin promptly to regulate them, since they were still mainly private carriers. Motor vehicle licenses were imposed, and laws were enacted to ensure safety in operation and to limit the maximum size and load; but little more than this was done. Soon organized companies put themselves forward as common carriers of passengers and freight from city to city and between states. Having no expense for the maintenance of roadways, these companies were able to offer lower rates than the railroads with which they competed. As the highways and vehicles were improved, longer and longer runs became possible. Regular schedules were established and followed. Passengers and freight could be picked up at locations convenient to travelers and shippers. Besides these common carriers there were "contract carriers," i.e., those who hauled goods only by special contract with large manufacturers and wholesalers. Various large business concerns operated large fleets of trucks for their own use. The results were cutthroat competition among these carriers and between them and the railroads, underpayment of truck and bus drivers in order to keep down expenses, failure to provide insurance against accidents, and a lowering of the standards of service all around. The railroads complained long and bitterly of this unregulated competition, the truck and bus companies themselves suffered losses, but the states did little or nothing about it. When they attempted to limit competition by denying permits to operate to companies that planned to do an interstate business, the Supreme Court declared this was beyond the power of the states.

National Regulation. In 1935 Congress passed the present act for the regulation of interstate bus and truck traffic. This law authorizes the Interstate

Commerce Commission to regulate this business in three respects. (1) All such carriers in interstate commerce must register with the commission, and the latter has power to issue, or to refuse to issue, certificates of convenience and necessity to new companies that propose to enter this field. (2) The commission is empowered also to regulate the safety and the service of these carriers and to require them to deposit bonds or insurance policies to protect the public against injuries. (3) Rates may also be regulated by the commission. Most of the operating companies are inclined to follow existing railroad rate schedules and to cut them just enough to attract business from the railroads.

State regulation of highway traffic was not ended by the enactment of the Motor Carrier Act of 1935. The length and over-all size of trucks, trailers, and buses, maximum loads, rates of speed, and other factors continue under state control, and state taxes are also applied to such carriers. The resultant state interference with over-the-road traffic was an obstruction to the war effort at a number of points until the states were induced to join hands with the nation in facilitating all war-necessary hauling. At the same time a nation-wide speed limit and other restrictions on road travel that were imposed by national war agencies in order to conserve tires and gasoline gave a foretaste of what may some day be needed—a national highway traffic code.

REGULATION AND PROMOTION OF CIVIL AVIATION

Limited Regulation of Air Transportation. Only after World War I did the state and national governments become sufficiently impressed with the importance of private and commercial aviation to provide for regulation. Following the proposal in 1922, a considerable number of states adopted the Uniform State Law for Aeronautics, which asserts the state's sovereignty over the air above it and provides for the responsibility of the operator of an airplane for damages caused to others. In 1926 Congress passed the Air Commerce Act to regulate commercial flights between states but exempted purely intrastate flights and those for mere pleasure purposes. Under this act the Bureau of Air Commerce of the Department of Commerce had the power to provide for testing and licensing aviators, to make rules as to air traffic, and to set standards for construction and safety of planes to be operated between states commercially. In order to bring about complete uniformity of regulation, the states have in most cases adopted the federal regulations as a part of their aviation codes, so that private flyers must in most states conform to exactly the same rules.

Subsidies and Other Aids to Aviation. The national government is still subsidizing air transportation and helping to promote its growth through the payment of liberal subsidies for the carriage of air mail. Prior to World War II the air transport industry was dependent upon mail revenues for much of its profit, but such dependence steadily decreased in the war period, and is likely to be far less important in the decades ahead. To promote aviation, national, state, and local governments have made extensive expenditures on airports, airways, and aviation research. During World War II the nation also made substantial improvements in numerous state and local airports and landing fields. It is expected that Congress will soon pass an act for grants-in-aid for airports just as was done a generation ago for improving the state highways.

Present Regulation of Civil Aeronautics. At the present time the Department of Commerce has the main responsibility for promoting and regulating civil aeronautics. The Administrator of Civil Aeronautics in the Commerce Department fosters the development of civil aeronautics and air commerce by establishing civil airways and landing fields, providing for the control and protection of air traffic, and promoting technical aeronautical progress. He also carries out safety regulations, administers the Civilian Pilot Training Act of 1939, and expands public airports and landing areas. The Civil Aeronautics Board, also in the Commerce Department, exercising quasi-legislative and quasi-judicial powers, prescribes safety standards and regulations, and may revoke or suspend safety certificates. It regulates the rates for the carriage of persons and property, prescribes compensation rates for the carriage of mail, and regulates the general financial setup of air carrier companies. It also investigates accidents and conducts special studies to reduce aircraft accidents.

TRANSPORTATION BY WATER

National Responsibility for Waterways. Navigable waters include practically all streams, canals, lakes, and other waters that can be made to float even a log or a canoe.[5] As the result of a number of Supreme Court decisions interpreting the commerce power and the jurisdiction of the federal courts in admiralty and maritime cases, the power of the national government over all navigable waters is complete and can be made exclusive if Congress so desires. All major waterways are dealt with in Congressional legislation. Cities and states make some expenditures to improve local harbors and waters, but on the whole they have been glad to let the national government bear most of this burden. Thus there is a long history of national legislation and appropriations for river and harbor improvements, together with a considerable body of regulatory measures. State and local governments get the consent of the national authorities for drawing water from lakes and streams and for making such improvements as bridges over them where navigability might be impaired.

Phases of National Activity. Congress has acted with respect to the four major groups of waters that are navigable. These are (a) rivers, canals, and lakes within the country, (b) the Great Lakes, (c) coastal waters, bays, and harbors, and (d) the high seas, the Panama Canal, distant dependencies, and foreign ports and shipping. Its actions may also be grouped under four headings: (1) The promotion of navigation and navigability of waters through the construction and maintenance of permanent public works, such as the deep-

[5] U. S. v. Appalachian Electric Power Co. (1940), 311 U. S. 377.

ening of harbors, lakes, and rivers, the construction and maintenance of light-houses, breakwaters, harbor improvements, etc.; the provision of floating aids to navigation such as lightships and buoys; and the study, mapping, and reporting of water depths, hidden hazards, and weather conditions. (2) The construction and maintenance of ships, and the promotion of their operation through grants of subsidies for carrying the mails, and in other ways. (3) The direct operation of ships both on the high seas and on the Mississippi-Ohio river system. (4) The regulation of shipping operations to protect the safety of persons and goods, to protect the workers in matters of pay and working conditions, to prevent excessive competition, and to regulate rates.

The expenditures of the national government on the improvement of harbors and waterways have run to a number of billions of dollars, far exceeding what it has spent on highways. It seems to be the general theory that waterways can be made to haul goods cheaper than railroads, and that internal waterways are needed partly to supplement other means of transportation and partly to provide a sort of competition that will keep down railroad rates. The expenditures on shipbuilding and on ship subsidies for ocean-going vessels have been defended as an aid to American exporters and importers and as providing a merchant marine for use as an auxiliary to the navy in time of war. To attempt here to describe the work of the Inland Waterways Corporation in hauling goods on our central river system, or the work of the Maritime Commission in promoting and regulating marine commerce generally, would require more space than can be allotted. An important provision of the Transportation Act of 1940 is the extension of the jurisdiction of the ICC to cover water carriers operating on all navigable waters. The act empowered the ICC to regulate the rates, services, and management of both common and contract water carriers.

A National Transportation System. The national legislation described above has been piecemeal and experimental. Under an act of 1933 Joseph Eastman of the ICC was appointed Federal Coordinator of Transportation. This was the first step toward the planning of a national transportation policy and system. In one of his reports the coordinator showed that public aids to transportation, amounting in all to billions of dollars, have created facilities that in some cases are of little public benefit, and that further aids might merely perpetuate uneconomic competition.[6] He suggested instead a careful planning of transportation facilities of all kinds in accordance with calculated needs. The Transportation Act of 1940, by extending ICC control over water and rail-and-water rates, filled one gap in federal transportation legislation, but the experiences of the coordinator and of the ICC in attempting to eliminate uneconomic units showed how difficult it is to achieve a national transportation plan in the face of the opposition of local and special interests. The interstate trade barriers that are so commonly encountered by truck lines

[6] Federal Coordinator of Transportation, *Public Aids to Transportation*, 4 vols., Washington, 1938-40.

operating between states are but another evidence of the same problem. When World War II again created a crisis in transportation and made necessary the full use and control of all transportation facilities, the ODT (also under Joseph Eastman) and the WSA (War Shipping Administration) proved rather conclusively the value of coordinated regulation and operations.

REGULATION OF COMMUNICATIONS

The telegraph, the telephone, and the radio are in this country conducted primarily as private businesses. Governments own and operate only such necessary facilities as police telegraph and radio systems for purely public purposes. Telephone service, at first unregulated, was next regulated only by the states through their public service commissions. Telegraph companies came for a time under the Interstate Commerce Commission. The radio, and particularly radio broadcasting, after some preliminary attempts at local regulation to prevent static and interference, was next regulated by the national government. It set up the Federal Radio Commission, now defunct, to assign wave lengths to different stations, to prevent interference, and to put some restrictions on advertising. The threat of censorship involved in any such regulation caused considerable concern for a time, and the acts of the commission in granting and withdrawing licenses brought it widespread unpopularity.

In its general reorganization of regulatory bodies and methods, the New Deal Congress in 1934 established a single authority, the Federal Communications Commission, consisting of seven members, to regulate the radio, telegraph, and telephone systems. Over radio broadcasting it has substantially the same powers as were possessed by its predecessor, the Radio Commission. Over telephone and telegraph lines it has the same authority as the Interstate Commerce Commission formerly had, including some control over telephone consolidations, and a right to enforce reasonable rates for interstate and foreign service. The control of the states over telephone companies and their local rates is specifically protected by the federal act.

The telephone industry is already so consolidated that a unified national service is available. The same is true of the telegraph industry today. Radio broadcasting presents some peculiar problems. Its revenues come largely from advertisers. The great chains provide the principal programs for the local stations, and the struggles between them for control over and access to the principal stations resulted in some restrictive and monopolistic practices. The FCC ordered the division into two systems of what was previously the largest chain of all, and required some modifications in the contracts between the chains and their affiliated stations, to permit the latter to have more freedom in the choice of programs and in the management of their own affairs.[7] The commission also licenses broadcasting stations, and revokes licenses, regulates

[7] See National Broadcasting Co. v. U. S. (1943), 319 U. S. 190.

wave lengths and the power of stations, and exercises some supervision over programs in order to avoid indecency and prevent imposition on the public.

THE POST OFFICE

The American people have not followed the English precedent of having a single, integrated, public system of communications under the control of a Post Office Department. Nevertheless, the Post Office is the oldest, and in annual revenues and expenditures still the largest, single agency of communication in the United States, although the telephone system runs it a close race. The Post Office Department is one of the largest businesses in the world, managing more than 44,000 post offices and employing over 300,000 workers.

Services of the Post Office. The power of Congress to provide for the postal system is complete and exclusive; the states have no share in it. Furthermore, Congress has the power to expand the service more or less as it sees fit and to make it a government monopoly, as it has done. The Post Office provides three different types of service to the people. (1) First is the mail service itself, including the collection, carriage, and delivery of letter mail, newspapers, magazines, and parcels. Special branches of this service are the railway mail service, the air mail service, the oceanic and international mail services, rural free delivery, city delivery, and the parcel post division. Of these all except the last may be classed as communication services. (2) Next come the financial and banking services, including postal savings banks, the transfer of money from place to place by means of money orders, and the sale of government bonds for the Treasury Department. These are not communication services, but are justified on the ground that the thousands of post offices in small communities can be utilized in these ways for the convenience of the people, especially where no local banks exist. (3) As noted in an earlier chapter, the Post Office Department also has law-enforcement functions under statutes passed by Congress to prevent the mailing of lottery tickets, obscene matter, threats, poisons, and advertising intended to obtain money by fraud. In addition to these main functions the Post Office has some incidental ones. It is in many respects the point of contact between the citizen and those services of the government in which he is particularly interested, such as the Civil Service Commission, and the recruiting services of the army and navy. It is of great assistance in connection with census work as well.

NATIONAL HIGHWAY FUNCTIONS

State and local governments carry on the principal activities in the provision of highways, roads, and streets. This is the result of public policy rather than of any want of power in the national government to take over a larger share of the highway functions. Under its commerce powers and war powers alone Congress could do a great deal more in this field, but what it already does is by no means insignificant. Through various administrative agencies it already provides thousands of miles of roads in military reservations, Indian reservations, national forests, and other nationally owned areas. Within the states its principal highway responsibilities are discharged by grants-in-aid. Through the leverage provided by these grants, the national government has been able to control highway routes, to influence the organization, personnel, and methods of state highway departments, and to set standards for proper highway construction and maintenance. The development of the present extensive and well-improved nation-wide system of highways could hardly have taken place without national aid. For this result not only Congress but also the Public Roads Administration in the Federal Works Agency deserve great credit. The nation's work in regulating interstate bus and truck traffic was mentioned previously.

PUBLIC UTILITIES

As in the case of highways, the principal responsibility for regulating public utilities rests upon the state governments. In recent years, however, the national government has undertaken, under various laws and through several administrative agencies, to supplement the work of both the states and private enterprise. The Federal Power Commission has a nation-wide responsibility for developing power projects in the public domain and on navigable waters, while TVA in its region, and the Reclamation Service in the Pacific Coast and mountain states area, have similar but more localized responsibilities. Rural electrification is promoted by the Rural Electrification Administration (REA).

The principal regulatory body of the national government for public utilities is also the Federal Power Commission. It exercises the power to regulate the rates and service of companies that (a) distribute natural gas across state lines, (b) operate pipelines in interstate commerce, and (c) transport electricity across state boundaries to sell in bulk to local distributors. The effect of this general line of national activity in this field is not to oust state regulation but to supplement it by promoting and regulating those parts of the production process that are effectively beyond state control or help. These parts include mainly interstate shipments of electricity and gas, and the production of power on the rivers and on lands that belong to the national government.

SUMMARY

Looking back over this brief chapter one can see in operation certain broad public policies. (1) Private ownership and operation are the rule for the railroads, bus, and truck lines, air lines, telephone, telegraph, and radio systems, and for most shipping by water. (2) In all these services, however, the need for national regulation has been recognized, at least to the extent of control over all interstate and foreign operations. In effect national regulation has become dominant. (3) Public ownership prevails entirely as to the postal system and the highways, roads, and streets, and it exists elsewhere for limited facilities to supplement those that are privately owned. (4) The state and local governments construct, maintain, and control most of the public highway system, while the national government provides financial aid sufficient to have a strong influence on the planning of major routes and on standards of construction and maintenance. (5) The interdependence of the various facilities of transportation and communication has been fully demonstrated. For example, despite the great increase in traffic by highways, water, and air, the railroads proved to be indispensable for the great bulk of traffic during World War II. Whatever developments take place in other facilities, therefore, the need for an efficient railroad system cannot be ignored.

Present indications point, indeed, to a tremendous expansion in airways and in highways in the years ahead. A national gridiron of superhighways is far along in the planning stage. Airport and air line developments are certain to come, to take advantage of the great technological improvements in airplanes that came during the war. Along with these and other progressive changes a further increase in national aid and national control is almost inevitable.

REFERENCES

G. Lloyd Wilson (ed.), *Railroads and Government, The Annals*, vol. 187, Philadelphia, 1936.

Federal Coordinator of Transportation, *Reports* of, 1934 ff., espec. report of January 21, 1935, House Document no. 89, 74th Congress, 1st sess.

——, *Public Aids to Transportation*, 4 vols., Washington, 1938-40.

Malcolm M. Willey and Stuart A. Rice, *Communication Agencies and Social Life*, New York, 1933.

Reports of Interstate Commerce Commission, Federal Communications Commission, Postmaster General, Federal Power Commission, etc.

U. S. Government Manual.

I. L. Sharfman, *The Interstate Commerce Commission*, 5 vols., New York, 1936.

Merle Fainsod and Lincoln Gordon, *Government and the American Economy*, New York, 1941, chs. 8, 9, 11.

L. H. Haney, *The Congressional History of Railways in the United States*, 2 vols., Madison, 1910.

E. R. Johnson, *Government Regulation of Transportation*, New York, 1938.

J. M. Herring and G. C. Gross, *Telecommunications*, New York, 1936.

National Planning Association, "The Crisis in Transportation," *Planning Pamphlets*, no. 7, Washington, Sept., 1941.

Works Progress Administration, Marketing Laws Survey, *Comparative Charts of State Statutes Illustrating Barriers to Trade Between States*, Washington, 1939.

H. G. Moulton, *The American Transportation Problem*, Washington, 1933.

J. S. Buck, *The Granger Movement, 1870-1880*, Cambridge, 1913.

Interstate Commerce Commission, *Interstate Commerce Commission Activities, 1887-1937*, Washington, 1937.

United States, 75th Congress, 1st sess., Sen. Rep. 1275, *Government Activities in the Field of Transportation*.

Robert D. Baum, *The Federal Power Commission and State Utility Regulation*, Washington, 1942.

Joseph E. Kallenbach, *Federal Cooperation with the States under the Commerce Clause*, Ann Arbor, 1942.

A. N. Christensen and E. M. Kirkpatrick, *The People, Politics, and the Politicians: Readings in American Government*, New York, 1941, pp. 827-40.

CHAPTER 30

Natural Resources and Agriculture

CONSERVING THE NATION'S RESOURCES

Nations need to take long views. In formulating their policies they must think not only of the present but also, and primarily, of the centuries upon centuries through which the national life is likely to be prolonged. This is true in international relations, and it is equally true in domestic policy. Individuals generally take short views—for a day, a year, a few years, or at most a single lifetime—but responsible leaders, conscious of the nation's almost unlimited duration, strive to make policies and to establish conditions that will promote the nation's welfare throughout the ages.

The present and future welfare of a people depends first upon themselves and second upon the natural resources available for their use. The latter consist primarily of (a) the land area and whatever fertility there may be in the soil; (b) the subsoil riches, such as metals, coal, oil, and gas; (c) the available waters, including streams and lakes within the country, and the adjacent lakes and sea; (d) the forests, the grass, and other vegetation that grow naturally upon the land; and (e) the game animals, birds, and fish that make the land their habitat. Some of these resources are not reproducible. Once the minerals, oil, and natural gas have been used up, or the soil has been destroyed by erosion, there is little more that man can do about it. A nation that is looking toward permanent greatness and happiness cannot afford to destroy today what future generations will need but cannot reproduce. Over many destructive forces of nature, such as earthquakes, hurricanes, cyclones, and excessive rainfall, man has little or no control. The best he can do is to prepare against their coming. But excessive flooding can be reduced to some extent by measures of flood control, drought by the storage of waters, and forest fires can be limited and to some extent prevented by due care. Destructive insects, birds, and animals can also be controlled to a very considerable extent—but what about careless and destructive man?

506

The American Domain. The founders of the national government of the United States did not have to think seriously about the nation's natural resources. Nature had supplied the thirteen states most bountifully. In addition to their own territories they had, as in a common fund, millions upon millions of acres of virgin lands and forests in the west, stretching all the way to a river called the Mississippi that few men had ever seen. As a matter of fact their immediate successors seemed to have even less need to worry. Before settlement on any significant scale had even reached the Mississippi the Louisiana Territory was purchased (1803)—another immense empire—and thereafter other areas were acquired until by 1852 the nation laid claim to all its present continental area, reaching from the Atlantic to the Pacific Ocean. What natural resources these lands would yield no man could possibly foretell. The lure of the unknown, the excitement of anticipated discoveries, and the hope of personal enrichment, drew wave after wave of explorers and pioneers into the vastness of the great American domain. It did not take long to bring the forests under the ax and the prairies under the plow—and it took but little longer to make Americans realize that natural resources are not inexhaustible.

Government Disposition of Land. The total land area of the continental United States, exclusive of Alaska and the Panama Canal Zone, is just under 3 million square miles, or about 1,900 million acres. This amounts to about 14 or 15 acres per capita. Three-fourths of this land has been at one time or another in the legal possession of the national government. Only the original thirteen states, together with Kentucky, Tennessee, and Texas, had legal title to the unappropriated lands within their limits. Of nearly 1,500 million acres once possessed by the national government, over 1,000 million acres, or more than half the area of the United States, have been sold or given away. What is left in the ownership of the national government is about 450 million acres, or more than a fifth of the nation's area.

Policy of Private Development. The great American objective was to acquire dominion of the land from sea to sea, and then to have the land brought into production as rapidly as possible by private exploitation. The national government first used the lands to pay off its Revolutionary War soldiers and others who had claims against it. Much land was sold to settlers and granted to homesteaders. Some was granted to the states to promote education and to foster the building of railroads and internal improvements; and the states granted away or sold these lands in much the same way as the national government did. The railroads, too, sold their lands as rapidly as possible. In the early decades of the republic, at least, the dominant economic and political philosophy was individualistic. The men who controlled public policy gave little or no thought to the desirability of maintaining public ownership and management of the nation's patrimony. How this policy worked out in the disposal of the public lands is clearly shown by the following approximate figures.

DISPOSITION OF THE PUBLIC DOMAIN, 1787-1931 [1]

	Acreage
Cash sales to individuals	310,000,000
Homestead entries by individuals	246,000,000
Grants to states for education, etc., later sold to individuals	182,000,000
Railroad and similar grants, largely sold to individuals	140,000,000
Bounty warrants, grants to soldiers, etc.	64,000,000
Private claims of individuals	35,000,000
Indian allotments to individuals	27,000,000
Other grants to individuals, corporations, municipalities, etc.	47,500,000
Total disposed of	1,051,500,000

Area and Value of Present Public Lands. A number of the states hold considerable acreages of forest land, parks, and tax-delinquent tracts, but the national government is by a wide margin the greatest landholder. It has over 175 million acres in national forests, 55 million in Indian reservations, and about 50 million in reclamation projects, national parks, and miscellaneous holdings. These millions of acres, equal to the whole northeast from Maine to Wisconsin and Illinois, are all permanently reserved against private exploitation. In addition there are about 175 million acres still open to private settlement or in process of being privately acquired. While the great bulk of this land lies in the Rocky Mountains and in semiarid regions of the West, it is nevertheless a patrimony of great potential value and one worthy of careful administration.

Nature of Disposal Policy. The policy of rapid disposal into private possession had much to commend it. It resulted in the speedy development of the country and the establishment of millions of self-supporting farm homes. Railroads spread rapidly over the land, and industries and cities grew. The defects in the policy that have since come into clearer view were largely the results of haste, lack of knowledge, the greed of exploiters, the ineffectiveness of government control over settlement, and the development of a get-rich-quick attitude that affected even many farmers. Inadequate knowledge of soil conditions and rainfall led hundreds of thousands of settlers to take up land that proved later to be unfit for successful farming. This was true in the mountains, in the forests of the Great Lakes region, and on the great plains. The railroads and the states that had lands to sell, and even the national government, over-advertised the land and thus stimulated men to undertake unwise settlement and tillage. Nevertheless, the lure of the land was the strongest factor in bringing on the many tragedies of wasted lives that resulted. The pressure on the national government to open ever new areas to homesteading was strong and persistent.

Timber and Mineral Exploitation. In addition to the settlers looking for farms, there were the lumber interests and the men who sought precious

[1] See Herman Stabler and others, *Rise and Fall of the Public Domain Exclusive of Alaska and Other Outlying Possessions*, Amer. Soc. of Civil Engineers, mimeographed, 1932, p. 8; *Statistical Abstract of the United States*, 1940, pp. 129-35.

metals, iron, coal, and oil. These were shrewder and even more insistent in their demands. Many of them were guilty of timber-stealing and claim-jumping. They invaded the public domain even before it had been opened. Once they found wealth in any form, they exploited it to the utmost. Very few had any regard for conservation. Timber cutters rarely felt obligated to leave the small trees for providing another crop, or to plant anew where they had harvested. The thing to do was to get the value out of what nature had provided—"to skin the country and move on," said Theodore Roosevelt.[2] Profit was almost the sole motive, and even the government did not adequately protect the public interest. Indeed, the close league between the exploiters of the land and government officials was shown up in many cases.

Beginnings of Conservation Movement. Long before 1900 there were men who saw that the natural resources of the country were not inexhaustible and who spoke in protest at the extravagant waste of resources. Their words fell on deaf ears.[3] At the turn of the century, Gifford Pinchot and Theodore Roosevelt carried on a dramatic campaign for conservation, but found that the members of Congress representing primarily local interests would not support them even to the extent of providing appropriations for studies of the conservation problem. Laws for the establishment of national parks and forests were obtained, however, and, by executive order, considerable areas of land were withdrawn from settlement. The fight for conservation went on through the following decades, but it took the depression, the droughts of 1934 and 1936, the dust storms, and the great floods of recent years to dramatize the conservation problem sufficiently to make many persons conscious of it. Americans have awakened in recent years to find their great forests practically gone, the grasslands of the great plains largely destroyed, their natural gas and oil supplies being rapidly depleted. Gold and silver production has declined, and iron mining has but a limited life left in the United States. Much the same can be said of other ores. Anthracite coal cannot last much longer, but there are still large supplies of softer coals. Game animals and birds and fish are more limited in supply than they should be, and would soon be gone entirely were it not for increasingly stringent game laws and public propagation of many species.

Results of Uncontrolled Individual Exploitation. The growing realization that American natural resources are not inexhaustible has raised the question as to what caused these losses and how they can be made up and avoided in the future. Clearly, individual freedom carried to excess results in great injury to the public. Each man who takes all the game he wants for himself creates a condition that prevents any man from filling his bag. Unbridled individual freedom results, then, in destruction of natural resources and in injury to the whole community. The fate of the public is sealed by the greed, the igno-

---

[2] Theodore Roosevelt, *The New Nationalism*, 1910, p. 51.

[3] For a brief account, see A. E. Parkins and J. R. Whitaker (eds.), *Our Natural Resources and Their Conservation*, 1936, ch. 1.

rance, or the carelessness of the individual. That more stringent public regulation is necessary in the interests of all can hardly be questioned.

What Is Conservation? The need for conservation is evident, but what is conservation? Is it merely keeping the public lands in public hands? That seems to be the idea of some. A broader concept is that it concerns both public and private lands and resources, that what is in private possession also needs to be considered, and that the question of public versus private ownership is wholly incidental. Even disregarding this question, there are a number of different ideas that may be thought of in connection with conservation. (1) Certainly useless, criminal, or negligent destruction of things is at the opposite pole from conservation. (2) A step removed from such destruction is ruthless exploitation, where the person concerned does get a profit for himself from the cutting of every tree in the forest, but wastes much and does nothing to ensure the continuance of the supply. (3) Next comes regulated development and utilization. Permission to utilize resources is sold or granted under reasonable restrictions. For example, the game bag is limited, or the number of cattle permitted to graze in a particular piece of forest is restricted so as to preserve the turf. By such means the supply may at least be maintained constant if not actually increased. (4) Fourth comes the idea of rebuilding or making up for the former depletion by planting and propagating more than the amount currently used. Another example would be the efforts to reclaim waste metals that might otherwise be irrecoverably lost. Since most private producers are unable to afford such work, it calls for public effort. (5) Finally, conservation in the sense of merely locking up resources and forbidding anyone to touch them is sometimes defensible, as in the case of holding certain oil fields for future supply of oil for national defense. This practice is applicable only to nonreproducible things, and then only for urgent reasons. True conservation generally involves the regulated development, utilization, and reclamation of natural resources. Resources exist for reasonable use, not for either destruction or hiding away.

Powers of National Government over Resources. The powers of the national government to conserve resources are not unlimited, but they are extensive. The Constitution says that "The Congress shall have Power to dispose of and make all needful Rules and Regulations respecting the Territory or other Property belonging to the United States; . . ." [4] Here is stated not only a power of sovereignty over the national lands but also a right of proprietorship. The nation is owner as well as ruler of the public lands. Hence it has the power to hold such lands as it desires and to dispose of them as it wills. It may retain mineral rights and water power while granting the surface rights to others, for example, or make any other disposition it sees fit.

By implication from its power to regulate commerce, the control of all navigable waters of the nation belongs to Congress. Thus the damming of rivers and the development of water power and the withdrawal of waters from

---

[4] U. S. Const., Art. IV, sec. 3, par. 2.

navigable rivers and lakes are entirely under Congressional control. It is said that Congress has in general no control over land owned by the states, the local governments, or private persons. Its attempts to regulate the production of coal and of oil on private lands were first checked by the Supreme Court,[5] but later legislation on both subjects has been upheld.[6] In fact it is difficult to see how Congress can be prevented from controlling private and state lands and resources if such control is deemed by Congress to be necessary for any national purpose. To protect the nation's monetary system Congress has assumed complete control over the nation's gold supply. To provide for the national defense may it not do the same with uranium and the mineral sources from which it comes? How else can national and international control over the atomic bomb be achieved? And if these things can be done, why cannot coal, oil, land, and other things that are necessary to provide for national defense, or to promote and regulate commerce, or to protect the national domain, be also controlled by the nation even though at present in private or state ownership?

There is no doubt about the power of Congress to spend money for the general welfare. Given this power it can certainly purchase whatever lands and resources it needs to use. And it can also take what it needs by condemnation under the power of eminent domain.[7] Furthermore, under the treaty-making power the national government may enter into conservation work in unexpected ways. The Migratory Bird treaty between the United States and Canada, though it relates to and controls the taking of game that belongs to the states, is valid, and Congressional legislation to enforce it has been sustained.[8]

In short, if Congress fails to provide adequately for the conservation of natural resources it is not because it lacks constitutional power. That issue seems to have been settled rather decisively in its favor. At the same time the states also have ample powers to provide for conservation in matters not clearly covered by acts of Congress.[9]

Practical Difficulties in Conservation. Granting that the need for conservation exists, and that national and state governments between them have ample legal powers for the purpose, there still remain difficulties to be faced. First of all, there are conflicting interests and purposes. Local and private interests everywhere wish to exploit the minerals, oil, timber, and game to the utmost. To them these resources offer hopes of immediate gain, whatever the national

[5] Carter v. Carter Coal Co. (1936), 298 U. S. 238; Panama Refining Co. v. Ryan (1935), 293 U. S. 388.

[6] Sunshine Anthracite Coal Co. v. Adkins (1940), 310 U. S. 381.

[7] Kohl v. U. S. (1875), 91 U. S. 367; City of Cleveland v. U. S. (1945), 323 U. S. 329.

[8] Missouri v. Holland (1920), 252 U. S. 416. On the powers of the national government over wild life see also Robert H. Connery, *Governmental Problems in Wild Life Conservation*, pp. 31-52.

[9] Wall v. Midland Carbon Co. (1920), 254 U. S. 300; Hudson County Water Co. v. McCarter (1908), 209 U. S. 349; but see also Pennsylvania v. West Virginia (1923), 262 U. S. 553.

or state interest may be in conserving them. Local governments, also, want the resources in private hands so that they can be taxed for local purposes. If this is denied them, and if national or state government holds the resources in public forests or similar reserves, the local legislative representatives bring in measures to compel the central government to pay taxes thereon to the local units, although these efforts have so far had little success.

In the second place there are separate levels of government concerned, and the question must be settled as to which is to act for conservation in each particular case. Because it has had a head start and the greatest financial resources, the national government has led in establishing public forests, for example, but the states have not always gladly acquiesced in such plans. Even separate agencies in the national government do not always see eye to eye on conservation policies.

When the decision has been made to create a state or national forest reserve or to carry out some other conservation plan, further problems arise. Within the affected area various parcels of land will be owned by national, state, and local governments, and by private individuals and corporations. It is an expensive and slow process in such cases for any government to acquire ownership of the whole area; and to get complete agreement on a conservation policy without unified ownership is even more difficult.

Then, too, the various elements of nature are closely interdependent and a policy to promote one interest may seriously affect another. The "balance of nature" can easily be upset. If swamp land is drained for farming, adjacent forests may be destroyed by drought and fire, with resultant ruin to game and grasses as well. A Middle Western state some years ago introduced German carp to its lakes as commercial fish only to find that they are seriously detrimental to game fish. The plowing of some lands leads to erosion by wind and water. In short it does not pay to go ahead thinking of nature in terms of a single purpose or factor. The entire group of interdependent natural factors must be considered, along with the groups of people who depend upon them, and the final plan needs to be a comprehensive one that provides for all major needs and contingencies.

This broad and inclusive conception of planning for the conservation of resources has become more fully accepted in recent years. Its acceptance warrants the hope that future conservation programs will be more effective than some of the more limited and scattered efforts of the past.

Conservation Laws and Administration. Congress has enacted many different laws dealing with the nation's natural resources and to provide for their conservation and development. These are administered by a number of agencies. It is characteristic of Congress to act in this way, on particular matters, one at a time, and without attempting even to attain complete consistency. The President's Committee on Administrative Management in 1937 recommended that the principal conservation activities on the public lands of the government be combined in the Interior Department and that its name be changed to Department of Conservation. This would have involved, among other things, the transfer of the Forest Service from the Department of Agriculture to the Department of Conservation. Strong opposition to the proposal soon developed. The Reorganization Act of 1939 failed to authorize the proposed change, but the President was able to shift certain services to the Interior Department so as to increase its importance as a department for the conservation of resources. Under the Reorganization Act of 1945 still more changes in this direction may be accomplished.

Department of the Interior. Established in 1849 as the Home Department, the Department of the Interior has grown by addition and expansion of functions into an outstanding agency for the conservation of publicly owned resources, while certain other functions, like the Office of Education, have been transferred to other agencies. Among the principal divisions of the department for conservation purposes are the following: [10] (1) the *General Land Office*, which supervises the survey, management, and disposition of federal public lands, adjudicates claims thereto, conducts land surveys, and engages in research respecting minerals and other resources on federal lands; (2) the *Geological Survey*, which investigates the national mineral and water resources, makes topographic and geological surveys, classifies public lands, and supervises oil, gas, and mining operations by lessees on public and Indian lands; (3) the *Grazing Service*, which controls and restricts grazing on the western public lands in order to conserve the turf and the soil; (4) the *Bureau of Reclamation*, which has charge of irrigation projects on federal lands, constructs and operates great works like Boulder and Grand Coulee Dams, and engages in a general development and conservation program on the semiarid western lands; (5) the *National Park Service*, and the (6) *Office of Indian Affairs*, which are well-known agencies of this department; (7) the *Fish and Wildlife Service*, a relatively new unit in the department that investigates wild life, fish culture, and other biological problems, and administers the laws concerning fisheries, migratory birds, and wildlife sanctuaries; (8) the *Bureau of Mines*, which is essentially a research agency dealing with mining engineering, mining economics, health and safety of miners, and the technical problems of fuel, helium production, explosives, and manganese; (9) the *Petroleum Conservation Division*, which administers an act of 1935 that forbids the shipment in interstate or foreign commerce of any petroleum or petroleum products that are produced in excess of state quota laws. It also makes studies and recommendations to prevent the waste of petroleum and its products.

The department has other conservation functions, also, and for about four years (1939-43) it administered the Bituminous Coal Act of 1937, a law that aimed among other things to stabilize the soft coal industry. This act expired in 1943.

The Department of Agriculture. This department also has important functions in the conservation of resources. (1) The *Forest Service* conducts forest

---

[10] See *U. S. Government Manual.*

research and demonstration projects and also administers 160 national forests containing about 178 million acres—nearly one-tenth of the nation's area. In these forests it practices selective cutting on a sustained-yield basis, provides protection against fire and insect pests, and engages in planting and other reforestation activities.

(2) The *Soil Conservation Service* carries out a program of demonstration and educational projects designed to assist private landowners (farmers) in preserving their soil and its fertility, and promotes extensive soil conservation activities through nearly 1,200 soil conservation districts that include about 3 million farms.

(3) The *Production and Marketing Administration* has taken over the work of the former AAA in providing subsidies to farmers for certain approved soil-conserving activities. This is primarily a subsidy and crop control program.

Many of the research and educational activities of the department also contribute to the conservation of the soil as well as to the improvement of crops and farm animals. At one time the department centered a great deal of its work around the concept of land planning and land utilization, but Congress withdrew most of the funds for this purpose.

Other National Agencies. The *War Department*, with its continuous work on flood control and river and harbor improvement, is an important national agency of conservation. So, too, are the *Federal Power Commission*, which controls the development of dams and water power on navigable waters and on public lands; the *Migratory Bird Conservation Commission*, connected with the Interior Department, which helps to select sites for new game refuges; and other agencies.

TVA and the Regional Approach. Most of the conservation work of the national government mentioned above represents the piecemeal or single-function approach to the conservation problem. One agency goes into water conservation, another into forestry, and so on. The Tennessee Valley Authority (TVA) represents a different approach—one that is functionally more comprehensive but limited to a single region. The TVA is a government-owned corporation that operates in the Tennessee River valley, an area comprising 41,000 square miles and including parts of seven states. Its purposes are to construct and operate dams and munitions plants in the interests of national defense, to improve navigation and control floods in the river system, and to develop fertilizers for agricultural use. In addition, the President has directed it to conduct studies and make recommendations leading to the conservation, development, and use of all the area's natural resources. It is in fact doing all these things, independently in part, and in part in cooperation with state and local governments, cooperative societies and associations of citizens. These activities are necessarily having an effect in raising the standards of living in the entire region.

There has been talk of establishing a number of "little TVAs" in other river basins throughout the country and something of similar scope has been definitely proposed for the Missouri valley and for the Columbia River basin. Terrific opposition has developed against these proposals—from the Army Board of Engineers, the Reclamation Service, and numerous private groups and individuals. The TVA remains distinctive in the size of its operations and in the fact that it is organized as a government corporation under a board of three directors. In recent years the board has carried on its work through a general manager whom it appoints and controls.

It is, of course, the state and local governments that have the police power necessary in most cases to achieve compulsory conservation of resources. Such federal agencies as TVA can control navigable waters, but for the rest they must rely on their financial resources (provided by Congress) and their powers of education and persuasion to get their plans adopted. No state has established any agency quite like the TVA, but a number have set up state land-use committees and have also authorized counties to adopt zoning regulations to restrict unwise agricultural development and to promote the best uses of land. The United States Department of Agriculture has promoted the organization of unofficial land planning committees composed of farmers and others in hundreds of counties. Thus in one way or another land-planning and conservation activities are moving forward constantly.

PROMOTING AGRICULTURAL WELFARE

Current Farm Prosperity Abnormal. Since the defense emergency of 1940 farm income in the United States has gone upward to unprecedented peaks. The world-wide war made food one of the most important products of the "arsenal of democracy." The demand for farm products was unusually heavy, prices were high and would have been higher if they had not been controlled, and the nation was fortunate in having several bumper crop years. Farmers were enabled to pay off a great deal of farm debt, and prevented from investing heavily in farm machinery, automobiles, and durable household equipment because of the shortages in these expensive items. The "cash position" of the farmers is, therefore, unusually favorable. Moreover, the farmers are also assured by the government of good prices for two years after the end of the war.

Farm Conditions, 1930-40. It would be a great mistake to think of this wartime and end-of-the-war prosperity as the normal situation for agriculture. The previous decade (1930-40) was certainly unusually bad, but it is worth while to recall the situation as an antidote for excessive optimism at present. At the worst period of the depression, about 1932-33, unemployment had reduced the demand for farm products to a very low point, prices for farm products were the lowest they had been for many decades, and farm mortgages were being foreclosed by the tens of thousands. Whereas today (1946) there is a world-wide food shortage, in the 1930s there were tremendous surpluses to depress the market—a time of poverty in the midst of plenty!

The decade 1930-40 saw not only the greatest depression for both agriculture and industry in American history, but also the greatest efforts ever made by the government to restore the farm population to a sort of economic parity with other sections of the population. At the end of the decade, there were just over 6 million farms in the country, or nearly 200,000 fewer than in 1930. The farm population dependent on these farms was also less than in 1930 in about the same proportions. At the same time the average size of farms had increased somewhat, from 157 to 174 acres, and the total acreage in farms had also increased, but the average value of farm land and buildings had decreased tremendously, from $7,600 per farm to $5,500. Despite these various changes, agricultural income in 1939 was almost exactly the same as in 1930, just over 8 per cent of the national income, although the farm population was nearly 20 per cent of the total. Is it surprising that there is an "agricultural problem"?

Some Characteristics of Farming. Farming is a highly competitive industry. Not only does every farmer compete to some extent with every other, and every producing area or country with every other, but there is always the potential competition of those workers in city and village who, at the first sign of farm prosperity, move out to take up unused land. The industry is frequently overexpanded, with more producers and more potential production than the market can absorb.

Marketing Problems. The market for agricultural produce, while fairly stable as a whole, is subject to many subtle and unseen changes. When tractors took the place of horses in farming, the feed-producing areas suffered a considerable loss. Millions of acres thus freed from feed raising were turned to producing for human consumption. In the meantime, an increasing urban population, engaged in less strenuous and fatiguing physical labors, has been reducing its consumption of foods in some directions and changing over to other kinds of foods, such as milk products, fresh vegetables, and fruit. The production of grains and meat in other countries also has a tremendous effect on the market, since there is a world market and a world price for many staples. Dependent on distant markets, both domestic and foreign, the farmer finds that freight rates are a tremendous factor in his costs. The inland wheat, corn, and cattle farmer who must use railroads and trucks for shipping long distances seems at a great disadvantage as compared with those who can ship mainly by water to the leading ports and markets. Attempts to assist the farmer by the imposition of protective tariffs on farm products have been largely futile with respect to the great staple crops of which there is normally an exportable surplus. A tariff helps ordinarily only when the domestic production is less than the domestic demand, when a certain amount must be imported with the tariff paid. On the other hand the farmer must buy many things manufactured in the cities that are protected by the tariff, and the prices of which are increased by the tariff.

Low and Uncertain Income. It thus happens that although about a fifth of the population is still dependent directly on agriculture in all its branches, the normal income of the agricultural population is less than a tenth of the national income. The farm family's income is thus normally comparable with that of the family of the city laborer or mechanic rather than with that of the small businessman or professional man in the city. But the farmer who is also a farm owner has a considerable investment in his land and buildings, estimated at nearly $5,500 per farm in 1940. On this investment he has a direct tax burden under the property tax laws, and he also carries some mortgage burden on it in the case of nearly half of the owner-operated farms. These are fixed charges that cannot be avoided or postponed indefinitely, whatever may happen to farm income. All farms are not owner-operated, however; in 1935 two-fifths of all farms in the United States, representing nearly a third of all farm lands, were operated by tenants, who were bound to pay rent either in cash or in the form of a share of the crop. The "sharecroppers" constitute a special problem in the South, particularly among the Negroes, but even in the North Central states the tenant farmers number from a fifth to a half of the total number. Add to these factors the uncertainties of wind and weather, the occasional droughts and recurrent floods, soil erosion and losses of soil fertility, the insect and animal pests, the plant and animal diseases, and one sees some of the problems of farming.

Agrarian Demands for Government Aid. It is not surprising that farmers' movements have arisen from time to time to demand that something be done by government for agriculture. The spread of knowledge of how things could be improved has made the movement stronger and more widespread. Governments yielded to agrarian demands at first reluctantly, and then with increasing sympathy and zeal for improving the lot of the farmer. It is sometimes remarked that the most individualistic of occupations, farming, is today dominated by the most collectivistic and even socialistic ideas. It does not follow that farmers as a class are particularly socialistic in their thinking. They are still fundamentally individualistic. They want private ownership and operation of farms. They want as little compulsory regulation by the government as is possible. They have votes and will use them to resist government encroachment. What they want instead is such a program of government *aid for agriculture* as will enable farmers to get better incomes and security, and such measures of government *regulation of others* who sell to the farmers and who handle farm products as will reduce the chance of farmers being cheated or imposed upon.

Congress and Agriculture. The national Constitution says not a word about agriculture. The framers of that document made no express provision for Congress to do anything directly to regulate farming. Lacking any express powers to aid agriculture, but being under pressure to do something, Congress began a little at a time to make use of its implied powers. But it was not until 1862 that Congress, on the suggestion of Lincoln, established the Department of Agriculture.[11]

Powers of Congress to Assist Agriculture. Congress has authority to collect (and therefore to spend) taxes for the general welfare. It has also a general borrowing power. It may thus provide funds for lending to farmers and farm organizations, for conducting research into agricultural problems, for carrying on statistical work, and for promoting agricultural education. Its control over interstate and foreign commerce enables it to control the principal traffic in agricultural products, and through this power it may also control those farming activities that clearly affect commerce. The power to establish post offices and post roads gives rise to systems of rural free delivery and aids for rural roads. A number of other powers incidentally contribute to the same ends; for example, in the TVA such purposes as control of navigation and the provision of nitrates for war purposes under the war power were mixed with other purposes related to the provision of fertilizers for agriculture, electric power for rural electrification, and a general attempt to raise the level of agricultural life in a whole large area. The constitutional difficulties that have arisen were connected especially with schemes of agricultural relief in which the attempt was made to regulate farming and not merely to aid it, but Congress has found ways to help farmers in spite of a few adverse court decisions, and the Supreme Court has recently sustained all important agricultural legislation.[12] As in most other functions undertaken by Congress, therefore, the question of constitutional power is no longer the important one. There is, of course, some chance that national legislation will conflict with that of the states, since the states also have power to regulate agriculture; but such conflicts can usually be resolved by mutual accommodation or, if necessary, by applying the rule of national supremacy.

National Agricultural Legislation. Very few persons not directly connected with the study or administration of agricultural laws and services have any conception of the distances to which the national government has gone in its direct and indirect provision for agricultural welfare. Prior to World War I it tried to satisfy the farmers mainly by the tariff, aids to agricultural research and education, the regulation of railroad rates, and some halfhearted attempts to enforce the antitrust laws against monopolies that hampered agriculture. The slump in farm prices and the agricultural distress at the end of that war coincided with the rise of more effective farmers' organization and the establishment in Congress of the "farm bloc."

In 1920 the farmers demanded governmental aid in adjusting the farm part of the national economy to the changes brought about by the war. The country was slow to unite on a remedy that would meet the new conditions. In

---

[11] Alfred Charles True, *A History of Agricultural Experimentation and Research in the U. S.*, p. 19. See also Lloyd M. Short, *The Development of National Administrative Organization in the U. S.*, p. 374.

[12] See footnotes 14 and 15 below.

1921 and 1922, two tariff acts were enacted raising the duties on farm imports, but the old remedy failed to work; the expected rise in prices of exportable farm products did not materialize. The new demand to "make the tariff effective for agriculture" continued from 1922 to 1928 and was actualized in the McNary-Haugen bill, twice passed by Congress and vetoed both times. The plan sought to set up a government corporation to buy American farm products and to resell them on the foreign market, even if at a loss to the government. In this way undesirable surpluses were to be removed.

An alternative proposal, the Agricultural Marketing Act, enacted and approved in 1929, provided for a Federal Farm Board to assist in promoting the effective marketing of the principal crops and to encourage the formation of farmers' cooperatives for marketing purposes. Under the act the board created a corporation to stabilize the price of grain by purchasing surpluses of wheat and taking them off to market. The board recognized the need of limiting domestic production but had no machinery to prevent overproduction or to ascertain the desirable amount for an individual farmer to produce. In a short time the plan broke down.

The AAA, 1933-38. The next great effort in this direction was the first Agricultural Adjustment Act, approved May 12, 1933. The act was a landmark in the history of American agriculture. Its primary objective was to bring about an increase in farm buying power by reducing surpluses and by bringing supplies into line with demand. Under the act a tax was levied on all processors of agricultural products in proportion to the amounts they produced, and the money thus taken in by the government was to be used to pay benefits to farmers who agreed to restrict production. The program of crop restriction was well under way when the drought of 1934 caused a still further decrease in agricultural production. Prices rose, and from 1934 through 1936 the financial condition of the farmers improved very substantially. A distinctive provision of the act was the carrying out of the production adjustments through county associations of farmers organized for the purpose in all parts of the United States. On the whole the act was well administered and was popular among those farmers who benefited from it.

In 1934 and 1935 the AAA program was supplemented by such measures as the Bankhead Cotton Control Act, which provided for compulsory restrictions on the marketing of cotton, and the Kerr Tobacco Act. Likewise in 1935 Congress enacted the Bankhead-Jones Act, which sought to improve the farmers' production efficiency by aiming agricultural research more directly at specific production problems, and by increasing federal support of land-grant colleges and cooperative extension work.

In January, 1936, the Supreme Court invalidated the processing tax provisions of the AAA as an attempt to regulate agriculture in violation of the reserved powers of the states.[18] While the decision did not affect the validity

[18] U. S. v. Butler (1936), 297 U. S. 1.

of the AAA marketing agreements or commodity loans, it did put an end to adjustment programs predicated upon contracts with producers.

In February, 1936, the Soil Conservation and Domestic Allotment Act became law. The act retained the AAA goal of an equitable balance between farm and industrial incomes, but sought to achieve the goal by a shift in emphasis from production adjustment to soil conservation. Money was appropriated to make payments to farmers for making more extensive use of soil-conserving and soil-building crops and practices. But the 1936 act was inadequate to meet farmers' adjustment needs. It provided no effective check on production.

AAA of 1938. The third phase of New Deal agricultural experimentation began with the passage of the Agriculture Adjustment Act of 1938. This act continued and strengthened the conservation program of 1936. It provided also for a program including (a) "conservation payments" to producers for planting less than their acreage allotments of soil-depleting crops and for carrying out soil-building practices; (b) "parity payments" to producers of corn, wheat, cotton, tobacco, and rice, who plant less than their allotments; (c) commodity loans to support farm prices and store reserves; (d) marketing control of surpluses when approved by two-thirds of the producers voting on the question; and (e) federal crop insurance on wheat. A Federal Crop Insurance Corporation was created to offer crop insurance to wheat farmers. The act also expanded the work of removing surplus commodities begun earlier by the Federal Surplus Commodities Corporation and now transferred to its successor, the Surplus Marketing Administration. In addition to administering the marketing agreement program provided for in the Agricultural Agreement Act of 1937, the Surplus Marketing Administration program included programs of surplus removal, export subsidy, and encouragement of increased domestic consumption. The most spectacular portion of this program was the Food Stamp Plan, which provided for government purchase of surplus foods, and the distribution of these foods to those persons in the population who were on relief or who were living at an abnormally low standard. This plan proved to be so popular with both grocers and relief clients that it was soon made nation-wide.

Uncertainty as to the legal status of farm legislation enacted since 1936 was largely ended in 1939 when the Supreme Court upheld both the marketing quota provisions of the Agricultural Adjustment Act of 1938 [14] and the marketing agreement provisions of the Agricultural Marketing Agreement Act of 1937.[15]

The Ever-Normal Granary Plan. The New Deal laws for agriculture briefly described above were incomplete and experimental. They tended in general toward the goal of "parity" in income between agriculture and industry on

[14] Mulford v. Smith (1939), 307 U. S. 38.
[15] U. S. v. Rock Royal Cooperative (1937), 307 U. S. 533, and Hood and Sons v. U. S (1939), 307 U. S. 588. See also Wickard v. Filburn (1942), 317 U. S. 111.

the basis of a supposed natural relationship between the two, a relationship
that was alleged to have been destroyed by a greater decline in agricultural
than in industrial and commercial income. The laws were also described as
providing for an "ever-normal granary," so that no one need ever want, and
yet farm income would not be depressed by surpluses resulting from a succession of good crops. The methods used to attain these ends were (1) restrictions on production of the major crops by agreements among the farmers concerned; (2) government payments to farmers for reducing their acreage in
production, and for practicing soil-improving methods of farming; (3) government aid also in the orderly marketing of farm produce, to avoid both gluts
and scarcities, with provision for public purchase and storage of surpluses to
the extent needed to protect the consumers; (4) crop insurance for major
crops like wheat; increased national expenditures for agricultural education
and research, and for rural highways ("farm to market roads") and rural electrification; loans at low interest to farmers to save them from losing their
farms to the mortgage-holders, and to enable them to acquire farms; rural
land planning and soil conservation projects; and various other measures that
helped to round out the total New Deal program for the farmers.

Wartime Changes in Program. By 1940 these various measures had made
substantial changes in the rural outlook. Then came the "defense emergency,"
and this in turn was soon followed by total war. The farm program had to
be changed almost overnight. Maximum production became the goal, and
selective production of high-nutrition, low-cost foods was also encouraged.
Large surpluses and low prices were no longer a problem. It was necessary,
indeed, to guarantee the farmers certain minimum prices, but it was also necessary to prevent a disruption of the war effort through runaway prices. For
most crops, therefore, the government set both floors below and ceilings above
the prices. To encourage increased production it seemed necessary also to
guarantee the farmers a certain minimum price (90 per cent of parity) for two
years after the war; otherwise the farmer might not feel it worth while to break
up additional acres and to acquire the new equipment needed. To ensure a
low price to consumers it seemed wise also to fix ceilings over the prices that
they would have to pay and to provide government subsidies for food processors and dealers so that they would not suffer loss. The whole scheme was
mixed up with army supply, Lend-Lease, rationing of some goods, and other
factors. It all looked very complicated, but it worked. Farm production sur-
passed all previous records despite shortages of help and equipment on the
farms.

Farm Credit and Farm Security. Government activity in farm credit dates
from the enactment of the Federal Farm Loan Act of 1916 providing a dual
system for supplying long-term mortgage loans, embracing twelve federal land
banks and private joint stock land banks. The Hoover administration employed certain new measures in an effort to alleviate some of the distress of
the depression. In 1933, all existing credit agencies were consolidated into the

Farm Credit Administration and the Emergency Farm Mortgage Act was passed to provide a program of farm debt refinancing. The general purpose of the Farm Credit Administration (FCA) is to provide a coordinated credit system for agriculture by making long-term and short-term credit available to farmers and by providing credit facilities for farmers' cooperatives, marketing, purchasing, and business service organizations. Agriculture credit is made available by dividing the country into 12 farm credit districts, each containing the following major credit agencies: (a) the Federal Land Bank, which makes long-term mortgage loans through the national farm loan associations; (b) the Production Credit Corporation, which supervises local production credit associations making short-term loans to finance all types of farm operations; (c) the Bank for Cooperatives, which makes loans to farmer cooperatives; and (d) the Federal Intermediate Credit Bank, which acts as a bank of discount to supply short-term funds required by production credit associations, private financing, institutions making loans to farmers, and farmer cooperatives.

Additional agencies in the FCA include the Federal Farm Mortgage Corporation, which carries out principally the farm debt refinancing plan begun in the spring of 1933; the Land Bank Commissioner, who is authorized to make farm mortgage loans of a more emergency character than those made by the federal land banks; the Emergency Crop and Feed Loans section, which lends money to applicants unable to procure needed funds from other sources; the Regional Agricultural Credit Corporations, which make direct loans to farmers and stockmen; and the Federal Credit Union section, which charters and supervises the federal credit unions.

In spite of the vast scope of the FCA, various disadvantaged classes, including tenants, sharecroppers, and farm laborers, continued to remain outside its purview. As the result of a report of a Presidential committee on farm tenancy in 1937, Congress passed the Bankhead-Jones Farm Tenant Act of 1937 authorizing the Farm Security Administration to make loans to competent farm tenants, sharecroppers, and farm laborers to enable them to become farm owners. In addition to farm tenant aid, the Farm Security Administration, created in 1937 as the successor to the Resettlement Administration, developed programs of rural rehabilitation, establishment of low-income farmers on homesteads, and migratory labor camps.

Most of this program was useful down to World War II, and some of it was also highly beneficial during the war because it provided the funds needed by farmers to expand production. What the main farm credit needs will be at the formal end of the war is hard to say. There will be needs, undoubtedly, but they may be much smaller and they may be somewhat different.

United States Department of Agriculture. To carry out its immense and complicated program of activities to benefit agriculture, Congress has created and developed the Department of Agriculture into one of the largest departments in the administration. It is also reputed to be one of the best operated departments, and it certainly has high standards of personnel. The department is difficult to describe, however, because it is almost always in the process of reorganization to meet some new and urgent need.[16] Despite frequent regroupings and reorientations, however, the component agencies of the department continue to be about the same. Below the Secretary, Under Secretary, and Assistant Secretary are several groups of units with rather distinctive purposes, as follows:

1. A group of bureaus and offices concerned with technological and scientific research, e.g., Agricultural and Industrial Chemistry; Animal Industry; Dairy Industry; Entomology and Plant Quarantine; Plant Industry, Soils and Agricultural Engineering; Human Nutrition and Home Economics; Office of Experiment Stations.

2. A group of agencies concerned with the planning and administration of the "action programs." Most of these are now brought together in the Production and Marketing Administration whose function it is to coordinate all production, pricing, and marketing activities of the department. In this administration there is a director for each commodity—livestock, dairy, poultry, grain, sugar, tobacco, etc.—together with others who are to see to food distribution, shipping and storage of crops, marketing facilities, farm labor, equipment and so on. This new arrangement in effect supersedes the War Food Administration and absorbs the functions of a number of special units like the old AAA and the Office of Marketing Services.

3. A number of other activities that are highly important but more miscellaneous and not all closely related include (a) Farm Credit Administration, (b) Rural Electrification Administration, (c) Farm Security Administration, (d) Forest Service, (e) Soil Conservation Service, as well as several others.

4. Another group of units is concerned with the operation of the department itself and all its field activities. It covers the usual administrative problems such as finance and budget, personnel, and information.

Cooperation with State and County Governments. A department of such great size and so many ramifications is hard for the outsider to understand. Indeed it has been questioned in what sense this great organization can be called a department.[17] Its unity consists in part of the fact that it is backed up so strongly by a great group of economic interests, all the producers of food and fiber in the nation. Its support in Congress is far out of proportion to the percentage of the population that is directly dependent upon farming for a livelihood.

In part, also, its strength depends upon the close ties that it has with state and county governments throughout the nation. Congress has provided continuing support for the state land-grant colleges, for the agricultural experiment stations, for various programs of public service within the states, like pest and rust control, for support of agricultural and home economics educa-

[16] See John M. Gaus and Leon Wolcott, *Public Administration and the United States Department of Agriculture*, Chicago, 1940.

[17] Gaus and Wolcott, *op. cit.*, chs. 1-5.

tion in the high schools, and for county agricultural agents in all the rural counties to carry on extension service to the farmers. The Department of Agriculture keeps in close touch with these activities, sets standards for their operations, and has some influence upon the selection of the state and county personnel who are to administer the aided services. No other regular department of the national administration, unless it be the Federal Security Agency, has anything like this closeness of contact with the states and counties.

Postwar Agricultural Policy. The present great prosperity of American agriculture must be looked upon as temporary. World-wide recovery will mean a restoration of agricultural production everywhere and a sharp reduction in the foreign demand for American farm products. What policy shall the nation then pursue? A prosperous agriculture is in every way better for the nation than rural poverty and depression, but how can it be achieved and maintained in times of peace?

The Agricultural Dilemma. The New Deal farm program checked at least temporarily the process of agricultural decay, but it left the basic problem of finding markets to absorb the productive capacity of American agriculture without solution.

The desire of the farmer to improve his lot drives him, as it drives others, to try to increase his income, and he can do this as a rule only by producing more and selling what he produces. Because of the relative inelasticity of the demand for farm produce, more production, at least when it is world-wide, means creating a surplus on the market and thereby lowering the price. If the farmers at and below the margin would then quickly stop farming, the price would soon correct itself, once more there would be increase of production by the remaining farmers, more farmers would drop out, and so on until those who were left farming, using their utmost efforts and the best known methods, could produce just enough for the market. This process of adjustment does not work smoothly or without great hardship. Farmers do not quit easily, even though they lose money for a year or two; more farmers are always entering the field; and in times of drought and war it is found that a previous surplus is a good thing to have for the emergency. Food shortage is above all things to be avoided in the interest of the whole population. The world-wide food crisis of 1946 strongly emphasizes the dangers in shortage.

There is, therefore, an inherent difficulty in all public measures to promote agricultural welfare. On the one hand great efforts are made by research and education to improve production methods, so as to increase and improve supply and to reduce costs of production; and on the other hand this very work of improvement tends to create overproduction and hardship for farmers as a class. Governments generally want to see the science and art of agriculture steadily improved, so that production will be ample and costs for farm produce relatively low, but they are responsible also for preventing suffering among the marginal and submarginal farmers.

Legislation and Agricultural Problems. To leave the subject at this point seems indefensible, and yet to try to describe and evaluate all the services of government for agriculture is beyond the scope of this volume. A few points, however, deserve comment.

1. *Agricultural Legislation.* The solution of all the problems of American agriculture is probably not going to be found in any single legislative plan such as those that were developed and enacted during the New Deal. Conditions change constantly, and new measures need to be devised from time to time.

2. *Accepting Production Restrictions.* If agriculture expects to get from government any sort of floor under prices, it will be necessary to accept along with it some restrictions on production. The taxpayers cannot sign a blank check that guarantees a minimum price no matter how much is produced.

3. *Flexibility in Legislation.* Whatever comprehensive plan of stabilization and price guarantees is adopted, it will be necessary to permit the President and the Department of Agriculture considerable latitude to change the rules from time to time. Changes occur too quickly for a slow-moving Congress to keep pace.

4. *Scientific Improvements and Reduction in Costs.* Agriculture like other industries needs continuously to reduce its costs of production because of the rapid advance of the arts, the rise of competing products, and the opening of new areas of production. The goal should be ample supplies for consumers at low prices with a reasonable average profit for farmers over a period of years. Therefore everything the state and national governments can do within reason to improve methods and lower costs of production should be done. The development of new species, of new methods of cultivation and breeding, and of every improvement that gives promise of keeping American agriculture abreast or ahead of the procession, should be encouraged.

5. *Tax Policy.* In addition, government can do something through changes in tax policies to reduce the farmers' fixed costs, and through reasonable downward adjustments of the tariff to increase somewhat the foreign market for American farm products and to reduce the cost to the farmer of some things he needs but does not produce. These efforts also help to reduce his costs.

6. *Expansion of Markets.* Foreign markets cannot be expected to be steady and large enough to be a permanent support for American agriculture. The home market is the most reliable market. That being true, farmers' organizations and representatives need to support every reasonable effort to provide for full employment in American industry. City dwellers cannot buy ample food supplies at good prices when out of work in large numbers. Intelligent efforts to improve the diet of industrial and office workers and their families should also be supported. And new industrial uses for agricultural products need to be discovered.

7. *Retirement of Submarginal Land.* When farm prices are going up there is always the danger of overexpansion on poor lands, with a resultant excess

of production that again forces the price down violently and dislocates the whole industry. By acquiring and retiring from agricultural use all submarginal land, governments can do much to protect farmers on good land from this "unfair competition." In the long run the bulk of the production must come from the better lands. Continued improvements in the agricultural arts will undoubtedly assure a people of nearly stationary population, such as ours will soon be, enough production without the occasional use of submarginal land for this purpose. In short, wise land-use planning and the practice of conserving soil fertility are indispensable to the long-run prosperity of American farmers.

REFERENCES

On Natural Resources

Herman Stabler, G. W. Holland, and J. F. Deeds (U. S. Geological Survey), *Rise and Fall of the Public Domain Exclusive of Alaska and Other Outlying Possessions*, 38 pp. and 10 figures, mimeographed, 1932. (Presented at Convention of American Society of Civil Engineers, July 6, 1932.)

A. E. Parkins and J. R. Whitaker (eds.), *Our Natural Resources and Their Conservation*, New York, 1936.

U. S. Committee on the Conservation and Administration of the Public Domain, *Report* of, January, 1931, Washington, 1931.

C. R. VanHise, *Conservation of Natural Resources in the United States*, rev. ed., New York, 1930.

B. H. Hibbard, *A History of the Public Land Policies*, New York, 1924.

Alpheus T. Mason, *Bureaucracy Convicts Itself*, New York, 1941.

Report of the Great Plains Committee, *The Future of the Great Plains*, Washington, 1936.

Russell Lord, *To Hold This Soil*, Washington, 1938.

John H. Bradley, *Autobiography of Earth*, New York, 1935.

Paul B. Sears, *Deserts on the March*, Norman, 1935.

National Resources Planning Board, *Report*, Washington, 1934.

——, *Energy Resources and National Policy*, Washington, 1939.

John W. Powell, *Report on the Lands of the Arid Region of the United States*, Washington, 1879.

U. S. Department of Interior, Division of Grazing, *The Grazing Bulletin*, Washington.

——, Bureau of Reclamation, *National Irrigation Policy—Its Development and Significance*, S. Doc. 36, 76th Cong., 1st Sess., Washington, 1939.

U. S. Department of Agriculture, *Soils and Men: Yearbook of Agriculture, 1938*, Washington, 1938.

——, *Land Policy Review*.

——, Forest Service, *A National Plan for American Forestry*, Washington, 1933.

Raphael Zon, *The Future Use of Land in the United States*, Washington, 1909, Forest Circular 159.

J. Cameron, *The Development of Government Forest Control in the United States*, Washington, 1928.

ON AGRICULTURE

John Gaus and Leon Wolcott, *Public Administration and the United States Department of Agriculture*, Chicago, 1940.

Donald C. Blaisdell, *Government and Agriculture*, New York, 1940.

Carleton R. Ball, *Federal, State, and Local Administrative Relationships in Agriculture*, 2 vol., Berkeley, 1938.

Gladys Baker, *The County Agent*, Chicago, 1939.

Alfred C. True, *A History of Agricultural Experimentation and Research in the United States, 1607-1925*, U. S. Department of Agriculture Miscellaneous Publication No. 251, Washington, D. C., 1937.

O. E. Baker, Ralph Borsodi, and M. L. Wilson, *Agriculture in Modern Life*, New York, 1939.

E. G. Nourse, J. S. Davis, and J. D. Black, *Three Years of the Agricultural Adjustment Administration*, Washington, 1937.

J. S. Davis, *On Agricultural Policy, 1926-1938*, Palo Alto, 1939.

C. C. Taylor, H. W. Wheeler, and E. L. Kirkpatrick, "Disadvantaged Classes in American Agriculture," *Social Research Report*, No. VIII, U. S. Department of Agriculture, Washington, 1938.

Report of the President's Committee on Farm Tenancy, Washington, 1937.

Brookings Institution, *Report* to the U. S. Senate Select Committee to Investigate the Executive Agencies of Government, Reports Nos. 10 and 11. Senate Committee Print, 75th Congress, 1st Sess., Washington, 1937.

U. S. Secretary of Agriculture, *Report* of, annual.

U. S. Department of Agriculture, *Report* on Agricultural Experiment Stations, annual.

——, *Yearbook*, annual.

——, *Land Policy Review*.

U. S. Government Manual.

Wesley McCune, *The Farm Bloc*, Garden City, N. Y., 1943.

Theodore W. Schultz, *Redirecting Farm Policy*, New York, 1943.

John D. Black, *Parity, Parity, Parity*, Cambridge, Mass., 1942.

——, *Food Enough*, Lancaster, Pa., 1943.

A N. Christensen and E. M. Kirkpatrick, *The People, Politics, and the Politician: Readings in American Government*, New York, 1941, pp. 939-963.

CHAPTER 31

Labor and Social Security

GOVERNMENTAL RESPONSIBILITIES AND POWERS

According to the 1940 census there were over 100 million persons in the United States who were 14 years of age or over. At that time 53 million were definitely employable at remunerative work, but only 45 million had regular jobs, while about 8 million others were unemployed or were engaged on public relief work. The defense emergency and the war quickly changed this situation. Unemployment was reduced to a minimum, and manpower shortages appeared in most industries. The total of all civilian employment rose to over 65,000,000. This number included millions of women and tens of thousands of minors not previously employed. Various estimates for the postwar period speak of from 55 to 60 million persons for whom there should be jobs. These millions live mostly in cities and villages, and are dependent upon employment at wages for their livelihood. They are not like farmers who have means of getting subsistence from the soil even when times are not good.

Government and Labor Conditions. Thinking of government in general, national, state, and local, what responsibility has it for the protection of workers against the vicissitudes of economic life and for the promotion of the general welfare of labor? What is government doing to discharge its responsibilities in this area? (1) The relationship between workers and their employers is a legal relationship, and since organized government is the maker and enforcer of the laws, it cannot escape having a duty to make the laws regulating labor contracts as just and fair as possible. (2) The government's responsibility for promoting the "general welfare" and its duty to take care of those who are without means of subsistence when thrown out of remunerative labor make it especially important that government regulate wisely the whole field of human employment. (3) There are particular duties imposed on government under state and national constitutions—duties to prevent slavery and involuntary servitude, to help the worker collect his wages when he has labored for another but has not been paid, and various other specific constitutional duties.

It is right to ask and to try to answer these questions about the government's responsibility because in general this nation is an individualistic one. The assumption is that every person has a duty to provide for his own support. There is at present no constitutional guarantee (although many persons think that there should be) of the right to a job. Remunerative employment, men used to think, was something that everyone must find for himself. Today many persons think that the government should underwrite a plan of providing jobs for all, or what is called "full employment."

Power of States to Enact Labor Laws. The early labor laws of this country were based upon English common law and statutes. First the colonial assemblies and then the state legislatures supplemented and modified the older laws, but in fact for many decades there was relatively little legislation on the subject. Private employment depended upon oral agreements or written contracts between employer and employee. Hours could be long and wages low, child labor was not forbidden, nor was safety in factories required by law. As legislation on these and related subjects began to appear, it was mainly state and not national legislation. In the federal division of powers it was simply assumed that labor legislation was for the states to enact.

The Power of Congress to Pass Labor Legislation. The Constitution makes no reference to labor legislation in the powers granted to Congress. In fact, however, Congress has come to have a dominant position in the field of labor law. How did this come about? It is a story of small and tentative beginnings, followed by more confident assertions of national power until at last, under the New Deal, Congress, urged on by the President and finally supported by the Supreme Court, suddenly occupied most of the field with sweeping legislation.

Here are some of the bases of Congressional authority to regulate the conditions of labor. (1) As the largest employer of workers in the country the national government can establish its own terms of employment and thus set standards for other employers. (2) It can also make all contractors who work for it conform to its own labor standards or else forego receiving contracts from the government.[1] (3) In the District of Columbia and in the territories Congress has complete power over labor legislation, subject only to the national bill of rights. (4) Employers directly engaged in foreign and interstate commerce (shipowners and railroads, for example) are also completely subject to Congressional regulation of their labor relations.[2] The Supreme Court has also sustained legislation by Congress that regulates hours and wages in industries engaged in the "production of goods for commerce."[3]

[1] Perkins v. Lukens Steel Co. (1940), 310 U. S. 113.
[2] Wilson v. New (1917), 243 U. S. 332.
[3] U. S. v. Darby Lumber Co. (1941), 312 U. S. 100. See also N.L.R.B. (Wagner Act) cases (1937), 301 U. S. 1, 49, 58, 103, 142; and Kirschbaum v. Walling (1942), 316 U. S. 517.

To these powers may be added others: the express power over immigration; the war powers; the treaty-making power; and the power to tax and spend for the general welfare of the United States. Congress and the President in the exercise of these various powers, and the Supreme Court in the interpretation of them, seem to have no serious doubts any longer as to the amplitude of national power over all the more important labor relations. It may be that the wages and hours of barbers and hairdressers, of schoolteachers and local plumbers, when engaged in work that does not seriously "affect" interstate or foreign commerce are beyond the direct reach of acts of Congress. But the present Supreme Court, noting that the economy as a whole has become national and interdependent, no longer attempts to obstruct Congress in its control over the major factors in the national economy—manufacturing, mining, wholesaling, retailing, agriculture, transportation, and communication. When facing organized labor that demands national action, Congress can no longer hide behind the Constitution. It must regulate labor conditions as it regulates other phases of the nation's commerce and industry. In what directions and how far it shall go in its regulations is partly a matter of policy, but in large measure these issues are settled by the necessary conditions of the American type of economic society.

AGENCIES OF LABOR LAW ADMINISTRATION

Department of Labor. The national government responded to the rising demand for a continuous consideration of the needs of labor in 1884 when the Bureau of Labor was created in the Department of the Interior. In 1888 the Department of Labor was organized, headed by a commissioner, but without full status as a department. In 1903, Congress created the Department of Commerce and Labor. Nevertheless the agitation of labor for a separate department continued until it was finally achieved in 1913.[4] In the organic act Congress declared its purpose to be "to foster, promote, and develop the welfare of the wage earners of the United States, to improve their working conditions, and to advance their opportunities for profitable employment."

Other Administrative Agencies. As in other fields of administration Congress has not seen fit to put all the agencies that carry out labor laws into a single department. In the early days when national government activities in the labor field were limited to research, publication, and mediation of disputes the Labor Department contained all the activities of importance. The stress of World War I brought some departure from this pattern, but the new administration in 1921 shifted things back to the department again. Then came the New Deal and the passage of a number of very sweeping labor laws. The administration of these was assigned almost entirely to new agencies. This was the case also with several new labor activities in World War II.

[4] Lloyd M. Short, *The Development of National Administrative Organization in the United States*, pp. 397 ff.

Indeed at that time the War Manpower Commission far overshadowed the Department of Labor. After V-J day, however, the President acted under his war powers to rehabilitate the department and to bring under its control a number of important activities. The labor agencies that are still separate will be noted later.

Present Organization of Department of Labor. Although reduced in total scope during World War II, the department then included the following bureaus and divisions:

1. Bureau of Labor Statistics, the outstanding research and statistical agency of the national government on all labor matters.

2. Division of Labor Standards, engaged in the study and promotion of improved labor practices.

3. United States Conciliation Service, for the peaceful and voluntary settlement of labor disputes.

4. Wage and Hour and Public Contracts Divisions, a combined agency to carry out the provisions of the Fair Labor Standards Act and the public contracts (Walsh-Healey) act.

5. The Women's Bureau.

6. The Children's Bureau.

By Executive Order 9617, September 20, 1945, the President placed under the Department of Labor most of the functions of the War Manpower Commission, and all those of the National War Labor Board, including the following:

7. The United States Employment Service, to be discussed hereafter.

8. The Apprenticeship Training Service.

9. The Training within Industry Service.

10. The National Roster of Scientific and Specialized Personnel.

LOCATING A JOB

The theory that every man must find his own job breaks down in a great national economy, where industry is highly specialized, calls for a variety of skills, is organized in many large and small units, and is scattered far and wide throughout the nation. Private employment agencies sprang up to serve as brokers in getting men for jobs and jobs for men, but numerous abuses, and the inability of any one agency to reach more than a small percentage of the jobs available, made this a very unsatisfactory arrangement. To provide the necessary mobility for labor, to get the right men in sufficient numbers for jobs throughout the nation, there was increasing need for a nation-wide system of employment offices with adequate information about the different jobs that were available. Such a system was set up during World War I, when there was an acute labor shortage and also maldistribution of available labor. This first United States Employment Service, opposed by the owners of private employment offices and by industrialists who did not like to see the government helping labor in this way, was discontinued upon the "return to normalcy" after the war. Then began anew the agitation for a coordinated federal and state system of employment offices. An act for this purpose passed Congress in 1931, but was vetoed by President Hoover.

Wagner-Peyser Act and USES. In 1933, as a part of the New Deal program, Congress passed the present Wagner-Peyser Act establishing the United States Employment Service. Under this law the new service was set up as a bureau in the Department of Labor, with a director at its head and an advisory council to assist in formulating policies. On July 1, 1939, the functions of the Service were consolidated with the unemployment compensation functions of the Social Security Board and were transferred to the Federal Security Agency. Under the terms of the Wagner-Peyser Act, the Bureau of Employment Security of the Social Security Board was charged with the promotion and development of a national system of employment offices for men, women, and minors who are legally eligible for employment. The national government granted funds which were matched by the states for the maintenance of the employment offices.

Up to September, 1942, the states administered the employment offices in conjunction with the unemployment compensation service, but at that time the President, under his war powers, took over the employment service as a national agency, and placed it under the War Manpower Commission. This left the unemployment compensation service with the states, but legally separated from the employment offices. The centralization of the employment service aroused great opposition in the states, and late in 1945 Congress attached a rider to an appropriation-reversion bill to return the employment service to them. However, the President vetoed the bill, his argument being, in part, that during the transition from war to peace national control of the service was indispensable. Unified control was highly desirable during the war period, but the return of the service to the states is to be expected sooner or later. In the meantime, as noted above, it has been placed in the Department of Labor.

As an entirety the service has become an important factor in the national economy. It maintains several thousand employment offices and placement centers throughout the nation, and it annually assists in placing millions of workers in employment.

THE LABOR OF CHILDREN, ALIENS, AND CONVICTS

The Child Labor Problem. Free, adult American citizens do not want jobs turned over to any competing groups. The forms of competition against which they have struggled most successfully are (a) child labor, (b) immigrant labor, and (c) unfree or prison labor. In the case of child labor there are, of course, powerful social, physical, and educational arguments for its abolition. The movement against it goes back for well over a century to a time when the full effects of the industrial revolution and the rise of the factory system were first being felt.

Although themselves slow to start, the states were first in enacting legislation to restrict the labor of children. As usual in cases of state legislation some states had advanced standards while others stood at lower levels down to a few that had practically no restrictions. Because child labor is cheap, certain industries tended to move to the states that were without restrictions on child labor. Eventually the national conscience was shocked by the reports of child labor conditions, and organizations arose to agitate for national legislation. In the vanguard of this movement was organized labor.

Attempted Legislation by Congress. From 1912 on both major political parties took the position that the national government should do something to put an end to child labor generally. Several different methods were tried, of which three were declared invalid by the Supreme Court. (1) Congress tried by legislation passed in 1916 to forbid the interstate shipment of goods made by child labor, and (2) in 1919 it imposed a punitive tax upon the employers of child labor in mines and manufacturing establishments. Both statutes were declared unconstitutional by the Supreme Court, primarily on the ground that they were attempts to invade the reserved powers of the states over manufacturing.[5] (3) In 1933 Congress enacted the NIRA, authorizing the President to approve codes of fair competition. The prohibition of child labor was a standard provision of all codes. When the Supreme Court held the NIRA invalid, this attempt to control the evil also was defeated.

Proposed Child Labor Amendment. (4) Congress in 1924 proposed to the states the adoption of an amendment to the Constitution to give Congress the necessary power. The proposed amendment, endorsed by all political parties, reads as follows:

> Sec. 1. The Congress shall have power to limit, regulate and prohibit the labor of persons under the age of eighteen years.
> Sec. 2. The power of the several states is unimpaired by this article except that the operation of state laws shall be suspended to the extent necessary to give effect to legislation enacted by the Congress.

In the face of the well-financed opposition by manufacturers' organizations, only 6 states had ratified the amendment by 1933. Up to January 1, 1942, 28 states had ratified this amendment, but the prospects of obtaining 8 more ratifications to make it effective are not very good. A number of state legislatures have definitely rejected it. Furthermore, interest in the amendment has waned since another approach to the difficulty has proved successful, as noted below. In 1939, the Supreme Court was asked to decide whether the child labor amendment was still open to ratification despite the lapse of years since

[5] Hammer v. Dagenhart (1918), 247 U. S. 251; Bailey v. Drexel Furniture Company (1922), 259 U. S. 20.

it was submitted by Congress in 1924.[6] It ruled that this was a matter for Congress to decide, but Congress has taken no action. Presumably the amendment is still before the states that have not adopted it.

Joint State and Federal Action on Child Labor. (5) Following the decision in the case concerning prison-made goods, discussed below, attention was turned to the possibility of Congress forbidding the shipment into any state of any goods the sale of which is forbidden in the state concerned. Legislation of this type now exists with respect to both liquor and goods made by prison labor. Several states also forbid the sale within the state of the products of child labor. If Congress should enact and provide for the enforcement of a law forbidding the shipment of such goods into these states, interstate shipment of child-made goods would be ultimately shut off from many states, and thus there would be little incentive left for any state to fall below any child labor standard that the national government might set. On further examination this proposal appeared to be unnecessarily clumsy and uncertain as to results.

The Fair Labor Standards Act. Leaders for child labor reform finally decided that the best thing to do was to try once more to use the national commerce power. The hope that new direct legislation by Congress on child labor would be upheld by the Supreme Court was strengthened by the great change in the Court's views that took place about 1937. In 1938 Congress enacted the Fair Labor Standards (Wage-Hour) Act applicable to interstate and foreign commerce. Under this law industries that produce for commerce may not employ children under 16 years, nor children under 18 years in occupations declared hazardous by the Children's Bureau of the Department of Labor. The provisions do not apply to children employed by their own parents in occupations other than mining or manufacturing, and the Children's Bureau is given power to permit children from 14 to 16 years old to do work (other than manufacturing or mining) that does not interfere with their schooling, health, or well-being. Establishments violating these provisions are forbidden to ship goods in interstate commerce. The act specifically exempts children in agricultural employment.

This act was put into effect at once with considerable effect. The Supreme Court upheld the act in a very strong decision.[7] Supplementing this act are several others, such as the Sugar Act of 1937 as amended in 1940, which also put restrictions on the employment of children in industry.

With the passage of these acts, the minimum age standard for employment has become an established feature of national legislation. It needs to be pointed out, however, that these laws do not reach all instances of child labor. Besides making a broad exemption in favor of agriculture, the act makes it possible for numerous enterprises that do not produce for commerce to continue to use child labor unless the state laws forbid.

[6] Coleman v. Miller (1939), 307 U. S. 433.
[7] U. S. v. Darby Lumber Co. (1941), 312 U. S. 100.

Tariffs, Immigrants, and Alien Workers. The competition of immigrants and foreigners with American labor is too broad a subject to be dealt with adequately here. It falls under three headings.

1. First comes the attempt through the imposition of protective tariffs against foreign-made goods to protect the American workman against lower-paid foreign labor, and thus to preserve the "full dinner pail" and "the American standard of living and wages" for the American worker. Many workers in industries had faith in this method over a long period of time, and no doubt that faith only awaits a period of depression to be revived again. At present, however, the policy of government is to reduce tariffs, and thus to take the shackles off production and to encourage importation as well as the export of goods. The belief today is that the United States can gain and hold a considerable foreign market for its industries through increased mechanization and decreased costs of production.

2. Next should be noted the attempts to restrict the immigration of foreign workers into the United States. At one time immigration into this country was almost unrestricted, and, as long as there was free land for homesteading to which men could go when wages and working conditions in the cities were unsatisfactory, the effect on the standard of wages paid was not perhaps very great. When this condition changed, industrialists still wanted immigration to be unrestricted. The foreigner did not know the prevailing rates of pay, and was willing to accept much lower wages. Thus the industrialists benefited from both the protective tariff and the free immigration of cheap labor. The American workman, on the other hand, began a drive to shut off immigration. Step by step the restrictions on immigration were increased until today, under the quota system that prevails, and with the policy of deporting undesirable aliens still in vogue, the net immigration into the country has been greatly reduced. During the war years the bars were lowered a little in order to admit some of the victims of Nazi persecution, but to offset this influx there have been years in which the numbers of those who left the United States exceeded the numbers of those who entered.

3. Finally comes the question of the right of immigrant aliens who are lawfully in the country to engage in employments in competition with American workers. In the manpower shortage period of World War II little was heard about this question, but it will arise again whenever there is considerable unemployment.

Naturally the native worker wants to restrict the rights of aliens when jobs are few. Facing the problem of low-paid Mexican labor, the state of Arizona some years ago enacted a law to the effect that employers of 5 or more persons must give at least 80 per cent of the jobs to American citizens. This statute the Supreme Court held unconstitutional as denying the equal protection of the laws to persons who are legally resident here.[8] Laws still exist, however,

[8] Truax v. Raich (1915), 239 U. S. 33. See also David Fellman, "The Alien's Right to Work," *Minnesota Law Review*, vol. 22, pp. 137-76, Jan., 1938.

requiring state and local government departments to employ only citizen labor on public works, and such laws have been upheld as constitutional. Since 1938 the national government has provided that no alien be given employment on federally aided work projects, and during World War II aliens were removed understandably from defense and munitions jobs. Aliens do not have complete equality of rights in employment, therefore, but as the proportion of aliens in the community declines still further this discrimination will be of less importance.[9]

Convict Labor. Convicts like other persons need regular and satisfying work. Many systems of employing prisoners have been tried: farm and maintenance work in the institutions, contracting out to private employers, work on the public roads, and definite prison industries producing useful goods that can be sold, and from which the prisoners can be paid a little money to save or to send home to their families. Organized labor has for a long time protested against prison-made goods being sold on the open market in competition with the products of free labor. Various states began years ago to limit the sale of goods made in their own prisons, and the amount of prison-made goods thus sold has for several generations been much less than one-half of 1 per cent of all goods. Nevertheless, organized labor wanted still further restrictions, and in 1929 Congress was induced to enact the Hawes-Cooper Act, effective in 1934, under which each state may put the same restrictions on the sale of goods made in outside prisons as it makes respecting goods made in its own prisons. The importation of goods made abroad by prison labor has been forbidden also. The Ashurst-Summers Act passed in 1935 required all prison-made goods offered for shipment in interstate commerce to be plainly marked as such, and forbade the shipment into states of any goods that are intended to be sold in violation of state laws. This act was held valid by the Supreme Court.[10] In 1940 Congress finally forbade all transportation in interstate commerce of prison-made goods except when produced for use by the national or state governments or by the District of Columbia.

WAGES, HOURS, AND SAFETY LAWS

Legislation Before New Deal. The more advanced states were considerably ahead of the national government prior to the New Deal in enacting and enforcing laws on hours of work, times and methods of wage payments, minimum wages, and the safety of workers. Most of the laws on hours related only to the work of women and children, because of the adverse view taken by the Supreme Court in 1905 on the attempt to apply such legislation to men,[11] while minimum wage laws also suffered several rebuffs from the Court.[12]

[9] See Henry R. Bernhardt, "The Right to a Job," *Cornell Law Quarterly*, vol. 30, pp. 292-317 (1945).
[10] Kentucky Whip and Collar Co. v. Illinois Central Railroad Co. (1937), 299 U. S. 334.
[11] Lochner v. New York (1905), 198 U. S. 45.
[12] Adkins v. Children's Hospital (1923), 261 U. S. 525; Morehead v. New York ex. rel. Tipaldo (1936), 298 U. S. 587.

Despite these discouragements Congress had enacted laws establishing the 8-hour day in railroad employment, and later fixing the wages of railroad workers during the emergency of World War I.[13] A first Employers' Liability Act providing rules for compensating workers who were injured in interstate commerce was held unconstitutional, but a revised act on the same subject was upheld.[14]

Early New Deal Laws. Prior to 1933 the federal government had made no attempt to establish a minimum wage for workers engaged in production of goods for interstate commerce. With the depression came new demands and new arguments for wages and hours regulation and the federal government embodied some regulations in the NRA code provisions. Following the demise of the NRA, Congress enacted the Guffey Act of 1935, which was soon declared unconstitutional because of its minimum wage provisions. Subsequent federal legislation included the Public Contracts (Walsh-Healey) Act of 1936 regulating minimum wages to be paid by concerns entering into a contract for furnishing supplies to or doing work for the national government; the Merchant Marine Act of 1936 authorizing the Maritime Commission to fix the minimum wage for officers and crews on vessels receiving federal subsidies; and the Sugar Act of 1937, authorizing the Secretary of Agriculture to fix a fair and reasonable wage to be paid by sugar concerns entitled to benefit payments under the act.

Fair Labor Standards Act. Encouraged by the Supreme Court's change of attitude in 1937, Congress in 1938 enacted a comprehensive measure regulating the hours of work and wages of all employees of establishments whose products are shipped in interstate commerce. The Fair Labor Standards (Wage-Hour) Act of 1938 establishes a maximum of 8 hours per day and a weekly maximum of 40 hours per week for the third year of the act and thereafter. The 40-hour week went into effect, October 24, 1940. The working week may be extended through collective bargaining agreements subject to a maximum of 1,000 hours for any 6-month period. Seasonal industries are allowed to employ labor up to 12 hours a day or 56 hours a week for not longer than 14 weeks in any one year. However, these limits may be exceeded provided compensation for overtime is made at the rate of not less than one and one-half times the employees' regular hourly rate of pay. During the war a 48-hour week was standard, but time-and-a-half pay applied to all time over 40 hours.

The act established a minimum wage rate of 25 cents an hour the first year of operation, 30 cents an hour for the next 6 years (1939-45), and 40 cents an hour thereafter. The administrator of the act, on recommendation of industry committees composed of representatives of the employers, employees, and the

---

[13] See Wilson v. New (1917), 243 U. S. 332.

[14] See First and Second Employers Liability cases—Howard v. Illinois Central Railroad Co. (1908), 207 U. S. 463; Mondou v. New York, New Haven and Hartford Railroad Co. (1912), 223 U. S. 1.

public, may establish for any industry a minimum wage between 30 and 40 cents an hour. These rates were absurdly low in World War II and were generally exceeded. Where in 1941, 17 per cent of all persons employed (exclusive of farm labor) received less than 40 cents an hour, in 1945 all but 20 per cent received more than 65 cents an hour, and the number of persons in manufacturing receiving less than 50 cents an hour fell from 3,000,000 in 1941 to 330,000 in 1945. The President has recommended increases to an ultimate minimum of 75 cents an hour.

Industries exempted from the application of the act include dairying, agriculture, fishing, and those retail or service establishments, the greater part of whose selling or servicing is intrastate. Employees engaged in executive, administrative, professional, or local retailing work are exempt. In affirming the constitutionality of the Wage-Hour Act, the Supreme Court said:

> It is no longer open to question that the fixing of a minimum wage is within the legislative power and that the bare fact of its exercise is not a denial of due process under the Fifth more than under the Fourteenth Amendment. Nor is it longer open to question that it is within the legislative power to fix maximum hours.[15]

There are substantial penalties for violations of the Fair Labor Standards Act. To enforce its provisions the Department of Labor has a nation-wide service with 13 regional and various local offices. Within its scope come the child labor and wage and hour provisions and also the Walsh-Healey Act with respect to wages and hours on public contracts.

UNIONIZATION AND THE RIGHT TO STRIKE

Unions and Strikes. The most spectacular phase of the labor problem relates to the right to form unions, to engage in collective bargaining, and to strike. The general tendency in the last few decades has been in the direction of removing restrictions on combinations of workingmen. In recent years, the relation of government to labor has been based upon the assumption that workers have a right to organize and to bargain collectively through representatives of their own choosing. Along with the right to organize unions have gone the rights of conducting strikes in ordinary, nonviolent ways, and of peaceful picketing and persuasion. Many legal difficulties have arisen, however, and under the New Deal the national government itself supported the side of the unions in order to establish a new order of relations between organized capital and organized labor.

Labor Unions and Antitrust Laws. The strikes, boycotts, and black lists of labor unions necessarily have the effect of upsetting and even shutting off trade for some concerns. Are they then subject to the antitrust laws and the

[15] U. S. *v.* Darby Lumber Co. (1941), 312 U. S. 100. See also West Coast Hotel Co. *v.* Parrish (1937), 300 U. S. 379.

laws forbidding restraints of trade? To the surprise and chagrin of many labor leaders, while the sugar trust escaped dissolution under the Sherman Act under an early Supreme Court decision, the acts of labor unions were held by the courts to violate the law when they resulted in such restraints upon commerce. The application of the antitrust laws to labor unions produced agitation for the enactment by Congress of the Clayton Act of 1914, one feature of which was the attempt to free the unions from this threat. As construed by the courts, the act did not materially change their situation, so that labor unions have continued to be subject to antitrust laws to a limited but uncertain extent.[16]

Injunctions in Labor Disputes. As a rule, however, labor unions are not incorporated like business concerns, nor do they all have great funds in cash or in fixed assets against which judgments obtained in civil suits could be assessed to give the damaged business any recompense for loss of business or destruction of property. Lawyers representing the employers in strike matters have applied to the courts for injunctions, therefore, to forbid the unions from doing certain things injurious to business during strikes. It has in all these cases been alleged that irreparable injury would result to the business, that suits against all the members of the union would be too difficult, and that there would be no remedy at law that could make good the losses. In the 1880s a few eastern state courts granted injunctions in such cases against the strike activities of the unions, and in the noted case involving Eugene V. Debs in the great railroad and Pullman strikes of 1894 the Supreme Court of the United States gave its approval to the injunctive method of judicial interference in strikes.[17] From that time on it was the regular thing for employers to seek injunctions against strikers. The objection of the strikers to this method of procedure was that there was inadequate opportunity for the workers to present evidence and testimony to the court, that temporary injunctions hastily issued tended to tie the hands of the unions permanently and made their strikes ineffective, that the injunctions issued covered almost every kind of strike activity, going in many cases far beyond what the unions thought was necessary, and that anyone who violated such an injunction became subject to fine and imprisonment by the judge alone, without a jury, for "contempt of court." Under the injunction procedure everything seemed to be stacked against the workers.

The Norris-La Guardia Act. In 1932 Congress passed a far-reaching anti-injunction act, the Norris-La Guardia measure, which specifically declared it to be the national "public policy of the United States" that the workers should have full freedom to organize and to join unions, without any interference by employers or others, for the purpose of collective bargaining, and

---

[16] Apex Hosiery Co. v. Leader (1940), 310 U. S. 469; U. S. v. Hutcheson (1941), 312 U. S. 219; U. S. v. International Hod Carriers, etc., (1941), 313 U. S. 539, and other memorandum decisions on same page.

[17] In re Debs (1895), 158 U. S. 564.

that the federal courts should not have the right to interfere by injunctions with a series of specified acts, including refusing to work, becoming a member of a union, paying dues, assembling peaceably, and peaceably advising and urging others to assist in these and other specified measures. This statute, besides putting many restrictions on the powers of the federal courts to issue injunctions in labor disputes, also provides that any person tried for contempt of court for violating any labor injunction that is issued shall have a right to a jury trial.

Section 7a of NIRA. Under the New Deal the national government sought further to encourage the organization of labor unions. One of the most famous provisions of NIRA (National Industrial Recovery Act of 1933, administered by NRA, the National Recovery Administration) was Section 7a which provided that every code of fair competition approved by the President must guarantee to workers the right to organize and to bargain collectively, uncoerced by employers. During its short life, this section gave a tremendous push forward to the organization of workers in all industrial lines, but conversely it acted as an incentive to a stronger organization of employers. The NRA was soon declared unconstitutional, but the drive for unionization and collective bargaining did not stop.

National Labor Relations Board. Even long prior to NRA the national government had provided for mediation and arbitration of labor disputes in the railroad industry; at various times the government had set up agencies for studying labor problems and for settling strikes or conducting arbitrations in other labor disputes. No sooner did the President begin to approve codes of fair competition under NRA than it began to appear that some agency would be needed to settle labor disputes that arose under the codes. Such an agency was created by executive order in 1933—the National Labor Board which represented both employers and employees. In 1934 it was discontinued, and a National Labor Relations Board was established, also largely on the basis of executive orders. Finally in July, 1935, the National Labor Relations Act created the National Labor Relations Board (NLRB), but most employers refused to be bound by it until its constitutionality was established by Supreme Court decision in April, 1937.[18]

This act is patterned after older laws and directly reflects the past experience of the government in controlling labor relations. It represents no radical departure from earlier legislation. The act clearly contains the most important expression of public policy encouraging and protecting labor's right to organize. Implicit or explicit in the law are certain basic propositions: (1) Workers must be free to bargain collectively without coercion or restraint. (2) Collective bargaining by workers is socially desirable. (3) The refusal of employers to bargain collectively induces strikes and industrial unrest. (4) "The inequality of bargaining power between employees who do not possess full freedom of association or actual liberty of contract and employers who are organized in

[18] NLRB v. Jones and Laughlin Steel Corporation (1937), 301 U. S. 1.

the corporate or other forms of ownership association substantially burdens and affects the flow of commerce. . . ." (5) "Protection by law of the right of employees to organize and bargain collectively safeguards commerce from injury . . . and promotes the flow of commerce by removing certain recognized sources of industrial strife and unrest, by encouraging practices fundamental to the friendly adjustment of industrial disputes and by restoring equality of bargaining power between employers and employees."

The act asserts that "employees shall have the right to self-organization, to form, join, or assist labor organizations, to bargain collectively through representatives of their own choosing, and to engage in concerted activities, for the purpose of collective bargaining or other mutual aid or protection." But the act goes beyond a general assertion of the rights of the workers to self-organization for the purpose of collective bargaining. It adds specific prohibitions against employer activities deemed incompatible with the right of labor to organize. Types of employer tactics listed as unfair are interference, restraint, or coercion of employees in unionizing and bargaining; the sponsoring of labor organizations by the employer; discrimination against employees because of union membership; the discharge of or discrimination against an employee because he has filed charges or given testimony under the act; and the refusal to bargain collectively. The act also specifically affirms that it is the majority of workers who are given collective bargaining rights. This provision is intended to prevent an employer from dealing with a minority group in order to avoid dealing with an organization that he does not like.

The NLRB consists of 3 members, appointed by the President with Senate consent, for 5-year terms, with salaries of $10,000 each. It is an independent agency, separate from the Department of Labor. The Board is given full power to enforce the act and to decide cases arising under it. It is empowered to decide in cases of dispute which of two unions really represents the workers, to determine the appropriate bargaining unit, to help employees to select representatives for purposes of collective bargaining, to investigate charges of unfair labor practices, and to order cessation of such practices. The Board's powers of enforcing its decisions are twofold: (a) the hearing of charges, and (b) the issuance of cease and desist orders which become final when affirmed by the federal Circuit Court of Appeals. The act applies to industries affecting interstate commerce, with the exception of agriculture, domestic service, employment by parent or spouse, government employment, and employment covered by the Railway Labor Act.

The Settlement of Labor Disputes. The NLRB was intended to protect the right to unionize and to promote fair labor practices, but not to settle ordinary labor disputes, including strikes. The United States Conciliation Service has existed in the Department of Labor since 1913 to conciliate labor disputes on a purely voluntary basis. It may deal with any type of labor dispute except those in transportation services (railways, Pullman and express companies, and air lines) which since 1934 have come within the jurisdiction of the National Mediation Board.

In 1941 the President created for the emergency the National Defense Mediation Board. When war came a new executive agency, the National War Labor Board (NWLB), took over the attempt to settle labor disputes that might impede the war effort, and it served until after V-J day. The NWLB served mainly as a policy-making board and board of appeals; the actual decisions in labor disputes were made in the first instance by the 12 Regional War Labor Boards. At first the NWLB and the regional boards had no authority whatever. They endeavored to settle all disputes amicably within the confines of a few basic understandings, namely, (a) that prices were not to be forced up; (b) that wages also were to be "frozen" for the duration except where they were subnormal and created real hardships, and except also that an approximate 15 per cent increase might be allowed based upon the already increased cost of living ("Little Steel Formula"); and (c) that organized labor would keep its pledge not to strike. In case the boards failed to obtain a settlement of a dispute, the President could seize any essential plant and operate it in the name of the government. By the War Labor Disputes (Smith-Connally) Act of June 25, 1943, the NWLB was authorized to settle labor disputes in essential industries by orders, but there was little attempt at coercion.

The Postwar Outlook. Just as soon as Japan had surrendered, and before the legal end of the war, wartime maladjustments between prices and wages and the pent-up feelings of large sections of organized labor brought on a large number of strikes, some of which were of nation-wide scope. As reconversion and the production of civilian goods were delayed, the President recommended legislation to set up fact-finding agencies to act in labor disputes, if possible before strikes ensued. A Republican-Southern Democratic group of Representatives forced through the House a bill to set up a new mediation board, to require a 30-day cooling-off period before strikes commence, to make unions as well as employers suable, and to provide for the punishment of acts of labor violence. This bill was viewed with outright hostility by organized labor. Nevertheless it passed the Senate during the railroad strike crisis of May, 1946, but was vetoed by President Truman and his veto was sustained by the House by the narrow margin of five votes.

The difficulty is in part connected with the national policy of trying to avoid postwar inflation by holding prices in line, and at the same time to settle labor disputes in the old way by free bargaining between employers and unions. Since wages are a major factor in production costs, and costs control prices to a large extent, the dilemma is a real one. If government could sit on the sidelines and not worry about rising prices, the two groups, unions and employers, could get together; wages could be increased; the employers could raise their prices; and the public could pay the bill. This may be an oversimplified explanation, but something like this has happened many times. It becomes increasingly clear that a government that wants to avoid inflation, that wants to hold the line on prices, cannot leave the fixing of wages entirely to the old system of free collective bargaining, which always implied some flexibility in prices. In short, the national government must either forego its attempts to control prices, or else set up some policy and public agency for the actual fixing of wages. This may be the next step in national labor legislation.

UNEMPLOYMENT COMPENSATION AND OLD-AGE INSURANCE

The New Deal took the nation into another field of action on behalf of labor. This was the provision of a sort of limited insurance against unemployment, and a separate scheme for old-age insurance for the great mass of workers. Both of these were provided by the Social Security Act of 1935.

Old-Age and Survivors Insurance. This is a nationally operated plan of old-age insurance or annuities provided as a matter of right to persons who have paid into the fund, and to their survivors. The agency responsible for administering the scheme is the Bureau of Old-Age and Survivors Insurance of the Social Security Board, a major unit in the Federal Security Agency.

The plan is designed primarily for wage and salary earners in ordinary business and industry. Over 39 million persons are covered, but—and this is a serious defect—nearly 30 million others who have received wages at one time or another since January 1, 1937, are not protected. These omitted persons included in 1945 large groups like agricultural laborers and farm owners (over 8 million), self-employed persons outside of agriculture (4.5 million), governmental employees (6 million), domestic servants (2 million), railroad workers (1.4 million, who are covered by a separate national retirement system), and over 10 million persons then in the armed forces.

A payroll tax is levied on earnings up to $3,000 a year for every person who is under the plan. The national government receives and administers the funds and makes annuity payments to persons past 65 years of age in amounts of from $10 a month for an individual (the minimum) to $85 a month for a family (the maximum). The actual amounts being paid in 1944-45 were under $15 a month for a single surviving parent, about $25 a month for a retired male worker, and $50 a month for a widow with three or more children. These averages will increase with time, but they are obviously rather low. All told, over a million and a quarter individuals were benefiting directly from annuity payments in 1945.

Unemployment Compensation. The provision of unemployment compensation is a joint national-state undertaking under the Social Security Act of 1935 and the various state laws on the subject. The national act offers 2 inducements to the states to cooperate in the plan. The first inducement is that the national government will pay the administrative costs. The second is a tax-offset plan that may be summarized as follows: A national tax to support unemployment compensation is levied by Congress upon all employers with 8 or more employees. If a state passes its own compensation act and levies its own payroll tax, the payment of this state tax will entitle the taxpayer to forego payment of up to 90 per cent of the national tax. Thus the state has almost nothing to lose by passing a compensation act, since the employer must pay the United States tax in full if there is no state tax; he pays little if any more if there is a state tax, and if there is a state tax its proceeds may be used within the state for an unemployment compensation plan. Needless to say, perhaps, that all states now operate schemes of unemployment compensation.

The actual administration of the compensation plan is left almost entirely to the states, under standards set nationally, and under the supervision of the Bureau of Employment Security of the Social Security Board. The proceeds of the state tax are paid to the United States Treasury which credits them to the state's unemployment compensation fund and pays them out to claimants who are approved by the state agency. In recent years the states have introduced considerable diversity into their compensation plans, with resultant weakening in some states of the reserves, and reductions in both the coverage and the amounts paid. There has arisen a great deal of demand, therefore, to have the system made completely national and uniform, and to raise the scale of unemployment compensation benefits, both in amounts and in the number of weeks of payment. Congress has recently been very cool to all such proposals.

MAXIMUM EMPLOYMENT, PRODUCTION, AND PURCHASING POWER ACT

After long debate and agitation Congress recently enacted a somewhat diluted version of the so-called "full employment bill." As originally introduced in 1945 by Senator Murray of Montana the bill declared it to be the responsibility of the national government to promote the private enterprise system and at the same time to foster business and lay plans so that all Americans able to work and desiring to work would be able to obtain remunerative employment. The measure called for advance planning under the President of an annual "national production and employment budget." In general the theory was that the national government should take the lead in maintaining full employment, without coercion on anyone, and that whenever employment fell below "full employment" by a significant percentage the national government should set in motion various measures, including public works, to provide for the unemployed. The bill was subjected to a great deal of adverse criticism and it underwent much change during passage. The words "full employment" were omitted, and so were the provisions for the annual production and employment budget and for a national guarantee of the right to work. Provision was made for a council of economic advisers to the President to assist in preparing "economic reports." Opinions differ as to whether the bill as finally passed in February, 1946, was a strong or a weak substitute for the original measure.

REFERENCES

John B. Andrews, *Labor Laws in Action*, New York, 1938.

Robert R. R. Brooks, *When Labor Organizes*, New Haven, 1937.

John R. Commons and John B. Andrews, *Principles of Labor Legislation*, 4th rev. ed., New York, 1936.

Merle Fainsod and Lincoln Gordon, *Government and the American Economy*, New York, 1941.

Lewis L. Lorwin and Arthur Wubnig, *Labor Relations Boards*, Washington, 1935.

Selig Perlman, *A History of Trade Unionism in the United States*, New York, 1922.

Joseph Rosenfarb, *The National Policy and How It Works*, New York, 1940.

Emanuel Stein and Jerome Davis (eds.), *Labor Problems in America*, New York, 1940.

Edwin E. Witte, *The Government in Labor Disputes*, New York, 1932.

Code of Laws of the United States, Title 29.

U. S. Secretary of Labor, *Annual Reports*.

U. S. Department of Labor, *Digest of State and Federal Labor Legislation*, annual.

——, *Proceedings of the National Conference on Labor Legislation*, annual.

——, *Labor Laws and Their Administration*.

——, *Handbook of Federal Labor Legislation*, Bull. no. 39, 1941, in 2 parts.

Raymond Atkinson, *The Federal Role in Unemployment Compensation Administration*, Washington, 1941.

S. E. Harris, *The Economics of Social Security*, New York, 1941.

U. S. Social Security Board (now in Federal Security Agency) *Reports*, Washington, annual.

U. S. Government Manual.

U. S. National Labor Relations Board, *Annual Reports*.

Encyclopaedia of the Social Sciences, various articles on labor.

A. N. Christensen and E. M. Kirkpatrick, *The People, Politics, and the Politician: Readings in American Government*, New York, 1941, pp. 841-69.

CHAPTER 32

Education, Health, and Welfare

THE ROLE OF THE NATIONAL GOVERNMENT

In 1787 the states already had rudimentary services in the fields of education, health, and poor relief, and it was the need for national provision for other functions—defense, foreign affairs, commerce and finance—rather than any demand for social services that led to the adoption of the Constitution. However, the national government has today a large and important program of activities in the services covered by this chapter, and more such activities seem to be on the way. The intention here is not to describe these functions in any detail but to outline them, suggest their significance, and try to forecast a little of their future development.

Powers of the National Government. The debates in the Federal Convention and the controversies over the adoption of the Constitution throw little light on the intention of the founding fathers respecting the functions here dealt with, and the Constitution itself yields very little. Public health, social welfare, and elementary and secondary education seem hardly to have been mentioned in the convention debates. A number of the leaders of the time, including Washington, felt that it was unfortunate that young Americans had to go to England and the Continent for higher learning. They thought, too, that a national university would be a great influence for drawing all parts of the United States closer together. C. C. Pinckney and James Madison proposed that the national government be given authority to establish a national university, and, Madison added, the power "to encourage by premiums and provisions the advancement of useful knowledge and discoveries." This was a suggestion for government support of research and advanced education. Gouverneur Morris thought, and perhaps correctly, that a specific power to establish a national university was not necessary, that the exclusive power of Congress over the seat of government would be sufficient. So the convention took no action, and Congress has never attempted to establish a national university.

The patent and copyright power conferred upon Congress is suggestive but rather restricted: "To Promote the Progress of Science and useful Arts, by securing for limited Times to Authors and Inventors the exclusive Right to their respective Writings and Discoveries." Perhaps the postal power and the authority "to fix the Standard of Weights and Measures" are also worthy of mention because they are related to research and the dissemination of knowledge. Most important is, however, the power to tax and to spend for the "general Welfare of the United States." This opens the door to national expenditure in a number of social fields.

Factors in the Nationalization of the Social Services. As we look at these meager and indirect statements of power, and contrast them with the tremendous program of work carried on by the national government in these fields, we are constrained to look for an explanation of the discrepancy. The national power of the purse has been highly important. State and local governments have gladly joined hands to place upon the nation some of the expense of public education, health, and welfare work. Then, too, the nation became more unified, and its various parts more interdependent as commerce, industry, and urbanism advanced. A rising standard of living and the broadened views that result from more education led men to think in national terms. The services of health and education, for example, have been fostered by nation-wide organizations that saw shorter roads to success in their reforms if the national government would act. And members of Congress had little or nothing to gain by opposing the new requests for national appropriations for the general welfare.

As a matter of fact much of what the nation does for these functions it does through granting funds to state and local governments. The programs are nationally supervised but locally performed. Since the national government does not itself administer many of the programs, only a brief sketch of them needs to be given here.

Administrative Organizations. In 1937 the President's Committee on Administrative Management recommended the establishment of a Department of Social Welfare with the following functions: "To advise the President with regard to social welfare," and "To administer federal health, educational, and social activities; to conduct research in these fields; to administer federal grants, if any, for such purposes; to protect the consumer; to conduct the federal aspects of federal-state programs of social security where need is the basis of payment to beneficiaries; to administer all federal eleemosynary, corrective, and penal institutions; and to administer probation and parole." This was a broad proposal that Congress did not approve. Instead of one department for all these purposes the following agencies now divide the work among them:

1. Federal Security Agency, including
   (a) United States Office of Education
   (b) Public Health Service
   (c) Social Security Board
       i—Bureau of Old-Age and Survivors Insurance
       ii—Bureau of Employment Security
       iii—Bureau of Public Assistance
   (d) Howard University
   (e) St. Elizabeth's Hospital
2. Veterans Administration
3. National Housing Agency
4. Department of Commerce
   (a) Bureau of the Census
   (b) Bureau of Standards
5. Department of Interior
   (a) Office of Indian Affairs
   (b) Bureau of Mines
6. Department of Agriculture
   (a) Graduate School
   (b) Extension Service
   (c) Agricultural Research Administration
       i—Bureau of Human Nutrition and Home Economics
       ii—Office of Experiment Stations

In these agencies, and they are not all, one senses the wide sweep of the nation's services to education, research, health, and welfare. The Veterans Administration and the Office of Indian Affairs include a wide range of services each, while others like the Bureau of Standards have only one principal function, in this case scientific research.

PUBLIC EDUCATION

The state and local governments retain primary responsibility for public educational policies, finance, and administration in the United States. The national government contributes funds and programs in particular fields (agricultural, mechanical, and home economics education, and vocational rehabilitation, for example), guidance, tuition, and support for the education of veterans, research and leadership in education generally (Office of Education) and scientific research on many subjects. Future developments in this field are likely to include (1) a new program for the promotion of scientific research, partly within the government and partly in universities and research institutes; and (2) substantial grants-in-aid to the states on the basis of need for the support of elementary and secondary education. It is known that some states of low average income are paying proportionately more than others to support education, and that they are still falling short of being able to compete with others in quality. When they see that their school graduates, educated by them at considerable cost, go in large numbers to other states to make their careers, these states feel that they have adequate reason for requesting more national support of education.

The proposals for a nation-wide program of scientific research to be supported by national government appropriations are an outgrowth of the experience in World War II. During that conflict the Office of Scientific Research and Development achieved marvels for the nation in developing radar, the proximity fuse, the atomic bomb, and many other less spectacular inventions, while other emergency agencies of the government did outstanding work in the social sciences and other fields. It is well known, however, that it was nip and tuck between German and American scientists as to which would first produce the atomic bomb, and that the Germans led in rocket bombs and in jet-propelled planes. Defense considerations alone argue strongly, therefore, in favor of national support for a program of research to keep this nation well in the lead in scientific progress. Most inventions will probably have more peacetime than wartime uses. Congress has shown a friendly interest in the proposals for scientific research, but has not yet agreed upon a definite bill. Its already generous support of research in agriculture and other fields makes it reasonable to expect that it will not long delay in passing some general research measure.

PUBLIC HEALTH

Beginnings of Public Health Work. Public health work began historically in the United States with the governments of towns and cities. They received powers even before 1800 to abate nuisances and to establish pesthouses and quarantine. In England this function reached the level where the national government provided for it in part in 1848, but in the United States it reached the state level for the first time in 1869 when Massachusetts established a state department of health. The national government had in 1798 established a Marine Hospital Service to look after the health of American sailors. The quarantine work with respect to ships entering American ports remained a local service, with some exceptions, until 1878 when it was assigned by act of Congress to the Marine Hospital Service. This service was given extended health functions and a change of name in 1902, and in 1912 it became the United States Public Health Service. Today, in addition to private associations that work in this field, organized public health work exists at all levels of government, national, state, and local.

National Agencies for Public Health. In the national government the principal agency concerned with the public health is the Public Health Service, now in the Federal Security Agency. This bureau carries on extensive surveys and investigations into the administration of public health measures, compiles and publishes excellent reports and statistics of use to all state and local health agencies, and enforces various quarantine laws and other statutes and regulations. It supplies, also, responsible leadership in national drives on particular diseases. The Food and Drug Administration, also in the Federal Security Agency, aids in preventing the sale of dangerous foods, drinks, and drugs. Under the Social Security Act, Congress has provided for substantial aid to the states for maternal and child health, and for the promotion of health education, health demonstration projects, and the training of public health personnel. Indeed the reorganization of 1939 and 1940 that created the Federal Security Agency has given the nation for the first time a strong unified organization to lead the fight on disease.

Postwar Public Health Measures. Congress has already enacted measures for a general revamping and improvement of the medical and hospital services for all men and women who served in the armed forces in World War II. These services will reach a considerable part of the population, but this is not all. The President has proposed a program of prepaid medical care under national government auspices for the entire nation, together with a scheme of insurance benefits during periods of sickness. In making his proposal he pointed out that nearly 5 million men were rejected for military service during World War II because of physical or mental defects, many of which might have been prevented or corrected by proper medical care. The President's plan is certainly an impressive one, but it will cost a great deal of money, and Congress does not appear to be ready for it.

SOCIAL WELFARE

Early Indifference of National Government. Throughout the long development of social welfare work as a local and state function the national government held somewhat aloof. The Indians were finally accepted as a national charge, the Red Cross was chartered, and the veterans of the wars were provided for; but the general population and its needs for welfare work fell outside the ken of the national authorities. One little measure raised the important question of principle. Congress in 1921 passed the Sheppard-Towner Act, making a small appropriation each year for 5 years to assist the state health departments in carrying on conferences, clinics, and instruction for expectant mothers, in order to reduce the toll of deaths of both babies and mothers. Most of the states entered heartily into the program, and with apparently good results. The Supreme Court sustained the act as constitutional against attacks by both private parties and a dissenting state.[1] The Court held that neither the taxpayer nor the state had any standing in Court to contest the government's expenditure. Nevertheless Congress apparently decided that this was no proper function of the national government, and the act was allowed to expire in 1926.

The great depression raised the question of the national government's responsibility in a new and burning form. President Hoover, recalling the stand

[1] Frothingham v. Mellon, and Massachusetts v. Mellon (1923), 262 U. S. 447.

taken 40 years earlier by President Cleveland, held that direct relief for the unemployed was the responsibility of state and local governments, and of private relief associations. The opposition argued that unemployment was national in its scope; that it was the result of the breakdown of the national economic system; and that the state and local governments simply did not have the resources to cope with the situation. Congress in 1932 authorized the RFC to lend money to the states for relief purposes.

The New Deal in Welfare Work. The Democratic party came into power in 1933 committed to a policy of national action to end the depression. Congress promptly authorized the loans necessary for a large national program of relief and public works. A quicker and more complete reversal of national policy has seldom been seen. The years 1933 and 1934 were notable for the provisions made for relief and public works expenditures, and the year 1935 marked a further step forward with the adoption of the Social Security Act. Finally, federal interest in adequate housing was expressed through a number of statutory enactments. Defending his social welfare program in 1934 President Roosevelt argued, "If, as our Constitution tells us, our federal government was established among other things 'to promote the general welfare,' it is our plain duty to provide for that security upon which welfare depends." [2]

FERA. In 1933 Congress authorized the creation of the Federal Emergency Relief Administration (FERA) under an administrator to be appointed by the President. Large sums, including what was left of the $300,000,000 that the RFC was to lend to states for relief purposes, were made available to this new unit. The administrator soon recruited a staff and issued regulations concerning the expenditure of the funds. Grants were made to the states from the federal funds. In part the states had to match the grants with equal or larger amounts; in part the grants were unrestricted, so as to take care of the most needy states. States had to submit their plans for spending the money granted, and were required to provide adequate personnel and investigators, i.e., social workers, to assist in the work in the counties and other local units. Millions of dollars soon began to flow to the states.

PWA. The National Industrial Recovery Act of 1933 provided an appropriation of over $3 billion for financing public works as a means of putting men to work. The national government used some of these funds directly, but in the main they went to state and local governments for highways, public buildings, utilities, and "self-liquidating projects." Housing was one of the things to be encouraged under these funds. Outright grants were made for approved public works up to 30 per cent of the cost; loans could be made for the additional 70 per cent. Wage and hour provisions were stipulated to protect those employed on the new public works. Difficulties were encountered in getting this program under way, and there was considerable delay in getting building projects started.

[2] Message to Congress, June 8, 1934, quoted in Josephine C. Brown, *Public Relief, 1929-1939*, p. 55.

Later Changes in National Relief Programs. Near the end of 1933, with millions of men still unemployed and needy, the President allocated additional millions to FERA for a Civil Works program (CWA) with the intention of putting a million or more men to work quickly on projects of local importance, though not necessarily permanent in their nature as in the case of PWA. Naturally there were many "made work" projects, but the desired result was quickly and effectively achieved. In the spring of 1934, CWA was discontinued, but Congress made additional appropriations for FERA. Other relief and works measures of 1933 and 1934 provided for Emergency Conservation Work (the Civilian Conservation Corps), and for drought relief, among other things. In short, from March, 1933, to the middle of 1935, the national government was principally concerned with measures of immediate attack upon unemployment. The decision was soon reached that PWA should be discontinued and that national help for direct relief should be ended also as quickly as the state and local governments could assume the burden. It was agreed, however, that the national government should continue with a program of employment for those capable of working. A new act passed in 1935 provided, therefore, for the Works Progress Administration (WPA).

WPA. With the liquidation of the FERA in 1935 the care of the unemployables was turned back to the states and localities. The WPA became the major unit in the national works program, undertaking to provide employment for the needy unemployed on useful projects at a so-called security wage. In practice the distinction between employables and unemployables was not strictly maintained largely because local and state funds for direct relief were inadequate. WPA employment reached 3 million at the beginning of 1936 and began to taper off. But the program expanded again at the end of 1937. After 1939, WPA was called Work Projects Administration. With defense employment increasing at that time, WPA appropriations were reduced and the works program restricted, and the President authorized its liquidation on December 4, 1942.

The Social Security Program. In 1935 Congress and the administration undertook the establishment of a permanent program of social security on a national scale. This program is intended to meet the permanent needs of the aged, the unemployed, mothers and dependent children, the blind, and several other classes. It also makes certain provisions for public health work. In the main the law provides for national aid to state governments to attain these ends, but one feature of the program, compulsory old-age insurance, is strictly a national measure. This program was discussed in the preceding chapter.

Assistance for the Needy Aged. The second method by which the Social Security Act provides for the security of old people is a plan of encouraging states by federal aid to provide assistance to the needy aged. While the contributory old-age insurance plan was nation-wide in scope, federally administered, and compulsory, the noncontributory old-age assistance plan benefits *needy* aged people only in those states that pass the necessary laws. The act provides a cooperative federal-state relationship in which the state initiates and administers the old-age assistance law and the national government pays half the cost of the assistance given, but not over $20 a month for each individual. In order to receive federal grants, the states must set up plans that conform to federal standards of procedure and administration, and to age, residence, and citizenship requirements for recipients. By the close of 1938 all states were administering old-age assistance under plans approved by the Social Security Board.

In addition to its $20 a month maximum for each case, the national government adds 5 per cent to its contribution to each state to help pay for the administration of the system. Naturally, as the principal contributor to the administrative costs of these state acts, the national government has laid down some rather definite rules about state personnel and about the tests of need and age that are to be applied to aged applicants for assistance.

Other Security Provisions. The provisions for old age and for unemployment are the principal and the most expensive parts of the whole social security plan. The law provides also for national grants to the states for aid to dependent children and mothers, to crippled children, to child welfare services, and to maternity and infancy services. Other provisions of the law cover national aid to the needy blind, to be administered through the states, and assistance to public health work and vocational rehabilitation services. In all these cases the appropriate national authorities have a right to insist that the states receiving the aid present and carry out acceptable plans of work, but it is the states that control actual expenditures.

Administration of New Social Welfare Laws. The social security program of the national government passed out of its experimental stage with the creation in 1939 of the Federal Security Agency.[3] Headed by one man who sits with the cabinet, this is a national social welfare department in everything but name. Brought together in this agency are those government units that are vested with responsibility to provide security against the hazards of old age, unemployment, illness, and accident as well as assistance for public health and education—the Office of Education, Public Health Service, Social Security Board, Food and Drug Administration, and several others.

National administration of the principal social security measures is vested in the Social Security Board of the Federal Security Agency. This board consists of three members appointed by the President with Senate consent. The standards of its administrative and personnel policies have been very high. In carrying out its duties, also, it has insisted on improved standards in the state governments that are to participate in the program. The states have been compelled in a number of cases to reorganize their welfare departments, to

[3] The constitutionality of the Social Security Act has been fully sustained by the Supreme Court. Steward Machine Co. v. Davis (1937), 301 U. S. 548, 57 S. Ct. 883; Helvering v. Davis (1937), 301 U. S. 619, 672, 57 S. Ct. 904. See also Carmichael v. Southern Coal and Coke Co. (1937), 301 U. S. 495, 57 S. Ct. 868.

create new state departments for employment security, to ensure better administration in the local units, and to adopt a merit system of employment. The years since 1933 have seen more important changes in state and local welfare organization than any comparable period in American history, and it cannot be doubted that most of the changes have been improvements.

Criticisms of Social Security. Aside from the administrative difficulties of a national-state system, the security program has been criticized on many grounds. From one side comes the criticism that the plan is wholly inadequate, that agricultural labor, domestics, and others should somehow be included, and that the amounts guaranteed and provided for different purposes are insufficient. There is, of course, never any end to demands of this kind, and yet there are ways in which the laws can be extended with some reasonable prospect of success. From another side come the criticisms that the payroll taxes are a burden on industry, and tend to reduce employment instead of helping it. Provisions for social and economic security, it is claimed, have a tendency to make for a static society, with lowered production and diminished chance of progress. Serious questions are also raised concerning the entire national budget and the public debt. Increased taxes and expenditures at this time for a future social security, think some, are of doubtful financial wisdom. Nevertheless the President and the Social Security Board find much support for their recent proposals for further extensions of the social security system and for increases in the amounts of various benefit payments. No one talks seriously of abandoning or even reducing the scope of the present social security and social welfare program.

PUBLIC HOUSING

The Housing Problem. In the early days of American expansion, housing concerned legislators mainly in terms of protection against fires and structural defects. Beyond such minimum and negative regulations, men could build houses and rent them pretty much as they pleased. In point of time, inadequate and unsafe housing for low-income groups has existed since the industrialization of the western world. The tremendous growth of cities was in part an accretion of ramshackle shanties and desolate tenements. Faced with the picture of immigrant populations huddled in such places, city governments began by the end of the Civil War to enact building codes prescribing permissible building standards. The codes did little or nothing to eliminate existing slums, and generally failed to prevent new ones from arising. In the latter years of the nineteenth century, the settlement movement under Jane Addams and Lillian Wald took up housing reform and the improvement of living conditions. Yet in 1930 more than one-half million families in New York lived in "old-law tenements" condemned 40 years previously by Jacob Riis as substandard and unfit. Private enterprise had failed to build dwellings for the urban poor; public regulation in itself could produce no low-cost housing.

Early Governmental Activities. Given the housing need, four possible methods or a combination of methods presented themselves: (a) to increase the real income of workers; (b) to reduce by voluntary methods the profits of builders; (c) to reduce building standards; and (d) to build houses with governmental aid. The feasibility of the fourth method was well demonstrated by New York, the city often called the American laboratory of low-rent housing, as well as by the national government in defense housing during World War I. With the enactment of the 1926 New York state housing law, an American governmental unit for the first time undertook positively to stimulate the building of low-cost houses. Despite the success of New York's attempts, no other state followed in its footsteps. Finally confronted with the full force of depression Congress in 1932 passed the Emergency Relief and Construction Act authorizing the Reconstruction Finance Corporation to make loans to limited dividend companies for the construction of low-cost housing projects. In the main, however, the object of the act was to stimulate employment. This indirect governmental attack on the housing problem has continued to be the typical American approach. The housing result of the 1932 act was practically nil. Slums continued to exact an increasing toll. Government surveys indicated that 1 out of 6 dwellings in cities was overcrowded, unsafe, or unfit for habitation according to the standard set. In rural areas, 1 out of 2 dwellings was inadequate in some important respect.

New Deal Legislation. Beginning in 1932, the national government turned toward the alleviation of the worst effects of economic collapse. The foreclosure of mortgages on homes had reached an appalling rate. In order to bolster the deteriorating home-financing system of the country, Congress created a number of agencies. (1) The Federal Home Loan Bank system was established to provide a credit reserve for home-financing institutions so that they might provide more adequate housing credit facilities. (2) Supplementing the long-run job of the Federal Home Loan Banks, the Home Owners' Loan Corporation was created for the immediate relief of distressed home owners. The HOLC was authorized to grant long-term mortgage loans at low interest rates to those who were in urgent need of funds for the protection or recovery of homes and who were unable to procure the money elsewhere. (3) The Federal Housing Administration was created to encourage new private home building and modernization by insuring lending institutions against losses on loans and by offering time-payment financing to the borrower at a low rate. (4) In 1937 the United States Housing Authority was created to eliminate unsafe and unsanitary housing conditions and to relieve the acute shortage of decent low-cost dwellings by subsidizing local public projects for slum clearance and low-cost housing that could not be supported on a commercial basis.

As a whole the New Deal housing program was designed to ease home financing, to prevent wholesale mortgage foreclosures on private homes, and to stimulate employment in the home construction industry. It achieved valuable results in these directions but failed to improve appreciably the housing standards of the lowest income groups. Not until the adoption of the United States Housing Act and the creation of the USHA in 1937 did Congress adopt a policy of aiding and encouraging local public housing agencies to provide for public slum-clearance and housing construction. The USHA made loans to local housing authorities on approved slum-clearance and housing projects. These loans bore interest at the "going federal rate" plus one-half of 1 per cent, and could run for 60 years. The local housing agency had to supply 10 per cent of the project cost. In addition USHA made annual subsidies over a period not exceeding 60 years to assist in achieving and maintaining the low-rent character of a housing project. To supplement annual federal subsidies, annual local contributions had to be made in an amount equal to at least one-fifth of the annual federal subsidy. Tenants for USHA projects were to be selected from families in the lowest income groups.

Congress authorized USHA to make loans to local housing authorities up to $800,000,000 total. Thereafter it failed to grant further appropriations, and the whole USHA program was slowed down. In 1940 the rehousing program under USHA had affected only 650,000 persons. Even immediate expansion would still have left large blocs of the population without adequate housing.

Defense and War Housing. Then came the defense emergency and World War II. This suddenly changed the focus and the tempo of national housing activities. Housing had to be provided at once for the defense industries and in boom town areas. Congress legislated promptly to liberalize loans to local housing authorities for defense housing, and it also authorized direct construction of defense housing by a new national agency, the Federal Public Housing Agency (FPHA). Because of the necessity for both speed and economy the new legislation authorized inexpensive types of housing that could be torn down again when the need for it had passed away after the war. At the same time, to protect the public generally OPA established controls over rents in all war production areas.

The Postwar Housing Situation. When the fighting had ended and the veterans began to return home nearly every urban center experienced an acute housing shortage. Moveable housing units like trailers were transferred from certain defense plant areas where industry had stopped but these at best provided very little relief. Once more the national government was called upon to act. The National Housing Agency, a creation of the war period, which drew into one organization the various national government agencies that are concerned with housing, was requested by the President to prepare generous plans to meet the housing crisis. On February 8, 1946, the President laid before Congress a plan to expedite the building in 1946 and 1947 of nearly 3 million new moderate-priced homes, mostly through private enterprise but with government subsidies to stimulate the production of the needed materials.

THE NEW SOCIAL ROLE OF THE NATIONAL GOVERNMENT

Even this hasty review of what the national government has done in a little over a dozen years of depression, war, and reconversion to promote the public welfare suggests what a revolution has taken place in national public policy. Whereas at one time the national government did almost nothing in the social welfare field, today it has a positive, comprehensive, and expanding program. Public education, public health, social welfare and social security programs, and both private and public housing have been quickened, expanded, and improved by national action.

It is not that the national government has moved in to occupy these fields in a monopolistic way. Quite the contrary, its main efforts have been to aid individuals to get on their feet and to assist state and local governments to carry their proper responsibilities. While giving aid the national government has insisted that the state and local governments meet certain minimum standards, but far from weakening state and local administrations this policy has actually strengthened them. They are assured, also, of regular financial aid for their services, and they know that in emergencies like the housing crisis of 1946 the nation stands ready to step in with more aid. This is indeed something new in American public policy. Its potentialities for the future are nearly unlimited.

REFERENCES

EDUCATION

American Council on Education, *Citizens Conference on the Crisis in Education*, Washington, 1933.

National Advisory Committee on Education, *Federal Relations to Education*, Washington, 1931.

E. B. Wesley, *Proposed: The University of the United States*, Minneapolis, 1936.

United States Office of Education, various bulletins.

Advisory Committee on Education, *Report of the Committee*, Washington, 1938.

PUBLIC HEALTH

W. G. Smillie, *Public Health Administration in the United States*, 2nd ed., New York, 1940.

J. A. Tobey, *Public Health Law*, 2nd ed., New York, 1939.

——, *The National Government and the Public Health*, Baltimore, 1926.

United States Public Health Service, various bulletins.

American Public Health Association, *American Journal of Public Health*, monthly.

SOCIAL SECURITY AND WELFARE

R. T. Lansdale, E. Long, A. Leisy, and B. Hipple, *The Administration of Old Age Assistance*, Chicago, 1939.

A. W. Macmahon, John D. Millett, and Gladys Ogden, *The Administration of Federal Work Relief*, Chicago, 1941.

Josephine C. Brown, *Public Relief: 1929-1939*, New York, 1940.

E. M. Burns, *Towards Social Security*, New York, 1936.

A. Epstein, *Insecurity, A Challenge to America*, 2nd rev. ed., New York, 1938.

P. H. Douglas, *Social Security in America*, New York, 1939.

Harry Millis and Royal Montgomery, *Labor's Risks and Social Insurance*, New York, 1938.

Social Security Board, annual reports.

Isabel Gordon Carter, ed., *Appraising the Social Security Program, The Annals*, vol. 202, Philadelphia, 1939.

Helen I. Clarke, *Social Legislation*, New York, 1940.

Maxwell Stewart, *Social Security*, rev. ed., New York, 1939.

R. C. White, *Administration of Public Welfare*, New York, 1940.

HOUSING

E. E. Wood, *Introduction to Housing Facts and Principles*, Washington, 1940.

Michael Straus and Talbot Wegg, *Housing Comes of Age*, New York, 1938.

Mabel L. Walker, *Urban Blight and Slums*, Cambridge, 1938.

Temporary National Economic Committee, *Toward More Housing*, Monograph no. 8, Washington, 1940.

William Ebenstein, *The Law of Public Housing*, Madison, 1940.

National Association of Housing Officials, *Housing Yearbook*, Chicago, annual.

Miles L. Colean and others, *American Housing, Problems and Prospects*, New York, 1944.

National Housing Administration, reports and bulletins.

Nathan Straus, *The Seven Myths of Housing*, New York, 1944.

THE CONSTITUTION OF THE UNITED STATES OF AMERICA[1]

WE THE PEOPLE of the United States, in Order to form a more perfect Union, establish Justice, insure domestic Tranquility, provide for the common defence, promote the general Welfare, and secure the Blessings of Liberty to ourselves and our Posterity, do ordain and establish this CONSTITUTION for the United States of America.

ARTICLE I.

SECTION 1. All legislative Powers herein granted shall be vested in a Congress of the United States, which shall consist of a Senate and House of Representatives.

SECTION 2. The House of Representatives shall be composed of Members chosen every second Year by the People of the several States, and the Electors in each State shall have the Qualifications requisite for Electors of the most numerous Branch of the State Legislature.

No Person shall be a Representative who shall not have attained to the Age of twenty-five Years, and been seven Years a Citizen of the United States, and who shall not, when elected, be an Inhabitant of that State in which he shall be chosen.

[Representatives and direct Taxes shall be apportioned among the several States which may be included within this Union, according to their respective Numbers, which shall be determined by adding to the whole Number of free Persons, including those bound to Service for a Term of Years, and excluding Indians not taxed, three fifths of all other Persons.] The actual Enumeration shall be made within three Years after the first Meeting of the Congress of the United States, and within every subsequent Term of ten Years, in such Manner as they shall by Law direct. The Number of Representatives shall not exceed one for every thirty Thousand, but each State shall have at Least one Representative; and until such enumeration shall be made, the State of New Hampshire shall be entitled to chuse three, Massachusetts eight, Rhode-Island and Providence Plantations one, Connecticut five, New-York six, New Jersey four, Pennsylvania eight, Delaware one, Maryland six, Virginia ten, North Carolina five, South Carolina five, and Georgia three.

[1] This version of the Constitution is that published by the Office of Education, United States Department of the Interior, in 1935. It follows the original document closely in matters of spelling and capitalization.

When vacancies happen in the Representation from any State, the Executive Authority thereof shall issue Writs of Election to fill such Vacancies.

The House of Representatives shall chuse their Speaker and other Officers; and shall have the sole Power of Impeachment.

SECTION 3. The Senate of the United States shall be composed of two Senators from each State, chosen by the Legislature thereof, for six Years; and each Senator shall have one Vote.

Immediately after they shall be assembled in Consequence of the first Election, they shall be divided as equally as may be into three Classes. The Seats of the Senators of the first Class shall be vacated at the Expiration of the second Year, of the second Class at the Expiration of the fourth Year, and of the third Class at the Expiration of the sixth Year, so that one-third may be chosen every second Year; and if Vacancies happen by Resignation, or otherwise, during the Recess of the Legislature of any State, the Executive thereof may make temporary Appointments until the next Meeting of the Legislature, which shall then fill such Vacancies.

No Person shall be a Senator who shall not have attained to the Age of thirty Years, and been nine Years a Citizen of the United States, and who shall not, when elected, be an Inhabitant of that State for which he shall be chosen.

The Vice President of the United States shall be President of the Senate, but shall have no Vote, unless they be equally divided.

The Senate shall chuse their other Officers, and also a President pro tempore, in the absence of the Vice President, or when he shall exercise the Office of President of the United States.

The Senate shall have the sole Power to try all Impeachments. When sitting for that Purpose, they shall be on Oath or Affirmation. When the President of the United States is tried, the Chief Justice shall preside: And no Person shall be convicted without the Concurrence of two thirds of the Members present.

Judgment in Cases of Impeachment shall not extend further than to removal from Office, and disqualification to hold and enjoy any Office of honor, Trust or Profit under the United States: but the Party convicted shall nevertheless be liable and subject to Indictment, Trial, Judgment and Punishment, according to Law.

SECTION 4. The Times, Places and Manner of holding Elections for Senators and Representatives, shall be prescribed in each State by the Legislature thereof; but the Congress may at any time by Law make or alter such Regulations, except as to the Places of Chusing Senators.

The Congress shall assemble at least once in every Year, and such Meeting shall be on the first Monday in December, unless they shall by Law appoint a different Day.

SECTION 5. Each House shall be the Judge of the Elections, Returns and Qualifications of its own Members, and a Majority of each shall constitute a Quorum to do Business; but a smaller Number may adjourn from day to day, and may be authorized to compel the Attendance of absent Members, in such Manner, and under such Penalties as each House may provide.

Each House may determine the Rules of its Proceedings, punish its Members for disorderly Behavior, and, with the Concurrence of two thirds, expel a Member.

Each House shall keep a Journal of its Proceedings, and from time to time publish the same, excepting such Parts as may in their Judgment require Secrecy; and the Yeas and Nays of the Members of either House on any question shall, at the Desire of one fifth of those Present, be entered on the Journal.

Neither House, during the Session of Congress, shall, without the Consent of the other, adjourn for more than three days, nor to any other Place than that in which the two Houses shall be sitting.

SECTION 6. The Senators and Representatives shall receive a Compensation for their Services, to be ascertained by Law, and paid out of the Treasury of the United States. They shall in all Cases, except Treason, Felony and Breach of the Peace, be privileged from Arrest during their Attendance at the Session of their respective Houses, and in going to and returning from the same; and for any Speech or Debate in either House, they shall not be questioned in any other Place.

No Senator or Representative shall, during the Time for which he was elected, be appointed to any civil Office under the Authority of the United States, which shall have been created, or the Emoluments whereof shall have been encreased during such time; and no Person holding any Office under the United States, shall be a Member of either House during his Continuance in Office.

SECTION 7. All Bills for raising Revenue shall originate in the House of Representatives; but the Senate may propose or concur with Amendments as on other Bills.

Every Bill which shall have passed the House of Representatives and the Senate, shall, before it become a Law, be presented to the President of the United States; If he approve he shall sign it, but if not he shall return it, with his Objections to that House in which it shall have originated, who shall enter the Objections at large on their Journal, and proceed to reconsider it. If after such Reconsideration two thirds of that House shall agree to pass the Bill, it shall be sent, together with the Objections, to the other House, by which it shall likewise be reconsidered, and if approved by two thirds of that House, it shall become a Law. But in all such Cases the Votes of both Houses shall be determined by Yeas and Nays, and the Names of the Persons voting for and against the Bill shall be entered on the Journal of each House respectively. If any Bill shall not be returned by the President within ten Days (Sundays excepted) after it shall have been presented to him, the Same shall be a Law, in like Manner as if he had signed it, unless the Congress by their Adjournment prevent its Return, in which Case it shall not be a Law.

Every Order, Resolution, or Vote to which the Concurrence of the Senate and House of Representatives may be necessary (except on a question of Adjournment) shall be presented to the President of the United States; and before the Same shall take Effect, shall be approved by him, or being disapproved by him, shall be repassed by two thirds of the Senate and House of Representatives, according to the Rules and Limitations prescribed in the Case of a Bill.

SECTION 8. The Congress shall have Power To lay and collect Taxes, Duties, Imposts and Excises, to pay the Debts and provide for the common Defence and general Welfare of the United States; but all Duties, Imposts and Excises shall be uniform throughout the United States;

To borrow money on the credit of the United States;

To regulate Commerce with foreign Nations, and among the several States, and with the Indian Tribes;

To establish an uniform Rule of Naturalization, and uniform Laws on the subject of Bankruptcies throughout the United States;

To coin Money, regulate the Value thereof, and of foreign Coin, and fix the Standard of Weights and Measures;

To provide for the Punishment of counterfeiting the Securities and current Coin of the United States;

To establish Post Offices and post Roads;

To promote the Progress of Science and useful Arts, by securing for limite Times to Authors and Inventors the exclusive Right to their respective Writings and Discoveries;

To constitute Tribunals inferior to the supreme Court;

To define and punish Piracies and Felonies committed on the high Seas, and Offenses against the Law of Nations;

To declare War, grant Letters of Marque and Reprisal, and make Rules concerning Captures on Land and Water;

To raise and support Armies, but no Appropriation of Money to that Use shall be for a longer Term than two Years;

To provide and maintain a Navy;

To make Rules for the Government and Regulation of the land and naval Forces;

To provide for calling forth the Militia to execute the Laws of the Union, suppress Insurrections and repel Invasions;

To provide for organizing, arming, and disciplining the Militia, and for governing such Part of them as may be employed in the Service of the United States, reserving to the States respectively, the Appointment of the Officers, and the Authority of training the Militia according to the discipline prescribed by Congress;

To exercise exclusive Legislation in all Cases whatsoever, over such District (not exceeding ten Miles square) as may, by Cession of particular States, and the acceptance of Congress, become the Seat of the Government of the United States, and to exercise like Authority over all Places purchased by the Consent of the Legislature of the State in which the Same shall be, for the Erection of Forts, Magazines, Arsenals, dock-Yards, and other needful Buildings;—And

To make all Laws which shall be necessary and proper for carrying into Execution the foregoing Powers, and all other Powers vested by this Constitution in the Government of the United States, or in any Department or Officer thereof.

SECTION 9. The Migration or Importation of such Persons as any of the· States now existing shall think proper to admit, shall not be prohibited by the Congress prior to the Year one thousand eight hundred and eight, but a tax or duty may be imposed on such Importation, not exceeding ten dollars for each Person.

The privilege of the Writ of Habeas Corpus shall not be suspended, unless when in Cases of Rebellion or Invasion the public Safety may require it.

No Bill of Attainder or ex post facto Law shall be passed.

No capitation, or other direct, Tax shall be laid unless in Proportion to the Census or Enumeration herein before directed to be taken.

No Tax or Duty shall be laid on Articles exported from any State.

No Preference shall be given by any Regulation of Commerce or Revenue to the Ports of one State over those of another: nor shall Vessels bound to, or from, one State, be obliged to enter, clear, or pay Duties in another.

No Money shall be drawn from the Treasury, but in Consequence of Appropriations made by Law; and a regular Statement and Account of the Receipts and Expenditures of all public Money shall be published from time to time.

No Title of Nobility shall be granted by the United States: And no Person holding any Office of Profit or Trust under them, shall, without the Consent of the Congress, accept of any present, Emolument, Office, or Title, of any kind whatever, from any King, Prince, or foreign State.

SECTION 10. No State shall enter into any Treaty, Alliance, or Confederation; grant Letters of Marque and Reprisal; coin Money; emit Bills of Credit; make any Thing but gold and silver Coin a Tender in Payment of Debts; pass any Bill of Attainder, ex post facto Law, or Law impairing the Obligation of Contracts, or grant any Title of Nobility.

No State shall, without the Consent of the Congress, lay any Imposts or Duties on Imports or Exports, except what may be absolutely necessary for executing its inspection Laws: and the net Produce of all Duties and Imposts, laid by any State on Imports or Exports, shall be for the Use of the Treasury of the United States; and all such Laws shall be subject to the Revision and Control of the Congress.

No State shall, without the Consent of Congress, lay any duty of Tonnage, keep Troops, or Ships of War in time of Peace, enter into any Agreement or Compact with another State, or with a foreign Power, or engage in War, unless actually invaded, or in such imminent Danger as will not admit of delay.

ARTICLE II.

Section 1. The executive Power shall be vested in a President of the United States of America. He shall hold his Office during the Term of four Years, and, together with the Vice-President, chosen for the same Term, be elected, as follows

Each State shall appoint, in such Manner as the Legislature thereof may direct, a Number of Electors, equal to the whole Number of Senators and Representatives to which the State may be entitled in the Congress: but no Senator or Representative, or Person holding an Office of Trust or Profit under the United States, shall be appointed an Elector.

[The Electors shall meet in their respective States, and vote by Ballot for two persons, of whom one at least shall not be an Inhabitant of the same State with themselves. And they shall make a List of all the Persons voted for, and of the Number of Votes for each; which List they shall sign and certify, and transmit sealed to the Seat of the Government of the United States, directed to the President of the Senate. The President of the Senate shall, in the Presence of the Senate and House of Representatives, open all the Certificates, and the Votes shall then be counted. The Person having the greatest Number of Votes shall be the President, if such Number be a Majority of the whole Number of Electors appointed; and if there be more than one who have such Majority, and have an equal Number of Votes, then the House of Representatives shall immediately chuse by Ballot one of them for President; and if no Person have a Majority, then from the five highest on the List the said House shall in like Manner chuse the President. But in chusing the President, the Votes shall be taken by States, the Representation from each State having one Vote; A quorum for this Purpose shall consist of a Member or Members from two-thirds of the States, and a Majority of all the States shall be necessary to a Choice. In every Case, after the Choice of the President, the Person having the greatest Number of Votes of the Electors shall be the Vice President. But if there should remain two or more who have equal Votes, the Senate shall chuse from them by Ballot the Vice-President.]

The Congress may determine the Time of chusing the Electors, and the Day on which they shall give their Votes; which Day shall be the same throughout the United States.

No person except a natural born Citizen, or a Citizen of the United States, at the time of the Adoption of this Constitution, shall be eligible to the Office of President; neither shall any Person be eligible to that Office who shall not have attained to the Age of thirty-five Years, and been fourteen Years a Resident within the United States.

In Case of the Removal of the President from Office, or of his Death, Resignation, or Inability to discharge the Powers and Duties of the said Office, the same shall devolve on the Vice President, and the Congress may by Law provide for the Case of Removal, Death Resignation or Inability, both of the President and Vice President, declaring what Officer shall then act as President, and such Officer shall act accordingly, until the Disability be removed, or a President shall be elected.

The President shall, at stated Times, receive for his Services, a Compensation, which shall neither be encreased nor diminished during the Period for which he shall have been elected, and he shall not receive within that Period any other Emolument from the United States, or any of them.

Before he enter on the Execution of his Office, he shall take the following Oath or Affirmation:—"I do solemnly swear (or affirm) that I will faithfully execute the Office of President of the United States, and will to the best of my Ability, preserve, protect and defend the Constitution of the United States."

SECTION 2. The President shall be Commander in Chief of the Army and Navy of the United States, and of the Militia of the several States, when called into the actual Service of the United States; he may require the Opinion in writing, of the principal Officer in each of the executive Departments, upon any subject relating to the Duties of their respective Offices, and he shall have Power to Grant Reprieves and Pardons for Offenses against the United States, except in Cases of Impeachment.

He shall have Power, by and with the Advice and Consent of the Senate, to make Treaties, provided two-thirds of the Senators present concur; and he shall nominate, and by and with the Advice and Consent of the Senate, shall appoint Ambassadors, other public Ministers and Consuls, Judges of the supreme Court, and all other Officers of the United States, whose Appointments are not herein otherwise provided for, and which shall be established by Law: but the Congress may by Law vest the Appointment of such inferior Officers, as they think proper, in the President alone, in the Courts of Law, or in the Heads of Departments.

The President shall have Power to fill up all Vacancies that may happen during the Recess of the Senate, by granting Commissions which shall expire at the End of their next Session.

SECTION 3. He shall from time to time give to the Congress Information of the State of the Union, and recommend to their Consideration such Measures as he shall judge necessary and expedient; he may, on extraordinary Occasions, convene both Houses, or either of them, and in Case of Disagreement between them, with Respect to the Time of Adjournment, he may adjourn them to such Time as he shall think proper; he shall receive Ambassadors and other public Ministers; he shall take Care that the Laws be faithfully executed, and shall Commission all the Officers of the United States.

SECTION 4. The President, Vice President and all civil Officers of the United States, shall be removed from Office on Impeachment for, and Conviction of, Treason, Bribery, or other high Crimes and Misdemeanors.

ARTICLE III.

SECTION 1. The judicial Power of the United States, shall be vested in one supreme Court, and in such inferior Courts as the Congress may from time to time ordain and establish. The Judges, both of the supreme and inferior Courts, shall hold their Offices during good Behaviour, and shall, at stated Times, receive for their Services a Compensation which shall not be diminished during their Continuance in Office.

SECTION 2. The judicial Power shall extend to all Cases, in Law and Equity, arising under this Constitution, the Laws of the United States, and Treaties made, or which shall be made, under their Authority;—to all Cases affecting Ambassadors, other public Ministers and Consuls;—to all Cases of admiralty and maritime Jurisdiction;—to Controversies to which the United States shall be a Party;—to Controversies between two or more States;—between a State and Citizens of another State;—between Citizens of different States;—between Citizens of the same State claiming Lands under Grants of different States, and between a State, or the Citizens thereof, and foreign States, Citizens or Subjects.

In all Cases affecting Ambassadors, other public Ministers and Consuls, and those in which a State shall be Party, the supreme Court shall have original Jurisdiction. In all the other Cases before mentioned, the supreme Court shall have appellate Jurisdiction, both as to Law and Fact, with such Exceptions, and under such Regulations as the Congress shall make.

The trial of all Crimes, except in Cases of Impeachment, shall be by Jury; and such Trial shall be held in the State where the said Crimes shall have been committed; but when not committed within any State, the Trial shall be at such Place or Places as the Congress may by Law have directed.

SECTION 3. Treason against the United States, shall consist only in levying War against them, or in adhering to their Enemies, giving them Aid and Comfort. No Person shall be convicted of Treason unless on the Testimony of two Witnesses to the same overt Act, or on Confession in open Court.

The Congress shall have power to declare the Punishment of Treason, but no Attainder of Treason shall work Corruption of Blood, or Forfeiture except during the Life of the Person attainted.

ARTICLE IV.

SECTION 1. Full Faith and Credit shall be given in each State to the public Acts, Records, and judicial Proceedings of every other State. And the Congress may by general Laws prescribe the Manner in which such Acts, Records and Proceedings shall be proved, and the Effect thereof.

SECTION 2. The Citizens of each State shall be entitled to all Privileges and Immunities of Citizens in the several States.

A Person charged in any State with Treason, Felony, or other Crime, who shall flee from Justice, and be found in another State, shall on demand of the executive Authority of the State from which he fled, be delivered up, to be removed to the State having Jurisdiction of the Crime.

No Person held to Service or Labour in one State, under the Laws thereof, escaping into another, shall, in Consequence of any Law or Regulation therein, be discharged from such Service or Labour, but shall be delivered up on Claim of the Party to whom such Service or Labour may be due.

SECTION 3. New States may be admitted by the Congress into this Union; but no new State shall be formed or erected within the Jurisdiction of any other State; nor any State be formed by the Junction of two or more States, or parts of States, without the Consent of the Legislatures of the States concerned as well as of the Congress.

The Congress shall have Power to dispose of and make all needful Rules and Regulations respecting the Territory or other Property belonging to the United States; and nothing in this Constitution shall be so construed as to Prejudice any Claims of the United States, or of any particular State.

SECTION 4. The United States shall guarantee to every State in this Union a Republican Form of Government, and shall protect each of them against Invasion; and on Application of the Legislature, or of the Executive (when the Legislature cannot be convened) against domestic Violence.

ARTICLE V.

The Congress, whenever two-thirds of both Houses shall deem it necessary, shall propose Amendments to this Constitution, or, on the Application of the Legislatures of two-thirds of the several States, shall call a Convention for proposing Amendments, which, in either Case, shall be valid to all Intents and Purposes, as part of this Constitution, when ratified by the Legislatures of three-fourths of the several States, or by Conventions in three-fourths thereof, as the one or the other Mode of Ratification may be proposed by the Congress; Provided that no Amendment which may be made prior to the Year One thousand eight hundred and eight shall in any Manner affect the first and fourth Clauses in the Ninth Section of the first Article; and that no State, without its Consent, shall be deprived of its equal Suffrage in the Senate.

ARTICLE VI.

All Debts contracted and Engagements entered into, before the Adoption of this Constitution, shall be as valid against the United States under this Constitution, as under the Confederation.

This Constitution, and the Laws of the United States which shall be made in Pursuance thereof; and all Treaties made, or which shall be made, under the Authority of the United States, shall be the supreme Law of the Land; and the Judges in every State shall be bound thereby, any Thing in the Constitution or Laws of any State to the Contrary notwithstanding.

The Senators and Representatives before mentioned, and the Members of the several State Legislatures, and all executive and judicial Officers, both of the United States and of the several States, shall be bound by Oath or Affirmation, to support this Constitution; but no religious Test shall ever be required as a Qualification to any Office or public Trust under the United States.

ARTICLE VII.

The Ratification of the Conventions of nine States shall be sufficient for the Establishment of this Constitution between the States so ratifying the Same.

DONE in Convention by the Unanimous Consent of the States present the Seventeenth Day of September in the Year of our Lord one thousand seven hundred and Eighty seven and of the Independence of the United States of America the Twelfth. In Witness whereof We have hereunto subscribed our Names.

G° WASHINGTON
Presidt and deputy from Virginia
[Other signatures omitted.]

ARTICLES IN ADDITION TO, AND AMENDMENT OF, THE CONSTITUTION OF THE UNITED STATES OF AMERICA, PROPOSED BY CONGRESS, AND RATIFIED BY THE LEGISLATURES OF THE SEVERAL STATES, PURSUANT TO THE FIFTH ARTICLE OF THE ORIGINAL CONSTITUTION.

[ARTICLE I.]

Congress shall make no law respecting an establishment of religion, or prohibiting the free exercise thereof; or abridging the freedom of speech, or of the press; or the right of the people peaceably to assemble, and to petition the Government for a redress of grievances.

[ARTICLE II.]

A well regulated Militia, being necessary to the security of a free State, the right of the people to keep and bear Arms, shall not be infringed.

[ARTICLE III.]

No Soldier shall, in time of peace be quartered in any house, without the consent of the Owner, nor in time of war, but in a manner to be prescribed by law.

[ARTICLE IV.]

The right of the people to be secure in their persons, houses, papers and effects, against unreasonable searches and seizures, shall not be violated, and no Warrants shall issue, but upon probable cause, supported by Oath or affirmation, and particularly describing the place to be searched, and the persons or things to be seized.

[ARTICLE V.]

No person shall be held to answer for a capital, or otherwise infamous crime, unless on a presentment or indictment of a Grand Jury, except in cases arising in the land or naval forces, or in the Militia, when in actual service in time of War or public danger; nor shall any person be subject for the same offence to be twice put in jeopardy of life or limb; nor shall be compelled in any criminal case to be a witness against himself, nor be deprived of life, liberty, or property, without due process of law; nor shall private property be taken for public use, without just compensation.

[ARTICLE VI.]

In all criminal prosecutions, the accused shall enjoy the right to a speedy and public trial, by an impartial jury of the State and district wherein the crime shall have been committed, which district shall have been previously ascertained by law, and to be informed of the nature and cause of the accusation; to be confronted with the witnesses against him; to have compulsory process for obtaining witnesses in his favor, and to have the Assistance of Counsel for his defence.

[ARTICLE VII.]

In suits at common law, where the value in controversy shall exceed twenty dollars, the right of trial by jury shall be preserved, and no fact tried by a jury, shall be otherwise reexamined in any Court of the United States, than according to the rules of the common law.

[ARTICLE VIII.]

Excessive bail shall not be required, nor excessive fines imposed, nor cruel and unusual punishments inflicted.

[ARTICLE IX.]

The enumeration in the Constitution, of certain rights, shall not be construed to deny or disparage others retained by the people.

[ARTICLE X.]

The powers not delegated to the United States by the Constitution, nor prohibited by it to the States, are reserved to the States respectively, or to the people.

[Amendments I-X, in force 1791.]

ARTICLE XI.

The Judicial power of the United States shall not be construed to extend to any suit in law or equity, commenced or prosecuted against one of the United States by Citizens of another State, or by Citizens or Subjects of any Foreign State. [1798.]

ARTICLE XII.

The Electors shall meet in their respective states and vote by ballot for President and Vice-President, one of whom, at least, shall not be an inhabitant of the same state with themselves; they shall name in their ballots the person voted for as President, and in distinct ballots the person voted for as Vice-President, and they shall make distinct lists of all persons voted for as President, and of all persons voted for as Vice-President, and of the number of votes for each, which lists they shall sign and certify, and transmit sealed to the seat of the government of the United States, directed to the President of the Senate;—The President of the Senate shall, in presence of the Senate and House of Representatives, open all the certificates and the votes shall then be counted;—The person having the greatest number of votes for President, shall be the President, if such number be a majority of the whole number of Electors appointed; and if no person have such majority, then from the persons having the highest numbers not exceeding three on the list of those voted for as President, the House of Representatives shall choose immediately, by ballot, the President. But in choosing the President, the votes shall be taken by states, the representation from each state having one vote; a quorum for this purpose shall consist of a member or members from two-thirds of the states, and a majority of all the states shall be necessary to a choice. And if the House of Representatives shall not choose a President whenever the right of choice shall devolve upon them, before the fourth day of March next following, then the Vice-President shall act as President, as in the case of the death or other constitutional disability of the President.—The person having the greatest number of votes as Vice-President, shall be the Vice-President, if such number be a majority of the whole number of Electors appointed, and if no person have a majority, then from the two highest numbers on the list, the Senate shall choose the Vice-President; a quorum for the purpose shall consist of two-thirds of the whole number of Senators, and a majority of the whole number shall be necessary to a choice. But no person constitutionally ineligible to the office of President shall be eligible to that of Vice-President of the United States. [1804.]

ARTICLE XIII.

SECTION 1. Neither slavery nor involuntary servitude, except as a punishment for crime whereof the party shall have been duly convicted, shall exist within the United States, or any place subject to their jurisdiction.

SECTION 2. Congress shall have power to enforce this article by appropriate legislation. [1865.]

ARTICLE XIV.

SECTION 1. All persons born or naturalized in the United States, and subject to the jurisdiction thereof, are citizens of the United States and of the State wherein they reside. No State shall make or enforce any law which shall abridge the privileges or immunities of citizens of the United States; nor shall any State deprive any person of life, liberty, or property, without due process of law; nor deny to any person within its jurisdiction the equal protection of the laws.

SECTION 2. Representatives shall be apportioned among the several States according to their respective numbers, counting the whole number of persons in each State, excluding Indians not taxed. But when the right to vote at any election for the choice of electors for President and Vice-President of the United States, Representatives in Congress, the Executive and Judicial officers of a State, or the members of the Legislature thereof, is denied to any of the male inhabitants of such State, being twenty-one years of age, and citizens of the United States, or in any way abridged, except for participation in rebellion, or other crime, the basis of representation therein shall be reduced in the proportion which the number of such male citizens shall bear to the whole number of male citizens twenty-one years of age in such State.

SECTION 3. No person shall be a Senator or Representative in Congress, or elector of President and Vice-President, or hold any office, civil or military, under the United States, or under any State, who, having previously taken an oath, as a member of Congress, or as an officer of the United States, or as a member of any State legislature, or as an executive or judicial officer of any State, to support the Constitution of the United States, shall have engaged in insurrection or rebellion against the same, or given aid or comfort to the enemies thereof. But Congress may by a vote of two-thirds of each House, remove such disability.

SECTION 4. The validity of the public debt of the United States, authorized by law, including debts incurred for payment of pensions and bounties for services in suppressing insurrection or rebellion, shall not be questioned. But neither the United States nor any State shall assume or pay any debt or obligation incurred in aid of insurrection or rebellion against the United States, or any claim for the loss or emancipation of any slave; but all such debts, obligations and claims shall be held illegal and void.

SECTION 5. The Congress shall have power to enforce, by appropriate legislation, the provisions of this article. [1868.]

ARTICLE XV.

SECTION 1. The right of citizens of the United States to vote shall not be denied or abridged by the United States or by any State on account of race, color, or previous condition of servitude—

SECTION 2. The Congress shall have power to enforce this article by appropriate legislation. [1870.]

ARTICLE XVI.

The Congress shall have power to lay and collect taxes on incomes, from whatever source derived, without apportionment among the several States, and without regard to any census or enumeration. [1913.]

ARTICLE XVII.

The Senate of the United States shall be composed of two Senators from each State, elected by the people thereof, for six years; and each Senator shall have one vote. The electors in each State shall have the qualifications requisite for electors of the most numerous branch of the State legislatures.

When vacancies happen in the representation of any State in the Senate, the executive authority of such State shall issue writs of election to fill such vacancies: *Provided,* That the legislature of any State may empower the executive thereof to make temporary appointments until the people fill the vacancies by election as the legislature may direct.

This amendment shall not be so construed as to affect the election or term of any Senator chosen before it becomes valid as part of the Constitution. [1913.]

ARTICLE XVIII.

[Section 1. After one year from the ratification of this article the manufacture, sale, or transportation of intoxicating liquors within, the importation thereof into, or the exportation thereof from the United States and all territory subject to the jurisdiction thereof for beverage purposes is hereby prohibited.

Section 2. The Congress and the several States shall have concurrent power to enforce this article by appropriate legislation.

Section 3. This article shall be inoperative unless it shall have been ratified as an amendment to the Constitution by the legislatures of the several States, as provided in the Constitution, within seven years from the date of the submission hereof to the States by the Congress.] [1919.]

ARTICLE XIX.

The right of citizens of the United States to vote shall not be denied or abridged by the United States or by any State on account of sex.

Congress shall have power to enforce this article by appropriate legislation. [1920.]

ARTICLE XX.

Section 1. The terms of the President and Vice President shall end at noon on the 20th day of January, and the terms of Senators and Representatives at noon on the 3d day of January, of the years in which such terms would have ended if this article had not been ratified; and the terms of their successors shall then begin.

Section 2. The Congress shall assemble at least once in every year, and such meeting shall begin at noon on the 3d day of January, unless they shall by law appoint a different day.

Section 3. If, at the time fixed for the beginning of the term of the President, the President elect shall have died, the Vice President elect shall become President. If a President shall not have been chosen before the time fixed for the beginning of his term, or if the President elect shall have failed to qualify, then the Vice President elect shall act as President until a President shall have qualified; and the Congress may by law provide for the case wherein neither a President elect nor a Vice President elect shall have qualified, declaring who shall then act as President, or the manner in which one who is to act shall be selected, and such person shall act accordingly until a President or Vice President shall have qualified.

SECTION 4. The Congress may by law provide for the case of the death of any of the persons from whom the House of Representatives may choose a President whenever the right of choice shall have devolved upon them, and for the case of the death of any of the persons from whom the Senate may choose a Vice President whenever the right of choice shall have devolved upon them.

SECTION 5. Sections 1 and 2 shall take effect on the 15th day of October following the ratification of this article.

SECTION 6. This article shall be inoperative unless it shall have been ratified as an amendment to the Constitution by the legislatures of three-fourths of the several States within seven years from the date of its submission. [1933.]

ARTICLE XXI.

SECTION 1. The eighteenth article of amendment to the Constitution of the United States is hereby repealed.

SECTION 2. The transportation or importation into any State, Territory, or possession of the United States for delivery or use therein of intoxicating liquors, in violation of the laws thereof, is hereby prohibited.

SECTION 3. This article shall be inoperative unless it shall have been ratified as an amendment to the Constitution by conventions in the several States, as provided in the Constitution, within seven years from the date of the submission hereof to the States by the Congress. [1933.]

Index